PUBLIC RELATIONS

PUBLIC RELATIONS

CANADIAN EDITION

TOM KELLEHER
ANNE MARIE MALES

OXFORD
UNIVERSITY PRESS

OXFORD

UNIVERSITY PRESS

Oxford University Press is a department of the University of Oxford.
It furthers the University's objective of excellence in research, scholarship,
and education by publishing worldwide. Oxford is a registered trade mark of
Oxford University Press in the UK and in certain other countries.

Published in Canada by
Oxford University Press
8 Sampson Mews, Suite 204,
Don Mills, Ontario M3C 0H5 Canada

www.oupcanada.com

Library and Archives Canada Cataloguing in Publication

Title: Public relations / Tom Kelleher and Anne Marie Males
Names: Kelleher, Tom (Tom A.), author. | Males, Anne Marie, author.
Description: Includes bibliographical references and index.
Identifiers: Canadiana (print) 20190161825 | Canadiana (ebook) 20190161833 |
ISBN 9780199029914
(softcover) | ISBN 9780199039166 (looseleaf) | ISBN 9780199029952 (EPUB)
Subjects: LCSH: Public relations—Textbooks. | LCSH: Public relations—
Canada—Textbooks. | LCGFT: Textbooks.
Classification: LCC HD59 .K453 2020 | DDC 659.2—dc23

Cover image: ©32 pixels/Shutterstock
Cover design: Sherill Chapman
Interior design: Laurie McGregor

Brief Contents

Contents

PART THREE
TACTICS   215

PART FOUR
CONTEXTS   271

Preface

The textbook you are holding now is an updated Canadian version of an American textbook written about four years ago. In just four years, plenty has changed—Internet links died, apps fell out of favour, celebrities stopped trending, new companies rose to fame, and some old ones went downhill or disappeared.

Public relations is like that—our profession continues to change and evolve at an almost dizzying pace.

When I began my career in public relations, press releases were distributed by mail; hours were spent folding documents and sealing envelopes. If it was a big mailing, the whole office would chip in to make sure we made the deadline and my colleagues would help me haul the heavy boxes down to the nearest Canada Post office.

As a newly minted public relations practitioner, folding and mailing was my job, along with looking after the clippings on behalf of our clients—a time-consuming job that involved hours of cutting out newspaper and magazine articles and wielding a glue stick to create the large binders that formed the backbone of our monthly reports to clients. And yes, we used AVEs (ad value equivalents). At the time, these were considered state of the art in public relations measurement.

When I mention this to my students, they inevitably snicker or look at me with vague, unknowing eyes—this is so far outside of their realm of experience as to be unimaginable.

Today, printed media releases are virtually unheard of, "clippings" are captured and tallied digitally, and AVEs have been all but put to bed with the creation of the first set of Barcelona Principles in 2010. Media relations, which was once the primary focus of our industry, is a smaller and smaller part of day-to-day practice as owned media grows in importance. Smartphones are quickly replacing the computers that replaced the IBM Selectrics that were once found on every PR practitioner's desk. The times, as they say, are a-changing.

With the rapid pace of change public relations (and most industries) face today, it's easy to image that 20 years from now the newest crop of would-be practitioners will hear about the Internet, smartphones, and the current crop of popular apps and shake their heads at the archaic nature of it all.

The Canadian Public Relations Society recently released a white paper looking at public relations megatrends that will, according to the paper, continue to challenge our profession. These trends included the rising business value of reputation and relationships, the empowered audience, fake news, a gap in wealth and trust, and artificial intelligence. What's a practitioner to do? How can any of us possibly keep up?

That same paper provides some of the answers. At the heart of our profession are relationships—the relations in public relations. Our job is to build positive relationships that help an organization achieve its goals. As Daniel Tisch, president and CEO of Argyle Public Relationships, points out, that aspect of our work is more important than ever. "We've heard the cliché that content is king; a better axiom for today is that relationships are royalty," says Tisch.

Today's consumers have much higher expectations when it comes to their relationships with the brands and organizations in their lives. Transparency and clear communication are no longer a "nice to have"; they are an absolute expectation. When consumers connect with your company via social media or other means, they expect an instant answer. They also expect that your values will align with theirs, and they are looking to you and your company to tell them about the positive impact you're having on the community and the planet.

All of this speaks to a need for public relations and the skills we bring to the table. Is it any surprise that this is a growing profession with more and better opportunities than ever before?

Welcome to public relations in Canada. This book will provide you with an overview of our profession and a solid base upon which you can continue to learn. Ours is an exciting, fast-moving, and varied career that will allow you to work in virtually any industry. Whether you choose agency, corporate, or the charitable sector, public relations will allow you to make a valuable contribution to your organization while building a valuable career for yourself.

While public relations practice in Canada and the United States are often very similar, this book is proudly Canadian in its approach. In it, you'll find plenty of Canadian examples and cases from brands and companies you know.

Acknowledgements

Many thanks to my husband, Dave, and my girls, Trinity and Ava. Working on this book sometimes required extra effort from them to keep the household going when I was against a deadline.

Thanks to everyone at Oxford University Press, especially Lauren Wing, who displayed infinite patience throughout the development process.

Many thanks to my colleagues in the Bachelor of Public Relations program at Humber College in Toronto, Ontario—Lydia Boyko, Andrea Tavchar, and Dan Schneider—you've always been so generous with your time, resources, and ideas.

Special thanks to my professors in the Master of Communication Management (MCM) program at McMaster University in Hamilton, Ontario—Alex Sevigny, Terry Flynn, Michael Meath, Dave Scholz, and Al Seaman—each of you contributed to my development and helped take my career in a completely different direction.

Many thanks to the following reviewers, along with those who chose to remain anonymous, for their useful comments:

Colin Babiuk	MacEwan University
Kenneth Bell	University of Regina
Gary Fowlie	British Columbia Institute of Technology
Colleen Hood	Mount Royal University
Tess Laidlaw	Mount Saint Vincent University
Veronique Mandal	St. Clair College
Evan Potter	University of Ottawa
Jackie Westelaken	Fanshawe College

— Anne Marie Males

Guided Tour of the Book

Oxford University Press is pleased to present *Public Relations*, a contemporary introduction to the foundations and changing landscape of public relations in Canada. This first Canadian edition showcases an outstanding set of features and pedagogy guaranteed to spark readers' interest and promote student learning.

Key Features

142   **PART TWO** Strategy

Avoid setting goals at one level (e.g., liking) when what you and your client really want is effectiveness at a greater level (e.g., acting).

Using McGuire's Hierarchy of Effects for Planning

While not every public relations program will address all nine of these outcomes, and the steps do not always happen in the same order, thinking through McGuire's list (McGuire and others have offered other steps besides these) can help your planning in a number of ways. First, the list will help you avoid the mistake of setting goals at one level (e.g., liking) when what you and your client really want is effectiveness at a greater level (e.g., acting).

Second, the list will help you identify specific objectives and tactics and remind you not to forget any key steps. The remembering step may cue you to include reminder emails or build an app feature that notifies publics when it's time to act. When you are evaluating your efforts, the list may help you diagnose what worked and what didn't. Maybe your campaign message was tremendously popular (lots of liking) but led to very low participation. You might then review whether people actually understood your key message (comprehending) and knew how to act (learning).

Third, the list serves as a reminder to be realistic about expected outcomes. Let's say you get your story placed in the *Toronto Star* and it contains your key messages just how you want them. Score! According to a recent survey the *Toronto Star* is read by 1,064,000 people.³ For simplicity, we might optimistically estimate the following:

- Over one million people are exposed to the message.
- Approximately one-third of those who are exposed pay attention (350,000).
- A fifth of those who pay attention are interested enough to read the story (70,000).
- Most of those who read it understand the key message (53,000).
- A third of those who understand the key message acquire the skills you want them to (18,000).
  - Half of those with the skills agree (8,500).
  - One in 10 of those who agree remember (850).
  - Half of those who remember finally act on the message (425).

Convincing 425 people to do something is excellent if you're leasing airplanes or seeking large donations to a non-profit, but it may not be as meaningful if you're selling smoothies or trying to get out votes for a federal election. And in either case, 425 is a far cry from the one million impressions—the measure of how many people were exposed to a message—that you may be tempted to claim as a metric of success.

Digital media allow for better tracking of steps, as well. For some steps, such as liking and proselytizing, subscribers can gather fairly specific data. Metrics available for online video sites like YouTube allow subscribers to see the number of unique views, the average view duration, the number of people who shared the material or commented on it, and the content of those comments. You may find that almost everyone who started

impressions A measure of the number of people exposed to a message.

Dozens of different organizations, including Barrick Gold, Loblaw, RBC, and Aeroplan, were mentioned in *The Globe and Mail* on one particular day.⁴

What kinds of outcomes might these organizations expect?

Public Relations for a Canadian Audience

Canadian examples, data, practices, and profiles provide an essential foundation for any Canadian student interested in pursuing a career in PR.

310   PART **FOUR** Contexts

the car companies that have *not* cheated on emissions tests. Think of all the restaurants that have *not* had *E. coli* outbreaks, or the student groups that maintained membership despite changes in leadership, or the non-profits that rode out bad slumps in the economy, and so on. In some cases, alternate models can be used to illustrate what would have happened if a crisis occurred and had been managed poorly. And this is a happy outcome! Managers, experts, and others with deep knowledge of an organization and its day-to-day and year-to-year options will appreciate knowing they avoided a boycott, illness outbreak, bankruptcy, product recall, lawsuit, embarrassing media scandal, or any other potential crisis. What's more important—and this may be the result of either an issue averted or a crisis that played out all the way—is that evaluation allows you to learn lessons from experience and develop strategies for the future. Evaluation of how one issue was managed informs the first efforts of monitoring for the next one.

Crisis Types

situational crisis communication theory (SCCT) Theory that proposes effective crisis communication entails choosing and applying appropriate response strategies depending on how much responsibility for the crisis is attributed to the organization by key publics.

organizational crisis A major threat to an organization's operations or reputation.

Not all crises are preventable, and how organizations respond to crises should depend on the degree to which people attribute responsibility for the crisis to the organization. Public relations scholars Tim Coombs and Sherry Holladay developed one of the most well-researched and practical theories for crisis management called *situational crisis communication theory* (SCCT). SCCT is a contingency theory that suggests that some writers may feel as they face the growth of image-based social crises depends on the situation. Coombs defines an *organizational crisis* as "a significant threat to organizational operations or reputations that can have negative consequences for stakeholders and/or the organization if not handled properly."[15] When people think that an organization is responsible for a crisis (e.g., Volkswagen), its reputation suffers, and the crisis leads to more anger, less purchase intent, and greater likelihood of negative word of mouth about the organization. While issues management focuses on how to prevent organizational crises, crisis management deals with how to repair damage and rebuild reputation.[16]

Who's to blame? That is the question at the heart of initial crisis assessment. Researchers have identified three main groups of crisis types: victim crises, accident crises, and preventable crises.

Victim Crises

When publics see the organization as a victim, they assign minimal responsibility for the crisis to the organization. Natural disasters such as hurricanes, tsunamis, and earthquakes are prime examples. People outside of an organization can cause victim crises too, such as cases of sabotage, terrorism, or product tampering.

One of the most famous examples of crisis management in the history of public relations stemmed from a victim crisis that arose because of prod[...] an organization. In 1982, news broke that six adults and [...] had died from cyanide poisoning after taking capsules of [...] tles of Tylenol capsules that had been tampered with had c[...] but were all purchased in the Chicago area, investigators [...] factories. Police suspected that someone had purchased th[...] capsules, and then returned the products to store shelves.

Tylenol's parent company Johnson & Johnson coop[...] expressing sympathy and sharing accurate information [...] ation's response. At a cost of more than $100 million, Jo[...]

---

10 Multimedia and Mobile   251

web ad or social video starts playing automatically on your device in an office, library, or classroom? Mute buttons get a lot of use these days, and descriptive text and subtitles become that much more important.

Images

"Uh oh, we're being challenged again," wrote Allen Mireles in an article for Cision. Cision is a public relations and social media software company. Mireles is described on the website as a wordsmith, and her words convey the anxiety that some writers may feel as they face the growth of image-based social media. "That's right, PR is being nudged away from the familiar comfort of text-based communications to more visual forms of communications, especially in our digital campaigns."[3] Photo-based platforms of social media have been built, adopted, and grown into central channels for public relations efforts. Snapchat, Instagram, and Pinterest wouldn't exist without images. And the vast majority of the images shared via these platforms wouldn't exist without mobile devices.

This isn't to say that working with images and photos is something new to public relations. In their 1984 text *Managing Public Relations*, Grunig and Hunt noted that photos and illustrations "represent a basic form of visual communication used in each of the four public relations models."[4] (The four models are defined in Chapter 2.) What's changed significantly is the technology.

When using photographs or images as public relations tactics, you have three options for obtaining them:

1. Create them yourself.
2. Hire a professional to take photos or create original images.
3. Buy images or obtain permission to use others' material.

Creating Your Own Images

Advances in digital camera technology have increased the accessibility of do-it-yourself photography. Your average smartphone camera can generate image quality that used to be reserved for only those willing to invest heavily in expensive digital cameras. But just because the phone in your pocket *can* capture amazing images at very high resolution doesn't mean your photos are automatically high enough quality for your organization's communication needs. Factors to consider in taking photos include lighting, composition, angles, background, and props. Yes, social media have widened our latitude for what we accept and expect in shared imagery. Hastily snapped selfies, for example, have found a place in our digital culture. But just as expectations for writing styles vary from one context to another,

This image was posted on the Dove Instagram account. What meaning does the photo convey to you? Now consider that the image was posted with the caption "'Beauty standards don't define me.' Teacher and aspiring model Meryem shows us that unique is beautiful, and the world is a better place when that's recognized."

What public relations purpose does the combination of picture and words serve?

---

98   **PART ONE** Foundations

lobbying Working to influence the decisions of government officials on matters of legislation.

government relations Management of relationships between an organization and government officials who formulate and execute public policy.

public affairs Management of policy-focused relationships between an organization, public officials, and their constituents.

corporate social responsibility (CSR) Companies' commitment of resources to benefit the welfare of their workforce, local communities, society at large, and the environment.

In Canada, the organization recently organize[...] sate, an ingredient in pesticides, which has been lin[...] They have also been involved in campaigns regardi[...] neutrality in Canada, and in supporting the Indigen[...] SumOfUs was also instrumental in helping the una[...] proposed solution on the plastic crisis including a[...] quently introduced by the governing Liberal Party o[...]

Government Agencies

Organizations of all types practise advocacy, also known as lobbying. Lobbying is the process through which individuals and groups articulate their interests to federal, provincial, or municipal governments in order to influence public policy or government decision-making. Lobbyists may be paid third parties who communicate on behalf of their clients or employees of a corporation or organization seeking to influence the government.

Lobbying is regulated in Canada under the Lobbying Act, and anyone lobbying must register with the Office of the Commissioner of Lobbying. The line between lobbying and government relations (the act of managing the relationship between an organization and government officials) is sometimes a blurry one; and so, some people who consider themselves government relations practitioners will register as lobbyists just to be on the safe side.

Chapter 11 covers some key regulatory agencies with which public relations practitioners should be familiar, and Chapter 2 discusses politics and government as part of the heritage and contemporary practice of public relations. One of the primary functions of government public affairs is the dissemination of information *to* constituents (i.e., public information). Another key function is advocating *for* those constituents.

In this chapter, and throughout the text, we see how the idea of building and maintaining relationships applies in the public sector. A government agency may be seen as either an organization or a public, depending on your perspective. In the school board example for media relations, we saw the public school board as an organization with a public relations person who was responsible for communicating with news media and other publics. With the Chicago surfer example, we saw how the case could be framed with Surfrider Foundation as the organization and the city park service as a public.

Ethics: Corporate Social Responsibility and Loyalty

Corporate social responsibility (CSR) refers to a company's commitment to allocate resources to benefit society and the environment. The contributions may come in the form of financial donations, employee time, or socially beneficial business practices. While non-profit organizations exist primarily to make a positive difference in their communities and the natural environment, for-profit businesses and corporations exist primarily to make money. If they don't make money, they eventually will not exist at all and cannot benefit anyone.

Ontario doctors recently lobbied the government to outlaw cosmetic eye tattoos.

In this case, are they acting as an organization, a public, or both?

Strong Coverage of Theory

Public Relations provides a comprehensive overview of communication theory, pairing important concepts with hands-on practice for a complete student learning experience.

Reflects the New Era of Digital and Social Media

Emphasizing new and social media, *Public Relations* explores the changing landscape of public relations while also providing a classic foundation, supplying students with a comprehensive introduction that reflects today's more participatory communication environment.

An Emphasis on Ethics

Critical for success in public relations, ethics is explored in dedicated sections included in every chapter, covering topics such as codes of ethics, transparency, corporate social responsibility, loyalty and diversity, privacy, and conflicts of interest.

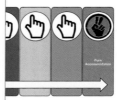

300   PART FOUR Contexts

Case Study

A Crisis Threatens the Future of Maple Leaf Foods: A Classic Study in Crisis Communication

The Arthur W. Page Society is a New York–based professional association for senior public relations and corporate communications executives and educators. Like the CPRS's (Canadian Public Relations Society's) Code of Professional Standards, the Page Society has a set of guidelines for practice. "Page Society members regard these principles as the guidelines by which they, and indeed all communications professionals, should undertake their role."

One of the seven principles is "conduct public relations as if the whole enterprise depends on it"; one of the best modern-day illustrations of this principle in action is the 2008 case of Maple Leaf Foods and how the organization handled the communications surrounding the incident.

In August 2008, Maple Leaf Foods was facing a major crisis. Listeria had been found in some of their food products, specifically cold cuts, and people were getting sick and dying. By the time the crisis was over, 22 deaths would be attributed to the contaminated products, and Maple Leaf Foods had a major crisis of confidence on its hands. How could Canadian consumers ever feel safe buying roast beef, corned beef, and other cold cuts for their families knowing Maple Leaf products had caused a number of deaths?

Maple Leaf Foods CEO Michael McCain was widely praised for how his company handled the crisis.

Can you think of other examples of crises that were well handled?

Issues and Crises   301

Continued

Are there situations when pure advocacy or pure accommodation might be appropriate, or are these merely theoretical constructs?

Case Studies and Real-World Examples

Dedicated "Case Study" boxes found in each chapter—featuring companies such as Maple Leaf Foods and Coca-Cola, and topics such as publicity stunts, net neutrality, and the Barcelona Principles—demonstrate real-life public relations applications of core concepts found in each chapter.

---

180   PART TWO Strategy

Voices from the Field

Jefferson Darrell

Image courtesy of Jefferson Darrell

Jefferson Darrell is an accomplished marketing communications professional with more than 15 years of brand strategy expertise, generating earned and owned media using both traditional and digital channels. He is highly effective in stakeholder relations, negotiating, and conceiving and cultivating mutually beneficial partnerships. Having worked on numerous integrated marketing campaigns on both the agency and client side, Jefferson brings a broad understanding of the entire marketing mix to every project.

In the diversity and inclusion space, Jefferson has been instrumental in educating and lobbying for diversity and inclusion in the marketing communications industry under his consultancy Breakfast Culture. He has delivered numerous talks and sat on panels about the importance of diversity and inclusion. He has been an active participant in diversity and inclusion conferences including the Institute of Communications Agencies' (ICA's) IDEA Summit (Inclusivity, Diversity and Equity in Advertising), P World's Global PR Summit, the Advertising Club of Toronto, the Canadian Public Relations Society, the Canadian Association of Science Centres, and Canada's first-ever White Privilege Conference at Ryerson University. He believes Peter Drucker's famous quote: "Culture eats strategy for breakfast," and challenges today's marketers to "break some eggs!"

Canada is one of the most ethnically diverse countries in the world—do you see that diversity reflected in public relations practitioners?
Agreed. Canada is a very ethnically diverse country. Anecdotally, one does see lots of diversity in terms of people studying and employed in the public relations (PR) industry at the junior and intermediate levels. Currently, that diversity clearly stops at the senior management levels. Many agencies have homogenous management teams that are primarily Caucasian and, in many cases, primarily male in a female-dominated industry. Again, this is anecdotally from observation when one looks at

the senior management teams on PR agency websites. Many of my colleagues of colour and I discuss our experiences and which Canadian PR agencies are not friendly for people of colour.

For a true measurement of how diverse the public relations industry is at all levels we need to incorporate data collection. I have been lobbying both the Toronto chapter of the International Association of Business Communicators (IABC) and the CPRS to incorporate diversity and inclusion metrics with their annual membership surveys to have data to learn just how diverse the public relations industry really is in Canada. My challenge to Canadian PR agencies: does your workforce, at all levels, represent the demographics of Canada and the markets where you operate?

Why do you think public relations doesn't reflect the diversity of Canada's population?
As a society we like to believe that Canada is a meritocracy, but we are not. Systemic discrimination plays a tremendous role in who gets hired, retained, and promoted. There are systemic issues, company and human bias and prejudices that prevent people from excelling during the hiring, promotion, and retention process. Companies often mask their bias and prejudices under the guise of "cultural fit." Look around the boardroom tables and see who "fits" and who doesn't. In diversity and inclusion theory we call this "insider-outsider dynamics." Again, data collection that not only looks at demographics but also questions the barriers faced by employees who may be different from the "insider group" will help to shed some light on this issue.

How do you make the business case for diversity in public relations?
There are numerous ways. Just about every management consultant organization has published a paper about the business case for diversity. In Rick Miner's 2014

Implementation   181

The fact that the Canadian PR industry is beginning to have the diversity, equity, and inclusion discussion is a major step in the right direction. However, we must move beyond what promises to be difficult discussions and transactional "fixes" (e.g., multicultural lunches) to actual action with companies making transformative changes (e.g., policies and procedures) to initiating programs to hire, retain, and promote historically underrepresented candidates.

How important is it for young practitioners to find mentors within the industry?
It is extremely important. For me, I didn't see people who look like me in senior roles in the PR industry. Sadly, I still don't see many similar faces in Canada. This is one of the reasons I go out of my way to mentor young practitioners.

In public relations we often talk about the importance of truth and authenticity. How does diversity fit in with those concepts?
Diversity fits in completely with this concept. If a person can bring their authentic self to work they will be more productive. For example, all of the energy that goes into "staying in the closet" if one is LGBTQ+, or "code-switching" if one is racialized, or constantly fighting to be heard and taken seriously if one is a woman, is energy that could and should be put towards business goals. If an employee is permitted to live their authentic self at work and be an individual yet also belong to a unique group, just imagine the possibilities. Let's break some eggs!

Voices from the Field: Q&As with Public Relations Professionals

Public Relations offers "Voices from the Field" boxes in each chapter, featuring interviews with practitioners from across Canada who offer students direct advice and insights from a range of public relations careers.

Public Relations Careers | Sports PR

Manager, In-Game Communications

For a die-hard hockey fan, this may seem like a dream job, but it would be a tough one to land and maybe even tougher to succeed. Would you be ready for it?

JOB TITLE
Manager, In-Game Communications, NHL

JOB DESCRIPTION
The Manager, In-Game Communications is a versatile writer who leads the NHL's In-Game Communications team in bringing to life the facts, figures, and story lines from more than 1,300 games each season. The Manager is responsible for guiding storytelling and research, leading and assisting a group of writers, and communicating relevant information to media, Rightsholders, Member Clubs, League executives, and fans in real time during all games.

SAMPLE DUTIES AND RESPONSIBILITIES
- Identify storylines and lead the writing, research, and editing of the NHL Morning Skate, a daily publication that pulls together the NHL's top editorial moments and highlights in a succinct, compelling manner
- Use a deep knowledge of hockey to guide in-game storytelling in real-time and act as the lead for all in-game communications from the public relations team
- Actively contribute to real-time coverage and end-of-night publications while leading 3-5 team members.

- Monitor trending topics and relay information to other members of the Communications team and/or League executives, as necessary

QUALIFICATIONS
- Proficient writer and editor who can work under tight deadline pressure in a fast-paced environment
- Excellent oral communication and interpersonal skills
- A strong understanding of the League's rule book and a passion for hockey
- Exhibit excellent attention to detail
- Experience with Adobe Photoshop or equivalent considered an asset
- Successful completion of post-secondary education in a relevant discipline
- 3-5 years demonstrable experience working in a similar capacity at a Club or League level or in another fast-paced, live environment
- Understanding of and aptitude for social media, with an emphasis on Twitter and Instagram

DISCUSSION QUESTIONS
How would you demonstrate an aptitude for social media? Which specific publics would you work with as part of the job?

Many political candidates and organizations hire agencies that specialize in political communication. If you're fired up about a candidate or a political cause, or if you think of yourself as a policy wonk and want to make a difference in the technical details of how government operates, political public relations may be for you.

Financial and Entrepreneurial

Financial public relations deals with investor relations, financial media relations, and disclosures of financial information, as discussed in Chapter 4 on relationship management. Employers range from Canada's banks, to large publicly held companies like Berkshire

Public Relations Career Boxes

Chapter 14, Careers, features sample public relations job titles, descriptions, duties, and qualifications — including spotlights on the BC Children's Hospital, the NHL, the Government of Saskatchewan, and PANDORA Canada—giving students insight into a range of PR career possibilities. Discussion questions encourage students to think of major daily responsibilities and challenges associated with each job.

11

Legal

Chapter contributed by Rachel Bellotti, lawyer and part-time professor at the Humber College Institute of Technology and Advanced Learning

At its core, practising law is no different than professional public relations practice. Both fields seek to address issues, target an audience, and cultivate a message that results in a positive outcome.

Key learning outcomes

11.1 Discuss why it is important to always run your work by in-house counsel or legal counsel.
11.2 Describe any limits to free speech, including libel and slander.
11.3 Describe the common types of intellectual property and the ways in which they are protected.
11.4 Identify where privacy comes into play in the role of public relations.
11.5 Identify and discuss agencies that guide and regulate public relations professionals.
11.6 Analyze ethical dilemmas public relations professionals face and what organization is in place to help guide a PR professional.

A ambassador806/iStock

...lations (PR), did you ever think that ...ot, right? You might even think it is odd ...to the law. The law and PR, however, are ...ationships a PR professional can make is ...d lawyers are dependent on one another ...al should attempt to be his or her own

...n their everyday tasks, there is a need for ...*Contentious Relationship between PR and* ...nd a lawyer sometimes requires balance. ...disagree with their legal team, but "both ...gh a crisis with its reputation and ability ...g PR and legal working together is in an

...ome a team? This partnership has become ...which technology has developed. The in-...ily has changed immensely, and now the ...h a crisis has been significantly reduced. ...onal and legal counsel has changed when ...is a higher demand for them to work to-...at in almost every relationship in which ...uestion of some kind will be at the core.[3] ...art, but lose in the eyes of the public, or, ...of the public. Which predicament would ...t think it is best to win in the eyes of the ...e what would happen if you lost in court. ...ation of a corporate client and ruin the ...to declaring bankruptcy and dissolving ...you answered "winning in the eyes of the ...mpany.

...cepts that you will come across in your

...ue someone who tweets something mean ...ng bad about someone you know? What ...initiated?
...?

...ion about a stock tip, are you able to share ...t?

...mation about a co-worker, are you able to

...essionals may deal with in the course of ...ws legislated by municipal, provincial, or ...and agencies. This chapter is to help you gain awareness of how important it is to cultivate a relationship with a lawyer.

A Dedicated Chapter on Canadian Law

A chapter on Canadian law features key information on the Canadian Charter of Rights and Freedoms, CRTC policy, various official Canadian guidelines and codes of ethics, as well as discussion of Canadian defamation, libel, copyright, and freedom of information law, providing students with crucial knowledge for successfully navigating the legal sphere of public relations.

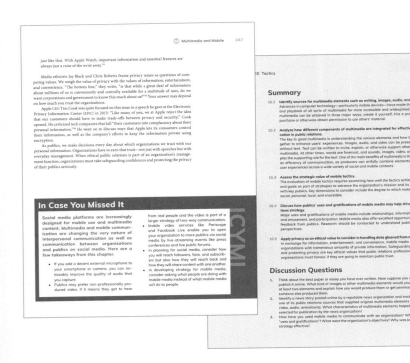

Extensive Pedagogical Features

A wealth of pedagogical features—including key learning outcomes, glossaries, summaries, discussion questions, further reading, and key terms—enhance student comprehension and provide easy navigation of concepts.

Resources for Instructors and Students

Online Supplements

Consumer Behaviour is supported by an outstanding array of ancillary materials for both instructors and students, all available in the book's Ancillaries Resource Centre (ARC).

For Instructors

- **An instructor's manual** includes chapter overviews, outlines, learning objectives, key terms, and class activities, as well as summaries and discussion activities connected to each case study found in the text.
- **A test bank** provides a comprehensive set of multiple choice, short answer, and essay questions to assess students' skills.
- **PowerPoint slides** summarize key points from each chapter.

For Students

A student study guide includes chapter overviews, flashcards, multiple choice questions, activities, and a list of articles and additional readings to enhance students' understanding of key consumer behaviour concepts.

PART ONE
Foundations

Principled Public Relations

"A little bird told me . . . ." What kinds of disclosure issues arise when a public relations professional is asked to tweet for a client?

Key learning outcomes

1.1 Define public relations in terms of organizations, publics, and the relationships between them.

1.2 Explain how public relations can serve as a management function.

1.3 Recognize key principles and values for ethical conduct in public relations.

1.4 Understand the importance of ethics in public relations.

1.5 Apply systematic ethical decision-making for public relations.

1.6 Identify international professional associations and become familiar with codes of ethics.

Engagement. Conversation. Influence. Transparency. Trust. These concepts pepper workshops, seminars, articles, and online discussions of what social and digital communication technologies mean for public relations. While essential for professional practice today, these concepts have been at the heart of good public relations long before Facebook, Twitter, and Snapchat.

This chapter introduces classic definitions of public relations as well as a modern description crowdsourced by the Canadian Public Relations Society (CPRS). By and large the crowdsourced, social-media–era definition matches the classics that have been used in the teaching and practice of public relations for decades. While keywords like *publics*, *organizations*, *communication*, and *relationships* may not be buzzworthy, they have stood the test of time as key components in any sound definition of public relations.

Defining Public Relations

Publics—it's not a term you hear every day outside of public relations classrooms and strategy meetings. We're all familiar with the word *public*, of course—it is most commonly used in front of other words like *library, transit,* and *opinion*, and in that context we know that it means everyone. *Publics*, which is plural of the term *public*, refers to a subset of *public*—in other words, not everyone. In public relations, **publics** are groups of people with shared interests related to organizations, and there are many different ways to define those publics.

General public—now here's a term you probably do hear every day. How is the general public responding to today's news events? What's the best way to get our message out to the general public? Can we engage the general public on this issue? The first two questions are nearly impossible to answer, and the answer to the third question is probably "no." That is the problem with the general public. In many cases the general public doesn't help us with strategy, and it doesn't help us identify any specific people with whom we want to communicate.

Engaging in public relations means communicating with people who are part of specific groups with specific interests. Some of these publics are groups that have an effect on the **organizations** for which we work. These include large corporations; small businesses; non-profits; schools; government agencies; **non-governmental organizations (NGOs)** organized at the local, national, or international level; and even clubs and student groups—pretty much any group of people organized to pursue a mission. Other publics are people who are affected by our organizations. Most publics fit both criteria in that the influence is mutual.

The Canadian Red Cross (organization) tweets out tips to help residents before, during, and after a flood in British Columbia. That's public relations. Representatives of a CPRS chapter (organization) make an announcement in an introductory communications class to recruit new members (public). That's public relations. Visit Florida, the state's official tourism marketing corporation (organization), posts photos and videos to its "Visit Florida" Facebook page and interacts with commenters (public) on the page. That's public relations. George Weston Limited (organization) posts a news release announcing its quarterly financial results and hosts a live conference call and webcast for investors (public) in order to satisfy Ontario Securities Commission (OSC—yet another public) regulations. That's public relations too. Notice that in none of these cases have the organizations set out to engage the general public. Instead, British Columbia flood victims, new communication majors, Facebook commenters, investors, and the OSC are identified as specific publics.

publics Groups of people with shared interests. An organization's publics either have an effect on the organization, are affected by the organization, or both.

general public A non-specific term that can refer to everyone in the world.

organization A group of people organized in pursuit of a mission, including businesses, non-profits, NGOs, clubs, churches, unions, schools, teams, and government agencies.

non-governmental organization (NGO) A group of people organized at the local, national, or international level, often serving humanitarian functions and encouraging political participation. NGOs can be large and involved in international development work such as CARE Canada or Médecins Sans Frontières / Doctors Without Borders Canada, or can be focused on a specific region or concern such as the Yukon Conservation Society.

Tim Hortons' online communication tools include their website, Twitter, Facebook, and Snapchat.

Are you part of one of Tim Hortons' publics? How could they communicate with you?

---

public relations
Management of communication between an organization and its publics, or the strategic communication process that builds mutually beneficial relationships between organizations and their publics.

The labels for publics and organizations are sometimes interchangeable. If executives from Enbridge Inc. (organization) organize a public meeting for British Columbia residents (public) to discuss a proposed pipeline project, that's public relations. And if residents then organize a coalition (organization) to oppose the pipeline (public), that's still public relations.

Completing a full definition of **public relations** requires more than just identifying organizations and publics. We still have to understand the second part of the term *public relations*—the relations.

Textbook Definitions

To define public relations, **consider organizations, publics, and the relations between them.**

Perhaps the most commonly cited definition of public relations is the one written by James Grunig and Todd Hunt in their classic 1984 public relations text *Managing Public Relations*: "the management of communication between an organization and its publics."[1] There's a lot to this business of managing communication, which is why so many other definitions of public relations abound. Another classic definition from another classic public relations text, *Cutlip and Center's Effective Public Relations*, defines public relations as "the management function that establishes and maintains mutually beneficial relationships between an organization and the publics on whom its success or failure depends."[2]

Naturally, people are wary, even skeptical, of textbook definitions. Ask people outside of the field of public relations what public relations is and you'll get quite different answers.

Outage Map

View Interactive Map

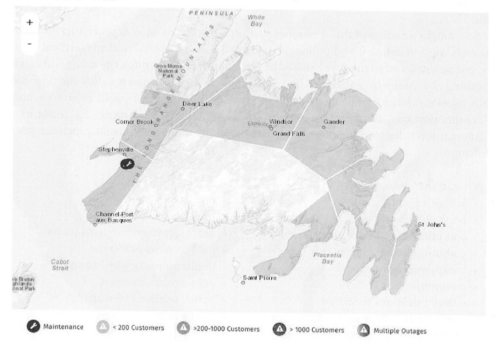

Maintenance   ⚠ < 200 Customers   ⚠ >200-1000 Customers   ⚠ > 1000 Customers   ⚠ Multiple Outages

Newfoundland Power uses a section of its website, including an interactive map, to report on current power outages.

Who are Newfoundland Power's key publics?

As an experiment, ask your family and friends to define public relations. Students who have undertaken this project in the past typically hear things like this:

> "It's about the media and getting publicity."
> "Honestly, I don't know. I know you're taking it in school but I don't really know
>   what it is except there's a lot of writing."
> "Damage control."
> "Spin."
> "You organize events and go to trade shows."
> "You have to be good with people."
> "It means you're the spokesperson for a company."
> "Scandal!"

ABC's *Scandal* is one of several television shows that features "PR" agents as key characters. Olivia Pope, the protagonist of ABC's hit political drama, is a former White House communication director who runs her own Washington, DC, crisis consulting firm. She "fixes" all sorts of political crises with clever deception and slick execution. Actress Kerry

Kathy Hutchins/Shutterstock.com

TV shows like *Scandal,* **which features Kerry Washington as crisis management consultant Olivia Pope, present an entertaining view of "PR."**

What messages do shows like this send about the field of public relations?

Washington, who plays Pope on the show, describes the character as glamorous but seriously flawed. "She's an entrepreneur, she's very smart, she has an amazing closet, and those are all things that I think are worthy of admiration," says Washington. "But she is nobody's role model."[3]

So what do we make of this disconnect between public relations as professors and professionals want to define it and public relations as *Scandal* viewers, students, critical bloggers, our parents, and so many others see it? It is tempting to just ditch the name and call it something else. Many organizations have done that, or they have never called the function public relations in the first place. Instead, they have departments of public affairs, corporate communications, community relations, and so on. The Government of Canada uses 83 different job titles to describe public relations and communications jobs including the following:[4]

- assistant press secretary
- author's agent
- book publicist
- communications adviser
- communications consultant
- communications expert
- communications officer
- communications specialist
- community information officer
- co-ordinator, information service
- co-ordinator, media relations
- fundraising campaign consultant
- information co-ordinator
- information officer
- media co-ordinator
- media events co-ordinator
- media relations co-ordinator
- media relations officer
- museum education officer

- officer, public relations
- press agent
- press secretary
- press secretary, public relations
- public affairs officer
- public affairs officer—military
- public relations agent
- public relations consultant
- public relations co-ordinator
- public relations officer
- public relations practitioner
- public relations representative
- public relations specialist
- publicist
- publicity agent
- publicity co-ordinator
- publicity information officer
- spokesperson
- tourism information officer

Specialized Areas of Public Relations

One possible explanation for the confusion around the definition of public relations might have to do with the wide variety of functions that may fall under the public relations umbrella. Two practitioners, both with the title "communications officer," may have jobs that are so different that it's hard to image that they are both in the same profession. One may spend most of his or her day dealing with the media, while the other writes speeches for the CEO and looks after employee communications. One may organize special events, while the other spends most of his or her day on social media. The variety is almost endless. The following specialized areas of practice are also part of modern public relations.

Issues Management

Issues management, according to Robert Heath, is an anticipatory, strategic management process that helps organizations detect and respond appropriately to emerging trends or changes in the socio-political environment.[5] In other words, it's about actively seeking potential problems and "heading them off at the pass" so to speak. A strong issues management program seeks to reduce the possibility of a crisis.

When Mountain Equipment Co-op (MEC) CEO David Labistour penned a blog post admitting the company had traditionally used white models for its ads[6] (thereby excluding people of colour), the company could be said to be engaging in issues management. No organization had, at the time of writing, challenged MEC's practices, but in the true spirit of issues management, the company realized times had changed and made the change on their own before it became a bigger issue or a crisis.

Crisis Communication

If problems aren't detected and solved at the issues stage, or, if a crisis develops suddenly, the communication function that deals with the situation is known as crisis communication. A crisis can be defined as "a significant threat to operations or reputations that can have negative consequences if not handled properly."[7] There are many examples of crises—natural disasters, fires, and chemical spills are all crises. CEO misconduct, financial impropriety, product defects, and social media blunders can also be crises for the organizations involved.

Crisis communicators help with the initial response, such as issuing a recall notice, and later work to help restore the organization's reputation that has been damaged by a crisis. Practitioners who specialize in crisis communication learn to expect the unexpected, as they can be called to a crisis at any time.

Community Relations

Community relations refers to the efforts made by an organization to build strong relationships with members of the immediate community. This may involve tactics such as communication materials, events, and meetings.

The University of Alberta, for example, has a community relations team. Their mandate is published on the university's website, as follows:

> The University of Alberta's strategic institutional plan, *For the Public Good*, articulates five goals: Excel, Build, Experience, Engage and Sustain. Community Relations focuses its work on the Engage goal. The goal as defined in *For the Public Good* is to engage communities across our campuses, city and region, province, nation and the world to create reciprocal, mutually beneficial learning experiences, research projects, partnerships and collaboration.
>
> Community Relations fosters institutional strategic connections with the communities it serves. Its goals are to build relationships and engage communities through two main areas of engagement: legislated processes in community consultation for campus planning and initiatives for community engagement and outreach.[8]

Crisis communication firms such as Navigator typically have a 24-hour hotline so that potential clients can get assistance right away.

Can you think of some examples where this might be necessary?

community consultation When an organization seeks input from community members who may be impacted by any decisions or actions taken by that organization.

government relations A specialized branch of public relations that helps organizations form better relationships with governments at all levels.

Community Consultation

The University of Alberta community relations mandate includes a reference to "community consultation." Community consultation means seeking input from community members who may be impacted by any decisions or actions taken by the organization.

In recent years, community consultation has been growing in importance, and there are many firms that specialize in this process.

In Canada, federal and provincial governments routinely consult with various communities, including Indigenous communities, on various initiatives. Consultation, however, does not always lead to agreement. The dispute between various Indigenous groups and the federal government around the expansion of the Trans Mountain pipeline in BC is centred around the concept of consultation. The Indigenous peoples who launched a court appeal against the pipeline claim that the Crown (the Canadian government) did not fulfil its constitutional duty to adequately consult with Indigenous groups whose territories and lives would be impacted by the pipeline.[9]

Event Management

While generally considered part of public relations practice, event management is also a separate discipline with its own education programs and professional association, the Canadian Society of Professional Event Planners.

Public relations practitioners should be able, however, to organize numerous special events including dinners, conferences, product launches, and community open houses. For large-scale events, it is not uncommon for public relations practitioners to work with professional event planners.

Government Relations

Government relations is another specialized branch of public relations. Government relations practitioners help an organization form better relationships

THE CANADIAN PRESS/Darryl Dyck

Chief Phil Lane Jr (centre) led the protest against the Trans Mountain pipeline expansion with other Indigenous elders and leaders.

Do you think a more extensive community consultation process could have led to greater support for the project?

with governments at all levels. A related practice is **public affairs**, which is generally a broader function that also deals with the public and special interest groups.

Crowdsourcing a Definition

The negative connotations and confusion over job titles have not been lost on those in the profession, and, in 2008, CPRS members Terry Flynn, Fran Gregory, and Jean Valin undertook a crowdsourcing project to arrive at an official definition for public relations in Canada. That definition, which is still in use today, is as follows:

> Public relations is the strategic management of relationships between an organization and its diverse publics, through the use of communication, to achieve mutual understanding, realize organizational goals, and serve the public interest.[10]

According to journalist and communications professor Ira Basen, the Public Relations Society of America (PRSA) rejected the CPRS definition because it included the phrase "serve the public interest," and in 2011 they set out to crowdsource their own definition.

public affairs A broader practice related to public relations that also deals with the public and special interest groups.

Courtesy of Social Signal

Social media skills are considered essential for many entry-level public relations jobs.

What does it really mean when someone claims to be a social media guru?

The PRSA crowdsourcing effort included consultation with 12 allied organizations, a blog with comments from readers, Twitter, and an online form for submitting possible definitions. *Oxford Dictionaries* defines the verb **crowdsource** as "obtain (information or input into a particular task or project) by enlisting the services of a number of people, either paid or unpaid, typically via the internet."[11] And that's exactly what PRSA did. By day 12 of the open submission period, the top 20 words submitted as part of suggested definitions for public relations were:

crowdsource To obtain information or input into a particular task or project by enlisting the services of a number of people, either paid or unpaid, typically via the Internet.

organization (mentioned in 388 submissions)
public (373)
communication (280)
relationship(s) (260)
stakeholders (172)
create (170)
mutual (158)
understand (153)
build (152)
audiences (147)

inform (144)
management (124)
brand (119)
company (116)
business (112)
people (100)
engages (94)
client (92)
awareness (88)
maintain (81)[12]

The task force then narrowed the field of definitions down to three finalists, opened a public comment period online, hosted a second "Definition of Public Relations Summit"

klenger/iStock

The CPRS definition of public relations includes the phrase "serve the public interest" while the PRSA definition does not.

Do you think "serve the public interest" belongs in a definition of public relations? Why or why not?

with partner organizations, revised the three definitions, and held a public vote to select the new definition. And the winner was . . . "Public relations is a strategic communication process that builds mutually beneficial relationships between organizations and their publics." You may have noticed that the crowdsourced and modernized definition of public relations isn't all that different from the classic definitions.

Principled Public Relations Management

Regardless of how you define it, good public relations requires excellent management. When an organization's communication is focused more on image and less on what the organization is actually doing, negative connotations like spin and damage control become unfortunately accurate descriptions.

The problem with communication strategies based on image and fluff, however, is that publics can see right through them. In sports and entertainment, the audiences may not mind. Sensationalism, snafus, public social media fights with other celebrities, and name changes are all part of what keep people interested in celebrities like Drake, Taylor Swift, Sean Combs, and Kim Kardashian.

But publics are ready to call you on it if you try to promote your organization in ways inconsistent with how your organization is managed. It is easier than ever for people to call out businesses for such inconsistencies. Greenwashing is a great example. Many organizations try to present themselves as eco-friendly to appeal to environmentally conscious publics but there are many consumer organizations ready to call them on the practice.

> Everyone's heard the expression "whitewashing"—it's defined as "a coordinated attempt to hide unpleasant facts, especially in a political context." "Greenwashing" is the same premise, but in an environmental context. It's greenwashing when a company or organization spends more time and money claiming to be "green" through advertising and marketing than actually implementing business practices that minimize environmental impact. It's whitewashing, but with a green brush.[13]

If your efforts at communication and promotion are not consistent with how your organization is managed, your organization will be seen far closer to the "bogus" end of the greenwashing index than the "authentic" end. Sites like the Greenwashing Index make it easy for people to collect and share their experiences. "If you've seen an ad promoting the environmental qualities of a product or company, post it here, rate it, then come back to see what other users say."[14]

Of course, publics have been discussing businesses and their authenticity since long before the Internet. Arthur Page, long-time vice-president of AT&T Inc., worked at the company from the 1920s through the thirties and forties and into the fifties. Page was one of the first public relations people to reach that level of management in an organization of that magnitude. He articulated and practised principles of public relations management that apply as well now as they did in the mid-twentieth century:

1. Tell the truth.
2. Prove it with action.
3. Listen to the customer.

spin Disingenuous strategic communication involving skewed interpretation or presentation of information.

greenwashing When an organization spends more resources claiming to be "green" through publicity, advertising, and marketing than actually implementing practices that minimize environmental impact.

authenticity The degree to which one communicates reliably, accurately, and true to his or her own character and the character of the organization that he or she represents.

4. Manage for tomorrow.
5. Conduct public relations as if the whole company depends on it.
6. Remain calm, patient, and good-humoured.
7. Realize the company's true character is expressed by its people.

Wisconsin Historical Society. WHS-55511

Arthur W. Page was an early proponent of authenticity and transparency in public relations.

Do Page's principles apply any more or less in the digital age?

> Even in cases that necessitate secrecy, tell the truth about what information your organization is protecting and why.

> Good public relations is based much more on what an organization does than on what it says.

Tell the Truth

It's one thing to not lie; it's another to proactively tell the truth. This principle can be equated with the idea of **transparency**.[15] Public relations researcher and ethicist Brad Rawlins has defined it as the opposite of secrecy:

> Transparency is the deliberate attempt to make available all legally reasonable information—whether positive or negative in nature—in a manner that is accurate, timely, balanced, and unequivocal, for the purpose of enhancing the reasoning ability of publics and holding organizations accountable for their actions, policies, and practices.[16]

Arthur Page realized that large organizations were particularly susceptible to public mistrust and suspicion when they overzealously protected secrecy. Governments, schools, churches, NGOs, and non-profits are all in danger of breeding fear, apprehension, dislike, and distrust when they shirk transparency. Of course, there are times when secrecy makes sense to publics, such as in times of national security crises or when businesses want to protect proprietary information to compete in markets, but, even in those cases, organizations can still "tell the truth" about what they are keeping secret and why.

Prove It with Action

You might call it the 90/10 rule. Page said that 90 per cent of good public relations should be determined by what an organization does, and about 10 per cent by what they say. Publicity is important, but only if it follows action. Swiss Chalet is always so good for so little. Disneyland is the happiest place on earth. Canadian Tire will let you give like Santa, save like Scrooge. KFC is finger lickin' good. Nike will help you just do it. These are all-powerful slogans for brands, but think about how much work goes into making the slogans resonate. The slogans are hollow if the organization isn't managed in such a way as to make the words ring true.

You won't see BP's "Beyond Petroleum" slogan on the list. In 2000, BP (formerly British Petroleum) introduced a new logo as part of a major re-branding campaign by its agency Ogilvy & Mather. The bright, new—and of course green—sunburst logo was a textbook example of branding. Literally. In Pavlik and McIntosh's *Converging Media* textbook, the authors defined branding as "the process of creating in the consumer's mind a clear identity for a particular company's product, logo, or trademark." To illustrate the concept in the second edition of that text, the logo was captioned "British Petroleum has successfully rebranded its company with a new logo and a public image as being environmentally friendly."[17]

But, according to contributors on the PR Watch website, "BP's investment in extractive oil operations dwarfed its investment in renewable energy."[18] Critics immediately began to question the campaign and there were accusations of greenwashing. Then, in the summer of

2010, when BP's Deepwater Horizon rig exploded, leading to one of the worst manmade environmental disasters in history, BP was hammered on social media. Online contests were introduced to see who could design the best logo mocking BP's green sunburst. A YouTube video portraying clumsy BP executives botching an attempt to clean up spilled coffee went viral, getting 10 times more views than BP's official YouTube channel headliner following the accident. More than 160,000 Twitter users followed a fake BP Twitter account spoofing the company.

Later, BP did make some commendable efforts as part of its continuing road to recovery. They used Twitter to send important information out as fast as possible when media inquiries were overwhelming their media relations staff. But, in terms of action, BP soon became seen as a classic case in how not to handle public relations. After interviewing experts, American journalist Elizabeth Shogren concluded that BP "failed to communicate the three key messages the public needed to hear: That BP was accountable for the disaster, was deeply concerned about the harm it caused and had a plan for what to do."[19] Not only were they not able to communicate well; they also weren't ready to prove it with action.

Listen to the Customer

Listening, or paying attention to and processing what others are communicating, is at the heart of **two-way communication**. For organizations with large publics, listening requires an investment in systematic research. It also requires management to be responsive to what the media and employees have to say. The press may pick up on public sentiment, and employees often have a very good sense of what people outside the organization think. In both technical terms and everyday language, listening is more than just hearing. While those managing an organization may hear what's being said about the organization in the news, at the water cooler, online, or out on the street, real listening means considering what the **feedback** means for the organization and what can be done about it. Page saw listening as an important part of public relations, and he saw the public relations person's role as one of keeping upper-level management and others inside an organization informed about public sentiment.

Counting headlines, Facebook likes, Twitter followers, phone calls, YouTube views, or keyword mentions gives some indication of what people are thinking and talking about, but good listening requires more careful and deliberate attention to what is being said and what that means for your organization and how it is managed. You can't manage a business on buzz alone.

Manage for Tomorrow

Be **proactive**. That's easy enough to say, but harder to do. After a crisis hits, it is much harder to engage in thoughtful dialogue with publics about what an organization can and should be doing. When public relations people are called in after a major screw-up to clean up the mess, their role is mostly **reactive**, limited to damage control, at best, or spin, at worst, unless they can report that the organization is taking real action to correct whatever problems have occurred. While even the very best-managed organizations are susceptible to surprise crises, some organizations simply miss opportunities to stave off disasters because they are not listening well to what is going on in their environment and considering the ethical implications. This kind of listening today requires traditional research as well as participation in and monitoring of online communities and forums.

Agencja Fotograficzna Caro/Alamy Stock Photo

BP's sunburst logo was designed to highlight the company's commitment to the environment.

What comes to your mind when you see the BP logo?

Winner of Greenpeace's Rebrand BP Competition. Designed by Laurent Hunziker

Following the BP oil spill, web users competed to design the best mock logo for the company.

Why do you think it was so easy to mock BP after the oil spill?

transparency
Deliberate attempt to
make available all legally
reasonable information
for the purpose of
enhancing the reasoning
ability of publics.

listening Deliberately
paying attention to and
processing what others
are communicating.
In public relations
and organizational
communication, this
means processing
feedback.

**two-way
communication** When
both parties send and
receive information
in an exchange, as
opposed to the one-
way dissemination of
information from an
organization to its publics.

feedback Information
returned from the
environment in response
to an organization's
action or communication
that can be used for
continuous adjustment
and improvement of the
organization.

proactive A
management style
that is anticipatory,
change-oriented, and
self-initiated to improve
the organization's
environment and its
future.

reactive A management
style that responds
mainly to problems as
they arise rather than
anticipating them and
averting them.

Page's proactive public relations—managing for tomorrow—means building goodwill, avoiding business practices that will lead to unfavourable business conditions, and anticipating how publics will respond to business decisions that will have negative consequences. This concept of proactive public relations is based on two big assumptions. First, public relations people have a role in managing the operations and policies of an organization. Second, public relations people are in a position to sense when major opportunities arise or when trouble is brewing.

Page acknowledged that the purpose of public relations isn't to try to answer every little complaint "because you can't run around and put salve on every sore that appears in the world." This is good news for those monitoring online product reviews. Rather, proactive public relations is tied to a broader strategy. University of Florida Professor Emeritus Robert Kendall defined proactive public relations as a "philosophy of public relations that takes the initiative in planning the nature of the relationships desired with publics and executes programs, campaigns, or activities designed to achieve the desired ends."[20] Strategic public relations is proactive.

Conduct Public Relations as if the Whole Company Depends on It

Page saw public relations as a **management function**, but he also realized that top managers were not the only ones responsible for public relations. In discussing leadership, he described how the role of a company president is "first to have the company intend to do the right thing by the public" and then to "get everyone in the company to do his part in carrying out the policy, effectively, reasonably and politely."

Employees have always been spokespeople for organizations, whether that was in their job titles or not. If we want to know what is going on with the big manufacturing plant in our community, we may read about it in the newspaper, but we also won't be afraid to ask our neighbours who work there. Airline flight attendants may be our windows into the workings of the larger airline. The mail carrier may be our source on the postal service. Public relations depends on all of these people, and all of these people depend on public relations.

No one wants to be part of an organization that is dreaded in his or her own neighbourhood. We want to go to schools, volunteer for non-profits, and join civic and religious organizations that are respected in our communities. We want to work for organizations that are managed well and proactive in public relations, and of course we want them to stay solvent and avoid crises too. To the degree that public relations supports these goals, we all depend on it even if we aren't officially working in public relations.

Remain Calm, Patient, and Good-Humoured

We love this one. Page reminds us not to forget the importance of being good-natured, even in dealing with stressful day-to-day situations and larger organizational crises. Publics resent organizations with rude people representing them and, all else being equal, are more forgiving of those that are pleasant. It's human nature.

Throughout the ages, good public relations people have known how important it is to maintain good relationships with reporters. "Never pick a fight with someone who buys ink by the barrel," the old saying goes. The same idea applies in this era of digital publishing and consumer-generated media. Review sites like Yelp and TripAdvisor and reviews on popular online shopping sites like Amazon.ca, Walmart.ca, and Costco.ca give all sorts of consumers a voice. No barrels of ink required.

In fact, the human element is even more important as many publics will to turn to peers online as sources of information about large organizations (and products) as opposed to major media institutions. A recent study by PWC found that nearly 40 per cent of Canadian consumers say that reading product reviews, peer reviews, or feedback on social media has an influence on their shopping behaviour—and that number jumps to 55 per cent when you look at the 18–24 age bracket.[21]

Academic research bears out Page's principle as well. In surveys and experiments, my colleagues and I have found that a variable called conversational voice is important in maintaining good relationships with publics online. This "voice" is gauged by asking people how much they agree with statements about how an organization communicates. Organizations with communicators who are perceived as making communication enjoyable, using a sense of humour, admitting mistakes, and even providing links to competitors rank higher on the conversational voice scale. And that conversational voice correlates with public relations outcomes such as satisfaction and commitment, as well as trust.[22]

PCWorld's Robert Strohmeyer offered sound advice in writing about how to deal with online critics:

> I like to think that most people are generally sensible, but the internet has an uncanny knack for transforming rational adults into raving, infantile morons. Yelp, doubly so. Once you accept this basic tenet, you can begin to view your online critics as the reasonable minds they probably are, rather than the juvenile half-wits they appear to be.[23]

An Ottawa student found herself on the receiving end of a letter from a lawyer demanding that she stop posting negative reviews and take down the existing reviews of CLV Group, an organization that managed an apartment she once lived in. The student had no idea how the company found her (she posted anonymously) and, concerned, took the reviews down fearing further legal action.[24]

Despite CLV's success in getting the student to take down the reviews (it did generate some negative press for them in the process), Strohmeyer maintains that flaming critics or threatening to sue them is the wrong approach. Instead, he recommends working within the Yelp toolset by signing up for a business account, which lets you claim your business's Yelp page. Once you've done that you can both encourage positive reviews (but don't insist on them!) and respond constructively and politely to critics, the same way you would if they were at your service counter or reception desk. Moreover, says Strohmeyer, "Have fun with it."

Realize the Company's True Character Is Expressed by Its People

Effective integrated communication means that publics form their beliefs and attitudes about organizations based on all their points of contact with an organization. Organizations are made up of people, and these people themselves are the most powerful points of contact that others have with the organization. "I am quite certain that the general body of our employees can be trained to represent the company effectively even on complicated

KEEP CALM AND CARRY ON

Shawshots/Alamy Stock Photo

The popular "Keep Calm" meme was derived from a World War II public safety poster in Great Britain and reached its peak of popularity in 2013.

What do you think drove the popularity of this meme? What memes are popular today and what drives their popularity?

To effectively listen in public relations, participate in and monitor online communities, in addition to using traditional research.

Sometimes the best way to handle tense situations is to stay engaged with the community and keep a sense of humour.

Would you be inclined to dine at this restaurant?

management function Part of an organization involved in its overall leadership and decision-making, guiding how the organization operates in its environment, rather than merely following the instructions of others.

conversational voice An authentic, engaging, and natural style of communication that publics perceive to be personable.

flaming Hostile communication among Internet users.

subjects," said Page.[25] As Harold Burson, founding partner of Burson-Marsteller, put it, "The thinking goes like this: public relations should permeate every corporate transaction—literally involving almost every employee—from the receptionist to the person at the check-out counter, those who sell the product and those who service it." In other words, "Public relations is now everybody's job."[26]

Social media have only amplified this idea. Managing relationships between organizations and publics means managing organizations in ways that encourage constructive relationships to arise from the countless interpersonal interactions online and offline between all the people who represent the organization and all those with whom they communicate in that role. While the idea of managing for effective **integrated communication** that is consistent across organizational functions goes way back before the Internet, social media have changed the game with new management challenges in an era in which people "like me" are becoming more influential, while mainstream media and large institutional sources are struggling for credibility. Particularly in online contexts, this requires managing **distributed public relations**, in which public relations responsibilities are shared among a broad cross-section of an organization's members or employees. People look for authenticity in online communication. They still read and view news stories told by journalists about organizations, but, more and more, publics communicate directly with all sorts of people from organizations online. When that happens, there is an opportunity for the organization to communicate its true character.

Ethics

Page's principles of public relations make sense on a practical level. It is not hard to understand why he had such a long and successful career. But these principles also show the importance of moral philosophy and ethics in public relations. Truth, action, empathy, and character give meaning to the day-to-day work of public relations. Put bluntly, damage control and spin are lame. Who wants to do that for a living? There are many good reasons to put ethics at the centre of your thinking about good public relations.

Reasons for Studying Ethics

You'll feel better about yourself. **Ethics** are moral principles that govern behaviour and are deeply personal. You'll wake up in a much better mood every morning if you know you are going to work for an organization with values congruent to your own. Strategic public relations means that the public relations tactics you perform are derived from solid goals and objectives, and that those goals and objectives serve the broader mission of your organization. This doesn't mean that you have to agree with every single action the organization takes. In fact, the very nature of ethics is dealing with competing values and gray areas. You may agree wholeheartedly with the mission of a non-profit that employs you, but that doesn't mean you agree with the way they go about pursuing that mission. Sometimes you have to take a stand in your own organization to make your case when you disagree, and you should feel empowered to do so. The important thing is that you can practise public relations in a way that feels right to you and in a place where you don't feel like you are selling your soul to get the job done every day. In a field like public relations your sanity may well depend on how you and those you work with handle ethical dilemmas and gray areas.

Of course, ethics aren't all about gut feelings. Good people make bad decisions all the time. Resolving ethical problems is a matter of the heart, but it is also an intellectual activity. As public relations practitioners move up in their careers, and as they earn more and more respect in management, the importance of their ethical decision-making becomes more important to the organizations they represent, and, ideally, they get better at ethics. This is why it is essential to study principles and systems for ethical reasoning now and to continue to brush up on your ethics throughout your career, which leads to the next point.

You'll be better at your job. Many ethical dilemmas arise out of interactions with reporters, clients, colleagues, and members of various publics. Solid relationships with reporters are built on trust, consistency, and mutual understanding of professional roles and responsibilities. Retaining clients and attracting new ones requires a reputation for fairness and integrity. Loyalty and expertise are among the keys to positive and productive relationships with colleagues. And transparency is essential in dealing with online communities when strategic communication is the essence of your job. Developing a solid ethical framework that you can explain to others will help you in all of those relationships, and those relationships are the stuff of which successful, fulfilling careers are made.

You'll be more important at work. As Shannon Bowen puts it, communication professionals must pay attention to ethics before they desperately need to. "Once a crisis of conflicting ethics or high media interest befalls the organization it is too late to begin searching for ethical guidance."[27] Bowen is a professor, ethicist, and member of the Arthur W. Page Society. In her research she has found that spotting ethical dilemmas is key to resolving issues before they become crises. Beyond just identifying ethical dilemmas, public relations people must be able to discuss the issues with members of their organization's dominant coalition. **Dominant coalition** is a term used to describe the group of people with the greatest influence in how an organization operates, including CEOs, presidents, board members, top managers, vice-presidents, and so on. The dominant coalition may or may not include public relations executives. However, these are the people who steer the organization at the highest levels, and a public relations person who is well versed in rational, defensible, ethical decision-making will be in the best position to inform this group in handling public relations issues before they become crises.

Competing Duties

Working in public relations means serving many masters. In their book *Public Relations Ethics*, Philip Seib and Kathy Fitzpatrick highlight the source of many ethical dilemmas as individual practitioners face them.[28] That source is competing duties. If you work in public relations, you have a duty to

1. yourself;
2. your client;

> Respond constructively and politely to critics online, the same way you would if they were at your service counter or reception desk.

integrated communication Communicating with publics consistently across organizational functions including public relations, advertising, marketing, and customer service.

distributed public relations Intentional practice of sharing public relations responsibilities among a broad cross-section of an organization's members or employees, particularly in an online context.

ethics Moral principles that govern a person's or group's behaviour.

dominant coalition Group of people with the greatest influence in determining how an organization operates and pursues its mission.

3. your employer;
4. the profession;
5. the media; and
6. society.

There are likely vegetarians who work in public relations agencies that represent steakhouses. There are almost certainly people who are deeply annoyed by cable news channels but still work hard to accommodate their TV producers prior to interviews. There's even a certain textbook author and professor who criticizes Walt Disney Co.'s massive media empire and then happily takes his kids to Walt Disney World. None of these folks are necessarily sellouts. The vegetarian may welcome the restaurant to his community to boost the economy while providing jobs, not to mention the business for his own agency, which supports his own financial stability. The public relations practitioner arranging the cable news interview may weigh the importance of free speech and vigorous debate as much more important in society than her opinion of the particular station's host and format. And your textbook author doesn't think a personal boycott of a major media conglomerate is a requisite for educating others about issues of media consolidation in society. On the other hand, there are times when public relations practitioners must say no to reporters. There are times when agencies should decline clients. There are times when a potential paycheque is not worth the dissonance it creates.

A Guide for Decision-Making

Addressing these apparent dilemmas ethically requires careful thinking. Fitzpatrick offers the following guide for public relations practitioners:

1. Define the specific ethical issue/conflict.
2. Identify internal/external factors (e.g., legal, political, social, economic) that may influence the decision.
3. Identify key values.
4. Identify the parties who will be affected by the decision, and define the public relations professional's obligation to each.
5. Select ethical principles to guide the decision-making process.
6. Make a decision and justify it.

In many ways, social media have made ethical communication easier. We get to speak in our own voices in forums in which direct, informal communication is valued. Social media give us means for discussing and resolving our professional issues with easy access to others' opinions and views. We get to experiment in mixing our personal and professional identities. This can lead to a

Clay Bennett / © 1998 The Christian Science Monitor (www.CSMonitor.com). Reprinted with permission.

Learning (and practising) ethics has value well beyond the classroom.

What do you see as the major benefits of studying ethics before working in public relations?

heightened sense of awareness of our consistencies and inconsistencies. At the same time, however, this breaking down of clear divisions between our personal and professional communication raises new dilemmas, and digital media technologies introduce new opportunities for deception.

Codes of Ethics

Most organizations of communication professionals offer codes of ethics to articulate their values and to guide their members. While it is debatable whether public relations is technically a profession, codes of ethics certainly encourage professionalism. One major factor keeping public relations from being recognized as a profession like law or medicine or architecture is licensing. You do not need a license to practise public relations. Anyone can call himself or herself a PR person. This is unfortunate, but the alternative, according to those opposed to professional licensing, would be a violation of our right to free speech. Imagine if you were not allowed to speak on matters of public concern in an official capacity because you did not have a license.

Criticisms of Codes

Lack of enforceability is one criticism of codes of ethics. If a member acts within the law but outside of the code of ethics, revocation of the person's membership is the most the association can do in response. The good news is that it doesn't happen very often (in fact, there is no record of it ever happening at CPRS).

However, this leads to a second criticism of codes of ethics, which is that they simply are not effective or even necessary as means of policing behaviour. Most members of these professional organizations practise public relations with good intention, and those few who do run blatantly afoul of the codes can probably take advantage of the subjective nature of interpretation and the relatively weak mechanisms of enforcement to evade any institutional consequences.

A third criticism is that codes of ethics can be vague and lack internal consistency. By definition, ethical dilemmas involve competing choices. Loyalty may run up against independence. Confidentiality may come at the expense of transparency. When codes of ethics call for all of the above, the member may be put in a pickle.

Advantages of Codes

First, codes of ethics help communicate the professional standards of an association's membership to both internal and external parties. Some of you reading this book may not pursue public relations as a career. You may go into advertising, marketing, or event management. Or you may become a dentist, deep-sea diver, or police officer. But if you read the codes of ethics or discuss them with anyone who knows them, you will come away with a much better idea of what members of these organizations do and what values they embrace. For better or worse, everyone is exposed to public relations in democracies like ours, and the more people understand what makes for good, ethical public relations the better.

"Tweeting under False Circumstances"

Todd Defren runs SHIFT Communications, a public relations firm specializing in digital and social media that has served clients including McDonald's, H&R Block, and Tyson Foods. Defren is also a highly influential blogger with a large number of readers of his "PR Squared" blog.[29] Defren has highlighted some new dilemmas unique to social media.

Let's use Fitzpatrick's process to walk us through one of Defren's cases, "Tweeting under False Circumstances."

Define the Specific Ethical Issue/Conflict

A client asked Defren and his associates to tweet for him at a trade show from the client's Twitter account. The client was adept at Twitter and prominent in his field. He had a significant number of loyal followers on his account who were used to hearing directly from him via that channel.

> He posts regularly, sometimes several times a day. He "gets" Twitter; he finds value in the dialogue and his followers appreciate that a well-placed exec from a Big Company is engaged with them online.

> Now, a big industry tradeshow is coming up. He'll be very active there, as a speaker and organizer. The executive wants his tweetstream to reflect his activity at the show, and to highlight other happenings at the conference, as well. He's very concerned that he won't be able to support this many to-do's.[30]

Identify Internal/External Factors

A big part of the appeal of Twitter as a form of social media is that followers have access to interesting and influential people with whom they otherwise would not be able to interact. The culture of social media is an external factor that must be considered, and the executive's commitment to authenticity in this environment is an internal factor.

> You can see how this request comes from a "good place." This executive's commitment to online engagement is so fierce, he doesn't want to abandon it even for an important event. He knows his followers would understand his absences, but he thinks there is going to be real value in tracking what's happening at the conference, and in responding to folks online throughout.[31]

Identify Key Values

Loyalty, transparency, expertise, and independence are among the key values in this case. Not only does Defren have to weigh his loyalty to the client, but he also must consider the loyalty and trust that the client's Twitter followers may have in the executive.

This loyalty brings transparency to the forefront because if those followers expect the executive to write all his own tweets and if he is planning on changing that without telling them, they may be deceived. The behind-the-scenes change would mean a lack of transparency. The client means no harm—his request comes from a good place, as Defren said—but part of what he is paying Defren and his firm for is expertise in knowing the lay of the land in social media and counselling on exactly this type of situation.

> While it's true he is asking us to misrepresent ourselves, he feels that it would still be authentic because of his trust in us.

Identify the Parties Who Will Be Affected

This is where those competing duties to various people come into play. This case appears to be a doozy because Defren has a duty to pretty much everyone in Seib and Fitzpatrick's list: himself, his client, the profession, the media, and society.

- **Duty to self**: As is pretty clear from his blog, which includes detailed analysis of ethical dilemmas like this one, Defren invests his own intellect, hard work, and time in his strategic communication practice. If he botches this, it could damage his reputation and lead to personal disappointment. There also could be financial consequences for him personally.
- **Duty to client**: Defren's firm has been hired to do a job. Yes, a big part of that job is to communicate for the client, but he also owes the client solid independent counselling based on his expertise and knowledge of social media.
- **Duty to the profession**: Not only will botching this job with poor ethical decision-making discredit Defren, but it also may reflect poorly on the whole field of public relations. Unfortunately, examples of misrepresentation and deception in public relations are not hard to find, as these cases tend to get called out and told and retold online. Mentioning public relations and ethics together in the same sentence will lead to rolled eyes and snarky responses in many circles. The only way to combat this is with performance.
- **Duty to the media**: The media in this case are mostly social media, Twitter users in particular. Just as relationships with reporters, editors, and producers are critical to effective communication via magazines, newspapers, radio, and television, relationships with Twitter users are the essence of effective tweeting. If Defren disappoints his client's followers, he has not only undermined his client's credibility and effectiveness, but he will also have taken something away from the utility of the medium as a whole.
- **Duty to society**: Social media have the potential to facilitate meaningful democratic dialogue and healthy economies by affording publics the opportunity to engage organizations in the honest exchange of ideas, currency,

Continued

products, services, and social capital. Social media also can provide a haven for misinformation, deceit, mistrust, cynicism, and generally shattered expectations. I'm guessing Defren wants to contribute to the former and not the latter.

Select Ethical Principles to Guide the Decision-Making Process

At this stage of the analysis it becomes fairly clear that openness, honesty, trust, transparency, and authenticity are at stake. **Deontological ethics** are systems of decision-making that focus on duties or rules. To the degree that the principle of duty is central to the decision on how to act in this case based on moral obligations to each of the parties, you could say that it guides our thinking. Of course, other principles apply too, and we will look at some of those in cases in the chapters that follow.

deontological ethics System of decision-making that focuses on the moral principles of duty and rules.

Make a Decision and Justify It

So what did Defren do?

> So we suggested a compromise. . . . Yes, we would tweet from his account, but with the following conditions:
>
> Prior to the event, he must tweet, "During the show some of my tweeting will be supplemented by our extended team."
>
> A reminder to that effect would go out, regularly, throughout the conference, i.e., every 10th tweet would remind followers that someone besides the executive might be "at the controls" of his Twitter account.
>
> When character spaces permitted, we'd add a #team hashtag to denote that the tweet was not published by the exec—but, honestly, this attribution fell away more often than not; we largely relied on the "every 10th tweet" approach to cover our ethical backsides.

In the end, the solution seemed easy, but this was largely due to Defren's expertise and careful ethical thinking. He was able to serve the client well with a compromise that didn't require compromising his ethics or causing harm to his business, his profession, or society. Defren and his client experienced no "pushback" from the tweets. Interestingly, Defren still had some ethical concerns and questions (about whether some people would still be duped despite the every-tenth-tweet approach), and was courageous enough to post the whole case as well as his follow-up concerns in a very public blog entry inviting feedback. When I checked last the vast majority of the comments were constructive and supportive. The very act of airing his case and concerns for open discussion honours the spirit of social media while also reinforcing Defren's commitment to ethical practice—the word *practice* meaning that we are all always working to improve in this area.

Voices from the Field

Eileen Tobey

Image appears courtesy of Eileen Tobey

Eileen Tobey is a successful public relations entrepreneur and communicator with more than 30 years of experience as a public relations leader and agency CEO. Her industry sector experience ranges from health care to not-for-profit, industry start-ups to packaged goods and beverage manufacturers as well as all three levels of government. She is a multiple-award winner of national and international PR awards, an Accredited Public Relations (APR) practitioner, Fellow (FCPRS), and Life Member (LM) of the Canadian Public Relations Society (CPRS). Eileen is also the first CPRS senior fellow in residence at Humber College School of Media Studies & Information Technology in Toronto where she mentors the next generation of public relations practitioners. Eileen has a keen interest in public relations ethics and their pragmatic application to modern public relations practice.

In general, do you think public relations is moving towards higher ethical standards?
Yes, I believe public relations is moving towards higher ethical standards especially in Canada where the Canadian Public Relations Society (CPRS) has been very instrumental in defining itself as an association whose members are recognized as leaders for ethical and strategic public relations. Two important research studies conducted by the CPRS over the past two years conclude that PR practitioners are seeking champions in ethical public relations and wanting specific professional development to help them navigate ethical issues and trends faced by the profession here in Canada and also around the world. In 2018, the Global Alliance (a confederation of the world's major PR and communication management associations and institutions) prepared global principles of ethical practice in public relations and communication management. The 2018 report was developed following a global review of codes of conduct and codes of ethics (including those from CPRS) and resulted in a list of 16 principles that are deemed to be both universal and fundamental, including guiding principles and principles of professional practice.

What kinds of ethical issues are entry-level public relations people likely to face?
If you consider the values and ethics listed in the Canadian Public Relations Society Code of Professional Standards—honesty, truth, accuracy, and integrity—then entry-level public relations practitioners will definitely face a variety of ethical issues that challenge those values depending on the stakeholders or publics they work with. Being asked to prepare misleading or untruthful content for a product or service, taking credit for work that isn't yours, or tracking and identifying a journalist's inaccurate and "fake" news story are a few of the many ethical issues they may encounter.

What kinds of new ethical dilemmas have come up with the growth of social media?
With the barrage of content appearing every minute on several social media channels, it is sometimes challenging to identify or critically analyze what's real and what isn't. Add to the fact that artificial intelligence (AI) and certain algorithms can detect your reading, posting, or sharing patterns means that inaccurate or demonstrably misleading material can be shared with millions in an instant.

Learning good critical thinking skills and analysis are key to addressing these issues and ethical dilemmas.

In what ways have new media contexts reinforced or challenged classic principles?
The speed at which information is shared challenges us but shouldn't cause the public relations professional to

Continued

waver, especially if they are familiar with the core values and principles of ethics listed by public relations organizations like the CPRS and the Global Alliance. Ethical behaviour in public relations contains overarching "classic" guiding principles such as working in the public interest, obeying laws and local customs, freedom of the media, etc., together with professional conduct, honesty and accuracy, trust, and integrity when dealing with publics and stakeholders.

How much can ethics be taught and learned in public relations, and how much does it just depend on the person's individual values?
Using case studies focused on real-life business and professional ethical issues is imperative when teaching public relations students about ethics in business.

Through case-based learning, students can review, discuss, and determine appropriate approaches to certain ethical behaviour in public relations. Students of public relations should learn that as professionals they have the potential to influence and inform publics that can help shape the success of a product, service, company, or government policy.

What is the most important guide that a public relations practitioner might use in trying to make ethical decisions?
The CPRS Code of Professional Standards offers practical guidance for public relations practitioners when tasked with making an ethical business decision during their public relations career. The Global Alliance also shares broad guidelines.

Accredited in Public Relations (APR) Credential awarded by CPRS and other professional communication organizations around the world to those who have demonstrated competency in the knowledge, skills, and abilities required to practise public relations effectively.

Communication Management Professional (CMP) Credential awarded by IABC to recognize communicators at the generalist/specialist level.

Strategic Communication Management Professional (SCMP) Credential awarded by IABC to recognize senior communicators who have reached an accepted standard of knowledge and proficiency in their chosen field.

Second, codes offer carefully articulated and professionally agreed-upon guidelines for decision-making and action. For example, the CPRS Code of Professional Standards contains nine clauses that clearly outline behavioural expectations for members.

Third, there are practical and reputational advantages to knowing and working with established codes of ethics. Professional communication associations such as the CPRS and the International Association of Business Communicators (IABC) offer voluntary accreditation, which allows practitioners to distinguish themselves among others in the field with a professional designation. CPRS grants the designation of **Accredited in Public Relations (APR)**, and the professional credentials for IABC are the **Communication Management Professional (CMP)**, designed for the generalist/specialist level, and **Strategic Communication Management Professional (SCMP)**, designed for highly skilled business communicators. You may also see practitioners using **Accredited Business Communicator (ABC)**, which was the IABC accreditation used in the past. Criteria for all these designations include demonstrated professional experience and evidence of knowledge, skills, and abilities, including ethics.

Professional Associations

In Canada, the two largest associations for professional communicators are the Canadian Public Relations Society (CPRS) and the International Association of Business Communicators (IABC).

The national organization of CPRS consists of a federation of member societies located across Canada. Each member society has its own local constitution and runs a program of professional development events, seminars, and networking opportunities for members. The local CPRS societies include:

- Vancouver
- Vancouver Island
- Prince George
- Calgary
- Edmonton
- Regina
- Manitoba
- Hamilton

- Toronto
- Ottawa/Gatineau
- La Société québécoise des professionnels en relations publiques
- New Brunswick
- Northern Lights
- Nova Scotia
- Newfoundland and Labrador

The IABC is an international association that has 14 chapters in Canada. Headquartered in San Francisco, 40 per cent of the IABC's members are from Canada. Like CPRS, the IABC also has a code of ethics for professionals. Both the CPRS Code of Professional Standards and the IABC Code of Ethics are included as appendices in this book.

For comparison, the International Public Relations Association (IPRA) Code of Conduct is included (see Appendix C). This code, adopted in 2011, represents a consolidation of three prior international codes (the 1961 Code of Venice, the 1965 Code of Athens, and the 2007 Code of Brussels). CPRS is affiliated with the IPRA, and you'll probably notice some consistencies between the CPRS code and the IPRA code, but it is also interesting to note the IPRA focus on human rights and dignity. The IPRA code also includes some language specific to online media and issues of trust, credibility, and privacy.

Regardless of whether you call it a field, a practice, or a profession, public relations can be defined best by both words and actions. While there is no denying the existence of poor public relations and shady practice, professional organizations stand to help bring our body of knowledge together with ethical and effective practice for the benefit of students, practitioners, and society.

Review and discuss organizations' codes of ethics to better understand the values that members embrace.

Accredited Business Communicator (ABC) An IABC credential used to recognize accredited communicators until 2013; it has now been replaced by the above credentials.

In Case You Missed It

If you tell people you're studying public relations, they may not know what you mean. Here are a few tips from the chapter to help you think about what public relations people do, just in case anyone asks.

- To define *public relations*, consider organizations, publics, and the relations between them.
- Even in cases that necessitate secrecy, tell the truth about what information your organization is protecting and why.

- Good public relations is based much more on what an organization does than on what it says.
- To effectively listen in public relations, participate in and monitor online communities in addition to using traditional research.
- Respond constructively and politely to critics online, the same way you would if they were at your service counter or reception desk.
- Review and discuss organizations' codes of ethics to better understand the values that members embrace.

ICYMI

Summary

1.1 Define *public relations* in terms of organizations, publics, and the relationships between them.

According to the CPRS definition, "Public relations is the strategic management of relationships between an organization and its diverse publics, through the use of communication, to achieve mutual understanding, realize organizational goals, and serve the public interest."

1.2 Explain how public relations can serve as a management function.

When public relations is practised as a management function, practitioners proactively communicate with an organization's publics, carefully consider what feedback means for the organization, develop strategy, and work with the organization's leadership to implement and evaluate both actions and communication.

1.3 Recognize key principles and values for ethical conduct in public relations.

Arthur Page's principles for public relations management (e.g., tell the truth; prove it with action) are as relevant today as they were in his time. Codes of ethics also articulate common values that have been vetted by professionals. Classic ethical principles and frameworks, such as duty, can be applied in public relations just as they are in other areas of life.

1.4 Understand the importance of ethics in public relations.

Ethical public relations practitioners can work with a cleaner conscience, but they also can work with a clearer sense of how to handle difficult situations with reporters, clients, colleagues, and various publics. In turn, ethical public relations practitioners are more valuable to the organizations that depend on them. Value to organizations results in greater job opportunities.

1.5 Apply systematic ethical decision-making for public relations.

Step-by-step guides such as Fitzpatrick's "Ethical Decision-Making Guide," cases like Defren's client tweeting example, and codes of ethics all offer good guidance for practising ethical decision-making offline and online.

1.6 Identify international professional associations and become familiar with codes of ethics.

CPRS and IABC are two major professional organizations offering codes of ethics, but they are not the only ones. See online resources for many more.

Discussion Questions

1. Describe the job of one public relations person you've seen in media (real or fictional). How does that job description compare to the formal definition of public relations presented in this chapter?
2. Name an organization that you have worked for or had direct experience with that does some form of public relations. Would you say that public relations is part of that organization's management function? Why or why not?
3. What would Arthur Page like most about Facebook?
4. Some people describe public relations as the conscience of an organization. Do you think that is a good way to define public relations? Why or why not?
5. Search online for another communication-related code of ethics such as one for journalism, filmmaking, blogging, or marketing. How are the values expressed in that code different from the values expressed in the CPRS code?

Further Readings and Online Resources

The Elevation of Public Relations

https://www.cprs.ca/getattachment/About/Who-We-Are/The-Future-of-CPRS/CPRS-
    Elevation_of_Public_Relations.pdf.aspx?lang=en-CA

In "Voices from the Field," Eileen Tobey references a document produced by CPRS called "The Elevation of Public Relations." This paper provides an overview of trends affecting public relations in Canada today and suggests some areas of opportunity for the future. The paper, authored by senior public relations practitioner Dan Tisch, is based on interviews with a number of industry notables and is intended to spark debate and discussion.

Code of Ethics, Global Alliance for Public Relations and Communications Management

https://www.globalalliancepr.org/code-of-ethics/

The Global Alliance for Public Relations and Communications Management (GA) is a confederation of the world's largest public relations associations and institutions, including CPRS. Representing 160,000 practitioners and academics around the world, the Global Alliance states their mission is to "unify the public relations profession, raise professional standards all over the world, share knowledge for the benefit of its members and be the global voice for public relations in the public interest." The GA recently created a set of 16 ethical principles designed to be universally applicable.

In reading these principles, do you see any that would be difficult to uphold in Canada? Are there countries in the world where you think these might be more challenging?

Ethical Decision-Making Guide

https://www.prsa.org/wp-content/uploads/2016/10/decisionguide.pdf

We all know we should be ethical, but how do we know when we are—or aren't— being ethical? The PRSA offers this guide for members to help them think through whether a decision or action is ethical.

Peer-Reviewed Academic Journal Articles

Bowen, S.A. (2008). A state of neglect: Public relations as "corporate conscience" or ethics counsel. *Journal of Public Relations Research, 20(3), 271–96.*

Peer-reviewed academic journals (also known as scholarly journals) contain articles written by experts in a particular field that are reviewed by other experts before being published to ensure their quality and accuracy. In the past, journals were printed like magazines. Today, almost all are available online and many are available only online.

If you're reading this textbook as part of a college or university public relations program, chances are your school's library offers you access to any number of public relations journals such as *Public Relations Review, Journal of Public Relations Research,* or *Journal of Communication Management.* In many cases, you will be able to access the articles in these journals online through your school's library website.

Each chapter of this book suggests one academic article to read for further insight, but why stop at one? There are dozens, and in some cases, hundreds, of interesting academic articles you can read to deepen your knowledge.

This article examines the idea that public relations practitioners are not only responsible for their own ethics but also have a role to play in ensuring that the entire organization is ethical by acting as an "ethics counselor."

Key Terms

Accredited Business
  Communicator (ABC)   24
Accredited in Public Relations
  (APR)   24
Authenticity   11
Communication Management
  Professional (CMP)   24
Community consultation   8
Community relations   7
Conversational voice   15
Crisis communication   7
Crowdsource   10
Deontological ethics   22
Distributed public relations   16

Dominant coalition   17
Ethics   16
Feedback   13
Flaming   16
General public   3
Government relations   8
Greenwashing   11
Integrated communication   16
Issues management   7
Listening   13
Management function   14
Non-governmental
  organization (NGO)   3
Organization   3

Proactive   13
Public affairs   9
Public relations   4
Publics   3
Reactive   13
Spin   11
Strategic Communication
  Management Professional
  (SCMP)   24
Transparency   12
Two-way communication   13

2

Public Relations Models through the Ages

It took much more than a stroke of luck for tobacco companies to convince women to smoke in the 1930s. Were the tactics they used ethical?

Key learning outcomes

2.1 Analyze public relations models on one-way/two-way and asymmetrical/symmetrical dimensions.

2.2 Demonstrate knowledge of key figures in public relations history.

2.3 Integrate knowledge of social history with knowledge of public relations.

2.4 Identify common motivations for strategic communication in history.

2.5 Apply knowledge of history to analyze modern public relations practices.

2.6 Distinguish public relations from journalism.

2.7 Discuss the ethics of transparency, objectivity, and advocacy.

▲ Lenscap/Alamy Stock Photo

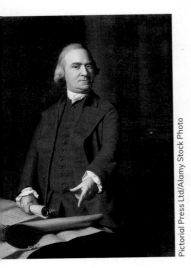

Pictorial Press Ltd/Alamy Stock Photo

In many public relations books, the Boston Tea Party is identified as one of North America's first publicity stunts. American colonist and founding father Samuel Adams is credited with creating this and other propaganda to oppose the British monarchy. Through his writings, he inspired the tax protest that came to be known as the Boston Tea Party. After that, Adams continued to promote the concept of independence from Great Britain.

Can you think of any recent publicity stunts that have caused a government (municipal, provincial, or federal) to rethink their plans?

In the opening pages of *Managing Public Relations*, right before defining public relations as the management of communication between an organization and its publics, Grunig and Hunt reflected on the problems of the times (early 1980s). They described public relations as a "young profession" with "roots in press agentry and propaganda, activities that society generally holds in low esteem."[1] They then charted a historical progression of public relations to frame the maturation of the profession by outlining four models of public relations in history:

1. Press agentry/publicity
2. Public information
3. Two-way asymmetrical
4. Two-way symmetrical

While the formal treatment of public relations as a field of study and practice may have been a twentieth-century development, historians have traced elements of public relations back through recorded history. Modern communication historians make the case that public relations activities are as old as religion, education, business, and politics.

Public Relations Models in History

Generations of public relations students have learned about the field's development through the lens of Grunig and Hunt's four models of public relations. However, these models also have been criticized for oversimplifying public relations and its history. What public relations people do doesn't fit neatly into four boxes, some say. This is exactly why Grunig and Hunt used the term *models*:

> We've chosen the term "models" to describe the four types of public relations that we believe have evolved through history, in order to emphasize that they are abstractions. In scientific usage, a model is a representation of reality . . . . If we construct models of public relations behavior by observing the most important components of that behavior, then we can make some sense out of the many diverse communication activities we call public relations.[2]

In the first two models, press agentry/publicity and public information, the communication is primarily one-way. In the second two models, two-way asymmetrical and two-way symmetrical, the communication is two-way (Table 2.1).

Press Agentry/Publicity

Born in Madagascar in 1674, Joice Heth arrived in America in her youth and was a slave to one Augustine Washington, father of George Washington. Heth was the first one to put clothes on the future father of America, and she basically raised the boy. In 1836, Heth was 161 years old and retained astonishingly good health, singing hymns, laughing heartily, and telling stories of the boy Washington. . . . Or so potential patrons were told in the billing of an attraction that began the press agentry career of showman extraordinaire P.T. Barnum.[3]

That not everyone bought the story about Joice Heth did not bother Barnum. On the contrary, he relished the attention that controversy brought. Can you think of any contemporary celebrities or politicians that seems to revel in controversy?

At the outset of my career, I saw that everything depended on getting the people to think, and talk, and become curious and excited over and about the "rare spectacle." Accordingly, posters, transparencies, advertisements, newspaper paragraphs—all calculated to extort attention—were employed, regardless of expense. My exhibition rooms in New York, Boston, Philadelphia, Albany, and in other large and small cities, were continually thronged and much money was made.[4]

Barnum will forever be associated with the **press agentry/publicity model**. Propaganda, attention getting, and less-than-accurate information (if not downright lies) are hallmarks of the press agentry model, which is as alive in this millennium as it was then.

In December 2015, KFC invaded an annual TV awards show in Hong Kong (the TVB awards—the equivalent to the Junos in Canada) by delivering boxes of fried chicken wings to the elegantly dressed celebrities in attendance. Brandchannel's Abe Sauer described the stunt as garish: "Hong Kong's TV royalty

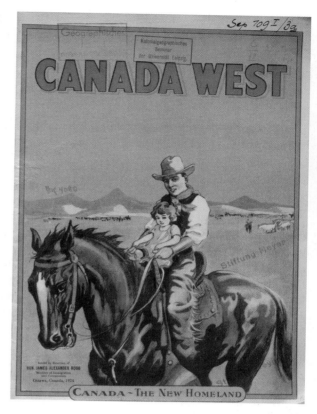

Posters were a key part of nineteenth-century publicity tactics. This one, promoting British immigration to western Canada, shows father and child riding a horse in the idyllic countryside.

Are there any ethical issues associated with this tactic?

press agentry/publicity model Model of public relations in which communication is mostly one-way, sometimes initiated by an organization with little concern for accuracy or completeness in order to gain the attention of publics.

TABLE 2.1 Four Models of Public Relations

Publicity/press agentry	Organization ↘ Publics	Communication is mostly one-way, initiated by an organization with little concern for accuracy or completeness
Public information	Organization → Publics	Communication is mostly one-way, initiated by an organization to inform publics with truthful and accurate information
Two-way asymmetrical	Organization ⇅ Publics	Communication is two-way but unbalanced, with the organization using research/feedback in an effort to persuade publics to change attitudes or behaviours
Two-way symmetrical	Organization ⇄ Publics	Communication is mostly balanced, with the organization as likely to change attitudes or behaviour as its publics

Pictorial Press Ltd/Alamy Stock Photo

One of the reasons P.T. Barnum remains a controversial figure is that his initial claim to fame involved a hoax. In 1935, Barnum purchased a blind slave, Joice Heth, who he claimed was the 161-year-old former nurse of George Washington. He called Heth "the most astonishing and interesting curiosity in the world," and put her on display in New York. Barnum created interest by spreading a rumour that Heth was actually a doll controlled by a ventriloquist. After her death in 1836, Barnum staged a public autopsy and charged 50 cents for admission. The autopsy revealed that Heth was likely no older than 80. There is no question that, by today's standards, Barnum's actions were exploitive.

Do today's reality television stars face similar exploitation in the name of entertainment?

Case Study

Publicity Stunts: The Reality of Gaining Attention in the Marketplace of Ideas

Publicity stunts, and the publicity/press agentry model in general, are still around because there is often a payoff in their use. As Press Officer Sadie Chapple reminds us "PR stunts are as old the Gladiators who battled in the coliseums and as new as a Hollywood socialite 'accidentally' releasing a sex tape. They are theatre; and, when used properly, they transcend the moment and become an effective tool to deliver your public relations message."

PR writer Shannon Peerless, head of PR ad agency 10 Yetis PR, has some guidelines for what makes a successful PR stunt:

In my opinion, a good PR stunt needs to be one (or more) of the following things: visual, clever, and reactive. Anything that is going to photograph well or that has good video content to support it is going to help a PR stunt along in the coverage stakes). A "clever" stunt is one that I would define as making other brands and PROs think "I wish I'd thought of that" or one where the beauty is in the simplicity of it all.

Chapple agrees that a good PR "stunt" should capture the attention of both the public and the media as well as having the ability to create buzz on social media. But buzz that doesn't connect to the brand has limited value. "The point of the stunt is to bring the values and story of your brand or organization to life. Too often, people remember the stunts, but not the people behind it. If a stunt doesn't connect back to the brand, even if it is a media hit, it hasn't met its objective."

Many PR bloggers and columnists point to a recent publicity stunt by Red Bull as one of the greatest PR stunts of all times. To promote the company's products and in keeping with its tagline "Red Bull Gives You Wings," the company sponsored a promotion that saw Austrian skydiver and base jumper Felix Baumgartner ascend 128,100 feet in a stratospheric balloon and make a freefall jump that saw him rushing towards earth at speeds in excess of the sound barrier before parachuting to the ground, shattering several world records in the process. The stunt, which involved more than 10 years of planning, garnered media attention around the world.

Of course, stunts don't have to be as elaborate or expensive to be effective. In August 2017, workers in Toronto's financial district were greeted by child-sized figures wearing empty, yellow children's raincoats as part of a promotion for the Ontario-shot film *IT*. Warner Bros. Canada set up the mannequins throughout the downtown core and invited passers-by to snap a photo with Georgie (the first victim in the Stephen King story-based film), and by posting the picture with the **hashtag** #WheresGeorgieTO on Twitter, they could win tickets to a private screening of the film.

Publicity stunts are frequently used to promote movies. In London, England, passersby were greeted by a massive Stay Puft marshmallow man rising up from the ground to promote the upcoming release of the rebooted *Ghostbusters*.

A&W scored a hit when they set up what they claim was the first ever "float through"—a floating "restaurant" on BC's Penticton Channel. The stunt, which was filmed as a commercial for the company's Facebook site, saw an A&W uniform-clad actor handing out burgers to those just floating by. The stunt delighted local "floaters," generated positive media coverage, and resulted in a video with more than two million views.

However, to be effective, stunts need to be carefully planned and thought through or companies run the risk of offending the very publics they were hoping to impress. Calgary radio station 90.3 AMP Radio found that out the hard way when they ran a promotion asking listeners to vote on whether $5,000 would be given to a lucky listener or burned. When the votes were tallied 57 per cent voted for burned, and the station obliged. A public and social backlash followed, with many people pointing out that the money could have been donated to charity instead of being wasted. Eventually, the station put another $10,000 on the line, and this time, the public voted in favour (91 per cent) of giving the money to a listener.

The AMP Radio organizers should have heeded the lessons learned in the now famous case of "Boaty McBoatface," which proved that public voting can sometimes yield surprising and undesirable results. In 2016, the Natural Environment Research Council (NERC) in England invited the public to suggest and vote on a new name for its polar research ship. When the polls closed, that number one choice was "RRS Boaty McBoatface." The NERC eventually decided to go with the fifth-place choice, *RRS Sir David Attenborough*.

A poorly thought-out stunt can do more than just arouse public outrage—it can also result in safety concerns. A summer promotion by Coors Light called Search and Rescue involved hiding 880 briefcases across Canada, which participants needed to find using an online map and Twitter clues. One of the cases, left at a busy intersection in downtown Toronto, was mistaken for a bomb and shut down a major intersection while emergency responders investigated.

hashtag A word or phrase (with no spaces) preceded by the hash symbol (#) that users can include in posts to categorize information online. Many social media platforms allow users to search or filter news feeds for information identified with the tag.

awkwardly accepted the greasy boxes thrust upon them and proceeded to gracelessly gnaw at fried chicken wings while the award show went on."[5] The stunt was reminiscent of the Oscars the year before when Ellen DeGeneres ordered pizza to be delivered for all the stars in attendance. DeGeneres's pizzas, however, were from a local Los Angeles pizza place called Big Mama's and Big Papa's, and the slices of pizza were much easier to serve and eat in formal attire than the KFC wings in Hong Kong. The franchise owner of Big Mama's and Big Papa's estimated a 500 per cent increase in sales following the Oscars.[6]

Public Information

Long before Bill Gates and Mark Zuckerberg dropped out of Harvard, Ivy Ledbetter Lee left graduate school at Harvard in the late nineteenth century, largely for financial reasons. Whereas Gates and Zuckerberg eventually changed the nature of personal media as we know them with Microsoft and Facebook, Lee started America's third public relations agency and went on to become the man many refer to today as the founder of public relations.

Before his stint at Harvard, Lee had graduated cum laude from Princeton in 1898 and had worked as a journalist for the Associated Press, the *Philadelphia Press*, and the *Chicago Record*.[7] And prior to starting the public relations agency Parker & Lee in late 1904 with George Parker,[8] he worked for *The New York Journal*, *The New York Times*, and *New York World*.[9] Parker & Lee's company slogan heralded a journalistic background—"Accuracy, Authenticity, and Interest"[10]—and it very much distinguished Lee's brand of public relations from Barnum's press agentry.

While the Parker & Lee agency lasted only a few years, Ivy Lee went on to represent some of the biggest names of the day in corporate America, including the Pennsylvania Railroad and the Rockefellers. While Lee's legacy is complex—he also counselled I.G. Farben, the German dye trust, on how to improve relations with Americans after the Nazis took control of the trust—his name is deeply associated with the **public information model** of public relations; in this model communication is mostly one-way, initiated by an organization to inform publics with truthful and accurate information. When he sent materials to the press, Ivy Lee was known to include his "Declaration of Principles," which stated:

> This is not a secret press bureau. All our work is done in the open. We aim to supply news. . . . Our matter is accurate. Further details on any subject treated will be supplied promptly, and any editor will be assisted most cheerfully in verifying directly any statement of fact. . . . In brief, our plan is frankly, and openly, on behalf of business concerns and public institutions, to supply the press and public of the United States prompt and accurate information concerning subjects which it is of value and interest to the public to know about.[11]

Transparency is a value we hear much of in the age of social media. Although the degree to which Lee was walking the walk is debatable, he was talking the talk of transparency a good century before the Internet. As Clive Thompson put it in *Wired* in 2007, "Transparency is a judo move. Your customers are going to poke around in your business anyway, and your workers are going to blab about internal info—so why not make it work for you by turning everyone into a partner in the process and inviting them to do so?"[12]

In the early 1900s, railroad accidents were not uncommon, and railroad companies would generally do what they could to keep the bad news under wraps. But when the Pennsylvania Railroad had a wreck near Gap, Pennsylvania, Ivy Lee went with a different strategy:

> Instinctively the railroad management put its news suppression machinery into motion. Just as quickly, Lee reversed it. Reporters were invited to travel to the scene of the accident at the railroad's expense. Lee promptly set up facilities for reporters and photographers.[13]

The resulting coverage was better than usual, and the Pennsylvania Railroad was later compared favourably to railroads that refused to adopt such an open-access policy.

Today, most public relations departments within organizations spend at least part of their time serving the public information function. Even when organizations are not seeking to gain extra attention, they still often need to get messages out accurately and reliably. In many cases, public communication is actually required by law. For example, publicly held corporations, which are organizations that have offered shares for trading in stock exchanges

public information model Model of public relations in which communication is mostly one-way, initiated by an organization to inform publics with truthful and accurate information.

Photo by ullstein bild/ullstein bild via Getty Images

Ivy Lee began his career as a journalist, and he carried journalistic values into his work for corporate clients.

How was Lee's work in public relations different from journalism?

Photo by Kirn Vintage Stock/Corbis via Getty Images

Rather than working to obstruct reporters, Ivy Lee encouraged them to cover accidents.

Why would a public relations practitioner want to communicate openly about an organization's crises?

or other public markets, are obligated to file certain reports and to make public certain information that may affect investors' decisions.

Annual reports and quarterly profit/loss statements are examples of material information that must be released in a timely, accurate, and fair manner. So even if Magna International or Air Canada have a bad quarter and don't meet their earnings goals, they still have to report that information in a way that ensures that anyone interested in buying or selling shares is properly informed as a result.

Public information is also a common practice in government work. At the federal level, these jobs are usually called communications officer or communications advisor. At the provincial level, a variety of titles are used, including communications officer, information officer, public affairs officer, and communications lead.

Check out the recent job posting for an information officer with the Government of Alberta on the next page:[14]

Notice that the role includes one-way communication: an effective "flow" of ministerial and program information. Public information and publicity/press agentry are both one-way models of communication, but the essence of the public information is quite different in character from press agentry in that the goal is much more focused on providing accurate information than attention-getting.

Public affairs officer is the standard title in the Canadian Armed Forces. Military public affairs officers attend 15 weeks of basic training at the Canadian Forces Leadership and Recruit School in Saint-Jean-sur-Richelieu, Quebec. The standard starting salary for a Canadian Armed Forces public affairs officer is $51,000.[15]

> *Organizations must get messages out accurately and reliably, even when they are not seeking to gain extra attention.*

Two-Way Asymmetrical Communication

Bernays is also credited (or blamed, depending on your perspective) with getting people to consume more bacon for breakfast. Bernays researched breakfast diets in the early twentieth century and found that for the most part people ate light breakfasts of "coffee, maybe a roll, and orange juice."[16] So he consulted with his doctor about the benefits of a heavier breakfast and, lo and behold, he found that "a heavy breakfast was sounder from the standpoint of health than a light breakfast because the body loses energy during the night and needs it during the day." He then asked that doctor to write to thousands of other doctors to confirm the benefits of a hearty breakfast. When about 4,500 of the 5,000 doctors to whom they wrote concurred with the conclusion, Bernays publicized the finding nationally.

Interestingly, the resulting news coverage not only headlined the benefits of a hearty breakfast as broadly endorsed by thousands of doctors, but also "many of [the newspapers] stated that bacon and eggs should be embodied with the breakfast, and as a result sales of bacon went up." How did Bernays know that bacon sales went up? Bartlett Arkell, founder and president of the Beech-Nut Packing Company, wrote him and told him as much. Arkell would know because bacon was one of Beech-Nut's primary products. And Beech-Nut was one of Bernays's clients.

What distinguishes Bernays's work from other publicity stunts is the use of research to understand publics, develop strategy, and even to evaluate the results. Bernays applied the social science of the times. He saw the role of the public relations counsellor as interpreting publics to clients as well as interpreting clients to publics.

Today's public relations professionals have access to more scientific research and huge amounts of online data to help them understand publics and to gauge the success of their efforts. Surveys, email responses, Twitter comments, usability studies, and focus groups are examples of ways organizations get to know their publics these days, as are less obtrusive sources of data that you as a consumer/Internet user may provide without even knowing it. Just check your web browser's cookies!

> Professionals today have access to more scientific research and online data to help them understand publics and to gauge the success of public relations efforts.

Case Study

Edward Bernays's "Torches of Freedom"

Picture this. On the crowded streets of one of the world's busiest cities, a group of influential young people does something carefully planned but also unexpected by the crowds around them. Behind-the-scenes organizers have worked social networks and even mainstream media to maximize coverage, and the perfectly choreographed event draws the attention of onlookers. Some are shocked. Some are delighted. But it becomes apparent that the event was staged for more than just shock value or entertainment. Some see it as the start of a social movement.

No, this isn't a reference to the 2010 Air Canada "Operation Snowflake" Christmas **flash mob**, which generated press coverage across the country and a YouTube video with millions of views. Nor does it have anything to do with the latest performance from Choir! Choir! Choir!, a Toronto-based singing "flash mob" with dozens of viral videos with millions of views to their credit.

Instead, the event described was the Torches of Freedom march; the "influentials" were New York debutantes; and the site was an Easter parade on Fifth Avenue in New York. The date, however, was 1930 and the man behind the scenes was Edward Bernays. Bernays competes with Ivy Lee for the legacy of being known as the father of public relations. Oh, and about those "torches of freedom": they were cigarettes marketed to women.

Bernays coordinated the Torches of Freedom event on behalf of his client George Washington Hill, president of the American Tobacco Company. Here is how Bernays recalls the project in his memoir *Biography of an Idea*:

> Hill called me in. "How can we get women to smoke on the street? They're smoking indoors. But, damn it, if they spend half the time outdoors and we can get 'em to smoke outdoors, we'll damn near double our female market. Do something. Act!"
>
> "There's a taboo against such smoking," I said. "Let me consult an expert, Dr A.A. Brill, the psychoanalyst. He might give me the psychological basis for a woman's desire to smoke, and maybe this will help me."
>
> "What will it cost?"
>
> "I suppose just a consultation fee."
>
> "Shoot," said Hill.
>
> [Bernays was no stranger to psychoanalysis. His uncle was Sigmund Freud.]
>
> Brill explained to me: "Some women regard cigarettes as symbols of freedom," he told me. "Smoking is a sublimation of oral eroticism; holding a cigarette in the mouth excites the oral zone. It is perfectly normal for women to want to smoke cigarettes. . . . But today the emancipation of women has suppressed many of their feminine desires. . . . Feminine traits are masked. Cigarettes, which are equated with men, become torches of freedom."

flash mob When a group of people plans and executes a surprise public event or performance that is usually organized via electronic media and unanticipated by those who are not participants.

Continued

PETRAS MALUKAS/AFP/Getty Images

Photo Courtesy of The Museum of Public Relations

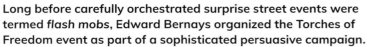

Long before carefully orchestrated surprise street events were termed *flash mobs*, Edward Bernays organized the Torches of Freedom event as part of a sophisticated persuasive campaign.

How did Bernays link smoking a cigarette with women's fight for equality?

In this last statement I found a way to help break the taboo against women smoking in public. Why not a parade of women lighting torches of freedom— smoking cigarettes?[17]

Bernays called friends at *Vogue* magazine to get a list of debutantes. Then he had his secretary, Bertha Hunt, sign and send a personalized telegram to each one. Think direct messaging, 1930s style:

In the interests of equality of the sexes and to fight another sex taboo I and other young women will light another torch of freedom by smoking cigarettes while strolling on Fifth Avenue Easter Sunday. We are doing this to combat the silly prejudice that the cigarette is suitable for the home, the restaurant, the taxicab, the theater lobby, but never no never for the sidewalk. Women smokers and their escorts will stroll from Forty-Eighth Street to Fifty-Fourth Street on Fifth Avenue between Eleven-Thirty and One O'Clock.[18]

It worked. Bernays reported that the event made front-page news in both photos and text and opened editorial debates in the weeks that followed in publications from coast to coast. As evidence of his success he cited newspaper reports in Massachusetts, Michigan, California, and West Virginia that women were smoking on the streets.* "Age-old customs, I learned, could be broken down by a dramatic appeal, disseminated by the network of media."[19] While Bernays's strategy was mostly intuitive and his reasoning was mostly theoretical, the case illustrates the power of public relations tactics as powerful tools for persuasion.

---

*Bernays's claims about the impact of national publicity resulting from the Torches of Freedom event were later called into question by historians.[20]

The torches-of-freedom stunt and bacon-and-eggs "study" had all the trappings of press agentry and publicity, but behind the scenes was evidence of a clever two-way model of communication designed to sell more cigarettes and bacon by leveraging an understanding of desires, diets, and deference to authority. The communication may have been two-way in that sense, but it was also clearly not balanced. As Grunig and Hunt put it, both Bernays and Lee "stressed the importance of communicating the public's point of view to management," but in actual practice, "both did much more to explain management's view to the public."[21] This two-way **asymmetrical model** of communication describes much of the work that modern public relations professionals practise as they advocate and work to persuade publics on behalf of organizations. Bernays may be criticized for promoting tobacco as liberating and bacon as healthy, but his idea of using two-way communication and research to persuade publics can (and is) just as likely to be applied by organizations with quite different perspectives such as the Canadian Cancer Society or the Heart and Stroke Foundation.

Bernays later regretted promoting tobacco, a sentiment he expressed plainly in his memoirs, claiming that the dangers of tobacco were not understood at the time. Historians, and Bernays himself, also made it clear that his work was produced in partnership with his wife Doris Fleischman, who retained her last name throughout her career. They worked together for 58 years from their marriage in 1922 until her death in 1980. Bernays lived until 1995 when he died at the age of 103.

Bernays is associated with the unbalanced two-way asymmetrical model in the same way that Ivy Lee has been associated with the public information model and P.T. Barnum has been associated with the publicity/press agentry model. Each has been painted with broad strokes here mostly for the purposes of providing colourful illustrations of models of public relations. It's worth noting that Edward Bernays himself is largely responsible for framing the history of public relations as a mostly twentieth-century progression from press agentry to a sophisticated two-way management function that helps corporations understand public interests. Among the benefits of Bernays's longevity in life and career was that he had decades to write and promote his take on the history of the field he helped define in his earlier years.

In his now famous 1947 essay, "The Engineering of Consent" (which was later expanded into a book), Bernays outlines some of the tools and techniques that should be used to gain consent from the public. He talks about undertaking research, including public opinion polls, before beginning any campaign and selecting tactics. Known today as formative research, this notion is widely accepted today but was considered revolutionary at the time.

While many of the tactics suggested in *The Engineering of Consent* seem benign by today's standards, some of Bernays's thoughts and suggestions were controversial:

> The engineering of consent should be based theoretically and practically on the complete understanding of those whom it attempts to win over. But it is sometimes impossible to reach joint decisions based on an understanding of facts by all the people. The average American adult has only six years of schooling behind him. With pressing crises and decisions to be faced, a leader frequently cannot wait for the people to arrive at even general understanding. In certain cases, democratic leaders must play their part in leading the public through the engineering of consent.

asymmetrical model Model of public relations in which communication is two-way but unbalanced, with the organization using research/feedback in an effort to persuade publics to change attitudes or behaviours.

Marian Weyo/Shutterstock.com

Edward Bernays used research and persuasive tactics to sell bacon.

Was this any more or less ethical than his use of research and persuasion to sell cigarettes?

Two-Way Symmetrical Communication

symmetrical model Model of public relations in which two-way communication is mostly balanced, with the organization as likely to change attitudes or behaviour as its publics.

Symmetry is balance. In a two-way **symmetrical model** of communication, organizations are just as likely to change as their publics. Historical examples are out there but are not as easy to come by as splashy stories of press agentry and persuasion. In the epilogue to his nearly 800-page authoritative volume on the history of public relations, *The Unseen Power: Public Relations, A History*, Scott Cutlip suggested that Earl Newsom's work on behalf of Ford Motor Company may fit the bill for an example of two-way symmetrical communication.[22] As principal of his own firm, Earl Newsom and Company, Newsom counselled some of America's largest and most powerful corporations of the mid-twentieth century such as Standard Oil, Merrill Lynch, Trans-World Airlines, CBS, and Ford Motor Company. According to Cutlip,

© Queen's Printer for Ontario, 2012

Every fall, provincial governments across Canada launch multimedia flu shot campaigns designed to convince Canadians to get a flu shot.

Which of the four models of communication best describes these campaigns?

Newsom did not consider himself an "agent" for clients, responsible for publicity and promotion. Rather, Newsom saw himself as a counsellor first and foremost, advising clients on management issues of public interest.

In the mid-1950s, Ford Motor Company, along with the rest of the auto industry, was taking heat for automobile safety, or lack thereof. Newsom counselled Ford to launch a safety campaign. The campaign, however, was much more than a publicity stunt or sales drive. It included a Ford-sponsored national safety forum attended by safety researchers, auto industry engineers, and law enforcement officials. Henry Ford II announced a $200,000 grant to Cornell University for the specific

Cornell Aeronautical Labs, Liberty Mutual Insurance, and Ford Motor Company partnered to develop the 1957 Cornell–Liberty Safety Car as one of the first auto concepts developed from crash testing.

Is the relationship between Ford and its publics symmetrical?

purpose of researching highway safety and injury prevention. The campaign also included short movies illustrating the research and development of dashboard crash padding, safety door latches, and more safely designed steering wheels. While much of Ford's reputation for safety unravelled in the decades that followed, the effort to use research and two-way communication between an organization (Ford) and its key publics (researchers, safety experts, engineers, and, ultimately, automobile owners) to the mutual benefit of both the organization and its publics illustrated the idea of two-way symmetrical communication. To the extent that Ford changed its operations and vehicle design in the interest of its publics, the relationship was more symmetrical than if they had just kept their research and development closed to outside influence and feedback and used the campaign only to promote later sales.

Arthur Page, whose principles for ethical management of public relations are outlined in Chapter 1, is also seen as an example of an upstanding practitioner with a symmetrical worldview. He saw winning public approval, confidence, and trust as essential to successful management. In his words, "All business begins with the public permission and exists by public approval."[23]

Yet, if there is a name associated with the two-way symmetrical model of public relations, it is not a public relations man, but a theorist, or actually two theorists. James and Larissa Grunig are emeritus professors at the University of Maryland. Together with many colleagues, the Grunigs developed and executed a decades-long program of research on excellence in public relations. Among the main ideas to emerge from these studies was that "using the two-way symmetrical or a combination of the two-way symmetrical and two-way asymmetrical model (called the mixed-motive model) almost always could increase the contribution of public relations to organizational effectiveness."[24] This line of research and theory, which started in the 1970s and 1980s, continues today.

Although we may not find any one contemporary organization or practitioner to serve as a model of pure and continuous symmetry in public relations, we do see plenty of examples of engaging public relations in which the engagement is fuelled by moments of good, balanced communication between two or more interested parties. Many of these examples come from non-profits and publicly funded institutions.

Hospitals, for example, have unique relationships with their publics. Whereas consumers may exercise some power in dealing with private companies through their purchasing

For more than 20 years, St Michael's Hospital in Toronto, Ontario, has involved patients and community members through four Community Advisory Panels (CAPs).

What advantages and disadvantages are there to practising symmetrical communication?

decisions, hospitals are publicly funded and residents cannot shop around for health-care services in the same way they might when purchasing a microwave oven or a pair of shoes.

Funding for health care in Canada, including hospitals, is provided by the federal government, which transfers funds to the provinces to run hospitals and fund other health-care services.

Many provincial governments require hospitals to consult or engage with their communities when making decisions about the services they provide, and this is done in a variety of ways across the country.

One hospital with a long tradition of involving community members and patients is St Michael's Hospital in downtown Toronto. In 1992, the hospital set up four specialized Community Advisory Panels (CAPs). These panels, made up of hospital staff, patients, and community members, provide advice to the hospital on priority populations, ensure continuous improvements, and advocate on behalf of the populations they represent. The CAPs focus on:

- Women and children
- People who are homeless or under-housed
- People with severe and persistent mental illness
- Aboriginal health

Since 1992, CAPs have maintained a crucial dialogue between St Michael's Hospital and our broader inner-city community. They bring the community voice into the hospital and take the hospital into the community. CAPs help to create and support inclusive services for those who are at-risk and have special needs.

According to the hospital, CAPs have contributed to 60 innovations in patient care and education and have had a huge impact on how the hospital provides care. For example, the Mental Health and Addiction CAP identified a need to respond more effectively to 911 calls that involved individuals experiencing a mental health crisis. After consultation with community groups and the hospital, they helped create a unique partnership between the hospital and the police called the Mobile Crisis Intervention Team, which includes a hospital nurse and a Toronto police officer. As part of the program, team members travel together in an unmarked car and respond to crisis situations involving mental health and addictions with the goal of de-escalating crises.

A Broader Social History of Public Relations

Historical portraits of Barnum, Bernays, and even Lee are coloured with a tint of infamy. But Barnum served as a mayor of Bridgeport, Connecticut, and founded Bridgeport Hospital. Bernays applied his expertise to promote education for minorities, Thomas Edison's invention of electric lighting, and the field of public relations itself. Ivy Lee worked for the

American Red Cross. Indeed, a different sample of cases and clients sets a different tone for the history of public relations. The tactics that each practitioner helped develop can, like any other instrument of communication, be used for good or evil.

Moreover, a broader, more inclusive, social history of public relations reveals that effective public relations was around long before the rise of twentieth-century business. Historians have debunked the "Big Bang Barnum" narrative as a comprehensive accounting of the birth of public relations.[25]

Historians Margot Opdyke Lamme at the University of Alabama and Karen Miller Russell at the University of Georgia culled through decades of literature on the history of public relations and found more than 70 articles, chapters, and books that focused on history prior to the twentieth century.[26] Besides business, they found public relations to have a rich heritage in three "deep veins" of history: religion; education, non-profit, and reform; and politics and government.

Religion

Lamme and Russell highlighted evidence of public relations as early as the first century. Although we wouldn't go so far as to say that St Paul was a PR guy, at least one public relations historian identifies Paul as "one of the most influential communicators in history." "In the contemporary language of public relations, he played all its roles: writer–technician, liaison, manager, and strategist," wrote Robert E. Brown of Salem State University with an admitted sense of anachronism in making the case.[27] In addition to authoring much of the New Testament, St Paul deftly segmented his publics (Jews and early Christians), tailored his rhetoric for his audiences, visited churches, and was effective enough in spreading his message to change the course of religion and world history. Today, religious leaders and organizations remain adept at both traditional and emerging public relations tactics.

Examples of religions using social media are everywhere. Rabbi Josh Yuter was celebrated by the National Jewish Outreach Program as a top-ten Jewish influencer for his use of social media: "Yuter is not only a pulpit rabbi. He's a popular blogger, tweeter, and podcaster (his Jewish-themed podcasts were downloaded more than 20,000 times last year.)"[28] The website Islamographic.com offers Islamic education through infographics.[29] The pope has a Twitter page (@Pontifex) and over five million followers on Instagram. (However, the pope's social media statistics pale in comparison to those of Selena Gomez, Ariana Grande, and Justin Bieber, who all have around 100 million Instagram followers.)

Education

College and university graduation ceremonies are a time of great pomp and circumstance, and whether you realize it as you sit there in your cap and gown, that's the point at which you "switch publics." You go from student to alumni member and potential donor. Before too long, you'll receive emails, direct mail pieces, magazines, or tweets encouraging you to support your alma mater.

While we may not know exactly when this practice started, Harvard College is known to have begun fundraising campaigns as early as 1641 when college representatives were sent to England to emphasize how the college was educating American Indians as part of a pitch for donations.[30] In the 1700s, Princeton and Columbia (at the time named King's College) both used **news releases** to publicize their commencement ceremonies.[31]

Effective public relations was around long before P.T. Barnum or Edward Bernays.

St Paul has been referred to as one of the most influential communicators in history.

Was St Paul practising public relations?

news release A statement of news produced and distributed on behalf of an organization to make information public. Traditionally news releases (aka press releases) have been issued to news media with the intent of publicizing the information to the news organization's readers, listeners, or viewers.

Khalil Aleker, Founder of Islamographic.com, explaining Islam to the world in the most simple way using graphics (infographics)

Religious organizations remain among the most spirited in public relations.

Why do you think that is?

Promoting a cause also means supporting a mission, which requires strategy beyond mere awareness.

Politics and Government

Lamme and Russell found examples of public relations–type activity dating back to Alexander the Great in the fourth century BCE. Tutored by Aristotle as a boy, Alexander went on to become not only a great warrior but also a great war reporter, or at least he saw to it that others sent stories of his exploits in battle back to Macedonian courts.

Early Canadian history is also full of communication strategies and tactics that today would be labelled public relations, such as the Canadian Government and Clifford Sifton's work in the late 1800s and early 1900s promoting immigration to Western Canada.[32]

In the years following Confederation in 1867, the Canadian government sought to increase the population and develop the national economy. Settling the West and creating a stable source of food and grains that could be exported became an important priority. As part of its public relations campaign, the government distributed over one million brochures to farmers throughout the UK, and thousands of posters were distributed to British post offices.

Working under then Prime Minister Wilfrid Laurier, Sifton mounted a media relations campaign to promote Canada as an immigration destination that included giving free trips to newspaper and magazine editors, and, at the St Louis World's Fair in 1904, over 200,000 pamphlets were distributed to fairgoers.[33]

Public Relations History in Canada

In the United States, the evolution of public relations was led by business, but in Canada, many of the early public relations efforts came from government. By 1900, some private institutions, such as Canadian Pacific, had embarked on full-time publicity operations.

In the years following World War II, public relations in Canada began to grow. Canada's first public relations associations were formed in 1948—one in Montreal and another in Toronto—and by 1953, they had merged to become the Canadian Public Relations Society (CPRS).

In an effort to document Canada's public relations history, the CPRS began the Jack Yocom Public Relations Profile Collection, an online resource that profiles 19 early practitioners. These include Jack Yocom, who developed one of the first public relations courses; Luc Beauregard, who founded NATIONAL Public Relations in 1976 (it is now one of Canada's largest public relations firms); and Ruth Hammond, who was the first woman to join the CPRS in 1956.

Advocacy and promotion are easy to spot. Coloured ribbons are prime examples: pink ribbons for breast cancer awareness, yellow to support troops, red to support the fight against AIDS and HIV, and even periwinkle to support research on stomach and esophageal cancers. Each ribbon is a symbol of a cause with organizations working on behalf of the cause. Of course, mere awareness is only part of the process of advocacy. Promoting a cause also means supporting a mission, which requires strategy beyond mere awareness. Fighting cancer requires money for research, physician involvement, preventive behaviour, and early detection of treatable conditions.

Major Motivations for Public Relations

Lamme and Russell's broader view of public relations history reveals several major motivations for public relations throughout the ages. These include recruitment, legitimacy, agitation, and advocacy, in addition to profit.

Recruitment

St Paul recruited for the Christian Church. The government of Canada recruited women to work in munitions factories during World War II. Your college or university may have recruited you. Today, public relations practitioners are involved in the recruitment of volunteers for non-profits, new members for political organizations, new hires for corporations, and, of course, new students for colleges and universities.

While the timeless tactics of face-to-face visits, meetings, and events are still the backbone of many recruiting efforts, today's recruiters are just as likely to use social networking sites and other forms of social media to carry out their work. In a survey of more than 1,400 people on a registered list of human resources and recruiting professionals conducted by *Jobvite* in 2015, 92 per cent of recruiters reported using social media to support recruiting efforts. Eighty-seven per cent said they used LinkedIn, 55 per cent said Facebook, and 47 per cent of those polled reported using Twitter.[35]

In a study of university officials, San Diego State University Professor Kaye Sweetser and Tom Kelleher (an author of this book) found that those communicators working in admissions and recruiting were among the most enthusiastic adopters of social media for public relations work. As one participant in the study put it, there's a "competitive advantage" in using social media "to attract and maintain a younger demographic, which is adept and attuned to social media." Another said, "If [students] are there and that is where they naturally are, then you have to go to [that] market. . . . We need to be there."[36]

Legitimacy

Öffentlichkeitsarbeit means "work for the public sphere" in German.[37] Scholars have found Öffentlichkeitsarbeit to date back as far as the tenth century when Austrian monarchs and statesmen disseminated coins, pictures, and pamphlets to legitimize their positions.[38] Lamme and Russell also highlighted studies showing how early Christian churches sought legitimacy, and later how members of the church were used to enhance the legitimacy of others' efforts.

In the eighteenth century when James Oglethorpe, who founded the American colony of Georgia, was looking to promote the settlement of Savannah, he leveraged the endorsement

A lawyer and politician, Clifford Sifton is best known for his aggressive promotion of immigration to settle the Canadian West. Between 1896 and 1905, the annual number of immigrants entering Canada rose from 16,835 to 141,465.[34]

Do modern-day immigrants to Canada have a more realistic set of expectations of what they will find here?

Today's recruiters are just as likely to use social networking sites and other forms of social media to carry out their work as they are more traditional tactics.

pseudo-event An event organized primarily for the purpose of generating media coverage.

status conferral When media pay attention to individuals and groups and therefore enhance their authority or bestow prestige to them.

organic search results Search engine results that are generated because of their relevance to the search terms entered by users and not resulting directly from paid placement as advertising.

search engine optimization (SEO) Process of improving the position of a specific website in the organic search results of search engines.

> Major news and search sites confer legitimacy by way of algorithms that take into account what users are searching for and linking to.

of the Archbishop of Canterbury. "Oglehorpe and his associates were well aware of the value of the staged event to attract public attention—the pseudo-event is sine qua non of today's promotion," wrote Scott Cutlip in one such historical recounting. Oglethorpe travelled to England to "rally for support" and brought an Indian chief and some of his warriors with him. To boost legitimacy, Oglethorpe's itinerary included a staged meeting with the Archbishop of Canterbury. The visit of Oglethorpe and the Indians generated lots of publicity, and Oglethorpe's travel party upon his return to Georgia included two shiploads of new colonists.

In the twentieth century, communication researchers identified a function of mass media that they called status conferral. Paul Lazarsfeld and Robert Merton wrote in 1948 that "the mass media bestow prestige and enhance the authority of individuals and groups by legitimizing their status."[39] For this reason, many public relations practitioners would consider it a crowning achievement to get their client or organization (or themselves) featured on the *Today* show, in *Time*, or on the front page of their major metropolitan newspaper. That type of coverage, provided it's positive, means instant legitimacy.

Today, Google, Yahoo, Bing, and other major news and search sites confer legitimacy by way of algorithms that take into account what users are searching for and linking to. In a sense, they crowdsource search results. Rather than a small group of editors acting as gatekeepers for what gets covered, decisions about what gets the top billing in organic search results depend on automated calculations. Organic search results are those that are not paid for as advertising or sponsored links. An entire field of practice known as search engine optimization (SEO) has sprouted, and public relations practitioners are among the most interested in sharpening their skills. The goal of SEO is to make your links rank as highly as possible in the results when someone does a keyword search for your client's name, products, or services. Having a client show up on the first page of Google results for their business's keywords is for many as much of a professional win as making the cover of a magazine or newspaper.

Internet power players confer legitimacy in other ways too. In November 2012, over the objections of Israel and the United States, the United Nations General Assembly voted to recognize the state of Palestine, upgrading its UN membership from "observer entity" to "nonmember observer state." Legitimacy was implied. But that legitimacy was bolstered significantly five months later in May 2013 when Google changed the name on www.google.ps from "Palestinian territories" to simply "Palestine." As noted in a follow-up story by NPR's Emily Harris, "Google didn't announce the name change, but it didn't have to. In a place where small gestures can carry great symbolism, Palestinians noticed right away."[40]

Agitation

Getting people fired up has long been a motivation of strategic communicators. In the early 1900s, organizations such as the Women's Christian Temperance Union used pamphlets, events, and a white ribbon campaign to successfully press provincial governments for prohibition of the sale of alcohol. (In most cases, the bans on the sale of alcohol were short-lived; by 1930 every province and territory had repealed their ban except Prince Edward Island, where alcohol sales were outlawed until 1948.)

Google confers status.

Why do you think Google recognition matters so much?

Protesters opposed to the Trans Mountain Pipeline used a variety of tactics, including online petitions and in-person protests, to spread their message.

Which do you think is more effective today: online activism or in-person activism?

Organized agitation evolved into new forms with the rise of the Internet. Gone are the days when organizers had to phone potential supporters one by one; today protests and events can be organized quickly online, and organizers use social media and other tactics to quickly spread their messages.

Advocacy

On the flip side of agitation is advocacy, which is the very first professional value listed in the PRSA (Public Relations Society of America) Code of Ethics. Whereas agitation has been used in history in opposition efforts, **advocacy** in the history of public relations has meant promoting persons, organizations, and nations. As an example of one of the longest-running promotional campaigns in history, Lamme and Russell highlight the Catholic Church's "1,000-year public relations campaign." Featuring St James as a patron saint to Spain, it promoted both the church and Spanish nationalism in the ninth and tenth centuries.[41] The very term **propaganda** derives from the work of the Catholic Church to propagate faith. Prior to the world wars of the twentieth century, the word did not carry the negative connotation it has today.

advocacy Public promotion of a cause, idea, or policy.

propaganda The spread of information used to promote or support a particular point of view. In modern use, the term usually refers to false, misleading, or exaggerated information.

Profit

Of course, generating revenue has been a major motivator for public relations throughout the ages, and not just for big corporations. Even non-profits such as churches, governments, foundations, schools, non-governmental organizations, and foundations have sought to raise

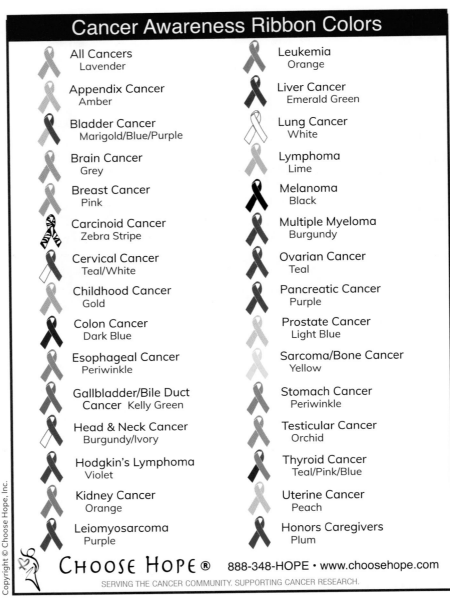

Cancer Awareness Ribbon Colors

All Cancers Lavender	**Leukemia** Orange
Appendix Cancer Amber	**Liver Cancer** Emerald Green
Bladder Cancer Marigold/Blue/Purple	**Lung Cancer** White
Brain Cancer Grey	**Lymphoma** Lime
Breast Cancer Pink	**Melanoma** Black
Carcinoid Cancer Zebra Stripe	**Multiple Myeloma** Burgundy
Cervical Cancer Teal/White	**Ovarian Cancer** Teal
Childhood Cancer Gold	**Pancreatic Cancer** Purple
Colon Cancer Dark Blue	**Prostate Cancer** Light Blue
Esophageal Cancer Periwinkle	**Sarcoma/Bone Cancer** Yellow
Gallbladder/Bile Duct Cancer Kelly Green	**Stomach Cancer** Periwinkle
Head & Neck Cancer Burgundy/Ivory	**Testicular Cancer** Orchid
Hodgkin's Lymphoma Violet	**Thyroid Cancer** Teal/Pink/Blue
Kidney Cancer Orange	**Uterine Cancer** Peach
Leiomyosarcoma Purple	**Honors Caregivers** Plum

CHOOSE HOPE ®   888-348-HOPE • www.choosehope.com
SERVING THE CANCER COMMUNITY. SUPPORTING CANCER RESEARCH.

Copyright © Choose Hope, Inc.

Coloured ribbons are prime examples of advocacy and promotion.

How many of these colours would you recognize? What are the benefits of this type of awareness?

money as seen in the examples discussed in this chapter. That said, one of the largest roles for public relations has been and always will be working in conjunction with advertising and marketing to promote the sale of products, services, and ideas. Chapter 3 will cover the differences and, perhaps more important, the integration of public relations with related functions such as marketing and advertising.

Voices from the Field

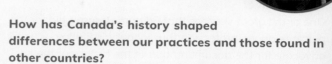

Amy Thurlow

Amy Thurlow, PHD, APR, FCPRS is a Professor of Communication Studies at Mount Saint Vincent University in Nova Scotia, where she teaches public relations management, communication studies, and organizational communication.

Amy's research interests focus on the areas of identity construction, critical historiography, and organizational communication. Grounded in an approach of critical theory, her work has looked at the impact of communication on organizational change strategies, the role of power and legitimation in the construction of organizational and individual identities, and the relationship between history and theory in understandings of knowledge production.

In most public relations textbooks, we read about public relations history from a US perspective. Is Canada lacking a public relations history?
Although the US history of public relations is certainly the dominant story of the public relations profession around the globe, we are starting to see some inroads into the establishment of more diverse histories from international perspectives. From the Canadian perspective, work on the history and historiography of public relations in this country has begun to produce a distinct literature in this area (e.g., Emms, 1995; Johansen and Ferguson, 2005; Thurlow, 2014; Thurlow and Yue, 2015; Wright, 2011). What we are seeing from this process is that the Canadian PR experience differs from the US history in important ways.

So, in answer to your question, I would say that Canada is not lacking a public relations history. There certainly exists a rich and interesting history within a Canadian context. The challenge is to find opportunities to surface this history within the dominant narrative of US public relations.

How has Canada's history shaped differences between our practices and those found in other countries?
The dominant history of PR globally is that of the US experience. The US perspective essentially constructs a linear history that is characterized by an American, corporate perspective and highlights the experiences of high-profile, mostly male practitioners of the twentieth century. This near hegemonic way of knowing our profession severely limits possibilities for PR scholars and practitioners in terms of imagining our professional identities. By that I mean, we have a very limited range of possible answers to draw from when answering the question, "What does good PR look like?"

In fact, a number of jurisdictions now have documented histories of the origins of PR in their areas, and these are beginning to create a multi-vocal history of the profession. This, of course, contains a variety of identities, practices, and theoretical approaches to the field.

For example, the main differences in terms of practice that have emerged between the US history of PR and our Canadian experience relate to, first, the focus on government and public policy, and, second, our historical relationship with journalists and media. Canadian public relations originated within a context of government and public policy. The focus was on immigration and settlement, not corporate reputation. Even today, the very strong presence of public relations practitioners within Canadian government and public information contexts reflects that history. Likewise, while journalists and public relations practitioners in the time of Ivy Lee and Edward Bernays were battling over ethical concepts and the definition of the term *propaganda*, Canadian journalists and PR practitioners had a much more collaborative and amenable approach to information sharing and the importance of public information campaigns. The friction

Continued

between media and PR in Canada did not really appear on a wider basis until after the mid-1940s.

Public relations history is often dominated by Edward Bernays. Do you think he deserves this central spot in the narrative?

One of the great services that Edward Bernays did for the public relations profession throughout his lifetime was to advocate for the documentation of the history of the profession. Naturally, he wrote from his own perspective and about things with which he was involved. And, as historical theorists have pointed out, history is an assemblage of narratives that reflect power, privilege, and the shaping of knowledge in a given time. The challenge is not that Bernays himself is a central character in the narrative; it is that there must be more narratives from a multitude of sources. PR students should have access to multiple versions reflecting many different experiences, a plurality of histories of PR experience that may be shared, learned, and written as part of the larger narrative. It is our role now as PR scholars and practitioners to surface those competing histories and privilege those voices as well.

The history of public relations is a required unit in most public relations courses at college or university. What practical benefit is there to studying public relations history?

The practical benefit to knowing one's history is immense. Ultimately, many of the challenges that face the public relations profession today are a result of the fact that we have adopted, for over a century, an ahistorical approach to the development of the profession. The nagging problems of public relations—no clear definition, a public stigma around the profession as unethical, blurring boundaries between content creation and "true journalism," etc.—have arisen because we are not grounded in historical understandings of the profession. Because the hegemonic narrative of how PR evolved gives us a linear, periodized understanding of theory and practice, we have been challenged to fully develop theoretical frameworks within our own discipline. We rely very heavily on Excellence Theory or the two-way

symmetrical model, which teaches us that PR was once (historically) bad (press agentry), and then it became better as time passed (two-way communication). This polarized view of the discipline limits our theoretical understanding of professional communication, of the role of PR in society, of the construction of our own identities within the field, and of almost every other dimension of public relations scholarship we can imagine.

Who is your favourite historical Canadian public relations figure, and why?

My favorite historical Canadian public relations figure is Ruth Hammond. She was a real pioneer in terms of Canadian PR. A former journalist, Ruth started her own PR consulting agency in Toronto, and in 1956 she was one of the first women in Canada to join the Canadian Public Relations Society. During the 1950s and 60s she worked extensively with clients from the non-profit sector, including the YMCA, the Girl Guides, and the United Way. And as a PR practitioner she was an important mentor for many other women entering the field in Canada at that time, and for years to come. Her career is profiled in the CPRS Yocum series at https://www.cprs.ca/About/Yocom-Public-Relations-Profiles/Ruth-Hammond.

What's the most important lesson from public relations history that a student can take into practice?

The most important lesson from public relations history that a student can take into practice is a critical approach to theory, practice, and the "way things are done." When we began to uncover multi-vocal histories of public relations, we also began to gain insights into our theoretical foundations. It became apparent that symmetrical communication, for example, was not an inevitable, historical evolution of public relations practice—it was one theoretical perspective that became woven into a specific historical narrative that supported one explanation of how PR evolved. This caused us to rethink our theoretical underpinnings, our historical understandings, and opened so many doors in terms of the study of PR history, theory, and practice.

Ethics: Transparency, Objectivity, and Advocacy

Disclosure and dissemination of information is a cornerstone of public relations ethics. Media ethicist Patrick Lee Plaisance argues that transparency is ethical not because of its strategic outcomes (e.g., reputation for doing the right thing), but because it is essential to human dignity.[42] He cites philosopher Immanuel Kant in building a case that the best reason to be transparent is respect for other people. By making available all relevant information, we respect others' autonomy in informed decision-making. Grunig and Hunt painted Ivy Lee as an exemplar of the public information model of public relations: "Lee viewed the public as made up of rational human beings who, if they are given complete and accurate information, would make the right decisions."[43]

As a former journalist, like many of today's public relations practitioners, Lee embraced the general idea of objectivity. We say "general idea" here because objectivity is a philosophically elusive concept. *Oxford Dictionaries* define the adjective *objective* as "not influenced by personal feelings or opinions in considering and representing facts."[44] But journalists, or any other human beings for that matter, struggle with total removal of feelings and opinions in selecting, interpreting, and reporting facts. You won't find objectivity specifically stated in the Canadian Association of Journalists (CAJ) Code of Ethics, but that doesn't mean they have abandoned the idea of pursuing truth. "Journalism does not pursue truth in an absolute or philosophical sense, but it can—and must—pursue it in a practical sense," according to the Pew Research Center's principles of journalism.[45]

Whereas Lee identified with journalists (and many journalists identified with Lee), Edward Bernays made it a point to define public relations as much more than a journalistic function. Bernays embraced advocacy, and in doing so unabashedly distinguished public relations from journalism. Today, there is little debate about advocacy's place in public relations. This is in sharp contrast to journalism, where advocacy is a no-no. The CAJ Code of Ethics, for example, instructs journalists to "serve democracy and the public interest by reporting the truth. This sometimes conflicts with various public and private interests, including those of sources, governments, advertisers and, on occasion, with our duty and obligation to an employer."[46]

The case has even been made that Edward Bernays did more to advance the ethical evolution of public relations than Ivy Lee because Bernays embraced advocacy and encouraged writing it into a code of ethics rather than trying to act as a journalist while on the payroll of a non-news organization. Genevieve McBride wrote in the *Journal of Mass Media Ethics* in 1989 that public relations' struggle towards professionalism would benefit from a view of history that embraces Bernays's "disassociation from the journalistic perspective" rather than Lee's "dysfunctional standard of objectivity."[47]

Whether you practise public information with a journalistic set of values or advocacy with a penchant for persuasion, the principle of transparency is critical. In a democracy, it is OK to advocate, as long as you are transparent about what you're doing, meaning that you respect others' autonomy in informed decision-making.

Transparency also offers a useful lens for studying public relations history. In what ways was Bernays's work for Beech-Nut ethical? Unethical? How about Ivy Lee's work with Nazis in Germany? Should Lee be let off the hook because he was transparent? Lee could (and did)

objectivity State of being free from the influence of personal feelings or opinions in considering and representing facts.

The principle of transparency is critical whether you practise public information with a journalistic set of values or with advocacy.

argue that his work in counselling Germans in the late 1930s was consistent with his respect for rational human decision-making. He said he was working to improve mutual understanding between Americans and Germans. In a congressional hearing in 1934, Lee testified that he counselled German propaganda minister Joseph Goebbels and other German leaders that "they would never in the world get the American people reconciled to their treatment of the Jews."[48] The same hearing revealed that Lee was receiving $25,000 a year from the German dye trust for his public relations counsel. Assuming Lee was upfront about his business arrangement, was his work ethical?

In Case You Missed It

While public relations tactics have been around since the dawn of civilization, our body of knowledge about the field has come a long way in the past few decades. Here are some time-tested truths, along with a slightly new perspective.

- Organizations must get messages out accurately and reliably, even when they are not seeking to gain extra attention.
- Professionals today have access to more scientific research and online data to help them understand publics and to gauge the success of public relations efforts.
- Effective public relations was around long before the rise of twentieth-century business.

- Promoting a cause also means supporting a mission, which requires strategy beyond mere awareness.
- Today's recruiters are just as likely to use social networking sites and other forms of social media to carry out their work as they are to use more traditional tactics.
- Major news and search sites confer legitimacy by way of algorithms that take into account what users are searching for and linking to.
- The principle of transparency is critical whether you practise public information with a journalistic set of values or with advocacy.

Summary

2.1 **Analyze public relations models on one-way/two-way and asymmetrical/symmetrical dimensions.**

One-way models of public relations are all about getting information out and, in the case of press agentry, getting attention. The public information model is one-way too, but it is more concerned with accuracy. Two-way models range from asymmetrical, in which organizations use research and feedback to persuade publics, to symmetrical, in which organizations and publics exhibit more mutual communication and change.

2.2 Demonstrate knowledge of key figures in public relations history.
Barnum, Lee, and Bernays are often associated with press agentry, public information, and scientific persuasion, respectively. But a fuller history recognizes the contributions of many other innovative communicators and strategists. The dominant history of PR globally is that of the US experience, however some attempts to establish more diverse histories from international perspectives have begun.

2.3 Integrate knowledge of social history with knowledge of public relations.
Business, religion, education, politics, and government are intertwined with public relations throughout history inasmuch as organizations and publics have communicated, persuaded, and adapted to one another over time.

2.4 Identify common motivations for strategic communication in history.
While the term *public relations* may not have existed in common use prior to the twentieth century, its functions and tactics have been applied in pursuit of recruitment, legitimacy, agitation, advocacy, and profit throughout human history.

2.5 Apply knowledge of history to analyze modern public relations practices.
Seemingly modern phenomena such as flash mobs, Internet activism, and radical transparency were preceded in history by events and actions built on the same general principles (e.g., publicity stunts, propaganda, and declarations of principles like Ivy Lee's).

2.6 Distinguish public relations from journalism.
Public relations values advocacy. Journalism values objectivity—or balance of coverage if objectivity isn't possible.

2.7 Discuss the ethics of transparency, objectivity, and advocacy.
Edward Bernays and Ivy Lee can be compared. Lee pursued journalistic integrity, but he still worked on the payroll of specific organizations to which he was loyal. Bernays embraced advocacy.

Discussion Questions

1. Some say that real-life public relations is better described with a mixed-motive model in which one-way and asymmetrical communication are used by the same organizations that are also practising symmetrical communication. Describe a relationship that you have as an individual that could be seen as mixed-motive.
2. Both Ivy Lee and Edward Bernays have been called the "father of public relations." Do either one of them deserve that title? Why or why not?
3. Name a Canadian historical event not mentioned in this chapter in which public relations played a key role, and explain how public relations was involved (even if it wasn't called public relations at the time).
4. How would P.T. Barnum use social media? Provide some specific examples.
5. Find an example of a blogger or social media influencer and describe how what they do is different from public relations.
6. Asymmetrical public relations is much more common in everyday practice than symmetrical. Does that mean most of the field is inherently unethical? Why or why not?

Further Readings and Online Resources

A Train Company Crashed Two Trains
https://www.smithsonianmag.com/history/train-company-crashed-two-trains-you-will-believe-what-happened-next-180964237/

This article by Lorriane Boissoneault examines an 1896 publicity stunt that involved deliberately crashing two locomotives. The result was an "unexpected" explosion that killed two people and injured dozens of others. Worst publicity stunt ever? See what happens next.

History of Public Relations Timeline
http://www.prmuseum.org/pr-timeline/
Yes, there is a public relations museum; it's in New York City. The museum's website provides a neat public relations timeline that starts with cave drawings and ends with virtual reality.

How different is PR in Canada versus the US?
http://marketingmag.ca/advertising/column-how-different-is-pr-in-canada-versus-the-u-s-93395/
This article, written for *Marketing* magazine by Canadian journalist Ira Basen, compares the history of public relations in both countries, and concludes that Canadian "PR is still generally seen as a more benign force than in the US." Read this article and see if you agree.

Peer-Reviewed Academic Journal Articles
Henry, S. (1997). Anonymous in her own name. *Journalism History*, 23(2), 51.
When we talk about pioneers in public relations, the names Ivy Lee and Edward Bernays immediately come to mind for most people. But there's another notable figure who remains largely unsung: Doris E. Fleishman, who, in addition to being a notable public relations practitioner and women's rights activist, was married to Edward Bernays. Read more about her fascinating career and life in this article.

Johansen, P. (2001). Professionalisation, building respectability, and the birth of the Canadian Public Relations Society. *Journalism Studies*, 2(1), 55–71.
Many Canadian public relations practitioners were journalists before they switched to public relations, and this article, which was published in a journalism journal as opposed to a PR journal, chronicles the early days of the CPRS. See if you agree with Johansen when he refers to public relations as a "semi-profession."

Key Terms

Advocacy   47
Asymmetrical model   39
Flash mob   37
Hashtag   32
News release   43
Objectivity   51

Organic search results   46
Press agentry/publicity
 model   31
Propaganda   47
Pseudo-event   46
Public information model   34

Search engine optimization
 (SEO)   46
Status conferral   46
Symmetrical model   40

Convergence and Integrated Communication

Is Red Bull an energy drink company that produces media content, or a media company that produces energy drinks?

Key learning outcomes

3.1 Define different forms of convergence.

3.2 Analyze how convergence affects public relations.

3.3 Discuss how functions of advertising and marketing may be integrated with public relations.

3.4 Distinguish public relations from advertising and marketing.

3.5 Discuss public relations' role in the free flow of information in society.

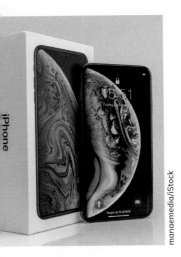

iPhone

manaemedia/iStock

ferrantraite/iStock

Black box fallacy: Multipurpose devices have not simplified life as much as some have hoped.

Why do you think that is?

Admit it. One of the very first things you do in the morning is check your media device. If not, then you are a better person than most of us. We accept updates to our apps. We check our social networking sites to see what clever memes our friends are propagating. We check business news and see how the latest round of mergers and acquisitions affects the products and services we use. Whether we realize it through the blur of our just-opened eyes, the world delivered to us by our bundled talk, text, and data plans has continued to converge and re-converge as we slept. There's a good chance many of your favourite TV shows, movies, music, and news sources are owned by the same big company. Your cultural interests increasingly overlap with people from all over the planet. This is the world you, your organization, and your publics inhabit. And it's ever more technologically, culturally, and economically converged every time you upload, download, like, snap, submit, share, or agree to yet another end-user license agreement.

Communication firms are merging and converging with one another in the global marketplace of ideas, while professional communicators continue to weigh the pros and cons of integrating public relations with advertising and marketing. Making sense of all this convergence and integration and what it means for public relations requires an understanding of the multiple dimensions of convergence, an appreciation for the workings of integrated communication, and a respect for classic principles of public relations that apply steadily as times and technologies change.

Convergence

Convergence is a concept that can be difficult to understand, in part because it has different meanings in different contexts. USC Professor Henry Jenkins recommends thinking about multiple processes of convergence.[1] Convergence can be a technological process, but convergence also describes cultural, economic, and professional processes.

Technological Convergence

We may be seduced by the idea that one day all of our media needs will be met with one elegant device. Jenkins calls it the black box fallacy. "Sooner or later, the argument goes, all media content is going to flow through a single black box into our living rooms (or, in the mobile scenario, through black boxes we carry around with us everywhere we go),"[2] but as he points out, it just doesn't work out that way.

For our author Tom Kelleher, it was the iPhone 3GS. He was one stoked customer walking out of the Apple store in the summer of 2009 with his brand-new device. In his hand, he held a phone, a compass, a GPS, a camera, a calculator, a news reader, a video recorder, a voice recorder, an audio player, a TV, and an app store that would let him turn the thing into his own portal to Twitter, Facebook, LinkedIn, or any other social network service he wanted. His mediated life was going to be simple and uncluttered. Or not. As the years go by, he and his family seem to be losing the war against technoclutter. Old tablets, phones, earbuds, cameras, wires, flash drives, charging wires, game consoles, iPods, Bluetooth devices, routers, printers, monitors, and remote controls litter his home, car, and office.

Make no mistake. Technological convergence is real. Technological convergence brings together formerly separate technical capabilities. As multiple forms of media content become digitized, opportunities for mixing and mashing them increase. "When words, images and sounds are transformed into digital information, we expand the potential relationships

Image courtesy of the Canadian Museum of Nature.

These interactive multimedia kiosks are part of a travelling exhibition on minerals produced by the Canadian Museum of Nature.

In what ways are kiosks like these a product of technological convergence?

between them and enable them to flow across platforms," wrote Jenkins in *Technology Review*.[3] We see technological convergence everywhere—on our smartphones, TVs, car dashboards, kids' games, and public kiosks.

But human uses, needs, and desires for media vary widely from person to person. There's no single solution for everyone. And there's no single media solution for any one person across every situation. This is why that magical black box doesn't exist, and it also is why public relations people must understand other dimensions of convergence beyond the technological ones.

Cultural Convergence

Just as technological convergence presents an apparent paradox (media are combining at the very same time that media technologies are proliferating), so too does cultural convergence. On one hand, we are witnessing vast cultural hegemony. Hegemony—now here's a term usually reserved for the most critical approaches to public relations.

Stemming from Marxism, cultural hegemony occurs when a ruling class imposes its social, political, or economic ideals on subordinate groups in society at the expense of cultural diversity. Public relations people are rarely portrayed as the good guys in these scenarios. "Americanization" or "McDonaldization" are examples, with "an increasing convergence on specific forms of artistic, culinary, or musical culture—usually, but not exclusively, moving from the United States, via newly global media, to the rest of the world," writes Yale Law Professor David Singh Grewal.[4] On the other hand, clearly, "cultural borrowing" increasingly works in other directions. McDonald's restaurants in India serve chicken and fish, as well as curry-infused options.

This kind of cultural borrowing can lead to accusations of cultural appropriation, which is the act of taking or using things from a culture that is not your own, especially without showing that you understand or respect that culture.

black box fallacy False notion that predicts most human communication needs will eventually be satisfied with a single device.

Technological convergence (aka digital convergence) When information of various forms such as sound, text, images, and data are digitized, affording communication across common media.

Public relations people must understand other dimensions of convergence beyond the technological ones.

cultural convergence When various forms of culture are exchanged, combined, converted, and adapted. On a global scale, this phenomenon has accelerated with the growth of digital media.

cultural hegemony The imposition of social, political, or economic ideals on subordinate groups in society.

cultural appropriation The act of taking or using things from a culture that is not your own, especially without showing that you understand or respect that culture.

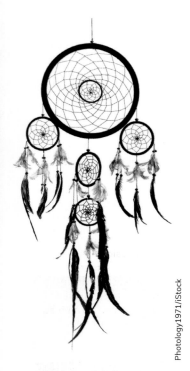

Dream catchers, which are believed to have originated from the Ojibwe nation, were traditionally used as talismans to protect sleeping people from bad dreams and nightmares. Today, they are ubiquitous and frequently created by children as a craft project.

Is this an example of cultural appropriation as some critics have suggested?

---

participatory culture
A culture in which private citizens and publics are as likely to produce and share as they are to consume; commonly applied in mediated contexts in which consumers produce and publish information online.

To the degree that successful public relations entails changes in human attitudes, knowledge, and behaviour, public relations people must work towards an enlightened understanding of their organizations' roles and their own personal roles in cultural exchanges. Jenkins describes cultural convergence as "both a top-down corporate-driven process and a bottom-up consumer-driven process."[5] Public relations people work where the two meet. They must understand and communicate from the standpoint of their organization's cultural values while understanding and interpreting their publics' cultures back to the organization, as well. Participating actively and transparently in public forums—constructively engaging **participatory culture**—is an important part of managing relationships, particularly in media environments characterized by cultural convergence.

Economic Convergence

Ketchum is a huge public relations agency with offices and affiliates in 70 countries, including Canada. Ketchum represents consumer-brand clients ranging from FedEx to Ikea to Kleenex to IBM.

If Ketchum is huge, Omnicom is huger. Omnicom acquired Ketchum as a subsidiary in 1996.[6,7] Omnicom is a global advertising, marketing, and communication services conglomerate that owns firms providing services in advertising, strategic media planning, digital marketing, direct marketing, and, of course, public relations. Omnicom serves 5,000 clients in more than 100 countries.[8] The vastness of this network entails not just public relations, but advertising, marketing, lobbying, and emerging digital and social media services, as well. This is **economic convergence**.

As with technological and cultural convergence, economic convergence presents a contradiction. At the same time that agencies are diversifying services, building networks, and opening global offices to serve geographically unique clients and publics in almost every corner of every continent, the overall number of major corporate players is dwindling. The Ketchum family tree is just one example that illustrates the size and scope of economic convergence in strategic communication. Omnicom, along with global conglomerates Interpublic and WPP, tops the list of holding firms ranked by revenues from public relations operations.

If you watched Super Bowl 50 in 2016, you saw Peyton Manning's last game as he and the Denver Broncos took down Cam Newton and the Carolina Panthers 24–10. But you also likely saw the most expensive advertising event of that year, in which $4.6 to $5 million was spent on each 30-second paid spot.[9] You might remember the Advil "Distant Memory" ad with a grandma doing yoga, or the NFL "Super Bowl Babies Choir," featuring fans born about nine months after their parents' favourite team won the big game.[10] The NFL also aired a "No More" ad against domestic violence. These three ads were products of the Grey New York advertising agency. Grey is owned by the holding company WPP. Or you may remember commercials for Colgate (owned by Colgate Palmolive), Butterfinger (owned by Nestlé) or Heinz (owned by Kraft Heinz Co.). These ads also came from agencies owned by WPP.

While public relations doesn't have a Super Bowl of its own, the case illustrates some of the pros and cons of economic convergence. Big companies have the capacity to produce excellent work. They have global networks that provide top-notch technical, creative, and strategic expertise to clients ranging from very specialized and localized organizations to mainstream companies reaching the widest possible audiences and publics. At the same time, the number of voices in the marketplace, when defined by corporate ownership, is shrinking.

For Super Bowl advertising, much of the marketplace is for commodities like candy bars, ketchup, and toothpaste. For public relations, which operates more in the marketplace of ideas than in the marketplace of commodities, the stakes may even be even higher. We may not lose sleep after learning that competing brands of pop and chips are represented by agencies that are owned by the same parent companies. But what if the clients are different national governments? How do you feel about a single communication firm representing both tobacco companies and health-care organizations? How do you feel about the NFL partnering with a non-profit organization to air anti-abuse ads during the Super Bowl? Economic convergence at the corporate level requires extra attention to public relations' role in society at large.

economic convergence When various media organizations and functions are merged under a single ownership structure. This form of media convergence is different from the term economists use to describe trends in world economies.

Professional Convergence

We can add professional convergence to the dimensions of convergence that matter most in public relations. One of the benefits of converged, multiservice agencies is that they can integrate communication functions strategically. Publicity and advertising can be used to support the marketing of consumer products. Marketing tactics can be used to support public relations. Public affairs and government relations benefit from good public relations with an organization's stakeholders. Healthy employee relations help customer service and sales. And so on, and so on.

The architects of multibillion-dollar mergers are not the only ones who must understand how all the functions go together. Each person working for each client must also understand how the functions integrate in order to manage, communicate, and counsel most effectively. From the intern to the account executive to the CEO, agencies operate best when everyone has a good sense of how their job fits into the larger mission and service to any particular client. Someone who places a hashtag in a paid TV advertisement should know what is going to happen when TV viewers jump platforms from their TVs to other screens. When the communication goes online, the company representatives monitoring the hashtag conversation should be in tune with the management of the organization hosting the exchange. The account executive, the media buyer, the advertising creative, the social media strategist, the online host, and the executives of the organization itself all need to work in concert.

Integration raises one more apparent paradox of convergence. Successful integration of functions of communication requires an understanding of, and respect for, the unique goals and contributions of each. This doesn't just apply to the big players on the world stage. Integration is equally important for in-house communications teams and for small organizations employing only a single communication specialist. In fact, if you are working alone

professional convergence When various functions of professional communication such as publicity, advertising, online services, and marketing are combined to improve strategy.

> On December 9, 2015, WestJetters came together to create 12,000 mini miracles in 24 hours.
>
> Watch what happened.

Courtesy of WestJet

Each year, West Jet spreads Christmas cheer to people across Canada and around the world through its "Christmas Miracle" campaign. Videos of this popular campaign, which have been viewed more than 50 million times since the first one was produced in 2012, can be viewed on West Jet's Christmas Miracle web page.

What types of employees and media people have to collaborate to make a campaign like this work? Are there any risks to consider in launching a campaign like this?

communicating for a small business or non-profit, you have no choice but to think through how all your communication and management functions gel together for a common purpose. Good public relations means recognizing both the differences and commonalities of advertising, marketing, and public relations.

Divergence

Using the term *paradox* to describe convergence sheds light on apparent contradictions, but, philosophically, it is not really that hard to reconcile ideas like professional diversity and integration. Divergence and convergence go hand in hand. The best chefs know the unique flavours of their individual ingredients well before they mix them together to serve the perfect dish. Chemists understand elements, compounds, and mixtures. Music directors know how each instrument plays in their ensemble. University of Amsterdam Professor Emeritus Betteke van Ruler studied communication management internationally and identified several typologies to classify types of public relations practitioners. One of those typologies is the "conductor" type of public relations person. The conductor is tasked with orchestrating different communication activities in much the same way that one leads a symphony. Before diving headfirst into integration, understand what exactly is being integrated and how public relations is fundamentally different in its goals from advertising and marketing. On the opposite side, van Ruler also identified a "town crier." Like the press agent/publicist, van Ruler's town crier is mostly seeking to be heard in the marketplace with little concern for listening to others outside of their organization. There's nothing wrong with working to gain attention in a crowded marketplace, but there is a point of diminishing returns in simply turning up the volume without stopping to listen to others. Sometimes even the best-intentioned voices do more to add to the cacophony than they do to bring clarity or understanding on the important issues they wish to discuss.

> If you place a hashtag in a TV ad, you should know what will happen when TV viewers jump platforms from their TVs to other screens.

> Before diving headfirst into integration, understand how public relations differs from advertising and marketing in its goals.

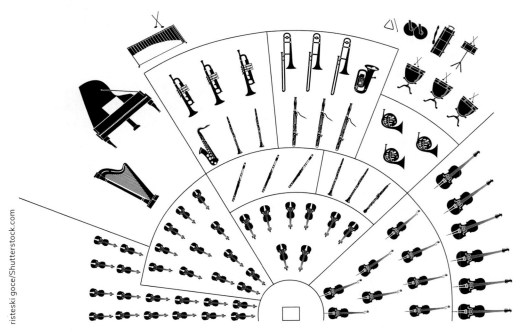

risteski goce/Shutterstock.com

Symphony orchestras offer a metaphor for integrated communication.

How is a conductor's role different from that of a town crier?

Advertising

Despite the explosion of innovation and change in media industries in recent decades, most media business models still rely on advertising dollars as a primary source of revenue. In traditional mass media, **advertising** is the paid media space that sponsors use to persuade audiences. The media space in broadcast media is measured based on time—for example, a 30-second radio or TV ad. Sponsors generally pay more for prime-time and wide-audience programming events like the Super Bowl, and less for time in local programming at off-peak times with smaller audiences. In printed newspapers or magazines, the space is sold based on lines or column inches or centimetres, or buyers may pay for the space based on the portion of the pages used such as a one-third-page ad, a half-page ad, a two-page spread, and so on.

Advertisement pricing formulas include not just the amount of time or space but also the estimated audience size, the demographics and influence of that audience, contract arrangements between the organization and the media outlet, and the context for placement and timing of the ad. For example, in 2016, the weekend circulation of *The Globe and Mail*, Canada's national newspaper, was 404,957 copies. The standard rate for advertising was $31.88 per line, and a full page was 2,800 lines, making the cost of a full-page ad almost $90,000. Meanwhile, a local ad in *The Bluffs Monitor*, a small newspaper circulated only in Scarborough, Ontario, is just $1,800. It makes a lot more sense for the local yogurt shop to advertise in *The Bluffs Monitor*. However, for an airline such as Porter, it may make more sense to advertise in *The Globe and Mail*.

One metric for calculating advertising value is **cost per thousand** (CPM) (the *M* in CPM is the Roman numeral for 1,000). A three-column-inch ad in a newspaper costing $42.60 to reach a circulation of 14,000 would yield a CPM of $42.60/14 = 3.04, or $3.04 per thousand readers. Public relations people sometimes use these calculations to figure an equivalent value for publicity when an organization is covered in the unpaid column inches of news and editorial content. This metric, known as **advertising value equivalency** (AVE), has been widely discredited as a measure of effective public relations. Proper evaluation of public relations requires much more careful thinking about the effects of communication than simply figuring what media coverage would have cost if you paid for it. The AVE issue is explored further in Chapter 8.

While newspapers and magazines make some money from subscriptions and single-copy sales, the majority of their revenue comes from advertising in the form of print advertising and online advertising paid for by marketers. (Some publications like student newspapers are free and depend almost entirely on advertising for their budgets.) Online advertising revenues are growing, while print advertising revenues are dropping.

For the price they pay, marketers get to choose the placement of their messages and design the message as they see fit for their purposes (within reason). Marketers hire advertising firms to strategically plan the precise words they want in the copy. The firms select fonts and colours that will work best. They choose the models and frame the pictures. In audio and video, they carefully design and produce the material to their own exact standards. In short, marketers buy not only media space but also the ability to control the content of that space.

Online, advertisers can buy **banner ads**, which display ads on a portion of web pages. Another option is **pre-roll advertising**, which is a commercial ad displayed for a few seconds as online video before the desired video is shown.

The CPM metric is commonly used with banner ads. Calculated based on the cost per thousand web page viewers, CPM is most similar to traditional advertising metrics for value.

advertising Media space purchased by sponsors to persuade audiences; or the practice of planning and producing this service.

cost per thousand (CPM) A measure of advertising reach that represents the cost of an advertisement relative to the estimated size of the audience.

advertising value equivalency (AVE) A calculation of the value of news or editorial coverage based on the cost of the equivalent amount of advertising space or time.

banner ads Advertisements on web pages designed to encourage users to click to reach an advertiser's site.

pre-roll advertising A commercial ad displayed as online video before the desired video is shown.

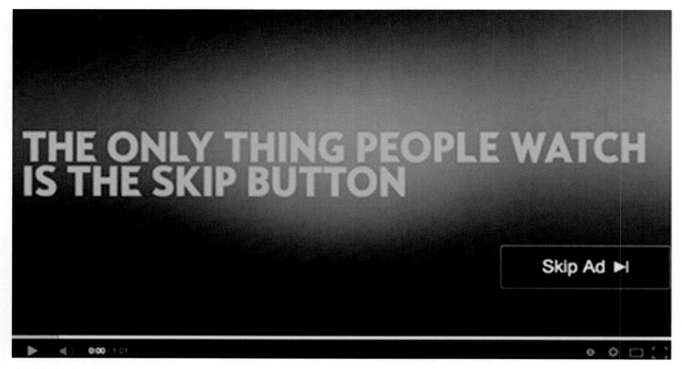

THE ONLY THING PEOPLE WATCH IS THE SKIP BUTTON

Skip Ad ▶❙

Banner ads and pre-roll ads are criticized for being annoying and ineffective.

What kind of evidence would it take to convince you these ads have value?

> *Analytics help track behaviour as users move from initial exposure to some target behaviour, such as making an online purchase.*

click-through rate
Percentage of users who view an ad on the web and click on it to reach an advertiser's site.

search advertising
Paid placement of advertising on search-engine results pages. Ads are placed to appear in response to certain keyword queries.

Of course, there are a lot more data that can be tracked online than with traditional mass media. **Click-through rate** is the percentage of users who view an ad and actually click on it. If a thousand people view a banner ad on a web page, and 15 of them click on the banner, the click-through rate is 1.5 per cent.

Newer media enterprises rely on advertising for revenue, too. Google, Yahoo, and Bing sell sponsored results that appear when users search for certain keywords. So, if you search for "yogurt," you'll find yogurt ads and links prominently displayed at the top of your results. **Search advertising** is a good deal for advertisers because they reach people who are searching for specific keywords related to their business, and the pricing is tied more closely to the behavioural results of the ad (e.g., clicking) than to the number of people assumed to be in the audience exposed to the ad. Even beyond clicking on the initial links, Google Analytics and similar services help track user behaviour as they move from initial exposure to some target behaviour such as making an online purchase or setting up an appointment to talk to a sales representative. **Analytics** is a term used to describe researching online data to identify meaningful patterns.

Media space also can be sold in the form of pop-up ads on mobile apps, promotional tweets on Twitter, banners towed behind airplanes, product placements in TV shows or movies, videos in Facebook news feeds, real billboards on the highway, virtual billboards on the highway in your video game, the hoods of NASCAR race cars, or the decks of skateboards, snowboards, and surfboards.

Organizations buy advertising to reach audiences, most commonly to persuade people to buy products or services. Effective advertising sparks a desire in people. It piques interests and persuades. People who buy an organization's products and services are certainly an important public with whom to build and maintain relationships.

But beyond seeking profit, advertising can also be used to recruit employees and members, advocate and agitate for causes, and legitimize organizations and their missions. As such, advertising is an important tool for public relations. Likewise, public relations efforts can work to support advertising.

Marketing

Of course, advertising is a tool for marketing, too. In a classic text first published in 1960, Professor E. Jerome McCarthy introduced a handy way to learn the basics of what he called the marketing mix.[11] McCarthy's four Ps include product, price, place, and promotion.

Product

The product is the thing to be sold. Very often, it is a tangible item like a car or a serving of ice cream or an electric toothbrush. Or the "product" can be a less tangible item like downloadable computer software or a service like a mobile voice, text, and data plan. Ideas and behaviours such as preventing skin cancer or registering to vote can also be marketed. Marketers are involved with the development and branding of products and product families, and they analyze product life cycles. A new product will be marketed differently from a "mature" product. T-fal, the cookware company, won a Canadian "Product of the Year" award for its new T-fal Multicook and Grains device. This digital, programmable cooker is white and square, and, at first glance, looks more like a piece of computer equipment than something you could cook your dinner with. This product obviously must be marketed differently from a mature product like one of their traditional non-stick pans. As a result, T-fal Canada has uploaded numerous videos on its YouTube channel explaining what the product is and how to use it.[12]

Price

Price is obviously an important consideration, as it determines the revenue a company receives from sales, and therefore the company's profits. Pricing is sophisticated business. A product must be priced somewhere in line with customers' perceived value and affordability. If a product is priced too low, the company will not make a profit, and, moreover, the product may be perceived as "cheap" in the negative sense of the word. Higher pricing may give the product some prestige, but if the product is not affordable, no one will buy it.

Understand that this is a gross oversimplification of pricing strategies. Many, many other factors come into play. For example, one pricing strategy is called market skimming,

Bob Leverone/NASCAR via Getty Images

Like many NASCAR drivers, Canadian Cameron Hayley has many sponsors that help fund his racing career.

How many ads do you see?

analytics Researching online data to identify meaningful patterns. In strategic communication, analytics often focus on how web traffic leads to behavioural results such as sharing information or making online purchases.

marketing Business of creating, promoting, delivering, and selling products and services.

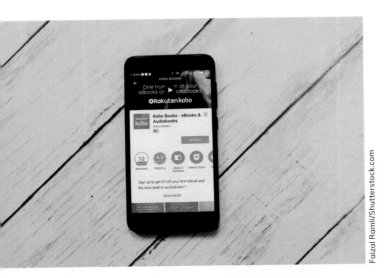

Faizal Ramli/Shutterstock.com

With digital media, the point of sale is often the same as the medium used to consume the media, such as music or audiobooks purchased on a smartphone.

How have digital media changed the way music, videos, and books are marketed?

---

market skimming
Marketing strategy that starts with higher prices for early adopters of unique products and services and then lowers prices later to sell to a broader base of consumers when competitors enter the market.

marketing mix
Combination of product, price, place, and promotion strategies in support of profitable exchange.

in which consumer products are priced higher at first when eager early adopters are willing to pay a premium for a new and unique product, but then priced lower later to appeal to broader, thriftier markets once the product is more mature in its life cycle and when similar competitors have likely entered the market. If Kwikset uses this strategy, they eventually may bring down the price of a Kevo lock into a more affordable range, especially as more lock companies start competing for business with similar products. Understanding pricing strategy requires knowledge of psychology and economics, among other social sciences. Like public relations, marketing involves research and theory to understand people and how they communicate with organizations and respond to their offerings.

Place

If you think of markets as places where buyers and sellers meet, you get a good sense of why distribution is such an important part of the **marketing mix**. You still can't download a pineapple or a pair of running shoes. Marketers have to figure out the best way to get products like these to their consumers. Produce has to be canned, frozen, or kept fresh during harvesting, packing, and shipping. Many stores and their shoppers now demand organic and locally grown foods, which means the logistics of packing and shipping interact with the appeal of the product itself. Food items are also marketed to restaurants and not just end consumers. Runners can order running shoes on the Running Room website, and they can return them for free, but many still prefer to go to an actual bricks-and-mortar store to try the shoes on and get personal advice from store staff before making a purchase.

That said, the Internet has opened many new markets and dramatically transformed others. Where do you buy music (if you buy music at all)? Probably not at a record store. At one time, most music was purchased in the form of tapes and discs, and people went to record stores to buy albums. Now most music is purchased digitally. This has changed the entire economic system of the music industry, and it has changed how music is marketed, too. Rather than focusing on how many CDs to burn and how to get the right number of those discs to the right stores where they will sell, and to the right DJs who might play them on the radio, modern music marketers pay closer attention to online downloads, playlist apps, and subscription streaming services. With digital media, the point of sale is most often online through sites like Amazon, iTunes, or eBay.

In marketing, like public relations, selecting the right channels is an important skill. Marketers choose channels of distribution to support their sales efforts. For media products like music, movies, books, and news, the channels for delivery and the channels for communication are often one and the same. You may use an e-book reader such as a Kobo or iPad to find your next novel, purchase it, and read it.

GEOFF ROBINS/AFP/Getty Images

Justin Trudeau's social media strategy is widely considered one of the deciding factors in his 2015 election win.

Why was Trudeau so successful on social media?

Promotion

If channels of distribution are the key to *place* in the marketing mix, channels of communication are the key to *promotion*. Ask a marketer what he thinks of public relations, and he will probably say he loves it as long as public relations people are not competing for control of his budget. From a marketer's perspective, public relations, like advertising, is a great tool for promotion.

Through the sales-focused lens of the marketing mix, public relations is sometimes reduced to tactics such as **publicity**. As a tool for both marketing and public relations, publicity can be defined broadly as activity designed to draw media attention. Publicity can be compared to advertising in three major ways: cost, control, and credibility.

In terms of *cost*, advertisers pay to guarantee media space, while publicity entails unpaid media coverage. Publicity happens when an organization, person, product, or service is covered as part of a news story, editorial, feature article, interview, or any other news format in broadcast, print, or online media. In this sense, publicity is "free," but there are many other costs in gaining good publicity, including staff salaries, production of multimedia content, planning and hosting special events, and managing an organization in a way that makes it newsworthy in the first place.

Advertisers get to *control* the message that they present in the media space that they buy. Promoters using publicity cede that control to editors, TV producers, journalists, analysts, bloggers, and any other third parties who bring news to audiences and publics.

Promoters promote. Advocates advocate. Salespeople sell. That's what they are supposed to do. Independent journalists, on the other hand, are expected to consider other perspectives

publicity Unpaid media coverage, or the practice of deliberately planning and producing information and activities to attract this coverage.

on the story. If you send a tech writer a sample of your new smartphone-enabled door lock with a news release about the product launch, she may rave about it in her column or on her blog. Or she may test it against competing devices and report that your product stinks in comparison. Or—and this is probably the most common response to attempts at publicity— she may just ignore you altogether. This is all part of media relations, which will be discussed more in Chapter 5.

Because advertisers pay to communicate the message, they may appear to have less *credibility*. One reason for giving up control of the message is that good publicity benefits from **third-party credibility**. If you (first party) are trying to persuade a potential customer (second party) to buy your product, the independent reporting of a third party may help your case. Of course, you think your product is great, and if you buy ad space, you're going to use it to say so. Consumers understand that. But when independent sources—such as tweeters, magazine columnists, or newspaper reporters—present your product in a positive light as part of a tweet, column, or news story, their opinions might carry more weight for the very reason that they don't come from the same party who is trying to profit from product sales.

Third-party credibility is not necessarily a law of nature. Research has shown that publicity isn't always more persuasive than advertising, but the general idea stands that publicity brings something to the mix that advertising doesn't. Even though publicity is not free, there are times when it is certainly more economical in reaching customers than advertising, and good publicity has the added benefit of being delivered by a source *independent* of your organization.

Marketers also use **word-of-mouth promotion**. The US Word of Mouth Marketing Association (WOMMA) keeps its definition simple: "any business action that earns a customer recommendation."[13] The third-party idea applies here too, except with word of mouth, the third party is more likely to be someone the customer knows and trusts on a more personal level. When you get information on a product or a brand from your friends chatting in class or posting on Instagram, that's word of mouth. When you turn around and share that information with others, you become the third party. WOMMA advocates word-of-mouth marketing that is

1. Credible: Marketing messages flow from businesses to customers and from customers to other customers and are honest and authentic;
2. Respectful: Businesses are transparent and earn consumer trust regarding privacy matters;
3. Social: WOM marketers encourage and engage in conversations about their products by actively listening and responding online and offline;
4. Measurable: WOM programs are well-defined, monitored, and evaluated in gauging success; and
5. Repeatable: A business repeats its WOM success over and over again to the point where it becomes a "truly talkable brand."[14]

Integration

Professional communicators must understand the differences among communication functions. As media systems converge, however, the lines between public relations, advertising, and marketing—as everyone else sees them—blur.

---

third-party credibility Assumption that information delivered from an independent source is seen as more objective and believable than information from a source with a vested interest in persuasion.

word-of-mouth promotion Passing of information and recommendations from person to person.

Word-of-mouth marketing should be credible, respectful, social, measurable, and repeatable.

Is the Canadian Tire pin board on Pinterest a tool for marketing or public relations? If Kleenex Canada runs a nuptial-themed series of Facebook videos timed to coincide with the summer wedding season and sees an increase in sales, is that advertising or public relations? When American Eagle's lingerie and apparel brand Aerie launched "The Real You Is Sexy" campaign to promote positive body images and encouraged users to post to Instagram or Twitter using #aeriereal to be featured on the brand's sites, was that public relations or marketing?[15] What about paying a Kardashian to retweet your content? Or the LEGO YouTube channel—do you consider that a tool for public relations or marketing?

These may be important questions for the sponsoring organizations as they budget for specific departments, but from a consumer's perspective, a brand should speak with one consistent voice. As consumers, we may understand that an organization is responsible for the communication, but we usually don't spend much time thinking about whether the communication is coming from an advertising or marketing or public relations department, or even from other consumers. This consistency and seamlessness in the minds of consumers and publics is a key outcome of effective integrated communication.

Integrated Marketing Communication

As a customer, you probably have a pretty clear idea how you feel about, say, your local grocery store. This feeling, or attitude, is based on your points of contact with the store, its products, and its brand. Sure, you're influenced by your previous shopping trips there, but also the coupons they mail you, advertisements you've seen on TV, the prices they charge, conversations with friends who worked there, a donation they made to your club, events they have sponsored, the way they let little leaguers sell candy bars out front, whether they buy produce from local farmers, their new app for your smartphone, and their membership card program. Whether you shop at the store depends on your beliefs and attitudes about the store, and in your mind that "clear idea" of how you feel is based on countless factors. As a customer, you don't lose sleep over what was public relations, marketing, or advertising. But for the people promoting the store and its sales, a major challenge is to coordinate all of these points of communication as smoothly and effectively as possible.

In generating sales revenue, **integrated marketing communication** is key. At times, public relations tactics may be applied in support of advertising, marketing, or sales promotion. At other times, the tools of advertising and marketing may be used as tools for public relations. In either case, effective convergence of organizational communication and management functions means smooth integration from the perspective of the organization's publics.

In the early 1990s, at the dawn of this digital age of participatory media, Bob Lauterborn called for a shift of thinking about the functions of advertising, marketing, and related communication functions. Lauterborn, a former advertising executive for large, US-based companies such as General Electric and International Paper Co. was an early proponent of integration. He recognized how the shifting landscape of media was changing the nature of communication between organizations and their customers: "In the days of 'Father Knows Best,' it all seemed so simple. The advertiser developed a product, priced it to make a profit, placed it on the retail shelf, and promoted it to a pliant, even eager consumer."[16] With the rise of digital media, consumer options for interaction with organizations increased. Communicators needed to think differently about the people with whom they were attempting to communicate. Those pushing for integrated communication advocated an

integrated marketing communication
Strategic coordination of communication functions such as marketing, advertising, and publicity to achieve a consistent concept in consumers' minds.

outside-in approach that started with people rather than products. In response to the four Ps, Lauterborn introduced the four Cs.

Consumer

Consumer wants and needs should replace product. "You can't sell whatever you can make any more. You can only sell what someone specifically wants to buy. The feeding frenzy is over; the fish are out of school," Lauterborn wrote in *Advertising Age* in 1990. The rise of mass media in human history accompanied the rise of mass production and consumption. As innovations of the Industrial Revolution made it easier for manufacturers to produce massive quantities of products (picture automobile assembly lines or truckloads of cases of identical cans of beer), mass media provided appropriate channels for promoting those goods (picture high-speed newspaper presses or Olympic-sized TV audiences). Henry Ford's famous quote sums up the relationship between the mass producer and his publics: "Any customer can have a car painted any colour that he wants so long as it is black."[17]

Of course, mass production and mass communication still define much of our world, but what Lauterborn and others noticed about the role of consumers changing in the 1980s and 1990s has only accelerated in this millennium.

Cost

Cost to satisfy wants and needs should replace "price." Beyond just dollars and cents that people pay for goods and services are many other costs. What are they giving up to make the

Photo by Popperfoto via Getty Images/Getty Images

Mass production led to mass promotion via mass media during the Industrial Revolution.

How has the relationship between organizations and the consumers they market to changed?

purchase? How much time does it take? Psychological factors come into play too. Lauterborn mentioned the costs of conscience and guilt. The dialogue of the satirical TV series *Portlandia* presents the polar opposite of Henry Ford's example in modern-era markets:

Waitress:	If you have any questions about the menu, please let me know.
Female diner:	I guess I do have a question about the chicken. If you can just tell us a little more about it?
Waitress:	The chicken is a heritage breed, woodland-raised chicken that's been fed a diet of sheep's milk, soy, and hazelnuts.
Male diner:	And this is local?
Waitress:	Yes, absolutely.
Male diner:	I'm going to ask you just one more time, and it's local?
Waitress:	It is.
Female diner:	Is that USDA Organic, or Oregon Organic, or Portland Organic?
Waitress:	It's just all-across-the-board organic.
Male diner:	The hazelnuts, these are local?
Female diner:	And how big is the area where the chickens are able to roam free? . . .

The questioning continues until the waitress leaves and comes back with the chicken's papers. ("His name was Colin.")[18] The humour in this sketch comes from its kernel of truth about the increasing level of responsiveness to and understanding of consumer wants and needs required to compete in modern consumer-centred marketplaces.

Convenience

Convenience to buy should replace "place." Our concept of marketplaces has followed a historical cycle similar to media and manufacturing. The local food movement is a throwback to times before the Industrial Revolution. Back then, if you didn't raise your own chickens or grow your own vegetables, you probably interacted with the farmer who did. People bought shoes from cobblers and not mall outlets. The Industrial Revolution added convenience in some ways, but most of that convenience was driven from the supply side. Supermarkets and big-box stores stand as evidence of that. Nonetheless, there are limits to what you as a consumer can find by going to a bricks-and-mortar Hudson's Bay, Walmart, or Roots store, and driving there to see what's available seems more and more inconvenient. "People don't have to go anyplace anymore," said Lauterborn, describing the era of catalogues, credit cards, and phone orders in 1990 that would soon become the era of eBay and Etsy.

Communication

Communication should replace "promotion." Perhaps this is the most profound change suggested. In *The Cluetrain Manifesto: The End of Business as Usual*, Internet visionaries Doc Searls and David Weinberger painted a nostalgic picture of early markets as real places "filled with people, not abstractions or statistical aggregates" that were alive with interpersonal conversations. Those conversations, they argued, were interrupted by the industrial era. Searls and Weinberger welcomed a return to richer, less promotional, interaction between people afforded by the Internet and social media, "where markets are getting more connected and more powerfully vocal every day."[19] With the growth of social media, other hybrids of journalism and marketing-related functions have arisen.

Hybrid Functions

It is no secret that a common career path for public relations people leads through a newsroom of some sort—a career track that dates back to Ivy Lee (Chapter 2). Some of the most skilled and influential people working in public relations have worked as journalists, and many college programs in public relations share academic space and curricula with journalism. Experience working with and training alongside journalists helps tremendously with the media-relations aspect of public relations.

You know those harsh deadlines and penalties for factual errors in your writing assignments in school? Those really do help train you for the "real world" of public relations. If you take a news writing class or work at your college or university newspaper or intern at a TV news station, you are also making contacts and building working relationships with people in the media who may help you throughout your career. Learning the news business and its core values and ethics gives you a tacit sense of where the line between journalism and public relations is drawn. Yet, even if you never work in the news media—and many of the best public relations people have not—understanding newsworthiness and practising storytelling are important for success in your job in public relations.

The most effective public relations people have always been good storytellers. Good stories, told well, make complex organizations and ideas understandable. That kind of communication helps build and maintain relationships between organizations and publics. Advertisers and marketers have always endeavoured to tell stories too, but their channels have been constrained to scarce paid space, and their focus has traditionally been tied to sales and customer loyalty. The concurrent trends of integrated communication strategy and increased channels for communication have set the stage for some interesting hybrids.

In **content marketing**, organizations develop media content to attract audiences and interact with publics. The content may be narrative stories, videos, photo memes, blogs, statistics, or infographics, but the idea is to make it interesting and engaging enough that people will seek it, consume it, and share it for its own information or entertainment value rather than see it as an interruption to some other media experience. People are bombarded with unrequested advertising and marketing messages all day every day, and they work hard to avoid and ignore them with DVR fast-forwarding, spam filters, and ad marginals. Content marketing is a counter-tactic, but not an adversarial one. Instead of being pushier, content marketers work to draw people to them on their own accord; this is also called **inbound marketing**. According to the Content Marketing Institute, "The essence of this content strategy is the belief that if we, as businesses, deliver consistent, ongoing valuable information to buyers, they ultimately reward us with their business and loyalty."[20]

By most definitions, the goal of content marketing is still pretty much straight marketing. The "targets" are still labelled customers, buyers, and audiences, but the fact that content marketing involves organizational storytelling and communication engagement

---

content marketing
Development and sharing of media content to appeal to consumers as part of an indirect marketing strategy in which consumers are drawn primarily to media content instead of directly to the product being marketed.

inbound marketing
Marketing strategy that focuses on tactics for attracting customers with useful, entertaining, or valuable information that customers find on blogs, search results, and other forms of online and social media.

> Good stories, told well, make complex organizations and ideas understandable.

Red Bull's Content Marketing Strategy

Imagine you're trying to write an assignment, but Red Bull is making it really hard for you to stay focused. You have just opened www.redbull.com to do some research, and find yourself seven minutes into a video of snowboarder Jeff Moore, watching him pull a front-side 360 off a three-story parking garage before being chased away by the building's security crew. You even have to skip an "ad" for Microsoft OneDrive to get to the video "content" on Red Bull's embedded YouTube channel. You can't tell the video series from the advertising from the marketing from the public relations. They've got fantastic photography, incredible videos, sharply written feature stories, and inspiring blogs by extreme athletes. Not only do they have the obligatory Facebook, Twitter, Instagram, YouTube, and Pinterest buttons, but the content is actually something you might want to share with your friends on these networks (or in your assignment). From a strategy standpoint, though, the most interesting part is that there is *no mention whatsoever* of the Red Bull beverage product unless you seek it out. In the far upper-right corner of the web page there are two small links for "Products and company" and "Shop." That's content marketing.

that likely reverberates well beyond sales makes it an important point of integration in an organization's communication efforts. Red Bull is a prime example. As *Mashable* tech writer James O'Brien put it, "Red Bull is a publishing empire that also happens to sell a beverage."[21]

The term **brand journalism** describes a similar strategy, but as the name indicates, the primary focus is on journalistic skills. Critics of content marketing are concerned that the practice will lead to backlash as the mad dash to provide content in support of sales will lead to poorer quality content and strategy. According to Christopher Penn of SHIFT Communications, "As content marketers struggle to keep up with the demands of creating content all the time that's high quality, increasingly they'll look to professionals who can maintain that pace without breaking a sweat—journalists."[22]

Chrysler Group LLC followed this strategy when it hired Ed Garsten, a veteran journalist with 20 years at CNN as correspondent, bureau chief, anchor, and producer, and experience as a national auto writer at the Associated Press and General Motors beat writer for *The Detroit News*. As head of Chrysler Digital Media, Garsten led a team that handled the Chrysler media website, broadcast communications, social media, and video production. "Most of us on the 8-person team have had actual television news and/or production experience giving us the background and skills to launch an in-house video operation for Chrysler Communications," blogged Garsten in describing the operation.[23] While Garsten and his team clearly brought journalistic talent to the job, the broader strategy is still one of marketing and public relations.

brand journalism Application of journalistic skills to produce news content for an organization to communicate directly with its publics without going through a third-party news organization.

Reproduced with permission of the Salvation Army

Sometimes ads are purchased to do more than sell goods or services.

How do these advertisements serve a public relations function?

How Public Relations Is Different at Its Core

In Chapter 1, we defined public relations as the management of relationships between an organization and its publics. In Chapter 2, we saw how public relations differs from journalism in that public relations people ethically advocate on behalf of their organizations, while journalists seek to report without bias favouring any one particular organization. In this chapter, we find that advertising and marketing overlap considerably with public relations. Many of the same tools and skills apply to all three endeavours, and all three work to promote an organization and its products, services, and ideas, but public relations differs in at least three ways: in its organization, publics, and relationships—the three main components of its core definition.

Organization (Beyond Offerings)

Marketing and advertising are primarily concerned with promoting an organization's offerings, and most often those offerings are products and services that the organization sells or exchanges to remain profitable. Public relations also promotes an organization's offerings, but, more important, *public relations promotes the organization as a whole*. There are exceptions to this general rule such as institutional advertising, which is paid advertising space that promotes an organization more than any of its specific products or services. However,

> When an ad serves an institutional goal beyond sales and marketing, it is acting as a tool for public relations.

when an ad serves an institutional goal beyond sales and marketing, it is acting as a tool for public relations.

Publics (Beyond Audiences)

In this chapter's discussion of advertising and marketing, you may have noticed that the groups of people who are targeted for advertising and marketing are referred to as audiences and not publics. The term **target audience** implies a carefully identified group of people who are chosen in strategy development for their propensity to buy an organization's products, services, or ideas. Marketers pay for advertising in the newspaper to reach readers who might buy yogurt or lease private jets. They buy ads on FM radio or Spotify to reach listeners who may purchase software. They sell insurance to Facebook users and medicine to TV news viewers. Readers, listeners, users, and viewers are all best described as *audiences* in this context because their primary relationship to the organization is one of financial exchange.

In advertising and marketing, organizations want to persuade audiences to buy stuff. These groups also fit the definition of publics because customers and consumers certainly have an effect on organizations, and organizations certainly have an effect on them. However, public relations people are responsible for building and maintaining relationships with publics even when the publics may never buy or sell anything from or to the organization. Neighbours, employees, students, volunteers, competitors, voters, taxpayers, disaster victims, beachgoers, and bicyclists may all be publics for certain organizations in circumstances in which no financial exchange is involved. The term *public* implies a more balanced two-way relationship than the term *audience*—one that is not predicated on the probability of a direct profit.

Relationships (Beyond Sales)

In advertising and marketing, relationships are a means to an end, and that end is usually sales. In public relations, maintaining relationships is an end in itself to the degree that an organization's success or failure depends on healthy working relationships with all sorts of publics beyond customers and those in the product supply chain. Media relations is a good example. Public relations people nurture relationships with journalists and editors in local, national, and global media. Yes, favourable publicity is a common goal, but the scope and duration of the relationship is much greater than any one promotional strategy. Because publicity in reputable news outlets cannot be bought like advertising, public relations people have to work to understand journalists and their interests in order to understand how to provide useful information to journalists as they do their work. Public relations people also need to build trust with the media.

Publicity isn't always welcome. During crises, public relations people work under great stress to preserve their organization's interests and resolve problems, while reporters are out to report what the organization has done wrong. Their roles are at odds, yet they still rely on each other. Public relations practitioners need journalists to help them communicate with their publics. Journalists need the public relations people to help them understand what happened. The greater the amount of mutual trust, the better each party will be able to perform during tense times. As we'll see in later chapters, trust is one important dimension of relationships, and news media are just one type of public with whom public relations people must maintain relationships.

target audience Group of people strategically identified for their propensity to consume an organization's products, services, or ideas.

> Building and maintaining relationships with publics is essential, even if they never buy from or sell anything to your organization.

> The greater the trust between public relations people and journalists, the better each party will be able to perform during tense times.

Voices from the Field

Sean Moffitt

Image courtesy of Sean Moffitt

Sean Moffitt is recognized as a business thought-leader, strategy advisor, digital innovator, keynote speaker, and author. After a number of executive strategy and marketing positions at Fortune 500 firms Procter & Gamble, Molson Coors, and Diageo, he founded Wikibrands (www.wiki-brands.com) and Agent Wildfire to deliver both consultancy and marketing services in a fast-changing digital marketplace. He recently launched The North Collective—a global, future-proofing solutions firm partnering with change-driven organizations—and CSW2—a services group connecting the dots of the crowd economy.

Sean has worked with hundreds of companies on digital strategy, culture, and marketing challenges, and acts as an executive advisor on a number of boards. As one of Canada's leading thinkers and practitioners on the digital marketplace, Sean keynotes and delivers workshops at dozens of events annually and has spoken in over 20 countries.

Do you see public relations as fundamentally different from marketing and advertising? Why or why not?
I think public relations is a fundamentally different skill set but perhaps not a distinct position in the future. We recently conducted a piece of research called "The Customer Zeitgeist" where we asked this question and 82 per cent of our panel agreed that the worlds of marketing, communications, PR, and even customer service are starting to blend together into one customer-focused discipline. In its current state, PR has a distinct set of characteristics around managing and defending a certain set of external stakeholders through content, outreach, and a variety of other outbound activities. The line will increasingly blur in the future as marketing customizes and personalizes its focus on external audiences while technology, new media, and artificial intelligence help shorten the gap between media, influencers, investors, customers, and stakeholders inclined to receive a brand's messages positively.

There's a great deal of discussion these days about "integrated marketing and communications." What does that phrase mean to you?
Integrated marketing and communications is the desired goal to treat their customer with experiences and activities positively and consistently across all their touchpoints and intersections with the brand. This means blending all marketing, PR, digital, media, and customer experience activities under one roof. It remains as an unrealized goal in most environments as companies struggle to build a single view of the customer, different corporate silos and leadership positions fail to align their efforts to the same goals, and various agencies and vendors act as a patchwork quilt of offerings that fail to work in concert with each other.

Is IMC a trend or is this a way of operating that's here to stay?
If you look at leading-edge companies, integrated marketing communications is a way of life. Leading tech companies and fast-growing SaaS (software as a service) companies both operate and appear as one integrated entity to their audiences. As these companies become the future benchmarks and hallmarks for great marketing and communications, and their staff leave to lead other less tech-related companies, their integrated practices will permeate other more traditional-minded and marketing-segmented companies and industries.

What about brand journalism or content marketing—how do they fit in?
The line between what is valuable content and what is marketing is being blurred. This development has both positive and negative implications. On a positive front, it's always been a paradox that the businesses funding content insert their ads and publicity that people have to suffer through to get to read, view, or watch what they want. Now some business-generated content is indecipherable from entertainment, user-generated content,

and journalism. The downside of this trend is that customers and audiences don't know when they are being sold to and in many cases, who is behind each message. As media entities continue to flounder in finding the revenue streams, the acceptance of advertorial and native advertising will become commonplace.

How do you feel about the merging of agencies into bigger and bigger conglomerates? Are clients being served better?

The benefits of scaling the size of agencies is simply not there. The basis of solid client–agency relationships and resulting good work is dependent on customer empathy and industry understanding, bespoke and customized service, and shared values. By making agencies larger and more global, the industry has become vanilla, more depersonalized, and more separated from client reality. With some notable exceptions (driven by efficiency), client service has suffered by the conglomeratization of agencies.

How about smaller firms or in-house communication operations? What kinds of challenges do they face in an age of convergence?

The trend is to bring services in house or contract services that were previously provided by agencies. To truly integrate content, media, and creative functions,

clients are realizing that these functions frequently need to be housed inside companies. Aided by technology, the services previously provided by agencies (e.g., media planning and buying, content and design development, analytics and insight) are being disintermediated and more efficiently handled by client staff.

Smaller agencies that have a specialized reputation or niche are surviving, with some thriving. Smaller agencies that are trying to be full service are being impacted by their ability to find strong and tech-literate talent and by clients who are challenging their fee structures. With a tenuous and mercurial environment, agency cultures are being buffeted between differing client and agency objectives, between agency management directives and less loyal front-line talent behaviours, and between account management and creative teams.

Any specific advice for the next generation of practitioners?

You are a business person first, PR person second. Your real and perceived value in the industry will be derived by how much you can advance or defend the value of the company you work for, not based on the calibre of your inputs. Increasingly in the future, your efforts will be more measurable, attributable, and linkable to your company/client bottom lines.

Ethics: Free Flow of Information

The Globe and Mail reported that some of the country's biggest television providers have been accepting payments from RT—the Kremlin-controlled news channel that is considered part of Russia's propaganda machine—in return for ensuring that it is widely available to Canadian households.[24]

RT has consistently responded to criticism of its reporting by positioning itself along a spectrum of news services that have a point of view, in the same way that Fox News represents a conservative interpretation of current events or, more broadly, the way that a Canadian perspective guides the operations of any Canadian news channel.

"This is not the CBC or the BBC we're talking about. Its deliberate mission is to politically undermine or destabilize Western countries . . . and to sow and encourage societal divisions," said Peter Van Loan, a Conservative MP who has raised concerns with the CRTC about RT's carriage deals with television providers.

As viewer habits shift, TV screens are not RT's only priority. The network has been working to expand its influence on social media and enjoys wide reach there, with nearly 2.8 million subscribers on YouTube, 4.8 million followers on Facebook, and nearly 2.7 million on Twitter for its main accounts. RT claims to be the "most watched news network on YouTube," if it combines views on all of its YouTube channels.

Transparency is certainly an issue to be discussed in the context of convergence. It presents yet another apparent paradox. On one hand, convergence has made identifying original sources of information a more complicated task. On the other hand, the distributed nature of communication makes transparency more of an imperative for effective relationship-building. If there is a single word to describe how the culture of emerging media differs from traditional mass media, it is *participation*.

Participatory media allow people to not only consume information but also to report and disseminate it. Blogging journalists who interact and collaborate with their readers as sources are taking advantage of the participatory nature of social media to do their research and to tell their stories. Cultural convergence in a digital media environment means that people from around the world can work together to participate in the news cycle by pooling resources to investigate stories. Public relations in this era means engaging participatory culture rather than fighting it.

When a huge public relations firm represents one of the largest nations on Earth as its client, economic convergence is definitely part of the story. Cultural convergence is too. In this case cultures clashed on two levels: first, the tension between nations and, second, the friction between layers of media.

As discussed in Chapter 2, advocacy is part of public relations; however, most codes of ethics also call for disclosure of information including naming their clients. Does this mean Ketchum should have done more to proactively disclose its work for Putin when it had Russia as a client?

Prime Minster Justin Trudeau has openly criticized Putin saying Russia needs to start playing a more positive role in the world on a variety of fronts.

What sort of conflicts of interest may arise when public relations firms represent national governments?

In Case You Missed It

To fully understand public relations, you must be able to zoom in on specific strategies and tactics and then zoom out to see the big picture of convergence and integration. Here are some snapshots from the different focal points in this chapter.

- Public relations people must understand other dimensions of convergence beyond the technological ones.
- If you place a hashtag in a TV ad, you should know what will happen when TV viewers jump platforms from their TVs to other screens.
- Before diving headfirst into integration, understand how public relations differs from advertising and marketing in its goals.

- Analytics help track behaviour as users move from initial exposure to some target behaviour, such as making an online purchase.
- Word-of-mouth marketing should be credible, respectful, social, measurable, and repeatable.
- Good stories, told well, make complex organizations and ideas understandable.
- When an ad serves an institutional goal beyond sales and marketing, it is acting as a tool for public relations.
- Building and maintaining relationships with publics is essential, even if those publics never buy from or sell anything to your organization.
- The more trust between public relations people and journalists, the better each party will be able to perform during tense times.

ICYMI

Summary

3.1 Define different forms of convergence.
Rather than being a single trend, convergence is better thought of as a number of processes that can be defined separately, including technological, cultural, economic, and professional convergence.

3.2 Analyze how convergence affects public relations.
Technological convergence affects the communication tools and tactics public relations people use. Cultural convergence means that understanding the interaction of organizational cultures and public cultures is an increasingly important task with more global contexts than ever before. As firms merge, economic convergence affects services on both a local and global level. Professional convergence is what happens when those services (and the jobs of the people who provide them) are integrated.

3.3 Discuss how functions of advertising and marketing may be integrated with public relations.
When integration is done right, advertising and marketing support public relations, and vice versa. In the minds of publics, an organization's management and communication efforts should be consistent.

3.4 Distinguish public relations from advertising and marketing.
Public relations is different from advertising and marketing in that it focuses on the overall relationship between the whole organization and many of its publics. Products are only part of what is promoted. Customers are only one public. Relationships are about much more than sales and profit.

3.5   Discuss public relations' role in the free flow of information in society.
Public relations practitioners advocate for organizations in the marketplace of ideas. Advocacy is a central value in democratic societies, but public relations people must remain transparent about their role and purpose.

Discussion Questions

1.   Do you have more or fewer media devices now than you did two years ago? How has techno-logical convergence changed your day-to-day media use?
2.   In 2017, Victoria's Secret was accused of cultural appropriation when its models came out dressed in lingerie "inspired by Indigenous African cultures." What is the difference between cultural convergence and cultural appropriation? If you make a dream catcher in art class is that cultural appropriation? What if you purchase one from the Whetung Ojibwa Centre near Peterborough, Ontario?
3.   Describe an advertisement you've recently observed that does not seem to be selling a par-ticular product or service. Who is the ad "marketing" to and why?
4.   Would you rather work for a public relations agency/department or an integrated communi-cation agency/department? Explain your preference.
5.   Do you think a public relations firm in one country should represent the foreign government of another country during times of conflict between the two nations? Discuss your ethical reasoning.

Further Readings and Online Resources

What is IMC? A Beginner's Guide to Integrated Marketing and Communications
https://learn.g2crowd.com/integrated-marketing-communications
This blogpost by Grace Pinegar includes some interesting examples of recent IMC campaigns.

Glossary of Terms
https://contentconnection.prsa.org/all-about-pr/glossary
The Public Relations Society of America (PRSA) publishes a handy glossary of public relations terms, which includes *advertising, marketing,* and *marketing communications.* Do you see how the lines between these functions might be blurred?

SickKids' $1.3 Billion Fundraising Supernova: VS Limits
http://cmolab.ca/media/sickkids-1-3b-fundraising-supernova-vs-limits/
The SickKids Foundation recently launched the largest fundraising campaign in the history of Canadian health care as they sought to raise $1.3 billion for a new hospital. This podcast, produced by CMO Lab, features an interview with Lori Davison, vice-president of brand, strat-egy, and communications at SickKids, and explains how integrated marketing and communi-cations was critical to the campaign's success.

Peer-Reviewed Academic Journal Article
Smith, B.G. (2013). The public relations contribution to IMC: Deriving opportunities from threats and solidifying public relations' future. *Public Relations Review, 39*(5), 507–13. doi:10.1016/j.pubrev.2013.09.012
This article suggests that integrated marketing communications, or IMC, has largely been led by marketing, but the field of public relations, with its unique view of stakeholders, needs to take part in the future development of IMC.

Key Terms

4

Relationship Management

As Kermit the Frog sang, "It's not easy being green." How does Coca-Cola balance its main business of selling soda with efforts to promote healthy living?

▲ creativep/Alamy Stock Photo

Congratulations! You made it. You're the vice-president of public relations. You're seated in a bright glass conference room, taking in a sweeping view of the city skyline with your counterparts in legal, accounting, and marketing. You've earned a coveted seat at the proverbial management table—the C-suite. But the mood darkens a bit when the CEO enters, takes a seat with the sun at her back, and says she needs to trim some expenses. She then asks everyone to justify their budgets.

The head of legal explains how his unit is winning lawsuits and keeping the organization in compliance with various laws to avoid costly penalties. The chief financial officer (CFO) presents impressive budget figures and forecasts. The chief marketing officer (CMO) draws a direct link between his department and sales revenue.

It's your turn. What do you say?

This is somewhat of a trick question because much of what you do in public relations is done in collaboration with the others. Excellent public relations helps resolve disputes before they become crises or end up in litigation. The CFO relies on public relations for help communicating in a timely and accurate manner with all financial stakeholders, including shareholders, employees, and analysts. And, as we saw in Chapter 3, public relations and marketing work together in support of sales and profit. But what does public relations do in its own right? In public relations, you manage the relationships that all of the other departments depend upon. This is your time to shine.

This chapter builds on a broader definition of public relations as the management of mutually beneficial relationships with publics. Relationships built around news, commerce, and contentious issues are all part of the field, and this chapter discusses jobs in those areas of public relations. At the highest levels of organizational management, however, relationships with all of an organization's stakeholders must be managed simultaneously and in balance. Corporate social responsibility is one strategy for reaching that balance, and this chapter includes an illustrative case from one of the world's largest companies. But regardless of the size or mission of your organization, the ethical, harmonious, and simultaneous management of all those relationships may be one of the toughest jobs there is.

Managing Relationships

If we want to understand organization–public relationships and explain how those relationships are beneficial, we have to think about real people and how they interact with one another. Starting in the 1980s, public relations educators and practitioners began to turn their focus from publicity to relationships. In 1984, the same year that Grunig and Hunt published *Managing Public Relations*, Professor Mary Ann Ferguson presented a key paper calling for public relations scholars to focus on relationships as the central idea for the field.

In the decades that followed, organization–public relationships became a more prominent topic for research and for understanding public relations in general. In 2000, Professors John Ledingham and Stephen Bruning published *Public Relations as Relationship Management*, a text that advocated turning away from the idea of public relations as mainly "a means of generating favorable publicity" and embracing "the notion that relationships ought to be at the core of public relations scholarship."[1] The ensuing shift in thinking rose concurrently with the rise of new ways for publics to communicate with organizations. Social media emerged as alternatives to mass media at the same time that we moved from seeing public relations as an overwhelmingly mass-mediated phenomenon to a more conversational, relationship-building one.

This illustration by Felipe Dávalos is of an Aztec marketplace.

How might relationships in digital marketplaces be similar to relationships in ancient marketplaces?

participatory media Media in which publics actively participate in producing and sharing content.

relational maintenance strategies Ways of building and sustaining mutually beneficial relationships between organizations and publics.

In heralding the rise of **participatory media**, social media enthusiasts welcomed a return to the more direct way of communicating that was common before industrialization and mass communication drove a wedge between organizations and their publics. They refocused on the importance of conversations in the marketplaces where organizations and publics meet.

For some insights on how to understand relationships between organizations and publics, scholars turned to interpersonal communication research. They sought to discover if what worked in relationships between spouses or between doctors and patients, for instance, might help us better understand the strategies that would succeed in organization–public relationships.

Taking Care of Relationships

Professors Dan Canary and Laura Stafford have studied interpersonal relationships for decades. In the early 1990s, they catalogued a number of successful **relational maintenance strategies**, which included the following:

- Positivity: expressing favourable attitudes, and interacting with partners in a cheerful, uncritical manner
- Openness: self-disclosure, directly discussing the nature of the relationship including its problems, and willingness to listen
- Assurances: covertly and overtly communicating the importance of the relationship and a desire to continue with the relationship
- Social networking: relying on the support of mutual friends and common affiliations
- Sharing tasks: performing one's responsibilities including routine tasks and chores; in a marriage or partnership, this may include cooking, cleaning, and managing finances

In research reports for the Institute for Public Relations, Professors Linda Hon and James Grunig took these strategies and recommended a shift to focus on public, rather than interpersonal, relationships.

- Openness would include disclosures about the nature of the organization and information of value to its publics.
- Assurances would include communication that emphasized the importance of publics in the relationship.
- Social networking would involve an emphasis on common affiliations between the organization and publics—on social networking sites, these links might take the form of shared Twitter followers, LinkedIn connections, or mutual likes on Facebook.

© Felipe Dávalos/Mexicolore

- Sharing tasks would include asking for public support or offering support when appropriate—as when an organization voices its backing for a cause, encourages employees to volunteer, or makes a donation.

Key Outcomes of Relationships

Depending on the specific goals and objectives of organization–public relationships, mutually beneficial relationships may come in many forms. The benefits may come as the result of **exchange relationships**, as when a customer buys a product or service. If the transaction goes well, the company earns sales revenue and the customer receives something of value in return. In investor relations, a publicly held corporation secures capital, and investors get a return by way of dividends or increased value of the shares they own. In contracts and legal actions, specific terms for exchanges are spelled out in detail.

According to Hon and Grunig, **communal relationships** are equally important, if not more important, to public relations people in the long run. "In a communal relationship, both parties provide benefits to the other because they are concerned with the welfare of the other—even when they get nothing in return."[2] Hon and Grunig highlighted four key outcomes of good organization–public relationships:

- Control mutuality: Although it may be unrealistic to expect steady and perfect symmetry, each side should have some sense of control and be comfortable with the balance of influence.
- Trust: Hon and Grunig identified three dimensions of trust: "integrity: the belief that an organization is fair and just. . . . ; dependability: the belief that an organization will do what it says it will do. . . . ; and competence: the belief that an organization has the ability to do what it says it will do."
- Satisfaction: In satisfying relationships, both parties have positive expectations and feel like those expectations are being met.
- Commitment: Is the relationship worth continuing? This question can be asked as a matter of time and effort or in terms of the emotional investment. How much does each party value the relationship relative to competing relationships?

Research has shown that these long-term relational benefits correlate with shorter-term communication effects like the achievement of specific strategic goals and objectives that may be on the table in a meeting with a CEO. That is, the better the long-term relationships

exchange relationships
Relationships in which each party gives benefits to the other with the expectation of receiving comparable benefits in return.

communal relationships
Relationships in which each party gives benefits to the other and a primary motivation for each is the other's benefit.

The better the long-term relationships between your organization and publics, the more likely you are to achieve your goals.

THE CANADIAN PRESS/Nathan Denette

Prince Harry surprised 20,000 elementary students when he made an appearance at Toronto's WE Day in 2017.

What type of relationship between the publics—in this case the WE movement and WE Day attendees—does this event support?

you cultivate between your organization and its publics, the more likely you are to be able to achieve your daily, monthly, and annual goals. Pursuing communal relationships may not on its own be enough to sustain most organizations in their missions, but when excellent public relations builds and maintains solid relationships in coordination with other organizational units doing their jobs well, the whole organization thrives. Healthy long-term relationships can save organizations money by reducing costs of strikes, boycotts, lawsuits, and lost revenues from dissatisfied customers who take their business elsewhere. On the positive side, strong relationships help garner support from donors, legislators, consumers, employees, volunteers, and shareholders.

Strong, positive relationships (or strong negative relationships) help form what's known as public opinion. Public opinion is generally defined as a collection of individual opinions on an issue of public interest. Public opinion is of great interest to politicians, who often base decisions on spending and legislation on public opinion. Public opinion is generally measured through polls.

Abacus Data conducted a survey prior to the legalization of cannabis in Canada, and found that 70 per cent of Canadians supported or could accept legalization. Twelve per cent were opposed, and 18 per cent were strongly opposed.[3] In this case, public opinion (the majority) supported legalization and it proceeded as planned.

There are two ways to think about interpersonal relationships and organization–public relationships. First, we can think of the interpersonal relationship as an analogy for the organization–public relationship. Relationships between organizations and publics are *like* relationships between individuals. Both require effective communication and mutual understanding. The same kinds of strategies work in both, and the outcomes sought are similar too. These relationships can be observed by asking people about their experiences with an organization as a whole.[4]

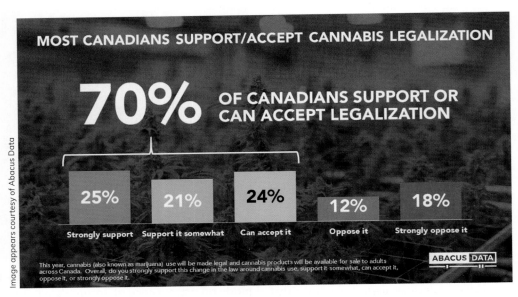

Image appears courtesy of Abacus Data

If polls showed that the majority of Canadians were strongly opposed, the government might have chosen to delay or cancel the planned legalization.

Do governments always make decisions based on popular opinion?

The image shows the exterior sign of a hospital building reading "The Hospital for Sick Children / SickKids", with directional signs: "THE SLAIGHT FAMILY ATRIUM", "THE GARRON FAMILY CANCER CENTRE", "PARKING", "170 ELIZABETH STREET", and "EMERGENCY".

JHVEPhoto/Shutterstock.com

The Hospital for Sick Children—SickKids—has some of the most loyal "fans" of any organization.

With which publics do they maintain relationships? What are some of the outcomes of these relationships?

Second, we can think of interpersonal relationships *as components of* organization–public relationships. The relationship between the two groups of people is made up of all the interpersonal interactions involved when individuals in organizations communicate with individuals in publics. For example, individuals may *trust* specific people in an organization with whom they've interacted. They may be *satisfied* with the interpersonal exchanges and *committed* to continuing conversations as long as they feel a sense of *mutual control* in the relationship.

Professor Elizabeth Toth pointed out early in the relationship-management literature that interpersonal communication is the foundation for analyzing organization–public relationships. She recommended a focus on relationships between public relations people and all of an organization's constituencies within various contexts.[5] For example, the context of media relations would call for looking at relationships with journalists and editors; the context of internal communications would mean looking at relationships with employees and members; and the context of issues management might mean thinking about communication with individual advocates and activists. Three major contexts for organization–public relationships are news-driven relationships, commerce-driven relationships, and issues-driven relationships.

elenabsl/Shutterstock.com

Organizational–public relationships have many parallels to interpersonal relationships.

How are your relationships with organizations on social media similar to your relationships with friends on social media?

News-Driven Relationships

Sharing news has been and always will be an important part of public relations. Whether it is editing a company newsletter, blogging about your organization's current events, or working to get coverage in national or international outlets, news is very much the currency of public relations practice.

Media Relations

Think about the term *media*, "the main means of mass communication (especially television, radio, newspapers, and the internet) regarded collectively,"[6] according to *Oxford Dictionaries*. When people speak of the news media, they are generally referring to the people who use these channels to write, produce, and deliver news—journalists, bloggers, analysts, editors, and producers. Relationships with these people are at the heart of media relations. Sometimes news media come to an organization for information, and other times the organization goes to the news media to get stories out. Over the course of a career in public relations, you will likely find yourself in both situations, often with the same people. The same person whom you pray will attend your organization's groundbreaking today may call you a year from now when your new building has a gas leak.

As public relations executive Peter Himler observed in a 2014 blog post that despite the increase in channels for communicating directly with publics, "One look at any PR job board will reveal that media relations remains the single-most sought-after competency by agencies of all stripes and most in-house communications departments."[7] Understanding modern media newsroom operations and the jobs of reporters, editors, bloggers, and TV producers is as much a key for career advancement in public relations as it has ever been.

Pitching

pitching When a public relations person approaches a journalist or editor to suggest a story idea.

Pitching is when public relations practitioners encourage the news media to cover stories involving their organizations. To keep up with industry trends, it's helpful to subscribe to several email and trade publication lists for public relations. Scarcely a week goes by when one of these sources doesn't include some form of advice on pitching—"Seven Ways to Think Like a Reporter," "Five Reasons Your Pitch Stinks," "How to Pitch TV News Reporters," "Pitching a Broadcast Story? Think Visual," "How NOT to Write a Pitch Letter," and "The Dos and Don'ts of Pitching Journalists on Social Media" are just a few examples. Pitching is one of the most common and challenging tasks that public relations practitioners face. A few themes emerge from these types of advice columns.

Know Newsworthiness

Journalists must make decisions every day about what qualifies as news. Depending on the size of their news organization and its audience, journalists may receive dozens, if not hundreds, of pitches for each news story they actually cover. Although much of the news you see in newspapers, online, and over the airwaves results from pitches made to journalists, much of it also happens without pitching. A public information officer for Parks Canada may spend a lot of time talking to reporters covering a wildfire, or a sports information director for a university may answer a sports reporter's request to interview a head hockey coach about a big win. A wildfire or a big win are both newsworthy—no pitch required.

Whether journalists find the stories themselves or become aware of them with the help of people working in public relations, newsworthiness is the criterion they use to determine what is worth covering as news and what is not. Five key elements of **newsworthiness** include timeliness, proximity, conflict and controversy, human interest, and relevance.[8] Others include novelty, shock value, impact, or magnitude and superlatives such as the first, largest, longest, oldest, or most expensive of some category.

Looking at stories in the news media and identifying what makes them newsworthy is usually pretty easy. What's trickier is understanding which news from your organization is newsworthy *from the perspective of journalists and their audiences.* If your CEO adopted three new puppies, it may be timely (happened yesterday), proximal (she is bringing them into the office), controversial (some office staff are allergic to dogs), interesting (they are *soooo* cute!), and relevant (new policy—everyone can bring their pets to work one day a week). By all means, put it in your employee newsletter or tweet about it for your personal networks. But does this "news" belong on tonight's local TV news or in the daily newspaper? How about national news?

The puppy story is a bit of a silly example, but look at the news releases streaming on services like CNW, PRNewswire.com, or Marketwired and you'll likely find examples that are even less newsworthy. A medical care management company was nominated for an award in workers' compensation case management,[9] an employee of a "healthy lifestyle company" achieved the rank of "2-star ambassador" within his own organization,[10] and a wood composite company announced that it was extending warranty coverage for its decking and railing materials up to five years. All of these news releases were pushed out over international media services in a 20-minute period on a Thursday afternoon.

Of course, context is important. If your CEO adopted the puppies as part of the launch of a major new partnership with your local Humane Society, the story may be newsworthy in your community beyond your organization. Likewise, the medical care award, the employee recognition, and the extended warranty may be newsworthy in some limited contexts. Newsworthiness is in the eye of the beholder. When you know a journalist and their beat, and you have newsworthy information to present in good form that is important to their readers (viewers, listeners, etc.), you will be set up for a win–win—the mutual benefit of helping the journalist with their job while benefitting your organization by getting its story out. But if you mismatch your news with the journalist, at best you will be ignored and at worst you will lose credibility and damage the relationship for the future.

newsworthiness
Standard used to determine what is worth covering in news media.

THE CANADIAN PRESS/Fred Chartrand

In 2013, Attawapiskat Chief Theresa Spence went on a hunger strike until then Prime Minister Stephen Harper agreed to meet her to discuss Indigenous issues. The strike garnered national media coverage.

Which elements of newsworthiness led to so much media attention in this case?

> Before pitching to reporters, read their news stories, watch their programs, and follow their social media accounts to better understand their style and the type of news they cover.

Empathize with Reporters

Finding an appropriate outlet for any story means really understanding the person to whom you are sending the news and, just as important, understanding their audience. A famous quote from Sun Tzu's *The Art of War* says, "To know your enemy, you must become your enemy." At the risk of framing the relationship between public relations practitioners and journalists as hostile (it shouldn't be), we may apply the same general idea. To know the news media, you must become the news media.

Advice from the trade press tells us to consider journalists' deadlines, to understand their business, and to answer questions such as "Why do I care?" and "Why now?" from their perspective. In other words, put yourself in their shoes. Experience working in newsrooms certainly helps. But even if you have never worked as a journalist, you can still empathize with what it's like to work on deadline and make an effort to understand the people to whom the journalist delivers the news. Read their news stories, watch their programs, and follow their social media accounts; all of these things will help you to better understand their style and the type of news they cover.

Make Yourself Useful

Good journalists do a tremendous amount of research, and public relations specialists are in a unique position to help with access to an organization's people and information. If you work for a school board, you may be one of the most important sources of information for an education reporter. You may be asked for information on test scores or teacher salaries even when those are not the stories you are hoping to communicate. Knowing what information you can share, and what information you are legally obligated to share, will help you help journalists. Even when you have to decline to share information, for example, because it is private human resources data or student information, being open about your constraints will help. Again, there may be no immediate benefit to you or your organization when you work with a journalist on a tough story, but building and maintaining a relationship will likely pay off in the long run with fair coverage and greater receptiveness when you do have positive news to share.

Another way to make yourself useful is to direct reporters to other people within your organization who can help as sources. Don't be offended if journalists want to skip right over you as a source. Remember: Put yourself in their shoes. If you were writing a news story about school district test scores, would you rather interview a public relations representative or a school board member, principal, or teacher?

Pavel Kapysh/Shutterstock.com

Online services like Cision help initiate source–reporter relationships.

How might relationships started from "media catching" be different from relationships started with pitching?

Interviews and source–reporter relationships can also be initiated more proactively. Many universities maintain experts databases that catalogue professors and researchers based on their areas of expertise and their willingness to work with journalists on related stories. The Internet has facilitated this on a global level with services like Cision's ProfNet or HARO (Help a Reporter Out), which connect reporters with sources. This practice has been called **media catching**.[11] It reverses the traditional flow of pitching from sources to reporters. Instead of public relations people pitching stories to journalists, journalists can post queries online to which any registered user with relevant information or expertise can respond.

While relationships are key to media relations, depending on the nature of your organization or clients, many, if not most, of your relationships with journalists may be best characterized as exchange relationships. You exchange information or access for news coverage. Especially early in your career, you may not have longstanding relationships with many of the journalists you pitch to. Nonetheless, in situations where you haven't worked with a journalist before, knowing newsworthiness, empathizing, and making yourself useful will not only help your chances of **story placement**; it also may set the stage for a longer-term professional relationship.

> **media catching** When journalists post queries online inviting public relations people or others with relevant information or expertise to respond. Public relations people "catch" these opportunities rather than "pitching" story ideas to journalists.

Networking Relationships

Pick up any public relations textbook or read any PR blog, and sooner or later you're going to come across an article about networking and how important it is to public relations professionals.

Many students are terrified by the thought of going to a professional event and talking to seasoned PR pros. "What if no one wants to talk to me? What would I say anyway?"

Happily, most students find out these fears are completely unfounded once they attend their first CPRS (Canadian Public Relations Society) or IABC (International Association of Business Communicators) event. Veteran members usually make a special effort to reach out to newbies (we were all there once!) and it's relatively easy to turn to the person beside you and say hello.

Before you attend your first networking event, think of a few questions you'd like to ask. If there's a speaker, make an effort to introduce yourself and tell him or her how much you enjoyed the event. If you have a good conversation with someone, be sure to send them a LinkedIn request the next morning.

A networking event is not, however, the place to aggressively search for an internship or a job. Do not hand out your resume—if someone asks, you can send it via email later on.

> **story placement** The outcome of a successful pitch, when a story involving a public relations practitioner's organization or client is covered in the news media.

Commerce-Driven Relationships

As we saw in Chapter 3, many of the relationships in public relations are driven by dollars. The most obvious examples are business-to-consumer relationships. Other important relationships driven primarily by commerce include business-to-business relations, employee relations, and investor relations.

B2C

B2C, or business to consumer, can describe software, types of organizations, or the relationships between organizations and publics. B2C software usually means e-commerce platforms in which an end user can initiate and complete a transaction online. If you buy an airline

> **Business to consumer (B2C)** The relationship between a business and the end users or consumers of its product or services.

ticket from an airline website, order a pair of shorts from a retail store online, or purchase software to download, you are working with B2C applications. In the context of the rise of e-commerce as a major sector in world economies, B2C is used to describe companies that sell products or services directly to consumers online. Prior to the dot-com boom, people probably wouldn't have thought to refer to their local bookstore as "B2C," but when Amazon rose to success selling books and other products directly to consumers via the Internet, the business model was seen as innovative. Amazon, along with countless other companies that have entered the direct-to-consumer market online, are referred to as B2C companies.

The term *B2C* also highlights the relationships between businesses and their customers. The four Cs of integrated marketing communication (consumer, cost, convenience, and communication) highlight important dimensions of those relationships. But, as any business person knows, financial success depends on relationships with a number of different publics in addition to customers. By definition, public relations people have an important role to play in maintaining relationships with any group of people on whom the organization's success or failure depends. In business, these publics include other businesses, employees, and investors.

B2B

Business to business (B2B) The relationship between a business and other businesses.

B2B stands for *business to business*. Like B2C, B2B is often used to describe technologies such as the platforms that businesses use to perform online transactions with one another. B2B also refers to the relationships between business people from different companies or organizations. For example, when a business hires another business for a service such as management consulting or accounting, that's a B2B relationship. In the context of marketing, the supply chain from raw materials to manufacturers to wholesalers to retailers involves many B2B relationships before products ever make it to consumers. If you purchase a new smartphone, think of all the transactions that are involved before the device ever reaches the palm of your hand. Silicon is mined or extracted from sand and purchased to make microchips. Microchips are assembled with touch screens, microphones, optical devices, and so on. The computer is then programmed with software, including multiple apps that enable multiple services and functions. For every smartphone that is sold, there are countless prior business transactions involving the raw materials, buying and selling of component parts, assembly, delivery, intellectual property, and so on.

Besides the sheer volume of transactions involved, a major difference between B2C and B2B is the nature of the buyers. B2B buyers shop as part of their job. The individuals and committees that make decisions about where to buy raw materials from for manufacturing products or which package delivery service to contract with are normally well-informed buyers. They are hired, retained, and promoted for their expertise in understanding the market and for making rational, highly informed purchasing decisions based on all the data available to them. They use computers and software programs to help them, but, like journalists in media relations, they are still people who make decisions in the context of interpersonal relationships.

georgejmclittle/123RF

Mobile technologies have changed the nature of many consumer purchases.

How is your relationship with online retailers different from your relationships with retailers that have physical stores? Where do you like to shop more often?

THE CANADIAN PRESS IMAGES/Larry MacDougal

Canada's largest B2B trade show is the Calgary-based Global Petroleum Show, which is attended by over 40,000 people each year. Exhibitors include international and regional manufacturers, distributors, and service companies providing technologies, equipment, and solutions for the oil and gas industry.

How are B2B relationships similar to B2C relationships?

Public relations people play a role in B2B relationships using many of the same tactics and channels of communication used for relationships with other key publics. Next time you walk through an airport, pay attention to the display ads and billboards. You'll notice that it's not just coffee and neck pillows being promoted, but also IT systems and consulting services.

Likewise, you've probably seen ads for B2B companies on TV, online, and in magazines, particularly if you pay attention to the same news and events as business people. Naturally, *The Globe and Mail* will carry B2B news and advertising, but business people also watch sports, go on vacations, and attend music festivals, which is why you may notice many events and venues bearing the name of B2B companies, that you, as a consumer, may not know about.

Social media provide additional vehicles for B2B communication. In a blog entry for "Social Media Today," Jennifer Hanford identified many good examples.

- Email marketing company Constant Contact maintains more than 100 Pinterest boards subscribed to by more than 20,000 followers featuring photos and images that communicate "'intangible' solutions on this visual platform by tapping into their creativity."[12]
- Global cloud computing company Salesforce.com uses its Facebook page to post company links, pictures, and news. They use the main Facebook page to respond to followers who comment and ask questions and to link to the other Facebook pages for the company's various divisions. They also include product demos and news on industry trends.

- Inbound marketing company HubSpot uses Twitter to strike "a good balance between tweeting content and audience engagement." With tens of thousands of followers, their social media team not only posts news but also asks questions of their followers to start conversations. They answer questions as well.
- Cisco Systems uses its YouTube channel to post videos for its tens of thousands of subscribers that "engage, educate, and inform without overtly selling."
- Dell uses LinkedIn groups to post company news, career information, and links to job openings, as well as to host business and product-specific discussions.

Employee Relations

internal publics Groups of people with shared interests within an organization.

external publics Groups of people with shared interests outside of an organization. These groups either have an effect on or are affected by the organization.

> *Healthy relations with internal publics, such as employees, are prerequisites for healthy relations with external publics.*

Internal publics are an important part of public relations. If we're talking about businesses and commerce-driven relationships, the internal publics are employees. Perhaps nowhere else in public relations are the relational outcomes of trust, satisfaction, commitment, and control mutuality so apparent. Trusting, satisfied, committed, and empowered employees are sure to be more productive and more attuned to and invested in the organization's mission. Moreover, in a world where employees are often the first line of communication with **external publics**, healthy internal relations are prerequisites for healthy external ones.

Internal trust is essential to the operating climate of most businesses, and that trust works both ways. When employees trust the organization and the organization's management trusts the employees, everyone benefits. On the employees' side, most indices of "best places to work" include trust as a central component. When *The Globe and Mail* partners with Great Place to Work Canada to pick the 100 best companies in Canada to work for, two-thirds of the score is based on the results of a trust index survey.[13] On the business side, Nan Russell writes in *Psychology Today* that organizational benefits of workplace trust include the following:

- greater profitability
- higher return on shareholder investment
- decreased turnover of top performers
- increased employee engagement
- heightened customer service
- expanded staff well-being
- more collaboration and teamwork
- higher productivity
- enhanced creativity and innovation[14]

Establishing and maintaining trust isn't always easy. In fact, it's really difficult to foster a trusting workplace when the relationship isn't already positive to begin with. Many variables come into play as part of the overarching organizational culture. Some of these, such as the personalities of the people involved, are outside of the scope and control of public relations, but others, particularly communication and policy, may be areas in which public relations people can offer some help.

uberfliphq [Follow]

616 posts   2,382 followers   1,336 following

Uberflip
Uberflip lets marketers create, manage & optimize content experiences at every stage of the buyer journey • learn about our amazing culture!🦋
startupong.com

summa fu...   learning!   fireside 🔥   2019!   🏆   pride🌈   customer ...

⊞ POSTS   ⓣ TAGGED

Image appears courtesy of Uberflip

Healthy relations with internal publics, such as employees, are prerequisites for healthy relations with external publics. Some B2B companies use social media to reflect or connect with their internal publics. Uberflip is a B2B platform that works with marketers to create digital content.

Who do you think follows Uberflip on Instagram?

In the digital age, BYOD (bring your own device) policies are a good example. Intel Corp. has such a policy and allows employees to use their own mobile devices to access the company's internal IT system. According to one report, about 30,000 employee devices are logged in daily.[15] This policy requires Intel's senior management to trust employees to properly handle and protect sensitive corporate information. It also requires employees to trust the company to keep their information private. The issue with BYOD policies, labelled a "trust gap" by researchers, is that employees often don't understand just how much personal information the employer can retrieve.

Intel Corp. handles the trust gap issue with communication. They post answers to frequently asked questions on their intranet, they train IT help desk employees to discuss BYOD monitoring, and they operate a 24/7 telephone support system. The results are mutually beneficial. On one side, employees get to use the devices with which they are most comfortable—in a one-year period the number of employees using their own devices at Intel increased from about 3,000 to about 17,000. On the other side, organizations get more productivity—Intel estimated that employees using their own devices produced an average of 57 more minutes of work a day than they would have otherwise.

Professor Linjuan Rita Men surveyed more than 400 employees of US companies across several industries to see which channels of internal communication were most effective. She found that email and direct face-to-face communication in traditional meetings and with direct managers facilitated information exchange, listening, and conversation. Social media, including social networking sites, blogs, instant messaging, wikis, and streaming audio and video channels were less commonly used, but they served to improve the organizational climate by boosting employee engagement: "In other words, the more often companies use social media to connect with employees, the more engaged employees feel. When employees are engaged, they feel empowered, involved, emotionally attached and dedicated to the organization, and excited and proud about being a part of it."[16] Print media such as newsletters, brochures, reports, and posters, though still important for disseminating information, had less of an effect on employee engagement in Men's study.

Investor Relations

investor relations
Management of relationships between an organization and publics in the financial community—for example, investors, analysts, and regulators.

If you use salary data as a measure of organizational importance, **investor relations** is one of the most valued functions among job titles that include the word relations. In 2016, the median salary for an investor relations manager in Canada was $80,918, and top IR officers at corporations make well over $100,000.[17] Even though investor relations managers are just as likely to come from backgrounds in business management, accounting, or finance as they are to come from communications or public relations, investor relations is very much a public relations function. The National Investor Relations Institute defines investor relations as "a strategic management responsibility that integrates finance, communication, marketing and securities law compliance to enable the most effective two-way communication between a company, the financial community and other constituencies, which ultimately contributes to a company's securities achieving fair valuation."[18]

> While financial information is tightly regulated, investor relations managers use many of the same channels of communication as any other public relations people.

Professor Alexander Laskin has researched investor relations as a subfunction of public relations. When Laskin interviewed investor relations managers, he found they overwhelmingly agreed that building relationships with investors and analysts is one of the most important things they do. Most cited the importance of good relationships in building trust that the company can do what it says. This leads to financial publics giving the company and its management the benefit of the doubt during times when they might otherwise second-guess their investments. In his panel study, Laskin developed the following statement on relationship-building in investor relations, which the participants endorsed.

The rewards of this relationship can be significant. Value gaps tend to diminish because investors believe management can accomplish what it says. Positive events and development earn higher stock gain rewards. A flat or down quarter isn't an automatic sell signal. . . . Patience is more likely to be accorded.[19]

While financial information is tightly regulated, as discussed in Chapter 11, investor relations managers use many of the same channels of communication as any other public relations person. These include face-to-face meetings, conference calls, media conferences, news releases, brochures, periodic (e.g., quarterly or annual) reports, websites, blogs, and online video.

IR managers have to understand financial markets in Canada and around the world.

How is investor relations different from other areas like media relations or consumer relations?

Issues-Driven Relationships

Social and environmental issues are big concerns for even the most profit-focused organizations. Relationships with customers, employees, investors, and other businesses may be driven by money, but they are also driven by where the organization stands on issues that affect human and natural resources. Some organizations, however, exist for the very purpose of addressing social or environmental issues. They focus specifically on issues for the sake of making a difference, with a much less direct link to any commercial motive.

Non-profit Organizations

The Nature Conservancy of Canada's mission is to lead and inspire others to "join us in creating a legacy for future generations by conserving important natural areas and biological diversity across all regions of Canada."[20] The Heart and Stroke Foundation exists to prevent disease, save lives, and promote recovery.[21] CARP's mission statement reads, in part, "CARP is a national, non-partisan, non-profit organization committed to advocating for a New Vision of Aging for Canada, promoting social change that will bring financial security, equitable access to health care, and freedom from discrimination."[22] With mission statements like these, non-profit organizations define themselves by a commitment to some sort of environmental or social benefit besides profit.

Of course, this doesn't mean non-profits don't need to generate revenue. They still need money to pursue their missions, but the relationships that they maintain with their publics are centred on the issues. Among the most important publics for non-profit organizations are volunteers and donors. Both support the missions of non-profits. Donors donate money, and volunteers donate time.

> Volunteers and donors are among the most important publics for non-profit organizations.

Volunteers

Managing relationships with volunteers involves a mix of external and internal communications. Recruiting volunteers means reaching out into the community and other organizations to find and initiate relationships with people who are likely to help your organization by volunteering time and effort. When college public relations campaign classes take on non-profit organizations as clients, a common initial goal for the campaigns is to recruit volunteers. Another common goal, which often emerges after students do some initial research, is *retaining* volunteers.

Donors

Although non-profits do make money from fees for services and goods, government grants, and other sources, they also depend on donors for revenue. Issues-driven organizations must work just as hard as—if not harder than—commerce-driven organizations to meet their financial goals. That said, those financial goals should not be confused with the greater social benefits the organizations exist to support. The money is only a means to an end. Thus, the most fruitful donor relationships are long-term and based on mutual commitment to the organization's mission. Research and practice both bear out the idea that "fundraising is less about raising money and more about building relationships."[23] PRSA (Public Relations Society of America) Fellow, former fundraising executive, and professor of public relations

Kathleen Kelly recommends stewardship as a key practice for success in non-profit public relations management. Four elements of stewardship have been found to influence how donors perceive their relationships with non-profit organizations. Kelly's four Rs are reciprocity, responsibility, reporting, and relationship nurturing.

- *Reciprocity*: When donors support an organization, the organization should respond with appreciation. This may be as simple as a handwritten thank-you note or recognition in a member magazine. In cases where someone has made a tax-deductible contribution, the organization can reciprocate with a written thank you and confirmation that will help the donor file for a deduction.
- *Responsibility*: If you make a donation to aid disaster victims, or to help feed local families in need, you want to be able to trust that the organization is using your donation for that specific purpose. Non-profits have a responsibility to do what they promise to do. However, all non-profits use at least a small part of their budgets for administrative functions, so non-profit executives need to work hard to make sure that donations are managed properly. Public relations people can serve to make sure that donors' wishes are clearly understood, communicated, and honoured in the management of funds.
- *Reporting*: The Internet has made it much easier for organizations to share tax forms, financial plans, audit information, and detailed information about programs and services that demonstrate social accountability as well as financial accountability.[24] The best non-profits are readily transparent.
- *Relationship nurturing*: This final R echoes the idea of communal relationships in which financial exchanges take a back seat to mutual respect and recognition. One measure of relationship nurturing is how often donors hear from an organization when they are *not* being asked for money.[25] As Kelly puts it, the best way to nurture a long-term relationship is simple: "Accept the importance of previous donors and keep them at the forefront of the organization's consciousness."[26] Include donors on email lists. Network with them on social networking sites. Send them copies of breaking news releases that are going to news media. Invite them to events. All of these are ways to keep them in the loop and in the organizational "consciousness."

issue An important topic or problem that is open for debate, discussion, or advocacy.

Photo by Carsten Koall/Getty Images

A volunteer at a Berliner Stadtmission shelter for refugees gives out clothing donated by Japanese brand Uniqlo. Germany has taken in more than 1.6 million asylum seekers since 2014.

What sustains the relationships between the charity that runs this shelter, its volunteers, its donors, and the migrants and refugees it serves?

When Publics Are Organizations and Organizations Are Publics

An **issue** is any important topic or problem that is open for debate, discussion, or advocacy.[27] If products, services, stocks, and money are the stuff of exchange in regular marketplaces, issues are what fuel exchange in the marketplace of ideas. When groups of people are organized on more than one side of an issue, the terms *organization* and *public* become interchangeable.

Activists

Larissa Grunig defines an *activist public* as "a group of two or more individuals who organize in order to influence another public or publics through action that may include education, compromise, persuasion, pressure tactics, or force."[28] In issues management and crisis management, activists are often defined from the perspective of one organization, but in thinking about two-way relationships, organizations themselves may be activists. Many non-profits and NGOs are just as organized, sophisticated, and effective in their public relations strategies as the other organizations with which they interact.

Take Chicago surfers, for example. Yes, real surfers—not the kind who browse websites but the people who ride freshwater waves in Lake Michigan. For the City of Chicago and the Chicago Park District, surfers did not constitute a public to be concerned with until 2008, when a surfer was arrested for surfing in Lake Michigan. At that point, surfing in Lake Michigan became a recognized *issue*.

SumOfUs is a global advocacy organization that campaigns to hold large companies accountable on social and environmental issues such as climate change, human rights, and freedom of information.

The organization is unique, in that it has no formal offices. Its 32 staff members live in 11 countries around the world, including Canada, and the entire organization relies on donations from individuals as opposed to corporations.

Image courtesy of SumOfUs, CC BY 3.0

SumOfUs was launched in 2011 with a campaign demanding better working conditions for suppliers to Apple and a campaign thanking Starbucks for supporting same-sex marriage.

When did this group become more of an organization than a public?

In Canada, the organization recently organized a petition to curb the use of glyphosate, an ingredient in pesticides, which has been linked to cancer, in Canada's food system. They have also been involved in campaigns regarding working conditions in BC mines, net neutrality in Canada, and in supporting the Indigenous struggle against fossil fuel projects. SumOfUs was also instrumental in helping the unanimous passing of Motion M-151, which proposed solutions on the plastic crisis including a single-use plastic ban that was subsequently introduced by the governing Liberal Party of Canada.

Government Agencies

Organizations of all types practise advocacy, also known as lobbying. Lobbying is the process through which individuals and groups articulate their interests to federal, provincial, or municipal governments in order to influence public policy or government decision-making. Lobbyists may be paid third parties who communicate on behalf of their clients or employees of a corporation or organization seeking to influence the government.

Lobbying is regulated in Canada under the Lobbying Act, and anyone lobbying must register with the Office of the Commissioner of Lobbying. The line between lobbying and government relations (the act of managing the relationship between an organization and government officials) is sometimes a blurry one; and so, some people who consider themselves government relations practitioners will register as lobbyists just to be on the safe side.

Chapter 11 covers some key regulatory agencies with which public relations practitioners should be familiar, and Chapter 2 discusses politics and government as part of the heritage and contemporary practice of public relations. One of the primary functions of government public affairs is the dissemination of information *to* constituents (i.e., public information). Another key function is advocating *for* those constituents.

In this chapter, and throughout the text, we see how the idea of building and maintaining relationships applies in the public sector. A government agency may be seen as either an organization or a public, depending on your perspective. In the school board example for media relations, we saw the public school board as an organization with a public relations person who was responsible for communicating with news media and other publics. With the Chicago surfer example, we saw how the case could be framed with Surfrider Foundation as the organization and the city park service as a public.

Ethics: Corporate Social Responsibility and Loyalty

Corporate social responsibility (CSR) refers to a company's commitment to allocate resources to benefit society and the environment. The contributions may come in the form of financial donations, employee time, or socially beneficial business practices. While non-profit organizations exist primarily to make a positive difference in their communities and the natural environment, for-profit businesses and corporations exist primarily to make money. If they don't make money, they eventually will not exist at all and cannot benefit anyone.

lobbying Working to influence the decisions of government officials on matters of legislation.

government relations Management of relationships between an organization and government officials who formulate and execute public policy.

public affairs Management of policy-focused relationships between an organization, public officials, and their constituents.

corporate social responsibility (CSR) Companies' commitment of resources to benefit the welfare of their workforce, local communities, society at large, and the environment.

THE CANADIAN PRESS/Justin Tang

Ontario doctors recently lobbied the government to outlaw cosmetic eye tattoos.

In this case, are they acting as an organization, a public, or both?

Voices from the Field

Kim Griffin

Image courtesy Kim Griffin

Kim Griffin leads Customer Service, Corporate Communications and Public Affairs for Maritime Electric Company Ltd, which supplies electricity to almost all of Prince Edward Island. Her diverse portfolio includes community investment, communications, media relations, stakeholder outreach, and corporate website and digital customer solutions, as well as customer contact centre operations. She is also the official corporate spokesperson for the company, frequently turning up in news stories and YouTube videos. In addition to her public relations work, Kim is an active and committed community volunteer and was recently named national co-chair of the Canadian Council on Mission, Priorities, Advice Science, & Technology for Heart & Stroke Canada.

I'm guessing you were taught that public relations can be defined as relationship management. How does that definition square with what you're doing now?

Relationship management or stakeholder management is about building open, honest two-way dialogues between organizations and members of the public. Working with stakeholders is a key part of the work I have been doing for over 20 years. I have worked for global brands in the beverage industry and have spent the last 10 years working and building strong relationships in the energy sector. Whether it is a project, media interview, or public consultation, understanding and working with various publics articulating the issue, understanding their concerns, and finding the medium to communicate the organization's message is fundamental. We need to connect with people. Where possible I strive for face-to-face meetings, but more often now people want an email reply or text and this tends to diminish the personal connection.

In the energy sector stakeholders often determine if a project moves forward. I work with rights holders, community leaders, residents, government, and regulators to foster an understanding of the need for our projects to supply a vital service to our customers. Many of these projects take years to complete, and this means building and maintaining positive working relationships, which is integral to their success.

What kind of challenges and rewards do you face in relationship management?

Truly understanding one's publics can be challenging and time consuming, but it can be very rewarding and meaningful. Some of my most rewarding projects have been in areas where there were significant opportunities for controversy. For the first time in my career I worked with First Nations communities in eastern Canada on a $142 million energy project, and those were the most rewarding relationships I have built in my career to date. I learned so much about respecting and planning seven generations ahead. We had elders share their personal stories and stories of the land and sea. They blessed our project, our workers, and were continually involved with our project team. The people, their genuine respect of the earth and each other, and the mutual respect we shared together working on this project has impacted me for a lifetime.

Do you change how you manage relationships when dealing with different audiences?

Of course! No two people are alike so in our profession there is a lot of customized work and messaging required to be effective. People have different drivers and perspectives so tailoring messages and pertinent information to various audiences is key.

Continued

What would you say is the most important factor in creating positive relationships?

Trust. Trust is everything, in what you say as a spokesperson for your organization, your project, and the work you do. I have been interviewed over 1,000 times in my career to date and have been treated fairly by media even when my message is negative because I strive to explain with clarity the issue and our response or plan. I deal with highly controversial issues and spend just as much time listening and trying to work with critics as I do working with our own team to be successful. I often say to journalists, "I don't expect a love story, just fairness that reflects both sides."

In what ways have you seen social media help or hinder public relations people manage relationships?

As public relations leaders we need to adapt to how our audiences want to communicate, and social media takes us to a new level in communication. There is certainly nowhere for corporate-speak in social media; people want unfiltered, instant, honest feedback on an issue or concern in real time. It's a useful communication tool but it takes a well-thought-out strategy to be effective for one's own organization. It can also elevate an issue instantly and garner a groundswell of exposure on issues that, at their worst, can damage reputation or leave a lasting negative impression. Where appropriate, when you are sincere with a client or customer, you can be highly effective.

What advice do you have for students as they manage the transition from classroom learning to professional careers?

I wake up every day and enjoy my work. It is a very busy and challenging profession that is often misunderstood, even today. There is always more to learn in our profession and examples in the public to study, reflect upon, and ask yourself, "How I would have handled this as a PR professional?"

My counsel for students just starting out is this: Get as much experience as you can. Contribute in your community through volunteering or at work to practise the profession and find the area you love most. At the same time, work to build a strong network both in and outside the profession. Seek out mentors along the way in the various stages of your career. Many will share their highlights, best practices, and mistakes.

> *Ethically balancing loyalties is one of the toughest jobs of public relations managers.*

Nobel Prize–winning economist Milton Friedman took this logic to an extreme in a famous 1970 article published in *The New York Times Magazine* titled "The Social Responsibility of Business Is to Increase Its Profits." Whether you agree with Friedman or not, he raises interesting ethical questions about how for-profit companies balance their need to make money with their responsibilities as corporate citizens. At the heart of the matter are competing loyalties. Companies may have loyalties to their communities and the natural environment, but they also must be loyal to their shareholders and employees who rely on them to remain profitable. Ethically balancing loyalties in a company's relationships with publics as diverse as environmentalists, government agencies, unions, employees, and stockholders is one of the toughest jobs of public relations managers.

Coca-Cola and Corporate Social Responsibility

Coca-Cola's position atop the branding world hasn't come easily, and its future there isn't guaranteed. In 2013, Coca-Cola slipped to third place behind Apple and Google on Interbrand's list of best global brands.[29]

In recent years, sugary drinks have been identified as culprits in the fight against obesity. Now being the number one soda brand in the world carries with it the risk of also being labelled as public enemy number one in the fight against obesity, particularly in North America. How can a company that relies on sales of sugary drinks that lead to obesity, diabetes, and tooth decay make a compelling case that it also cares deeply about the health of consumers?

Elon University student and PRSSA (Public Relations Student Society of America) president Heather Harder won the 2014 Arthur W. Page Society case study competition with her analysis of how Coca-Cola has managed its precarious position. She summarized the company's strategy as one of corporate social responsibility. "By acknowledging the obesity issue and spending millions of dollars on anti-obesity efforts, Coca-Cola is demonstrating corporate social responsibility—if not in its products, then at least in its community involvement."[30]

In late 2012 and early 2013, Coca-Cola launched a campaign called "Coming Together" that included a theme that "all calories count." The theme emphasized logic that consumers should balance the number of calories taken in with the number of calories they burn, and that calories from Coke products are essentially the same as calories from any other source. Coca-Cola used a variety of tactics to support the theme including

- videos aired on mainstream media;
- a crowdsourced effort that invited consumers to email comingtogether@coca-cola.com with personal stories;
- online video via http://www.coca-colacompany.com/coming-together/; and
- the announcement of several "commitments to fighting obesity" including offering low- or no-calorie options in every market,
- more prominently displaying calorie information on product labels,
- funding physical activity programs worldwide, and
- adopting more responsible marketing practices that avoid targeting children under the age of 12.[31]

The campaign ran in Canada, as well as the US, Brazil, France, and the UK.

The CPRS definition of public relations suggests that practitioners must act in the public interest. In this case, those working in public relations for Coca-Cola must balance their responsibility to their employer with their responsibility to many publics with varying interests.

Continued

Bychykhin Olexandr/Shutterstock.com

Coca-Cola's brand faces threats as sugary drinks are seen as a public health problem.

How can a pop company promote its main product while simultaneously working to be socially responsible?

Andrew Matthews/PA Wire URN:20953612 (Press Association via AP Images)

Coca-Cola has begun offering more low-calorie options including Coca-Cola Life, which is made with stevia, a plant-based sugar substitute.

To which publics is Coca-Cola loyal in this marketing effort?

According to Harder, "The challenge is for Coca-Cola to find a way to be taken seriously as a player in anti-obesity efforts while simultaneously increasing sales and offering consumers the products they love." Harder's conclusion highlights the importance of relationships with several key publics in defining the success of the CSR efforts.

Critics and Activists

Perhaps the most vocal opposition in this case came from members of the health-care community. Dr Yoni Freedhoff, the director of the Bariatric Medical Institute in Ottawa, was quoted by CBC news as calling sugar-sweetened beverages the number one single contributor of calories to North American diets. "I think what Coca-Cola is trying to do, is to be able to say to the world: 'Look, we're part of the solution, we're not part of the problem, and we don't need things like soda taxes, and cup size limits because we are already working on it.' So this is their way to try to avoid further legislation that would affect their sales."[32]

Consumers

Let's face it. People don't drink Coke for their health these days. If you work for Coca-Cola, you can be loyal to your consumers in a lot of ways with a lot of different products, but it would be a stretch to imply that your signature cola equates to a healthier food option. That said, research shows that consumers pay attention to CSR. In 2015, Nielsen surveyed more than 30,000 consumers in 60 countries. Sixty-six per cent of them said they would be willing to pay more for goods and services from socially responsible companies, up from 55 per cent in 2014 and 50 per cent in 2013.[33]

Investors

To preserve excellent investor relations with its thousands of shareholders around the world, Coca-Cola must maintain a profitable business model. Can you imagine what it would mean to shareholders—and even entire economies—if Coca-Cola just stopped selling soda because the product was unhealthy? The **golden mean** is an ethical principle in Aristotelian, Buddhist, and Confucius philosophies, which holds that the most ethical course of action lies between extremes. A golden CSR strategy for Coca-Cola undoubtedly lies somewhere between shuttering its flagship product line to allay the concerns of its critics and ignoring its critics altogether with an uninhibited drive for profit. In fact, CSR may help with profitability, as is evident in research suggesting a link between charitable giving and corporate revenues.[34]

golden mean Ethical doctrine holding that the best courses of action are found between extremes.

Employees

Positive relationships with employees are an important part of the equation linking social responsibility with profitability. It is not hard to imagine how companies with satisfied, committed, trusting, and empowered employees (i.e., those with excellent relational outcomes) are more likely to profit in business. CSR trends include programs that encourage employees to participate in service such as pro bono work or paid release time to volunteer in their communities.

Policymakers

Legislative relations also come into play, and Coca-Cola invests strategically in its own advocacy. The company lists corporate taxation, environmental policy, and product-specific policies including taxes and regulation as areas for investment. In 2016, Canada's senate called for a tax on sugary drinks, but so far, the recommendation has not been adopted or widely supported.

legislative relations Management of relationships between an organization and lawmakers, staffers, and others who influence legislation.

"The only thing a sugar tax will make thinner are Canadians' wallets," said Aaron Wudrick, the federal director of the Canadian Taxpayers Federation, in a release. "Good intentions do not always translate into good policy, and the record of these types of taxes in other jurisdictions leaves much to be desired."[35]

The Canadian Beverage Association, understandably, also did not support the idea.

"This has been tried in other jurisdictions and it has failed. It didn't reduce obesity. It increased the price of groceries, and resulted in job losses in the food and beverage sector," said Jim Goetz, president of the Canadian Beverage Association, in a release.[36]

Managing an organization requires managing relationships with all sorts of publics. Ethical issues arise when loyalty to any one public risks damage to mutually beneficial relationships with others. Those who work in public relations for Coca-Cola, like people in organizations of all sizes all over the world, face ethical challenges in remaining faithful to those they represent while honouring their obligation to serve the public interest. Corporate social responsibility can be both a strategy for and an outcome of careful relationship management in public relations.

Continued

Giving in Numbers 2018: What's Trending?

CECP, in association with **The Conference Board**, produces the largest, most robust, industry-leading, and internationally recognized research on corporate social investment, *Giving in Numbers*. This year, 300+ multi-billion dollar companies with aggregate revenues of over $7 trillion participated. Leading companies are increasing giving; focusing on signature programs with fewer yet bigger community investments; expanding employee volunteer programs; and contributing greater cash towards Disaster Relief. For more information, please contact CECP at **info@cecp.co**.

INCREASE IN TOTAL GIVING

6 out of 10
companies increased total giving, 2015 to 2017

+15%
Growth of median total giving, 2015 to 2017

DEEPER IMPACT OF GRANTS

22%
fewer grants are being written, but

19%
larger total grant amounts, 2015 to 2017

INTERNATIONAL GIVING

2 out of 10
giving dollars go to international-end recipients

10%
of international giving goes to Disaster Relief

CAUSES

306% +
Higher median cash giving for Disaster Relief vs. three years ago (2015)

6%
of total giving goes to Disaster Relief

+5pp & +3pp*
in percentage of companies reporting STEM and Workforce/Employment as top-priority focus areas, respectively, 2015 to 2017

TRENDS IN COMMUNITY INVESTMENTS

EMPLOYEE ENGAGEMENT CREATING VALUE & IMPACT IN SOCIETY

51% → 55%
Percentage of companies offering open matching-gift programs, 2015 to 2017

$1.3 MILLION
Median dollar amount raised from employee payroll deductions

MEASUREMENT OF OUTCOMES/IMPACTS

9 out of 10
companies are measuring the social outcomes/impacts of their programs

GROWTH OF CONTRIBUTIONS TEAMS

4%
increase in overall corporate employee headcount, 2013 to 2017

15%
increase in contributions teams' headcount, 2013 to 2017**

Notes: Unless noted, 2017 data collected in 2018. N values vary for each measure. Additional definitions available in the CECP Valuation Guide.
* 'pp' refers to percentage points.
**Notes: Same group of companies for overall corporate employee headcount and contributions teams headcount.

CECP is a CEO-led coalition that believes that a company's social strategy—how it engages with key stakeholders including employees, communities, investors, and customers—determines company success. Founded in 1999 by actor and philanthropist Paul Newman and other business leaders to create a better world through business, CECP has grown to a movement of more than 200 of the world's largest companies that represent $6.2 trillion in revenues, $18.4 billion in societal investment, 13 million employees, and $15 trillion in assets under management. CECP helps companies transform their social strategy by providing customized connections and networking, counsel and support, benchmarking and trends, and awareness building and recognition.

CECP (Chief Executives for Corporate Purpose) is a coalition of CEOs who believe that societal improvement is an essential measure of business performance. In 2018, they released this infographic highlighting trends in corporate societal engagement.

Is there a causal relationship between corporate giving and increased revenue? Why or why not?

In Case You Missed It

Effective public relations means managing relationships between an organization and its publics. Social skills and business skills both come into play, as highlighted in some of the key takeaways from this chapter.

- The better the long-term relationships between your organization and publics, the more likely you are to achieve your goals.
- Before pitching to reporters, read their news stories, watch their programs, and follow their social media accounts to better understand their style and the type of news they cover.
- Healthy relations with internal publics, such as employees, are prerequisites for healthy relations with external publics.
- While financial information is tightly regulated, investor relations managers use many of the same channels of communication as any other public relations person.
- Volunteers and donors are among the most important publics for non-profit organizations.
- Ethically balancing loyalties is one of the toughest jobs of public relations managers.

Summary

4.1 Apply knowledge of interpersonal relationships to organization–public relationships.
Many of the same relationship strategies that work in personal relationships—positivity, openness, assurances, social networking, and sharing tasks—also work in maintaining relationships between organizations and their publics. The outcomes are similar too: trust, satisfaction, commitment, and a sense of mutual control.

4.2 Discuss the concept of relationships as central to public relations.
Relationships between organizations and publics can be thought of at the group level where the relationships between one group of people (organization) and other groups (publics) are analogous to interpersonal relationships. These relationships can also be thought of as the aggregate of all the interpersonal interactions between individuals in the organization and individuals in publics. Either way, managing the relationships for mutual benefit of all parties is at the heart of public relations.

4.3 Identify broad categories of stakeholders with whom public relations people build and maintain relationships.
Public relations people build and maintain relationships with media (journalists, editors, producers, bloggers, etc.), financial publics (investors, analysts, regulators, etc.), internal publics (employees, members, etc.), and an array of external publics such as consumers, donors, government officials, community leaders, and activists, including those who oppose the organization.

4.4 Define different areas of public relations practice by identifying the publics with whom relationships are built and maintained.
One way to categorize the different areas of public relations is news-driven, commerce-driven, and issues-driven. Although there is much overlap, common jobs in public relations align with these categories. Media relations and publicity are news-driven. Investor relations, marketing communication, customer relations, and employee relations are mostly commerce-driven. Public affairs, legislative relations, and issues management are mostly issues-driven.

4.5 **Evaluate corporate social responsibility as a strategy for balancing the interests of diverse publics (stakeholder analysis).**

The Coca-Cola case illustrates how one company has attempted to balance the varying interests of investors, employees, consumers, activists, lawmakers, and global communities. The CSR strategy involves committing resources to benefit society and the environment while also seeking profits. The question for analysis is how effective the company is in building and maintaining simultaneous relationships with a range of stakeholders with very different interests.

Discussion Questions

1. Relationships can be complicated. Discuss a love–hate relationship that you have with a particular organization. What does that organization do well in the relationship? What does that organization do that causes frustration?

2. Describe another organization for which you think of yourself as a key public (for example, as a student at a university, as a taxpayer, as a customer for a business, or as a volunteer for a non-profit). What is the role of public relations in the relationship? Do the people performing that role have titles other than "public relations"?

3. Search for an advertised public relations job (public affairs, investor relations, etc.) at an organization where you'd like to work. From the job ad, what publics does it appear you would work with most in that position?

4. Name a for-profit company that you admire as socially responsible. What do they do that makes you admire them? How do you think their socially responsible activities help or hurt their profits?

Further Readings and Online Resources

Where Public Relations Is Headed in the Modern Era
https://www.forbes.com/sites/forbesagencycouncil/2016/11/28/where-public-relations-is-headed-in-the-modern-era/#706b07524d70

This article from *Forbes* magazine discusses PR's evolution from an emphasis on media relations to today's emphasis on relationships and reputation.

Canadian Investor Relations Institute (CIRI)
https://www.ciri.org/AboutCIRI/Policies/PracticeGuidelines.aspx

Investor relations is a specialized branch of communications with its own professional association in Canada known as the Canadian Investor Relations Institute or CIRI. Explore CIRI's website including CIRI's definition of investor relations. How does this differ from common definitions of public relations?

How B2B PR differs from B2C PR, and why should brands care?
https://www.the-cma.org/about/blog/how-b2b-pr-different-from-b2c-pr-and-why-should-brands-care

This blogpost published on the Canadian Marketing Association website compares B2B public relations (business to business) to B2C public relations (business to consumer), and features an interview with Janine Allen, senior vice-president, general manager, and partner at Kaiser Lachance Communications.

Peer-Reviewed Academic Journal Article
Reeves, H. (2016). Defining public relations' role in corporate social responsibility programs. *Public Relations Journal*, 10(2).

This article explores public relations' role in CSR programs and suggests that PR needs to be involved in CSR programs but in a supportive, complementary role.

Key Terms

PART TWO
Strategy

5

Research

Why is research the first step in public relations planning?

In politics, it is sometimes said that a new campaign starts the day after election day. Although we hope that our elected officials will focus more on getting their new job done than on getting re-elected, there is quite a bit of truth here for campaign strategists. An election is like a survey of voters, and fresh election results yield all sorts of new data to kick off planning for future campaigns.

Strategic planning is a cyclical process. Whether a student is planning one semester's budget based on the prior semester's spending, a volleyball coach is reviewing last season's performance to plan for the next season, or a campaign strategist is analyzing the results of one campaign to plan for the next one, the process is similar. Successful planning begins, ends, and begins again, with research (Figure 5.1). In between are planning (Chapter 6) and communication or implementation (Chapter 7). This chapter explains how strategy starts with research. Public relations campaigns and programs with research-based goals and objectives lend themselves to proper evaluation (Chapter 8). Proper evaluation helps you make a case for the value of your work. Being able to demonstrate the value of your work gets you hired and promoted.

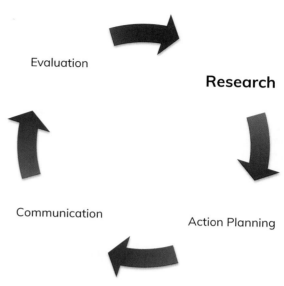

FIGURE 5.1 The RACE Cycle campaign begins, ends, and begins again with research.

What are some of the very first questions campaign planners should ask, and what kind of research helps answer them?

Research in the RACE Cycle

For years, public relations students studying for exams and practitioners reviewing for CPRS (Canadian Public Relations Society) accreditation interviews have referred to the four-step process of research, action planning, communication, and evaluation of programs (RACE). Other acronyms that start with R have also served as trusty mnemonic devices across public relations. RPIE,[1] ROPE,[2] and ROSIE[3] are three common examples: RPIE stands for research, planning, implementation, and evaluation. ROPE stands for research, objectives, programming, and evaluation. The ROSIE process includes research, objectives, strategies, implementation, and evaluation. Not only do they all start with an *R*, but they all end with an *E* for evaluation, which is a type of research in and of itself.

If we think of strategic public relations as a dynamic and cyclical process, it makes sense that the evaluation of one action, program, or campaign feeds back into the next. In fact, evaluation can happen at any point in a strategic program, not just at the end.

Evaluation can happen at any point in a strategic program, not just at the end.

Formative Research

When research comes at the beginning of the planning process or during the implementation of a plan, it is known as **formative research**. The information acquired during formative research helps you formulate your program or campaign and its components, including goals, objectives, strategy, and tactics. On one hand, formative research, or formative evaluation, can be casual and unscientific. If you call a few reporters to pitch a news story idea and they all decline abruptly, you may want to step back and reformulate your approach based on that information before you call anyone else. That's *informal* formative evaluation. However, informal trial and error on its own does not constitute strategic public relations.

formative research Research conducted at the beginning of the planning process or during the implementation of a plan.

On the other hand, formative research and evaluation can be carefully planned and sophisticated. Public relations professionals may begin campaigns or programs with detailed web **analytics**, carefully collected survey data on key publics or formally designed interviews. They also may continue to track those analytics, re-administer the surveys, and interview people for the duration of the campaign or program, using the live feedback to make corrections to strategy.

Summative Research

Summative research is when you've reached an end or stopping point in your campaign and you want to answer the question, "Did it work?" One way to differentiate between a campaign and an ongoing program is that a campaign has a defined beginning and end. A political campaign ends with an election. A year-end fundraising campaign ends on 31 December. A product-launch campaign ends when the product is fully available in the market, or at some specific date determined by the campaign's planners. In identifying an end-date for a campaign, planners make themselves accountable for specific outcomes at a specific point in time. Yes, those summative results can and should inform ongoing work and future campaigns, but as final evaluations, they answer the question of whether and to what extent the campaign achieved its goals (e.g., won the election, raised the target amount of money, or met sales projections for a new product).

When the *E* is placed at the end of an acronym like RACE or ROPE, it suggests summative evaluation. Remember, however, that research and feedback are important throughout the entire process of public relations work. This chapter focuses mostly on research as part of the planning process. Chapter 8 delves into specific methods for measurement, including evaluation research designed to quantify results of campaigns. One method to begin planning is to organize research into three major areas: (1) situation, (2) organization, and (3) publics.

Situation

Good public relations cases read like good stories, and good stories rely on an interesting setting. The setting provides the context for the problem or opportunity from which the public relations goals arise. At the very beginning, the situation may be only vaguely stated or implied (e.g., "We need to raise awareness"), but, with research, the situation can be analyzed more carefully to initiate strategic planning. Public relations case studies and write-ups for public relations case competitions such as PRSA's (Public Relations Society of America) Silver Anvil awards normally include a **situation analysis** at the beginning. Table 5.1 provides some examples of situation analysis starters from award-winning campaigns.[4]

Each of the cases described in Table 5.1 begins with a narrative presentation of the situation. The impetus for a public relations effort is either a problem, an opportunity, or some combination of the two. And, getting started means doing research to first identify the problem or opportunity and then to understand it well enough to create a narrative.

An effective situation analysis leads to a clear, concise **problem or opportunity statement** with which the client or organization and the team representing them agree. In their text *Strategic Communications Planning*, Brigham Young University's Laurie Wilson and Joseph Ogden write that a core problem statement can be written in a single sentence.[5] Others recommend a paragraph or two. Because it captures the essence of the situation

---

analytics A field of data analysis used to describe, predict, and improve how organizations communicate with publics; commonly refers to tracking of website traffic and resulting behaviour.

summative research Research conducted at the end of a campaign or program to determine the extent that objectives and goals were met.

situation analysis A report analyzing the internal and external environment of an organization and its publics as it relates to the start of a campaign or program.

problem or opportunity statement A concise written summary of the situation that explains the main reason for a public relations program or campaign.

and determines the scope and value of your proposal, your core problem or opportunity statement may well be one of the most carefully constructed sentences or paragraphs you write in all of your work in public relations. Distilling a vague, complex, and ambiguous context down to a brief statement that everyone involved can agree upon requires careful analysis.

SWOT Analysis

One common approach for structuring the analysis is the SWOT analysis. *SWOT* stands for strengths, weaknesses, opportunities, and threats.

Strengths are factors internal to your organization or client that will help you reach your goals or fulfill your mission. If your client is the faculty of a local university, some strengths might be a range of faculty projects that benefit local communities or a record of faculty involvement in community organizations as part of their professional service. It would take research to learn what these projects and organizations are and understand who benefits.

Weaknesses are internal factors that make it harder for your organization or client to do what it wants to do. In the university example, weaknesses may be a lack of training or professional incentive for faculty to communicate their scholarship outside of their peer groups. Or, perhaps there is a gap in communication between university faculty and the professional communicators representing the school. Again, it would take research to obtain an accurate sense of the internal communication environment.

Opportunities and threats are external variables. A relatively close-knit university town where there are few degrees of separation between citizens and the people working in the university could be an opportunity for word-of-mouth communication. A decreasing revenue projection that will put greater scrutiny on the university's budget may be a threat.

As with strengths and weaknesses, opportunities and threats are often two sides to the same coin. Greater scrutiny of an organization's budget may be perceived as a threat. Programs could be cut or jobs could be at risk. But at the same time, close attention to an organization's budget may provide an opportunity to communicate the value of the organization's work. In addition to educating students, colleges and universities employ thousands of people, generate revenue in patents and licenses, and provide launching pads for start-ups. Discovering strengths, weaknesses, opportunities, and threats and listing them in a table is an appropriate start, but the actual analysis of that information requires closer examination

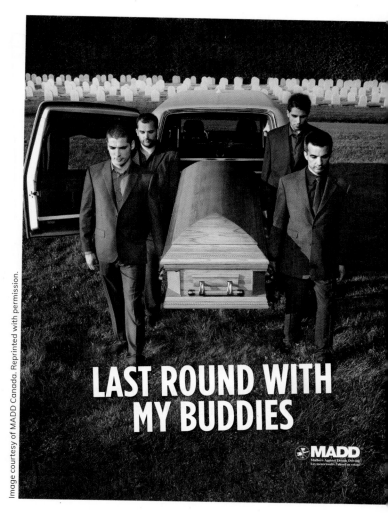

Image courtesy of MADD Canada. Reprinted with permission.

MADD Canada has created numerous campaigns to encourage Canadians not to drink and drive.

What kind of research could they do to know if the campaign efforts have worked?

SWOT analysis
Description and discussion of an organization's internal strengths and weaknesses and its external opportunities and threats.

Courtesy of Dave Carpenter

"I must say, your hindsight on this project was far more accurate than his foresight."

Evaluation of one project can serve as insight for the next one.

How does public relations research help turn hindsight into foresight?

> Gaining a deeper understanding of a situation requires digging for information of substance beyond an Internet search.

and discussion. Prioritizing the most relevant information, deciding what *not* to focus on, and understanding how different factors relate to one another and to your organization's mission are all part of the work you do in getting ready to tell the story.

Resources for Situation Research

In all likelihood, situation research starts with an Internet search and conversations with the clients. However, gaining a deeper, more analytic, and more nuanced understanding of the situation than what the client already knows from their own quick Google search requires digging deeper for information of substance. Here are some potential resources for researching the situation:

- Summaries of relevant media coverage, including stories placed in print, broadcast, or online media. The organization may already have reports on file or may subscribe to media monitoring services (see Chapter 8) that generate such reports.
- Copies of any organizational documents related to the problem that the client is willing to share, including policies, reports, archived correspondence, and web or intranet material.
- Collateral material from prior campaigns and programs (brochures, web content, product information, etc.), news releases, and ads.
- Any available statements, reports, or information from or about the organization's competitors that is relevant to the situation.
- Calendars or schedules of related events.
- Copies of relevant laws, regulations, budgets, or pending legislation that are publicly available through government web pages or upon request from government agencies.
- Any research already conducted and reported (surveys, interviews, content analyses, communication audits, message testing, and usability studies, etc.).
- Web analytics reports, which track website traffic such as the number of unique visitors to a site, the number of page views, how much time people spend on a site, the percentage of people who leave after seeing only one page (bounce rate), or indicators of other objectives such as the number of registrations or downloads (see Chapter 8).
- Prior marketing, advertising, and public relations plans.

As a cohesive narrative analysis of the situation comes together, and as that brief problem or opportunity statement begins to take shape, it's crucial to stay in touch with the client

TABLE 5.1 Examples of Situation Analysis Starters in Award-Winning Campaigns

Campaign	Situation
Hill+Knowlton and Plan International Canada's "Girls Belong Here"	"Girls face unique barriers that prevent them from being seen and heard. Millions still bear the brunt of poverty, are denied an education, are forced into marriage, and are subjected to violence—simply because they are young and female. . . . Turning this around by investing in girls will have huge benefits for everyone. And that is why Plan International Canada started its groundbreaking Because I am a Girl movement."
MSLGROUP, Leo Burnett Toronto, and SMG's "Always #LikeAGirl: Turning an Insult into a Confidence Movement"	"When a new Always-sponsored survey found that the start of puberty and first periods mark the lowest moments in confidence for girls, Always determined that empowering girls during this critical life stage should become our mission. We discovered that somewhere between puberty and adulthood, women had internalized the phrase 'like a girl' to mean weakness and vanity. So, we took 'like a girl' and transformed its negative power to mean 'downright amazing.' "
SickKids' "SickKids VS Launch"	"The philanthropic pie in Canada is not growing—giving behaviour remains flat among the SickKids' core donor base of females aged 45+. In order to drive future growth for SickKids Foundation, we needed to broaden our appeal to new audiences, including more men and more millennials as the next generation of donors. Our marketing communications challenge was to jolt the community into taking notice and attract the attention of potential donors who are sitting on the sidelines."
LDWWgroup's "Carnival Corporation: Navigating the World's Leading Cruise Company to Smoother Waters"	"A series of high-profile incidents in 2012 and 2013, including the sinking of the Costa Concordia resulting in the deaths of 32 passengers and the infamous Carnival 'poop cruise,' shook consumer confidence in Carnival Corporation and its nine cruise lines. Not surprisingly, bookings dropped, revenue sagged, and the reputation of the corporation and its brands suffered after the incidents with brand perception dropping by as much as 50 points. A new leadership team was put in place and the corporation brought in long-time PR professional Roger Frizzell to help tackle head-on the recovery of the company's reputation."

or organization's management to ensure you are on the right track. For example, consider the problem/opportunity statement for Ogilvy Public Relations Worldwide and DuPont's "Welcome to the Global Collaboratory" campaign:

> DuPont was challenged by its "chemical company" reputation, despite being a long-time global contributor to food production, nutrition and safety. It also confronted a landscape with a chief competitor, Monsanto, espousing a strong, public POV [point of view] that biotechnology is the primary answer to the problem. DuPont retained Ogilvy to develop a campaign to showcase to the global food influencer community its commitment to bringing together key audiences who can create solutions to ensuring global food security.[6]

An organization and its publics are embedded in the situation and must, therefore, be researched concurrently. Although practitioners may start with a general background and broad context for strategic public relations efforts, delving deeper makes apparent the need for research specifically focusing on the organization and its publics.

SWOT ANALYSIS

	Helpful	Harmful
Internal origin	**S** Strengths	**W** Weaknesses
External origin	**O** Opportunities	**T** Threats

marigranula/123RF

SWOT analyses help you identify key factors in planning for public relations.

How might researching factors of internal origin (strengths and weaknesses) be different from researching factors of external origin (opportunities and threats)?

in house When public relations people are employed directly within an organization rather than working for an external agency or contracted as independent consultants.

mission statement A formal statement of an organization's steady, enduring purpose.

vision Often aspirational, this is a vivid description of the organization as it effectively carries out its mission.

values Ideally, the core priorities in the organization's culture; they represent how people should act in the organization.

Organization

Perhaps the best place to start understanding an organization is its mission. The mission is the organization's steady, enduring purpose. For example, a college or university's mission may entail research, teaching, and service. Even if you are working **in house** or are already familiar with a client, you may still find it useful to review the organization's **mission statement**, **vision**, and **values**, if these are available.

Mission Statements

A for-profit corporation's mission may be quite different from the mission of a non-profit or NGO. For example, compare Wawanesa Insurance's mission statement

> "Earning your trust since 1896". . . . As a policyholder-owned mutual insurance company, we will continue to earn trust by providing quality products and services at the lowest price which supports long-term growth and financial stability.[7]

to the much shorter mission statement of the Girl Guides of Canada:

> To be a catalyst for girls empowering girls.

Not all organizations publish a mission statement, but you can still find evidence of an organization's broadest guiding principles and philosophy in key publications such as annual reports, or even the "About Us" section of a website.

These resources also give researchers a sense of the organization's values and culture. Given the amount of effort and levels of review that these major organizational statements often require before being published, they should be taken seriously as indicators of the reason the organization exists and deeper purpose of why people work there.

Resources for Organization Research

Other written documents to seek in learning about an organization may include the following:

- any written history
- the organization's charter and bylaws
- a flow chart or other description of the organizational structure
- product or service descriptions

- biographies of or interviews with key executives and board members
- summary budget reports, and other summary data on staffing, profits, stock values, and so on
- social media account profiles, posts, and networks, including individuals and other organizations
- organizational communication policies and social media policies, if available
- any prior research reports or audits of internal communication channels or programs

Of course, researchers cannot rely on formal written material alone to understand what makes an organization tick. Reviewing a company's web page, publications, and archives is not sufficient to gain tacit knowledge of something as intangible as organizational culture. Designing a public relations campaign with an appreciation for organizational culture in the context of a particular situation (or a situation in the context of an organizational culture) requires astute observation of not just written evidence but also people and their behaviour.

organizational culture
The unique character of an organization composed of beliefs, values, symbols, and behaviours.

Publics

In conducting research on the situation and organization, you gain a good understanding of the benefits that an organization seeks from public relations campaigns and programs. Public relations professionals use that research, along with research on publics, to develop goals and objectives that serve the organization's broader mission. But remember that the best relationships are mutually beneficial. This means you have to work to understand not just the interests of your own organization but also the interests of your publics. What are they going to get out of the relationship? This kind of understanding requires thinking about research as part of a larger process of two-way communication. The RACE process is very much a cycle of interactive communication between organizations and their publics. Just as your richest interpersonal communication happens when you listen as much as you talk, organization–public relationships flourish when public relations people spend as much energy trying to understand publics as they do trying to get their messages out.

Organization–public relationships flourish when you spend as much energy trying to understand your publics as you do trying to get your message out.

Internal and External

Publics can be either internal or external to the organization, and that designation may depend on the context. Employees and members are almost always thought of as internal publics, and as such they can be reached via internal channels such as face-to-face meetings, company email lists, hallway bulletin boards, intranets, and even the organizational grapevine. To the degree that these channels are used for gaining feedback, they can be used for research and evaluation.

While an organizational chart may offer a relatively simple map for reference when identifying internal publics, it is important to think about the definition of a public when identifying and prioritizing internal publics. Remember, publics are groups of people with shared interests who have an effect on an organization or whom the organization affects. Most people internal to an organization will fit both these criteria, but specific situations will mean prioritizing internal publics differently. If a university is working to gain

internal publics Groups of people with shared interests within an organization.

THE CANADIAN PRESS/Justin Tang

Canadian federal employees in British Columbia took to the streets to protest the government's Phoenix pay system, which caused employees to be underpaid, overpaid, or not paid at all.

In this situation, were the protestors internal or external publics for the government?

external publics Groups of people that exist mostly outside of an organization and have a relationship with the organization.

funding based on its faculty research and community service, faculty members will be a key internal public. In a campus nighttime safety campaign, university police and resident assistants may be more important. Alumni, who share an identity with the school, may be considered internal or external, depending on the situation.

External publics are outside of the organization and are generally reached via channels such as mass media, direct mail, and the Internet. Each of these channels also can serve as a resource for feedback and research. Even though mass media such as TV, newspapers, and radio are mostly one-way forms of communication, audience data from services like Nielsen TV ratings, responses to radio promotions, coupon codes from print ads, or traffic data from web pages can all be useful in researching external publics.

Of course, there are limitations on how precisely publics can be segmented based on the media they use. The most massive of mass media will certainly reach internal publics. You can bet employees are as affected by a Super Bowl commercial for their company as their global customers are—hopefully in a positive manner. Favourable cable news coverage or a front-page story in the news may have a similar effect. For internal publics, a well-received, big-time mass media hit may provide a boost in morale or give employees extra confidence that people have heard of their company when they pursue a sales lead or introduce themselves at a meeting.

Likewise, even the most interpersonal channels can reach external publics. This has always been the case with word-of-mouth communication, and it is more pronounced with social media.

Online, the lines between internal and external communication are increasingly blurring. In 2006, when corporate blogging was becoming a trend of interest for public relations research, our author Tom Kelleher surveyed a sample of people who had read and commented on blogs posted by people who worked at Microsoft and found that more than 30 per cent of the commenters also worked at Microsoft. The blogs were clearly channels for both internal and external communication. In this case, the effects looked to be beneficial because the respondents reported high levels of trust and satisfaction in their relationship with the organization.[8]

But it can go the other way too. When Yahoo CEO Marissa Mayer wanted to roll out a new strategy discouraging Yahoo employees from working remotely, HR director Jackie Reses sent out an internal memo introducing the new policy. It was marked "PROPRIETARY AND CONFIDENTIAL INFORMATION—DO NOT FORWARD."[9] The memo was immediately forwarded anyway, and within hours the story was all over social media and mainstream media alike. Yahoo management certainly received much more feedback than they sought.

Social media blur the lines between an organization's internal and external communications.

Latent, Aware, Active

According to Kurt Lewin, a pioneer in social and organizational psychology, "There is nothing so practical as a good theory."[10] A good example of practical theory in public relations is James Grunig's situational theory of publics. The theory applies easily to practice, in that it helps us identify and strategize about publics in the context of a situation analysis and the planning that follows. The situational theory of publics basically says that publics range from latent to aware to active based on their levels of involvement, problem recognition, and constraint recognition.

Marissa Mayer's Work-From-Home Ban Is The Exact Opposite Of What CEOs Should Be Doing

🕐 02/23/2013 04:18 pm ET | Updated Apr 25, 2013

7.1 K   [f] [𝕏] [𝕡] [✉]   [f] Like 24K

👤 Lisa Belkin
Senior Columnist, The Huffington Post

When Yahoo CEO Marissa Mayer rolled out a new work-from-home policy, the company received more feedback than it anticipated or likely wanted when it was forwarded externally.

How do social media blur the lines between an organization's internal and external communications?

Other Ways of Segmenting Publics

Depending on the context, public relations strategists may choose to segment publics in a number of other ways. For clear prioritization, publics may be labelled as primary, secondary, and tertiary. Suppose you are planning a shoreline clean-up project in conjunction with The Great Canadian Shoreline Cleanup. You may decide that young volunteers are your **primary public**. In planning, you would also want to develop strategy to communicate with their teachers and parents, as elementary-school-aged participants will require supervision and transportation. Parents of small children would also be primary publics, but you might decide to label parents of older teenagers and teachers who might encourage participation as **secondary publics**. Additional groups, known as **tertiary publics**, could include city officials, sponsors, or private waste removal companies as well as other shoreline users who will benefit.

> **primary publics** Groups of people identified as most important to the success of a public relations campaign or program.

In cases involving competition or divisive issues, publics may be segmented into proponents, opponents, and uncommitted. Campaign strategy, especially in political campaigns, often focuses on the uncommitted. While it is important to reinforce the attitudes of supporters, and occasionally those may be won over in an election, the greatest gains in many campaigns come from undecided or independent voters. The same logic applies outside of politics. Some people will support your efforts even without a public relations program, and others will never get involved; however, you can make progress with publics that are somewhere in between, moving them from latent to aware to active.

Sergei Bachlakov/Shutterstock

Planners need to consider many publics that will be involved in various ways with an event like this shoreline clean up in Thunder Bay, Ontario.

Can you name some primary, secondary, and tertiary publics for this event?

Applying the Situational Theory of Publics: Net Neutrality

situational theory of publics The theory that the activity of publics depends on their levels of involvement, problem recognition, and constraint recognition.

net neutrality When data transmitted on the Internet is treated equally by governments and service providers in a way that does not slow down, speed up, or manipulate traffic to create a favourable business environment for some organizations or users over others.

latent publics People who are affected by a problem or issue but don't realize it.

problem recognition When people detect a problem or situation in their environment and begin to think about it.

aware publics People who recognize that they are affected by a problem or issue in their environment.

The case of net neutrality offers an example of how the **situational theory of publics** can be applied. **Net neutrality** "means that Internet service providers may not discriminate between different kinds of content and applications online," according to Free Press's "Save the Internet" Campaign at www .savetheinternet.com. The issue, as described by the group is this:

> The biggest cable and telephone companies would like to charge money for smooth access to web sites, speed to run applications, and permission to plug in devices. These network giants believe they should be able to charge Web site operators, application providers and device manufacturers for the right to use the network. Those who don't make a deal and pay up will experience discrimination: Their sites won't load as quickly, and their applications and devices won't work as well. Without legal protection, consumers could find that a network operator has blocked the Web site of a competitor, or slowed it down so much that it's unusable.[11]

The Free Press organization advocates for net neutrality, and in doing so opposes Federal Communications Commission (FCC) regulations that would allow for a tiered system supported by telecommunications companies. In 2014, the FCC considered adopting a rule that would allow Internet service providers to offer a "fast lane" on the Internet for companies that are willing and able to pay for it. Under this rule, Netflix might have paid Comcast or AT&T to improve streaming speeds of its video material relative to other content providers. There was certainly more than one side to this issue, and the legal, technological, economic, and societal issues underlying the debate were rather complex. For example, Netflix's CEO actually strongly supported net neutrality for "democratizing access to ideas, services, and goods," and also because ISP interconnection fees will ultimately lead to "a poor consumer experience," he blogged in 2014.[12] Were you part of a latent, aware, or active public for the issue? The answer depends on three questions.

Problem Recognition

How often do people stop to think about the issue? If people haven't detected an issue, they won't think about it much. This doesn't mean they aren't affected or don't have a say. They may well still be part of a key public. They just don't realize it. Think of all the Netflix viewers, YouTube uploaders, and online gamers who never stopped to think about net neutrality before 2014. These are **latent publics**, because even though they can be defined as a public, they themselves don't recognize it. Once they do recognize the issue—**problem recognition**—and start thinking about it, they become **aware publics**. Most strategic public relations efforts involve not just mere awareness but also some level of understanding of the issue and, beyond that, behaviour.

Level of Involvement

How connected do people feel to the issue? A key factor in whether people will become **active publics** on an issue is their **level of involvement**. People who used the Internet primarily for low-bandwidth activities like checking email or occasional light web browsing may have been aware of the net neutrality issue, but they just didn't see a strong enough connection between the issue and their personal situations to get active on the issue.

From a public relations planner's perspective, research on demographics and psychographics is useful in identifying involved publics. Research on **demographics** answers questions like how old these people are and where they live. Research on **psychographics**, on the other hand, answers questions about variables such as the personality types of heavy Internet users and their preferences for online content. The psychographic profile of a potential active public in the net neutrality debate is one of a heavy data user who combines personal and social use of bandwidth.

Constraint Recognition

What, if anything, can people do about the issue? Let's say your public now really understands net neutrality and they're good and angry about it being taken away (high problem recognition) because of how badly that change will mess up their Internet experience if they are not willing to pay more to access high-quality content (high level of

active publics People who behave and communicate actively in response to a problem or issue.

level of involvement The degree to which people feel or think that a problem or issue affects them.

demographics Data describing objective characteristics of a population including age, level of income, or highest educational level obtained.

psychographics Data describing psychological characteristics of a population including interests, attitudes, and behaviours.

Courtesy of Giving Tuesday Canada

The goal of this message that made the rounds on Facebook and other social media sites appears to be to move publics from latent to aware or from aware to active.

What types of research do you think led to this tactic?

Giving Tuesday Canada is a social movement encouraging Canadians and Canadian organizations to establish the day after Cyber Monday as Giving Tuesday, a day dedicated to giving and generosity of all kinds.

How many specific ways can publics become active from this web page?

Continued

constraint recognition When people detect a problem or situation in their environment but perceive obstacles that limit their behaviour to do anything about it.

involvement). What are they going to do about it? The answer depends on **constraint recognition**, and a smart public relations plan will have a response to that question ready for publics at this stage. Free Press told web users they had options. "Share this page to spread the word to stop them from selling out Net Neutrality!" was one option. Signing an online petition to the FCC was another.

In 2015, instead of adopting rules providing for a fast lane, the FCC sided with millions of people who took an active stance on the issue. The FCC adopted rules to protect the open Internet: "America's broadband networks must be fast, fair and open—principles shared by the overwhelming majority of the nearly 4 million commenters who participated in the FCC's Open Internet proceeding."[13] The Free Press organization called the decision the "biggest victory for the public interest in the FCC's history."[14]

secondary publics Groups of people who are important to a public relations campaign or program because of their relationship with primary publics.

tertiary publics Groups of people who indirectly influence or are indirectly affected by a public relations campaign or program.

Some people will support your efforts without a public relations program, and others will never get involved, but you can make progress with publics that are somewhere in between.

Sometimes it makes sense to segment publics based on their role in the communications process. For example, you may want to think about the sources for your messages such as employees or members of your organization; the intermediaries such as reporters, community leaders, or social media influencers; and the target publics who will receive and respond to the message. Keep in mind that in two way-communication, senders and receivers will have interchangeable roles. For example, company representatives may be expected to send information out, but having those same people positioned to receive and respond to feedback is important too.

Resources for Research on Publics

The following are useful resources for conducting research on publics:

- *Results of prior surveys.* These may be conducted either by the organization or by others who have sampled from populations that overlap significantly with key publics.
- *Publicly available databases, including census data.* Funded by the government, Canadian Census data are free to access, and allow for searching and analysis based on geography and topics such as education, economy, health, and business.
- *Market research reports.* These generally cost money if you want data tailored to your specific questions about key publics, but they can be useful and fascinating if your budget permits them. For example, the Strategic Business Insights' VALS™ (values, attitudes, and lifestyles) system offers demographic and psychographic profiles of consumers.
- *Media lists.* These include journalists and other opinion leaders (e.g., columnists, editors, commentators) and online influencers (e.g., Instagram influencers, bloggers, and other actively engaged social media users).
- *News stories or online reports about key publics.* For example, if you search for "Great Canadian Shoreline Cleanup" you will find information about shoreline clean-up projects across the country, include media coverage and Facebook pages. More controversial situations usually generate even more media coverage, including descriptive information about proponents and opponents. News stories or prior research reports may also include perspectives gained from interviews that offer richer perspectives than are available from statistical reports.

- *Social media accounts of representatives of key publics.* Blogs, Twitter accounts, public Facebook groups, and Instagram accounts can offer a better understanding of a public's motivations, concerns, and general culture from a first-person perspective.
- *An organization's past communication records with key publics.* Look around for collections of comment cards, email folders with public feedback, archived comments or replies to social media posts, minutes from public meetings, guest lists for special events, and even logs of incoming phone calls (including complaints). As a customer, you may actually want to be told that your call to a company "may be recorded." It can give you hope that your concern will be taken seriously (though somehow we doubt those call recordings are listened to very often).

Find latest data from the 2016 Census

Place name:

⦿ Search 2016 Census Profile
◯ Search all 2016 Census data, analysis and maps

Search

Census of Agriculture ➡

Census Datasets (1991 — 2016) ➡

Census data are freely available online.

How might these type of data be useful in a public relations program?

Quantitative Research

When numbers and statistics accompany the results of research, it is considered quantitative research. In a blood drive, quantitative data could include demographic statistics on blood donors and non-donors in a county, the number of email accounts that are known to have received an invitation, the percentage of people who click on a link in an email invitation, the number of people who respond to a Facebook invitation, the number of retweets of a Twitter announcement, other more sophisticated analytics of the pattern of social media activities, the number of people who make an appointment to donate blood, the number of people who actually board the bloodmobile on a given day, and, perhaps most important, the amount of blood actually donated. Surveys and experiments are common methods for quantitative research.

quantitative research Research that results in numerical or statistical data and analysis.

Surveys

Questionnaires that are administered online, on printed paper, or face to face allow researchers to gather data from respondents that can be presented in quantitative form. Reports can include the number or percentages of people who answered questions in certain ways (yes, no, maybe, strongly agree, etc.) and more sophisticated statistics such as correlations and tests of the significance of interactions between variables.

For example, researchers who surveyed a sample of Polish university students with questionnaires administered in lecture rooms found that 19 per cent had considered blood donation and that 37.9 per cent had not decided about donating blood or had never even thought about it. They also reported that religious obligation (measured with a numerical scale of agreement with the statement "My religious beliefs encourage me to help other people") correlated with another item that measured "definite consideration of blood donation."[15] A positive correlation in this case means that people who reported stronger religious beliefs were more likely to consider donating blood.

Experiments

treatment group A group of subjects or people in an experiment that receive or are exposed to a treatment.

Experiments allow researchers to test predictions based on controlled differences between groups. For example, researchers working with the Swiss Red Cross and the Zurich Blood Donation Service sent three different invitations out to people who were registered in the blood donation service's database. Recipients of the invitations were randomly assigned to one of three groups. Members of one group, a **treatment group**, were offered a lottery ticket as an incentive to donate. A second treatment group was offered a free blood screening. The third group, known as a **control group**, was offered no special incentive. Because more than 10,000 donors were part of the study and participants were assigned to groups randomly, any difference between groups could reasonably be attributed to the different invitations and incentives. The researchers found that "offering a lottery ticket increases usable donations by 5 percentage points over a baseline donation rate of 42 percent."[16]

control group A group of subjects or people in an experiment that do not receive or are not exposed to a treatment for the purpose of comparison.

Content Analysis

content analysis A systematic method for analyzing recorded information such as audio, video, or text.

Content analysis does not involve direct interaction or questioning of people but, rather, analyzing the content of people's communication. Any type of recorded communication—from newspaper articles to TV shows to YouTube comments to Instagram feeds—can be systematically analyzed.

In planning a blood drive, it may be useful to analyze the content of comments on the organization's Facebook page, news stories that mention the organization by name, letters and emails written to the organization, or internal communication such as memos and newsletters. University of Miami Professor Don Stacks identified four types of units of analysis that can be quantified.[17]

1. *Words or symbols.* How many times has the word *bloodmobile* been used in the local newspaper in the past year? How many times during a drive was #bloodmobile used on Instagram? How many arm selfies appeared?
2. *Characters.* These are the people involved or the roles that they play. How often do stories include *volunteers, donors, doctors,* or *recipients*?
3. *Time and space.* How many minutes of news coverage does a blood drive get on TV? How much space does the announcement get in a company email newsletter?
4. *Items.* An item is the message itself. How many tweets? How many comments? Even the number of likes on Facebook could count as items.

ArtBabii/Alamy Stock Photo

Social media allow countless ways for people to communicate.

What are some useful units of analysis that can be quantified in a medium like Facebook?

Content analysis also can reveal themes and underlying messages in communication. Stacks calls this *latent* content. A careful analysis of blog entries about donating blood may, for example, reveal a theme of interpersonal influence if bloggers regularly mention key people who motivated them to donate.

Convenience, guilt, safety, or altruism could also show up as themes. Exploring deeper themes and meaning, however, is much more of a qualitative endeavour than quantitative. Therefore, content analysis can be quantitative or qualitative.

A/B Testing

A/B testing, also known as split testing, is a research technique designed to test a single variable. Let's say you want to test different news release headings as links on one of your organization's web pages. You could set up two versions of the web page—an "A" version with one news release heading and a "B" version with another heading. These are basically two conditions in a simple experiment. Your website can then be programmed to randomly display either A or B to a sample of visitors over a period of time. A/B testing programs allow you to compare the two conditions against each other to see, for instance, whether the A version or the B version generates more clicks through to the full text of the news release. The independent variable (the cause) is the type of headline, and the dependent variable (the effect) is click-through behaviour. When software and computer programs are used to automatically test digital messages, marketing and advertising researchers call this **automated copy testing**.

Qualitative Research

Qualitative research answers open-ended questions that can't be answered with numbers alone. What motivates people to donate blood? What fears, concerns, or misconceptions do potential donors have? What differences have volunteers observed between one-time donors and donors who give blood repeatedly? Interviews, focus groups, and direct observation give researchers and strategists a deeper understanding of human behaviour.

Interviews

While it is interesting and useful to know that researchers have found a statistical correlation between religious beliefs and consideration of blood donation, much more can be learned about what potential blood donors are thinking and feeling by sitting down with them (or talking on the phone or Skype, for example) and asking carefully considered open-ended questions. In-depth interviews allow respondents the opportunity to elaborate, sometimes revealing answers the researcher may have never even considered. Perhaps the connection between religion and blood donor attitudes has something to do with deep-seated personal values. Or is it just convenience if the blood drives are organized at churches? Or is it a combination of these factors? Interviewing people is a good way to find out. Interviews enable respondents to answer questions in their own terms instead of merely agreeing or disagreeing with statements

The hashtag #Bloodmobile aggregates an interesting sample of user-generated content related to blood drives.

How might you use Instagram in the research process for planning a blood drive in your community?

A/B testing Experiment in which one group of participants is randomly assigned to see one version of a message and another group is randomly assigned to see a second version. Results are then compared to test the effectiveness of message variations.

automated copy testing Using computer programs to automate the process of testing digital messages such as promotional copy.

qualitative research Research that results in in-depth description and understanding without relying on the use of numbers or statistics to analyze findings.

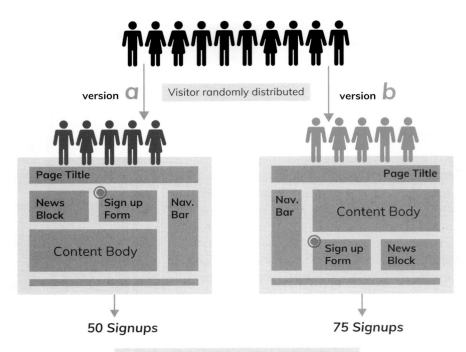

FIGURE 5.2 This example shows how different page layouts (independent variable) can be compared to see which delivers more signups (dependent variable).

What other independent and dependent variables can be tested with A/B testing?

Source: Developed by Sparsh Gupta (CEO, VWO).

in surveys or answering questions within the constraints of short-answer questionnaire formats. Interviews can focus on facts and biographical information, beliefs, feelings, motives, behaviours, perceived norms, and conscious reasoning for feelings and behaviour.[18]

Focus Groups

In public relations, we are very often interested in how people think, feel, and act in groups. Focus groups are essentially group interviews. Instead of sitting down with an individual, you would arrange to interview a small group of 6 to 12 people together. While each person may not have the opportunity to articulate his or her own insight at length the way he or she would in a one-on-one interview, the conversation among people in a focus group may yield results that more closely approximate the way people form and express ideas in social settings.

A well-moderated focus group will allow group members to explore points of agreement as well as areas in which members diverge in their attitudes, beliefs, and behaviours. In his book *Focus Groups as Qualitative Research*, sociologist David Morgan wrote about how focus groups can bring to life topics that may be mundane or difficult to explore in depth with any one individual: "I once watched a marketer with a background in sociology conduct a lively demonstration focus group of professors and graduate students who discussed their use of bar soap."[19] Indeed, it would be hard to imagine sitting down with one person for an hour

Focus groups were commonly used by advertising firms in the *Mad Men* era of the 1950s and 1960s to test ad concepts, and they have been widely adopted in social sciences in recent decades.

How can public relations researchers use focus groups?

or so to talk about a bar of soap. Imagine what a skilled group moderator could do with the right group of people from one of your key publics discussing a topic like blood donation.

Direct Observation

Of course, what people say is not always consistent with what they do. Therefore, do not overlook direct observation as a form of research. Two types of direct observation are participant and non-participant observation. In **non-participant observation**, the researcher does not interact with the people being observed. A researcher might sit unnoticed a few feet away from volunteers who are staffing a blood drive registration table or out of the way in the back of a bloodmobile and watch what people do and say. In **participant observation**, the researcher interacts with those being observed, sometimes for very long periods of time. You may have seen documentaries dealing with anthropologists who go to great lengths to become part of the cultures they wish to understand. Research in public relations planning likely will not require such an intense personal commitment. If your organization is a local blood bank, you could learn a lot by serving as a volunteer or by going through the blood donation process yourself while observing others.

Direct observation can also reveal important variables to measure in other types of research. For example, a blood bank may decide to do further research on factors that influence donors, such as cleanliness of facilities, the comfort of waiting areas, food and drink options, and donor interaction with counsellors.

non-participant observation Research method in which the researcher avoids interaction with the environment or those being observed.

participant observation Research method in which the researcher deliberately interacts with the environment and those being observed.

Secondary and Primary Research

secondary research
Collection, summary, analysis, or application of previously reported research.

Many of the resources for research listed earlier would be considered secondary research, which is the re-use of research and data that have already been collected. When public relations strategists explore census data, read market research reports, search for blogs or news stories online, or review research from past case studies, they are conducting secondary research. Consider how much you can learn about blood drives (situations), blood banks (organizations), and blood donors (publics) without even stepping away from your computer. In writing this chapter, every single resource on blood drives consulted was available online. But if I wanted to plan my own blood drive here in my own hometown, I would still have some specific questions that would require primary research to answer.

primary research
Systematic design, collection, analysis, and application of original data or observation.

Primary research involves designing research and collecting your own data for communication planning. One clear benefit of primary research is that it allows you to tailor research to your own specific purposes. While you have learned that lottery tickets were an effective incentive to convince people to donate blood in Switzerland and that college students in Poland are motivated in part by religious beliefs, you may want to test other incentives with your own research.

> Primary research allows you to tailor your research to your own specific purposes.

Formal and Informal Research

As mentioned near the beginning of this chapter, research in public relations ranges from casual and unscientific to carefully planned and sophisticated. In other words, the options range from informal research to formal research. The more carefully that public relations strategists design research with clear rules and procedures for the collection and analysis of information, the more formal the research.

In addition to the census, Statistics Canada undertakes numerous other research projects. Here are just a few facts gleaned from some of the research studies undertaken by Statistics Canada:

informal research
Research conducted without clear rules or procedures, which makes the findings difficult to replicate or compare to other research or situations.

- In 2016, Canadian households spent an average of $30 on peanut butter and other nut butters and $14 on jams, jellies, marmalades, and similar preserves (from the 2016 Survey of Household Spending, 2016).
- In 2016, 7.4 billion table eggs were produced in Canada (Census of Agriculture, 2016).
- The most popular outdoor activities for Canadians in 2016 were hiking and backpacking (General Social Survey, 2016).
- Forty-three per cent of Canadians eat poultry on any given day (Canadian Health Survey, 2015).
- Three in ten Canadians aged 18 and over reported using some form of opioid in the past five years (Survey on Opioid Awareness, 2017).

formal research
Research designed with clear rules and procedures for collection and analysis of information.

While many of the nuggets of information from these various surveys would make for interesting questions in a trivia contest, it is easy to imagine how the research would be useful in strategic planning for anyone practising public relations. The research yields a wealth of data on the situation and the publics with whom these organizations are most concerned.

The main issue with formal research is that it doesn't come cheap. Let's say you don't have a couple hundred million in your budget, but you still need to do some research. Informal research can be designed and conducted for practically free. If you were researching drug and alcohol issues, you could ask your friends and family about drugs and alcohol (informal interviews or focus groups), create a quick online questionnaire or Surveymonkey survey and post it on your organization's page (informal survey), compare a few different types of brochures to see if they have different effects on people (informal experiment), or skim local newspapers for drug- and alcohol-related stories (informal content analysis).

Of course, asking a few friends some questions and conducting national surveys that cost millions of dollars represent extremes on the spectrum from informal to formal research. Deciding on research that best meets your organization's needs and budget means weighing costs and benefits. Two of the biggest factors driving decisions about research are reliability and validity.

Reliability refers to how well a particular research technique can be applied multiple times and yield comparable data. Consider this scenario: In getting ready for a long trip, you lift your suitcase and estimate how much it weighs because you don't want to get dinged with a $25 fee for overweight luggage if your bag weighs more than 23 kilograms. You zip your bag closed and lift it a few inches off the ground. "About 18 kilograms," you figure. "No problem."

Two hours later, you unload your luggage from the car to the curb at the airport. You lean way into the back of the car to heave your bag out. "Oh no," you think this time. "This thing has got to weigh at least 25 kilograms." In reality, your bag weighs the same at the airport as it did at home, but your guestimate is not reliable.

You get to the ticket counter for the moment of truth. "Please put your bag on the scale," says the ticket agent. The digits on the display scramble and then settle in on the reading—24 kilograms. "D'oh!" You take your bag off the scale, pull a jacket and a book out, and heave it back on the scale. The digits on the scale scramble again as you wait for the new reading . . . 22 kilograms. "Woohoo!" No one argues with the scale. We assume it is reliable. If you place the same bag with the same contents on the scale multiple times it should give the same reading. That's reliability. If you get a different reading on a second measure, you assume that the weight of the suitcase actually changed, not that something is wrong with the scale. Again, the assumption is that the scale is reliable.

One of the goals of the Canadian Tobacco, Alcohol and Drugs Survey (CTADS), a biennial general population survey of tobacco, alcohol, and drug use among Canadians aged 15 years and older, is to track changes in drug and alcohol use. The formal research methods employed are designed for reliability so that if the results show a change in drug or alcohol use among a certain population, researchers can be confident that the change in results is due more to actual changes in the population than to errors in the survey as a measurement tool. Smaller (and less expensive) research designs can be reliable too if they are designed well.

Validity refers to the accuracy of a measurement or observation in reflecting what the researcher intends to measure or observe. After the agent checks your bag at the ticket counter, it rides on a conveyor belt and disappears into another part of the airport, likely to

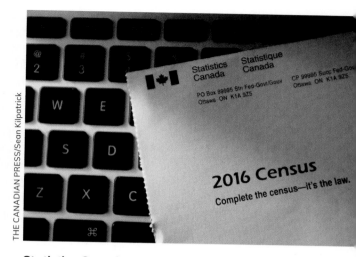

THE CANADIAN PRESS/Sean Kilpatrick

Statistics Canada spends millions of dollars each year on primary research projects. The most recent census, which was conducted in 2016, cost an estimated $715 million.

Why is this research so expensive?

reliability Consistency and precision of a particular research technique.

validity Accuracy of a particular research technique in measuring or observing what the researcher intends to measure or observe.

go through an X-ray machine or pass by bomb-sniffing dogs. The scale at the ticket counter may offer a reliable reading of weight in kilograms, but no validity in representing the contents of the bag. From the weight scale, the agent would have no idea whether the bag contains 22 kilograms of books or 22 kilograms of clothes or 22 kilograms of pineapples.

Validity in public relations research and social science research can be particularly tricky because we often try to measure and observe things that are much harder to define than books, clothes, or pineapples. When the concepts to be measured include intangibles like attitudes towards an organization, involvement with an issue, or behaviour that is not easily observed in public, validity is a big concern. Even in a very reliable survey of alcohol use, for example, we have to wonder about validity. Consider the following findings from the 2015 Canadian Tobacco, Alcohol and Drugs Survey:

- In 2015, 77 per cent of (or 22.7 million) Canadians reported consuming an alcoholic beverage in the past year, a prevalence unchanged from 2013 (76 per cent or 21.9 million).
- There was a higher prevalence of males than females reporting past-year alcohol use (81 per cent or 11.8 million males and 73 per cent or 10.9 million females).
- The rate of alcohol use among young adults aged 20 to 24 (83 per cent) was higher than among youth aged 15 to 19 (59 per cent) and adults aged 25 years and older (78 per cent). The prevalence of alcohol use among age categories (i.e., youth, young adults, and adults 25 years and older) was statistically unchanged compared to 2013.
- Provincial rates of alcohol use in the past year ranged from 73 per cent in Prince Edward Island (or 88,000 Prince Edward Island residents) to 82 per cent in Quebec (or 5.6 million Quebec residents). For all provinces, the prevalence of alcohol use remained unchanged compared to 2013.
- Young adults (aged 20 to 24) had riskier patterns of alcohol consumption compared to youth (aged 15 to 19) and adults older than 25 years. Twenty-eight per cent (or 542,000) of young adult drinkers exceeded the guideline for chronic risk. In comparison, 16 per cent (or 185,000) of youth drinkers and 19 per cent (or 3.6 million) of adult drinkers exceeded this guideline.

After reviewing the research methods, we read this report and are fairly confident in the reliability of the results. We're confident that there are, on a percentage basis, more drinkers in Quebec than Prince Edward Island. But we're a little less confident in how well the data from a self-reported drinking survey conducted by telephone represents the complexity of alcohol use and abuse.

Another example is campus crime safety campaigns. If you organize a campus safety campaign that emphasizes the importance of reporting suspicious activity, how would you feel about an increase in calls to police on your campus? Would you be disappointed because this indicates more suspicious activity? Or would you welcome the news that more suspicious activity was actually reported? Or would you need more information to draw a conclusion? This is a question of validity and requires a deeper understanding of the information available. You may obtain that information from further quantitative data (number of actual convictions or data on property loss) or you may obtain it from qualitative research (in-depth interviews with law enforcement, riding along with police on their beats, etc.).

No single research method, no matter how formal, is perfect. There are always trade-offs. The strengths of a large-scale national survey with tens of thousands of participants can become limitations in understanding deeper social phenomena. Careful observation or

Voices from the Field

Susan Paul

Image courtesy of Susan Paul

Susan Paul is an associate vice-president with Leger Research working out of their Calgary office. A marketing research professional with over 15 years of experience in strategy and research, she began her career in Edmonton in the food and beverage industry, where she led research and development activities for various companies in Canada, USA, Asia, and Europe. Susan has worked extensively on brand strategy research, reputation research, stakeholder engagement, public opinion research, user experience research, usage and attitudes research, and advertising and communications testing. She is also a skilled moderator and has more than 1,000 hours of hands-on facilitation experience.

Susan applies her research insights to help her clients solve their branding, marketing, and business challenges. Her industry experience includes oil and gas, utilities, financial services, education, health services, automotive, retail, consumer packaged goods, public sector, and not-for-profit.

Research is the first step in the RACE process. How important is research to the practice of public relations?
Research in the first step of the process is critical and it drives strategy. It allows for fresh perspectives and inspiration; it can also offer a broader perspective and serve to prevent the PR practitioner from developing ideas from within their personal vantage point. A strong PR practice is a two-way process and includes both listening and receiving communications. Research is the "listening" part of this equation and helps us understand who the receiver is, what they care about, what to say to them, and how to reach them. Without this first step, you are standing on the street corner with a megaphone and people aren't listening.

Public relations research very often entails social science research. In what ways have you seen traditional social science research best applied in public relations?
It's best applied when the research uses two independent samples of stakeholder groups and the results from each group are compared. For example, we look at how

physicians say they treat patients and how patients feel they are treated. This type of work can reveal wide disparity in perspectives, and public relations communications can use this as an opportunity to provide messages to physicians, so they can communicate better with patients in a way that improves the physician–patient relationship.

We hear a lot about new methods for evaluating social media efforts with digital metrics, but in what ways are strategists using digital resources for formative research?
Digital resources have been great at helping define audiences: who they are, where they are online (i.e., which websites, groups, social media, etc.), what they care about, and what they are talking about. It also shows us the specific words and phrases they use to describe their lived experiences, which in turn helps the public relations professional "speak their language."

Are digital media making research cheaper and easier for public relations people?
Yes and no. On a basic level, it is much easier to see how a campaign is shared and distributed online among key stakeholder groups. By this I mean we can easily track metrics such as likes, shares, up votes, clicks, etc. On the other hand, a more meaningful evaluation of a campaign involves measuring outcomes such as changes in attitudes, behavioural changes, and increased market share. These two sets of metrics—"likes" and "bottom line data" are not necessarily correlated, and you still need to do primary research with your stakeholders to get the complete picture.

What specific research skills will help entry-level job candidates in the job market, and how can they acquire these skills?
I can think of two important skills, and they are related to each other. The first is understanding bias in research. Bias can occur at any phase of a research project: sampling, data collection, analysis, interpretation,

Continued

and publication. Bias can be intentional or unintentional, and it's important to be able to identify bias, because it can lead to incorrect conclusions and misleading audiences. The most common form of bias that we see is in the data collection phase—and starts with the way that questions are written. So, the second important skill is learning how to write questions. The key to this is asking yourself what you need to know about your audience, instead of thinking about what you want to be able to say to them. There are many ways to acquire these skills: by learning what types of bias exist, by reading fake news versus real news, by reading research reports and asking yourself where the bias could exist, and by taking a basic course in writing survey questions.

Have you ever been completely surprised by something you discovered through research?
I am always surprised at least a little bit by the research we do. I think surprise is where the insights come through, and it's where we deliver value to our clients. If we aren't surprised at all by our research, we're probably asking the wrong questions.

in-depth interviewing can reveal rich information to help you understand your organization and publics and their deeper motivations, attitudes, and behaviour, but reliability becomes an issue with this type of research because it would be difficult to repeat with consistent results.

A research methods course will help you design and evaluate research for reliability and validity. Even if you end up performing secondary research or hiring others to conduct research, understanding the different types of research and the strengths and limitations of your options is a critical part of planning for strategic public relations and for reporting the results of your work with confidence.

Ethics: Utilitarianism

Research helps us make informed decisions. Public relations practitioners use research not only to inform their own thinking and strategy but also to inform and persuade their organizations and publics. Contributing to the marketplace of ideas in a way that informs citizens in democracies is one of the highest ideals of public relations. One of the most common ways that public relations professionals engage the marketplace of ideas is to present research data.

In democracies, ideas are often judged based on the question of which course of action will do the greatest good for the greatest number of people. In philosophy, this approach to decision-making is called **utilitarianism**. Nineteenth-century English philosopher Jeremy Bentham and one of his students, political economist and philosopher John Stuart Mill, spelled out utilitarianism as an ethic of consequences. That is, they wrote that you can decide on an ethical course of action by determining which actions will have the best consequences. Take into account all the good and bad consequences of competing actions, and determine which action does the most good and the least bad, and then you are ready to act ethically.

Ethics of consequences can be applied in everyday decision-making. In deciding how to handle media interview requests when bad news breaks, which stories to include in newsletters, what photos to pin on Pinterest, and even which employee tweets to retweet, public relations practitioners think through the consequences of their actions in an effort to make the right decisions every day. But when dealing with large-scale issues of public concern,

> No single research method, no matter how formal, is perfect. There are always trade-offs.

utilitarianism Principle that the most ethical course of action is the one that maximizes good and minimizes harm for people.

> Research the consequences of competing actions and determine which action does the most good and the least bad. That's utilitarian ethics.

research is often brought into the mix to help organizations decide on their positions and then advocate appropriately.

Take, for example, the issue of raising minimum wages, which many provincial governments have announced in recent years. It's an interesting and difficult political and economic issue, and we have organizations with paid professionals ready and willing to help us sort out the best course of action.

In Ontario, the minimum wage increased to $14 an hour in 2018; in Alberta, the minimum wage increased to $15 in 2019. In the wake of these announcements, many organizations released reports detailing possible negative impacts. The Bank of Canada, for example, suggested that the increase could cost 60,000 jobs across the country. Their data suggested that even though some people would benefit from raised wages, others—particularly the least skilled and least experienced employees—would suffer because there would be fewer jobs.[20] The thrust of that report, and other reports drafted by banks and other institutions, suggests that *not* raising minimum wages would do the greatest good for the greatest number of people.

Of course, there is another side to this issue. In the wake of the Bank of Canada report, economists began to question the bank's assumptions, and some went so far as to suggest that the minimum wage increase would have a positive impact on the economy and people who make minimum wage.

Writing in *Maclean's* magazine, economist Armine Yalnizyan explained how an increase in the minimum wage would lead to an economic boost:

> When higher income households see wage gains, some of it goes to savings. Additional consumption also often flows to vacations and luxury goods, often imported. In other words, a non-trivial part leaks out of the local economy.

Everett Historical/Shutterstock.com

John Stuart Mill advanced the ethics of utility—making decisions based on expected consequences.

How can research help public relations practitioners practise utilitarianism?

Steve Russell/Toronto Star via Getty Images

Workers in Toronto protest for a higher minimum wage.

In what ways could reasonable people disagree about the consequences of raising minimum wages?

The Coalition for Gun Control use research to argue in favour of gun control in Canada, while opposing organizations, such as The Canadian Shooting Sports Association, use research to argue against gun control.

How does this example illustrate the limitations of utilitarianism in applied research ethics?

When lower-income households see a sustained rise in incomes, they spend virtually all of it. Most goes to food (more nutritious food or eating out), better health care, and more education. Sometimes it also goes to rent (moving to a better neighbourhood). Almost all of this spending stays in the local economy. So boost the minimum wage and you boost the economy from the bottom up.[21]

As the minimum wage case shows, determining the most ethical answers to public-interest questions by trying to maximize positive and minimize negative outcomes can be difficult. Philosophers call it utilitarian calculus, and it has its limits. In the minimum wage case, much of the confusion stems from the fact that the organizations promoting the research have very different political and business agendas.

Perhaps the moral of the story for public relations is to avoid confusing the use of research for advocacy and profit with the process of utilitarian ethics. As public relations scholars Shannon Bowen and Don Stacks point out, a primary weakness of utilitarian ethics is that the person who applies them can use them "to sanction whatever he or she wants to maximize in their *personal* good outcomes, as opposed to maximizing the greatest good for the greatest interest in the public interest."[22]

In 2012, the Institute for Public Relations measurement commission adopted a statement on ethical standards in public relations research and measurement that promotes many core values beyond utilitarianism: "All research should abide by the principles of intellectual honesty, fairness, dignity, disclosure, and respect for all stakeholders involved, namely clients (both external and internal), colleagues, research participants, the public relations profession and the researchers themselves."[23]

In Case You Missed It

The very first thing most of us do when we need an answer to a new question is hit the search button. But research in public relations is about so much more than online searching and re-searching. To develop effective strategy and achieve worthwhile outcomes, we have to ask the right questions and understand the best methods for answering them. Here are some tips to consider as you get started with your programs and campaigns, maybe even before you open Google.

- Evaluation can happen at any point in a strategic program, not just at the end.
- Gaining a deeper understanding of a situation requires digging for information of substance beyond an Internet search.
- Organization–public relationships flourish when you spend as much energy trying to understand your publics as you do trying to get your message out.
- Social media blur the lines between an organization's internal and external communications.
- Some people will support your efforts without a public relations program and others will never get involved, but you can make progress with publics that are somewhere in between.
- Primary research allows you to tailor your research to your own specific purposes.
- Validity is a big concern when trying to measure intangibles like attitudes towards an organization or involvement with an issue.
- No single research method, no matter how formal, is perfect. There are always trade-offs.
- Research the consequences of competing actions and determine which one does the most good and the least bad. That's utilitarian ethics.

Summary

5.1 Explain the role of formative and summative research in the RACE cycle.

Formative research is conducted before and during a campaign or program to develop and fine-tune strategy. Summative research is conducted at the end to answer the question, "Did it work?" However, one campaign or program normally leads to another, so what may be considered summative for one effort may become formative for future strategy. Research and evaluation can be thought of as connected parts of a cycle rather than the beginning and end of a linear process.

5.2 Describe the contents of a situation analysis.

In writing a situation analysis, the planner researches and reports on the strengths and weaknesses of an organization along with the opportunities and threats in the organization's environment (i.e., SWOT analysis) as they relate to the motive for a public relations program or campaign. The narrative analysis leads to a concise problem or opportunity statement that clearly articulates the reason for planning a public relations program or campaign and sets the stage for campaign goals.

5.3 Strategically segment publics.

Publics can be identified and researched on several dimensions. Some categories for segmenting publics are (1) internal and external; (2) latent, aware, and active; and (3) primary, secondary, and tertiary. Demographic and psychographic information can help researchers understand publics.

5.4 Compare the costs and benefits of various research methods.

Researchers must weigh the relative costs and benefits of different research options including primary and secondary research, formal and informal research, and quantitative and qualitative research. Secondary research is generally cheaper and easier than primary research, but primary research yields custom results that are directly applicable to the situation at hand. Informal research is easier than formal research, but formal research is conducted with rules and procedures that allow for more confidence in the results. Quantitative research allows for clear numerical reporting and analysis of large amounts of data. Qualitative research allows for richer description and deeper understanding of the people or content studied.

5.5 Differentiate between reliability and validity.

Reliability refers to the consistency and precision of a research technique: "Does the instrument produce the same or comparable results in repeated trials?" Validity refers to the accuracy of the technique: "Are you measuring what you think you're measuring?"

5.6 Evaluate utilitarianism as an ethical principle for public relations research.

Utilitarianism is a useful ethical principle to the extent that the person applying it makes unbiased and informed decisions based on a clear understanding of the relative harm and benefit of competing courses of action. When researchers work with a biased perspective on the data available, they tend to calculate benefit and harm in ways that support their own opinions or agendas rather than society at large.

Discussion Questions

1. Recall an event or activity that you've planned and conducted in the past year. What kind of research, if any, did you do? How could evaluation of that effort help you next time you do a similar event or activity? What kind of research would you do next time?

2. Think of a public relations campaign idea that would be helpful to a familiar organization. Quickly jot down relevant strengths, weaknesses, opportunities, and threats that come to mind. What kinds of research would you need to do to more formally develop your SWOT analysis for that organization?

3. Name an organization that's facing an issue trending in the news. Who are the organization's internal and external publics? Who are the latent, aware, and active publics for the issue? Who are primary, secondary, and tertiary publics?

4.   Have you ever conducted a survey, focus group, or other type of social research? Aside from cost, what are some advantages and disadvantages of doing research yourself versus paying for research services?

5.   Using an example, explain the difference between reliability and validity. (Bonus if you can use your explanation to show a measure that is reliable but not valid, or valid but not reliable.)

6.   Name a decision that a politician made that you don't agree with. Make a utilitarian argument for why you would make a different decision. What kind of research supports your case (and his or hers)?

Further Readings and Online Resources

Primer for PR Research

Stacks, D.W. (2017). *Primer for public relations research* (3rd ed.). New York: Guilford Press.

This book is considered by many to be the book on public relations research, and is used as a textbook in many university and college PR courses. It is a great source for understanding PR research basics.

Creative Ways to Research Your Target Audience

https://www.prdaily.com/6-creative-ways-to-research-your-target-audience/

This blogpost was published on the "Ragan's PR Daily" site and suggests some interesting ways to do formative research.

How Original Research Can Bolster Your PR Efforts

https://www.prdaily.com/how-original-research-can-bolster-your-pr-efforts/

This article, which is another blogpost from "Ragan's PR Daily," suggests a completely different use for research—using it to generate media coverage for your organization or client.

Jim Grunig: Why He Does Research, His Toughest Audiences, and His Favorite Rock and Roll Music

http://www.themeasurementstandard.com/2016/01/the-measurement-life-interview-with-jim-grunig-why-he-does-research-his-toughest-audiences-and-his-favorite-rock-and-roll-music/

James (Jim) Grunig is one of PR's leading academics and theorists. In this interview with Bill Paarlberg for *The Measurement Standard*, Grunig discusses the importance of starting with research (among other topics).

Peer-Reviewed Academic Journal Article

Watson, T. (2012). The evolution of public relations measurement and evaluation. *Public Relations Review*, 38(3), 390–8. doi:10.1016/j.pubrev.2011.12.018

Today, research is a major part of public relations, but it wasn't always so. This article tracks the evolution of measurement and evaluation over the last 110 years.

Key Terms

A/B testing   125
Active publics   121
Analytics   112
Aware publics   120
Automated copy testing   126
Constraint recognition   122
Content analysis   124
Control group   124
Demographics   121
External publics   118
Formal research   128
Formative research   111
Informal research   128
In house   116
Internal publics   117

Latent publics   120
Level of involvement   121
Mission statement   116
Net neutrality   120
Non-participant observation   127
Organizational culture   117
Participant observation   127
Primary publics   119
Primary research   128
Problem or opportunity statement   112
Problem recognition   120
Psychographics   121
Qualitative research   126

Quantitative research   123
Reliability   129
Secondary publics   119
Secondary research   128
Situation analysis   112
Situational theory of publics   120
Summative research   112
SWOT analysis   113
Tertiary publics   119
Treatment group   124
Utilitarianism   132
Validity   129
Values   116
Vision   116

Planning

Convincing people to wash their hands more is a universal challenge. How do international organizations collaborate to change behaviour and measure success?

Key Learning Outcomes

6.1 Analyze strategic communication outcomes.

6.2 Map public relations strategy from mission to tactics.

6.3 Write SMART objectives.

6.4 Distinguish between outputs, outcomes, and impacts.

6.5 Develop basic timelines to organize tasks in a strategic public relations program.

6.6 Identify key categories of public relations budget items.

6.7 Apply consequentialism to make ethical decisions about setting and achieving public relations objectives while enhancing the profession.

The ALS Ice Bucket Challenge went viral in the summer of 2014 and raised more than $100 million in 30 days.

What makes a campaign like this go viral? What is the role of planning?

planning Forethought about goals and objectives and the strategies and tactics needed to achieve them.

Evaluation

Research

Communication

Action Planning

FIGURE 6.1 In the RACE cycle, planning is preceded by research (including evaluation of past programs and campaigns) and drives implementation.

How does research help planners write better goals and objectives?

Jackpot! When the Ice Bucket Challenge went viral in the summer of 2014, it raised massive awareness for the Amyotrophic Lateral Sclerosis (ALS) Association. Facebook users posted more than 2.4 million related videos, while Instagrammers hashtagged some 37 million videos #ALSicebucketchallenge or #icebucketchallenge.[1] Many criticized the campaign for encouraging people to dump ice water on their heads to avoid making donations, but others were quick to point out that the campaign raised more than $100 million in 30 days.[2] There's no way the ALS group, or any other organization, can predict exactly how a viral campaign of this magnitude will play out. Luck played a role, no doubt, but a quote attributed to Roman philosopher Seneca puts that role in perspective: "Luck is what happens when preparation meets opportunity."

Public relations **planning** is preparation for opportunity (Figure 6.1). Planning is the forethought about goals and objectives and the strategies and tactics for achieving them. Studying outcomes of past campaigns and programs can help us develop goals and objectives for future ones. There are a number of steps that take place between noticing ice buckets being dumped over people's heads in your Instagram feed and writing a cheque to support ALS research. This chapter discusses those steps as well as the key components of plans to achieve them: goals, objectives, timelines, and budgets.

A Hierarchy of Outcomes

There are times when a client or organization knows they need help with public relations but they have a hard time specifying exactly what it is that they want you to do. Your job as the public relations professional is to convert fuzzy thinking into a strategy that will lead to meaningful results for the organization.

One of the most common client requests is "Help us raise awareness." Awareness may be part of the desired results, but more often than not, awareness is only an intermediate step in a larger process to reach some other goal. Awareness of a cause, a new product, or an app is only part of the process in leading people to donate, purchase, or download, and to continued involvement or use beyond that.

Planning for public relations means considering a number of outcomes beyond awareness. Even in the most balanced of organization–public relationships, public relations practitioners need to think strategically about communication. That is, they need to think about the specific outcomes of their actions and communication.

Yale social psychologist William McGuire developed a hierarchy-of-effects model that outlines key steps in public communication campaigns (Figure 6.2): tuning in, attending, liking, comprehending, learning, agreeing, remembering, acting, and proselytizing.

Tuning In

Before communication can have any effect at all, people must be exposed to the messages. Think of all the messages you see and hear every day: advertising, announcements, posters, flyers, email, social media posts, and so on—you get the picture—even the most tuned-in media users are exposed to much more messaging than anyone can possibly pay attention to. While exposure is necessary in communication, it is only the first step in effective communication.

Attending

Attention is the next challenge. Take almost any hallway bulletin board near a university classroom or lecture hall. Watch as people walk by the posted flyers day after day. They are all exposed to the message if they even glance at the bulletin board, but how many of them actually pay attention? Next time you listen to ads on a streaming music service like Spotify (assuming you haven't subscribed to the ad-free version), pay attention to how you pay attention. Do you notice the first ad or two more than the ones that come on after you've been listening a while?

Liking

On Facebook, we can signal our "likes" with a thumbs-up. It's one of many emotions we can express. According to McGuire, "liking" in particular is an important step in message processing because people must maintain interest in a message in order to process it further. In public relations, our messages are often more complex than a Facebook photo, a hallway flyer announcing an event, or a streaming radio ad for tacos. Our publics may not love the idea of donating blood, eating more vegetables, or joining a community discussion on a controversial issue, but if we are going to convince them to participate, our communication has to keep them engaged. If they dislike or are not engaged by a message, they are unlikely to process it in a meaningful way.

Comprehending

Sometimes people like a message, but they just don't get it. In public relations, goals and objectives for communication often depend on publics understanding complex ideas or considering different sides of multidimensional issues. A clever post or credible spokesperson may get lots of "likes," but effective communication requires comprehension.

The Government of Canada's old food rainbow to promote balanced eating suggested an almost unlimited number of carbs, and maybe a nice steak and a milkshake. In hindsight, that's probably not what Health Canada was really trying to communicate.

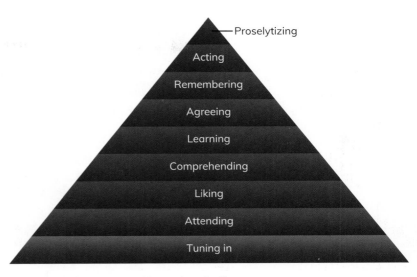

FIGURE 6.2 McGuire's hierarchy of effects.

Why might digital media marketers sometimes refer to this process as a funnel?

Awareness of a cause, new product, or app is only one step in leading people to donate, purchase, or download.

There's evidence of limited success with this hallway flyer because some of the contact tabs have been taken.

When someone takes a contact tab, which steps to persuasion are complete? Which still remain?

Over the years, the Government of Canada has used a variety of images to communicate eating guidelines to Canadians, including a rainbow, a circle design, and a chart. Today's food guide uses a plate to show the elements of a healthy diet.

What makes this design effective?

The round plate design suggests a more balanced approach, whereas the chart is very specific in its direction.

Learning

Helping publics acquire relevant skills is one of the more difficult goals to achieve in public relations. Consider campaigns to get people to save for retirement, properly separate recyclables, or maintain safe privacy settings on social media accounts. Public relations basically becomes an act of teaching. However, instead of the students sitting captive in a classroom, the primary public may be new employees who are overwhelmed in their first week on the job, tired residents taking their trash out, or distracted teenagers uploading to their Instagram accounts. Reaching and teaching each public will require different tactics. New employees may be asked to view an online video about retirement plans at their leisure before registering for benefits. Instructions for recycling might be placed right on the bins. Teens' parents may be recruited to review privacy settings before signing cell phone contracts (although teaching parents may be harder than teaching their kids).

Agreeing

So let's say you've taught your public how to open a retirement account, where to dispose of pizza boxes, or how to revoke access to third-party websites when posting photos on mobile apps. That still doesn't mean they will agree to do so. Attitude change is at the heart of persuasion.

Remembering

McGuire reminded communicators that publics must both store what they've learned in memory and later retrieve that knowledge and attitude at the right time. Even with the best intentions, people often forget to do what it is they learned and agreed to do. When was the last time you actually reviewed your privacy settings on your social media accounts? Would a reminder help? Building reminders into public relations campaigns makes sense.

Acting

A lot of work goes into using communication to change knowledge and attitudes, but the most important results are usually behavioural. Consider this annual flu shot scenario. Each fall, Tom *views*, *reads*, and *hears* messages about flu season and the importance of getting a flu shot. He *pays attention* because he hates getting sick. He wouldn't say he loves the messages, but they do hold his *interest* as he thinks about how vaccines work and the risks and benefits for individuals and communities. He *understands* what getting a flu shot entails, that he is eligible, and that he should get one each fall. He *learns* that all he has to do is walk in to a clinic on a Monday through Friday, sign a form, and roll up his sleeve. He *agrees* it's a good idea. Then he gets an email *reminder* on a Tuesday afternoon when he has no other appointments. But none of this matters to him, his immune system, or the general state of public health in his community if he doesn't actually walk into the clinic and get the shot. *Behaviour* is what matters most.

Proselytizing

Some of the very best campaigns and communication efforts go beyond a two-step communication flow from sender to media and from media to receivers. They go viral like the ALS Ice Bucket Challenge. People not only learn, agree, and act, but they also encourage others to do likewise; this is referred to as **proselytizing**. Proselytizing may be the secret sauce of viral social media, but it also is key to the endurance of historical social movements in religion, education, and politics.

> When campaign goals include helping publics acquire relevant skills or knowledge, public relations basically becomes an act of teaching.

proselytizing When members of publics advocate or promote to others the goals and objectives of a communication strategy. Proselytizing is a key part of campaigns going viral.

Using McGuire's Hierarchy of Effects for Planning

While not every public relations program will address all nine of these outcomes, and the steps do not always happen in the same order, thinking through McGuire's list (McGuire and others have offered other steps besides these) can help your planning in a number of ways. First, the list will help you avoid the mistake of setting goals at one level (e.g., liking) when what you and your client really want is effectiveness at a greater level (e.g., acting).

Second, the list will help you identify specific objectives and tactics and remind you not to forget any key steps. The remembering step may cue you to include reminder emails or build an app feature that notifies publics when it's time to act. When you are evaluating your efforts, the list may help you diagnose what worked and what didn't. Maybe your campaign message was tremendously popular (lots of liking) but led to very low participation. You might then review whether people actually understood your key message (comprehending) and knew how to act (learning).

Third, the list serves as a reminder to be realistic about expected outcomes. Let's say you get your story placed in the *Toronto Star* and it contains your key messages just how you want them. Score! According to a recent survey the *Toronto Star* is read by 1,064,000 people.[3] For simplicity, we might optimistically estimate the following:

- Over one million people are exposed to the message.
- Approximately one-third of those who are exposed pay attention (350,000).
- A fifth of those who pay attention are interested enough to read the story (70,000).
- Most of those who read it understand the key message (53,000).
- A third of those who understand the key message acquire the skills you want them to (18,000).
- Half of those with the skills agree (8,500).
- One in 10 of those who agree remember (850).
- Half of those who remember finally act on the message (425).

impressions A measure of the number of people exposed to a message.

Convincing 425 people to do something is excellent if you're leasing airplanes or seeking large donations to a non-profit, but it may not be as meaningful if you're selling smoothies or trying to get out votes for a federal election. And in either case, 425 is a far cry from the one million **impressions**—the measure of how many people were exposed to a message—that you may be tempted to claim as a metric of success.

Digital media allow for better tracking of steps, as well. For some steps, such as liking and proselytizing, subscribers can gather fairly specific data. Metrics available for online video sites like YouTube allow subscribers to see the number of unique views, the average view duration, the number of people who shared the material or commented on it, and the content of those comments. You may find that almost everyone who started

THE CANADIAN PRESS/Graeme Roy

Dozens of different organizations, including Barrick Gold, Loblaw, RBC, and Aeroplan, were mentioned in *The Globe and Mail* on one particular day.[4]

What kinds of outcomes might these organizations expect?

a video watched it all the way through or that almost no one who clicked on it actually watched it or shared it.

Digital marketers, who are focused on sales as a final outcome, sometimes refer to the process outlined in McGuire's model as a **funnel**. The funnel represents a customer's journey from exposure to purchase (and eventually post-purchase loyalty and sharing/proselytizing). In Google Analytics, the basic process is termed a *conversion funnel*. "With this funnel in place, you can see whether users navigate from one page or screen to the next," as explained on a Google Analytics support page.[5] Any online action that can be tracked electronically then becomes a measurable step in the process. For example, a marketer might track the number of people who find their business's home page from a Google search, then the number of those people who click on a promotion, then those who fill in a form, and then the number of people who make a purchase online. Similar processes can be tracked for organizations with goals of recruiting new members, getting petitions signed, or registering people for online discussion forums.

For now, it's important to think specifically and realistically about the outcomes of strategic communication. Chapter 8 will delve more into measurement at various levels of outcomes.

Strategic Planning

Tactical decision-making refers to daily management and communication without consideration of the strategic objectives, goals, and mission of an organization. **Strategic decision-making**, on the other hand, means that public relations tactics are planned and implemented to help an organization pursue its mission and goals.

A public relations person posting a short, looping video on the microblogging service Tumblr may be doing so as part of a broader strategy. For example, General Electric (GE) curates beautiful photos and video clips of wind turbines on a Tumblr page. Some were taken by drones, while others are part of a five-photographer offshore photo trip. Sure, these seem like cool tactics, but these are really part of a bigger strategy that connects to GE's goal of being a leader in power generation.

If, however, you are working in public relations and you find yourself posting a video just because you think it would be cool to post a video or because it seems like a trend you should be following, your decision-making may be more tactical than strategic. In an article about using Tumblr, Neil Patel of KISSMetrics offers some questions strategic communicators should ask themselves before diving in:

Why do you want to create a Tumblr blog? Just because everyone else is isn't a good answer. Do you want to build awareness to your brand? Another blog? Do you want to create revenue? Do you want

funnel A model for tracking how people move from exposure and awareness to action, particularly in online marketing where the goal is to convert a large number of web page viewers to sales leads or purchases.

tactical decision-making Daily management and communication tactics implemented without consideration of the strategic objectives, goals, and mission of the organization.

strategic decision-making Daily management and communication decisions made with mindfulness of the objectives, goals, and mission of the organization.

Chris New for @generalelectric

General Electric uses images like this on its Tumblr page as part of its broader strategy to be known as a leader in power generation.

What makes this tactic strategic?

1933bkk/Shutterstock.com

Pounds of recycled material may be used to define a campaign goal.

What kinds of public relations tactics and objectives could be used to achieve such a goal?

tactics Specific actions taken and items produced in public relations.

FIGURE 6.3 In strategic public relations, a mission drives goals, goals drive objectives, and objectives drive tactics. Think about what you're doing right now (reading this book).

Are you being strategic or tactical? If strategic, what are your own larger objectives, goals, and mission?

to educate customers? Or improve customer service relations? Your answers will help you create a sustainably successful Tumblr blog.[6]

Tactics are the specific actions you take and items you produce in public relations. Video clips, news releases, websites, flyers, special events, press conferences, infographics, TV ads, email messages, hashtags, and apps are all tactics. Indeed, public relations isn't public relations without tactics. However, absent a broader strategy, it's hard to say what value tactics have for your organization. *Example of a tactic: The development of an app that allows high-school students to record, upload, and post a running total of the amount of material they recycle.*

Objectives are the specific measurable steps that you must achieve to accomplish larger goals. Video views, people in attendance at a special event, coverage in news media of a press event, placement of recycling bins at key locations, a minimum percentage of social media followers who use a particular hashtag, or number of app downloads all could be quantified and measured as evidence of objectives being met. Objectives are valuable to organizations when they help meet broader goals. *Example of an objective: To achieve 1,000 downloads and registrations of the recycling app by high-school students in the Winnipeg School Division by 15 February.*

Goals are desired outcomes that directly help an organization pursue its mission. Dollars donated, percentage of the population registered to vote, products sold, and pounds of waste recycled are all examples of goals that could be set at various levels to contribute in a meaningful way to an organization's mission. *Example of a goal: Winnipeg high-school students will recycle ten tons of plastic by 1 June.*

An organization's **mission** is the overall reason the organization exists. The mission should guide all management and communication. Finding the cure for a disease, sustaining democracy, making money, or preserving the environment may be central to various organizations' missions.

Of course, many tactics go into achieving an objective, multiple objectives are normally required in order to attain a goal, and organizations perpetually work towards goals in pursuit of their missions (Figure 6.3). **Strategy** is the underlying logic that holds a plan together and offers a compelling rationale for why we expect a plan to work. A campaign can have one overarching strategy as well as several smaller strategies that work in conjunction to support various dimensions of success. *Example of a strategy: High schools will compete to see which school logs the most recycled material by the end of the school year, with progress posted online and publicized on social media, and the winner will receive a full day off for an eco-fair and picnic at the end of the school year.*

Global Hand Washing Day: Goals, Objectives, and Outcomes

Did you know that 15 October is Global Hand Washing Day? The Water Supply and Sanitation Collaborative Council (WSSCC) is a global partnership organization based in Geneva, Switzerland, that is affiliated with the United Nations. Partners include NGOs, private companies, and government agencies. In its mission statement, WSSCC lays out its vision "of a world where everybody has sustained water supply, sanitation, and hygiene."[7] From that mission and vision, the organization has adopted a broad strategy to contribute "substantially to global efforts to improve sanitation and hygiene for vulnerable sections of society, with a special focus on communities in Africa and Asia."

UNICEF, a key partner with WSSCC in sponsoring Global Hand Washing Day, has published a toolkit for hand washing campaign planners, which outlines major goals for hand washing campaigns. These goals are derived from the larger missions of WSSCC and UNICEF and provide the strategic rationale for objectives that determine appropriate tactics. Program planners want to see behaviour change. They want more people to wash their hands and to sustain that behaviour. This, in turn, leads to the ultimate goal of public health impact, including reducing diseases such as respiratory infections and diarrhea.[8]

Specifically, the UNICEF toolkit presents the following goal: "Increase, improve and/or sustain good hand washing behaviour and form good hand washing habits."[9] This is a great goal. We should all wash our hands more. And it clearly serves the missions of WSSCC, UNICEF, government health ministries, soap companies, and any other organization affiliated with Global Hand Washing Day. However, campaign planners need more than a well-stated and well-intentioned goal. Success in strategic public relations means being able to demonstrate the results of your work. A goal like this can be achieved by identifying and accomplishing objectives as steps along the way.

SMART Objectives

Well-designed objectives are SMART objectives. SMART stands for **s**pecific, **m**easurable, **a**ttainable, **r**elevant, and **t**ime-bound.

Specific

Well-written objectives state exactly what the strategic communicator plans to accomplish in a way that makes the outcome clear to all who see it. A goal to improve hand washing behaviour is general. It is also debatable. A seven-year-old boy and his father may have very different opinions about what counts as good hand washing, and a trained public health worker might have advice for both. An objective serving the goal of improving hand washing would need to be more specific about what is meant by *improvement*. Does improved hand washing mean people will wash their hands more often? At specific times? Using more soap? Perhaps all three of these are

Continued

objectives Statements that indicate specific outputs or outcomes desired. In strategic public relations, objectives are specific

goals Statements that indicate a desired result for public relations efforts. In strategic planning, goals are more specific than the organization's mission but more general than objectives.

mission Overall reason an organization exists.

strategy Underlying logic that holds a plan together and offers a rationale for why it will work.

important outcomes needed to achieve the larger goal. In that case, each would be the basis for a separate specific objective. Multiple objectives may serve each goal.

Measurable

Can the results be observed and measured in a way that shows actual change? A clear objective sets a standard that will define success. This could be the number of times people report washing their hands in a day, the percentage of people who are observed washing their hands before meals, or the pounds of soap used in a community centre in a month.

Attainable

Although you want to be ambitious in setting objectives, it's important to be realistic. Research and past experience may guide planners in finding that balance between ambitious and attainable. In a hospital staffed by professional health-care workers, it might be realistic to aim for 100 per cent participation in an effort to get doctors and nurses to wash their hands thoroughly before contact with patients, but would it be realistic to try to get 100 per cent of children in a remote village to wash their hands three times a day?

Relevant

Do the objectives relate clearly to the goal and mission? An objective to generate a certain number of re-blogs on a Tumblr site dedicated to hand washing may be specific, measurable, and attainable. But if your goal is to increase hand washing in specific communities in Africa, you would need to be able to explain how that Tumblr blog is relevant where it matters.

Time-Bound

Timing is a critical part of strategy. Setting a deadline for accomplishing an objective adds accountability. It also aids planning, as deadlines for specific objectives become milestones for achieving larger goals in the broader campaign timeline. A goal for a certain percentage of children to wash hands in school in October may be preceded by an objective to guarantee donations of soap to the schools by the start of the school year.

Sample objectives in the UNICEF toolkit include the following. Do you think they are SMART?

- Increase knowledge about the benefits of hand washing with soap among primary school-aged children in 100 primary schools within one year.
- Increase the number of primary school-aged children that wash hands with soap before eating in 100 primary schools within one year.[10]

Outputs, Outcomes, and Impacts

In writing goals and objectives, it is important to think beyond what you plan to do and to think about what you plan to *accomplish*. While it makes sense that a strategic plan outlines **outputs**—tasks completed—a plan without goals and objectives

outputs Tasks or work attempted and completed, including communication tactics produced. Outputs can be completed without necessarily leading to meaningful results (i.e., outcomes).

that specify the results of those efforts will fall short on strategy. Output objectives focus on the tangible efforts of public relations such as the number of tweets posted, news releases sent, events sponsored, or schools visited by experts. As Professor Ronald Smith puts it in his text *Strategic Planning for Public Relations*, "Measure outputs if you wish. They can provide useful assessment of what has been done. But don't stop there."[11]

Beyond outputs, **outcomes** identify the results of public relations work. How many people retweeted your tweet? How many news organizations covered the story in your news release? How many schools reported participating in Global Hand Washing Day as a result of invitations from health experts? How many students were observed washing their hands?

In the big picture of public relations campaigns and programs, planners may want to account for impact. **Impacts** are the broadest and furthest-reaching results of public relations efforts. They also are the hardest results to attribute to the specific efforts of a particular program. You may never know if your recycling program affects global climate change, but you may be able to at least estimate the amount of energy conserved or landfill space saved. These would be impacts beyond the outcomes of the number of people who report recycling, which may follow the output of distributing recycle bins. Here are samples from the UNICEF hand washing program:

- Output: Number of door-to-door visits by hygiene promoters to discuss with caregivers the role of hand washing in nurturing children.
- Outcome: Proportion of primary caregivers who report washing hands with soap and water at two critical times during the day.
- Impact: Reduced prevalence of illness among children younger than five years old living in the household observed.

outcomes Observable results of public relations work.

impacts The broadest and furthest-reaching results of public relations efforts, often stated in terms of societal benefit.

Timelines

In the RACE (**r**esearch, **a**ction planning, **c**ommunication, and **e**valuation) model, research leads to goals and objectives, which lead to strategies and tactics, which are monitored, adapted, and evaluated with further research. The process is cyclical, but it also happens in a logical order, and a timeline for that order puts each step in chronological context. At the most basic level of management, a good timeline determines when to spend resources (such as time and money) on what. Key steps in a public relations plan timeline include formative research, client/management meetings, implementation of management and communication tactics, production of media and communication materials, events, and evaluation.

A good timeline determines when to spend resources (such as time and money) on what.

Formative Research

Once you have a general idea of your goals and how they fit into the organization's larger mission or vision, you'll want to start thinking about two types of formative research. The

benchmarking Process of setting a point for comparison with eventual program results in order to observe change over time. (Benchmarking can also be used to make performance comparisons with other organizations or industry standards.)

first is benchmarking. Benchmarking research defines your starting points for accomplishing goals and objectives. While it's impressive that ALS raised $100.9 million between 29 July and 29 August 2014, what gives that figure real meaning in gauging the success of the Ice Bucket Challenge is the fact that ALS had raised $2.8 million during the same time period the year before. In a hand washing campaign like the one in the UNICEF example, you would want to do research in the early stages of planning to determine the proportion of primary-school-aged children who wash hands with soap prior to eating *before* you start so that you can later determine your program's success in "moving the needle," so to speak. If 75 per cent of children are found to wash hands before eating in the 100 schools under observation, then that would be your benchmark, and 95 per cent or even 100 per cent might be a reasonable goal. If, however, you learn that only 5 per cent of children currently wash hands before eating, then that would be your benchmark, and a goal of 50 per cent (a 10-fold increase) might be more realistic.

In management by objectives (MBO), planners consult with their organizations and clients to determine appropriate objectives for which they will be accountable. For both social and scientific reasons, a 50 per cent success rate in a hand washing campaign may or may not be a desirable outcome. Benchmarks can be used for broad program goals or at the level of any specific objective. Any of the steps in McGuire's model can work as a place to gather benchmark data for later comparison to determine the effectiveness of strategic communication.

McGuire's steps also work in formative *evaluation*. The purpose of formative evaluation is to monitor program efforts to enable corrections based on feedback; it may be used at any time in a campaign and may be built into a timeline as a periodic or ongoing effort. For example, social media analytics allow communicators to monitor real-time feedback in response to any post. Review of annual, weekly, daily, or even hourly reports of social media activity can be built into program timelines. Which Facebook posts are getting the most views (tuning in)? Which tweets are "favourited" the most (liking)? Which Tumblr blog entries are re-blogged (proselytizing)? You can check if certain times of day, sources of information or types of content such as replies to others, humour, personal narrative, or rational argument are working or not working well and adjust your social media strategy accordingly based on that diagnosis. Formative evaluation works for any form of communication strategy and not just social media.

> Social media analytics allow communicators to monitor real-time feedback in response to any post.

Client/Management Meetings

Public relations campaigns and programs are often initiated in a meeting with a client or with management in your own organization. After that initial meeting, public relations planners forecast the timeline for their proposed project. In cases in which an agency is trying to win new business, the agency will then develop a competitive campaign proposal to try to win the business. If you've ever watched *Mad Men* or other portrayals of a client pitch, you can imagine the amount of preparation that goes into the proposal. Winning new business or management approval requires a clear articulation of strategy and mutual agreement about how that strategy will be implemented. Beyond the initial meeting and pitch, plans should include an outline of how often those implementing the campaign will meet with clients or management.

Action and Communication Tactics

Communication should be planned around organizational action. Sometimes the communication must precede action, as when an electric company consults with communities via town hall meetings prior to installing new power lines. Communication also is planned concurrently with action, as when commuters and customers are notified in real time about construction that may interfere with traffic or electric service. Communication also may follow the project to promote the improved service or to explain increases (or decreases) in electric bills that occur as a result. Two-way communication that results in mutually beneficial relationships between organizations and publics happens throughout the process. In your timeline, that communication may be labelled as research in early stages and evaluation in later stages as you gather feedback.

Production of Media and Communication Materials

Print tactics require lead time for copywriting, design, printing, and distribution. Audio, video, and multimedia communications need time for scripting, production, and editing. Interpersonal and social media channels need to be established and relationships need to be developed as part of an ongoing process of relationship building and maintenance. Program timelines should take all of this prep time into account.

Events

Some programs are planned around a single major event such as an election or a grand opening. In planning these programs, the event date becomes the focal point around which all other tasks are scheduled. How far in advance do announcements need to be made? How much time should be allotted to the production and placement of those announcements? Who will live-tweet the event as it happens? How soon after the event will results of the program be evaluated?

Other programs include multiple events. Event types include holiday celebrations, speeches and panels, press conferences, celebrity appearances, carnivals, contests, building dedications, and so on. Events can be geographically dispersed (broadcasts, webcasts, virtual conferences). They can be dictated by tradition or law (homecoming, the Canadian Census). They can even be participant-driven, such as **unconferences**—conferences organized for active peer-to-peer exchange of ideas and information—meet-ups and grassroots rallies. But if events are to be part of a larger public relations plan or program, their place on the calendar must be considered carefully in planning.

unconferences
Meetings or conferences organized by their participants for active peer-to-peer exchange of ideas and information. Unconferences are less structured and more participatory (e.g., fewer one-to-many presentations) than traditional conferences.

SMART objectives make it clear when, what, and how evaluation should be conducted.

Erik Kabik Photography/MediaPunch

Special events, like this grand opening concert for T-Mobile Arena in Las Vegas featuring The Killers, are focal points in public relations calendars and timelines.

How does an event like this support broader public relations goals?

Evaluation

Strategic communicators who write SMART objectives realize they've done themselves a favour when it's time for evaluation. If objectives are specific and measurable what needs to be measured will be clear (e.g., number of primary caregivers who report washing hands or pounds of recyclable material collected). If objectives are attainable, relevant, and time-bound, the right time to measure results also will be readily apparent. Furthermore, if benchmark research is designed well, conducting evaluation research will largely be a matter of repeating earlier research and comparing results.

Planners have several options for timeline formats. Gantt charts are types of bar charts that show project timelines including the start and duration times of tasks. Looking at each task (normally presented in horizontal rows), a planner can consider how long a task will take or how often it needs to be repeated. Looking at any particular time (normally presented in vertical columns), a planner can consider which tasks will occur at the same time and which resources will be needed. Gantt charts can be relatively simple, like the sample presented in Figure 6.4 that was created with standard spreadsheet software. Planners can design more advanced interactive Gantt charts using relatively inexpensive project management software available online.

Other options for timelines are to use a standard calendar or to develop a bulleted list that is organized based on times relative to a focal event. For example, the list may start with what should be done 6–11 months before the event, include monthly and weekly tasks leading up to the event, and end with what needs to be done in the days and weeks after the event has passed (Figure 6.5). Simple checklists of tasks with due dates also are helpful in planning.

Sample Plan

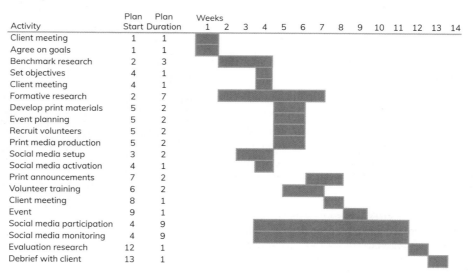

Activity	Plan Start	Plan Duration	Weeks
Client meeting	1	1	
Agree on goals	1	1	
Benchmark research	2	3	
Set objectives	4	1	
Client meeting	4	1	
Formative research	2	7	
Develop print materials	5	2	
Event planning	5	2	
Recruit volunteers	5	2	
Print media production	5	2	
Social media setup	3	2	
Social media activation	4	1	
Print announcements	7	2	
Volunteer training	6	2	
Client meeting	8	1	
Event	9	1	
Social media participation	4	9	
Social media monitoring	4	9	
Evaluation research	12	1	
Debrief with client	13	1	

FIGURE 6.4 Gantt chart for a 14-week plan with primary event in week 9.

What advantage is there to using a Gantt chart as opposed to a checklist?

Example of Basic Fundraising Event Planning Timeline

6–11 months out

- Final decision on chairs/co-chairs
- Develop event committees (fund development/marketing/auction/volunteer)
- Discuss & determine event theme
- 1st meeting w/co-chairs

3–6 months out

- Select event date & book event venue
- Evaluate vendor needs & requests for proposals (REPs) for catering, rentals, A/V, printing
- Develop, print, and compile silent auction/corporate sponsorship solicitation packets
- **Media:** Send calendar listing to society "glossies" (at least 4 months out)

3 months out

- Distribute corporate marketing and program book packet to potential sponsors/advertisers
- Mail underwriter letters to identified targets
- Develop detailed budget for event and review with event stakeholders
- Create payment portal for tickets
- Draft contracts/finalize RFPs for services
- Start collecting email addresses from event stakeholders for "Save the Date"

2–3 months out

- Follow-up on all corporate sponsorship/silent auction/program ad solicitations
- Update web page event information
- **Media:** Define media/publicity strategy (coordination of advertising, PR, and social media)
- Event site visit
- Create Save the Date & email
- Start collecting snail-mail invitation lists from all event stakeholders

6–10 weeks out

- Start recruiting volunteers for the night of duties
- Send invite to printer
- **Media:** Distribute calendar release 8 weeks out and full press release to media targets 6 weeks out

4–6 weeks out

- Finalize event web page info
- Mail formal invitations
- Have silent auction committee develop a silent auction check-out procedure
- Identify banner/signage needs, design & send to printer
- **Media:** Follow up with media targets to secure event coverage/coordinate email/social media invites

2–3 weeks out

- Finalize budget
- Finalize silent auction and program (with ads) and design forms/programs
- Create first draft of run of show (event schedule & script) and review with chairs
- Create list of all vendors to be paid day/week of event
- Review volunteer duties
- Program book, silent auction listings to printer
- **Media:** Encourage all event stakeholders to distribute personal email invitations

Week of event

- Create vendor day-of point person list (with emails & cell phone numbers)
- Create a detailed load in/sound check schedule
- Create sorted guest lists (seating charts/table assignments)
- All printing (programs/silent auction forms/labels) & signage picked up
- **Media:** Send digital reminder to all contacts and those of event stakeholders

Immediate follow-up

- Close-out (All income/expenses collected and logged)
- Confirm all receivables paid

2–6 weeks after (closeout, evaluation, & stewardship)

- Committee and attendee acknowledgments
- Special "thank-you's" to corporate sponsors, underwriters, and silent auction donors
- Thank-you event for volunteers
- Close out receipt of income and payment of expenses and create closing financial report
- Share event results with all event stakeholders

FIGURE 6.5 List of tasks for a one-year plan culminating in an event at the end with follow-up.

What are some of the challenges in trying to do this kind of planning?

Budgets

Achievable goals and objectives depend on the budget, and the budget depends on the resources needed to achieve the goals and objectives. In some cases, the budget is set in advance, and the planner works to develop a program within that budget. In other cases, the planner develops a proposal and then requests or negotiates a budget to carry out the plan. Either way, gaining budget approval and then achieving the goals and objectives within that budget indicate professionalism in public relations. Both processes entail reaching agreement with clients or management on the value of your work and having them invest valuable resources in getting the work done.

Three key resources to consider in any public relations budget are personnel, administrative costs and supplies, and media. These three categories overlap. For example, if you hire an influencer to use Snapchat to promote your product at a music festival, that could be considered either a personnel expense or a media expense. If you buy paper and colour toner to produce posters or flyers, that could be categorized as administrative or as media in the budget. And if you hire translators for an international conference, that could be considered either an administrative expense or a personnel expense. The key is to organize your budget in a way that makes sense to the person or people funding it and to make sure that you carefully think through the categories, so you don't leave out any major expenses.

> *Organize budgets in a way that makes sense to the people funding them.*

Personnel

Even in programs with no budget, people invest time and depend on others to do so as well to achieve public relations goals. Class projects and **pro bono** work for non-profit organizations often are planned and conducted with almost no financial resources, but this doesn't mean that people aren't investing. In such cases, it is important to note the time required. Although the hours worked by volunteers, students, or employees with salaries paid for by other sources may not show up as dollar figures, those hours should be acknowledged in the plan as required resources.

pro bono Public relations work conducted as a public service without fee or payment.

On the other end of the accounting spectrum for personnel costs, agencies often apply very specific billing formulae to account for their employees' time working on client accounts. Our author Tom Kelleher will always remember the first time he saw a billing sheet. "I was working in an unpaid summer internship during weekdays and operating a driving range golf-ball picker on nights and weekends for $6.50 an hour. My supervisor at the internship was just a few years older than me. He asked me to review a project budget, and I just about fell out of my chair when I saw that he was getting $150 an hour for his work. I did the math and figured he must be making more than $300,000 a year. How could this be? Why wasn't he driving a Ferrari?"

billable rate Amount that an agency or firm charges clients per hour of an employee's time.

When agencies bill clients for their work, they often include **billable** hourly rates as a major part of the budget, but the amount billed is considerably larger than the amount the employee gets paid. Public relations author and consultant James Lukaszewski offers the following example.[12] Suppose an account supervisor at a public relations agency earns a salary of $65,000 a year. Assuming the employee is paid for 40 hours a week over the course of 52 weeks, her hourly pay comes out to $31.25. However, the agency also pays for her benefits, including costs such as health insurance and retirement contributions. These fringe benefits can cost the firm up to 30 per cent or more of her base pay. With 30 per cent fringe added, her

PUBLIC RELATIONS BUDGET   HubSpot

Fill in your **projected expenses** here.
(Those "$100" entries are placeholders.)

Fill in your **actual expenses** here.
(Those "$100" entries are placeholders.)

	Jan-17 Budget	Jan-17 Actual	Feb-17 Budget	Feb-17 Actual	Mar-17 Budget	Mar-17 Actual	Q1 Budget	Q1 Actual	Amount Left	Apr-17 Budget	Apr-17 Actual	May-17 Budget	May-17 Actual	June-17 Budget	June-17 Actual
SUBSCRIPTIONS															
Press release service (e.g. PRWeb)	100.00	100.00	100.00	100.00	100.00	100.00	300.00	300.00	0.00						
Research/contact service (e.g. Cision)	100.00	100.00	100.00	100.00	100.00	100.00	300.00	300.00	0.00						
Reputation monitoring software (e.g. Vendasta)	100.00	100.00	100.00	100.00	100.00	100.00	300.00	300.00	0.00						
CONTENT															
Press releases	100.00	100.00	100.00	100.00	100.00	100.00	300.00	300.00	0.00						
Newsletters	100.00	100.00	100.00	100.00	100.00	100.00	300.00	300.00	0.00						
Reports	100.00	100.00	100.00	100.00	100.00	100.00	300.00	300.00	0.00						
Guest posts	100.00	100.00	100.00	100.00	100.00	100.00	300.00	300.00	0.00						
EVENTS / TRADESHOWS															
Admission	100.00	100.00	100.00	100.00	100.00	100.00	300.00	300.00	0.00						
Transportation	100.00	100.00	100.00	100.00	100.00	100.00	300.00	300.00	0.00						
Accommodations	100.00	100.00	100.00	100.00	100.00	100.00	300.00	300.00	0.00						
Meals	100.00	100.00	100.00	100.00	100.00	100.00	300.00	300.00	0.00						
MEDIA RELATIONS / AWARDS															
Dinners	100.00	100.00	100.00	100.00	100.00	100.00	300.00	300.00	0.00						
Gifts	100.00	100.00	100.00	100.00	100.00	100.00	300.00	300.00	0.00						
Award entry fees	100.00	100.00	100.00	100.00	100.00	100.00	300.00	300.00	0.00						
AGENCY															
Retainer fees	100.00	100.00	100.00	100.00	100.00	100.00	300.00	300.00	0.00						
Expenses	100.00	100.00	100.00	100.00	100.00	100.00	300.00	300.00	0.00						
Other	100.00	100.00	100.00	100.00	100.00	100.00	300.00	300.00	0.00						
TOTAL	$1,700.00	$1,700.00	$1,700.00	$1,700.00	$1,700.00	$1,700.00	$5,100.00	$5,100.00	$0.00	$0.00	$0.00	$0.00	$0.00	$0.00	$0.00

Year-to-Date Summary	Budget	Actual	Amount Left
SUBSCRIPTIONS	$900.00	$900.00	$0.00
CONTENT	$1,200.00	$1,200.00	$0.00
EVENTS / TRADESHOWS	$1,200.00	$1,200.00	$0.00
MEDIA RELATIONS / AWARDS	$900.00	$900.00	$0.00
AGENCY	$900.00	$900.00	$0.00
TOTAL	$5,100.00	$5,100.00	$0.00

Your year-to-date totals will automatically populate here.

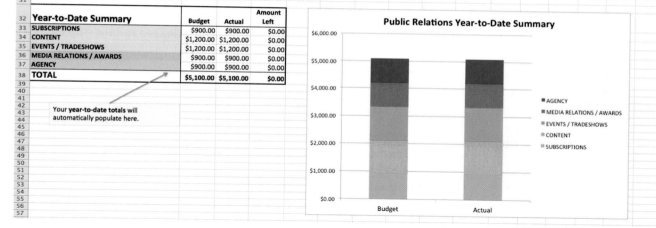

Public Relations Year-to-Date Summary

Legend: AGENCY; MEDIA RELATIONS / AWARDS; EVENTS / TRADESHOWS; CONTENT; SUBSCRIPTIONS

This budget template from HubSpot.com opens as an Excel file and can be customized for any public relations program.

How are the categories of personnel, administrative costs and supplies, and media included in the template?

hourly cost to the agency is $40.63 per hour. Of course, agencies wouldn't make any money if they charged their clients only their actual costs, and they have many other expenses to cover besides those payroll costs, so they bill clients at a rate of three or even four times the cost of paying the account executive. Using a multiple of three, the billable rate for the account supervisor would be $121.89 per hour. Using a multiple of four, the billable rate would be $162.52 per hour, even though she is earning an annual salary of $65,000 and not $338,000. Now it's clear why Tom's internship supervisor was driving a nice Toyota but not splurging on an Italian sports car.

overhead expenses
Costs of running a business that are not directly related to the product or services delivered.

media planning Choosing media channels to achieve strategic communication goals and objectives. Media planning drives advertising purchases.

reach Percentage or number of people exposed to a message at least once via a specific communication channel during a defined period of time.

We can see how important it is to factor in the amount of time people will spend on particular projects when developing budgets. While an agency's HR and accounting departments may handle all the specifics of salaries, fringe, and billing, planners must still provide an estimate of how many people will work on which projects and for how long. Other staff-related costs to consider include hiring freelance writers and editors, photographers, artists, spokespeople, social media influencers, or any type of temporary workers such as event security staff for a concert or drivers to take nurses to remote communities in an international health-care campaign.

Administrative Costs and Supplies

In agencies or established businesses, regular and ongoing administrative costs such as electricity, paper, and Internet services are often considered overhead expenses, meaning public relations planners normally wouldn't need to account for them specifically in developing a campaign strategy or program budget (though clients pay for them indirectly with marked-up prices for services). Beyond those costs, or if you are working independently, you have to think about budgeting for any items that you will need for your campaign that you don't plan on having donated or paying for out of your own personal funds. These costs may include anything from specialty items like coffee mugs or T-shirts, to nametags, pizza and drinks, soap for hand washing, bins for recycling, computers and tablets—you name it. If you are organizing an event as part of a larger program, you may estimate the total cost of the event in your initial program proposal rather than getting too specific with each line item. Other major nonmedia expense categories include travel, facility rentals, speaker fees, and research costs.

Media and Communication Expenses

Advertising and promotion are important costs to consider in most public relations programs. For traditional media, price quotes can be obtained to get an accurate estimate of how much to budget for advertising. As with print media, advertising sales representatives from radio and TV stations can give you quotes for media space (e.g., a 30-second spot during prime time). Someone budgeting for a national branding campaign may have to choose between, say, spending their $100,000 budget on a full-page colour ad in *The Globe and Mail* or two 30-second TV spots during a Stanley Cup playoff game. Of course, many factors go into such decisions, and when the stakes are high, professional media planners are part of the process. Media planning entails considering factors such as strategy and audience demographics to make sure that advertising budgets are spent wisely and in line with SMART objectives. Reach (the percentage or number of people exposed to a message) and frequency (the average number of times people in an audience are exposed to a particular message in a given period) are two of the most important variables. Media planning is a career path in and of itself.

Advertising in digital and interactive media has evolved into new models of buying and selling media. Programmatic media buying, for example, involves automated real-time bidding (RTB) that is pre-programmed by marketers and

OK, who ordered pizza? Even smaller expenses like food and snacks for events add up when you are working independently.

Where might you find pizza in a public relations budget?

automated to buy space when certain criteria are met. In programmatic media sales, publishers use software called supply-side platforms (SSPs), and buyers use demand-side platforms (DSPs). Twitter product developer and executive Ameet Ranadive explains the process with an example:

> Based on its knowledge about this user (e.g., the user recently searched for flights to Hawaii on a travel website), a DSP will bid on the right to serve an ad to this user. The RTB exchange will then run an auction for the ad impression generated by this user. The winning DSP will serve a creative—potentially a dynamic display ad with personalized content, perhaps including the recently browsed flight details, price, and image of the destination—to the user.[13]

Programmatic media buying can be used for everything from basic ads on news websites to promoted tweets to Google search returns to sponsored posts in Facebook. Again, this type of media planning requires specialized expertise, but understanding the basics will help public relations planners work with media planners in buying space in digital and interactive media.

At this point, you may be thinking, what about "free" media? You can write your own newsletter, distribute your own flyers, or set up your own Twitter account, Facebook group, or Tumblr blog for free, right? It's true that these communication tactics don't incur advertising costs, but you will have other costs to consider. An effective social media presence requires time and effort—in other words, personnel costs. If you are including flyers in your budget, you should include the cost of designing and printing.

For professionalism with just about any communication tactic, public relations planners must also consider the costs of production. The American Association of Advertising Agencies stopped tracking the costs of TV ad production in 2012, but in their last report in 2011, they calculated the average cost of production for a 30-second TV commercial at $354,000.[14] Obviously, that figure could be much higher if you involve high-priced celebrities or state-of-the-art special effects. For a basic event flyer, you might design it yourself or buy lunch for a talented friend to design it. Even so, you'll want to check with a local printer on printing prices if you don't have access to a good copy machine with a full supply of paper and toner. For example, to print in full colour, Staples charges $20 for 50 copies and $350 for 1,000 copies. These numbers undoubtedly vary (and the Staples quote probably won't apply anymore by the time you read this), but it goes to show how important it is to think about production costs and to build them into your budget.

frequency The average number of times people in an audience are exposed to a particular message in a defined period of time.

programmatic media buying Automated media buying that is preprogrammed so that advertising purchases are completed when certain criteria set by buyers (marketers) and sellers (media) are met. Programmatic media buying commonly occurs via computer-run, real-time auctions.

A social media presence may be "free" of advertising costs, but it still requires personnel costs.

Gene Blevins/ZUMA Wire/Alamy Live News

Social media command centre war rooms like this one allow for 24/7 monitoring of client mentions and trends.

Setting up social media accounts may be free at first, but what other expenses need to be considered in budgeting for continued operation?

Voices from the Field

Charzie Abendanio

Image courtesy of Charzie Abendanio

Charzie Abendanio is the corporate communications manager at Maple Leaf Sports & Entertainment (MLSE), which owns the Toronto Maple Leafs (NHL), Toronto Raptors (NBA), Toronto FC (MLS), Toronto Argonauts (CFL), Toronto Marlies (AHL), Raptors 905 (NBA G League), TFC II (USL), and Raptors Uprising Gaming Club (NBA 2K League). MLSE also has a charitable arm, MLSE Foundation; owns and operates Scotiabank Arena and two digital channels, Leafs Nation Network and NBA TV Canada; and has a partnership with Live Nation. A relatively recent graduate of Humber College's public relations degree program, Charzie describes herself as a storyteller, and is determined to make her mark in the industry and one day impact public relations in a meaningful way.

What has been your career path thus far?
I'm currently the corporate communications manager at MLSE and have been in this role for about a year. Prior to MLSE I worked alongside PR practitioners at APEX PR, a Toronto-based agency with clients from the corporate, tech, and consumer industries. In 2016, I was a consultant in Alberta with the Regional Municipality of Wood Buffalo in the communications department. This municipality oversaw the evacuation, re-entry, and rebuilding of Fort McMurray, the town that was damaged by the wildfires in May 2016. I've also interned at several other PR agencies in Toronto while in school.

Do entry-level practitioners need to be concerned with strategic planning, or can they get by early in their careers by just being good with tactics?
As an intern or junior practitioner, you are not expected to build a communications plan with objectives and strategies on your own. A great workplace will have colleagues that will mentor you and help develop your strategic thinking skills and also challenge you to exercise this way of thinking. It's also important to be aware of other successful and unsuccessful marketing/PR campaigns to use as inspiration and provide real-life examples when ideating

tactics for new campaigns. Learn everything you can from those colleagues because sooner or later (hopefully sooner!) you'll find yourself in a more senior role where you do need to develop strategy. Strategic planning is at the heart of all successful public relations campaigns.

How important are specific objectives?
Specific objectives are vital. Your clients or, if you're working on the corporate side, your bosses expect to see how your work contributes to the goals of the organization. This can only be demonstrated by setting appropriate measurable objectives. Counting "likes" on a social media post isn't good enough—you have to demonstrate how your work contributed to the bottom line.

If your campaign looked good, received a lot of coverage, or generated discussion, it's important to determine that these results were the original goals by outlining your objectives earlier in the planning stages.

Are there times when it makes more sense just to wing it and go with instinct, or do you always need to have a plan?
There are times where you will need to decide quickly, but usually that is during execution. And depending on the event/campaign, planning will help mitigate those moments where a decision needs to be made quickly without seeking advice from your colleagues or project manager. In the planning process you should be considering the potential situations that may happen and how to respond to them. Arming yourself and your team with that knowledge will ensure you are not in a position where you need to "wing it."

What's the coolest campaign outcome you've achieved in your career thus far?
The Raptors winning the 2019 NBA Championship and being a part of that has been a highlight in my career. My team and I helped organize the media coverage during the parade and rally and after a short summer we started

working on the 25th Anniversary campaign to celebrate a milestone in the team's history, which included the Championship Ring Ceremony at Home Opener on October 22, 2019. Part of that campaign was to build anticipation around the 25th season celebrating the Toronto Raptors, a special art installation at Nuit Blanche, and all the amazing activities happening at the first regular season game. It has been incredible to own a part of how we share the story with our fans, the country, and globally as well.

What advice do you have for new practitioners?
The first couple of years in your career is the best time to make mistakes and learn, and to do that you need a manager that is willing to give you those opportunities. Don't be afraid to take risks and put your hand up to take on projects where you may not have the skills or knowledge to execute but you've built enough trust with your manager who will guide you through that process.

Ethics: Beware of Zombies; Enhance the Profession

When public relations strategy includes a social media platform like Instagram, a common element of SMART objectives relates to the number of followers, likes, or comments the account receives. As you know if you have ever started a social media account, the first batch of friends and followers comes relatively easily.

That first batch of friends and followers may be all you need if you're keeping your account for personal reasons. Your network may grow slowly and organically from there as you discover new friends and others discover you. That's how most of us expect social media to work. So when we see that @beyonce has 117 million followers on Instagram but follows no one, we know a different pattern of influence is in process. The communication is one-way. However, in between small interpersonal accounts and pure mass-communication-by-Instagram, there are many ways that strategic communicators build social media influence into their plans.

One way to harness influence in social media is to work long and hard to build a large and lasting base of friends and followers. Over time, working to provide content that people enjoy and find useful enough to like and share will earn you or your organization followers and clout. Consistent and regular interaction (i.e., two-way communication and relationship-building) with others online is also a big part of what it takes to be successful in building online social networks.

As noted in the budget section, social media aren't really free. Success with social media requires an investment over time in providing valuable content and building relationships. The return on that investment in public relations comes when it's time to get the word out about your recycling drive, to introduce your company's new product, or to remind voters to go to the polls in support of your cause on Election Day. From tuning in to going viral, a large and well-maintained social media network can support each and every one of the steps in McGuire's model of strategic communication.

Now, what if we were to offer you a shortcut? A site called iDigic offers 500 followers for USD $6.95 or 5,000 followers for USD $39.95. Another site, Buzzoid, has similar prices—USD $6.99 for 500 followers or USD $39.99 for 5,000 followers. It is widely acknowledged that these followers are not the same as the real people who would otherwise follow your account out of

It's possible to pay for fake followers on social media accounts.

What are the pitfalls of buying zombie followers?

real interest in you or your organization. What these services offer are "zombie" followers. The companies operate thousands of fake accounts that exist for no other purpose than to follow other accounts. Other packages include automated "like" and commenting functions. One Dutch blogger who paid for a service told how real commenters called out an automated comment that said "Nice pic" when the actual post was a video. It's safe to say that zombie followers are not high on anyone's list of primary publics. This ain't *The Walking Dead.*

Buying followers sounds like an ethical violation, but let's run through Kathy Fitzpatrick's guide for ethical decision-making (see Chapter 1) to see if it really is.

Define the Specific Issue/Conflict

Buying followers may be a quick, inexpensive, legal, and effective way to boost quantitative results (followers, likes, comments, etc.) for social media objectives. However, the followers aren't real people. The benefit of buying followers is one of perception—accounts with more followers *appear* to be more credible, reliable, and popular. But they aren't real people! You aren't building relationships.

Identify Internal/External Factors

Major internal factors include program budget, goals, and objectives. An important strategic question is whether purchased followers will actually contribute to the larger goals of a campaign. External factors include the perceptions of external publics who may be impressed with large numbers but feel deceived and lose trust if they were to learn that the account holder had paid for zombie followers. Could you report to a client with confidence and good faith that thousands of purchased followers would help you achieve a goal to get more people to buy a product, make a donation, or volunteer time?

Identify Key Values

> A big part of what makes social media social is that people are motivated to engage other real people.

Authenticity, transparency, and expertise are key values. A big part of what makes social media social is that people are motivated to engage other real people. Authenticity matters in any social context (not just online media). Touting fake friends or followers is not an authentic approach to self-presentation in any type of communication. Most people keep the practice hush-hush and would feel "busted" if the word were to get out that they had paid for followers. If you were to buy followers as part of a public relations strategy, would you want people to know? Probably not, and wanting to keep something a secret indicates a lack of transparency. Building a base of followers for an organization by creating engaging content and maintaining mutually beneficial relationships requires expertise. That expertise is what employers and clients pay public relations people for. Employers and clients might feel duped if they knew you "earned" your money with cheap shortcuts.

Identify the Parties Involved

Again, one party is the employer or client. The practitioner himself or herself is another. We may not count the zombie followers as a party, but people in real publics who see the social media account and make decisions based on perceptions of that account would be another party. At the broadest level, anyone working in public relations whose reputation may be damaged by unethical practices in this area is also a party.

Select Ethical Principles

In Chapter 1, we applied deontological (duty-based) principles to decide whether ghost tweeting was ethically defensible for a public relations practitioner. In Chapter 5, we applied the principle of utilitarianism to evaluate how public relations research is presented. Utilitarianism focuses on the results of one's actions. For this case, let's consider consequentialism—a results-based system of ethics that holds that the best ethical decision is the one leading to the best outcomes or impacts.

consequentialism
Results-based system of ethics that holds that the best ethical decision is the one leading to the best outcomes or impacts.

What are the consequences of buying followers? A very narrow view would be that buying followers results in short-term success in meeting objectives. One might even expand this into an ethical argument by saying that buying followers is ethical if it leads to larger, more important consequences. For example, if you bought followers for an NGO account, and those followers led to more real followers, and those real followers donated money, and that money was used to fight the Zika virus spreading in El Salvador, preventing birth defects would be the result. Preventing birth defects would certainly be an end that one could use to justify the means of buying followers. But come on. You could drive a truck through the logic of that strategy. The following consequences are more likely:

1. Nothing happens. You spend part of your budget buying followers and no one even notices.
2. It kind of works. You buy followers and it somehow makes your account look more legit. A few real followers ensue, but they are deceived in the process because they assume you are producing content and communicating in a way that others have found worthwhile.
3. It backfires, and you get called out on it. This happens. Services like Twitter Audit and Socialbakers' fake followers app make it easy to check your own or others' social media accounts for fake followers. Your client may get mocked online for doing this because the lack of authenticity and transparency runs directly counter to the values listed earlier. This hurts your client's reputation and your own credibility as a professional. It also drags down the reputation of public relations as a profession in general.

Make a Decision and Justify It

Although buying followers may offer a quick and inexpensive way to meet short-term social media objectives, there are plenty of ways to justify the decision not to do so. In all likelihood, the consequences will not be positive or productive. Real expertise and professionalism in public relations means being willing and able to put in the time and effort required to build relationships. The Canadian Public Relations Society (CPRS) Code of Professional Standards directs that "a member shall practice the highest standards of honesty, accuracy, integrity and truth, and shall not knowingly disseminate false or misleading information." Buying followers is a clear violation of that principle.

Professionalism in public relations means being willing and able to put in the time and effort required to build relationships.

In Case You Missed It

Public relations professionals are some of the busiest people in business, but mere busyness is a waste of time without planning. These tips from the chapter will help you see day-to-day activities as ways to serve the broader missions of organizations in society.

- Awareness of a cause, new product, or app is only one step in leading people to donate, purchase, or download.
- When campaign goals include helping publics acquire relevant skills, public relations basically becomes an act of teaching.
- Avoid setting goals at one level (e.g., liking) when what you and your client really want is effectiveness at a greater level (e.g., acting).

- A good timeline determines when to spend resources (such as time and money) on what.
- Social media analytics allow communicators to monitor real-time feedback in response to any post.
- SMART objectives make it clear when, what, and how evaluation should be conducted.
- Organize budgets in a way that makes sense to the people funding them.
- A social media presence may be "free" of advertising costs, but it still requires personnel costs.
- A big part of what makes social media social is that people are motivated to engage other real people.
- Professionalism in public relations means being willing and able to put in the time and effort required to build relationships.

ICYMI

Summary

6.1   Analyze strategic communication outcomes.
Planning for public relations means considering a number of levels of outcomes. McGuire developed a hierarchy of effects model that outlines key steps in public communication campaigns: tuning in, attending, liking, comprehending, learning, agreeing, remembering, acting, and proselytizing. Beyond exposure and attention/awareness, strategists must think about steps leading to behaviour change and proselytizing when communication goes viral. Minding these outcomes helps planners set goals, identify appropriate objectives and tactics, and be realistic about expected outcomes.

6.2   Map public relations strategy from mission to tactics.
Strategic decision-making means that daily action and communication tactics can be tied with specific objectives, which help achieve broader goals, which serve an organization's mission. When public relations action and communication are implemented without this context, decision-making is more tactical than strategic.

6.3   Write SMART objectives.
SMART objectives are specific, measurable, attainable, relevant, and time-bound. SMART objectives add accountability and enhance professionalism in public relations practice.

6.4 Distinguish between outputs, outcomes, and impacts.
Outputs describe the tangible efforts of public relations practitioners—what people *do*. Outcomes describe the results of that work—what people *accomplish*. Impacts are the broadest and furthest-reaching results of public relations.

6.5 Develop basic timelines to organize tasks in a strategic public relations program.
As with SMART objectives, which are time-bound, timelines foster accountability in the management of strategic programs and campaigns. Key steps to consider include formative research, client/management meetings, implementation of tactics, production of communication materials, events, and evaluation.

6.6 Identify key categories of public relations budget items.
Three key resources to consider in any public relations budget are personnel, administrative costs and supplies, and media. These three categories overlap.

6.7 Apply consequentialism to make ethical decisions about setting and achieving public relations objectives while enhancing the profession.
Consequentialism entails thinking through the outcomes of one's actions in making ethical decisions. The case of whether to buy followers on Twitter or Instagram raises questions about consequences such as misspent budget or ineffective strategy. More important, ethical decision-making in this case means considering broader consequences such as deception of publics and damaging (rather than enhancing) the profession.

Discussion Questions

1. When was the last time you changed your behaviour as a result of an organization's strategic communication? Which of McGuire's steps did you go through?
2. Search for an organization that (a) has its mission statement posted online, and (b) has conducted a public relations tactic that you think was effective. Describe how the tactic might help achieve an objective, which helps with a goal, which supports the mission. What's the strategy?
3. Name a goal that you have for this year. Write three SMART objectives towards that goal.
4. Draw or chart a timeline that shows how the objectives mentioned in question 3 lead towards the goal over time.
5. When was the last time you saw public relations have a real impact (as impact is defined in this chapter)? What was the organization, and how did it make a difference on a broad level?
6. Suppose you are the leader of a student or community organization that is given a budget of $1,000 to compete with other similar groups to recycle the largest number of plastic bottles in your community. How would you allocate your budget between personnel, administrative costs and supplies, and media?
7. Not all fake followers on social media are bought. Almost every account is susceptible to at least a small percentage of unwanted fake followers (in the same way that we get spam via email). Should public relations people be responsible for removing these fake followers for clients? Why or why not?

Further Readings and Online Resources

Earned Media Uprising: Quantifying PR's Contribution to Business
instituteforpr.org/earned-media-uprising-quantifying-prs-contribution-to-business/
The Institute for Public Relations (IPR) is a non-profit foundation dedicated to research in, on, and for public relations. This essay by Mark Weiner, posted on IPR's website, explores how earned media helps an organization meet its business objectives.

The Difference between Goals & Objectives
rapidbi.com/the-difference-between-goals-objectives/

Struggling to remember the difference between goals and objectives? This blogpost by Mike Morrison makes it crystal clear.

Microsoft Excel Beginners Tutorial
www.youtube.com/watch?v=k1VUZEVuDJ8

What does public relations planning have to do with Microsoft Excel? Plenty, as it turns out. Many agencies and organizations put their plans in Excel and use it for other functions such as managing contact databases. "Proficient in Microsoft Excel" is a great line to add to your PR resume. If you're not proficient, there are many free online tutorials to help you out, like this one.

Peer-Reviewed Academic Journal Article
Spence, J.C., Brawley, L.R., Craig, C.L., Plotnikoff, R.C., Tremblay, M.S., Bauman, A., . . . Clark, M.I. (2009). ParticipACTION: Awareness of the ParticipACTION campaign among Canadian adults—Examining the knowledge gap hypothesis and a hierarchy-of-effects model. *The International Journal of Behavioral Nutrition and Physical Activity*, 6(1), 85–5. doi:10.1186/1479-5868-6-85

McGuire's hierarchy of needs is frequently used in campaigns with a health message. This article explores the hierarchy of needs by examining Canada's long-running ParticipACTION campaign.

Key Terms

Benchmarking   148
Billable rate   152
Consequentialism   159
Frequency   154
Funnel   142
Goals   144
Impacts   147
Impressions   142
Media planning   154

Mission   144
Objectives   144
Outcomes   147
Outputs   146
Overhead expenses   154
Planning   138
Pro bono   152
Programmatic
  media buying   154

Proselytizing   141
Reach   154
Strategic decision-
  making   143
Strategy   144
Tactical decision-making   143
Tactics   144
Unconferences   149

7

Implementation

Before Chipotle had to deal with their food safety crises, they faced some challenges trying to stay green. How did the restaurant chain handle the heat?

Key Learning Outcomes

7.1 Explain how organizational action is the foundation for credible communication.

7.2 Analyze cases of action and communication in the implementation of effective public relations.

7.3 Outline media options on a continuum from controlled to uncontrolled.

7.4 Differentiate among owned, paid, shared, and earned media.

7.5 Describe the relationship between the values of loyalty and diversity.

7.6 Summarize the benefits of implementing diversity initiatives.

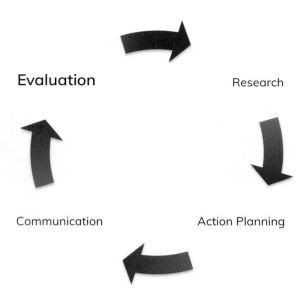

Evaluation

Research

Communication

Action Planning

FIGURE 7.1 In the RACE model, a well-planned, research-based public relations program ends with the evaluation of outcomes.

What kind of outcomes would an organization like Chipotle measure, and how would these compare to those measured by an organization like the Canadian Red Cross?

> Excellence in the field of public relations is based on meaningful action.

diversity Inclusion of different types of people and different types of views.

> Organizations must bring something beyond talk to their relationships with publics.

After research and action planning, it's time to implement programs and manage the communication that goes along with them. The third step in the RACE (research–action planning–communication–evaluation) process is communication, which can include a combination of organizational action and communication (Figure 7.1). As important as communication is in public relations, excellence in the public relations field is based on meaningful action.

We've all heard spokespeople use buzzwords about "maximizing potential," "taking it to the next level," "providing thought leadership," or "giving 110 per cent." But what do those phrases mean, especially if they can't be tied to anything specific that the organization is actually doing? "Actions speak louder than words," the old adage goes. The same logic applies in the implementation of public relations plans. It's one thing to say your organization values **diversity** and inclusion, for example. It's another to manage the organization in a way that proves it.

Taking Action

Recall from Chapter 1 that Arthur Page said principled management of public relations means you have to "prove it with action." The Red Cross doesn't just send thoughts and prayers when disaster strikes. They send aid workers with blankets, water, and first aid.

In Chapter 2, on the history of public relations, we saw how public relations matured when organizations started taking it seriously as a management function based on action. With the counsel of Earl Newsom, Ford Motor Company didn't just talk about the importance of auto safety in the 1950s; it actually funded research on safety and changed its operations and vehicle design in the interest of its publics.

In Chapter 3, on convergence and integration, we explored the link between public relations, marketing, and advertising based on the shared communication function of the three fields. We also learned that promotion is just one of the four Ps, along with product, place, and price. Kwikset enjoyed great publicity for its technological savvy when its Kevo deadbolt (which enables you to unlock doors at home using a Bluetooth-enabled smartphone) was named product of the year. But that publicity resulted only after the company did the heavy lifting of research and development to bring the new product to market.

"What have you done for me lately?" could have been the theme for Chapter 4 on relationships. Relationships with employees, investors, media, and other organizations and publics are all predicated on organizations bringing something beyond talk to the relationship.

Chapters 5 and 6 on research and planning bring us to the doorstep of action. A well-planned, research-based public relations program will be implemented in line with the organization's mission and broad goals. But living up to these ideals and "walking the walk" can be tough, as Chipotle Mexican Grill can attest.

Case Study

Pulled Pork: Chipotle's Challenge to Act on Its Principles

Chipotle Mexican Grill endured one of the toughest restaurant food-safety crises in US history in 2016 when multiple locations across several states were investigated as sources of *E. coli* outbreaks. Chipotle's crisis response is covered in Chapter 12, but one of the main factors in Chipotle's ability to withstand the initial shock of that massive crisis was its organizational history of building and maintaining strong relationships with its publics based on both action and communication.

Chipotle's "Food with Integrity" program outlines the company's commitment to using only quality ingredients and respecting the welfare of farmers, animals, and the environment. They communicate this commitment and move beyond platitudes and into specific policy for managing their operations:

> It means serving the very best sustainably raised food possible with an eye to great taste, great nutrition and great value. It means that we support and sustain family farmers who respect the land and the animals in their care. It means that whenever possible we use meat from animals raised without the use of antibiotics or added hormones.[1]

For pork in particular, Chipotle works with farmers whose pigs are raised outdoors or in pens that meet specific criteria. They buy from farmers who raise pigs on a vegetarian diet without using antibiotics. "It's the way animals were raised before huge factory farms changed the industry. We believe pigs that are cared for in this way enjoy happier, healthier lives and produce the best pork we've ever tasted."[2] And Chipotle didn't just talk the talk. They walked the walk, sourcing 100 per cent of their pork from farmers who abided by their strict guidelines.

Of course, maintaining these standards comes at a cost, but the business model worked for Chipotle—up to a point. The chain surged in growth between 2001 when it began implementing the policy and 2014 when Chipotle shares jumped 37 per cent. In 2015, analysts projected Chipotle's first-quarter profits would grow 49 per cent compared to those of McDonald's, which was facing a 12 per cent decline according to the same analysts.[3] Chipotle was soaring in the markets and in public relations, minding investors, customers, and even pigs, all at the same time.

But that beautiful balance was knocked off-kilter in early 2015 when Chipotle discovered that one of its major pork suppliers was not complying with the humanitarian guidelines. So what did they do? They pulled the pork from about a third of their restaurants. This was a huge management decision for a burrito chain known for its *carnitas*.

In a way, Chipotle was a victim of its own success. Its eco-friendly business model became harder and harder to sustain as the chain grew. While farms that met Chipotle's standards still made up a relatively small percentage of food suppliers,

Continued

Chipotle had grown into one of the nation's largest fast-food chains. "Those two realities could eventually prove untenable, because . . . they simply don't add up,"[4] wrote *Washington Post* blogger Roberto Ferdman. This was the public relations challenge for Chipotle.

Chipotle, however, stuck to its principles. "This is fundamentally an animal welfare decision and it's rooted in our unwillingness to compromise our standards where animal welfare is concerned," Chipotle communications director Chris Arnold told Ferdman. As the case continued, Chipotle management had to make tough decisions to balance their own interests with the interests of their publics. They resorted to rotating their restaurant menus periodically so that no one restaurant would go without carnitas for any extended period of time.

Of course, Chipotle still has its critics. The case even gave rise to the hashtag #carnitasgate, while "pork-ocalypse" trended on Twitter. Some speculated that the whole ordeal was a conspiracy to sell more of its meatless, tofu-filled "sofritas," which were introduced at about the same time.[5]

Any way you slice it, this case illustrates how much management goes into real public relations. Anyone can slap a web page up, post some tweets, or send out news releases claiming that an organization is green and sustainable, but living up to the promise while growing an organization's bottom line entails a lot of hard work (i.e., implementation).

Image courtesy of Joseph Brewster

Yes, we have no carnitas.

How do you think pulling a major menu item affected Chipotle's reputation? How do you think it affected their sales?

Choosing Channels

Two-way communication and relationships are the heart of public relations. Most of what you can expect to do on a day-to-day basis in public relations is indeed communication. In between meetings, phone calls, and presentations, you'll spend your time on email and social media. You'll probably chat like mad—both in person and via instant messaging. Skyping, blogging, tweeting, posting—even old-fashioned reading and writing—are all forms of communication. In managing relationships, you have to make smart choices about when to send a text, when to "reply all" in an email, when to call someone on the phone, when to tweet, when to send a photo, and, perhaps most important, when to turn off all your devices and pay attention to the people in the room with you.

A lot of these decisions are not unique to public relations. Most people working in modern organizations have to make these same decisions as they manage their professional interactions. What makes public relations different is that we also have to manage the communication that we plan and do on behalf of the organizations that we represent. In implementing public relations programs, we are expected to make wise and informed decisions about which channels of communication to use, when, and for what purpose. When communicating to meet specific goals and objectives, we have to carefully analyze the pros and cons of various media for communications between organizations and publics.

How Do You Choose the Right Tactics?

Choosing the best tactic for your public relations program has everything to do with how well you know your audience or stakeholders. What do they do for a living? Are they married or single? Where do they live? How do they consume media? Do they watch cable television or just Netflix? Do they listen to the radio? Do they commute or take public transit? Knowing the answer to all these questions (and more) will help guide your decision-making process.

Selecting the channels for communication is a big responsibility.

What factors are most important to consider before launching social media efforts?

Some decisions are obvious—you wouldn't hold a launch party for a new line of children's toys at a nightclub, for example. But make sure you are making decisions based on research and data, not just your assumptions.

Let's imagine that you are launching a new skincare and make-up line for one of your best clients. This new line is intended for men and women aged 55 and older. You might assume that a social media campaign is not the way to go given the demographics of your target audience, and, a few years ago, you might have been correct. But recent data shows 64 per cent of consumers aged 50–64 are using social media. Provided you choose the right platform (again, research will point you in the right direction), social media could be an important part of your launch campaign.

Public relations tactics must be chosen to suit the audience, not the practitioner. You might have great Instagram skills, but if your target audience doesn't use it, you have to pass.

> Make wise and informed decisions about which channels of communication to use, when, and for what purpose.

Controlled and Uncontrolled Media

Traditionally, public relations practitioners have thought about media in terms of how much control they have (or how much control they give up) when using various channels and tactics for communication. Internal newsletters or television ads would be thought of as controlled media because communicators may write and edit, or create and produce, messages exactly how they want them. They also control where and to whom the messages are sent. If you edit your own newsletter, you choose exactly what stories you want to include, you choose the images and layout, you define the angle on the stories, and you decide whose mailboxes the newsletter lands in. If you are paying for a TV spot, you are buying control of the message. You can make creative and strategic decisions about how the message is produced (or at least you contract the people who do). You also decide where, when, and how often the ad airs. Recall the concepts of reach and frequency from Chapter 6.

Uncontrolled media includes newspapers, TV and radio news, and external websites, as well as blogs and social media that are not produced internally.[6] You can spend days crafting a news release to perfectly align with your organization's goals and objectives, but the second that you attach it to an email to a journalist or blogger and hit "send," you lose control. It's up to the journalist how (and if) to tell the story after that.

Most communication falls somewhere in between entirely controlled or uncontrolled. Real, interactive, and two-way communication doesn't allow one party or another total control. Press conferences and interviews are good examples. Following his election as the leader of the Ontario Progress Conservative Party, Doug Ford faced a number of challenging media scrums and one-on-one media interviews, such as this one with CBC Radio's Robyn Bresnahan in Ottawa:[7]

controlled media
Channels of communication that allow public relations practitioners to write, edit, produce, and distribute messages as they see fit.

uncontrolled media
Channels of communication that are outside of the control of public relations practitioners.

Bresnahan: Are you Ontario's version of Donald Trump?

Ford: No. I guess the media wants to always pump that up, but that's the only person I've heard and I've talked to tens of thousands of people and it's never come up.

Bresnahan: In 2013, *The Globe and Mail* ran an article that stated you sold hashish in Etobicoke in the 1980s and you threatened to sue them at the time. If these allegations are untrue, why haven't you taken legal action against the *Globe* to clear your name?

Ford: Well, you know something, Robyn, it's funny, you want to hash up something (excuse the pun, by the way), bring this up, something in high school that is absolutely false, that I'm going to waste my time going up against the richest man in, one of the richest people in the entire world to wear me down and spend millions of dollars? I'm sorry, you know something, you can dig stuff up, 40 years ago, which is absolutely false, which is absolutely 100 per cent false. . . .

Bresnahan (interrupts Ford): But it has to do with trust, doesn't it? I mean, for instance, you initially denied that your brother Rob used illegal drugs, specifically crack cocaine.

Ford: I was on the understanding that . . . Rob never did drugs in front of me, Robyn. And I appreciate you bringing his name up because Rob was one of the best civic servants there ever was. But I appreciate this. . . .

Bresnahan: But the main point is I understand you think I am attacking you. But the main point is. . . .

Ford: I would never think you're attacking me, Robyn, neither would your listeners.

Bresnahan: But the main point is how can people trust you?

So why would any strategic communicator want to mess with uncontrolled media? Well, for starters, money is a factor. You don't pay for the space for a newspaper story that runs as the result of a news release or an interview with your CEO that airs on national TV. When press events go well, organizations receive a lot of good publicity; this means that they reach publics via mass media that otherwise would be prohibitively expensive. Some also see credibility as a big advantage for uncontrolled media. When your message is vetted by a journalist or editor and told as part of a news story, it may carry more credibility.

Think about the Chipotle story. What's more compelling—a statement directly from Chipotle's communications director or a story in *USA Today*? The actual effectiveness of **third-party credibility** is the subject of academic debate and very much depends on the context.

In most situations, like the Chipotle case, public perceptions of and relationships with organizations are the result of a converged mishmash of communication and experience with those organizations. A news report consists of a mix of the reporter's story and quotes from her sources. Readers will consider that story along with everything else they have heard about the organization. Of course, they also will think about any first-hand experience they have had. In implementing public relations programs, we have to consider what our organizations are doing as it affects publics (action), what we are saying (communication), and what others are saying about us (third-party communication).

Paid, Earned, Shared, and Owned Media

Another way to think about the spectrum of media options is in terms of paid, earned, shared, and owned, also known as the PESO model. Public relations people and their organizations have always had options for all four. But new technologies have changed the way media are owned and paid for. Social media in particular have changed how we share information. And today's public relations professionals seek to earn followers, fans, likes, search engine rankings, and positive reviews, in addition to earning news coverage.

third-party credibility Tendency of people to attribute greater trustworthiness or expertise to a source other than the original sender of a persuasive message.

AP Photo/Alan Diaz

Rafael Nadal pauses during a news conference following his opening-match loss at a tennis tournament.

In what ways are press conferences controlled or uncontrolled as media events?

PESO (or PESO model) refers to the mix of paid, earned, shared, and owned content

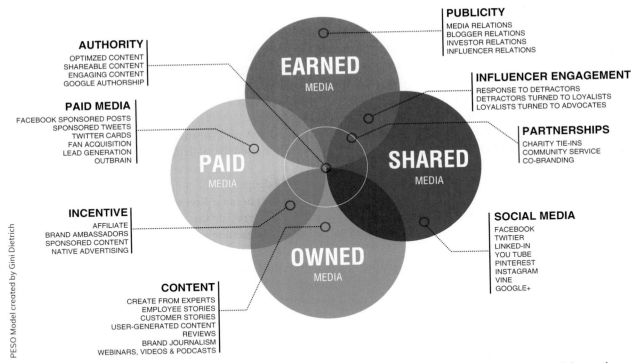

AUTHORITY
OPTIMZED CONTENT
SHAREABLE CONTENT
ENGAGING CONTENT
GOOGLE AUTHORSHIP

PAID MEDIA
FACEBOOK SPONSORED POSTS
SPONSORED TWEETS
TWITTER CARDS
FAN ACQUISITION
LEAD GENERATION
OUTBRAIN

INCENTIVE
AFFILIATE
BRAND AMBASSADORS
SPONSORED CONTENT
NATIVE ADVERTISING

PUBLICITY
MEDIA RELATIONS
BLOGGER RELATIONS
INVESTOR RELATIONS
INFLUENCER RELATIONS

INFLUENCER ENGAGEMENT
RESPONSE TO DETRACTORS
DETRACTORS TURNED TO LOYALISTS
LOYALISTS TURNED TO ADVOCATES

PARTNERSHIPS
CHARITY TIE-INS
COMMUNITY SERVICE
CO-BRANDING

SOCIAL MEDIA
FACEBOOK
TWITTER
LINKED-IN
YOU TUBE
PINTEREST
INSTAGRAM
VINE
GOOGLE+

CONTENT
CREATE FROM EXPERTS
EMPLOYEE STORIES
CUSTOMER STORIES
USER-GENERATED CONTENT
REVIEWS
BRAND JOURNALISM
WEBINARS, VIDEOS & PODCASTS

EARNED MEDIA

PAID MEDIA

SHARED MEDIA

OWNED MEDIA

PESO Model created by Gini Dietrich

In her "Spin Sucks" blog, Gini Dietrich offers the PESO model, which classifies tactics that work in each media category, as well as overlaps between categories.

Can you name an organization (or organizations) using the range of tactics effectively?

Owned Media

brochureware Web pages that present essentially the same material as printed materials such as brochures.

In traditional media, owned channels include newsletters, corporate video, brochures, direct mail, and even voicemail messaging systems. Since organizations own the channels, they more or less control the message and its dissemination, as well as the opportunity for feedback or two-way communication. With the advent of the Internet, owned options expanded to include intranets and web pages. While intranets allow for two-way communication on organization-owned platforms, public-facing web pages allow organizations to communicate externally.

Most early organizational web pages were designed primarily for delivering messages in a one-way fashion. Many websites still fit this description. Think Web 1.0. These websites are sometimes referred to as brochureware because they basically present the same information that can be delivered in traditional media, like brochures. They enable organizations to disseminate information, potentially to worldwide audiences. *Potentially* is a key word here because—let's be realistic—people in Kazakhstan or Kenya probably won't search online for a judo club in Moose Jaw. For websites to reach their potential, they need to be part of a communication strategy that drives people to them. After all, websites don't get delivered to targeted publics in the same way that brochures, newsletters, or in-house videos do. People have to actively search them out and find them.

Organizations can enhance the utility of owned media when they give up some control and allow for feedback and sharing.

Owned media include newer and emerging channels for communication as well. Podcasts, webinars, text messaging systems, blogs, apps, and online video can all be owned. But like web pages in general, their utility to users is often enhanced when organizations give up some control and allow for feedback and sharing. This brings us to a more profound implication of the Internet for public relations—the way it has opened new channels for two-way communication and interaction between organizations and publics.

Contents - Government of Canada's primary site is the Internet electronic access point through which Internet users around the world can obtain information about Canada, its government and its services. Direct links are also provided from this site to government departments and agencies that have Internet facilities.

About Canada | Government Overview | Federal Institutions
Programs | What's New | Search | Comments | Other Governments
Français | Telephone Directory

Paid Media

Advertising is probably the first thing that comes to your mind when you think about paid media, and rightly so. As defined in Chapter 3, advertising is the stuff that fills paid media space. That space could be column inches in a newspaper, page portions of a magazine, seconds on the radio or TV, or pixels on a computer monitor or a giant high-definition LED display at a sports arena. Product and brand advertising are designed primarily to help sell products and services. **Corporate advertising** or institutional advertising is designed more to promote the organization as a whole.

Paid media also include banner ads, Google AdWords, targeted email distribution, or pay-per-click services. LinkedIn, for example, sells ads that will appear on profile pages, in users' inboxes, on search results pages, and in LinkedIn group pages. You can target your ads based on job titles, geography, age, gender, or company size. Then you set up your account to **pay per click**—whereby the sponsor of an ad pays each time an ad is clicked—starting at $2 per click and going up to whatever maximum you set in a bid.[8]

Native advertising, another paid option, is ads that match the format of the primary content of the medium or channel. A sponsored column or **advertorial** in a newspaper or magazine, a promoted tweet, a sponsored Facebook post, or an in-feed ad—they're all paid media. And they can get expensive. When Snapchat first offered companies the opportunity to buy one day's worth of ads to appear in users' "recent updates" feeds, they reportedly charged $750,000 US. Apparently, it was worth it to big brands like Samsung, McDonald's, and Universal Pictures, which used the new paid service to promote the film *Dumb and Dumber To*.[9]

Whenever you see the words "Sponsored content" or "You may also like" on a web page or in an app, you're very likely looking at native advertising. A word of caution: this type of communication risks being deceptive. Stealth advertising that is designed and placed to trick people into thinking they are seeing third-party news, reviews, or editorial content is a bad idea if your goal is to build and sustain trust between your organization and its publics.

Low resolution and a distinct lack of visual appeal are the best descriptions for the federal government's first website back in 1996.

How different is today's website? What improvements have they made?

corporate advertising
Paid media designed to promote an organization as a whole rather than sell a particular service, product, or product category (also sometimes called institutional advertising).

pay per click Model of media sales in which advertisers, marketers, or sponsors pay an online publisher or website owner for each time the sponsored message or advertisement is clicked.

Paul McKinnon/Shutterstock.com

Bus wraps get attention.

Is this owned, paid, shared, or earned media?

native advertising Paid advertising that is presented in the form of the media content that surrounds it. Advertorials are a type of native advertising, as are promoted tweets, sponsored posts, and so on. Native advertising should be labelled as "advertising," "paid content," "sponsored," etc.

advertorial Paid advertising that is presented in the form of editorial content.

Shared Media

Years ago, our author Tom Kelleher was fortunate enough to take a public relations management course from the late Jack Felton, who was the recipient of just about every major award in American public relations. Mark Weiner, CEO of PRIME Research, remembered Felton as "a bridge to the 'Mad Men' era of public relations" who taught people how public relations "focused on personal relationships, great ideas and service to others."[10]

One of the most important lessons Tom learned from Felton was the value of sharing media. Felton taught that when you see an article or story that you think a client or colleague would find interesting, you should clip it, attach a quick note, and share it. At the time, he was talking about actually using scissors to clip articles from newspapers and magazines, handwriting a note, physically attaching the note with a real paper clip, and sending it with a stamp and envelope or dropping it into a co-worker's mailbox. It was good advice then, and it is good advice now. But the big difference is that you can do all this in seconds on your phone or computer with a simple click on a "share" button and a few strokes of the keyboard. Social media have made it much easier.

This ease of sharing also has big implications for organizations when they are the source or subject of stories and links being shared online. Think about your own social media use. How often do you "share" your own original content, and how often do you share stories, memes, photos, videos, and other content from organizations that may consider you a member of one of their publics? Organizations invest a lot of resources in developing content that they hope will be shared. When broad sharing is a goal, the biggest successes are the posts that go viral.

Hey @Pharrell, can we have our hat back? #GRAMMYs.

When social media director Josh Martin famously tweeted these eight words and one hashtag on behalf of Arby's during the 2014 Grammys, he instantly achieved the stuff of social media legend. Sometimes success in going viral is as much luck and timing as it is pre-planned strategy. His tweet—one of the most viral ever—took "just a few seconds" to compose and post, but by the Monday morning following the Grammys, his post had been retweeted more than 70,000 times.

The tweet was a joke referring to singer–songwriter Pharrell Williams's oversized brown hat that had an uncanny resemblance to the Arby's logo. Martin posted it just as millions were watching the Grammys on TV and wondering what was up with the hat. Of those millions, a big percentage apparently also was on Twitter. "It took longer to find Pharrell's handle and make sure I spelled his name correctly" than it did to actually write and post the tweet,

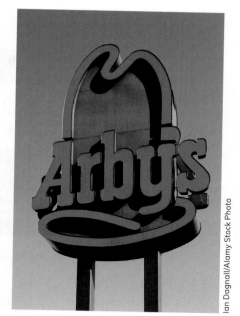

WENN Rights Ltd/Alamy Stock Photo

Ian Dagnall/Alamy Stock Photo

Arby's social media director Josh Martin scored big when his tweet about Pharrell Williams's hat at the Grammys was shared and re-shared among tens of thousands of Twitter users.
Do you think planning or luck played a bigger role?

Martin later told *Adweek*. "It came to me organically."[11] While this was no accident—Martin was on duty that night doing "social listening" and monitoring the Grammys chatter for Arby's—no one could have predicted the success. It could be said that Arby's and Martin worked to create their own luck that night.

In fact, successful efforts to share (and be shared) are often very carefully planned and implemented. GoPro's YouTube strategy is a good example. GoPro is a company that makes HD, waterproof video recording devices. With more than 7.7 million subscribers as of this writing, a big part of the company's strategy is the way it facilitates sharing among its subscribers. "Subscribers provide velocity," writes *Econsultancy* blogger Christopher Ratcliff. "YouTube loves velocity," he continues. "They'll watch it, they'll share it and your video will end up in more places."[12]

To be sure, it doesn't hurt that the nature of GoPro's product line lends itself perfectly to a social media site that is built on the concept of amazing videos. But GoPro leverages the medium particularly well by providing a forum for users to determine which videos are the best by viewing, liking, sharing, commenting, and discussing. Most of the sharing is between and among the organization's publics, and GoPro representatives are careful and strategic about how they get involved. For instance, they may select and post a user video of the day, offer a few comments on popular videos, or occasionally answer product-related questions in the discussion section of their YouTube channels. However, the biggest act of sharing may be the way GoPro shares its platform by letting users provide some of the content and dominate the discussions.

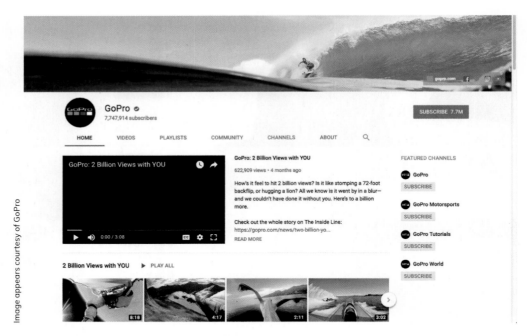

Image appears courtesy of GoPro

GoPro's YouTube channels have millions of subscribers.

Why is GoPro so successful in leveraging shared media?

Just as you give up control of a story as soon as you send a news release, you give up control of information when you share it with your publics on social media.

In communication strategy, sharing can refer to either the sharing of content such as a tweet or a video, or the sharing of a forum or channel, such as a discussion page or YouTube channel. Either way, sharing means ceding some control.

It's just as easy to find examples of organizations that have gone viral for regrettable reasons when the shared communication about them spun out of control. If you need a study break, just Google "public relations hashtag fail" for some comic relief. You'll find all kinds of examples, like when Qantas Airlines introduced #QantasLuxury asking fliers to tweet about their "dream luxury in-flight experience." The problem was that Qantas launched the effort one day after failed labour negotiations led to its fleet being grounded. Predictably, sarcastic and snarky customers had a field day on Twitter: "BREAKING NEWS: Qantas introduce #QantasLuxury class. Same as standard class, but the plane leaves the ground," tweeted a user with the handle @PuppyOnThe Radio.[13] As described in a Reuter's story, the "ill-timed public relations campaign" left the Australian airline "red faced."[14]

In the same way that public relations practitioners give up control of a news story as soon as they send a news release to journalists, they also give up control when they share information with publics on social media. Quick-witted comments and thrilling videos may generate shares and open conversations, but some of the most meaningful public relations outcomes still depend on earning the respect of influential media gatekeepers.

Earned Media

Just as advertising may be the first thing that people think of when they think of *paid* media, publicity may be the first thing that comes to mind for public relations practitioners when they think of *earned* media. *Publicity* is defined as "information from an outside source that is used by the media because it has news value" and "an uncontrolled method of placing messages because the source does not pay the media for placement."[15] In other words, publicity isn't bought. Publicity is earned.

A classic example is a newspaper story that is written and published as the result of a news release. If an organization has done something newsworthy, its public relations person will have a higher probability of success getting the story reported in the paper than if the news release is mostly spin and deemed by editors to have little news value. As discussed in Chapter 4 on relationships, effective public relations people understand how journalists think. They understand news value. They know when their organizations have done something that merits media coverage. When public relations people work in a management role, they help organizations perform in the public interest, and they also help organizations tell that story by garnering media coverage. They help organizations *earn* media attention.

Of course, the concept of media attention today is much broader than making news in newspapers, magazines, television, and radio. In addition to traditional editors and producers, today's **media gatekeepers** are social media influencers, everyday media consumers, and even computer algorithms. Having a picture of your product pinned on a top Pinterest board, trending on Reddit ("the front page of the Internet"), getting retweeted by a celebrity, or showing up at the top of organic search results on Google are all forms of earned media.

Wikipedians define *search engine optimization* (SEO) as "the process of affecting the visibility of a website or a web page in a search engine's 'natural' or unpaid ('organic') search results."[16] While you can buy placement at the top of search results with programs like Google AdWords, effective SEO requires earning that placement by offering useful information, designing your site well, and building relationships with other sites that may link to yours. On the last point, Google rewards earned links more than self-placed ones. Google treats a link from an external page as a "vote" by that page for the page to which it links. In Google's algorithms, "votes cast by pages that are themselves 'important' weigh more heavily and help to make other pages 'important.'"[17] In the same way that news operations draw a line between paid advertising and editorial content (sometimes referred to in publishing lingo as the separation of "church and state"), search engines take care to separate paid and unpaid results to protect the relevance of their search results and the credibility of their service.

> **media gatekeepers**
> People or processes that filter information by deciding which content is published, broadcasted, posted, shared, or forwarded.

> *Today's media gatekeepers include social media influencers, everyday media consumers, and even computer algorithms.*

Mixed Media

In the universe of owned, paid, shared, and earned media, communications functions and effects mix and overlap considerably. Content from an owned channel like a company blog, Pinterest board, or Twitter timeline can easily be shared with a re-post, re-pin, or retweet. Paid advertising, including native advertising and paid search results, can complement earned coverage in those same channels.

"Canada's cannabis law makes headlines worldwide." This CTV News story posted online originated with a Government of Canada news release.

Who are the gatekeepers determining whether the news makes its way from source (Government of Canada) to receiver (CTV website users)? How did the Canadian government earn the coverage?

The Magic Mix: Dell's Integration of Owned, Paid, Shared, and Earned Media

When owned, paid, shared, and earned media converge just right, it's "pure magic," according to *Mashable* contributor and public relations technology strategist Rebekah Iliff.[18] Iliff points to Dell Inc.'s annual release of the Global Technology Adoption Index (GTAI) during its Dell World event as a prime example.

Dell hosts the Dell World convention in Texas each year for industry partners, tech media, and thousands of customers. Think about the range of publics and types of public relations that are involved in such an endeavour: media relations, employee relations, investor relations, B2B relations, and consumer relations, to name a few.

To leverage attention and communication opportunities beyond the event itself, Dell conducts an annual study of major tech adoption trends in the areas of security, big data, cloud computing, and mobility. This type of information has value to a range of Dell's publics. But rather than parsing out its communication efforts into separate tactics, Dell integrates its communication across the whole owned–paid–shared–earned spectrum.

In a sense, Dell both *owns* and *shares* the conference and its online presence, and it uses both types of tactics to promote the GTAI. Founder and CEO Michael Dell announces the GTAI at the Dell World event press conference, which is of course a push for *earned* media, and Dell *pays* for advertising space, as well. Dell's senior vice-president of global marketing Monique Bonner explains the strategy as one of integration in which the GTAI study is converted into "a variety of digital assets . . . all of which point back to specific Dell digital properties."[19] These include the following:

- an owned website
- share-friendly social media platforms including Dell's LinkedIn page, Facebook account, and Twitter feed (#DellGTAI)
- promoted posts on LinkedIn and Twitter paid for by Dell
- shareable infographics, presentation decks, and online video that can also be used in earned media placements
- pitches for earned placement in international and business media and tech sites
- paid native advertising in *The New York Times*

Iliff summarized the "magic" like this: "Technology enables a company to draw in the customer; then directs them to an ecosystem of content, allowing them to learn, explore, interact, and ultimately make a buying decision."[20] The ecosystem is not just composed of content, however; the ecosystem is also made up of relationships and interaction between and among the organization and its many interrelated publics.

Continued

Matthew Busch/Bloomberg via Getty Images

Dell promotes its annual Dell World event with hashtags like #DellWorld and #DellGTAI.

How does this case illustrate the interplay of owned, paid, shared, and earned media?

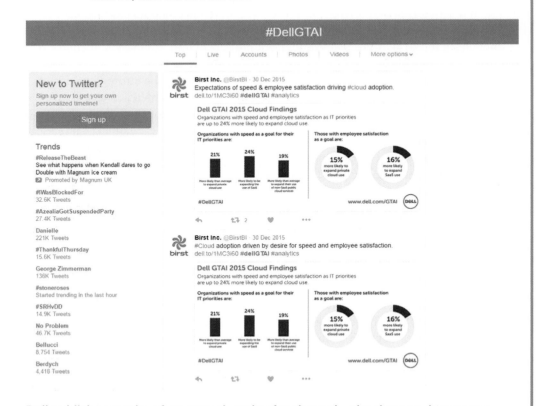

Dell publishes results of an annual study of major tech adoption trends across a variety of channels.

Which of Dell's publics would find this information valuable?

Ethics: Loyalty and Diversity in Communication and Action

Just as communication without action produces meaningless spin, diversity initiatives without loyalty amount to window dressing or a "misguided attempt to gain political correctness points,"[21] as media critic Eric Deggans puts it. A key step in the process of ethical decision-making is identifying the diverse parties who will be affected by a decision and defining the organization's loyalty to each.

The Canadian Public Relations Society's (CPRS's) official definition of *public relations* embeds the notion of diversity, but it refers specifically to diverse publics rather than diversity within the profession:

> Public relations is the strategic management of relationships between an organization and its diverse publics, through the use of communication, to achieve mutual understanding, realize organizational goals, and serve the public interest. (Flynn, Gregory, & Valin, 2008)

Canada is widely recognized as one of the most ethnically diverse countries in the world, but little research has been done to examine diversity within the field of public relations in this country. What work has been done tends to focus on traditional gender (male/female) diversity and has not explored issues related to ethnic diversity.

The CPRS's counterpart in the United States, the Public Relations Society of America (PSRA), has made diversity a key area of focus moving forward.

In response to a 2011 *PRWeek* editorial titled "Agencies Must Find Answers for a Lack of Diversity,"[22] PRSA Chair and CEO Rosanna Fiske wrote that PRSA had "made increasing diversity in the profession a core tenet of our mission." Fiske noted that PRSA, along with the Arthur W. Page Society and the Council of PR Firms, among others, had identified diversity as a priority to "engender not only greater diversity within our ranks, but higher value for our services."[23] So what does diversity have to do with loyalty, and what does this ethical question have to do with implementation?

In their book *Doing Ethics in Media*, ethicists Jay Black and Chris Roberts write that we expand our empathy as we grow personally and professionally. At earlier stages of moral development, we tend to be loyal to ourselves and to those who have power over us such as parents, teachers, and bosses. But as we mature in life and in our professional careers, we expand our worldview and our empathy with "people who are not like us—people different in race, ethnicity, physical ability, religion, sexual orientation, age, economic class, etc."[24] In public relations—a field defined as the management of relationships with all sorts of publics—empathy and loyalty go hand in hand with diversity. The more diverse decision-makers within an organization, the more effective the organization will be in relating to its various publics. Diversity initiatives that are implemented as part of an organization's mission and loyalty to both internal and external publics are more than window dressing. They are the implementation of good strategy.

When Prime Minister Justin Trudeau formed his first cabinet in 2015, he created the first gender-balanced cabinet in Canada's history. However, that cabinet included only five visible minorities and two Indigenous peoples—an improvement over the previous government's cabinet that included one Indigenous person and three visible minorities, but still not truly reflective of Canada's ethnic diversity.[25]

loyalty A sense of obligation or support for someone or something, including both organizations and publics.

The more diverse the decision-makers within an organization, the more effective the organization will be in relating to various publics.

Voices from the Field

Jefferson Darrell

Image courtesy of Jefferson Darrell

Jefferson Darrell is an accomplished marketing communications professional with more than 15 years of brand strategy expertise, generating earned and owned media using both traditional and digital channels. He is highly effective in stakeholder relations, negotiating, and conceiving and cultivating mutually beneficial partnerships. Having worked on numerous integrated marketing campaigns on both the agency and client side, Jefferson brings a broad understanding of the entire marketing mix to every project.

In the diversity and inclusion space, Jefferson has been instrumental in educating and lobbying for diversity and inclusion in the marketing communications industry under his consultancy Breakfast Culture. He has delivered numerous talks and sat on panels about the importance of diversity and inclusion. He has been an active participant in diversity and inclusion conferences including the Institute of Communications Agencies' (ICA's) IDEA Summit (Inclusivity, Diversity and Equity in Advertising), P World's Global PR Summit, the Advertising Club of Toronto, the Canadian Public Relations Society, the Canadian Association of Science Centres, and Canada's first-ever White Privilege Conference at Ryerson University. He believes Peter Drucker's famous quote: "Culture eats strategy for breakfast," and challenges today's marketers to "break some eggs!"

Canada is one of the most ethnically diverse countries in the world—do you see that diversity reflected in public relations practitioners?
Agreed. Canada is a very ethnically diverse country. Anecdotally, one does see lots of diversity in terms of people studying and employed in the public relations (PR) industry at the junior and intermediate levels. Currently, that diversity clearly stops at the senior management levels. Many agencies have homogenous management teams that are primarily Caucasian and, in many cases, primarily male in a female-dominated industry. Again, this is anecdotally from observation when one looks at the senior management teams on PR agency websites. Many of my colleagues of colour and I discuss our experiences and which Canadian PR agencies are not friendly for people of colour.

For a true measurement of how diverse the public relations industry is at all levels we need to incorporate data collection. I have been lobbying both the Toronto chapter of the International Association of Business Communicators (IABC) and the CPRS to incorporate diversity and inclusion metrics with their annual membership surveys to have data to learn just how diverse the public relations industry really is in Canada. My challenge to Canadian PR agencies: does your workforce, at all levels, represent the demographics of Canada and the markets where you operate?

Why do you think public relations doesn't reflect the diversity of Canada's population?
As a society we like to believe that Canada is a meritocracy, but we are not. Systemic discrimination plays a tremendous role in who gets hired, retained, and promoted. There are systemic issues, company and human bias and prejudices that prevent people from excelling during the hiring, promotion, and retention process. Companies often mask their bias and prejudices under the guise of "cultural fit." Look around the boardroom tables and see who "fits" and who doesn't. In diversity and inclusion theory we call this "insider–outsider dynamics." Again, data collection that not only looks at demographics but also questions the barriers faced by employees who may be different from the "insider group" will help to shed some light on this issue.

How do you make the business case for diversity in public relations?
There are numerous ways. Just about every management consultant organization has published a paper about the business case for diversity. In Rick Miner's 2014

report, "The Great Canadian Skills Mismatch," examining population growth from Canadian census data, by 2031 Canada will have an overall worker shortage of 1.9 million people. The ICA diversity study reports that "the Canadian population is undergoing a profound transformation" with visible minorities more than doubling from 11.6 per cent in 1996 to 22.7 per cent in 2006 and this will continue in a "steep and upward trend."

When we look at recent marketing and public relations gaffes from major brands, consumers are reacting with negative sentiments and/or closing their wallets. Many of these gaffes could easily have been avoided had there been more diversity at the decision-making table. These gaffes have affected stock prices. The market has even seen stock prices rise when companies "do the right thing" in the name of diversity and inclusion. I call this "woke marketing."

As an industry, do you think we're making progress on the diversity front?

For me that is a loaded question. As a person who is senior in his career and has hit a glass ceiling, the progress cannot happen fast enough. One thing I have learned on my own diversity and inclusion journey is that this will take time. Canada is years behind the United States on the diversity and inclusion front. Many of the top PR firms in the US have senior managers and C-suite level executives who focus on diversity and inclusion in their firms. Many of these successful organizations incorporate accountability for diversity and inclusion in their KPIs (Key Performance Indicators) that are tied to executive bonuses and compensation, and many of them are reaping the financial rewards of diversity and inclusion in their firms.

The fact that the Canadian PR industry is beginning to have the diversity, equity, and inclusion discussion is a major step in the right direction. However, we must move beyond what promises to be difficult discussions and transactional "fixes" (e.g., multicultural lunches) to actual action with companies making transformative changes (e.g., policies and procedures) to initiating programs to hire, retain, and promote historically underrepresented candidates.

How important is it for young practitioners to find mentors within the industry?

It is extremely important. For me, I didn't see people who look like me in senior roles in the PR industry. Sadly, I still don't see many similar faces in Canada. This is one of the reasons I go out of my way to mentor young practitioners.

In public relations we often talk about the importance of truth and authenticity. How does diversity fit in with those concepts?

Diversity fits in completely with this concept. If a person can bring their authentic self to work they will be more productive. For example, all of the energy that goes into "staying in the closet" if one is LGBTQ+, or "code-switching" if one is racialized, or constantly fighting to be heard and taken seriously if one is a woman, is energy that could and should be put towards business goals. If an employee is permitted to live their authentic self at work and be an individual yet also belong to a unique group, just imagine the possibilities. Let's break some eggs!

However, there is a debate about whether a cabinet that truly reflects Canada's ethnic diversity is necessary or achievable. "A cabinet that includes no one of Italian or Chinese origin, a cabinet without Arabs, a cabinet without a single black person—while Sikhs (who comprise about 1.4 per cent of the Canadian population) hold four cabinet posts—is not a true portrait of Canada. Not that I mind," wrote *The Globe and Mail* columnist Lysiane Gagnon. "The last thing a modern government needs is a cabinet that would reflect the exact ethnic makeup of the population. That's because it's impossible to achieve: Ministers are chosen from a caucus that results from the vagaries of politics and doesn't correspond to demographic reality."[26]

Case Study

Doing Good by Doing Well: Kimberly-Clark's Efforts to Promote Diversity

When Kimberly-Clark Corp. named Sue Dodsworth to the role of vice-president and chief diversity officer, they communicated all the right things. "Diversity and inclusion is critical to the success of our business," [27] said Chairman and CEO Thomas J. Falk in the news release. With global brands like Huggies, Kotex, Kleenex, Scott, and Pull-Ups, it didn't take advanced analytics to understand that many of Kimberly-Clark's most important publics are women. Data available at the time showed that 85 per cent of the company's customers were female.[28] While naming Dodsworth to this post sent a message, Kimberly-Clark needed more for any lasting effect. "We must build a more diverse and inclusive global organization that looks, thinks, and behaves like the people that use our products," said Falk. Dodsworth had her work cut out for her.

Research and planning came first. In sharp contrast to the demographics of its customers, only 17 per cent of Kimberly-Clark's upper-level (director-level or higher) employees were women. In closer analysis of HR data, Dodsworth found two **glass-ceiling** points in women's careers at Kimberly-Clark. Many women were "stuck" in the position they attained right after their first promotion, and others were stuck just below the director level.[29]

A company like Kimberly-Clark often promotes managers from areas like manufacturing or millwork that traditionally may not include many women. Dodsworth and her team analyzed hiring and promotion data and interviewed employees. They learned that women were deterred by leadership job descriptions that mentioned

glass ceiling Metaphor used to describe a present but unseen barrier to promotion for women and minorities.

Kristoffer Tripplaar/Alamy Stock Photo

Kimberly-Clark claimed, "We're changing more than just diapers around here."

How did the company's efforts to promote diversity also promote the company's business interests?

years of experience in these areas as desirable qualifications. As Dodsworth explained in a *Fortune* article, "When we asked why, it was, 'Because of these 10 things that I need for the role, I've only got eight.' Whereas when I talked to the men who applied, they had five and they were going for it."

Dodsworth and her team then developed and implemented a strategy that focused on career development. Dodsworth asked hiring managers writing job postings to focus more on skills that could be transferred to new positions than on accumulated years of past experience. Other actions included global networking forums, mentoring programs, hiring policies that were more amenable to work–life balance, and the implementation of specific business plans for recruiting and developing more women leaders. As reported in a news release announcing that Kimberly-Clark had won a 2014 Catalyst Award, the results were impressive:

- The number of women who held director-level or higher leadership positions globally increased by 71 per cent.
- The number of women with racially or ethnically diverse backgrounds in "director-plus" positions at Kimberly-Clark in the United States doubled.
- Internal promotions of women to "director-plus" jobs increased from 19 per cent to 44 per cent.

Catalyst is a non-profit organization dedicated to advancing business leadership opportunities for women. The Catalyst Award "annually honours innovative organizational approaches with proven, measurable results that address the recruitment, development, and advancement of all women, including diverse women."[30]

While some may see the award and the publicity it earned as "great PR," that recognition is less important to the success of the organization than the role of public relations as part of the way the organization is managed. As Dodsworth reported in the *Forbes* article, "This started as an initiative, but now it's the way we work."

In Case You Missed It

Communication in public relations will ring hollow without action to back it up. Here are some key points from the chapter to help you hit the right notes in implementing a successful public relations plan.

- Excellence in the field of public relations is based on meaningful action.
- Organizations must bring something beyond talk to their relationships with publics.
- Make wise and informed decisions about which channels of communication to use, when, and for what purpose.

- Organizations can enhance the utility of owned media when they give up some control and allow for feedback and sharing.
- Just as you give up control of a story as soon as you send a news release, you give up control of information when you share it with your publics on social media.
- Today's media gatekeepers include social media influencers, everyday media consumers, and even computer algorithms.
- The more diverse the decision-makers within an organization, the more effective the organization will be in relating to various publics.

Summary

7.1   Explain how organizational action is the foundation for credible communication.
You have to walk the walk if you are going to talk the talk, and actions speak louder than words. Both of these common sayings speak to the idea that the implementation of solid public relations programs requires the management of organizational action. Communication that is not based on meaningful action is spin.

7.2   Analyze cases of action and communication in the implementation of effective public relations.
Chipotle's pork issue illustrates how an organization implemented public relations with both action and communication.

7.3   Outline media options on a continuum from controlled to uncontrolled.
Media like brochures, newsletters, intranets, and advertising fall on the controlled end of the spectrum because the public relations practitioner can, to some extent, control the production and distribution of content. Social media and publicity are considered uncontrolled because public relations practitioners cede control to social media users, news editors, and producers. The most uncontrolled media often provide better options for two-way communication, credibility, and influence.

7.4   Differentiate among paid, earned, shared, and owned media.
Paid options include advertising and other media services that require payment for placement and distribution of information. Earned media include traditional publicity as well as coverage by third parties online (i.e., influencers). Shared options are more common in social media, where users share by re-posting, retweeting, tagging, linking, and so on. Owned media include organizational web pages, newsletters, intranets, and other controlled media that organization employees own and operate. These channels often overlap, and integrated strategies may use all of the media types for implementing common goals.

7.5   Describe the relationship between the values of loyalty and diversity.
At more advanced stages of professional and moral development, we expand our empathy to people who are different from us, thereby expanding our loyalty to more diverse groups.

7.6   Summarize the benefits of implementing diversity initiatives.
Understanding an organization's obligations to and relationships with diverse publics informs ethical decision-making and management of an organization. The more that diversity of public relations staff and internal publics reflects the diversity of an organization's external publics, the better suited the organization will be for building and maintaining mutually beneficial relationships, as illustrated in the Kimberly-Clark case.

Discussion Questions

1.   Name an organization that you believe lives up to high standards. What does the organization do to earn your respect, and how does the organization communicate about those actions?

2.   Name an organization that you feel relies on spin for promotion. Give an example of why you think the organization doesn't back its communication with action.

3.   Provide an example of a case when an organization benefitted from something going viral, and compare that to a case in which viral communication harmed an organization. To what degree did the organizations have control of the channels in each case?

4. Pick a (non-news) organization that is often featured in both your social media feeds and in traditional media. Review its online communication to identify examples of owned, paid, shared, and earned media.

5. We often think of race and gender as types of diversity. What other kinds of diversity can benefit organizations in public relations, and how?

Further Readings and Online Resources

What the PESO Model Got Wrong
www.axiapr.com/blog/what-the-peso-model-got-wrong
The PESO model (paid, earned, shared, and owned) that appears in this chapter has been widely adopted by public relations practitioners. This blog post by Noell Ochieng questions one element of this model as it applies to PR.

Why Are There So Few Men in PR?
www.ragan.com/why-are-there-so-few-men-in-pr/
In North America, public relations is a female-dominated industry. This post by Arik Hanson examines this trend by exploring why fewer men than women pursue careers in PR.

What It's Like to Be Black in PR
www.prweek.com/article/1456118/its-black-pr
This mini-documentary, produced by PR Week, asks professionals what it's like to be black in PR. Watch it, and/or read some of the articles and commentary the film inspired.

Peer-Reviewed Academic Journal Article
Tindall, N.T.J., & Waters, R.D. (2012). Coming out to tell our stories: Using queer theory to understand the career experiences of gay men in public relations. *Journal of Public Relations Research*, 24(5), 451–75. doi:10.1080/1062726X.2012.723279
When we think of diversity, we usually think about ethnic diversity first. This article explores another aspect of diversity: sexual orientation and the experiences of gay men in public relations.

Key Terms

Advertorial   171

Brochureware   170

Controlled media   168

Corporate advertising   171

Diversity   164

Glass ceiling   182

Loyalty   179

Media gatekeepers   175

Native advertising   171

Pay per click   171

PESO (or PESO model)   169

Third-party credibility   169

Uncontrolled media   168

Evaluation

What counts in public relations measurement?
The Barcelona Principles (2.0!) will get you up to speed.

Key learning outcomes

8.1 Explain how evaluation research can be used in public relations program development and message testing.

8.2 Describe how media monitoring services have evolved in the digital age.

8.3 Discuss how digital technology has expanded our ability to track and analyze data in evaluating public relations programs.

8.4 Evaluate public relations research practices using industry standards for research (i.e., Barcelona Principles).

8.5 Identify tools for measuring online and traditional public relations outcomes.

8.6 Analyze the relationship between independence as a core value of public relations and the ethical conduct of research, measurement, and evaluation.

▲ Courtesy of AMEC

Evaluation is the process by which we determine the value of our work. When we invest time, energy, and budgets in both short- and long-term projects, we use evaluation to understand our return on investment. We also use evaluation to demonstrate to employers and clients the value they receive when they invest in us and our programs. From determining whether it's worth it to update an Instagram feed daily to pitching a million-dollar campaign proposal, evaluation is how we know—and show—the value of our work.

Knowing what to evaluate is something you decide back in the planning stage. If you set measurable objectives, the evaluation stage is where you determine if you met, missed, or exceeded those objectives.

The *E* (evaluation) may come last in the four-step RACE formula (Figure 8.1), but, as we've discussed throughout the book, evaluation and research go together, and both are used continuously throughout strategic public relations programs. In the introduction to Chapter 5, we described research as a cyclical process. Evaluation of prior programs can be useful right at the very beginning of a new campaign or program. In Chapter 6 on planning, we discussed the concepts of formative research and benchmarking. In planning goals and objectives, it's important to understand the current state of your organization, situation, and publics so that you can measure your progress against that baseline or starting point. Then, in Chapter 7, we looked at how the media landscape for implementing public relations programs has changed. Digital and social media have not only expanded our options for communication; they have also expanded our ability to track and analyze activity across owned, paid, shared, and earned media. In this chapter, we examine what we count as successful communication and our metrics for understanding that success.

FIGURE 8.1 In the RACE model, evaluation demonstrates the value of what was planned and communicated, but it also helps current and future planning and communication.

How can evaluation of one program or campaign serve as formative research for the next?

Old and New Methods

All of the major research methods described in Chapter 5—surveys, experiments, content analysis, interviews, focus groups, and direct observation—are just as useful now as they have been through the history of social science. The purposes for these methods haven't changed much. For example, surveys are still conducted to gather data that describe demographics and what people think, feel, and do. In addition, as a method for evaluation, the data from surveys conducted before a campaign can be used as a baseline for comparison to data collected during and after a campaign to assess changes in cognition, attitudes, and behaviour.

Of course, online survey tools make it much easier to collect and analyze data than it was in the days when most surveys were conducted using paper and pencil. However, online surveys still serve much the same purpose as paper surveys. In fact, for some research with some populations, you may receive a higher response rate and a more representative sample of participants with a survey sent by snail mail or handed to respondents in person. Nielsen still mails pen-and-paper surveys to collect data on household TV-viewing behaviour.

However, there has been significant innovation in research methods. Also, Nielsen and other media tracking firms have developed **digital watermarking** technology that enables

digital watermarking
Information embedded into digital audio and video signals that can be used to track when and where the content is delivered.

audio and video to be tracked with digital information woven into the signals that carry programming content. This helps copyright owners protect their information, and it also helps companies like Nielsen track which signals reach your TV and mobile devices. This digital research technology has the advantage of providing more accurate accounting for what content is delivered, but, unlike paper surveys and diaries, the watermarking technology can't tell researchers whether you are actually paying attention.

In a laboratory setting, communication researchers might use eye-tracking software, or even functional magnetic resonance imaging (fMRI), to observe how people pay attention to and respond to messages. Virtual reality headsets are becoming more commonly available to everyday gamers and consumers. And with new technology for communication comes new ways to measure and evaluate the experiences. Every virtual movement can be recorded and analyzed.

Whether you use traditional or new research technology, and whether you evaluate traditional or new public relations efforts, your research decisions should be driven by the specific purpose of your evaluation. Three major areas for evaluation research are message testing, media monitoring, and measurement of outcomes (i.e., metrics and analytics).

eye tracking Process of measuring eye movements to determine where people are focusing; often used in website testing.

functional magnetic resonance imaging (fMRI) Tests that use magnetic fields to generate images of brain activity, including responses to communication and media stimuli.

Message Testing

As a way to evaluate your tactics for communication, message testing can range from informal to formal and from qualitative to quantitative. Ever type a tweet and then quickly show it to a friend before posting? That's message testing: you are doing a tiny bit of evaluation research to see how others will receive your message before you send it. Other examples of ways to test messages with more rigour include focus groups, readability tests, and experiments.

Focus Groups

Focus groups have been a popular method of message testing in advertising, entertainment, and public relations for decades. Focus groups can be formal. Trained moderators may lead discussions with small groups of carefully recruited participants who must respond to campaign concepts. Organizers of a health campaign may run focus groups to see what types of messages and appeals resonate most with high school students. A start-up tech company getting ready to launch a new app may invite early adopters to focus groups to discuss the design of the app's icon or various display pages.

Readability Tests

Every time an editor or reviewer reads through copy and offers feedback, they are helping with message testing. This feedback is normally qualitative in the form of editorial suggestions and comments, either

Michael Short/Bloomberg via Getty Images

Attendees at a Facebook developer's conference try virtual-reality glasses.

How might virtual reality be evaluated as a public relations tactic?

written or oral. But message testing also can be quantitative. For example, if you paste the text from the previous paragraph into a readability tester window on the site www .readability-score.com, the software will tell you that the paragraph has five sentences, 94 words, 156 syllables, and 484 characters, with an average of 1.7 syllables per word and 18.8 words per sentence. The software calculates that this all adds up to an average readability score, or a grade level of 11.2. So, if you've graduated high school, we should be OK. However, this little bit of message testing reminds me to try to keep my sentences short.

Courtesy of Kristi Camera and Kelly Logan

Even informal message testing can be useful as formative evaluation in public relations.

What kind of message testing have you conducted?

Media Monitoring Services

Monitoring media is another area of evaluation that has sped up considerably in the digital age. In the days before Google (and Google alerts), interns and other entry-level employees used to get paper cuts and calluses from paging through stacks of newspapers and magazines every morning looking for mentions of a client's name or product. After finding a story, they would review it to see how relevant it was and whether it was primarily positive, negative, or neutral (a very basic form of content analysis). Then they would use scissors, a glue stick, and a copy machine to create pages for the clip book. The clip book was a three-ring binder that included all the print media coverage they had found and categorized.

Evaluating TV coverage was another issue. In some offices, VCRs would be programmed to tape-record the morning and evening news programs whenever the public relations person expected coverage of his or her organization. Another option was to contact TV stations directly to request copies of the coverage. The cassettes or transcripts would be saved for later analysis, reporting, and presentation.

But that was for do-it-yourselfers. Bigger agencies and organizations with larger budgets subscribed to **clipping services**. Clipping services monitored print and electronic media for mentions of clients in local, national, or international media. Their menu of services included monitoring coverage in different types of media, capturing related content, and conducting content analysis of news and editorial mentions. They would also calculate numbers like total number of impressions. In fact, they still do. Fortunately, media monitoring services have evolved with digital media and are among the most useful tools in digital public relations because of the way they support public relations professionals in the collection, analysis, and reporting of media data for evaluation.

Aside from the obvious advantage of automating the process of scanning, "clipping," compiling, and sorting media coverage, media monitoring services have also expanded the range of evaluation available. While legacy clipping services of the twentieth century included opinion pieces and editorials, the content was limited to what was published or

A/B testing, as discussed in Chapter 5, can be used to quickly compare the effects of different digital content and messages.

clipping services Businesses that monitor print and electronic media for mentions of clients in local, national, or international outlets; see also media monitoring services.

media monitoring services Vendors that assist public relations practitioners in the collection, analysis, and reporting of media data for evaluation; see also clipping services.

ferlistockphoto/iStock

Before digital tracking was easily accessible, the clip book—a binder of press clippings—was a common way to show off the results of publicity efforts.

How has computer technology changed the nature of media monitoring?

Media monitoring services help you analyze social media content that is actively produced, discussed, and shared by publics online.

broadcasted, not how people responded to the content. Old clipping services measured earned media and not shared media. They offered little evidence of what publics were thinking, feeling, or doing as a result of the coverage. Today's media monitoring services still measure publicity, but they also monitor online conversations and facilitate the sharing of information.

- Cision's social software "searches millions of posts and mines the data that will help you monitor the performance of key brand attributes and engagement, target emerging brand value and market drivers, and make informed business decisions easily and efficiently."[1]
- Meltwater's software allows users to track a story in all channels and "stay on top of 30 billion articles, 30 million blogs, and a continuous stream of Facebook, Twitter, and YouTube posts—from 205 countries in 87 languages."[2]
- LexisNexis Newsdesk allows you to "search an unmatched, global-content collection—from a single dashboard—improving your ability to monitor the buzz on companies, brands and competitors around the world."[3]
- MRP (media rating points) is a popular method for reporting on traditional earned media campaigns in Canada. Developed by the CPRS Measurement Committee, MRP is designed to measure, evaluate and report the results of media relations campaigns including print, broadcast and online. The system analyzes coverage by tone and other criteria, and calculates reach using up-to-date data.[4]

As defined in Chapter 5 on research, content analysis is the systematic analysis of any type of recorded communication. Media monitoring services enable large-scale content analysis of both traditional and social media. Social media content that is actively produced, discussed, and shared by publics online can now also be monitored and analyzed, giving public relations people access to a new dimension of mediated content. That said, many of the most important goals and objectives of public relations programs—affecting what people think, feel, and do—cannot be measured with only content analysis.

Metrics, Analytics, and Data

Metrics and analytics are essentially synonyms for measurement and evaluation. It's not unusual for people to append the words *real time*, as in *real-time analytics*, to emphasize the immediacy of digital measurement. Large media organizations with high-traffic websites can run countless A/B tests in any given day to optimize their content. These simple experiments are just the tip of the analytics iceberg. Planners and editors who have a good handle on computer programming and statistics can develop **algorithms** to test various combinations of factors (e.g., message selection, message placement, image selection, headline styles, colour) leading to various outcomes (e.g., click-through rates, time spent on page, sharing behaviour). This type of algorithm-building is what made BuzzFeed founder Jonah Paretti so successful in building that "viral-content machine" into one of the most powerful information sources on the Internet.[5] It's what makes a site like Mashable competitive with *The New York Times* online.

While *The New York Times* employs an army of more than a thousand journalists, editors, designers, and coders, Mashable gets its tens of millions of site visitors and social media

algorithm A formula or set of steps for solving a problem. A computer algorithm can be the series of steps used in automated message testing and placement.

followers with a team of about 60 reporters, according to Jim Roberts. Roberts had worked as an editor at *The New York Times* before joining Mashable as its executive editor and chief content officer. Mashable's front page is primarily algorithm-driven. A computer program decides which stories to promote and demote on the page based on real-time analysis of which stories get the most views, shares, and clicks at different times of day. "Data," he says, "is our friend—in fact it is our lifeblood at Mashable."[6]

While the term big data means many things to many different people, this is one example of what people are talking about when they use the term. *Forbes* contributing writer Lisa Arthur defines *big data* as "a collection of data from traditional and digital sources inside and outside your company that represents a source for ongoing discovery and analysis."[7] You can collect this information directly from your organization's or client's publics through cookies or registrations. This is known as first-party data because you collect the information yourself—the "first party" is you. You can also buy third-party data from vendors who collect and aggregate data from other sources and then sell you more data about your publics than you may even know what to do with. That's something to consider very carefully. There are so much data available that people don't really know what to do with it all.

Running a series of message-testing experiments that may have taken weeks or months to set up a few years ago can now happen almost instantly, in real time, so to speak. The problem with running 45 A/B tests in one day is that anyone doing that probably hasn't put much thought into exactly what they're testing and why. Testing messages with data from experiments is just one type of *analytics*. As defined in Chapter 5, the term refers to any analysis used to describe, predict, and improve how organizations communicate with publics online. According to researcher Seth Duncan, two common applications of analytics are particularly useful in public relations: tracking visitor behaviour and segmenting referring sources.[8]

Tracking Visitor Behaviour

The first important use of web analytics in public relations is tracking the behaviour of website visitors. When someone visits your web page, searches for a word or phrase, or clicks on an ad or other link, all that information can be recorded and analyzed. The data available from this process include number of unique visitors to a page, number of visits, number of page views, how long a user stays on a site, and bounce rate, which is the percentage of visitors who go to your site but then leave the site instead of continuing towards other goals you may have established. Specific goals that can be tracked include downloads, registrations, completed forms, electronic petition signatures, donations, or purchases.

Once you have identified your measurable goals, you can calculate a conversion rate, which is the number of goals reached divided by the number of unique visitors to your site. Let's say you are trying to

big data Large amounts of data from traditional and digital sources that can be used for ongoing discovery and analysis of media content and human behaviour.

cookie A text file stored on a user's computer that is used to track and remember the user's activity online.

first-party data Data on user or consumer behaviour that is collected by an organization from the people who use the organization's websites or online services.

Cyberstock/Alamy Stock Photo

What's new," "what's rising," and "what's hot" on Mashable's home page are largely determined by algorithms.

What kinds of data do you think feed the computer's decisions? How would this type of data be useful to marketers and public relations planners?

third-party data Data on user behaviour that is collected or aggregated by one organization and sold to another organization.

bounce rate In online strategy, the percentage of visitors who visit a site but then leave the site instead of continuing towards other goals as defined by the strategist.

conversion rate In online strategy, the number of goals reached divided by the number of unique visitors to a site.

get people to sign an online petition to make a statement to your local lawmakers. The goal is to have people sign the online petition. You track 1,000 unique visitors to your website. The data show that 700 visitors to your site leave right after seeing the first page, but 150 of them actually click through to the petition and "sign" it. Your bounce rate is 70 per cent and your conversion rate is 15 per cent.

Segmenting Referring Sources

A second important use of analytics outlined by researcher Seth Duncan is segmenting the referring sources for web visitors. Web analytics enable you to know whether people found your site online by directly typing in the URL (direct traffic) or as a result of organic search results or paid search results (e.g., Google AdWords). You can also find out what keywords people used in those searches. Other referring sources that public relations people track include clicks from email campaigns, banner ads, native advertising, social media posts, and coverage by news media. Notice how these could be classified as owned, paid, shared, and earned, respectively (see Chapter 7).

Parsing Big Data

Again, the availability of data in digital research and evaluation is usually not the problem. It's figuring out what to do with that data. Researchers aren't the only ones facing this challenge. Those working on the creative side of public relations also can be overwhelmed by how to develop communication strategies for large-scale campaigns when such huge amounts of data are available.

Traditionally, campaign messages have been tailored for relatively general demographic profiles. A political TV ad may be created for soccer moms or blue-collar workers, for example. But with the abundance of data available now, demographic profiles easily can be segmented into hundreds, thousands, or even millions of unique profiles. Think about your own social media profile. Are you a female in a relationship who shares certain BuzzFeed content, lives in Vancouver, "likes" Justin Trudeau, prefers JJ Bean's coffee to Starbucks, and shops for just about everything on Amazon? Instagram, which is owned by Facebook, probably knows that. Or are you a male who lives in Halifax and tweets about the Habs, goes to StFX, and regularly travels to Mexico? Twitter probably knows that. Facebook and Twitter and all sorts of third-party companies collect, buy, and sell data that can be used for targeting messages for marketing and political campaigns.

All of these new options have created new challenges for public relations professionals. How do you measure the results of your work in this changing digital landscape? That's where the Barcelona Principles come in. These principles provide useful instructions for keeping it real in the digital age when it comes to metrics (i.e., measurement), analytics (i.e., analysis), and evaluation.

Barcelona Principles

By 2010, public relations had matured into a field that was global, digital, and relationship focused. Social media was blowing up, and organizations worldwide had to figure out what to do about it—how to demonstrate the value of public relations in a new era of media. It was one of those opportunity-or-threat moments for the whole field. In order to earn and keep their seats at management tables, public relations executives would have to tackle the question of how to do research that would not only drive success but also demonstrate public relations' contributions to organizational missions. That was the stage for the 2nd European Summit on Measurement in Barcelona. The group was convened by AMEC, the International Association for the Measurement and Evaluation of Communication, and IPR, the Institute for Public Relations. By the end of that meeting, delegates from 33 countries had agreed to the Barcelona Declaration of Research Principles, which was billed as the first global standard of public relations measurement.[9]

In 2015, AMEC updated the principles to "reflect the significant changes we have seen in the media landscape and the emergence of integrated communications," according to David Rockland.[10] Rockland is a partner and managing director at Ketchum and past chairman of AMEC, who led both the 2010 discussion and the international effort to update in 2015. The Barcelona Principles include seven key items. You may notice that most of these ideas resonate with other key points we've covered in prior chapters on the RACE (research, action planning, communication, evaluation) formula.

Principle 1: Goal Setting and Measurement Are Fundamental

You may recall from Chapter 6 that good goals are supported by SMART objectives, and that the *M* in SMART stands for measurable. *Measurable* implies *quantifiable*. For example, you can count (i.e., quantify) the number of followers on Twitter, snaps on Snapchat, people who physically attend an event, real dollars donated to a cause, or downloads of applications. However, the strategic importance of those metrics depends on what they tell you about your progress towards a goal. Is 5,000 followers a good thing? It depends on your organization and its goals. For a local non-profit that started a campaign two months ago with 25 followers, a count of 5,000 followers could be fantastic news, showing evidence of exceeding goals. For an international coffee brand or a national political candidate, 5,000 followers may be a depressingly low number. It's the combination of the number and the goal that yield actual strategic value. As stated in the original Barcelona Principles,

> Fundamentally important, goals should be as quantitative as possible and address who, what, when and how much impact is expected from a public relations campaign. Traditional and social media should be measured as well as changes in stakeholder awareness, comprehension, attitude and behaviour.[11]

Notice that the last part doesn't focus on communication tactics or media coverage, but on what people feel, think, and do as a result of public relations efforts. This leads us to a second principle. . . .

Principle 2: Measuring Communication Outcomes Is Recommended

As discussed in Chapter 6, outputs are tasks that you complete, but the outcomes of public relations programs are changes in knowledge, attitudes, and behaviour. **Cognitive**

cognitive Having to do with mental processes such as thinking, knowing, perceiving, learning, and understanding.

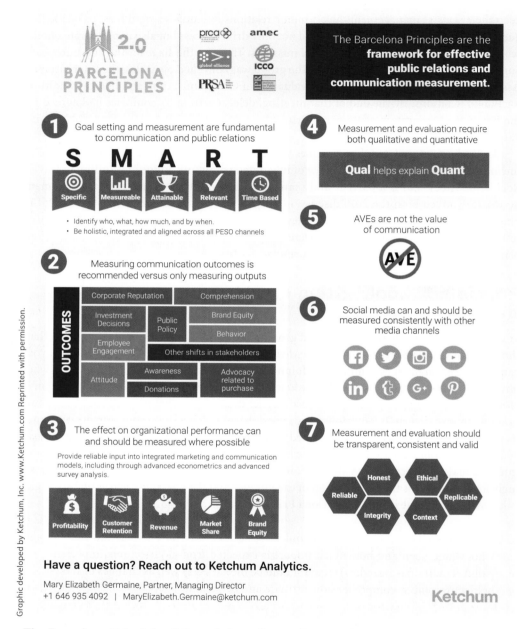

Graphic developed by Ketchum, Inc. www.Ketchum.com Reprinted with permission.

The Barcelona Principles 2.0 apply broadly to all sorts of communication, media, and organizations.

How will applying these principles benefit the status of public relations as a field?

attitudinal Having to do with affect, emotion, favour or disfavour towards an organization, brand, product, service or idea.

outcomes may include understanding an organization's position, learning how to do something, or comprehending a complex issue. **Attitudinal** outcomes may be related to advocacy, reputation, trust, commitment, satisfaction, and feelings of control mutuality (see Chapter 4). The last four (trust, commitment, satisfaction, and control mutuality) are key indicators of relational outcomes. If we define public relations as the management of relationships between organizations and publics, these four outcomes are as important as any. Behavioural outcomes include purchases, donations, healthy activities, volunteerism, public policy actions, financial investment, and so on.

Measuring outcomes requires defining them specifically. Measurement forces you to think about what you are actually accomplishing with your efforts. Measurement is an antidote for ambiguity. Think about the term *engagement*, for example. There's no doubt that engagement is of huge importance in public relations. But the specific value of engagement depends on how you define it. And how you define it determines how you measure it.

Engagement can be defined as attitudinal and based on emotions—how your publics *feel* about your organization and what it is doing. This kind of outcome might be observed with qualitative interviews or measured with a quantitative questionnaire that includes Likert-type items, which ask respondents how much they agree or disagree with statements about the organization. It is extremely common to see employee engagement surveys that include questions such as, "I am proud to work for X" and "I would feel comfortable referring a good friend to work for X."

Engagement also can be cognitive and based on what people think, learn, and know. Can people recall your hashtag? Do they understand how to register for your service? Will they remember your brand name when they do a keyword search? Cognitive engagement can be measured with questionnaires or even quizzes and tests. But cognitive engagement may also be inferred from metrics like how much time people spend reading a web page (or how far they scroll down), the number of people who watch a YouTube clip from beginning to end, or the keywords they use when searching for information.

Beyond implying cognitive activity, reading, scrolling, viewing, and searching also can be considered behavioural outcomes because these activities indicate that people are *doing* something as a result of your public relations efforts. When you host a web page, curate information for a social media presence, send a news release, or post a Vimeo video, those are outputs. When people scroll and download information from the web page, comment on and share your social media posts, write about your news, or watch and recommend your videos, those behaviours are outcomes. The Barcelona Principles remind us about the importance of measuring outcomes, but we also need to remember that not all behavioural outcomes are equal when it comes to achieving our goals. This leads us to a third principle. . . .

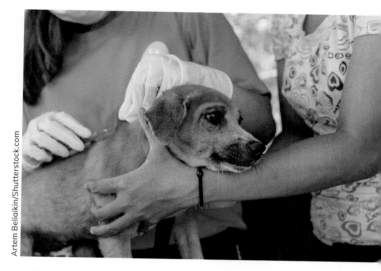

Artem Beliaikin/Shutterstock.com

Following an outbreak of rabies in Bali, Indonesia, the World Society for the Protection of Animals (WSPA) and the Bali Animal Welfare Association (BAWA) began a mass vaccination program to inoculate 350,000 of the island's dog population.

For this program, what kinds of cognitive, attitudinal, and behavioural outcomes could be measured among Bali's (human) residents?

behavioural Having to do with observable human action.

Likert-type items Questionnaire items that ask people to respond to statements with a range of defined response options such as the range from "strongly disagree" to "strongly agree."

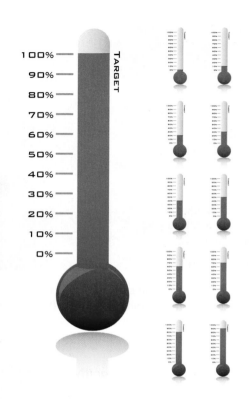

FUND RAISING TARGET

Non-profit organizations often share progress towards fundraising goals as part of their strategy.

Which of the Barcelona Principles apply to this tactic?

Programs like Google Analytics and Brand Lift can help measure both sales and non-sales-driven organizational performance.

Principle 3: The Effect on Organizational Performance Should Be Measured

Collecting data that show that 80 per cent of people who open a video watch it to the end or that people spend an average of four minutes reading your story online definitely indicate levels of attention and behaviour as outcomes, but these metrics don't necessarily mean success in supporting your organization's goals and mission. When goals are marketing based, the metrics should include the steps involved in the conversion funnel discussed in Chapter 6. The funnel entails traceable steps like searching for key terms, clicking on links, browsing product offerings, and making purchases.

Programs like Google's Brand Lift allow marketers to run A/B testing with video ads on YouTube. As part of this service, Google randomly selects two groups of people that fit the profile of campaign target demographics. An *A* group is served a specific video ad from the campaign, and a *B* group sees unrelated ads. In other words, *A* is the treatment group in the experiment and *B* is the control group. Then Google tracks those same users later to see which exact words they use when doing searches. Any significant differences in searches between the groups can be attributed to the campaign video. After a few days, if the *A* group searches for the specific brand name or related keywords more than the *B* group, Google calls that a "lift in brand interest," and it's one of many ways the company monetizes its data by packaging it for marketers, advertisers, and public relations people who use their paid services.[12]

Programs like Google Analytics and Brand Lift are designed specifically with marketers in mind, but there's clearly a role for public relations in the marketing mix, and the same measurement tactics can be applied on non-sales-driven organizational performance. "Our field is growing in its service to NGOs, charitable organizations, governments, the military; organizations that fall outside the business perimeter," said Ketchum's John Paluszek, who is a past chair of the Global Alliance for Public Relations and Communication Management. "We should be talking about 'organizational results' instead of only 'business results.'"[13]

Principle 4: Measurement and Evaluation Require Both Qualitative and Quantitative Methods

Among the many videos posted on the Starbucks brand channel on YouTube is a video from June 2017 titled "How to Make Stovetop Espresso." This slick, how-to video has high production values and features Starbucks' products in a starring role.

Was the video a success? That question may be answered in both quantitative and qualitative terms. A quick look at the YouTube page revealed that in July 2018, the Starbucks channel on YouTube had 174,919 subscribers and this particular video had been viewed 17,305 times.[14] It had just three comments, as follows:

1. "Say what you want about Starbucks, I think that what they do is awesome and they're a force for change in the industry. Plus, they make cute, informational videos."
2. "I love it."
3. "Omg that ice cream idea looks really good. Never thought of that."

Given the size of Starbucks as an organization and the professional production quality of the video, it would be hard to say that this YouTube video on its own yielded significant return on investment. Quantitatively, 17,305 views and just three comments, even though they are positive, is an outcome that probably falls well short of expectations. But we should also keep in mind that Starbucks' goals for this campaign are much larger than what we can observe looking at a single YouTube video page and the publicly available analytics for it. Remember that determining the real value requires a combined understanding of both the metrics and the goal in the context of the organization's broader strategy.

In analyzing the content of comments and other forms of communication, qualitative analysis can include assessments of tone (negative, positive, neutral) and credibility of the source, channel, and message. Other important dimensions identified in the Barcelona Principles are evidence of effective message delivery, inclusion of third-party spokespersons, prominence of media channels, and visual aspects.

> The goals for a public relations campaign are usually much larger than what can be observed from evaluating the metrics for just one video or promo piece.

advertising value equivalency (AVE) A calculation of the value of news or editorial coverage based on the cost of the equivalent amount of advertising space or time.

Principle 5: Advertising Value Equivalencies Are Not the Value of Communications

AVE stands for **advertising value equivalency**, which is a calculation of the value of news or editorial coverage based on the cost of an equivalent amount of advertising space or time. If a public relations person places a story in a newspaper or magazine, she can measure the column inches and total space occupied by the story and then figure out what it would cost to buy an ad in the newspaper taking up the same amount of space. Likewise, if her organization is covered in a TV news story that lasts 30 seconds, she can look up the price of a 30-second advertisement during the program. Then, when she's ready to illustrate the value of her campaign, our public relations pro can compute a dollar value for all the publicity and—*voila!*—she shows success.

Monkey Business Images/Shutterstock.com

Students are being taught to avoid AVEs (advertising value equivalencies).

What was the original purpose of AVEs?

However, there are limits to the AVE approach of evaluating public relations programs. The first problem with AVEs is that they falsely indicate reach based on media placement and do not measure attitudes, knowledge, or behaviour. Second, they use multipliers. **Multipliers** are formulae applied to circulation numbers for print media based on the assumption that more than one person on average will read each copy of a publication, or that being covered as part of a news story is more valuable than paid advertising in the same media space. So, for example, a public relations person might argue that for each copy of a magazine that goes into circulation, four people will have the opportunity to read it. They may also propose that editorial coverage in the magazine is worth twice as much as advertising because of third-party credibility. Such a practitioner would reason that since four people have an "opportunity to see" (OTS) each magazine article and that each of those four people is twice as affected by the editorial content than they would be by a normal advertisement, then the multiplier should be $4 \times 2 = 8$. If their organization, brand, or cause is mentioned in a news magazine with a circulation of 100,000, they would apply the multiplier of 8 and calculate the AVE as the rate it costs to advertise for 800,000 impressions.

In addition to problems introduced in Chapter 6 with measuring campaign success based on mere exposure/impressions, the assumption that a mention in a print story has eight times the effect of a paid advertisement is at best not supported by science and at worst seriously delusional. The Barcelona group called multipliers flat-out "silly" unless they can be proven valid for a specific set of circumstances.

Principle 6: Social Media Should Be Measured Consistently with Other Media Channels

Of course, the scope of public relations is much larger than communication on social media, but digital media and media monitoring services certainly present new opportunities to use data to improve the evaluation of public relations programs. As with the measurement of most public relations outcomes, social media metrics should be tied to clearly defined goals and objectives. Compared to other more traditional and one-way media communication, social media measurement should focus more on "conversations and communities" and less on "coverage." The Barcelona group also emphasized the importance of technology-assisted analysis.

Principle 7: Measurement and Evaluation Should Be Transparent, Consistent, and Valid

The final Barcelona principle emphasizes the importance of maintaining integrity in the design, conduct, and reporting of evaluation research. **Transparency** in research means that researchers are open and not secretive about their methods. If someone says that a campaign generated 100 million media impressions or that they achieved a 30 per cent lift in brand interest, they should be open about how they calculated those figures. We might be suspicious of a campaign that boasts 100 million impressions if we learn that the researcher applied a multiplier of 8. On the other hand, if someone uses well-defined methods of analytics to show how keyword queries in a treatment group differed significantly from a control group in an A/B test, we would have more confidence in the researcher's results. This is especially true if we felt like we could run the same test and achieve consistent

multipliers Formulae applied to circulation or other media reach numbers based on assumptions that more than one person will be exposed to each copy of a message or that being covered as part of a news story is more valuable than paid advertising in the same media space.

Your evaluation of social media metrics should be clearly tied to defined goals and objectives.

transparency In research, openness in describing and explaining methods.

The Barcelona Principles: Somebody Had to Do It

In 2014, Andy Hopson launched The Agency—an integrated communications firm led by industry professionals and staffed by students at the University of Florida College of Journalism and Communications. Hopson, who had played key leadership roles at a number of leading public relations firms before joining the university, scored quickly in recruiting an entrepreneurial and digitally dialed-in group of students for the inaugural team.

Hopson's first hire was UF junior Ryan Baum, who, along with college faculty and staff, led a week-long recruitment campaign that garnered more than 270 applicants. Working all-nighters in an intensive review process, Hopson and Baum narrowed that list down to 57 star students. That highly qualified and eclectic first group came from public relations, advertising, journalism, telecommunications, psychology, and economics, among other majors and academic backgrounds. Most were in their final year.

The start-up quickly built momentum in its first semester, signing clients that included the Florida Department of Citrus, Mexican theme park Experiencias Xcaret, and the American Institute of Certified Public Accountants. As Dean Diane McFarlin said in a news release midway through the first semester, "The Agency is already carving out a national niche in millennial marketing. Staffed by an ever-fresh team of UF students on a campus with 50,000 young adults, The Agency is well positioned to help guide the industry on this topic."

However, as a good portion of the start-up staff began to make plans for graduation, The Agency faced one of its biggest challenges and toughest clients. That challenge was recruitment, and the "client" was their own organization. With his extensive agency experience, Hopson was no stranger to quick-turnover personnel situations. But ensuring continuity in new business development and national and international client service while building a sustainable revenue model in an academic environment presented a problem/opportunity that few (if any) had ever faced before.

As discussed in Chapter 5, strategic planning involves using research to develop a situation analysis and articulate a focused problem or opportunity statement that helps define goals and objectives. When Hopson, Baum, and other strategists analyzed the situation, an opportunity statement emerged: "Off to a fantastic start, The Agency must establish a strong means of maintaining ever-fresh talent by recruiting the very best available students." They decided the best way to do that was to exceed the application numbers from the initial recruiting campaign (recall that 270 had initially applied before 57 were chosen). Exceeding prior application numbers became the goal.

After further research and creative development, the students launched The Agency's new web page at theagency.jou.ufl.edu/ with the following notice:

Somebody had to do it.

Merging the industry with the classroom presents so many opportunities. The opportunity for students to excel alongside professionals. The opportunity to

Continued

provide national brands with original insights from millennial minds. The opportunity to do what needed to be done, although nobody had.

Led by professionals, staffed by students and inspired by faculty. The Agency was established to offer an immersive learning experience to public relations and advertising students and to provide them with the competitive advantage necessary to excel in the job market.

Looking back, the problem was clear. But it took fresh minds to reimagine an industry. . . .

Are you #TheSomebody we've been looking for? Only one way to find out. All it takes is a five-minute app to throw your hat into the ring.

Somebody had to do it. With you, we'll do more.

In addition to the web page launch, tactics included a Facebook page, Twitter and Instagram hashtags, a customized BuzzFeed quiz, email announcements through departmental lists, posters, and promotional events at the agency during high-traffic periods of the class day. The face-to-face recruiting events lent themselves well to plenty of selfies and Snapchat snaps. Agency members replaced their social media profile pictures with photos specifically composed for the campaign theme.

Perhaps the most impressive parts of the campaign, however, were the results and how the students tracked them. Near the end of the campaign, Baum sent this update to the college's leadership:

Courtesy of Kristi Camera and Kelly Logan

As part of a recruitment campaign, agency members replaced their social media profile pictures with themed photos including hashtags.

How could the success of this social media tactic be measured?

Hey all,

I just wanted to check in and report on a highly successful recruitment campaign. After getting over 270 applications last time, I was afraid we peaked early, but the numbers are in and over 356 applications were submitted in only five days. I haven't yet corrected for people submitting to multiple pillars, but we easily cleared 300 unique applicants—even with a fourth of the college graduating and ineligible to apply.

Some other fun numbers:

- *#TheSomebody had 318 posts from 223 unique Twitter handles over the five-day period, with over 192,136 impressions.*
- *Our Buzzfeed quiz (shout out to Chlo) had over 1,100 views with students, faculty and family members taking it throughout the week.*
- *Our Facebook posts reached the news feeds of 6,508 people, and 655 people directly engaged with them.*
- *It took the recruitment team only five days to pull this campaign together from scratch.*

On that note, it wouldn't have happened without an incredible team [Baum acknowledges team members].
Though we are losing a great team after only a semester, their hard work has established a legacy The Agency will be feeling for quite some time.
Let me know if any of you have any questions about recruitment or hiring!
Best,
Ryan Baum
Executive Assistant, The Agency

These students managed a campaign that bodes well for the future of The Agency, but, moreover, their campaign holds promise for the future of public relations research and evaluation. See how the Barcelona Principles apply?

1. Goal setting and measurement are fundamental to communication and public relations. The team set a clear and measurable goal at the outset: exceeding application numbers from the prior campaign. It's worth noting that the evaluation research of a prior campaign became benchmark research to start this program.

2. Measuring communication outcomes is recommended versus only measuring outputs. Baum's report goes beyond saying how many tweets the team sent, how many Facebook updates they posted, how many hours they worked at events, or how many different visual concepts they developed. Instead, the metrics focus on what their key public did as a result of these efforts: posting, sharing, tweeting, taking the BuzzFeed quiz, and ultimately applying for positions in the agency.

3. The effect on organizational performance can and should be measured where possible. While this campaign did not directly serve the business

Continued

goals of an external client, recruiting new talent is definitely an important result to track as part of The Agency's own organizational success.

4. Measurement and evaluation require both qualitative and quantitative methods. One of the unique aspects of the campaign was how applicants could "throw their hats into the ring" by tweeting with the hashtag #TheSomebody. "I am #TheSomebody who perseveres & is not afraid to roll-up their sleeves. I want to be #TheSomebody who inspires."[15] "I'm #TheSomebody who will be the first in my family to graduate college—and from the greatest in America no less."[16] Reviewing the tweetstream showed evidence of positive creativity and interest (and quite a bit of humour in the photos), and no evidence of hashtag hijacking. Likewise for the other social media tactics.

5. AVEs are not the value of communications. Students got an A on this one. Aside from mentioning reach and Twitter impressions, which looks to be explained as a calculation based on the number of followers of people who tweeted the campaign hashtag, they eschewed AVE-type metrics in favour of outcomes like viewing, posting, and submitting applications.

6. Social media can and should be measured consistently with other media channels. And clearly social media were measured in this case.

7. Measurement and evaluation should be transparent, consistent, and valid. At the outset of this campaign, Baum and his team benefitted from the accounting they did of results from the inaugural membership drive. Then, with the new campaign, they carefully tracked and documented their success in a way that enables them to hand over the data and methods for collecting it to their successors.

ll.studio/Shutterstock.com

Tools like Hootsuite allow you to track social media activity including the use of a hashtag in a campaign.

How does this help transparency and replicability?

results. Replicability is the ability to perform a research procedure or experiment repeated times to attain comparable results. While a lot of research results in competitive business environments may be justifiably proprietary, public relations researchers should still be able to explain their methods and results clearly and transparently to those who are paying for their services.

replicability The ability to perform a research procedure or experiment repeated times to attain comparable results.

Measuring the Right Outcomes

Andre Manning and David Rockland wrote the following for *The Public Relations Strategist* in early 2011:

> If we don't use AVEs, then what are the right metrics? And, since social media is the hottest thing going on in public relations, and the Barcelona Principles specifically address its measurement, how do we make sense out of all the different approaches that the approximately 300 suppliers of social media measurement are pushing?[17]

Measurement consultant and author Katie Delahaye Paine is widely recognized as a pioneer in social media measurement as it relates to public relations. Her answer to the question of how we can make sense of it all can be gleaned from her book *Measure What Matters*. In the book, she advocates measuring what people are saying, what people are thinking, and what people are doing (Table 8.1).

In a similar approach, social change agency Fenton recommends a *see–say–feel–do* model for social media metrics (Table 8.2).

These approaches are not too dissimilar from the basic psychology of attitudes, cognition, and behaviour applied earlier in this chapter and the discussion of engagement. The outcomes also align loosely with McGuire's steps in the persuasion process covered in Chapter 6.

Table 8.1 Katie Paine's "Measure What Matters"

Outcome to Be Evaluated	Description	Measurement
What Your Marketplace Is SAYING.	What people are saying about your organization in print, broadcast, or online in social networks, blogs, or communities	Media content analysis including analysis of visibility, tone, messages, sources, and conversation type
What Your Marketplace Is THINKING.	People's opinions, awareness, preference, perceptions of relationship with your organization, or engagement	Facebook likes and shares, retweets, email forwards, re-blogs on Tumblr, recommends on Medium
What Your Marketplace Is DOING.	Whether the behaviour of your publics has changed as a result of your efforts	Careful study of specific programs conducted by your team and systematic analysis of changes in awareness, web traffic, and sales; analytics

Source: Adapted from Katie Delahaye Paine, *Measure what matters: Online tools for understanding customers, social media, engagement, and key relationships* (Hoboken, NJ: John Wiley & Sons, 2011).

Table 8.2 Fenton's "Social Media Metrics That Matter"

Outcome to Be Evaluated	Description	Measurement
See	Exposure to brand and messaging	Page views and likes on Facebook, followers on Twitter, website traffic, email signups, RSS subscriptions, advertising impressions, Medium views and reads, and YouTube views
Say	Sharing information within and across social networks	Facebook likes and shares, retweets, email forwards, re-blogs on Tumblr, recommends on Medium
Feel	When people "engage with your messages or content, internalize your messages, and add their two cents"	Facebook comments or shares with comments, retweets with personalized messages, blog comments, and YouTube comments
Do	The conversion goal: "the thing you want people to DO"	Donations, advocacy actions, event attendance, membership, volunteerism, and sales

Source: Adapted from "Social Media Metrics Guide," Fenton, accessed May 14, 2015, http://www.fenton.com/new/wp-content/uploads/2013/04/social-media-metrics-guide.pdf.

Voices from the Field

Fraser Likely

Image courtesy of Fraser Likely

Independent public relations consultant Fraser Likely is considered one of Canada's leading authorities on public relations measurement.

Fraser is an Emeritus Member of the Institute for Public Relations Measurement Commission (IPRMC), and a Fellow of the International Association for Measurement and Evaluation of Communication (AMEC), having been a member since its inception. He has led a number of significant research projects and is currently managing an international research project examining PR measurement models with the goal of developing a standard model for measurement. In 2018 he won the Public Relations Society of America's Jackson, Jackson, & Wagner Behavioral Science Prize honouring his longstanding body of academic research.

A sought-after speaker, Fraser has presented at numerous conferences and has taught public relations at Royal Roads University and the University of Ottawa. He is also a Fellow and a Life Member of CPRS.

Evaluation is the last step in the RACE formula. When we talk about evaluation in a public relations context, exactly what should we be evaluating?
Evaluation is a broad term. It means finding the value or worth of something. In public relations, we can measure and from those measures evaluate communication

messages, products, and channels or media. We can measure and thus evaluate communication campaigns and stakeholder relations programs. We can measure and thus evaluate the contribution that public relations makes to organizational goals, reputation, and corporate social responsibility. We can measure and thus evaluate the quality of the services a public relations department offers, and we can evaluate the quality of the employees in that department. To ensure that we know the full value that comes from an organization investing in public relations, we should conduct all of these evaluations.

So, every public relations campaign or project should contribute to the organization's overall goals?

A public relations department should practise strategic communication. Therefore, a public relations department should not produce any message, product, channel, campaign, or program that does not directly support a business unit's or the organization's strategies that in turn further organizational goals.

Is there a standard way public relations practitioners should be doing evaluation?

Public relations academia and practice are developing best practices for measuring communication messages, products, channels, and campaigns. Unfortunately, work to date on developing standards has not been fruitful. Indeed, for a number of reasons—one, for example, is that research firms and public relations agencies want to have their own proprietary measurement approaches and don't want to be tied to a standard approach, even though their proprietary approach is not very different from any other competitor—the push to develop measurement standards has yet to reach critical mass. These days we hear a great deal about the importance of social media and online metrics. How important are these in the overall evaluation process?

It seems that the anecdotal evidence would suggest that social media and online measurement—measurement to find their effectiveness—is used more as formative research rather than evaluative research. It is used more as a planning tool for the next message, product, or campaign rather than as a tool to see if it helped the organization meets its goals. Measuring social media outputs (reach) and outtakes (response such as a like; share of voice; awareness) is only a first step in evaluation, but it seems that's the only step that most practitioners take. Therefore, while much time and money is spent on social media and online measurement, it is perhaps the least important of the various methods for evaluation.

In some ways, it sounds like evaluation is part of "selling" the results to senior management. Why is that important?

Again, it is a question of whether the public relations department practises strategic communication. By practising strategic communication, the public relations department's mission, goals, and strategies are aligned with the organization's mission, goals, and strategies, and the department communicates "purposely" to directly support those strategies. To determine if the department is indeed strategic, in that its communications help make the organization's strategies a success, the department must evaluate and then show senior management by way of its evaluation results that it brings value to the organization through its support of organizational strategy.

Despite the Barcelona Principles, some practitioners continue to use AVEs. Why do you think they're reluctant to let those go?

AVEs are typically used by public relations practitioners who are not very good at strategic communication. They feel that measuring AVEs will give them a "number" to show to management just how good they are. Fortunately, more and more senior management teams are seeing through the inappropriateness of the AVE number. The AVE number does not show the overall value or worth of the public relations department. For most of these public relations practitioners, it is just a matter of time before management asks them to defend the full value of their department—and they won't have a complete answer. Bye-bye that job!

Ethics: Independence

"There are lies, damned lies, and statistics." This quote, often attributed to Mark Twain, was the source of sociologist Joel Best's book title *Damned Lies and Statistics: Untangling Numbers from the Media, Politicians, and Activists.*[18]

independence In public relations ethics, the value of autonomy and accountability in providing objective counsel.

spambots Computer programs that automatically send unsolicited email or post comments in online forums.

Statistics, then, have a bad reputation. We suspect that statistics may be wrong, that people who use statistics may be "lying"—trying to manipulate us by using numbers to somehow distort the truth. Yet, at the same time, we need statistics; we depend upon them to summarize and clarify the nature of our complex society.[19]

Public relations can easily be lumped in with media, politicians, and activists according to Best's book title. In fact, one of the most critical books on public relations is subtitled *Lies, Damn Lies, and the Public Relations Industry.*[20] Yet, at the same time, we *need* statistics in public relations; we *depend on* statistics in public relations to summarize and clarify the nature of our complex society.

As discussed in Chapter 2, advocacy is a longstanding value in the history and current practice of public relations. The ethics section at the end of Chapter 2 discussed the tension between the ideal of advocacy in ethical persuasion in public relations and the elusive ideal of objectivity in journalism. Transparency was recommended as a way to deal with this tension, particularly in media relations and communicating with external publics. But public relations people also have to avoid excess in advocacy in their roles as counsellors to clients and organizational leadership. In public relations counselling, practitioners must balance advocacy and loyalty with **independence**.

Summarizing and clarifying the nature of complex society and of the data that we use to interpret human attitudes, knowledge, and behaviour are essential parts of the internal counselling function. Remember that two-way communication means public relations people interpret the organization to publics *and* interpret publics to the organization.

There are many traps that a public relations person could fall into in the interpretation and reporting of data to their clients and organizations:

John Morris/www.Cartoonstock.com

"That's what I want to say. See if you can find some statistics to prove it."

Ethical public relations requires balancing advocacy and loyalty with independence.

How would you respond to a request like this?

- A computer program may code sarcastic comments as positive.
- **Spambots** and zombie followers (Chapter 6) could inflate numbers for comments and followers.
- Some channels could be left out and others included in analyses, making public relations results look better.

- In global and cross-cultural campaigns, some languages or keywords could be left out and others included in analyses.
- News releases could be counted as media coverage.
- And, of course, AVEs and multipliers could be misused.

As critics of public relations like to point out, unbridled advocacy and subjectivity in collecting and analyzing data can lead to lies—even damned lies—and these traps only make it harder for a loyal advocate to keep numbers straight. Public relations researchers and ethicists have hashed this out carefully and recommend industry-wide standards for research to help practitioners perform "in a true counselling function rather than simply as an advocate for whichever client is paying the bill."[21]

One prominent group working to standardize research practices in public relations is the Coalition for Public Relations Research Standards. They have drafted standards for measuring social media, traditional media, the "communications lifecycle" (e.g., awareness, knowledge, interest, relationships, behaviour), and financial return on investment (ROI). One example of their early efforts is a Sources & Methods Transparency Table that assists researchers in consistently reporting where they obtain their social media data and how they analyze it.

Courtesy of the Institute for Public Relations

Some public relations agencies have developed their own proprietary measurement systems.

Why would a public relations practitioner or agency pledge to support research standardization?

The coalition's charter members include the Council of Public Relations Firms, Global Alliance for Public Relations and Communication Management, Institute for Public Relations, International Association for Measurement and Evaluation of Communication, and the Public Relations Society of America. Among the first major client organizations that pledged to abide by voluntary standards were General Electric, General Motors, McDonald's USA, and Southwest Airlines.

Abiding by a clearly stated set of standards in research, measurement, and evaluation empowers public relations researchers to conduct research that is both transparent and replicable. It allows them to maintain their independence as counsellors in presenting research with integrity.

Evaluation in Action

The following excerpt from an award-winning communications plan, created by DDB Public Relations for the Royal Canadian Legion, is a good illustration of the RACE formula in action and demonstrates how evaluation is woven into the planning process.

The *R* in RACE, research, is evident in many sections of the plan. Research helps to identify the organization's needs and to learn more about the target audience. Notice how most of the objectives in this plan are measurable, making it easy to determine if the plan achieved its goals.

The evaluation section (*E* in RACE) relates directly to the goals/objectives. For each goal, specific measurements are used, including measuring traditional media coverage and determining social media reach.

In this plan, DDB talks about specific business results, making the impact of public relations on the organization very clear. This plan resulted in an increase in the average donation from $1.40 to $14.10.

2019 CPRS TORONTO ACE AWARD SUBMISSION

Entrant's name: Martine Lévy
Organization name: DDB Public Relations
Division/Category: Best Digital Communications Campaign
Title of Entry: Digital Poppy Launch
Time Period of Project: October 2018 to November 2018

EXECUTIVE SUMMARY

SITUATION ANALYSIS: Each year from the last Friday of October to Remembrance Day, 11 November, millions of Canadians proudly wear a bright red poppy on their lapel as a visual pledge to honour Canada's veterans and never forget those who served and sacrificed for its freedom. The Royal Canadian Legion, as a part of its mission, endeavours to consistently inspire Canadians to remember and pay tribute to those who have served and continue to serve the country today. Additionally, every year, the Legion embarks upon their national Poppy Campaign, supported by thousands of legionnaires and cadets who volunteer to distribute poppies within their communities and raise donations for the Legion's Poppy Fund. The Poppy Fund supports Canada's veterans and their families through a variety of community-based programs and services. In 2018, facing on-the-street donation stagnation amplified by emerging new media technologies, dwindling volunteer sales' forces, and an increasingly cashless society, the Legion was ready to challenge the not-for-profit fundraising status quo—all they needed was an innovative approach that would bring a new generation of donors into the fold.

RESEARCH: DDB PR was brought on board to work alongside digital badge developer, Basno Canada, who had identified a unique opportunity to modernize the Legion's current approach to fundraising. Proprietary research and analysis, including audience profiling, focus groups with current and potential donors, a review of past Poppy campaigns, and one-on-one interviews with Legion volunteers helped the agency and its partners to determine that a digitally focused campaign would have the most impact and success in reaching new, younger donors. The team developed an innovative campaign that would bring the Legion into the twenty-first century, and the first-ever "digital poppy" was born. For the first time in Canada's history, the iconic poppy would also be available digitally, and Canadians would be able to donate to the Legion's Poppy Fund online. Available for download at www.mypoppy.ca, the digital poppy, along with the dedicated Poppy Fund donation opportunity, provided the Legion with a new, modernized platform for fundraising. All that was needed was a strategic communications program to help publicize the Digital Poppy Launch Campaign and bring it all to life.

AUDIENCE: Using the agency's strategic planning process and access to proprietary research, it was determined that the Legion's new approach needed to resonate with Canadians between the ages of 20 and 45—millennial-aged and millennial-minded individuals, those highly active on social media, who engage with and feel connected to social causes (e.g. Ice Bucket Challenge, Humboldt Strong, #PrayForParis, etc.). Stakeholder analysis and research identified that the one thing that most motivates this group is that they are recognized as people who do good and support causes, initiatives, and charities. Influenced by others who are engaging on social media (family, circle of friends, social influencers) as well as online news (*BuzzFeed, Huffington Post,* etc.) this audience would likely be most interested in an exciting cause-related campaign with the potential to "go viral."

STRATEGY: The first of its kind worldwide, the Digital Poppy Launch Campaign was especially designed with younger audiences of potential donors in mind—those who recognize and embrace the impact and power of social media-based initiatives. While the digital poppy on its own, as a new and exciting element to the traditional Poppy Campaign, would make an impact, the agency knew that the program would need an extra push—influencers and celebrity ambassadors who would carry the message across traditional media platforms and into the social realm. With just three weeks to launch, DDB PR developed a robust communications and public relations program, including strategic approach, launch media relations, social media, and influencer activities.

QUANTIFIABLE OBJECTIVES: Through media and influencer relations, the agency set out to support the 2018 Digital Poppy Launch Campaign and position it as a new and innovative extension of the Royal Canadian Legion's annual Poppy Fund. We set out to build awareness and drive publicity for the Digital Poppy Launch Campaign elements including the mypoppy.ca website, online donations, and social sharing, while positioning the campaign as a modernized approach towards fundraising. Leveraging celebrity endorsement and personal stories to drive the "feel-good" aspect of the campaign, the program also needed to ensure the national PR program supported overall Remembrance Day messaging as well as regional Royal Canadian Legion efforts, wherever possible.

Specific measurable objectives (using the MRP system):

- Secure a minimum of 15 million media impression for the campaign, with a cost-per-contact of $0.03 or less (per the industry standard). DDB PR conducted the Digital Poppy Launch Campaign pro bono.

- Create partnerships with a maximum number of influencers and ambassadors to reinforce the importance of the Legion's role in honouring and supporting Canada's veterans.

- Obtain a qualitative MRP score of 80 per cent with MRP messaging criteria including: brand mention, call to action (visit mypoppy.ca to download and donate), image inclusion, and key message inclusion.

TACTICS: To fortify the launch and give it cachet, a number of high-profile Canadian personalities, athletes, and organizations agreed to lend star power and social media support to the cause. Campaign ambassadors included recording artist Justin Bieber; artistic luminaries Margaret Atwood, Sandra Oh, and former Mrs. Universe Ashley Callingbull; Hockey Night in Canada's Don Cherry and Ron MacLean; members of the National Hockey League Players' Association; the Teamsters Union of Canada; Ancestry.ca; and corporate sponsor TELUS. The agency also leveraged their strong personal relationships with Canadian social media influencers, including Do the Daniel, Janette Ewen, Christian Dare, and Mark Munroe, to help push out digital poppy messaging to their followers on launch day, all pro bono. The agency crafted a national comprehensive media relations program, targeted to news, assignment, and city beats across broadcast (TV and radio), print, and online platforms, with materials that included internal key messages and Q&A, a wire release, a fact sheet about the Legion and the Poppy Fund, celebrity quotes and dedication stories, and hi-res images of the digital poppy and celebrity ambassadors with their digital poppy. To ensure cohesive messaging across all platforms and to support ambassador and corporate partner social content pushes throughout the campaign, the agency developed and disseminated a social media and influencer playbook. The playbook included messaging for pre-launch teasers, from campaign launch day to Remembrance Day. On launch day, celebrity ambassadors and members of participating organizations helped kick things off online by posting their own personalized digital poppies along with dedication stories and photos, pushing their fans and followers to visit www.mypoppy.ca.

BUDGET/RESTRAINTS: The campaign was conducted pro bono by the agency, with minimal budget allocated to essential hard costs such as wire releases and translation fees. There were no media dollars available or donated for traditional advertising support and no paid influencer programming, and we had little access to internal communications resources at the Legion, beyond official spokespeople. Not only did we need to publicize the new Digital Poppy Launch, but we had to help drive downloads and online donations. Beyond the lack of budget and constricted timelines, we were challenged by strict protocols around the official announcement and campaign launch timing. Traditionally, the Legion's Poppy Campaign cannot be publicly announced before the official presentation of the first ceremonial poppy (and for the first time in 2018, a digital poppy) to Canada's governor general in Ottawa—a ceremony that would take place (and no doubt garner media attention) on the last Monday of October. To further complicate matters, the Legion's two-week Poppy Campaign, including public poppy distribution and fundraising efforts, would begin, as it does every year, on the last Friday of October. DDB PR was challenged to devise a digital poppy–focused media relations launch strategy that would complement the governor general's announcement at the beginning of the week, successfully infiltrate Poppy Campaign launch stories throughout the week, *and* generate new coverage that would include pertinent details about the digital poppy throughout the two-week campaign in-market timing.

EVALUATION: The Digital Poppy Launch media relations program delivered stellar results that far exceeded initial quantitative and qualitative goals. The program resulted in:

- **142 media stories** and a total reach of **80,260,018** (the initial goal was 15 million) and with no associated budget spend, a zero MRP cost-per-contact
- An MRP quality score of **90 per cent** (the initial goal was 80 per cent), demonstrating successful inclusion of brand mention, the call to action and mention of the mypoppy.ca website, images of the digital poppy, and other campaign key messages
- Coverage in tier-one national media outlets including the *Toronto Star, The Globe and Mail*, the *National Post, Yahoo! News, Huffington Post*, Global News, CTV News, and CBC Radio
- Influencers and campaign ambassadors helped generate **99,836,927 social media impressions**, stirring hundreds of follower comments and engagement on the Royal Canadian Legion, Remembrance Day, Canada's veterans, and our pledge to never forget

Digital Poppy was a massive fundraising success garnering **10 downloads for every lapel poppy purchased** in addition to increasing donations by the same margin (**$14.10 vs $1.40**). As well, close to **15,000 stories and photos** were posted on social media. And, while the Royal Canadian Legion is unable to disclose Poppy Fund amounts raised via online donations, it has revealed that the Digital Poppy Campaign is one of the most positive and successful initiatives undertaken to date, with results far exceeding expectations. The digital poppy has been accepted as a long-term program for the Legion and will expand substantially in future years. They also anticipate that other countries that currently honour Remembrance Day will look to initiate similar digital programs, given the success seen in Canada.

In Case You Missed It

Digital technologies have not only expanded our options for communication; they have also profoundly enhanced our ability to track and analyze social media activity. Here are a few takeaways from this chapter.

- You can use A/B testing to quickly compare the effects of different digital content and messages.
- Media monitoring services help you analyze social media content that is actively produced, discussed, and shared by publics online.
- Use programs like Google Analytics and Brand Lift to measure both sales- and non-sales-driven organizational performance.
- Remember that the goals for your public relations campaign are usually much larger than what can be observed from evaluating the metrics for just one tactic such as an online video or promo piece.
- Your evaluation of social media metrics should be clearly tied to defined goals and objectives.

ICYMI

Summary

8.1   Explain how evaluation research can be used in public relations program development and message testing.

Evaluation of prior programs can be useful at the start of a new program for formative research and benchmarking to understand the current state of the organization, to assess their situation, and to set a baseline for measuring progress. Informal and formal message testing research, including focus groups, content analysis, and automated copy testing, can be used for message and strategy development throughout a campaign or program.

8.2   Describe how media monitoring services have evolved in the digital age.

The process of monitoring media coverage has sped up considerably. Traditional clipping services monitored print and electronic media for mentions of clients in local, national, or international media. Today's media monitoring services still measure publicity, but they also monitor online conversations and facilitate the analysis and sharing of information all day every day in real time.

8.3   Discuss how digital technology has expanded our ability to track and analyze data in evaluating public relations programs.

Data analytics are particularly useful in public relations for tracking online visitor behaviour and segmenting referring sources. Media monitoring services present new opportunities to use data to improve the evaluation of public relations programs with social media components. Compared to traditional media, social media measurement can focus more on conversations and communities and less on coverage.

8.4 **Evaluate public relations research practices using industry standards for research (i.e., Barcelona Principles).**
Seven principles for evaluating public relations research, measurement, and evaluation provide a working template for understanding industry standards: goal setting and measurement are fundamental to communication and public relations; measuring communication outcomes is recommended versus only measuring outputs; the effect on organizational performance can and should be measured where possible; measurement and evaluation require both qualitative and quantitative methods; AVEs are not the value of communications; social media can and should be measured consistently with other media channels; and measurement and evaluation should be transparent, consistent, and valid.

8.5 **Identify tools for measuring online and traditional public relations outcomes.**
Tools ranging from traditional surveys and direct observation to advanced technology for content analysis and behavioural tracking can be applied in the measurement of media content, attitudes, knowledge, and behaviour as outcomes of public relations programs.

8.6 **Analyze the relationship between independence as a core value of public relations and the ethical conduct of research, measurement, and evaluation.**
Public relations counsellors must balance advocacy and loyalty with independence. Independence in this context means providing objective counsel and being accountable for actions including proper conduct and reporting of research. Industry standards empower public relations researchers to conduct research that is both transparent and replicable. Abiding by such standards helps practitioners maintain their independence as counsellors in presenting research with integrity.

Discussion Questions

1. Discuss your experience with message testing. If you haven't been part of formal message testing, how have you seen it portrayed on TV or in movies, books, and so on?
2. How do media monitoring services assess *publicity* (mentions in news media)? Review online services to identify at least one quantitative and one qualitative example. Here are some possible sites to check:
   a) www.cision.ca/pr-software/
   b) www.meltwater.com/
   c) www.lexisnexis.ca/en-ca/home.page
3. How do media monitoring services assess *online conversations*? Review services to identify at least one quantitative and one qualitative example.
4. Find a public relations case study online that illustrates some or all of the Barcelona Principles and describe how each of the principles is (or is not) evident in the case. Here are some possible sites to check:
   a) www.prnewsonline.com/category/case-studies/
   b) prcouncil.net/resource/pr-case-studies/
   c) www.prweek.com/us/the_work
5. Describe one tool or app for measuring attitudes or behaviour online, and explain how it can be used in public relations.
6. Identify a case when an organization had to release bad news (perhaps a news story about an organizational crisis). Discuss what kind of research was involved and how you think the public relations person balanced advocacy and independence.

Further Readings and Online Resources

Public Relations Metrics
Paine, K.D. (2011). *Measure what matters: Online tools for understanding customers, social media, engagement, and key relationships.* Hoboken, NJ: John Wiley & Sons.

> Katie Delahaye Paine is widely acknowledged as the queen of public relations metrics, and her book, *Measure What Matters,* is considered required reading. For the latest in measurement news, check out her blog: painepublishing.com/katie-paines-measurement-blog/

Statement of Best Practice in Measurement and Evaluation
www.cipr.co.uk/content/awards-events/statement-best-practice-measurement-and-evaluation

> The Chartered Institute of Public Relations (CIPR) in the UK has guidelines regarding measurement. This includes a good explanation of the differences between inputs, outputs, outtakes, and outcomes.

How to Organize and Facilitate an Effective Focus Group
studentexperience.uwo.ca/student_experience/reporting__evaluation/focusgroup.pdf

> Focus groups can be a powerful tool for public relations practitioners. Western University has put together this handy how-to guide.

Peer-Reviewed Academic Journal Article
Watson, T. (2013). Advertising value equivalence—PR's orphan metric. *Public Relations Review, 39(2),* 139–46. doi:10.1016/j.pubrev.2012.11.001

> Despite being "outlawed" years ago, AVEs continue to be used by some practitioners. This academic article outlines the history of AVEs and suggests some reasons why they remain so hard to shake.

Key Terms

Advertising value equivalency (AVE)   197
Algorithm   190
Attitudinal   194
Automated copy testing   000
Behavioural   195
Big data   191
Bounce rate   191
Clipping services   189

Cognitive   193
Conversion rate   191
Cookie   191
Digital watermarking   187
Eye tracking   188
First-party data   191
Functional magnetic resonance imaging (fMRI)   188
Independence   206

Likert-type items   195
Media monitoring services   189
Multipliers   198
Replicability   203
Spambots   206
Third-party data   191
Transparency   198

PART THREE
Tactics

9

Writing

Telling the NCAA's stories means writing about more than just sports. How do they do it?

▲ Al Sermeno Photography/Shutterstock.com

Love 'em or hate 'em, listicles are part of the online media landscape. The term *listicle* is a portmanteau word, combining *list* and *article*. (*Spork* is another portmanteau, combining *spoon* and *fork*.) You've no doubt run across many listicles in your online browsing: for example, "8 Simple Things You Have Been Doing Wrong Your Whole Life,"[1] or "The 6 Most Ridiculous Things People Claimed to Legally Own,"[2] which had 1,362,519 views before I became number 1,362,520.

Critics complain that listicles are lazy writing, that they simply recycle content, and that they encourage shallow reading and thinking in an age of shrinking attention spans. If you look up *listicle* on Wikipedia, you will find the definition along with a cross-reference to clickbait.[3] Like popsicles—another portmanteau, come to think of it—listicles can be sweet and appealing, but not very substantive and nourishing.

But elsewhere, listicles get more love. In "Five Reasons Millennials Love Listicles," *Forbes* millennial contributor Steph Denning writes that the rise of listicles "reflects a more profound reality that we need a way to filter and process the information being thrown at us."[4]

Taking the writer's perspective, Arika Okrent describes listicles as literary form in *The University of Chicago Magazine*: "The true essence of the list form is consecutive order, taking a mass of stuff and finding a way to break it into pieces and lay it out in a line," she writes. "That also happens to be, in a way, the essence of language."[5]

The debate over listicles draws our attention to the challenges of public relations writing in a digital age. Actually, the debate over listicles draws our attention to the challenges of public relations writing in *any* age. At times, we must draw attention, but we don't want to cheaply bait readers with fluff. We write to communicate important and useful information with both form and substance. As representatives of complex organizations in society, we also have a responsibility to curate important information. We are charged with filtering and processing. We have to take a "mass of stuff" and make sense of it.

Public relations practitioners use a number of writing tactics to do their jobs. From features and factual news to tweets and texts, this chapter will cover some of public relations' most common writing assignments. But why not start with a list?

listicle An online article presented in the format of a numbered or bulleted list.

clickbait Promotional or sensational Internet content designed primarily to entice users to visit another website.

Five Reasons to Write Well in Public Relations

Writing is one of the most sought-after skills that employers screen for when hiring public relations talent. Many aspects of public relations work can be taught on the job, but writing takes a lifetime of learning and improvement. You probably had to demonstrate that you could write well to be admitted to college or university. If you're enrolled in a public relations program, you will have to write even better to earn your degree. The bar will be set even higher after graduation. Why is writing so important in public relations? What follows are discussions of five of the most important reasons.

piosi/Shutterstock.com

The Ten Commandments may be one of the best-known lists of all time. Imagine Moses on BuzzFeed.

Why have listicles grown in popularity as a style for online writing?

Relationships

In any kind of writing, but especially in professional writing, the best writers have a good sense of who their readers are. A great news release speaks to the journalist or the editor running the story as well as to the readers of their publications. A clever tweet resonates with followers who may be inclined to retweet. A persuasive PSA (public service announcement) script convinces a teenager to second-guess risky behaviour. A thoughtful thank-you note plants the seed for a donor to consider a larger gift in the future.

While writing tactics like these appear to be one-way communication, two-way communication is the essence of their larger context. Each tactic requires the writer to understand readers, listeners, watchers, fans, or followers. Remember that when you write for public relations, you are writing to build and maintain relationships.

Influence and Persuasion

Simply because you engage in two-way communication doesn't mean you can't use influence and persuasion. Think about your personal relationships with friends and family. From small decisions, like where to eat lunch or what to wear, to big decisions, like where to live and whom to associate with, you and your closest friends and family influence each other. At times you may be persuaded, and at other times you are the one doing the persuading. It's the overall balance of your relationships, however, that determines whether or not they are symmetrical.

Courtesy of Scott Hampson

Social Media is great because you don't actually have to be good at anything....

AGENT-X COMICS WWW.AGENT-X.COM.AU

A common misperception of social media management and public relations is that anyone can do it.

What kinds of expertise are needed to write well for social media?

The same idea applies in public relations. The most influential "influentials" in social media engage their publics. They don't use megaphones. Instead, they interact with their readers, which helps them write in ways that earn them respect and credibility. Good research in strategic planning, as discussed in Chapters 5 and 8, is another tool that helps writers understand their publics' thoughts, feelings, and behaviours, thereby making it easier for writers to influence those publics.

Goals and Objectives

It takes clear writing to articulate your goals and objectives as part of a public relations strategy. Write crisp, clean proposals and you'll get business. Write clear reports and you'll demonstrate results. Sharp technical writing convinces readers of the value of what you plan to do, the way in which you are going to do it, and the success that you will have when you're finished. But you also have to do the work you propose. In order to achieve those goals and objectives and to implement that brilliant strategy, you have to pull off the tactics. In public relations, that means writing well.

OK—I know what some of you may be thinking now. "Wait, what? I'm going to do most of my work in meetings and on the phone. I'm going to shoot videos and shake hands and talk to people. Where's the writing in that?" There's some truth to that. However, those meetings will lead to reports and news stories. Those phone calls will be followed up with emails. Handshakes may turn into deals that need to be formalized in writing. And those videos may need scripts and captions and written responses to the comments they generate on YouTube. Go ahead and include that little "Excuse-my-typos-I-wrote-this-with-my-phone" disclaimer on your email signature, but there's only so far you can go in achieving the communication goals and objectives for your organization without doing some good writing.

Reputation Management

Charles Fombrun, one of the leading experts on reputation, defines *corporate reputation* as

> a collective representation of a firm's past actions and results that describes the firm's ability to deliver valued outcomes to multiple stakeholders. It gauges a firm's relative standing both internally with employees and externally with its stakeholders, in both its competitive and institutional environments.[6]

While the practice of **reputation management** includes many activities such as planning, analyzing feedback, and evaluating an organization's reputation, a major component also entails writing. Think about the reputation of big brands like Apple or Toyota. Think about the reputation of your school. And think about the reputation of smaller organizations to which you belong. No doubt a big part of those reputations is based on their actions (Chapter 7), but what people write about these organizations also is important.

Reputation management can happen through paid, owned, or earned media. As search engines have become primary portals for publics to learn about organizations, *writing* for search engine optimization (SEO) (Chapter 7) has become an important part of reputation management, too.

reputation management Acting and communicating—often in writing—to influence an organization's reputation as part of a process that includes planning, analyzing feedback, and evaluating.

Impression Management

Social, mobile, and multimedia venues provide us with new ways to communicate and extra latitude in our writing styles. Some contexts allow you to write less formally than others, and some contexts have new grammar that you'll know better than your professor or boss. For example, the website Urban Dictionary lists multiple definitions for *cray cray*. One definition explains that the term stems from the word *crazy*, but a second definition may be more apt: "A desperate attempt to say 'crazy' made by some adult trying to be cool."

Closely related to the concept of reputation management is **impression management**. Most college students don't talk to their parents the same way they talk to their friends, which is quite different from how they may speak during a class presentation or a job interview. Psychologists will tell you that this is all part of being a well-adjusted adult. I can only imagine the response I would get if I spoke with my dean in the same way I talk trash with my surfing buddies or play around with my seven-year-old after school. The same goes for writing. The most effective writers understand the contextual difference between a text, a tweet, a cover letter, a news release, an annual report, and so on. Successful public relations

impression management Process in which people influence perceptions of themselves or their organizations by regulating and controlling information in social interactions.

people also realize that how they present themselves in social media requires a mindful balance between being authentic and being professional.

Impression management involves presenting yourself in ways that help you achieve your goals and aspirations in social interactions. When you work in public relations, you are responsible for managing the impression of your organization as well as your own impression. In face-to-face interactions, this may come naturally, but it takes careful attention and deliberate practice in writing. People will look to you for expertise in writing across all the media that serve as channels of communication between your organization and its publics. In order to be hired and promoted, you'll need to demonstrate fluency and flexibility in how you write across all the different contexts.

Storytelling

When you think of storytelling, you may think of sitting around a campfire, reading to a child, or even open mic night at a coffeehouse, but storytelling is serious business for anyone who works in professional communications. Journalists tell stories for a living, as do advertisers, social justice advocates, and international diplomats. In public relations we tell stories—nonfiction stories—that help us represent our organizations and build mutual understanding with publics. Brian Solis and Deirdre Breakenridge, authors of *Putting the Public Back in Public Relations*, describe the importance of storytelling in discussing blogger relations. They write that excellent public relations in social media contexts has less to do with the mechanics of online publishing and "more to do with storytelling, an understanding of what you represent, why it matters to certain people, and a genuine intent for cultivating relationships."[7]

Writing compelling stories candidly and credibly is tricky in any context, but doing so as part of a deliberate communication strategy may be one of the toughest jobs in public relations. It's easy to fall back to the relative safety of a corporate voice to conservatively deliver your organization's key messages. But, ironically, writing conservatively can also be a risky strategy. Writing trainer Ann Wylie advises public relations professionals to drop the corporate "'At XX, we . . .' construction." With tongue in cheek, she outlines three reasons:

1. It's patronizing. "At Wylie Communications, we don't believe our insurance company *really* understands us."
2. It's formulaic. "At Wylie Communications, we feel that this cliché might make us vomit."
3. It's off target. "At Wylie Communications, we prefer that you write about us instead of about your organization and its beliefs, understanding and knowledge."[8]

Wylie recommends focusing on the reader. She says you should write with more "you"s and fewer "we"s. This is pretty solid advice for any kind of persuasive writing. Tell readers what's in it for them. In public relations, however, you inevitably will have to tell your organization's story (or side of a story) at times. When you have to do that, one option is to tell an interesting story. Human interest is what's in it for your readers. The NCAA wants publics to know that "nearly 20% of all student–athletes are first-generation college students" and that

Telling the NCAA's Story—One Athlete at a Time

"Mikal McKoy was assigned two jobs when he moved in with his father in 2009: Get an education, and don't get caught in the streets."[9]

Are you wondering what this opening sentence has to do with public relations? What's the purpose? Or are you more interested in finding out who Mikal McKoy is and what happened to him? Either way, the goal is to get your attention and engage you. Telling a story is one of the best ways to do that. As writing god William Zinsser wrote, one of the best approaches to writing is to just tell a story. "It's such a simple solution, so obvious and unsophisticated, that we often forget it's available to us."[10] But success in public relations writing means telling stories with a *purpose*.

McKoy did both of those jobs that his father had assigned him. He earned a 3.7 GPA and admission into Albion College. "But by the second semester of his freshman year, the first-generation college student was back home in Muskegon, Michigan, living with his father and working at a metal factory that made automotive parts." The narrative arc continues. One of his best friends was shot and killed, and that friend was someone with whom he shared dreams of returning to school, playing college football, and earning a degree.

"After those conversations, it opened my eyes," McKoy said in the story. "We made this commitment. Now, I have to do it."[11] The first-generation college student returned to Albion the next year, working two campus jobs to pay for school and earning a spot on two of the college's teams—football and track. He went on to study psychology and get involved in mentoring programs for underrepresented elementary and middle school boys.

The story, as told by Rachel Stark, features emotion, direct quotes, and visual details. Stark writes for NCAA *Champion* magazine. In telling McKoy's story, Stark is telling the NCAA's story. Interviewed for *Public Relations Tactics* about her job as assistant director of strategic initiatives for the NCAA, Melissa Kleinschmidt, APR, said, "My goal is to tell the stories of how college sports give student–athletes the skills they need to succeed on the playing field, in the classroom and throughout life."[12]

"their athletic ability positions them to succeed beyond their collegiate experience."[13] Telling stories like McKoy's is one way to get the job done.

Features

Feature stories like those published in NCAA's *Champion* have long been a primary tactic in public relations writing. Rather than plainly reporting facts and information, a feature story digs deeper into some angle of an event, a person's life, an organization, or a place.

feature story A story that explores some angle of an event, a person's life, an organization, or a place.

Among the crazy array of media I've consumed in the past 24 hours are a memoir in *The New Yorker*, "Off Diamond Head: To Be Thirteen, with a Surfboard, in Hawaii,"[14] a *BBC News* story, "Godzilla Finally Gets Citizenship in Japan,"[15] and a customer testimonial video by an audience research vendor called Instant.ly, "How Bumble Bee® Seafoods Took Concept Testing to the Next Level."[16] All are features. At first I thought it would be a stretch to call *The New Yorker* piece a public relations tactic. Then I learned the article is the first chapter of the author's forthcoming book—it's part of a promotional strategy for book sales. "Godzilla" and "Bumble Bee" are also quite strategic.

The third example of a feature story that caught our attention is an online video feature. The one-minute, 44-second Instant.ly video features Bumble Bee Seafoods' director of innovation talking about how the company has used the online research services to test brand concepts. It's safe to assume it won't go viral. It's not funny or shocking, but it is a feature, and it's probably the most strategic of the three examples. I watched the video because Instant.ly sent me an email that read

> How are major brands innovating in today's fast-paced marketplace? Kara Sterner, Director of Innovation at Bumble Bee Seafoods shares how using new tools like Instantly Concept Test™ helps the company prioritize new ideas and make faster, educated decisions about what consumers are most likely to purchase.

They sent me the email because I'm on their mailing list as someone who has used their services recently. They know there's a fair chance I'll consider using their services again in the future, and getting me interested in another client's success story is one way to keep me on the hook. When I clicked on the link, I'm sure they tracked that data. After watching the video online, I had the opportunity to click to "request a demo." In other words, they're moving me through their funnel, and the script for the Bumble Bee testimonial is a feature written for a specific audience with specific goals. That's what makes it strategic.

In *Writing PR: A Multimedia Approach*,[17] Meta Carstarphen and Richard Wells list the following as feature types that public relations writers may produce:

1. how-to features
2. personal profiles
3. first-person accounts
4. opinion and editorial
5. humour or satire
6. historical writing
7. round-up stories with perspectives from multiple sources
8. photo essays
9. stories about products or services
10. trend articles

human interest
A personal or emotional storytelling angle that focuses on the human condition.

What they all have in common as basic elements, according to Carstarphen and Wells, are human interest and timelessness. **Human interest** stories have a personal or emotional angle. By *timeless*, they mean that these stories maintain their relevance and

Case Study

Godzilla Earns Citizenship; Shinjuku Earns Publicity

The Godzilla story, as it was told on the BBC website, has an interesting start:

> Most residents of Tokyo's pulsing Shinjuku ward, home to the busiest railway station in the world, are of the homo sapiens variety. Shinjuku has a population density of about 17,000 people per square kilometre but undeterred by this it has granted citizenship to a new resident, who only goes by one name—Godzilla.

Notice that the "why?" of this story is missing from the first few sentences. The **delayed lead** is common in feature writing. The first sentence's job in a story like this is to make the reader want to read the second sentence. Then, every sentence should do the same, "each tugging the reader along until he is hooked," according to Zinsser. Well, I was tugged along far enough in this one to learn that Godzilla earned his honorary citizenship for his role in promoting tourism.

Although the story byline in this case goes to BBC Asia writer Heather Chen, public relations people from Japan and Shinjuku likely did much of the legwork. When you work in public relations, your role in producing feature stories often happens in the background. You may write queries to media about their interest in the story, write the supplemental materials (in this case Godzilla's citizenship certificate), or even write full drafts of the story to send to reporters to use as they wish.

delayed lead A style of beginning a story without summarizing the story's main points in a way that entices readers to continue reading.

AP Photo/Shizuo Kambayashi

When Shinjuku granted Godzilla honorary citizenship in Japan, traditional and online media all over the world reported the story.

Why did this story have such broad appeal? What public relations goals did it accomplish?

Continued

The Godzilla story ended up all over the world in all kinds of media, including international wire services, national newspapers, local TV stations, newspapers, and online-only media like *Gawker*, *BuzzFeed*, and *Elite Daily*. There's no telling how many authors edited the story and put their own bylines on it, and the public relations team was likely thrilled about all the earned media even though their names were not mentioned. This isn't to say that you never get credit for writing feature stories in public relations. You are more likely to put your own name in the byline when you write for paid, owned, or shared media (Chapter 7) such as native advertising, internal newsletters, or your organization's social media sites.

And, yes, storytelling happens via social media too. Godzilla's story flew across Facebook and Twitter as people added their own voices. "Japan appointing Godzilla as its official tourism ambassador fills my heart with terrible, destructive love," tweeted Marjorie Liu (@marjoriemliu) to her more than 16,000 followers.[18] Twitter user and gaming magazine content manager Matt Bertz (@mattbertz) added his voice to the story too: "If Japan and Godzilla can mend fences, maybe there is hope for the middle east after all."[19]

Transmedia storytelling is an important context for public relations writing. When shared/social media are added to the storytelling mix, stories have more of a chance of going viral because readers and users have the opportunity to become part of the storytelling process as well. Granting citizenship to Godzilla turned out to be just the right kind of stunt to generate lots of media attention and participation in platforms that thrive on user-generated content.

It is important to remember, though, that both traditional news media and social media are uncontrolled. On the whole, the Godzilla story was received, reported, and shared in good fun. However, for every success story like this, there are several more that get almost no attention, and a few that backfire altogether. The best strategy for feature writers is to know readers and publics well enough to have a sense of what will be perceived as interesting, funny, or even shocking enough to draw attention and participation, but to avoid tastelessness, insensitivity, or offensiveness.

> When readers and users have the opportunity to become part of the storytelling process, stories have a better chance of going viral.

transmedia storytelling Telling a story across multiple platforms like games, web pages, apps, social media, and traditional media.

value long after they have been told. Of course, features can have a chronology or be tied to particular events in time, but they do not need to be timely in the same way that breaking news does.

It's difficult to nail down an exact definition of *feature story*. One approach is to define it with examples (as I've tried to do with the Godzilla and Bumble Bee Seafood features). Another is to distinguish features from the second major type of storytelling in public relations: straight news.

News

direct lead A style of beginning a news story that summarizes the story's main points (e.g., who, what, where, when, why, how) in the first sentence or two.

Whereas a feature writer may delay the most important points while appealing to human interest and emotion, straight news stories get right to the business of reporting the news with a **direct lead**. Even if readers never read past the first paragraph, they can get the gist of the content from direct leads. In the first sentence, reporters will often tell readers many, or even all, of the key story elements: the *who, what, when, where,* and *why* of the story. This news style of writing is often called the **inverted pyramid** because all of the most important information in the story is presented at the broad top of the story, and the narrower supporting details are written below as the story continues to the bottom. Figure 9.1 illustrates the structure.

The inverted pyramid has played an important role in defining an era of journalism. Although the exact history of the inverted pyramid is murky, most journalism historians seem to agree that the convention grew with the rise of technologies for mass communication. One story maintains that reporters during the US Civil War learned to place all of the important information in the first line or two in case telegraph lines were cut during wire transmission. The inverted pyramid also made sense as multi-page newspapers grew in size and popularity because many readers would not turn past the front page to finish reading complete stories that continued on inside pages.

In any case, traditional mass media technology encouraged the telling of succinct, fact-based stories without a lot of fluff or extraneous information, and news readers came to expect that. Concise writing became a news virtue, and if public relations people wanted to work with journalists to get their stories out through mainstream media, they needed to understand the function of a good news lead and the type of information required to support it. The same values apply today when it comes to telling stories in direct news style. Online news feeds, blog rolls, email preview panes, and search engine results all favour writers who know how to write a good lead.

As with features, sometimes the public relations person's role in telling news stories resides in the background, setting up the press conference or interview, compiling the fact sheet, or even drafting the entire news story with a direct lead and supporting details. In media relations, your job is to help others tell your organization's story (or your organization's side of the story) in their outlets. To do this, you need to understand news values and the way that journalists write and organize their stories.

At other times, you will have the opportunity to tell your organization's news stories directly to your publics. The Internet has increased these opportunities to serve as a direct source for news about your organization.

Writing for Intermediaries

Public relations writers can earn attention online beyond their direct networks through three main intermediaries: traditional news media gatekeepers (i.e., earned media), social media (i.e., shared media) and search engines. The three overlap considerably, but public relations writers must use different writing strategies and tactics for success in each.

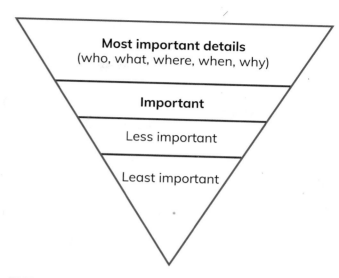

FIGURE 9.1 The inverted pyramid has defined a generation of journalistic style.

How has communication technology influenced the way we tell stories?

inverted pyramid A style of newswriting in which the most important information is presented at the broad top of a story and narrower supporting details are written below.

Online news feeds, blog rolls, email preview panes, and search engine results favour good leads.

Writing for News Media

In the gatekeeping model of media relations, publics find stories based on what editors and producers decide is newsworthy. Back when people obtained their news primarily by reading daily newspapers and watching 30-minute newscasts, publics relied on the editorial judgment of the gatekeepers in these news organizations to decide what news they should read or watch. In this model, people let others serve as the first filter of what news and information they should pay attention to.

To some extent, this gatekeeping still happens online. People still go to news websites without knowing exactly what the editors will deliver. They still count on editors to decide what's important. And that's why news releases, backgrounders, and fact sheets written primarily for journalists and editors are still key public relations tactics, even as their channels for delivery have moved online. Writing for these media requires attention to traditional news values, **Canadian Press (CP) style**, and other conventions of news writing.

News Releases

A **news release** is basically a news story, written in news style, by a public relations practitioner writing on behalf of an organization or client. News releases are often referred to as press releases because historically they were written for distribution to members of the press. With a news release, a public relations writer drafts and edits a news story, pitches it to reporters and editors, and hopes that various news media will retell the story. In other words, news releases are tools for seeking earned media (Chapter 7). **Video news releases** (VNRs) serve the same function for TV media, providing broadcast journalists with pre-produced news packages including audio and video material. **Social media releases** (SMRs) adopt the conventions of social media to include sharable online material such as useful chunks of text, quotes, photos, infographics, suggested tweets, social media handles, hashtags, and embeddable multimedia elements.

With the web, releases are more likely to reach nonmedia publics directly from the organization. The "press" may or may not be involved as intermediaries in the distribution of an organization's news. Therefore, in today's media environment, *news release* is probably a better term than *press release*. In any case, public relations writers should keep two key characteristics in mind when they produce news releases: format and newsworthiness.

Format is important, so that the news looks like news. In pitching a straight news story to journalists or editors in news organizations, public relations writers should do the following:

- Start with a good headline and **dateline**.
- Write using the inverted pyramid style.
- Include important factual information that the journalists would need to support the main points of the story.

For traditional print news releases, public relations writers follow certain conventions, such as including "For Immediate Release" with a date at the top. Many news release writers still include the word "-more-" at the bottom of the page if the release continues to another page, and "-###-" or "-30-" at the end of the story to let journalists know they've reached the last page. These symbols are a bit archaic, but in the right context, they signal

Canadian Press (CP) style Rules of writing (including grammar, capitalization, and punctuation) published by the Canadian Press news agency. These rules are the standard for public relations writing in Canada.

news release A news story, written in news style, by a public relations practitioner writing on behalf of an organization or client.

video news release A news release that provides broadcast journalists with pre-produced news packages including audio and video material.

social media release A news release that applies the conventions of social media and includes content designed for social media distribution and sharing.

dateline Text at beginning of news story that describes when and where a story occurred (e.g., "BEIJING, 16 June —").

that you understand the news business and its traditions. Check with your client or employer for templates, or work with them and news media to develop a consistent format for your news releases.

With most traditional news media, you'll want to write with CP style. If you ever have taken a news-writing or editing course in a journalism program, you know that journalistic training includes some tough lessons on editing. In some of the best J-schools, journalism students are slapped with 50-per-cent-off grade penalties for fact errors and harsh point reductions for CP style errors. Students who graduate from these programs are sharp writers, but they also are sharp critics of others' sloppy newswriting. Don't let your news be discarded because you overlook simple CP style editing rules. As discussed in Chapter 4, the best way to understand the needs of journalists is to develop solid working relationships with them.

The more important factor in whether your news release gets traction with third-party media is the actual newsworthiness of the information it delivers. Newsworthiness, also covered in Chapter 4, means that a story includes elements of timeliness, proximity, conflict and controversy, human interest, or relevance. But there's no direct formula for calculating news value. To understand which news from your organization is newsworthy, you need to understand the perspective of journalists and their audiences.

The news release on the following pages from Tim Hortons (distributed by Cision/CNW) contains many of the elements that are standard in a modern release. The headline and subhead are designed to give readers a good feel for what the story is about. This is nothing new; these elements were part of the very first press release written by Ivy Lee back in 1906. What is new are all the links to additional information, including the company's social channels (Facebook, Pinterest, Twitter, and LinkedIn), a link to the company's website, another link to the contest website, and a third link, which takes the reader to all previous Tim Hortons releases issued through Cision. The paragraphs about Tim Hortons and Jeep Brand at the end of the release are what's known as boilerplate—standard paragraphs that are generally included in every release.

(Note: This sample general press release will help increase awareness about flu shots. Please complete and send it to local media even if you don't have a specific event.)

Contact: (Your Name)
(Telephone Number)

(Insert Date)
For Immediate Release

The (Insert State) Diabetes Control Program
and CDC Encourage People with Diabetes to Get a Flu Shot
Despite Vaccine Delays

Recent reports about flu vaccine delays should not discourage millions of Americans from trying to get their annual flu shot, particularly if they have a chronic illness such as diabetes, say the Centers for Disease Control and Prevention and the **(Insert State)** Diabetes Control Program.

About 16 million people in the United States have diabetes and **(Insert state data here)** in _____. Failure to get vaccinated could leave many of them at risk for life-threatening influenza and pneumonia infections.

"This year it is more important than ever for people with high-risk conditions like diabetes to get vaccinated because they are more likely to have problems associated with flu and pneumonia," said Dr. Frank Vinicor, director of CDC's Division of Diabetes Translation. "Despite reports of the vaccine delay, we are recommending that people at high risk request vaccinations from their physicians as early as possible in the flu season. Physicians with no vaccine should direct patients to places that have a supply such as public health clinics or other private sources," Dr. Vinicor added. (The CDC website for supply information is www.cdc.gov/nip.)

According to CDC, deaths among people with diabetes increase 5 to 15 percent during flu epidemics and people with diabetes are three times more likely to die with complications of the flu and pneumonia. Despite these alarming figures, only half of the people with diabetes receive an annual flu shot and two out of three have never been immunized against it.

Organizations often create templates for news releases.

What are the advantages and disadvantages of writing with templates?

Fact Sheets

Fact sheets can accompany news releases or be presented on their own. They present factual information about an organization or its events, people, products, or services. They may be presented as frequently asked questions (FAQs), advice sheets, infographics, or even listicles.

fact sheet Short (often one-page) document that presents factual information in concise format.

Headline →

Start working out your thumbs, Canada! Tim Hortons® legendary Roll Up The Rim To Win® is back on February 6, 2019 Français Français

NEWS PROVIDED BY
Tim Hortons →

Dateline →

Feb 01, 2019, 06:00 ET

SHARE THIS ARTICLE

Subhead →

For the first time ever, Canadians can roll up for the chance to win one of 40 Jeep® Compass compact SUVs

TORONTO, Feb. 1, 2019 /CNW/ - Get excited Canada - on February 6, Tim Hortons Roll Up The Rim To Win contest is back and better than ever. For the first time, Tim Hortons has partnered with Jeep®, giving Canadians the opportunity to win one of 40 new Jeep Compass compact SUVs.

Tim Hortons® Roll Up The Rim To Win® is back February 6 with new cups featuring prizes surrounded by colourful confetti. (CNW Group/Tim Hortons)

Quote →

"Each year, our goal is to make Roll Up The Rim more exciting for our guests," says Jorge Zaidan, Head of Marketing, Tim Hortons Canada. "Whether it is through exciting prizes with new partners or highlighting moments that celebrate all Roll Up The Rim has to offer, we're excited to make this year the most exciting – and legendary – yet."

"We're thrilled to be teaming up with Tim Hortons and combining two iconic brands in a contest that has become a highly-anticipated Canadian tradition," said Bill Levasseur, Vice President, Sales & Marketing, FCA Canada. "This year's contest participants will have a chance to win one of 40 Jeep Compass SUVs. Redesigned as a best-in-class, global sport utility vehicle, Compass now resonates even more strongly with Canadians thanks to its trademark blend of all-weather 4x4 capability, style, technology and advanced safety features."

The Roll Up The Rim cups have had a makeover this year. They still feature the bold, yellow Roll Up The Rim To Win logo, but a new design features the prizes more prominently on the cup, surrounded by colourful confetti.

Thumbs Workout

To complement the 2019 launch of Roll Up The Rim To Win, Tim Hortons has released a fun thumb work out video on their social channels today. The video features different exercises set to music to get Canadians' thumbs in peak physical condition for roll up season.   → Body

The full 2019 Roll Up The Rim To Win campaign launches on February 6th with new advertising and fun new creative for social media.

Roll Up The Rim To Win runs from February 6 until April 17, 2019, or while cup supplies last. Prizes can be redeemed until May 3, 2019. Contest rules, odds of winning and prizing information can be found at participating Tim Hortons Restaurants or at RollUpTheRimToWin.com. Join the conversation online by using #RollUpTheRim.

About TIM HORTONS®

Tim Hortons®, part of Restaurant Brands International, is one of North America's largest restaurant chains operating in the quick service segment. Founded as a single location in Canada in 1964, Tim Hortons appeals to a broad range of guest tastes, with a menu that includes premium coffee, hot and cold specialty drinks (including lattes, cappuccinos and espresso shots), specialty teas and fruit smoothies, fresh baked goods, grilled Panini and classic sandwiches, wraps, soups, prepared foods and other food products. Tim Hortons has more than 4,800 system wide restaurants located in Canada, the United States and around the world. More information about the company is available at www.timhortons.com.   → Boilerplate

About Jeep Brand

Built on more than 75 years of legendary heritage, Jeep is the authentic SUV with class-leading capability, craftsmanship and versatility for people who seek extraordinary journeys. The Jeep brand delivers an open invitation to live life to the fullest by offering a full line of vehicles that continue to provide owners with a sense of security to handle any journey with confidence.

The Jeep vehicle lineup consists of the Cherokee, Compass, Grand Cherokee, Renegade and Wrangler. To meet consumer demand around the world, all Jeep models sold outside North America are available in both left and right-hand drive configurations and with gasoline and diesel powertrain options.

SOURCE Tim Hortons

For further information: or to arrange an interview, please contact: Meghan Giffin, North Strategic: Meghan.Giffin@northstrategic.com; LouAnn Gosselin - FCA Canada, Louann.gosselin@fcagroup.com   → Contact Information

Related Links

http://www.timhortons.com

But rather than applying a news story or feature narrative style, they focus more on the delivery of useful information. With just one or two clicks or taps, a reporter—or anyone else interested in the story—can access all sorts of related facts and background information written by people working in public relations.

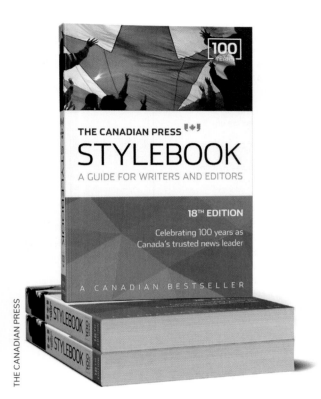

Knowing CP style is a necessity in media relations.

CP released a new 18th edition in 2017. What updates did it include?

---

morgue Storage space for archived files of old stories, notes, and media materials kept by news organizations.

media kits Packages of information assembled by public relations people for news media. Common contents include news releases, fact sheets, backgrounders, position papers, photos, graphics, and so on.

backgrounder Writing tactic used to give depth and context as background information for news stories.

Backgrounders

Picture practising public relations before the Internet. If you sent a news release to a journalist, she may have needed additional information on your organization or its key people. Without Google, she could have gone to the library or to her news organization's **morgue** (storage space for archived files), but chances are she wouldn't have had that background information at her fingertips unless she regularly covered your organization. So, you would have provided it, or at least had it available upon request.

For bigger media events, public relations people developed (and still develop) **media kits** that include news releases, fact sheets, and backgrounders, as well as photos, graphics, position papers, and anything else that might be useful for a reporter researching and producing a story. As technology advanced, public relations people began producing electronic media kits on CD-ROMs that could include all of the above plus audio, video, and interactive components. Today, all this information can be shared online with less need for printed materials and physical discs, but reporters still need background information for context. Regardless of the medium, it still makes sense to package background information in an easily accessible format for whoever is writing about your organization. Three useful tools are backgrounders, bios, and profiles.

Backgrounders provide the stories behind the straight news stories. They often are written as features and give depth and context to news stories by explaining the history—or background—of an organization or one of its events. Like fact sheets, backgrounders deliver information that will be useful to anyone writing a story about the organization, but backgrounders use a narrative structure that connects the factual information in a meaningful way that explains context. For example, the Transportation Safety Board of Canada (TSB), an independent agency set up to investigate serious transportation issues and accidents, regularly issues media releases, such as one with this lead:

> Today, the Transportation Safety Board of Canada (TSB) released its investigation report (M16P0378) into the causes and contributing factors that led to the October 2016 grounding and sinking of the US-registered tug *Nathan E. Stewart* in British Columbia. The report underlines the need to effectively and reliably manage the risk of fatigue in the marine industry.[20]

That's the start to the news release. The website with the news release also includes statements from TSB officials, a report on the investigation, webcast links, videos, social media links, and other relevant information. But what if a reporter isn't familiar with the *Nathan E. Stewart* in the first place? A TSB backgrounder tells the story, starting with this lead:

> On 13 October 2016, shortly after 0100 Pacific Daylight Time, the articulated tug-barge composed of the tug Nathan E. Stewart and the tank barge DBL 55 went aground on Edge Reef near Athlone Island, approximately 10 nautical miles west of Bella Bella, British Columbia, in the Heiltsuk First Nation's traditional territory. The tug's hull was eventually breached and approximately 110 000 litres of diesel fuel were released into the environment. The tug subsequently sank and separated from the barge. It was removed from the environment 33 days after the occurrence. Seven 208-litre drums of diesel oil-soiled absorbent pads were collected from the site.[21]

Note that this backgrounder provides all the relevant facts, including dates and times, that a reporter might need if covering the story.

Regardless of the medium, you should package background information in an easily accessible format.

Bio (or Biographical Profile)

A biographical profile, or bio, is essentially a backgrounder for a person.

The Royal Bank of Canada recently released the following:

> TORONTO, July 3, 2018 — Royal Bank of Canada (RBC) is announcing the launch of *RBC Reach*, a corporate accelerator that opens the door to a commercial deal with RBC for select post-seed to pre-series A startups. The program, which is accepting applications now, also provides companies with an initial investment and coaching to help them grow their businesses.
>
> Startups from across Canada and around the globe are invited to apply for a spot in the first cohort of the accelerator program, which will focus on delivering solutions that go beyond banking to solve challenges faced by RBC's business clients to help them thrive.[22]

The news release included a quote from Mike Dobbins:

> This is a unique approach to corporate accelerator programs," said Mike Dobbins, Chief Strategy & Corporate Development Officer at RBC. "Over the course of the program, the selected companies will collaborate with RBC executives, our own intrapraneurs and venture specialists from Highline BETA to address real challenges experienced by our clients. Our ambition is to create an expedited path to a commercial agreement with RBC, as well as solutions in market that could transform the way our clients do business.[23]

But what if the reporter has never heard of Mike Dobbins? The RBC media web pages include a biography of Dobbins and all the RBC executives:

> As Chief Strategy & Corporate Development Officer, Mike is responsible for working with Group Executive to develop RBC's overall strategic plan as well as providing leadership for mergers and acquisitions. Mike also chairs RBC's Innovation

Council which, in addition to overseeing investments in strategic partnerships, has responsibility for coordinating RBC's Innovation Labs which focus on research and the development of advanced capabilities in the areas of data, security and client experience. Mike is also Chairman of RBC Bank US, a director of City National Bank and is responsible for RBC's auto finance business. As a member of Group Executive, he is one of nine executives responsible for setting the overall strategic direction of RBC.[24]

The bio goes on to outline Dobbins's professional career and accomplishments. A photo is also provided.

Writing for Social Media

> *Before jumping into an online conversation, first you need to know how people are talking and what people are talking about.*

With social media, people find organizations online via links and referrals from other people. They can then read, comment, share, or create their own stories related to these organizations. They can participate, and they can interact. This is the essence of social media. Public relations writers must observe carefully before diving in. You wouldn't just walk into a room at a party and try to lead a discussion without first getting to know who was in that room, what they are talking about, and how they are communicating. The same goes for online communication. You must work to understand both the social and technological contexts first. Then, you can join the conversation. "The most important lesson in social media," write Solis and Breakenridge, "is that, before engaging anyone, you must first observe and understand the cultures, behaviour, and immersion necessary to genuinely participate in the communities where you don't already reside."[25]

blog Online post (or web log) with reflections, comments, and often links provided by the writer.

360b/Alamy Stock Photo

The Warby Parker blog provides a forum for employees to write about new styles of glasses, but also community service projects, travel, and books that employees recommend.

How do corporate blogs help "humanize" a company?

Blogs and Longer Form

Blogs were among the first social media writing forms adopted on a wide scale by public relations practitioners. They remain primary vehicles for longer-form writing in social media. Blogs are sort of the old-timers of social media, but, in 2004, they were a hot new thing. *Blog* was the most sought-after new word in Merriam-Webster's online dictionary that year.

Merriam-Webster's 2004 Word of the Year, *blog*, was defined as "a Web site that contains an online personal journal with reflections, comments, and often hyperlinks provided by the writer."[26] Compared to other forms of published writing, blogs were easy to update. The reverse-chronological order of most blogs made it easy for writers to regularly add new posts and accumulate serial content. Linking enabled blogs to be more social, too.

Public relations writers quickly recognized the potential utility of blogs for communicating with stakeholders and publics. However, to realize that potential would require some adaptation of traditional corporate writing. Dave Winer, who developed much of the software that enabled blogging to catch on in the 1990s, suggested that the only real requirement in identifying a blog was that the "personalities of the writers come through."[27]

Writing with personality was—and still is—a big part of blogging well. It is also still a tough challenge for many businesses and other types of organizations. Technology journalist Erica Swallow has outlined 10 tips for successful corporate blogging:[28]

1. *Establish a content theme and editorial guidelines.* While you can write about anything you want on your own personal blog, readers of an organization's blog should know what to expect, and the general theme should be closely related to what your organization does. Guidelines will help different writers from within the organization work together to support this theme.

2. *Choose a blogging team and process.* This team does not have to all come from the communications department. You want good writers, but you also want authentic voices that represent different parts of your organization.

3. *Humanize your company.* As Dave Winer advised, let the personalities of writers come through. Let your team tell their stories (and their co-worker's stories) as they relate to the theme of the blog. Use the blog and its comments section to have real conversations.

4. *Avoid PR and marketing.* Um, yeah, about this one, it depends on how "PR" is defined. Swallow equates PR with salesmanship. You do want to avoid that on blogs. It's a different story altogether, however, if you define public relations as building and maintaining relationships.

5. *Welcome criticism.* Criticism is part of human communication, and it's also a great opportunity to respond to constructive feedback.

6. *Outline a comments policy.* Of course, not all criticism is constructive. Guidelines for handling comments will make it transparent to both bloggers and readers which comments will be deleted and why.

7. *Get social.* Take advantage of social media affordances to connect your blog to your organization's other social media activities and to encourage sharing among your publics.

8. *Promote your blog.* Even if your blog has great content, you'll still need to drive people to it via other channels. Post new blog headlines to your other feeds with links back to the blog. Promote the URL in your email signature. Remind employees about it when you see them face to face.

9. *Monitor mentions and feedback.* Comments and feedback on your blog are not limited to the comments section of the blog. People will also comment on their own blogs and other forums. Google alerts and other search services can be set to monitor for specific terms and links, and notify you when your blogs get mentioned.

10. *Track everything.* In other words, use analytics. While number 9 on Swallow's list refers mainly to qualitative feedback, this last item reminds us to set up systems for tracking quantitative data. "At the minimum, make sure you're tracking site traffic, where referrals are coming from, and traffic-wise which posts are doing best," advises Swallow.

microblog A shorter blog post limited by space or size constraints of the delivery platform.

Most, if not all, of this advice applies to **microblogs** as well.

Microblogs and Shorter Form

Microblogging, according to *Canadian Oxford Dictionary*, is "a social media site to which a user makes short, frequent posts." Wikipedia editors define *microblogging* as "the practice of posting small pieces of digital content—which could be text, pictures, links, short videos, or other media—on the Internet." Under that definition, you can count Instagram, Facebook, Twitter, Tumblr, Snapchat, Yik Yak, and China's Sina Weibo, which claimed 130 million active users ahead of its initial public offering in 2014, as microblogging platforms. But before you dive in to reach all those users, you'll want to think about your public relations strategy and the technology and culture of each.

For example, let's compare Twitter to China's Sina Weibo. Like Twitter's original restrictions, Weibo users are limited to 140 characters per post. Also, like Twitter, Weibo's active user base is considerably smaller than its total population. According to one study, the number of users actually posting original content on Weibo was about 5 per cent.[29] Reposting is a common activity on both platforms. Like Twitter, Weibo also includes hashtag functions and shortened URLs.

However, since Chinese characters convey so much more information than Roman characters, that 140-character limit may be less of a constraint on Weibo than Twitter, which increased the character limit from 140 to 280 in 2017.

Perhaps the most obvious difference between Weibo and Twitter is that most Twitter users log in from countries like the United States, Brazil, and Japan, while most Weibo users are in China. But before you hire a translator to expand your social media reach into China, consider some of the cultural differences.

In comparing the two social media platforms, Edelman Digital's Cathy Yue noted that Weibo and Twitter present content differently, follow different business models, and attract different demographics (users are generally younger on Weibo than Twitter). Censorship is also a big factor. You would want to do a lot of research and work with people who really understand both the technology and the context of a platform like Weibo before representing your organization there. Yue concludes, "In order to successfully engage on Sina Weibo as a brand, it's important to keep in mind a classic Chinese saying, 'Precise knowledge of self and precise knowledge of the threat leads to victory.'"[30]

Imaginechina via AP Images

Sina Weibo is one of the largest social media platforms in the world.

What cultural differences would you research before starting a Weibo account?

Writing for Search Engines

Sometimes, we have to write for robots.

As public relations writers, we must understand newsworthiness and the conventions for newswriting, if we plan to get our stories out via news media. We must understand the cultures and contexts of social media, if we plan to write for social. And, if we want publics to find our organizations and stories when they do Internet searches, we must understand how to write for search engines. Whereas journalists act as gatekeepers in news media, and everyday Internet users serve as influencers in social media, *computers* are the intermediaries when we write to reach publics via search technology.

Search engine optimization (SEO) was defined in Chapter 7 as "the process of affecting the visibility of a website or a web page in a search engine's 'natural' or unpaid ('organic') search results."[31] In the same way that people rely on news media to select the most newsworthy information in the day's news or friends in their social networks to provide feeds of interesting information, they count on search engines to filter for the content that is most relevant to their search queries. So, what do these robots look for?

Although all search engines operate differently, with different rules (i.e., algorithms) for how search results are produced, some common elements that factor into most searches are keywords (of course), headlines, meta tags, links, and URLs.

Keywords

If you want your page to be found when people search for keywords, include those words on your page. It sounds obvious, but it takes planning to integrate keywords with your writing. If your company sells beach umbrellas, your decision would be fairly straightforward. You would want to make sure you mention "beach umbrellas" on your page. On second or third references, you would want to write "beach umbrella" instead of "our product." Research on other words that people use also will help. Maybe "shade" and "sun protection" make sense as keywords too. But don't go overboard to the point of ridiculous repetition. If you mention beach umbrellas 15 times in two paragraphs, you'll come across as annoying to human readers, and the computers will figure out your trick too. There's a point of diminishing returns—search engine algorithms actually punish excessive repetition. Google calls it *keyword stuffing*, and warns against filling your pages with duplicate words because it "results in a negative user experience and can harm your site's ranking."[32]

Headlines, Page Titles, and Descriptions

In print media, headlines capture attention and make the difference between whether someone reads a story or not. The same applies online, except potential readers have to go through the extra step of clicking or tapping on your headline from all the other ones that are going to be really similar in search results. Experts recommend aiming for 8–12 words.[33] For example, eBay's beach umbrella headline is simply "Beach Umbrella | eBay," and the page description reads, "Find great deals on eBay for Beach Umbrella in Outdoor Umbrellas and Stands." Rio Brands' headline reads, "Sun Protection and SPF Umbrellas | Rio Brands," and the page description says, "Rio Brands' line of SPF beach umbrellas and multi-position sun shades offer sun protection up to 99.8% of UVA and UVB rays." Notice that the Rio Brands title and description have more words, but that they also add some important keywords including "sun protection," "SPF," "UVA," and "UVB."

The headline also helps you distinguish your page from others with similar keywords but different purposes. The Skin Cancer Foundation hosts a page that is highly ranked on Google with the title "How to Hit the Beach Safely." The descriptive text reads, "Before a day

> Keep your web page headlines short—8 to 12 words; you need them to stand out from among the multitude of similar search results.

at the beach, you need strategies to keep from returning browned or burned by solar ultra-violet rays (UVR). Here's our five-step plan to make sure your next beach trip isn't just fun, but also sun-safe."

Meta Tags and URLs

meta tags Text used to describe a web page to search engines.

Meta tags are the snippets of text that you use to describe a web page to search engines. When you post a web page you should enter the page title and description as meta tags. Your webmaster or IT people can help if you are not the one who actually uploads the web pages, but you will want to work with them to make sure they include the right words. For titles, avoid default tags like "Untitled" or "New Page 1." The page description and specific keywords should also be entered as meta tags. Google recommends using different titles and descriptions for each page.

> To earn natural links, nurture relationships with other sites by offering information they will find valuable.

Another recommendation is to include keywords in the URL. Remember that the URL also shows up in search results pages, and many people decide whether to click based on the URL structure. There's a lot of information about the broader website's content with a URL. Think about how much information there is in comparing the two web pages in Table 9.1.

Links

anchor text Clickable text that provides a hyperlink.

Like public relations itself, linking is a two-way street. Search engines reward pages that have good relationships with other pages. When you link to other pages, avoid generic **anchor text** like "click here." Instead, choose the words carefully that you use to link to other pages (including other pages on your own website).

backlinks Incoming links that direct web users to a web page from another web page.

On the other side of the street are inbound links, or **backlinks**, which are links on others' pages that direct people to your pages. Search engines count these kinds of links as votes for your page, and the more you have, the higher your pages will rank in

TABLE 9.1 Meta Tags for Two Related Web Pages

Title	"How to Hit the Beach Safely," SkinCancer.org	"Golf: You've Got Skin in the Game," SkinCancer.org
URL	www.skincancer.org/healthy-lifestyle/outdoor-activities/how-to-hit-the-beach-the-sun-safe-way	www.skincancer.org/healthy-lifestyle/outdoor-activities/sun-safety-tips-for-sports-enthusiasts
Keywords	sunburn, sun protection, skin cancer prevention, UVA, UVB, sun protective clothing, UV-blocking sunglasses, sun hats	sun protection, sports enthusiasts, sunscreen, sun protective clothing, sun hats, UV-blocking, sunglasses
Description	Before a day on the beach, you need strategies to keep from returning browned or burned by harmful solar ultraviolet rays (UVR). Here's our five-step plan to make sure your next beach trip isn't just fun, but also sun-safe.	How do you play it safe in the sun? The Skin Cancer Foundation asked several athletes who are uniquely qualified to advise readers—they're also dermatologists. As skin experts, all of them take certain general precautions and recommend you do the same: Avoid outdoor athletics between the peak sun hours of 10 AM and 4 PM; wear protective clothing, hats and UV-blocking sunglasses.

search results. That said, search engines are designed to sift out "unnatural links," which are "placed there specifically to make your site look more popular to search engines."[34] Earning **natural links** means nurturing relationships with other sites by offering information that the writers and designers of those sites will find valuable. This brings us back to the core of good writing: useful and original information and good storytelling. Even in writing for robots, we have to think about the humans who will take interest and see value in what we write.

natural links Hyperlinks to a web page that are provided by other people who see value in the content of the page, as opposed to links that are posted for the primary purpose of manipulating search engines.

Academic Writing

Public relations students often struggle with the different types of writing they are being asked to produce, including academic writing. Academic writing refers to any work you need to do specifically to fulfil the requirements of your diploma or degree, such as essays, reports, or a thesis. Even though you are studying public relations, not everything you write will be written using PR writing skills and CP Style.

Your school probably has a specific format in which they want you to write and cite sources, such as APA, MLA, or Chicago. Before starting an assignment, make sure you understand which format you need to use.

Business Writing

While not unique to public relations, emails, memos, proposals, and old-fashioned letters on letterhead are a major part of the writing you will do in public relations. Every time you write something as an employee of your organization, you are managing your own impression as well as that of your employer or client. Business writing often calls for more formal structure and style. As with any of the types of writing mentioned in this chapter, you'll want to observe the norms. Train yourself with practice, peer feedback, and adaptation.

code-switching Alternating between two or more languages or cultural styles.

Being able to **code-switch** from the syntax of text messaging and Instagram to the formalities of an interoffice email or a client status report is a critical career skill. If you have a vacation planned that is going to delay a client project, you probably don't want to LOL about it or include #SorryNotSorry in the email to your boss or client. *And u r smart 2 not get too cute w txt punctuation and emojis!!!* ☺ With careful observation and practice, you may notice other more subtle conventions that apply, depending on the context. A few examples are contractions ("we will" or "we'll"?), salutations ("Hi Tom," or "Dear Dr. Kelleher:"?), formal titles ("UVic" or "University of Victoria"?), and punctuation ("." or "!!"?). When in doubt, CP's *Caps and Spelling* is an excellent fallback, but many organizations also publish their own style guides for consistency in organizational

G-Stock Studio/Shutterstock.com

We present ourselves differently in different contexts.

What are the major contexts for which you write in an average day, and how do you adjust your style for each?

communication. In fact, public relations writers are often tasked with developing these style guides for in-house use.

Just because you are writing formally does not mean you have to sacrifice your voice. As Zinsser reminds us, "It's what stockholders want from their corporation, what customers want from their bank, what the widow wants from the agency handling her social security. There is a deep yearning for human contact and a resentment of bombast." Write for clarity. Be concise. Remember your reader.

Voices from the Field

Dave Bourne
Image courtesy of Dave Bourne

Dave Bourne is an award-winning communications leader who has been helping businesses build key relationships, reputation, and brand loyalty for the past 25 years. By combining his affinity for language, design, and the power of strategic communications, Dave has created engaging projects that successfully transformed audience behaviours and achieved measurable results.

An early advocate of social media, Dave helped build some of Canada's first large online health-care communities. He continues to explore the power of digital engagement and using technology to bridge time and geographic barriers.

Most PR courses in college and university really focus on writing. How important is writing to modern public relations?
The ability to write clearly, effectively, and professionally is the most important tool a PR practitioner can possess, and should be considered a core competency. A great writer can learn how to be a strategic communicator, but it doesn't always work the other way around. On any given day, practitioners need to be able to pivot between different styles of writing for specific tactics. For example, speeches, media releases, and social media posts all require unique voices, even when the subject matter is essentially the same.

Has public relations writing become easier with the rise of social media or harder?
If anything, social media has made writing more challenging. Social posts must be more succinct than other communication methods, yet still have the ability to attract attention and convey key messages amidst the clutter of competing posts. It is also essential to reflect the voice of the company or client's brand, both in posts and in responses to comments, criticisms, or inquiries.

What role does writing play in social media success?
The mistake some students or young practitioners make is assuming that visual social media channels such as YouTube don't require strong writing to be successful. Good video content still requires a carefully crafted script, and writing for video is a special skillset that comes only with practice. The secret to good video is a compelling story and strong narrative—and that requires a carefully written script. For other social channels such as Twitter and Facebook, writers need to make effective use of keywords to allow messages to be easily discovered by the right audiences. And regardless of the social channel, brand voice and attention to grammar and spelling are essential.

Are there any forms of public relations writing that have become obsolete in recent years?
The tools used in public relations have evolved over the years, and PR practitioners have had to adapt their writing as a result. A notable example would be traditional media pitches or releases. The days of issuing a media release and waiting for eager journalists to call are long gone. Newsrooms have fewer resources, and getting

reporters interested in your pitch may now require much more effort. Today we commonly see media releases supplemented with the use of fact sheets, videos, infographics, social posts, and other creative approaches that can help demonstrate the value in your pitch, and can give reporters the content they need to tell your story.

How is new technology helping or hurting the quality of writing you see from new graduates and young practitioners?

There is a tendency for younger practitioners and PR graduates to be much more informal in all aspects of their writing. As digital natives who grew up with texting and social media, the use of acronyms and abbreviations has been normalized, for instance. While that may be acceptable when communicating with friends, it has no place in professional public relations. Grammar, spelling, and well-crafted writing never go out of style.

What is your favourite new convention in public relations writing? What annoys you most?

While it's not entirely new, content marketing has become a significant trend in public relations. The creation of online content that could include blogs, social media posts, and videos that do not explicitly promote a brand has proven to be a successful way to build trust and loyalty with customers or stakeholders. Online users have become mistrustful of overt advertising messages, and instead search for content that answers key questions they may have. Audiences tend to spend more time engaging with this content, making it an important focus for PR initiatives.

A convention that annoys me is influencer marketing, which is essentially the use of online influencers to post positive content about your product or service. The practice sometimes makes it hard for the public to differentiate between legitimate reviews by real customers and paid influencers, which I think can decrease brand trust.

Ethics: Professionalism, Honesty, and Writing for Mutual Understanding

The most effective writers know their readers. Public relations writing, in particular, depends on expertise in fostering mutual understanding. By definition, public relations is building and maintaining mutually beneficial relationships between organizations and publics.

The Canadian Public Relations Society (CPRS) Code of Professional Standards is very clear on honesty in communication:

A member shall practice the highest standards of honesty, accuracy, integrity and truth, and shall not knowingly disseminate false or misleading information. Members shall not make extravagant claims or unfair comparisons, nor assume credit for ideas and words not their own.

This part of the Code of Professional Standards raises some interesting questions. It directs that we don't knowingly disseminate false or misleading information—but what if misleading information is disseminated through unclear or inaccurate writing? Is that an ethical violation?

Words Matter: A Strange Choice for an Agency Name

As one US-based public relations firm learned, reciprocity takes research and planning, and getting one important turn of phrase wrong can spell disaster, especially if you make that turn of phrase the name of your firm.

> *Southern trees bear strange fruit,*
> *Blood on the leaves and blood at the root,*
> *Black bodies swinging in the southern breeze,*
> *Strange fruit hanging from the poplar trees.*[35]

These haunting lyrics from a 1937 poem by Abel Meeropol about racism and lynching in the US South entered the American psyche on the voice of jazz legend Billie Holiday, who recorded the song *Strange Fruit* in 1939. Throughout the century that has followed, *Strange Fruit* has served as a painfully important cultural reminder of one of the nation's ugliest memories. In 2012, two public relations practitioners starting a firm in Austin, Texas, "thought the name would be perfect for a hospitality PR firm that specializes in food and drink."[36]

This Twitter user mocked @StrangeFruitPR for lack of expertise in public relations.

What does expertise have to do with public relations ethics?

It's hard to imagine a scenario in which "strange fruit" would be an appropriate name for anything outside of serious racial dialogue. Of course, not everyone is familiar with the reference and history, and it would be understandable if someone used the term in everyday conversation without awareness of its deeper cultural significance. But if you are naming a new business, that is not everyday conversation. That single word or phrase should be as carefully conceived as any you ever write.

Strange Fruit Public Relations founders claimed they Googled the term when they thought of the name and found the Billie Holiday song, but figured it was not at all related to their firm and that "it wouldn't be top of mind in the public consciousness." For a period of

Sorry, that page doesn't exist!

Thanks for noticing—we're going to fix it up and have things back to normal soon.

@ StrangeFruitPR   Search

Bahasa Indonesia Bahasa Melayu Deutsch English Español Filipino Français Italiano Nederlands
Português Türkçe Русский हिन्दी 日本語 简体中文 繁體中文 한국어

© 2013 Twitter   About   Help   Status

The @StrangeFruitPR account on Twitter was removed, as were the firm's website and Facebook page.

In what ways does removing the accounts help rectify the problem? In what ways is damage from an incident like this irreversible online?

time after they named the firm in 2012 that reasoning appeared to hold up. But then in early December 2014 @StrangeFruitPR became a thing on Twitter.[37] As Twitter user @BlackGirlDanger put it: "You named your hospitality PR firm after a song about black people hanging from trees, @StrangeFruitPR? Really?"

The firm first tried to explain on Twitter: "Our passion is telling the stories of hospitality professionals. We chose our name bc these incredibly talented artists stand out in a crowd." They also tried to ingratiate on Twitter: "We believe in hospitality. Including all. No exclusion. The author & its famous singer hoped for a world where that would be a possibility." Ultimately, however, the company's principals shut down the @StrangeFruitPR Twitter account along with the company's website and Facebook page.

They eventually emailed a longer statement to the *Austin American-Statesman*: "We were wrong. . . . We extend our deepest and sincerest apologies for the offense caused by the name of our public relations firm. . . . We now know we were naïve to think that, and should have known better."[38]

Words matter.

And what about extravagant claims or unfair comparisons? We've all seen advertisements for products using descriptors like "beautiful" and "one-of-a-kind." Do those words belong in public relations writing? If your writing describes a 400-square-foot condo as "spacious," have you done a disservice to your public of potential condo buyers?

Someone assuming credit for ideas and words not their own raises the issue of plagiarism. Plagiarism can be defined as using someone else's words as your own, and it's easily done in this digital age. Chances are your college or university has a published policy on plagiarism including penalties like a grade of zero on an assignment or suspension. But plagiarism isn't just an academic issue—it's something that PR practitioners, who write so often, have to be conscious of on a daily basis.

Consider the unfortunate case of Chris Spence, who was the head of the Toronto District School Board. He was asked to write a personal essay in the *Toronto Star*, and it was later discovered that he had plagiarized certain passages in it. Journalists then began investigating, and discovered that he had also plagiarized parts of his PhD dissertation. Spence was forced to resign and his reputation suffered.

Media ethics scholars Jay Black and Chris Roberts note that almost every major world religion, political culture, and philosophical system includes some version of the ethic of reciprocity, or the **golden rule**.[39] In Christianity, "Do unto others as you would have them do to you." In Confucianism, "Do not do to others what you would not like yourself." In Islam, "Hurt no one so that no one may hurt you." In Judaism, "Love your neighbour as yourself."

golden rule Ethic of reciprocity—treat others as you would like to be treated yourself.

We all know the golden rule, and we learn it very early in life: "How would you feel if someone did that to *you*?" It's an important lesson on the kindergarten playground, and just as important in the business of managing relationships between organizations and their publics. In public relations, you have an ethical responsibility to work hard to understand publics.

In Case You Missed It

While principles of good writing apply across all media, writing for social media requires understanding both technology and culture. Here are a few takeaways from this chapter.

- When presenting yourself in social media, balance being authentic with being professional.
- Excellence in social media requires good storytelling—understanding your organization's stories and why those stories matter to your publics.
- When readers and users have the opportunity to become part of the storytelling process, stories have a better chance of going viral.

- Online news feeds, blog rolls, email preview panes, and search engine results favour good leads.
- Regardless of the medium, you should package background information in an easily accessible format.
- Before jumping into an online conversation, first you need to know how people are talking and what people are talking about.
- Keep your web page headlines short—8–12 words; you need them to stand out among the multitude of similar search results.
- To earn natural links, nurture relationships with other sites by offering information they will find valuable.

ICYMI

Summary

9.1   List five key purposes of good writing in public relations.
Five of the most important reasons to write well in public relations are to build and maintain relationships, to influence and persuade, to strategize (to both identify and achieve goals and objectives), to manage your organization's reputation, and to make your own impression as you build your professional identity.

9.2   Analyze news and feature styles of storytelling.

In straight news writing, writers report on the facts of a story (who, what, where, when, why, how), usually in inverted-pyramid style with the most important information in the lead and the narrower supporting details later in the story. Feature writers dig deeper into some angle of an event, a person's life, an organization, or a place. Feature stories are more likely to be told with a delayed lead.

9.3   Discuss the role of news media, social media, and search engines as intermediaries between public relations writers and publics.

In news media relations, publics find an organization's stories based on what editors and producers decide is newsworthy. In social media, people find organizations online via links and referrals from peers or others in their social networks. With respect to searches, they count on search engines to filter for the content that is most relevant to their queries. The three overlap considerably, but different writing strategies and tactics are necessary for success in each.

9.4   Apply writing tactics for news media, social media, and search engines.

Tactics for news media include news releases, fact sheets, backgrounders, bios, and so on. Examples of each are easy to locate online. One way to think about tactics for social media writing is to consider longer-form blogs and shorter-form microblogs that are common on platforms like Twitter, Instagram, Snapchat, and Tumblr. Writing for SEO requires thinking about keywords, headlines, titles, meta tags, and links, as well as original content that others will find valuable.

9.5   Compare and contrast styles for social media writing and business writing.

Although writing for social media requires understanding many conventions (hashtags, reposts, etc.), writing for social media is generally less formal than business writing. Both benefit from clarity, conciseness, and authenticity.

Discussion Questions

1. How would it help or hurt your job prospects if a potential employer reviewed all your social media profiles online right now?
2. Find a feature story that you think a public relations person had a role in writing. What kinds of strategy, goals, and objectives does it serve?
3. Imagine you are announcing your own graduation and getting hired at your dream job. Write (a) a text to your best friend, (b) a microblog post for your own personal account, (c) the headline for a blog entry on LinkedIn or another job-focused site, and (d) the headline for a news release to send to your hometown newspaper. How are the four similar and different?
4. Do you feel like you are sacrificing authenticity when you change your voice for different contexts (e.g., texting, blogging, business writing)? Why or why not?
5. Will CP style be important to you in your career? Will you write in inverted-pyramid style? Why or why not?
6. What's the worst public relations mistake you've seen written online? (You can search for one if none come to mind.) Was information removed from the web, and did that help? What might the writer have done differently to avoid the mistake?

Further Readings and Online Resources

Writing Tips for Young PR Pros
www.prdaily.com/8-writing-tips-for-young-pr-pros/
This blogpost by Michelle Garrett contains some practical tips for day-to-day PR writing.

The Ultimate Guide to Storytelling
blog.hubspot.com/marketing/storytelling
> Storytelling is one of the top trends in public relations today. This five-part blog outlines the hows and whys of storytelling in business.

Writing a PR Speech
reputationtoday.in/features/writing-a-pr-speech/
> Public relations practitioners are expected to be able to write in a variety of forms, and speechwriting is just one of them. This blogpost provides some handy tips for speechwriting in a public relations context.

Peer-Reviewed Academic Journal Article
Kent, M.L. (2015). The power of storytelling in public relations: Introducing the 20 master plots. *Public Relations Review*, 41(4), 480–9. doi:10.1016/j.pubrev.2015.05.011
> This article outlines 20 master plots, including quest, rescue, and revenge, and explores how they might be used in public relations writing.

Key Terms

Anchor text   236
Backgrounder   230
Backlinks   236
Blog   232
Canadian Press (CP) style   226
Clickbait   217
Code-switching   237
Dateline   226
Delayed lead   223

Direct lead   224
Fact sheet   227
Feature story   221
Golden rule   242
Human interest   222
Impression management   219
Inverted pyramid   225
Listicle   217
Media kits   230

Meta tags   236
Microblog   233
Morgue   230
Natural links   237
News release   226
Reputation management   219
Social media release   226
Transmedia storytelling   224
Video news release   226

10

Multimedia and Mobile

Can Snapchat work for more than selfies? See which major sports league was early to the game in giving it a shot.

Key learning outcomes

10.1 Identify sources for multimedia elements such as writing, images, audio, and video.

10.2 Analyze how different components of multimedia are integrated for effective communication in public relations.

10.3 Assess the strategic value of mobile tactics.

10.4 Discuss how publics' uses and gratifications of mobile media may help drive public relations strategy.

10.5 Apply privacy as an ethical value to consider in handling data gleaned from mobile media.

Even in the days when most news was printed on paper, when tweets were sung by birds, when a snap meant something broke, and when chatting was something you did with the person in front of you, your average human couldn't pay attention to all of these stimuli at the same time. The Internet hasn't helped matters.

In the digital age, it may appear that people focus intently as they stare into their smartphones, but, actually, as they swipe and tap on their devices, they must rapidly make decisions about what to pay attention to and what to ignore. They must also decide whom to communicate with and whom to ignore. This is **selective attention**, and every time you scroll and stop on a news feed, click on a link in a tweet, or view a snap on Snapchat, you select what to pay attention to in the virtual world.

So how do public relations professionals get and keep people's attention in this environment? How do we maintain relationships and engage in interactive communication without being annoying? As discussed in Chapter 9, telling a compelling story is one way. Elegant use of technology is another. But knowing what will make a story compelling and what will make technology elegant from the user's perspective hinges on understanding publics and their use of media.

No doubt you already have experience creating and communicating with mobile and **multimedia**. You've more than likely written captions for photos on Instagram, dropped a music track to a video clip or slideshow, or showed off your creativity with friends using Snapchat. Experience using social media creatively is certainly a plus for anyone entering the

selective attention
Process of filtering information by focusing on some stimuli in the environment while ignoring others.

multimedia The combination of any two or more forms of media such as text, graphics, moving images, and sounds.

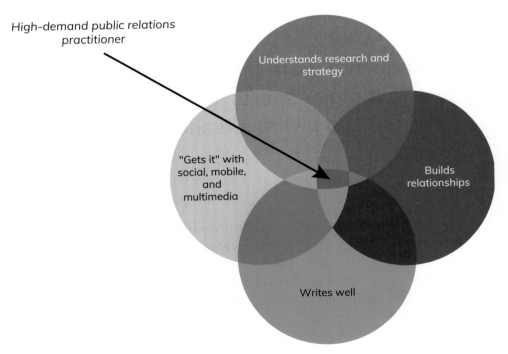

FIGURE 10.1 Young public relations practitioners may be at an advantage in experience with new media, but that's only part of the recipe for career success.

How can you improve in other areas?

field, but to manage effective public relations, that first-hand experience must be combined with professional knowledge.

As illustrated in Figure 10.1, some of the most in-demand communicators in public relations are those who understand current and emerging communication technologies but who also have a firm grasp on research, strategy, and relationship-building. Chapter 9 covered writing, based on the idea that the best writers understand both their strategy and their readers. Whereas excellent writers demonstrate a command of words and sentences, excellent multimedia and mobile communicators master the various elements of sight, sound, and motion in digital media.

Multimedia

The ability to combine media elements in meaningful ways is one of the most powerful aspects that drove early growth of the Internet and the web.[1] Today, in societies in which mobile communication technology is widely available, multimedia is changing the very nature of interpersonal communication as well as communication between organizations and publics.

Technically speaking, multimedia is simply the combination of any two or more forms of media such as text, graphics, moving images, and sounds. A slideshow with music is multimedia because it combines images and sound. A web page with video clips is also multimedia if it combines text and video. Regular old television is multimedia because it combines audio and video. However, advances in computer technology—particularly mobile devices—have made the production and playback of all sorts of multimedia far more accessible and widespread. Anyone with a smartphone can capture audio, photos, and video just about anywhere that their devices will function. And mobile allows us to consume multimedia just about anywhere. The key to creating good multimedia is understanding text, graphics, audio, and video and how they work together to enhance users' experiences.

> To create good multimedia, you must first understand how text, graphics, audio, and video work together to enhance users' experiences.

Text

Text may be the last thing we think of when we think of multimedia, but writing is a media element just like images, audio, or video. We write words in emails, tweets, posts, and pitches to introduce media content. We write words in infographics. We write words to serve as captions and subtitles for images and videos. We write copy for advertising and PSAs, bullet points in presentation decks, and reviews and descriptions of music and movies. Even our long-form writing is more likely to integrate media, as more materials are digitally produced, delivered, and consumed.

Texting, Tweeting, and Pitching

Robert Wynne, principal of a public relations firm in Manhattan Beach, California, and regular *Forbes* contributor on public relations topics, explained the importance of words and text in multimedia:

> You are trying to convince the media, the public, your employees, your vendors, shareholders, someone, to do something—change their opinion, reinforce their attitudes, write about or film your client, vote for your issue or candidate, or purchase

your service or product. Sometimes this is done in person, sometimes over the phone. But the majority of communications are done via words, whether in email, Twitter or online media. It all starts on the page or screen. With words.[2]

Words may be used to draw attention, as when a public relations person tweets to invite people to interact with multimedia. The art of the pitch—persuading someone to read, listen, or watch further—is still very much a word-based endeavour. Sometimes you write words to explain other elements of multimedia. Other times words are foremost, and sounds, images, video, and animation play the supporting role for the text. Social media news releases, for example, are built mainly around text with the accompanying multimedia elements to help tell the story. *Who, what, where, when,* and *why* are still at the heart of news releases, even if abbreviated to a brief lead sentence or a bulleted list of key points.

Infographics

infographics Visual presentations designed to communicate information simply and quickly with combinations of images, charts, tables, or text.

Infographics, which include a mix of words, images, and numbers, can further the central message of a press release or other public relations tactic and highlight components that bring text to life.[3] One of the main benefits of infographics is they enable writers to deliver critical information with concise text, while adding colour, context, and detail with other media. A downside to infographics is that they often don't display well on mobile devices. Although infographics are a relatively static form of multimedia, **user-centred design**—design deliberately focused on the end-user experience—is a key concern.

Captions and Subtitles

user-centred design Process by which media, messages, and other products and services are developed with continuous and deliberate attention to how end users will experience them.

When you post a picture on social media, the words you use to describe that image enhance the context and the meaning. As *The Wall Street Journal*'s Elizabeth Holmes put it, "A picture may be worth a thousand words, but on social media you need a caption."[4] Part of the beauty of mobile photo-sharing apps like Facebook and Instagram is that they allow users to tag people and indicate locations without using the caption for that basic descriptive purpose. However, this has "put creative pressure on photo sharers" to tell stories and add meaning, says Holmes. Your goal for captioned pictures should be for the image and the writing to complement each other. Your viewers will probably look first at the image. (Think of how you scan images as you scroll through your social media feeds.) If the image gets their attention, they will look to the caption for more information. If the caption is written well, they will look again at the image, perhaps from a different perspective with new focus on a particular part of the image or a new understanding of what they see. A good caption encourages this loop of engagement.

autoplay Feature that enables automatic playing of videos or other multimedia elements on users' devices.

NSFW Shorthand for "not safe/suitable for work."

In addition to captions presented below or alongside images and video, the growth of digital and social media has led to an increase in captions placed on top of images and video. Snapchat and other apps make it easier than ever to add words and drawings to images. Closed captioning (text that presents spoken words on screen during a video) has always been recommended for accessibility for hearing-impaired viewers. However, as more people view video on mobile devices in noisy or public places, subtitles become crucial for helping viewers understand what they're watching. Captioning is also useful for **autoplay** videos. Have you ever experienced that moment of panic when a **NSFW** (not safe/suitable for work)

SOCIAL MEDIA PRESS RELEASE
TEMPLATE, VERSION 1.0

CONTACT INFORMATION:

Client contact	**Spokesperson**	**Agency contact**
Phone #/skype	Phone #/skype	Phone #/skype
Email	Email	Email
IM address	IM address	IM address
Web site	Blog/relevant post	Web site

NEWS RELEASE HEADLINE
Subhead

CORE NEWS FACTS
- Bullet-points preferable

LINK & RSS FEED TO PURPOSE-BUILT DEL.ICIO.US PAGE
The purpose-built del.icio.us page offers hyperlinks (*and PR annotation in "notes" fields*) to relevant historical, trend, market, product & competitive content sources, providing context as-needed, and, on-going updates.

PHOTO e.g., product picture, exec headshot, etc.	**MP3 FILE OR PODCAST LINK** e.g., sound bytes by various stakeholders	**GRAPHIC** e.g., product schematic; market size graphs; logos	**VIDEO** e.g., brief product demo by in-house expert

MORE MULTIMEDIA AVAILABLE BY REQUEST
e.g., "download white paper"

PRE-APPROVED QUOTES FROM CORPORATE EXECUTIVES, ANALYSTS, CUSTOMERS AND/OR PARTNERS
Recommendation: no more than 2 quotes per contact. The PR agency should have additional quotes at-the-ready, "upon request," for journalists who desire exclusive content. This provides opportunity for Agency to add further value to interested media.

LINKS TO RELEVANT COVERAGE TO-DATE (OPTIONAL)
This empowers journalist to "take a different angle," etc.
These links would also be cross-posted to the custom del.icio.us site.

BOILERPLATE STATEMENTS

RSS FEED TO CLIENT'S NEWS RELEASES

"ADD TO DEL.ICIO.US"
Allows readers to use the release as a stand-alone portal to this news

TECHNORATI TAGS/"DIGG THIS"

SHIFT Communications's model for a social media news release offers a different template from the traditional release featured in Chapter 9.

What are the advantages and disadvantages of this social media news release compared to traditional releases?

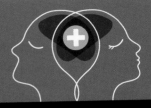

MENTAL HEALTH-RELATED DISABILITIES IN CANADA, 2017

The Canadian Survey on Disability covers Canadians **aged 15 years and over** who experience limitations in their everyday activities because of a **long-term condition** or **health-related problem.**

OVER 2 MILLION

Canadians aged 15 years and over have a mental health-related disability. This represents **7%** of Canadian adults and youth.

Four of the most frequently reported mental health-related conditions are:

ANXIETY | DEPRESSION | BIPOLAR DISORDER SEVERE STRESS DISORDERS

4 IN 5

Canadians with a mental health-related disability **also** have **at least one other type of disability.**

63 PERCENT

of those with a mental health-related disability also have a pain-related disability.

Among youth, **women** are twice as likely as **men** to have a mental health-related disability.

Youth aged 15 to 24 years

11%

WOMEN   **MEN**   5%

Nearly half of employed Canadians with a mental health-related disability feel that one or more of their conditions makes it difficult to change or advance in their job.

Of these, **1 in 4** believe it is due to **discrimination** or **stigma.**

OVER 1 MILLION

Canadians with a mental health-related disability say they require counselling services from a **psychologist, psychiatrist, psychotherapist,** or **social worker.**

519,400 received some counselling but require more

286,400 required counselling but did not receive any

Note: Persons with a mental health-related disability are identified as those who experience limitations in their daily activities because of difficulties with an emotional, psychological or mental health condition (e.g., anxiety, depression, bipolar disorder, substance abuse, anorexia, etc.).

Source: Canadian Survey on Disability, 2017.

Catalogue Number: 11-627-M
ISBN Number: 978-0-660-29139-0

Statistics Canada, Catalogue Number 11-627-M

Statistics Canada   Statistique Canada

www.statcan.gc.ca

Canadā

Since 2014, Statistics Canada has made extensive use of infographics to help explain study results. Infographics support key messages by bringing text and data to life.

What elements make an infographic effective?

web ad or social video starts playing automatically on your device in an office, library, or classroom? Mute buttons get a lot of use these days, and descriptive text and subtitles become that much more important.

Images

"Uh oh, we're being challenged again," wrote Allen Mireles in an article for Cision. Cision is a public relations and social media software company. Mireles is described on the website as a wordsmith, and her words convey the anxiety that some writers may feel as they face the growth of image-based social media. "That's right, PR is being nudged away from the familiar comfort of text-based communications to more visual forms of communications, especially in our digital campaigns."[5] Photo-based platforms of social media have been built, adopted, and grown into central channels for many public relations efforts. Snapchat, Instagram, and Pinterest wouldn't exist without images. And the vast majority of the images shared via these platforms wouldn't exist without mobile devices.

This isn't to say that working with images and photos is something new to public relations. In their 1984 text *Managing Public Relations*, Grunig and Hunt noted that photos and illustrations "represent a basic form of visual communication used in each of the four public relations models."[6] (The four models are defined in Chapter 2.) What's changed significantly is the technology.

When using photographs or images as public relations tactics, you have three options for obtaining them:

1. Create them yourself.
2. Hire a professional to take photos or create original images.
3. Buy images or obtain permission to use others' material.

Hind Bouqartacha/Getty Images

This image was posted on the Dove Instagram account. What meaning does the photo convey to you? Now consider that the image was posted with the caption "'Beauty standards don't define me.' Teacher and aspiring model Meryem shows us that unique is beautiful, and the world is a better place when that's recognized."

What public relations purpose does the combination of picture and words serve?

Creating Your Own Images

Advances in digital camera technology have increased the accessibility of do-it-yourself photography. Your average smartphone camera can generate image quality that used to be reserved for only those willing to invest heavily in expensive digital cameras. But just because the phone in your pocket *can* capture amazing images at very high resolution doesn't mean your photos are automatically high enough quality for your organization's communication needs. Factors to consider in taking photos include lighting, composition, angles, background, and props. Yes, social media have widened our latitude for what we accept and expect in shared imagery. Hastily snapped selfies, for example, have found a place in our digital culture. But just as expectations for writing styles vary from one context to another,

The NBA Gets in the Snapchat Game Early

With new ways of posting and sharing photos come new ways of telling stories. The NBA was an early adopter of Snapchat. For example, to help tell the story of Kevin Durant's 2014 Most Valuable Player award sponsored by Kia Motors Corp., the NBA made use of the Snapchat's "Stories" feature. With a series of three photos posted to the app, they encouraged fans on Snapchat to also watch on NBATV. com and NBA.com as Durant accepted the award.[7] The first snap showed the lectern where the MVP would soon stand, with the words "4:30 pm/et on NBATV & NBA.com. KD!" running across the image. The second snap showed Durant sitting for an interview with NBA legend Grant Hill and the words "The 2014 #KiaMVP & Grant Hill!" The final snap featured Durant at the lectern with the trophy on a pedestal in the foreground, and "Kevin Durant, the 2013–14 #KiaMVP!"

The NBA benefitted from being one of the first organizations to use Snapchat.

What new apps are novel right now as ways for organizations to communicate with publics?

It's not unusual for early-adopter organizations to get lots of attention when they use emerging platforms like Snapchat was in 2014, but that success can be fleeting if the attention doesn't lead to longer-term relationships. Amid the fast growth of Snapchat's popularity in 2014, one research firm reported that 77 per cent of college students were using the app at least once a day. The researchers also asked college students what they were using it for, and "creativity" was the most common answer, chosen by 37 per cent of the respondents. More important for public relations practitioners, though, were the findings in the same study that 73 per cent of college students said they would open a snap from a brand they knew, and almost half said they would open a snap from an organization even if they'd never heard of the brand.[8]

At the same time that the then-new Snapchat was wooing brands, the effectiveness of Instagram and Pinterest advertising was dropping fast, as demonstrated by a 2015 Forrester Research study. Keeping up with the rapidly changing social media landscape continues to be a challenge for public relations professionals. Assuming one's own social media usage is reflective of the broader public is a dangerous assumption, as is assuming that American statistics apply directly to Canada or other countries. Researching and understanding the media consumption habits of your publics is an important part of the communications planning process. Timing, context, and content are all important factors in using mobile and multimedia to engage publics, and it takes careful strategy to convert short-term attention to long-term relationships.

it is important to carefully consider the appropriate image style depending on the purpose and public.

Each social media platform has its own written and unwritten rules and unique cultural and technological dimensions. Some of the main differences are technical, including how long the images last, who gets to see them, what type of editing is available, and so on. For example, images sent via Snapchat will last from just 1 to 10 seconds before they disappear, while images uploaded to Instagram will last until you delete them. Other big differences are social and cultural. Just look at the different profile pictures people post on Twitter, Facebook, and LinkedIn. In discussing LinkedIn profile pictures, Entrepreneur.com's Kim Lachance Sandrow writes, "Here's a friendly reminder, particularly for the 39 million students and recent college grads lurking on LinkedIn: It's not for Man Crush Monday, not for swiping right and not for stalking your 8th grade crush."[9]

public domain Works of intellectual property for which the copyright has expired, the creator has forfeited rights, or copyright laws do not apply, making the works freely available for public use.

Hiring Photographers and Using Others' Images

For LinkedIn, you may want to consider hiring a professional photographer or at least working with a friend or colleague capable of taking a photo that you feel is high enough quality to represent you on your profile as you wish to be seen by potential employers. The same logic applies to photos that will represent your organization to potential publics.

Very often, the best image for your public relations needs already exists, but just because that .JPG, .PNG, or .GIF file is only a right-click away doesn't mean you can grab it and paste it into your blog post or newsletter without permission. Chapter 11 will discuss common copyright issues in more detail, but the good news is that there is an abundance of great imagery available online that can be used legally and with good karma, if you pay attention to copyright and permission requirements.

Public domain images are "free" images, including images produced by government entities, those that are so old that the copyrights have

D. Anschutz/Getty Images

This stock photo, "Girl playing soccer with grandfather in wheelchair as goal keeper," made BuzzFeed's list of "50 Completely Unexplainable Stock Photos No One Will Ever Use."

When might it be appropriate to use stock images in public relations?

expired (e.g., the *Mona Lisa*), or those that the original creators have explicitly released for public use. Be careful, however, in making unchecked assumptions. Use of government logos or seals such as the ubiquitous black and red Canada wordmark used by the federal government, a photograph or modified version of the *Mona Lisa* as it is presented in a copyrighted book, or certain types of Creative Commons licenses are restricted.

Many images are available for sharing as long as you obtain permission, properly attribute the image to its source, and, in some cases, link back to that source. Even Getty Images, one of the world's largest for-profit stock image providers, permits free use of its images online, as long as the images are embedded with the proper HTML code:

> Embedded images will include photographer attribution and, when clicked, will link back to www.gettyimages.com where the image can be licensed for commercial use. This will provide people with a simple and legal way to utilize content that respects creators' rights, including the opportunity to generate licensing revenue.[10]

Audio

Audio is often underappreciated in the world of social media. When you think of the most sharable and influential content online, you probably remember certain images you have seen, stories you have read, or videos you have watched. Of course, you can find and listen to your favourite music online, but audio's role in the business of strategic communication and storytelling in public relations is often a rather quiet one.

Two big factors working against audio in social media are simply structural. First, audio lends itself well to background tasking but not so much to sharing. You can listen to the radio or an e-book or podcast while you walk or drive because you don't have to look at anything. You can just hit the play button and get on with whatever you are doing. But that advantage becomes a disadvantage when it comes to sharing. "When you're driving a car, you're not going to share anything," said public radio show host and podcaster Jesse Thorn, when interviewed by Stan Alcorn for an article asking the question, "Why doesn't audio go viral?"[11] The second issue Alcorn identified was skimming—or rather the fact that audio can't be skimmed like text and video. Your news feed or search results are made up of chunks of text, still images, and videos. The Internet hasn't offered the equivalent sampling of audio. But while audio isn't as sharable as its counterparts in multimedia (text, photos, and video), it's still critical in public relations.

Radio Is Still Huge

Are you one of those people who doesn't listen to the radio anymore? Do you stream all your music? In Canada, you are in the minority. A recent government report suggests that we still listen to an average of 15 hours of radio a week. Traditional radio is still a force to be reckoned with in Canada, with 88 per cent of Canadians regularly listening to AM or FM radio content.[12]

According to the study of 400 English-speaking Canadians, 80 per cent of radio listeners still listen to their content through an AM/FM receiver such as a home or car radio; whereas online radio streaming penetration in Canada has risen to 22 per cent.

More than half of Canadians (56 per cent) listen through a receiver only (no online or satellite listening). Multiplatform listeners tended to be heavier consumers than receiver-only

Creative Commons Non-profit organization that encourages fair and legal sharing of content by helping content creators make their work available with clear terms and conditions. https://creativecommons.org/licenses/by-nc-sa/2.5/ca/

stock images Images that are professionally produced for selling or sharing, commonly available in searchable databases.

listeners—the receiver-only group listened to an average of 10.5 hours per week; while combined receiver and online listeners listened to 16.4 hours per week; and receiver, online, and satellite listeners reported 9 hours of consumption per week.[13]

Radio must still be considered as an option in any public relations campaign. Pitching your client as a potential radio interview candidate is a similar process to that used to try to get media coverage in print or on television. Start by identifying radio shows that book guest experts like your client, and do research to identify the show's producers or bookers. Then, prepare a targeted pitch offering your client as an informative expert—not just someone pushing a product or service.

Another option for gaining radio coverage, especially if you're a non-profit organization—is a radio PSA—public service announcement. Radio stations typically offer free airtime to organizations that have messages that are in the public interest. These are aired at the discretion of the station, so they are not a sure thing but may provide a good opportunity for exposure for minimal cost. The Huntington Society of Canada has a whole page on their website dedicated to PSA samples, including ones crafted for radio.

Can Audio Go Viral?

When we talk about something going "viral" it is most often video we're talking about. While not as common, audio can also go viral, usually in the form of a podcast.

One example is the podcast *Serial*, which debuted on iTunes in October 2014. The first 12 episodes featured host Sarah Koenig exploring the nonfiction story of the 1999 Baltimore murder case of 18-year-old victim Hae Min Lee and the trials of her possibly wrongfully convicted boyfriend Adnan Syed. By February 2015 the podcast had been downloaded 68 million times, and Syed had been granted an appeal. Koenig's powerful storytelling and investigation cast doubt on the original case, and many speculated that the podcast and the publicity it generated were at least part of the reason an appeal was granted after *Serial* put this case so prominently in the public eye (or should we say public ear?).[14] Widely described as "addictive," the weekly instalments of the podcast weren't exactly public relations tactics, but they did illustrate the power of audio as a medium for storytelling.

Serial is widely credited with increasing the popularity of podcasts. A 2017 survey revealed an estimated 10 million Canadians (34 per cent of the country's adult population) have listened to podcasts in the past year. More importantly, podcast listeners appear to be more educated and affluent than those that watch/listen to other forms of information and entertainment, making podcast listeners an important demographic for many organizations.

Audio in the Multimedia Mix

Professional producers of multimedia have always had an appreciation for the power of audio when combining multimedia elements. You can really get a sense of the importance of sound when you see **mashups** of video clips with incongruent audio, often with really funny results. Many who work in public relations think of the recording, mixing, and reproduction of sound as something best left to the professionals. That may be changing, however, with more user-friendly multimedia software. While you still want to hire skilled producers

mashups Media presentations created by combining two or more pre-existing elements from different sources.

If you add a decent external microphone to your smartphone or camera, you can noticeably improve the quality of audio that you capture.

for higher stakes, bigger-budget productions that need to command a tone of professionalism, much of an organization's more conversational multimedia can be produced in-house. Adding a decent external microphone to your smartphone or camera can noticeably improve the quality of audio you capture. Using basic consumer-grade software to add audio to your visual media can also enhance effectiveness. Have you ever noticed how much greater impact a slideshow has when the right music or narration is added? In the same way that a picture may convey very different meaning depending on the words used to describe it, the meaning of a video clip or slideshow can vary dramatically depending on the audio. With a little practice and training, and some affordable hardware and software, you can up your multimedia game.

Video

If audio is an underappreciated member in the ensemble of multimedia production, video is still the star of the show. As Cutlip and Center pointed out in their classic text *Effective Public Relations,* television was "*the* communications phenomenon of the 20th century," unrivaled in its capacity as a publicity medium to "provide a window on the world,"[15] and recent data show that TV is still a top source for people to get their news. The 24/7 nature of cable news creates opportunities for public relations professionals to pitch their clients as possible guests, especially if they have a product or message that ties into a current news story. While it's fair to say the Internet has supplanted TV as *the* communications "phenom" so far in the twenty-first century, excitement about video keeps cranking.

original digital video Video that is recorded, produced, and uploaded digitally for sharing online, as opposed to video originally produced for other channels like television or theatres.

The growth of services like YouTube and Vimeo that made it easy for users to convert, upload, share, and watch video online was obviously part of the movement. By the end of the first decade of the millennium, billions of video streams were being watched by hundreds of millions of unique users each month, and the largest video service by far was YouTube. In 2017, the service claimed more than 1.57 billion users with an average viewing session of 40 minutes—a 50 per cent increase year over year.[16]

In the same way that the culture of consumer-generated media has made amateur photography acceptable in many contexts of organization–public communication, publics are often more accepting of video produced and uploaded by everyday smartphone users, if the content is meaningful or entertaining enough. In 2018, Snapchat reported that more 400 million Snapchat stories are created each day— more than the number of users, which is just over 300 million.[17] An Interactive Advertising Bureau (IAB) survey of more than 1,000 US viewers in 2014 found that original digital video was perceived as more mobile, edgy, and unique than TV. In public relations, publics may prefer non-professionally produced video, if it means that they are getting real perspectives from real people within an organization and if the video is a part of a larger strategy of two-way communication. You may also create a video strategy where you, the public relations practitioner, appears in the videos as the company spokesperson. These can then be used in a variety of ways—posted on your website, tweeted to followers, or broadcast live, on location.

Publics may prefer non-professionally produced video, if it means they get to hear from real people and the video is part of a larger strategy of two-way communication.

If you choose a professional producer, he or she can create powerful messages using techniques of filmmaking and video production that cannot be matched by your average public relations person who pulls out a smartphone and shoots a quick clip for upload to Instagram, Facebook, Pinterest, or LinkedIn. As with still images and photos, you have the option of shooting and editing videos yourself or hiring a professional to produce them.

Producing Videos Yourself

If you have a quality video camera and multimedia editing software and know how to use them, that will be your best bet for making videos. But it also means you probably don't need video tips from an introductory public relations text. For the rest of us, here's some basic advice from a few experts.[18]

- **THE BEST CAMERA IS** the one you have with you. When asking a tech-savvy neighbour about the benefits of his iPhone 3GS in 2009, he said the best new feature was the video camera—not because of the superiority of the video quality but because it meant always having access to the camera for impromptu recording and capturing unexpected events. "Whether shooting video of my kids taking their very first bike rides or recording quick interviews with guest speakers for students in other classes, having quick access to a camera was crucial."

  A public relations person may shoot quick video to respond to questions from online publics, to demonstrate a product or process—sometimes called an **explainer video**, to showcase employees doing their jobs behind the scenes, or to interact with communities at music festivals.

- **CONSIDER UPGRADING YOUR EQUIPMENT.** Even if your main camera is on your mobile device, you can upgrade the quality of your video considerably with accessories. As mentioned previously, an external microphone will allow you to capture clearer audio and eliminate background noise, which is especially important when shooting videos outside or at crowded events. Investing in a tripod designed to work with your device will eliminate shaking. And mounting a light on your phone or using a portable light will help if you think you'll be shooting in a darker location or room with bad lighting.

- **PUT SOME THOUGHT INTO COMPOSITION.** Try to find interesting backgrounds that aren't too distracting. Putting an interviewee in front of a blank white wall will only provide viewers with a dreadfully boring talking head. Also avoid shooting video of people in front of windows—you want to make sure natural light works in your favour and not to obscure your interviewee into a mere silhouette. "Unimaginative visuals are the hallmark of bad corporate video," wrote Martin Jones, CEO of March Communications.[19] Consider interviewing people outside, or inside with an interesting background that will give viewers a sense of place without distracting them from the subject. Test a few different angles, if necessary, until you find one that works well for your purpose, which—by the way—should be

Explainer video Video produced to demonstrate a product, service, or process.

Photo by Brooks Kraft LLC/Corbis via Getty Images

US representative Jesse Jackson Jr used his phone to shoot video of a demonstration in front of the US Capitol.

Under what circumstances do you think it is more effective for high-profile communicators to use mobile video in lieu of professionally produced video?

Mobile video services like Periscope and Facebook Live enable you to live-stream events and thereby open your organization to more publics. Leading platforms including Facebook, Twitter, and YouTube are making it easier and easier to live-stream from your computer or mobile device.

consistent with your broader communication strategy. Are you using the video to contribute to a conversation, make transparent some inner working of your organization, or invite new members to join your organization? You can imagine how the video set for a fundraising message from your CEO would be composed differently from, say, a demonstration of how to install a replacement part that your company shipped to consumers following a safety recall.

- **TRY TO MATCH CONTENT TO CHANNELS.** In sharing videos on Pinterest, for example, content strategist Jamie Wallace suggests pinning video infographics, humour videos, and how-tos. "People share content (including pins) for the same reasons they decorate the inside of their school lockers, hang art in their homes, and decorate their offices with postcards, funny sayings, and family photos. These things provide a visual representation of the person, her ideas, and her ideals," says Wallace.[20] Matching video content to channels also means considering technical aspects, which continue to evolve and change. Originally, Snapchat was designed to allow only 10-second videos but users soon discovered a hack to extend that time. Even the age-old advice to always shoot video in a **landscape orientation** for best viewing on TV and computer screens for YouTube and Vimeo has changed. It used to be that **vertical video** (video framed in a tall, portrait orientation) was seen "as the mark of an amateur," according to *The New York Times'* Farhad Manjoo.[21] But that all began to change with vertically oriented smartphones, tablets, and the video apps that became popular with them. Differences in opinion about the aesthetics will probably never be resolved. However, in 2015, Snapchat reported that vertical performed "up to nine times better" than landscape on many of its engagement metrics. In that same time frame, YouTube tweaked its mobile apps to allow for vertical and Facebook began allowing full-screen playback of vertical videos.[22]

- **THINK BEYOND BASIC RECORDED VIDEO.** If you're feeling creative and are comfortable with the software, you might consider creating animations or video infographics. Another option is live-streaming video, which allows online viewers to watch whatever you point your camera at live. Live video streaming has been available since the turn of the millennium, but its everyday usability has improved as bandwidth and connection speeds have increased. Since the mid-2000s, services like Ustream, Twitch, Bambuser, and Google Hangouts made it possible for organizations to offer live video feeds to online users, but the rise of mobile-friendly services like Twitter's Periscope and Facebook Live led to renewed interest among public relations practitioners in adding live-streaming to their quiver of online communication tactics.[23] So what are some uses for apps like Periscope and Facebook Live in public relations? Public relations practitioners use live-streaming services to host press conferences, open corporate events to outside audiences, launch new products, and engage in live public forums. These direct-to-public channels for communication do afford organizations more control,

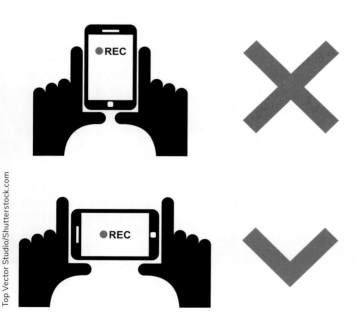

There are many online "PSAs" against shooting vertical video.

When might this advice not hold?

but in comparison to traditional coverage by third-party media, reach and credibility may be issues, as discussed in Chapter 7.

Hiring Experts

Depending on your budget and needs, you may choose to farm out video production work. With a quick keyword search, you can find companies that specialize in explainer videos, PSAs, television commercials, and the integration of video into digital multimedia presentations. **Freelancers** for video production can be paid by the hour or hired by the project. Services include scripting, basic video production, 2D and 3D animations, talent, video editing, and **post production**.[24] On sites like upwork.com you can find video contractors who have produced videos for as little as $11 all the way up to international companies that handle multimillion-dollar projects. The world's largest media companies are now investing in the production of videos for social media. Disney's Maker Studios, for example, describes itself as follows:

Dumb Ways to Die is considered the world's most shared public service announcement (PSA). The campaign was launched by Metro Trains Melbourne to promote rail safety in 2012 and the video went viral through YouTube. The Dumb Ways to Die channel on YouTube amassed over 200 million views, and has spawned several popular game apps.

What factors do you think contributed to this video's popularity?

> Entertainment is changing. Millennials are living a mobile, social, on-demand life. Maker is the global leader in short-form video reaching this diverse, tech-savvy group. With 55,000 independent creator partners from more than 100 countries, Maker is home to top digital stars, channels, and content. With growing scale driven by a robust technology platform and direct-to-consumer distribution, Maker is dedicated to developing talent, creating premium programming, and building lasting brands with engaged audiences.[25]

Maker is an interesting case of convergence in every sense of the word as discussed in Chapter 3: technological, cultural, economic, and professional. The very same media (e.g., YouTube) that seemed to challenge mass media (e.g., TV) based on a model of user-generated content and social sharing are now integral parts of the business plans of the most mainstream of mainstream media companies like Disney. Video was the essence of TV as *the* communication development of the twentieth century. Now it's in everyone's hands.

Mobile

In delivering a keynote address to an annual online video conference in 2015, YouTube CFO Susan Wojcicki revealed the media giant's three top priorities: "mobile, mobile, and mobile." There was perhaps no greater illustration of the importance of mobile to multimedia (and vice versa) than the revelation that the company that revolutionized the process of both

landscape orientation
Images or video framed so that width is greater than height, like traditional movies

vertical video Video framed in an orientation in which height is greater than width

freelancers People who work on a project-by-project basis instead of working more permanently for a single employer (e.g., freelance writers, photographers, video producers).

post production Process in media production that occurs after raw audio, video, or images have been recorded—includes editing, combining media elements, transitions, and special effects.

In planning for social media, consider how you will reach followers, fans, and subscribers but also how they will reach back and how they will share content with one another.

uploading and downloading video via social media changed its whole operating model to accommodate mobile trends. Wojcicki noted that a majority of video views were coming from mobile devices and that YouTube's revenue from mobile was growing at a rate of 100 per cent from year to year.

While the business models of online media companies have shifted to accommodate the profound increase in communication via mobile devices, the very grammar of online communication has changed too. Public relations practitioners have had to learn new techniques for composing images, producing live video, delivering audio, and writing short messages.

Will you use Periscope or Facebook Live? How long should your podcast segments last, and how many should you include in a series? How can you condense that 280-character tweet down to an even shorter Snapchat caption? When should you apply that Instagram filter? Depending on your experience with social and mobile media, you may be a step ahead of some of your more senior public relations colleagues when it comes to answering these types of questions.

However, there is so much more to effective public relations than personal experience with emerging platforms and technology. Multimedia and mobile are tactics. In the bigger picture of effective public relations, tactics are driven by strategy, and strategy is designed to achieve goals and objectives that are developed from research (see Chapters 5 and 6). Without proper management and strategy, pumping out explainer videos, live streams, and mobile app notifications is no more indicative of effectiveness or relationship quality than faxing press releases or placing flyers on car windshields. Implementing mobile tactics means weighing their advantages in light of strategy. Key dimensions to consider include the extent to which mobile tactics are social, personal, local, and—to some degree—snackable.

Social

The combination of mobile and social media use hit a tipping point in Canada in 2014 when the average number of minutes that Canadians spent with digital media on mobile devices was equal to the amount of time they spent on desktop computers. Not surprisingly, the 25–34 demographic was spending the most time online, averaging around 110 hours a month across various devices, more than half of it on a mobile device.

According to a 2017 a study done by Leger Research, Facebook remains the most popular social media, while Instagram, Snapchat, and YouTube continue to grow. With this in mind, you can see how it would be difficult to develop a mobile strategy that doesn't build on social uses of the technology.

Communication via social media means considering not just how you will reach your organization's followers, fans, and subscribers but also how they will reach back to your organization and how they will share multimedia content with one another. Think about how your organization can become part of the social conversation. What kinds of mobile content will people respond to and share, and why? How will your organization respond to that shared content? Social means interactive, and interactive means that individuals in your organization have the opportunity to communicate with

The Starbucks app recalls customers' previous orders in recommending future orders.

How might this type of personalization be used to support public relations goals besides sales and marketing?

individuals in your publics. That back and forth is very likely to happen via mobile media, so make sure any tactics you plan make sense for the devices on which the communication will happen.

Personal

Mobile media also allow for a tremendous amount of personalization. Marketers were among the first to mine user data to figure out new ways to personalize communication as they sought to sharpen their sales pitches. They learned to use individual data that are available from apps, registrations, and browsing histories to reach mobile consumers with messages tailored to their individual profiles.

When you use your mobile device to shop for plane tickets, download an audiobook, or put in a coffee order for pickup, there's a good chance that the app you use will present you with options based on your prior purchases and browsing history. Public relations practitioners can work with app developers and marketers who have developed loyalty programs to obtain a better understanding of their publics' uses of mobile and to coordinate on communication strategy. Public relations people can also personalize communication by engaging individuals with one-to-one conversation or by facilitating forums for the interaction of individuals within organizations and publics using mobile media.

Local

Localization is basically the geographic version of personalization. Unless you deliberately disable **geolocation** functions in your mobile apps, many apps you use will track your location and apply that to your communication preferences. Geolocation makes apps like Uber or Yelp much more convenient as you try to arrange a ride across town or find a local restaurant when travelling. The ads that you hear on Pandora or Spotify also can be localized, allowing both national and local marketers to reach you based on your registered location.

In developing public relations strategies, you should know where you plan to reach your publics and communicate with them. Mobile media offer you the opportunity to engage publics almost anywhere they go, provided they opt in to communication that they feel is worthwhile. Snapchat's **geofilter** service allows individuals and organizations to send messages and promote events to other Snapchat users in a specific geographic location.[26] For example, if you were planning a grand re-opening of a newly renovated community garden, you could set up a geofilter for everyone using Snapchat in that area at that time. This would enable you to communicate with them, and them to communicate with one another. The service is free for public places such as parks and landmarks and can be purchased for businesses and brands.

Snackable

What do you do with that little bit of extra time you have waiting in line, sitting in a doctor's office or passing time during a break between classes?

geolocation Function of communication devices that identifies the specific geographic location of the device.

geofilter Feature of social media (particularly Snapchat) that encourages communication among users within a specified geographic area by allowing users to post images with location-specific overlays.

Snapchat's geofilters allow users to share place-themed messages and promote events in specific geographic locations.

What kinds of organizations can benefit from the combination of social and local mobile content?

Snack Attack: An Iconic Brand Faces Fallout for Going Digital

Snackable content may have a place in public relations strategy, but planners should be attentive to how digital tactics serve objectives and goals. To extend the snack metaphor, we want to do more than deliver empty calories. Interestingly, one of the best examples comes from a real snack brand.

digitalreflections/Shutterstock.com

Some Cracker Jack fans were disappointed when in-box surprises were replaced with digital apps for mobile.

Did the brand take digital tactics too far, or might the tactic make sense in light of a broader public relations strategy?

Frito Lay's Cracker Jack brand has been known for more than a century as an iconic snack of caramel-coated popcorn and peanuts. It's featured in the lyrics to *Take Me Out to the Ballgame*, and it has become part of our language as an adjective describing exceptionally positive qualities (e.g., "That crackerjack public relations grad can get a job in any city she wants."). But, perhaps most important of all to generations of snackers, Cracker Jack's unique selling proposition has been "A Prize in Every Box." Millions of kids and adults have puzzled over how the little decoder ring, temporary tattoo, or plastic figurine always seems to end up at the very bottom of the box. There's even a Cracker Jack Collectors Association (www .crackerjackcollectors.com) "dedicated to the collecting of Cracker Jack prizes and related items." So, when Cracker Jack decided to leap into the business of digital snacking by replacing its toy surprises with virtual ones, many of its most loyal publics went nuts.

As announced in a Frito Lay news release, the company decided to "contemporize" its logo and packaging and, as part of that move, began offering digital prizes instead of physical ones. "The new Prize Inside allows families to enjoy their favourite baseball moments through a new one-of-a-kind mobile experience, leveraging digital technology to bring the iconic Prize Inside to life," said senior director of marketing Haston Lewis.[27]

"Totally disappointed," one commenter said on Facebook.[28]

"Huge baseball fan, huge computer guy, but this? Nope," commented another.[29]

Within days a Facebook community emerged, called "Put the PRIZE back in Cracker Jack," and garnered the attention of mainstream media such as NPR and PCWorld. The Chicago Tribune ran an editorial with the sarcastic heading, "Cracker Jack Prizes Go Digital: More Staring at a Screen? What a Treat!"[30]

The downloadable apps included one called "Dot Dash" and another called "Dance Cam" that enabled users to simulate experiences baseball fans know from ballpark video boards. Another one, "Get Carded," allowed users to create their own autographed trading cards, in digital format of course.

In fairness, the apps sounded pretty cool, but do you think they made sense as part of a larger strategy to maintain relationships between the organization and its publics? As with all public relations tactics, the evaluation of digital apps requires assessing how well they achieve objectives and goals as part of strategies to advance the organization's mission and its relationships with key publics.

Maybe you quickly check Facebook or swipe through some Snapchat stories? Can you ignore the little notification alert button telling you there's something you haven't seen? Like tasty snacks, these little morsels of content—text updates, photos, GIFs, videos, live streams, and so on—are hard to resist. While information snacking is not unique to mobile media, trends in mobile media use have resulted in increased consumption of snackable content. Snackable content refers to those easy-to-consume pieces of content that are available on the go. On the one hand, mobile media have led to a *decrease* in our attention spans as we squeeze more and more communication tasks into the rest of our daily lives. On the other hand, carrying our devices with us also means we *increase* the total hours of the day that we pay attention to media.

snackable content
Easy-to-consume pieces of content that are available on the go.

uses and gratifications
Approach to studying communication that focuses on how people use media and the gratifications they seek from media, as opposed to studying the effects of media on people as passive audiences.

Uses and Gratifications of Media

In media research, when communication scientists want to understand *what people do with media*, as opposed to *what media do to people*, they have applied an approach called uses and gratifications.[31] The user-oriented approach of uses and gratifications is particularly well suited to the study of new communication technologies.

Public relations researcher Ruth Avidar and her colleagues explored how and why 21- to 31-year-old Israelis were using smartphones.[32] The results imply that some major reasons people choose mobile media are for instrumental purposes (uses) and for pleasure (gratifications): relationships, information, diversion and amusement, and participation.

Avidar et al. found that uses and gratifications such as staying in touch with friends and family, sending personal messages, and acknowledging others were most important. In other words, *relationships* were the top reason these young Israelis used smartphones. *Information* was the second-highest rated reason found in this study and included obtaining news updates, seeking information, and managing information. Information was followed by *amusement* and *diversion*, which included gaming, relaxation, passing time, and fighting

In developing strategy for mobile media, consider asking what people are doing with mobile media instead of what mobile media will do to people.

Voices from the Field

Sandra Chiovitti
Image courtesy of Sandra Chiovitti

Sandra Chiovitti is the director of public relations at SickKids Foundation, where she has worked for more than a decade, following a number of roles on the PR agency side.

She leads the strategy for earned and owned content, and her responsibilities include media relations, issues management, internal communications, content production, social media and influencer programs, and the patient and celebrity ambassador program. Her PR team is part of an integrated Brand Strategy and Communications team of about 30 people building the number one charity brand in Canada.

Prior to SickKids Foundation, Sandra worked at three different PR agencies where her client work was focused on the consumer packaged goods sector. She also did a stint in corporate communications at Canada Post.

How are you using multimedia tactics in your day-to-day practice?

At SickKids Foundation, we are at a place where we think digital first. When we're briefed on a new project or campaign, we approach it from the perspective of digital strategy.

We look at a full 360-degree marketing communications mix and use all channels possible—from traditional media like print, radio, and TV, to organic and paid social media, to digital programmatic media buys, to e-newsletters and e-blasts to donors, to Instagram influencer programs. We produce a lot of video. Video storytelling is a powerful way to capture our community's attention and inspire them to donate to The Hospital for Sick Children (SickKids).

Yet, there's still that one old standby we haven't been able to eliminate yet—we still produce a hard-copy annual report. It's fully available online and emailed to our donors, but there's still a certain demographic of donors who really appreciate a printed copy.

What multimedia skills do new public relations practitioners need to have?

You need to be familiar with the different digital channels available to you to communicate your messages and which one to use to reach your various target audiences.

You need to know how to write for each—whether it's writing for web, short and pithy content for social media posts, or writing and producing an interactive and dynamic podcast.

[You need] the ability to conceptualize a story idea, narrative, and arc in a short, compelling, and visual way. Even if you're not producing or directing it, and even if you don't have a big marketing budget, you need to be able to brief a freelancer (or whoever you're hiring to do the work) on a conceptual idea—and then know how to chase the idea and package it so that it works for your organization and your audience—whether that's customers, employees, donors, or media.

How has mobile media changed public relations practice?

It means we're always on. Like, always on. With people engaging on social media 24/7, it means we're doing social community management every day of the week, before and after regular business hours, in order to be responsive to our donors and prospective donors—which, in the case of SickKids Foundation, is just about anyone (who wouldn't want to help improve children's health?).

It also means that something you may think is nothing could turn into something very quickly—sometimes great and sometimes less than great. We've had tweets that have turned into news stories in a very short time frame. If it's a slow news day, what wouldn't typically be an issue could turn into one quite quickly. On the flip side, if a fun video that's a bit surprising for SickKids Foundation to release happens to get noticed and retweeted or posted on an influencer's channels, we just watch our phones light up with notifications on the likes, comments, and shares. (That never gets old—it's exciting every time!)

Sometimes we amplify the reach and the buzz by putting some budget behind a video or social post and boosting it so we reach more people—and hopefully inspire more people to make donations to SickKids. Even though we're a charity, when it comes down to it, we're competing for disposable income and share of wallet like most other brands. And, in 2019, we know that means our donors and prospective donors expect to interact with us and have a user experience that's similar to how they interact with brands in their personal, day-to-day lives whether that is Airbnb and Amazon or Uber and Wealthsimple. We strive to be *that* digitally forward thinking.

What's the coolest multimedia public relations campaign you've seen or worked on? What made it so successful?

Of course, I am biased but the launch of the SickKids VS brand platform is by far the coolest campaign I have ever seen—and, yes, I worked on it, together with an integrated team of marketers, creatives, my PR colleagues, our senior management team, and our agency of record, Cossette. It was such a bold change in the look, feel, and tone of voice, and it really struck a chord with our audiences internally at the hospital (among patients and staff) and in the community in Toronto, throughout the province, and across the country. It went viral and global, generating media coverage and social engagement in about 20 countries during launch month in October 2016. We set out to reach new, younger, and more male audiences and set ambitious fundraising and engagement goals. SickKids VS outperformed every metric we anticipated and overdelivered during its first year. It continues to do that now as we're wrapping up year three.

What advice do you have for students about leveraging their familiarity with digital and mobile media for public relations career success?

Become familiar with all the various social media channels and be active on them. It's okay to pick a favourite (mine is Twitter since my primary role is media relations), but try to understand how they all work and what purpose each serves from a business perspective.

boredom. Interestingly, *participation* was rated lowest in this study of how and why millennials use mobile media.

Think about your own use of mobile devices. What kinds of apps do you use for maintaining relationships, obtaining information, amusing yourself, seeking diversion, and participating in online activities? And what role do organizations practising public relations have in those experiences? Are they the subjects of those news feeds? Do they provide the news? Do they provide the apps? How do you communicate directly with them via mobile?

While thinking about your own experiences with organizations is a good exercise to help you develop questions to drive your planning, it's not normally a good idea to think of yourself as representing your organization's publics. It takes research to understand your publics from their perspectives.

Benoit Daoust/Shutterstock.com

It seems like anywhere people wait, mobile media are being used.

How do you use mobile media when you're waiting in line? What kinds of organizations attempt to communicate with you in that time?

Ethics: Privacy and Safeguarding Confidences

Internet of things (IoT)
Global network of physical objects that are connected to one another in a way that enables them to communicate with one another and the Internet at large.

end-user license agreement (EULA)
Legal agreement between a software provider and the person using the software.

It's not just our tablets and phones on which we communicate. We also communicate more than we realize on the **Internet of things (IoT)**. Although experts haven't yet agreed on a single definition, the basic idea of IoT is that more and more objects in our environment are connected to each other in a way that enables them to communicate via a network, and by extension the Internet at large.

"The premise behind the IoT," according to eMarketer, "is that any object, whether natural or manufactured, can gain the ability to transmit data over a network."[33] Cars with built-in GPS are on the IoT. Home security systems that can be activated remotely and that report activity are on the IoT. My running watch can transmit data about my workout over the Internet, and I can share that with other users including running groups and organizations that may want to advertise running-related products and services to the group and me. Even my dog has a small microchip, which was implanted at the same time he received immunizations as a puppy. If he gets lost, he can be scanned for a unique ID number from the chip, which can be reported to a pet-finding service to match his number to my contact information in a database.

As members of publics, we often communicate without even trying. When was the last time you checked your privacy settings for location services on all your apps? Do you actually read the **end-user license agreements (EULA)** you agree to when you register for new apps? Most of us skim those EULA screens and trust that the organizations won't do anything evil with our data. From a public relations standpoint, this trust may indicate a healthy relationship between the end user and the organization using the data. But it also raises the stakes for the organization we entrust.

Safeguarding confidences is a key provision in the CPRS Code of Professional Standards. "A member shall protect the confidences of present, former and prospective employers / clients. Members shall not use or disclose confidential information obtained from past or present employers / clients without the expressed permission of the employers / clients or an order of a court of law."

Apple Computer Inc. is as big of a player as any in the global arena of mobile, multimedia, big data, and the Internet of things. That company knows more about its customers than their customers know about themselves. Think of all the data it holds from people running apps, using Apple Pay, making purchases with their Apple IDs, and working on their desktops, laptops, iPads, and iPhones. Think carefully about the pitch for its first-generation Apple Watch:

To wear it is to love it.

Receive and respond to notifications in an instant. Track your daily activity. Control your music using only your voice. Pay for groceries

charnsitr/Shutterstock.com

These apps offer a lot of information, entertainment, and convenience, but they require trusting organizations with private information.

Which organizations do you trust with your private data and why?

just like that. With Apple Watch, important information and essential features are always just a raise of the wrist away.[34]

Media ethicists Jay Black and Chris Roberts frame privacy issues as questions of competing values. We weigh the value of privacy with the values of information, entertainment, and convenience. "The bottom line," they write, "is that while a great deal of information about millions of us is conveniently and centrally available for a multitude of uses, do we want corporations and government to know this much about us?"[35] Your answer may depend on how much you trust the organizations.

Apple CEO Tim Cook was quite focused on this issue in a speech he gave at the Electronic Privacy Information Center (EPIC) in 2015: "Like many of you, we at Apple reject the idea that our customers should have to make trade-offs between privacy and security," Cook opened. He criticized tech companies that lull "their customers into complacency about their personal information."[36] He went on to discuss ways that Apple lets its consumers control their information, as well as the company's efforts to keep the information private using encryption.

As publics, we make decisions every day about which organizations we trust with our personal information. Organizations have to earn that trust—not just with speeches but with everyday management. When ethical public relations is part of an organization's management function, organizations must take safeguarding confidences and protecting the privacy of their publics seriously.

In Case You Missed It

Social media platforms are increasingly designed for mobile use and multimedia content. Multimedia and mobile communication are changing the very nature of interpersonal communication as well as communication between organizations and publics on social media. Here are a few takeaways from this chapter.

- If you add a decent external microphone to your smartphone or camera, you can noticeably improve the quality of audio that you capture.
- Publics may prefer non-professionally produced video, if it means they get to hear from real people and the video is part of a larger strategy of two-way communication.
- Mobile video services like Periscope and Facebook Live enable you to open your organization to more publics via social media by live-streaming events like press conferences and live public forums.
- In planning for social media, consider how you will reach followers, fans, and subscribers but also how they will reach back and how they will share content with one another.
- In developing strategy for mobile media, consider asking what people are doing with mobile media instead of what mobile media will do to people.

Summary

10.1   Identify sources for multimedia elements such as writing, images, audio, and video.

Advances in computer technology—particularly mobile devices—have made the production and playback of all sorts of multimedia far more accessible and widespread. Content for multimedia can be attained in three major ways: create it yourself, hire a professional, or purchase or otherwise obtain permission to use others' material.

10.2   Analyze how different components of multimedia are integrated for effective communication in public relations.

The key to good multimedia is understanding the various elements and how they work together to enhance users' experiences. Images, audio, and video can be presented with or without text. Text can be written to invite, explain, or otherwise support other elements of multimedia. At other times, words are foremost, and sounds, images, video, and animation play the supporting role for the text. One of the main benefits of multimedia is that they allow an efficiency of communication, as producers can artfully combine elements for the best user experiences across a wide variety of social and mobile contexts.

10.3   Assess the strategic value of mobile tactics.

The evaluation of mobile tactics requires examining how well the tactics achieve objectives and goals as part of strategies to advance the organization's mission and its relationships with key publics. Key dimensions to consider include the degree to which mobile tactics are social, personal, local, and snackable.

10.4   Discuss how publics' uses and gratifications of mobile media may help drive public relations strategy.

Major uses and gratifications of mobile media include relationships, information, diversion and amusement, and participation. Mobile media also offer excellent opportunities to obtain feedback from publics. Research should be conducted to understand publics from their perspectives.

10.5   Apply privacy as an ethical value to consider in handling data gleaned from mobile media.

In exchange for information, entertainment, and convenience, mobile media users entrust organizations with tremendous amounts of private information. Safeguarding confidences and protecting privacy are key ethical values that public relations professionals and their organizations must honour, if they are going to maintain public trust.

Discussion Questions

1.   Think about the best paper or essay you have ever written. Now suppose you were asked to publish it online. What kind of images or other multimedia elements would you add? Identify at least two elements and explain how you would produce them or get permission to do so, if someone else produced them.

2.   Identify a news story posted online by a reputable news organization and track that story to one of its public relations sources that supplied original multimedia elements (e.g., images, video, audio, animations). What characteristics of multimedia elements helped the story get selected for publication by the news organization?

3.   How have you used mobile media to communicate with an organization? What were your "uses and gratifications"? What were the organization's objectives? Why was (or wasn't) their strategy effective?

4. Thinking more about your experience interacting with an organization via mobile, what specific information do they now have about you? What makes you confident (or not confident) they will handle it properly?

Further Readings and Online Resources

How to Use Instagram as a PR Tool
spinsucks.com/social-media/instagram-pr-tool/
> This post from popular PR website Spin Sucks provides practical advice on how to use Instagram in a PR campaign.

How Multimedia Enhances Your PR Campaigns
www.cision.ca/best-practices/how-multimedia-enhances-your-pr-campaigns/
> Multimedia is growing in importance in public relations. This blogpost by Canadian media monitoring company Cision makes a strong case for including multimedia elements in every campaign.

17 Incredible Tools for Creating Infographics
www.creativebloq.com/infographic/tools-2131971
> You don't need to be a graphic designer to create professional-looking infographics. This blogpost reviews 17 free (or nearly free) tools and apps you can use to create infographics and other graphic elements for your projects.

Peer-Reviewed Academic Journal Article
Whiting, A., & Williams, D. (2013). Why people use social media: A uses and gratifications approach. *Qualitative Market Research*, 16(4), 362–9.
> Do you know someone who is constantly on social media? Uses and gratification theory might explain that behaviour, an idea that's explored in this article.

Key Terms

PART FOUR

Contexts

11

Legal

Chapter contributed by Rachel Bellotti, lawyer and part-time professor at the Humber College Institute of Technology and Advanced Learning

At its core, practising law is no different than professional public relations practice. Both fields seek to address issues, target an audience, and cultivate a message that results in a positive outcome.

Key learning outcomes

11.1 Discuss why it is important to always run your work by in-house counsel or legal counsel.

11.2 Describe any limits to free speech, including libel and slander.

11.3 Describe the common types of intellectual property and the ways in which they are protected.

11.4 Identify where privacy comes into play in the role of public relations.

11.5 Identify and discuss agencies that guide and regulate public relations professionals.

11.6 Analyze ethical dilemmas public relations professionals face and what organization is in place to help guide a PR professional.

When you entered the field of public relations (PR), did you ever think that you would need to understand the law? Probably not, right? You might even think it is odd that this textbook has an entire chapter dedicated to the law. The law and PR, however, are heavily intertwined. One of the most important relationships a PR professional can make is with a lawyer. For the most part, PR professionals and lawyers are dependent on one another in the industry, and no public relations professional should attempt to be his or her own lawyer.[1]

In order for PR professionals to be successful in their everyday tasks, there is a need for day-to-day legal consultation.[2] According to *The Contentious Relationship between PR and Legal*, the relationship between a PR professional and a lawyer sometimes requires balance. During a crisis, public relations professionals might disagree with their legal team, but "both PR and legal want the organization to make it through a crisis with its reputation and ability to continue to do business intact."[3] Therefore, having PR and legal working together is in an organization's best interest.

You may be thinking, when did PR and legal become a team? This partnership has become increasingly important given the fast-paced rate at which technology has developed. The increasing speed at which we can communicate globally has changed immensely, and now the amount of time a company or person has to deal with a crisis has been significantly reduced. Accordingly, the relationship between a PR professional and legal counsel has changed when it comes to working together to solve issues.[4] There is a higher demand for them to work together faster and more efficiently. It's a safe guess that in almost every relationship in which a PR professional and lawyer is concerned, a legal question of some kind will be at the core.[5]

Consider these statements: you can win in court, but lose in the eyes of the public, or, conversely, you can lose in court, but win in the eyes of the public. Which predicament would you rather be in? Although a PR professional might think it is best to win in the eyes of the public—as protecting image is paramount—imagine what would happen if you lost in court. Losing in court could seriously damage the reputation of a corporate client and ruin the client's balance sheet, which could potentially lead to declaring bankruptcy and dissolving the company as a whole.[6] Therefore, think again if you answered "winning in the eyes of the public," as legal ramifications can easily destroy a company.

As a PR professional, there are many legal concepts that you will come across in your daily practice. For example, consider the following:

- *Defamation*: Whom can you sue? Can you sue someone who tweets something mean about you? What about if they tweet something bad about someone you know? What if you retweet something that someone else initiated?
- *Copyright*: Can you use an image exclusively?
- *Business regulations*: If you find out information about a stock tip, are you able to share it with your friend? What if only you act on it?
- *Privacy*: If you come across interesting information about a co-worker, are you able to share that information?

These are just a few examples of what PR professionals may deal with in the course of their jobs. Many of these legal issues are based on laws legislated by municipal, provincial, or federal governments and are enforced by regulators and agencies. This chapter is to help you gain awareness of how important it is to cultivate a relationship with a lawyer.

Photo by Creative Touch Imaging Ltd./ NurPhoto via Getty Images

Michael Wheatley / Alamy Stock Photo

rblfmr/Shutterstock.com

Freedom of Expression protects free speech and is considered a fundamental freedom. But not all forms of speech are protected.

Which of these signs gets the least legal protection and why?

The Charter of Rights and Freedoms: Freedom of Expression

Canada is founded upon principles that recognize the supremacy of God and the rule of law: The Canadian Charter of Rights and Freedoms guarantees the rights and freedoms set out in it subject only to such reasonable limits prescribed by law as can be demonstrably justified in a free and democratic society.[7]

Generally speaking, freedom of expression is a fundamental right afforded to those who are part of a democratic society. Public relations is a profession that manages and transmits information between individuals or an organization and the public. The role of a PR professional is to communicate on behalf of a client to the public. Therefore, as a PR professional, the right to freely express is an important part of the profession.

In Canada, freedom of expression is protected as a fundamental right under section 2(b) of the Canadian Charter of Rights and Freedoms. Freedom of expression covers "freedom of thought, belief, opinion and expression, including freedom of the press and other media of communication."[8] However, freedom of expression is not absolute, and, as such, there are reasonable limits in place to protect against certain actions. In other words, we are restricted, to a certain extent, on what we can and cannot say.

Two areas that usually gain a significant amount of attention by media and public disclosure are hate speech and obscenity. For example, in *R v. Keegstra*, high school teacher Keegstra was charged under the Criminal Code with wilfully promoting hatred against an identifiable group by communicating anti-Semitic statements to his students.[9] The Supreme Court upheld the "*Criminal Code's* prohibition of the wilful promotion of hatred against identifiable groups. Dickson CJC took into account the dim prospect of the promotion of hatred contributing to the democratic process, or the search for truth."[10] Some other limits on freedom of expression could include defamation; regulations put in place by government agencies, such as the Canadian Radio-television and Telecommunications Commission (CRTC).

Limiting free speech has often created a point of contention, as some people feel that these limits are an act of control by the government. But there are also those who believe that these limits are necessary. Therefore, when it comes to limiting free speech, there needs to be a valid justification for it, as stated in section 1 of the Canadian Charter of Rights and Freedoms. Section 1 states that the government can pass laws that limit free expression so long as the limits are reasonable and can be justified in a free and democratic society.[11] In a sense, a freedom is governed by law. According to the Supreme Court of Canada, the approach to free expression has been that when deciding whether a restriction on freedom of expression is justified, the harms done by the particular form of expression must be weighed against the harm that would be done by the restriction itself.[12] As a public relations professional, your job could entail coming up with a publicity campaign, writing or marketing materials on behalf of clients, creating story pitches, and generating positive press coverage, among many other roles. And through these various roles, your speech could be limited depending on the nature of what you are trying to convey.

Defamation

One of the ways that someone can hit the legal limits for free speech is to infringe on someone else's reputation. **Defamation** is any false communication that injures someone's reputation. **Libel** and **slander** are both types of defamation. Libel refers to written words with a permanent record (e.g., in a newspaper or in a broadcast).[13] Slander, on the other hand, refers to "the publication of a defamatory statement by means of an oral communication."[14] In order to claim slander, however, you must prove you suffered some sort of financial loss. Otherwise, you must fall into one or more of the following four categories:[15]

1. You are accused of a crime (unless the accusation is made to the police).
2. You are accused of having a contagious disease.
3. Someone makes negative remarks about you in your work, profession, trade, or business.
4. You are accused of adultery.

The law will protect your reputation against defamatory statements, and you can sue for money (also called damages). In a libel, the defendant can possibly limit the amount of damages they will have to pay by publishing or broadcasting an apology right away. But an apology or retraction does not prevent the libelled party from suing. There is also a limitation period. A **limitation period** starts when the defamatory statement has caused damage, and a plaintiff has within two years of that date to sue.[16] When it comes to republication, "each publication is a separate and distinct libel and will be subject to its own limitation period."[17] Therefore, each time someone republishes the defamatory statement, it will be considered a new publication and start its own two-year limitation period from the date the publication was established. In other words, if you repeat a defamatory statement, you will face the same liability as the person who originally published it.[18] The common law has established a "repetition rule," and therefore "where there is a republication the republisher is directly responsible to the individual harmed, whether or not the original publisher has liability for the republication."[19]

In public relations, avoiding defamation is a regular task. This applies whether you are handling a competitive or political advertising campaign or building and protecting the reputation of a client, regardless if they are individuals or corporations. Public relations practitioners must be aware at all times when publishing online content because laws are continuously changing and online materials can be accessed at all times.

Defamation has evolved since the emergence of the Internet and social media. Among the most popular social media networks, Instagram, Twitter, YouTube, and Facebook make up the top four means of communicating on social media in Canada—and these are all platforms that can injure someone's reputation if not used carefully. This means that Facebook posts, Instagram and YouTube posts, and tweets are subject to libel and slander laws. In fact, there's even an informal term for Twitter libel.

The word *Twibel* rose in public consciousness after fashion designer Dawn Simorangkir sued punk rocker and actress Courtney Love for libellous Twitter statements. Following a dispute over payments for wardrobe items, according to the libel complaint filed by Simorangkir, Love tweeted to her tens of thousands of followers that Simorangkir was a "nasty lying hosebag

defamation False communication that harms someone's reputation.

libel False written communication that injures someone's reputation.

slander False oral communication that injures someone's reputation.

limitation period The two-year interval within which a plaintiff is able to sue for libel.

thief," and that police should "haul her desperate cokes [*sic*] out ass to jail" because "she has a history of dealing cocaine, lost all custody of her child, assault and burglary."[20] The parties later settled out of court for $430,000 (USD). Had Love spoken these statements in person instead of tweeting them, the defamation case would have been one of slander instead of libel.

After Love paid to avoid becoming the first-ever celebrity to go to trial over tweets, she ended up back in trouble with Simorangkir after taunting the designer's lack of followers on Pinterest and again accused her of theft. Love talked about the first lawsuit on Howard Stern's radio show when her Twitter habits came up, and Stern admonished her: "You can't just blurt things out."[21] Thus came Simorangkir's second lawsuit.

In Canada, we have yet to see any celebrity tweeting and blogging feuds at a level similar to the United States.

Although most social media websites have their roots in the US, "Both Twitter and Google have established Canadian based subsidiaries to specifically target the Canadian market. Their direct presence in Canada establishes a better position from which to collaborate with Canadian media outlets."[22] Social media have created a communication platform that complements any commercial endeavour and as a "public relations tool, social media provides opportunities that cannot be found in traditional advertising mediums: a deeper level of engagement."[23] However, with this evolution comes many legal issues.

Defamatory comments can now be made instantaneously on the Internet. This is called *Internet defamation* or *cyber libel*. **Cyber libel** is essentially traditional libel in an online context. Defamatory statements can be shared on comment boards, social media, criticism platforms, complaint sites, or elsewhere online.[24] Online users often assume that their audience is the small group of family, friends, or acquaintances they have "allowed" into their cyber world, but that world is now open to millions of people across borders and waters.

In order to bring a claim for defamation, there are certain requirements that must be met:

cyber libel Libel in an online context.

1. *The defamatory statement harms one's reputation.* The harmful statement must lower the person's reputation in the eyes of a "right-thinking" person.
2. *The defamatory statement must be made to a third party, not just to the person targeted by the statement.* The statements can be made about an individual, group, business, or organization.
3. *The statements made must be false.* In other words, a true statement cannot be considered defamation.
4. *Defamation is, for the most part, considered a strict liability tort.* This means that the defendants will be liable whether they meant to act intentionally or not when making those defamatory statements to a third party.

Photo by Nick Ut-Pool/Getty Images

Courtney Love Cobain became the first celebrity sued for defamation on Twitter ("Twibel") in 2009. In this photo, she arrives at court for an unrelated case.

Do you think suing someone for what they tweet is a violation of their right to freedom of speech?

Mudford v. Smith, 2009 CanLII 55718 (ON SC)

Peter Smith and Michael Smith were a father and son duo that owned Toronto Nitelife Inc. In 2003, Michael Smith hired Carey Mudford, who owned and operated Carey Mudford Interior Design (CMID), to provide design services for his personal residence, a loft, and a new restaurant business.

The restaurant was completed in October 2004, but when the restaurant opened, many of the chairs—21 of 100—either were broken or needed repair. Carey Mudford tried unsuccessfully to persuade the supplier, Furniture Toronto, to replace the chairs, so Peter Smith arranged for Furniture Toronto to repair them instead and then sued Furniture Toronto in Small Claims Court for the repair costs.

Peter Smith asked Carey Mudford for an affidavit of events to support the claim against Furniture Toronto, but Mudford's lawyer explained a written account of the events would be sufficient and provided that instead. Peter Smith was not happy with the ways in which Carey Mudford (or her lawyer) handled the situation or Peter's request for an affidavit and in retaliation named CMID as co-defendant to the suit.

In 2007, the court found Furniture Toronto responsible for the defective chairs and also required CMID to pay $18.30 because they had overcharged the Smiths when calculating the cost of chairs by rounding up to an even dollar amount.

In 2006, Michael Smith began a second lawsuit in Small Claims Court against CMID for the cost of repairing the hardwood floor in his personal residence. Months after the project was completed, Michael Smith claimed that the floors were damaged after CMID held a photo shoot for a magazine at the residence. CMID claimed that the damage was done before the photo shoot but eventually agreed to repair the damaged floor at its own expense. Unfortunately, Peter Smith was not happy with the repair job and sued CMID for $6,632, the amount it cost to refinish the floors for the second time. On 3 August 2007, a Small Claims Court judge granted judgment against CMID for $5,088 including costs. Carey Mudford paid for all judgments brought against her.

The feud between CMID and the Smiths did not end there. In late 2007, Peter Smith posted comments on a website about GTA-area businesses and renovation services. He wrote, "Carey Mudford Interior Design in my view has no integrity. I had to sue her in the court to receive damages and costs. Despite the judge awarding me a judgment and costs, she still has refused to make restitution!" He went on further to create a website on which he continued to defame CMID. In particular, he wrote

> Two separate Judges ruled that in two separate contracts that Carey Mudford entered into, SHE FAILED TO COMPLY WITH HER CONTRACTUAL [sic] OBLIGATIONS. . . . Despite the judgements which included costs, Carey Mudford has refused to pay restitution to date (1st Nov 2007).

Continued

along with this final message:

BE WARNED BE WARNED BE WARNED.[25]

A prospective client discovered the reviews and website notified Mudford, who was mortified to discover the critical website and the two postings. She sued Peter Smith for defamation.

At trial, there was no dispute that the defendant, Peter Smith, published these defamatory statements. What became the issue was whether there was a possible defence to excuse his actions. Peter Smith attempted to use the defence of truth, stating that all the accusations made were in fact true. However, the defence did not hold up. Justice Belobaba noted,

> *Proof that statements are literally true will not be sufficient if the words reasonably convey an overall impression that is false. The defendant will not be permitted to defend by justification if he or she has omitted facts . . . which, if reported, would create an entirely different impression from the reported facts taken alone.*

Peter Smith failed to establish any of his potential defences and therefore was found liable for defamation. Justice Belobaba awarded Mudford general damages of $30,000 and $5,000 for aggravated damages. Furthermore, because Mudford won the lawsuit, she was also entitled to her costs, which were fixed at $30,500 plus GST for a total judgment of approximately $67,000.

The Internet is not a safe haven for free speech. Users cannot feel comfortable or confident hiding behind a screen. There is no longer anonymity. Canadian judges are increasingly ordering Internet service providers to disclose the identity of people using pseudonyms to criticize others. "Canadian courts have already acknowledged both the permanency and the breadth of cyber-libel, which judges consider in awarding damages."[26] As Peter Smith learned, it's important to be careful when criticizing others online.

In Canada, the courts have not shown any leniency over defamatory comments made online versus defamation in print. Both are equally dangerous and both are held accountable. Once the above four requirements are proven, the action will succeed unless there is a defence. Some possible defences to defamation include

Truth (also known as justification)—if the statement made is in fact substantially true.[27]
Fair comment—we are all free to comment, even harshly, as long as we make it clear that the comments are opinions and not fact.[28]
Qualified privilege—allows a person to make defamatory statements towards another person while performing a public or private duty. The duty can be legal, social, or moral. For example, fair criticism in a review may fall under qualified privilege.[29]
Absolute privilege—allows people to make false and defamatory statements in criminal, quasi-judicial, and judicial proceedings, and in parliament.[30]

Responsible communication on matters of public interest—"Journalists should be able to report statements and allegations—even if not true—if there is a public interest in distributing the information to a wide audience. It will apply if: the news was urgent, serious and of public importance, and the journalists used reliable sources, and tried to get and report the other side of the story. Journalists for this context includes bloggers and anyone else publishing material of public interest in any medium."[31]

Consent—An individual cannot complain of a publication to which they have consented.[32]

Canada is considered to have the most plaintiff-friendly defamation laws in the English-speaking world. This is in contrast to the United States, which is considered less plaintiff-friendly, making them less attractive for managing online defamation.[33]

Defamation through Republication

In copyright law, **publication** means any act which can have the effect of transferring defamatory information to a third person.[34] Canada embraces the **multiple publication rule**, which states that "each sale or delivery of a single copy of a newspaper, magazine or book was a separate publication for which the injured plaintiff had a distinct cause of action."[35] In other words, a multiple publication rule allows for a new cause of action each time a defamatory statement is published.[36] This idea of multiple publications has been amended slightly in the case of *Thomson v. Lambert*, where the Court established that because

> there can be a potential injustice if a plaintiff is allowed to mount a series of lawsuits based upon a single article, the Courts have the power using their abuse of process jurisdiction to deal with such a course of action.[37]

In other words, if the court finds that there are multiple complaints being made about the same issue, courts will consider this an abuse of process and put a stop to it. However, courts will always consider republication of a defamatory statement within the necessary time limits outlined by the Ontario Libel and Slander Act.

In the United States, the single publication rule is favoured, which only allows for a new cause of action for each mass publication, instead of book, issue, or copy.

Hyperlinking

In Canada, hyperlinking does not constitute defamation. If you provide a link to a website or page that contains something defamatory, the hyperlink itself will not be considered defamation. In the landmark case *Crookes v. Newton*, Crookes was a victim of several defamatory comments and was in the process of bringing a number of defamation claims against various individuals and organizations, alleging that he had been defamed in several articles on the Internet. Newton was the owner and operator of a website that published articles on various political issues, including freedom of speech and Internet control. After the defamatory actions brought by Crookes commenced, Newton posted an article on his website that commented on the implications of Crookes's defamation suits for operators of Internet forums. Newton's article also contained hyperlinks to the material that allegedly defamed Crookes. Crookes sued Newton for defamation, claiming that by including the hyperlinks in

publication Any act which can have the effect of transferring defamatory information to a third person.

multiple publication rule In defamation, each sale or delivery of a single copy of a newspaper, magazine, or book is a separate publication for which the injured plaintiff has a distinct cause of action.

his article, Newton was publishing the allegedly defamatory material and was therefore liable for it. In the end, it was held that online context hyperlinking does not constitute publishing or communication for the purposes of establishing defamation.[38] Therefore, "organizations cannot use defamation law against any other organizations that 'share' defamatory material initially published elsewhere by posting links to the original source, if they do not provide additional commentary."[39] However, if additional commentary is provided alongside the hyperlink, then it will constitute defamation.

Keep in mind, defamation needs to harm someone's reputation. Simply harming someone's feelings does not constitute defamation. In public relations, you are primarily protecting the reputation of your client, whether it is an individual or a corporation.

Intellectual Property

As a public relations professional, you might be hired by a client to do some work that requires original content. But the question is, who owns the work—you or your client? Similarly, what if you had the opportunity to pitch a new client? Who owns the ideas—the client or you? This is where things get complicated.

intellectual property is the creation of the mind and includes inventions, literary and artistic works, designs, symbols, and names and images used in a business. Intellectual property can be protected through a trademark, patent, copyright, industrial design, or integrated circuit topography.[40] You think, why does someone need protection of their intellectual property? Well, for the most part it will prevent competitors from copying or closely imitating their products or services. However, as a PR professional, you too must be careful not to violate another person or company's intellectual property.

For the purposes of this chapter, we will focus only on copyright and trademarks, as they are the most prominent types of intellectual property that affect PR professionals.

Copyright and Trademark

In public relations, copyright and trademarks are two of the biggest intellectual property issues you will face during your career. Generally speaking, public relations involve creative works. As a PR professional, original material is always being created for your client. For example, you could be creating a brochure or annual report, a new logo, or a video. All of these types of works must be protected accordingly.

Copyright is the exclusive legal right to produce, reproduce, publish, or perform an original literary, artistic, dramatic, or musical work.[41] In order for you to own a copyright, it must be an original work, which is then automatically protected by copyright law. Because the protection is automatic, you do not have to register it. However, should you choose to register, you will receive a certificate issued by the Canadian Intellectual Property Office. An unregistered trademark is represented by ™ and a registered trademark is represented by ®. Once protected, the copyright will exist in Canada during the author's lifetime plus 50 years following their death.[42] After that, the work moves into public domain, and anyone can use it.[43] Once you own a copyright, you are in full control as to how you and others can use it.

Trademark protects a combination of words, sounds, or designs used to distinguish your goods or services from others' in the marketplace. For example, when consumers hear the well-known phrase "RRRoll up the rim to win" on the radio, they generally associate the

intellectual property The creation of the mind.

copyright A form of intellectual property that gives one exclusive legal rights to produce, reproduce, publish, or perform an original work.

trademarks Words, sounds, or designs used to distinguish goods and services from those of others in the marketplace.

phrase to a promotional contest held at participating Tim Hortons restaurants. In Canada, a business obtains rights in a trademark, including exclusive rights across Canada, by applying to the Canadian Intellectual Property Office for a registration. As long as the mark is "continuously, exclusively, and properly" used in Canada, a trademark owner can have perpetual rights to that trademark.[44]

A trademark is a business's most powerful form of intellectual property, not only because it protects its image but also because it could potentially last forever.[45] It could also be argued that there is more value in a trademark than in the business assets. That being said, there could be a lot of legal issues attached to a trademark, so public relations professionals must take the most appropriate steps and work with legal professionals before choosing or creating a new trademark for their client.[46]

shaunl/iStock

Trademarks are everywhere.

Can you identify the Canadian trademark in this photo? Is it registered or just trademarked?

Plagiarism

As a student, you've learned the importance of proper attribution. If you present someone else's specific ideas or words as your own, that's **plagiarism**. Digital media have made it much easier to "borrow" someone else's words, but that same technology makes it easier to identify plagiarism. Just put quotes around a sentence or excerpt of text and run a web search for that quoted material, and if the words have been plagiarized, there's a good chance you'll uncover an earlier source. Services like Turnitin, which boasts the ability to search more than 45 billion web pages, 337 million student papers, and 130 million academic articles, offer automatic checking for possible plagiarism.[47]

However, building on the contributions of others is essential to good scholarship. The key to avoiding plagiarism, then, is proper attribution. When words or specific ideas are not your own, you must let your instructors and anyone else reading your work know where those words and ideas come from. Give credit where credit is due.

Plagiarism is an issue outside of the classroom too. As a public relations professional, you may come across problems within your field dealing with clients who have plagiarized. For example, if a CEO uses someone else's words or thoughts in a public atmosphere and does not credit the originator, that can become a public relations problem. You may have read about high-profile politicians or commencement speakers who have been called out for lifting major parts of their speeches from other sources without attribution. When this happens, an opportunity for public honour turns into a case of public shame. In 2013, Chris Spence, head of the Toronto District School Board, resigned after a number of plagiarism allegations. In 2016, Mr Spence's teaching licence was revoked. In 2017, Mr Spence was found guilty of plagiarizing parts of his PhD dissertation.[48] In 2018, he was officially stripped of his degree. Mr Spence had knowingly copied paragraphs and sentences into his 1996 thesis.

Plagiarism can happen in social media, too. Easy sharing and re-posting of others' ideas, words, images, and works of art are essential parts of what makes social media

plagiarism Presenting someone else's words or ideas as one's own.

The key to avoiding plagiarism is proper attribution. Give credit where credit is due.

work, but that spirit of sharing and free-flowing information doesn't excuse plagiarism. Skye Grove, a rising "celebrity Instagrammer" in South Africa who had reached more than 40,000 followers on her Instagram account, was featured on national TV and successfully began selling her photography online. That all came to a stop when another Instagram user contacted the internationally popular technology news website Memeburn to report suspicions that Grove had plagiarized many of her images, including some that she had sold.[49] Memeburn investigated and found evidence of several suspected instances of plagiarism.

A week later, Grove's Instagram and Twitter accounts had disappeared, although it is unclear whether she deleted them voluntarily or whether they were removed for violating terms of service. Grove also was suspended without pay from her job as a communication manager for the NGO Cape Town Partnership.[50] Before deleting her Instagram account, Grove explained:

> For a long time I didn't believe my work was good enough. I wanted to impress people with my photography but didn't believe I was good enough. So, from time to time, I posted photos that didn't belong to me but that I claimed as my own. The more I honed my skill, the more I became compelled to be true to myself.[51]

In an email to Memeburn, Cape Town Partnership CEO Bulelwa Makalima-Ngewana explained that she had no reason to believe that Grove's mistakes were made as part of her official duties at the organization, but she also noted, "Personal and professional reputations are intertwined in the current social media climate."[52] With that hard lesson learned, Grove returned to both social media and her job later in the same year. While it may seem like it won't happen to you, plagiarizing on your personal social media pages *can* happen unless you cite the original source. So, remember to always cite the source.

Copyright Infringement

copyright infringement Use of protected works without proper permission from the copyright holder.

While attribution of words or ideas to a specific source is often enough to avoid plagiarizing, plagiarism is different from **copyright infringement**. According to the Copyright Act, a *copyright infringement* is "for any person to do, without the consent of the owner of the copyright, anything that by this Act only the owner of the copyright has the right to do."[53] If you want to include the full lyrics to a Maya Angelou poem on your for-profit Etsy page, use a Kendrick Lamar song as the soundtrack to a video you will distribute via paid downloads, or take an image from ESPN.com to put on T-shirts to sell at homecoming, attribution is not enough. Even if you make that attribution clear on the web page or video or T-shirt, you need permission to use the copyrighted material, because that material is someone else's intellectual property. Profiting from someone else's work or taking it out of context without permission can be treated as a form of stealing. You can get in trouble for copyright infringement even if you've cleared yourself of plagiarism.

Have you ever tried to download a video online from an unknown site? Downloading a video is considered illegal, but what about simply streaming the video for a one-time watch? Does that have the same repercussions? Matters like streaming versus downloading are at the core of issues considered to be copyright infringements. According to the Office of Consumer Affairs,

Those accessing the streams are unlikely to be infringing copyright, however. The law exempts temporary reproductions of copyrighted works if completed for technical reasons. Since most streaming video does not actually involve downloading a copy of the work, users can legitimately argue that merely watching a non-downloaded stream does not run afoul of the law.[54]

Recently, live streaming has become more prominent. Through media sources such as Twitter, Periscope, and Facebook Live, PR professionals have begun employing live streaming for events, Q&A sessions, behind-the-scenes views, and product launches.[55] Therefore, a PR professional must always be aware of whether they are simply streaming the content, which would not be infringement of copyright, or downloading video content, which would be considered a copyright infringement.

G7 Stock/Shutterstock.com

Give credit where credit is due.

When have you sought permission from something copyrighted?

In *Rains v. Molea*, Malcolm Rains was an artist who created large oil paintings featuring "white crumpled paper in still life form on an undefined base against a dark background."[56] Lucien Molea was also an artist whose interest in painting crumpled paper stemmed from a previous preoccupation of creating a virtual reality. Rains claimed that Molea infringed his copyright in using crumpled paper in a painting. In court, however, it was decided that there was in fact no substantial copying of Rains's paintings by Molea and therefore no copyright infringement. The judge found that the case involved "two artists who had the same (and not unique) idea to paint crumpled paper in a realistic way using conventional painting techniques. Their motivations are different. Their processes are different. Their resultant expressions are different."[57]

In the United States, copyright infringement has a takedown system under the Digital Millennium Copyright Act. This is the automatic takedown of web pages with infringing materials through the use of notifications to the website hosting the material.[58] This American statute is available to Canadian organizations, but only if the infringing material is posted through an American service provider.[59] Unlike the United States who "take down" those infringers, Canada has a "safe harbour" scheme. On 2 January 2015 Canada implemented a Notice and Notice provision in the Copyright Act, which was created as an aim to discourage online copyright infringement and give copyright owners more control over the use of their online works.[60] In other words, Canadians who download online content may receive a notice that they are being suspected of copyright infringement, and that's as far as it goes. Ultimately, it's up to the Internet service provider (ISP) to decide whether to notify its customers of suspected copyright infringement.

Copyright Notice:
Eastlink has received notice that your Internet service may have been used to illegally downloaded or shre copyrighted material. This message is being forwarded to you in accordance with canada's copyright legislation. **See Notice Here**

Eastlink is a cable television and telecommunications company based in Halifax. The company sends this notice to customers suspected of copyright infringement.

Are notices like this effective? Why or why not?

Fair Dealing

If you're essentially selling someone else's property for a profit, chances are they are going to want a cut. But, you may ask, what if you're not trying to make a profit? How can we participate in the marketplace of ideas if the only way to work with someone else's ideas is to obtain their permission and pay for the right? There is a solution: the Copyright Act provides certain exceptions to copyright infringement so that you can use works without obtaining consent from the copyright owners—this is known as **fair dealing**. Fair dealing can be used as an exception for the purpose of research, private study, education, parody, satire, review criticism, or news reporting.[61] For example, if you copy up to 10 per cent of a book or journal article as part of a news report, the copied text would be considered fair dealing and not copyright infringement; however, it is still important to cite your copied source to avoid plagiarism.

A two-step inquiry to determine fair dealing was outlined in *CCH Canadian Ltd v. Law Society of Upper Canada:*[62]

Whether the dealing was for an allowable purpose
Whether it was fair

Under this exception to copyright law, a "large and liberal interpretation are to be given in order to ensure that users' rights are not unduly constrained."[63]

fair dealing An exception to copyright laws for the purposes of research, private study, education, parody, satire, review criticism, or news reporting.

Public and Private Information

Intellectual property laws apply to information and ideas that can be claimed as privately owned by people and organizations. As discussed in Chapter 9, some works have entered the public domain, meaning that copyrights have expired, been forfeited by the owner, or otherwise do not apply. If you work in public relations for a publicly funded or government organization, you may find that laws that determine what you *must* communicate are much more a part of your day-to-day work than laws about what kinds of information you can claim and protect.

With the evolution of social media and the Internet, collecting personal information has become a lot more accessible. **PIPEDA (Personal Information Protection and Electronic Documents Act)** is a federally created piece of legislation that applies to "organizations that collect, use or disclose personal information in the course of commercial activity in provinces without substantially similar legislation."[64] It was "drafted broadly and in a technological neutral manner in order to apply equally to the electronic collection, use and disclosure of personal information in the course of commercial activity."[65] Did you think the Internet was a safe place to unleash your personal information? You did agree to all their terms and conditions, so why would you think otherwise?

In *R v. Spencer*, Spencer—while living with his sister and using her name—downloaded child pornography through an Internet file-sharing service. The police came across a public sharing folder containing the illicit material and contacted Shaw, the Internet service provider, to trace the address and name attached to the folder. The police did most of their searching through information that was publicly available. However, once more information was needed, the police required Shaw's cooperation, which further allowed them to obtain a search warrant and arrest Spencer on possessing child pornography.[66]

PIPEDA (Personal Information Protection and Electronic Documents Act) A federally created piece of legislation that applies to organizations that collect, use, or disclose personal information in the course of commercial activity in provinces without substantially similar legislation.

Privacy

As individuals living in a free and democratic society, we all value our privacy. Today, privacy can be harder to protect due to the easy access of the Internet and electronic databases. Before the Internet, private information was kept in paper files. Now it's possible for someone to "assemble detailed information about us, within minutes, without our knowledge."[67] Our society, businesses, organizations, and governments all have a responsibility to promote and protect privacy. Similarly, a PR professional must preserve their clients' privacy. It is a key component in PR, whether you are dealing with employee communication, releasing photos, product publicity, or any advertising and media inquiries about clients.

As your level of responsibility grows in an organization, so does your access to information about internal and external publics. Depending on the type of organization you work for, you may have access to employee performance evaluations, student academic records, volunteer contact information, and even photos of your colleagues with their families from their Instagram accounts. In addition to the obvious legal and ethical issues that may arise if you release negative information about someone, you must be careful even when your intentions are positive. If you write a biography of an employee or student who is receiving an award, you should check with that person to make sure it is accurate and that the person consents to the information being released. Likewise, if you pull a photo of someone from a social media account, you'll want to obtain permission before using that photo on your company web page.

Externally, **customer relationship management (CRM)** describes the process of tracking and forecasting customers' interactions with an organization. Huge amounts of data can be collected and analyzed to better serve customers with personalized experiences that are customized to their browsing history and preferences. These relationships—facilitated by data and technology—can be mutually beneficial. Customers gain customized experiences and convenient service. Organizations obtain lots of data to support their business decisions. Think about the organizations that offer you the most convenient and customized services. Maybe Google? Amazon? Netflix? How about your online news sources or favourite retailers for shopping? Your school? Your bank? Your hospital? You as a customer (or student, or patient, etc.) put an enormous amount of trust in these organizations. Public relations people have to be very careful with that trust.

In many cases, the right decisions about privacy of both internal and external publics can be made with good business sense and careful ethics, but you must also be aware of the legal rights and responsibilities of people inside and outside your organization.

> **customer relationship management (CRM)** Process of tracking and forecasting customers' interactions with an organization, often leveraging data for sales support.

Invasion of Privacy

Prior to 2012, Ontario did not recognize an action for breach of privacy. If someone accessed your private records and disclosed them, you would have no course of action. Since then, privacy actions can now be attributed to a landmark case known as *Jones v. Tsige*.

Both Jones and Tsige were employees in different branches at the Bank of Montreal. Jones had a personal bank account with her employer. Although the two women did not know each other, Tsige was in a common-law relationship with Jones's former husband.

Over a span of four years, while working at the bank, Tsige viewed Jones's personal banking activity. This conduct was done without authorization and for solely personal reasons. When Jones discovered that Tsige had repeatedly gained access to her confidential information, she brought an action for invasion of privacy. At first, the court rejected Jones's claim because there was no law that recognized an invasion of privacy. However, on appeal, the Court of Appeal overturned the lower court's ruling in favour of Jones and recognized a new common law tort called "intrusion upon seclusion."[68] This new tort is a subset of the broader invasion of privacy, and the recognition for this new tort was due in part because of "the power to capture and store vast amounts of personal information using modern technology."[69]

Since the *Jones v. Tsige* decision, several class actions have used this new tort. In order to make a claim for intrusion upon seclusion, an individual must establish[70]

1. the individual's conduct was intentional or reckless;
2. the individual invaded, without lawful justification, the plaintiff's private affairs and concerns; and
3. a reasonable person would regard the invasion as highly offensive, causing the plaintiff distress, humiliation, or anguish. (Anguish and suffering are generally presumed once the other elements have been established.)

Since deciding this landmark case, this new tort has the potential to dramatically impact society, media, and our core conceptions of individual privacy.[71]

Just as this new tort of invasion of privacy protects an individual's right to privacy, and PIPEDA protects private sector organizations from collecting, using, and disclosing personal information, the **Freedom of Information and Protection of Privacy Act (FIPPA)** was put in place so that the government can protect the privacy of an individual's personal information existing in government records. It also gives individuals whose personal information is kept the right to request access to government-held information, including general records and records containing their own personal information. FIPPA applies to Ontario's provincial ministries and most provincial agencies, boards, and commissions, as well as community colleges, universities, local health integration networks, and hospitals.

Financial Information

As discussed in Chapter 4, investor relations (maintaining relationships and communicating with financial publics such as current stockholders, potential investors, and financial analysts) is an important sector of public relations.

Investor relations (IR) is considered a sub-sector of public relations. Investor relations deals mainly with a public company and specifically how a company communicates with investors, shareholders, government authorities, and the overall financial community. Investor relations professionals need to be well equipped and familiar with the different regulatory requirements surrounding the financial disclosure requirements of a corporation. Their main purpose is to "ensure that a company's stock is being traded fairly through disclosure of key facts that allow all investors to assess

Freedom of Information and Protection of Privacy Act (FIPPA)
A Canadian law passed to ensure that the government makes its information accessible to citizens.

s_bukley/Shutterstock.com

Martha Stewart served five months in prison, five months of house arrest, and two full years of probation.

Do you think this was a fair sentence? Why or why not?

whether a company is a good investment or not."[72] Unlike public relations, an investor relations professional must work very closely with a corporation's accounting department, legal department, and top executives such as the chief executive officer (CEO), chief financial officer (CFO), and chief operating officer (COO). In comparison to public relations, investor relations has a much more regulatory role.[73]

The **Ontario Securities Commission (OSC)** regulates communication activities with investors, including **initial public offerings (IPOs)**. IPOs are highly choreographed financial events in which private companies first offer sale of stocks to public investors. As they would in any new corporate initiative or offering, public relations people play a role in the successful launch of IPOs.

For example, at the same time Uber Technologies Inc. ("Uber") was launching its UberX ride in Toronto, Uber was dealing with a legal challenge against the taxi industry. There was a lot of negative publicity and backlash about how Uber had hired drivers without commercial licenses. At the time, Uber did not have a PR team. Start-up tech companies are often unconvinced about PR and don't realize its importance until they find themselves in a PR crisis. In this case, a PR professional could have helped salvage the company's reputation: "Uber learned the hard way that PR is an important part of a business strategy."[74]

As a PR professional, if your client is a corporation, you may take a crucial role either before or after the potential IPO and have access to sensitive information known as **material nonpublic information**, which is any information that could influence the market value of a company or its products. This information is confidential in nature and usually only someone who is working closely with or is an employee of the company would have knowledge about such information.[75] While working closely with a corporate client, you will be likely exposed to plenty of material information that is not available to the public. The following are examples of the types of events and information that could be considered material:

- changes to the corporate structure or capital structure of the company
- financial results
- business operations, acquisitions, or dispositions

All of these could lead to a significant impact on the company.

Due to the sensitivity of the information that public relations professionals will be exposed to, they must be careful not to use this confidential information for their own advantage or pass off this information inadvertently to family or friends. If they do and a receiving party acts on this information to purchase shares of the company in the public market, this may be considered **insider trading** and could have serious consequences.

In November 2009, Canada held its first criminal conviction for illegal insider trading. Gil Cornblum and Stan Grmovsek went to law school together. When they graduated, they collaborated in a deliberate and prolonged illegal insider-trading scheme. Cornblum was working at a number of law firms in New York and Toronto when he received some material nonpublic information in his role as counsel to certain issuers on pending corporate transactions. He even went as far as to use the night secretarial staff's temporary password to search for information in the databases. Once he obtained this information,

Ontario Securities Commission A Canadian regulatory body that administers and enforces compliance with securities legislation.

initial public offering (IPO) Financial event in which a private company offers sale of stocks to public investors for the first time.

material nonpublic information Any information that could influence the market value of a company or its products.

insider trading When a company's employees or executives buy and sell stock in their own organization or share information with others who buy or sell before the information has been made public.

he passed it onto Grmovsek who executed the trades. They made a profit and split the profits between them.

In Canada, Grmovsek was charged with three offences: fraud, illegal insider trading, and money laundering. He was sentenced to 39 months in jail. Cornblum committed suicide a day before he was scheduled to plead guilty. The OSC's settlement agreement with Grmovsek stated that "Cornblum and Grmovsek provided extensive cooperation in assisting all regulatory authorities and law enforcement agencies involved in identifying the depth and breadth of the conduct at issue."[76]

Regulating the Business of Public Relations

Canadian Radio-television and Telecommunications Commission (CRTC) The administrative tribunal that regulates and supervises broadcasting and telecommunications in the public interest.

The **Canadian Radio-television and Telecommunications Commission (CRTC)** is an administrative tribunal that regulates and supervises broadcasting and telecommunications in the interest of the public.[77] The CRTC oversees more than 2,000 broadcasters, including TV services, am and FM radio stations, and the companies that bring these services to you (e.g., Rogers Communications). They also regulate telecommunications carriers, including major telephone companies.[78]

As regulators, the CRTC can be seen as the police of broadcasting. The CRTC puts out rules and regulations that must be followed in order to "enhance the safety and interests of Canadians by promoting compliance with the Unsolicited Telecommunications Rules (UTRs)."[79] For example, if you live in Canada and you want to reduce the number of telemarketing calls you receive, you can register your phone number on the National Do Not Call Registry—run by the CRTC.

Canadian anti-spam legislation (CASL) Law that protects Canadians from spam messages, hacking, malware, harmful software, and any other forms of privacy invasion.

Similarly, **Canadian anti-spam legislation (CASL)** is anti-spam legislation put into place to protect Canadians from spam messages, hacking, malware, harmful software, and any other form of privacy invasions. The CASL oversees and regulates any **commercial electronic messages (CEM)** sent to Canadian residents.[80] In other words, any business that sends any form of electronic messages to Canada should review the rules of CASL in order to abide by the guidelines.

commercial electronic messages (CEM) Any electronic message that encourages participation in a commercial activity, regardless of whether there is an expectation of profit.

Any CEM sent within Canada must have either the express or implied consent of the recipient. *Express consent* is where recipients have said they want to receive information from you.[81] If express, the consent needs to be clear-cut and straightforward. *Implied consent*, on the other hand, is slightly trickier in that you already have an ongoing business relationship within the last two years, the email address is publicly available, or the recipient voluntarily shared their contact information.[82] The onus is on the sender to prove whether express or implied consent has been received. Since CASL came into effect, it has made communication challenging, especially for those in public relations.

For a public relations professional, something as simple as sending out invites to a promotional party will require the guidance of CASL. Unless those invites are being sent to individuals who have consented to be on the email chain, everyone else is receiving an email in violation of CASL. This piece of legislation in Canada is enforced by the Competition Bureau of Canada, the CRTC, and the Office of the Privacy Commissioner. Similar to CASL is Europe's newly implemented legislation known as General Data Protection Regulation (GDPR), created to protect personal data.

Voices from the Field

Tyler Burns

Image Courtesy of Tyler Burns

Tyler Burns leads the investor relations function at Canopy Growth, a Canadian-based cannabis company that grows, processes, and distributes medical and recreational cannabis.

Based in Smith Falls, Ontario, Canopy was the first cannabis company to be listed on the Toronto Stock Exchange and remains the only cannabis company to be a member of a major global stock market index, in this case the S&P/TSX Composite Index. Most recently it was the first cannabis-producing company to be listed on the New York Stock Exchange. Tweed, a Canopy Growth subsidiary, was the first Canadian producer to be approved to export dried cannabis to Germany, and the company continues to offer an ever-increasing variety of products for sale through German pharmacies.

Burns is a recognized leader in marketing, public relations, and investor relations with over 15 years of experience in international business. His diverse background in product marketing, international standards, financial markets, and investor relations brings a fresh perspective to his work at Canopy. An aerospace engineer by training, Burns's resume includes time working at an Internet consulting firm and a Bluetooth semiconductor manufacturer.

What has been your career path up to now?
Well, it certainly wasn't a normal trajectory! I trained as an aerospace engineer, and when I graduated there just weren't any jobs in that field. I started an Internet consulting firm because there were lots of opportunities there. Later, I co-founded a semiconductor company; that's where I really began my investor relations work. Later, I led the investor relations function at WiLan, an Ottawa-based telecommunications company.

What do you do in investor relations? Who are your stakeholders?
Obviously, our shareholders are an important stakeholder, but I consider prospective shareholders equally important as we look to expand our shareholder base. Other important stakeholders include US and Canadian security regulators, customers, employees, and the communities in which we work.

I work closely with the directors of communications and government relations to determine the messaging. Because we are a publicly traded company, there are many regulations about disclosing information. Essentially, we can't disclose any material information about the company unless we share it publicly, through media releases. The rules are designed to provide a fair market, so that no investor has an unfair advantage.

What is a typical day like for you at Canopy?
There is no typical day. The company is growing so fast right now it's really a seven-day-a-week job. When I started with Canopy three years ago there were maybe 75 or 80 cars in the parking lot. Now there are more than 1,000 people (at the Smith Falls location) and you can't find anywhere to park.

What about CSR (corporate social responsibility)? Is that a big part of your work?
CSR as a concept is important to Canopy. We've made significant investments in research, education, and the communities in which we operate. But my stakeholders are primarily interested in the financial information.

What is the most exciting part of your job?
It's all exciting—I pinch myself every day when I get to work. Cannabis is a brand-new industry. I feel like we're in the first inning of a nine-inning game; the growth potential

Continued

is huge. According to Stats Canada, there are three or four million active cannabis users in Canada today, and countries around the world are legalizing or considering legalization. In Canada we have the opportunity to lead this industry globally, without significant competition from the US. That's a once-in-a-lifetime opportunity.

Every day, there's something new happening. We're hiring 20 or 30 people a day. We're building new facilities. The business is evolving so quickly that it's like a brand-new company every three months.

What recommendations do you have for students who may be interested in a career in investor relations?
If you're going to do IR, it's not enough to have communications skills and training—you really should take a business course of some kind so that you understand capital markets and accounting. CIRI (Canadian Investor Relations Institute) has some excellent courses, including a certification program that covers accounting and finance, capital markets, regulation, and strategy.

Ethics: Finding a Balance with the Law

At this point in your life, you have probably heard the saying that just because something is legal doesn't make it ethical. As a public relations professional, privacy is one area in which you may need more than a legal interpretation to make ethical decisions.

As a PR professional, the CPRS is your guide on how to act ethically in your profession. In becoming a member of the CPRS, a "pledge to maintain the spirit and ideals" of the CPRS must be taken. By pledging your oath as a PR professional, you are agreeing to abide by all the rules and regulations including the code of professional standards (or code of ethics). The overall code of the CPRS states the following:[83]

1. A member shall deal fairly and honestly with the communications media and the public, and
2. A member shall practice the highest standards of honesty, accuracy, integrity and truth, and shall not knowingly disseminate false or misleading information.[84]

In the same manner as lawyers, PR professionals are always faced with ethical dilemmas. PR professionals are meant to maintain the delicate balance between their clients' needs and the collective good of the public by working in accord with other professional counsel, the media, and the public. In doing so, they strive to benefit from open multidirectional communications. Ethics is at the forefront of a PR professional's career.

trade secret Business information that is not generally known to the public and not readily available to others who could profit from its disclosure or use.

In business law, a **trade secret** is information that is not generally known to others and not readily available to others who could profit from its disclosure or use.[85] Often trade secrets are valuable, as they can be anything from new technology to a creation of a unique recipe. For example, the formula for Coca-Cola or the recipe for a Big Mac are both considered trade secrets. The recipes and formulas are what keep the company valuable, and thus extremes are taken to protect the confidentiality of the trade secret."[86] As much as PR professionals are encouraged to be ethically honest and open regarding their client, there needs to be a balance and focus on the privacy of their client, too.

Case Study

R v. Ghomeshi, 2016 ONCJ 155

As a public relations practitioner, you expect your clients to be open and honest with you about any situation. Firms that are in the business of public relations or crisis communications require the full story so they can manage the situation with full knowledge and understanding. So, knowing that the profession is based on honesty, what would you do if your client lied to you?

Jian Ghomeshi was the host of a CBC television show called PLAY. Prior to PLAY, he was the host of a CBC radio show called Q, which featured interviews with prominent cultural and entertainment figures. By the early 2010s, Ghomeshi had achieved moderate celebrity status; he was a prominent and well-known personality in the arts and entertainment community in Canada. In 2014, rather abruptly, the CBC publicly terminated him in the midst of several sexual assault allegations.[87]

In 2014, Ghomeshi was charged with five criminal offences related to four separate events, involving three different complainants (some of the women remained nameless, under a publication ban, during the trial). Specifically, he was charged with four counts of sexual assault and one count of overcoming resistance by choking. He was granted bail and his lawyer claimed he would plead not guilty. After all the women had testified and explained what had happened to them, Ghomeshi did not step into the witness box to testify on his own defence. Ghomeshi's lawyers argued that the complainants were inconsistent witnesses who all lied under oath and that the Crown failed to prove its case beyond a reasonable doubt. Ghomeshi was found

THE CANADIAN PRESS/Mark Blinch

Mr Ghomeshi was found not guilty.

Do you think as a PR professional you could salvage Mr Ghomeshi's career?

Continued

not guilty, as the judge agreed that the complainants' testimony was "less than full, frank, and forthcoming."[88]

Before the trials began, PR firms Rock-it-Promotions and Navigator were helping Ghomeshi. In assisting with his public image, both firms dealt with false statements from Ghomeshi himself. He lied about the allegations against him. He explained, "It was a jilted ex-girlfriend who had manufactured lies" that Ghomeshi was abusive.[89] However, after more than eight women came forward alleging assault or sexual harassment, the two firms decided that they would no longer represent the CBC radio star.[90]

In a statement released by the Canadian Public Relations Society (CPRS), "As an industry association representing public relations practitioners in Canada, the Canadian Public Relations Society adheres to the premise that everyone deserves public relations and communications counsel."[91] Should Ghomeshi have received continued counsel from PR firms regardless of the fact that he had lied? Morally and ethically, is this right? The statement from the CPRS went on to read, "We pursue these goals with the firm belief that PR must always benefit and protect the public interest."[92] Therefore, having a client that lies to their PR firm is in strict violation of the CPRS code because PR professionals must always benefit and protect the public interest.

In some cases, people have argued that your Facebook profile or Twitter account is also a trade secret. In order for your account to constitute a trade secret, "The information must not be publicly known, actively kept secret by the business, valuable to the business and competitors, and not easily duplicated by independent effort."[93] Sometimes the lines get blurred when it comes to an organization and a social media account. Who do you think owns the account: the employer or employee?

The court recognized in *Thoi Bao Inc. v. 1913075 Limited (Vo Media)* that social media has value. Mr Vo was employed by Thoi Bao Inc. to perform various roles, such as TV cameraman, editor, supervisor, and webmaster. Their principal web presence was through the website thaoibaotv.com, which streamed audio, video, television shows, and other newscasts. During his employment, Mr Vo registered the domain name www.thoibaotv.com and, through a numbered corporation doing business as Vo Media, offered Vietnamese programming from the site, including online news and media services. Mr Vo did this without the knowledge of or approval of his employer, Thoi Bao Inc. Mr Vo was fired from and sued by Thoi Bao Inc. alleging a range of causes of action including trademark infringement, passing off, depreciation of goodwill, and copyright infringement. The federal court ordered Mr Vo to transfer to Thoi Bao Inc.

ownership and all rights of access, administration and control for and over the domain name (registered by Mr Vo) together with any other domain name, Facebook account, Twitter account, or other social media accounts registered to or in control of Mr Vo containing Thoi Bao, TBTV or ThoiBao TV or any confusingly similar trademark.[94]

This type of debate has become more common with the rise of the Internet. Ownership rights to a company's social media account have become increasingly debated in the courts.

Creating social media data is considered a powerful marketing tool for companies whether they are big or small. Companies mitigate the risk of misappropriation of their social media accounts by having an employer policy on social media accounts, clearly specifying in employment agreements any rights to social media accounts, registering the name of the social media account in the name of the company, and considering the social media account when acquiring another business.[95] Although in most cases the ownership rights lend itself to the employer, in some cases employees can own the rights to their social media accounts (for example, if you were hired specifically to create a social media account and manage it).

Based on recent case law, there is a strong indication that if a company's social media profiles are visible online, they can receive trade secret protection.

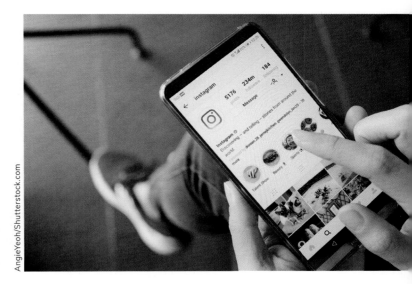

A social network could be considered one of an organization's "trade secrets."

How can public relations professionals ethically balance personal and professional uses of social networks?

In Case You Missed It

Social media have been called the Wild West of the Internet, a place where participants make up the rules as they go. While it is true that technology often advances faster than the law, some standard legal rules still apply.

- It is advisable to work alongside or consult a lawyer before proceeding to do anything.
- Libel (or slander) claims are equally as harmful whether they are in print or online. If you republish a defamatory statement, you are just as liable as the person initiating the defamation or reporting the defamation.

- Always give credit and source those whose work you are using; otherwise you will be subject to plagiarism.
- Intellectual property requires proper protection. Copyright and trademarks are the most prominent types of intellectual property within the public relations profession.
- Always obtain permission before disclosing any private information about a client.
- Your social media account can be considered a trade secret.
- Ethics should be the core value in your profession.
- Consent is a defence, if obtained.

Summary

11.1 Discuss why it is important to always run your work by in-house counsel or legal counsel.
As you try to protect your client's image, you also need to protect them legally. If they lose a battle in court, it could potentially bankrupt them. However, an image can, more often than not, be restored.

11.2 Describe any limits to free speech, including libel and slander.
Freedom of speech rights can be limiting in certain situations; for example, when they infringe upon another's reputation, intellectual property, financial interest, or privacy. Defamation is any statement that injures someone's reputation. Libel and slander are both types of defamation. Slander refers to the spoken communication, while libel refers to the written or recorded communication.

11.3 Describe the common types of intellectual property and the ways in which they are protected.
Intellectual property includes writing, inventions, logos, images, designs, and all combinations thereof. Some common types of intellectual property include copyright, trademarks, and patents.

11.4 Identify where privacy comes into play in the role of public relations.
As a PR professional, you need to take extra precaution that you are not sharing or divulging information about a client that is an invasion of their privacy.

11.5 Identify and discuss agencies that guide and regulate public relations professionals.
Depending on your area of public relations, you will need to become familiar with various government agencies that are responsible for protecting your key publics. There are many federal agencies that could influence your role, depending on who your client is. In Canada, the Competition Bureau focuses on ensuring compliance with the Competition Act in advancing consumer protection measures. Both the CFIA (Canadian Food Inspection Agency) and the Department of Health Canada regulate food and health-related industries. The OSC regulates financial information.

11.6 Analyze ethical dilemmas public relations professionals face and what organization is in place to help guide a PR professional.
When dealing with a corporation or client, there are certain measures that come into play, such as what you are allowed to disclose about the client versus what you are allowed to disclose about the corporation. Making sure these principles do not override each other is important. Safeguards and codes of ethics are at the forefront of the PR profession. The main organization used as a guiding principle is the Canadian Public Relations Society (CPRS).

Discussion Questions

1.   Describe an incident in which you think a PR professional would need the help of legal counsel. Why would legal counsel be necessary?

2.   Identify a defamatory statement (either in your own life or in the general news). What are the potential defences of the statement?

3.   Identify a piece of your own intellectual property that you would consider publishing online (perhaps a photo, essay, blog entry, song, or artwork). What type of intellectual property would it be considered? Would you need a license for it? Why or why not?

4.   Do you think that our current government initiatives to protect people's private information are sufficient? If so, why? If not, what could the government and taxpayers do to tighten up security?

5.   What branch of PR interests you most? Assuming you land a position, what regulatory agencies would you need to become more familiar with and why? (If the answer is none, explain why your work would not be regulated by any agency.)

6.   Again, assume you landed your dream PR job. Your new employer asks you to sign an agreement that allows the company access to any social media accounts you use for any tasks related to your job. How would you handle the situation?

Further Readings and Online Resources

How a PR Professional Can Refrain from Defamation
Downard, P.A. (2018). *The law of libel in Canada* **(4th ed.). North York, ON: LexisNexis Canada.**
> This book examines the various ways in which people can protect themselves from defaming others in publications.

How Social Media Has Impacted Public Relations
DiStaso, M., & Mccorkindale, T. (2012). Social media: Uses and opportunities in public relations. *GlobeMediaJournal,5(2),75–82.***www.researchgate.net/publication/259563914_Social_media_Uses_and_opportunities_in_public_relations**
> The evolution of technology has really changed the dynamics within public relations. PR professionals are now able to communicate with the public in differing ways.

How PR Professionals Can Protect Their Creative Works
Hutchinson, C. (2016). *Digital copyright law.* **Toronto, ON: Irwin Law.**
> This book examines the many ways in which PR professionals can protect their creative work in the digital world.

Ways in Which PR Professionals Can Navigate Their Social Media within the Internet
Lomic, P. (2018). *Social media and Internet law: Forms and precedents* **(2nd ed.). Markham, ON: LexisNexis Canada.**
> This book examines the ways in which PR professionals can use social media to navigate the Internet. It also gives an introduction to important legislation, privacy issues, and IP.

Peer-Reviewed Academic Journal Article
Myers, C. (2016). Apology, sympathy, and empathy: The legal ramifications of admitting fault in US public relations pra`ctice. *Public Relations Review,* **42(1), 176–83. doi:10.1016/j.pubrev.2015.10.004**
> This article explores the issue of apologies used by corporations who have done wrong in the eyes of their stakeholders. In some US states and Canadian provinces, saying "sorry" is not an admission of guilt, whereas in others it can be used against the company in court. This article makes the point that PR practitioners have to know the law in their jurisdiction before issuing an apology.

Key Terms

Canadian anti-spam legislation (CASL)   288
Canadian Radio-television and Telecommunications Commission (CRTC)   288
Commercial electronic message (CEM)   288
Copyright   280
Copyright infringement   282
Customer relationship management (CRM)   285
Cyber libel   276

Defamation   275
Fair dealing   284
Freedom of Information and Protection of Privacy Act (FIPPA)   286
Initial public offering (IPO)   287
Insider trading   287
Intellectual property   280
Libel   275
Limitation period   275
Material nonpublic information   287

Multiple publication rule   279
Ontario Securities Commission (OSC)   287
Personal Information Protection and Electronic Documents Act (PIPEDA)   284
Plagiarism   281
Publication   279
Slander   275
Trademark   280
Trade secret   290

12

Issues and Crises

How was one of the most iconic brands
in the automobile industry brought to its knees?

Key learning outcomes

12.1 Analyze responses ranging from advocacy to accommodation in public relations conflict cases.

12.2 Identify stages in the issues life cycle.

12.3 Describe how issues management can prevent or lessen the impact of crises.

12.4 Discuss how traditional media, social media, and offline word of mouth interact in the spread of crisis information.

12.5 Assess competing values in ethical conflicts of interest in the context of public relations issues and crises.

▲ rvlsoft/Shutterstock.com

Much of this book so far has been about how to conduct public relations as part of a management function that helps organizations meet goals and avert crises. However, even the very best public relations professionals working for the most responsible organizations face issues and crises. Some crises, such as natural disasters, are unavoidable, while other crises are not. One of the toughest jobs in public relations is being called on to help organizations navigate crises they created themselves. Before delving into ways organizations respond to crises, this chapter covers how issues evolve and how issues may be identified and managed proactively to minimize the need for crisis management.

Managing Conflict

"My god they're throwing guitars out there!" Though not quite as legendary as Paul Revere's "The redcoats are coming!" this exclamation from a passenger in the window seat of a United Airlines airplane started a bit of a revolution. Baggage handlers at Chicago's O'Hare International Airport had picked the wrong guy's guitar to toss around. The result was a flashpoint case illustrating the power of individuals to confront large powerful organizations on social media.

After hearing the startling observation from the back of a plane, Dave Carroll and fellow Halifax-based band members of *Sons of Maxwell* looked out to see that, indeed, their instruments were being heaved carelessly by United Airlines luggage handlers. Concerned about his $3,500 Taylor guitar, Carroll immediately brought the issue to the attention of a flight attendant. The flight attendant referred him to a "lead agent" in the terminal who said he needed to talk to another lead agent and dismissed his request before she disappeared into a crowd. Carroll then spoke to a third employee, who referred him to a fourth at his next airport.[1] This all-too-familiar storyline of poor customer service goes on and on. Carroll's guitar was smashed, and for nine months he tried and failed to reach an acceptable resolution with the airline.

The narrative was so ridiculous it was almost funny, and so Carroll decided to tap into that sentiment with the YouTube music video "United Breaks Guitars." The video featured a catchy tune and clever lyrics describing the whole experience, and it struck a chord with millions of frustrated passengers. In fact, the video went viral during the summer of 2009. Eighteen million views later, Carroll's bio describes him as not only a singer–songwriter but also a master storyteller, professional speaker, and social media innovator.

On the other side of the story, United Airlines saw its market value drop $180 million in the four days after Carroll's video was uploaded to YouTube. While a claim that Carroll's social media attack was the main reason for the financial loss would be hard to prove, the damage to the airline's reputation was "undeniable" according to a *Huffington Post* business report.[2]

United Airlines wasn't the first airline to feel the impact of social media in managing issues, conflicts, and crises. And it certainly wouldn't be the last. In 2013, Twitter user Hasan Syed slammed British Airways for losing his luggage. His tweets reached a mere 400 followers, which in most cases would have been the end of the story. However, then Syed paid $1,000 for another 50,000 users to see the tweets as part of Twitter's promoted tweets advertising service. In doing so, he demonstrated the power of paid advertising as a social media tactic available to individuals.[3] Although Syed paid for the promoted tweets, his investment went

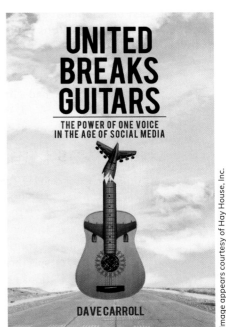

Image appears courtesy of Hay House, Inc.

Musician Dave Carroll became famous for launching a musical protest on social media with his YouTube hit "United Breaks Guitars."

How do social media change the way organizations and customer publics interact in conflict?

Hasan Syed drew international media attention when he paid to reach 50,000 people with this tweet complaining about British Airways, largely because he was the first customer widely known to have used this tactic.

Would you ever pay for a promoted tweet (or Facebook post or Snapchat story, etc.) to complain about an organization? What would make it worth/ not worth the cost?

Respond quickly and appropriately to challenges on social media to prevent issues from becoming crises.

contingency theory
A theory that proposes that the best course of action in any situation depends on the specifics of the situation.

pure advocacy Stance in issues management in which a public relations practitioner firmly pleads an organization's case without compromise.

much further than the 50,000 exposures delivered by Twitter when international media such as *Time, The Guardian, BBC, Mashable, The Australian,* and *NBC News* picked up the story.

Beyond airlines, any organization with publics online has had to come to terms with a shift of communication power when issues arise. Brandon Stanton, a photographer known for his Humans of New York photography project, declined an offer of $50 per photo from New York–based fashion powerhouse DKNY to display his work in their stores. When Stanton found out that DKNY had gone ahead and displayed his photos in a store window in Bangkok without his permission, he posted the following on his Facebook page: "I don't want any money. But please REBLOG this post if you think that DKNY should donate $100,000 on my behalf to the YMCA in Bedford-Stuyvesant, Brooklyn." [4]

Recognizing that it was facing both a legal and a public relations issue, DKNY responded with the following statement: "DKNY has always supported the arts and we deeply regret this mistake. Accordingly, we are making a charitable donation of $25,000 to the YMCA in Bedford-Stuyvesant Brooklyn in Mr. Stanton's name."

Stanton accepted the apology: "We are going to take them at their word that it was a mistake and be happy that this one had a happy ending." Even legal issues can be raised—and settled—on social media.

Dave Carroll versus United Airlines. Hasan Syed versus British Airways. Brandon Stanton versus DKNY. Each case presents a conflict that played out on social media and, therefore, played out in the public eye. Managing conflict, especially public conflict, is a major function of public relations. Public relations scholars have studied how public relations people in all sorts of organizations (not just big corporations like airlines and fashion companies) make decisions on how to communicate with publics when two-way relationships become contentious.

To help understand this decision process, University of Missouri professor Glen Cameron and his colleagues developed a contingency theory of conflict in public relations.[5] A **contingency theory** suggests that the best course of action in any situation depends on the specifics of the situation. In conflict, the action or communication tactic that a public relations person chooses depends on factors internal and external to the organization. Internal factors may include an organization's size, structure, and culture, as well as the autonomy of a public relations department within an organization and the level of practitioner experience. External factors may include the threat of litigation, business competition, political support, and the size and power of publics. Contingency theory also describes response options ranging from **pure advocacy** (firmly pleading the organization's case without compromise) on one side to **pure accommodation** (completely conceding to a public's demands) on the other side (see Figure 12.1). In many cases, social media have given publics greater power relative to organizations. But that doesn't mean public relations people have to always accommodate publics, nor do they always have to go to battle and advocate hard on one side of an issue.

United Airlines and DKNY had to consider very different contingencies. If you have ever actually read all the fine print in an airline passenger contract, you'd probably *not* be surprised to learn that United Airlines did *not* have to reimburse Carroll. In contrast, DKNY

Image appears courtesy of Humans of New York/Brandon Stanton

pure accommodation
Stance in issues management in which a public relations practitioner fully concedes to a public's demands.

DKNY displayed a New York photographer's work in this storefront window in Bangkok without his permission. The photographer called DKNY out on Facebook.

Did DKNY handle the situation well by apologizing and donating $25,000 to a charity? Why or why not?

faced a legitimate legal challenge based on Stanton's claim to intellectual property. United Airlines customer service agents had no reason to believe that Carroll would find an audience of millions for his complaint (especially on YouTube in 2009). DKNY likely realized that Stanton already had quite a following on Facebook and other social media.

The two organizations also offered very different levels of accommodation. United Airlines pretty much refused to accommodate Dave Carroll, while DKNY accommodated Brandon Stanton by apologizing and offering a $25,000 charity donation. Although the case had a happier ending for DKNY than it did for United Airlines, this doesn't mean that more accommodation is always better. In fact, that's the point of contingency theory. Sometimes you should advocate, and other times it makes more sense to accommodate.

You will probably never see a YouTube video of an airline passenger singing about his luggage that arrived undamaged or a viral Facebook campaign celebrating a company for attaining proper permissions for artwork. Most small business owners won't get 15,000 hits and national media attention for sticking up for their employees. In fact, the vast majority of issues will not rise to the level of a major public issue or crisis. It's also important to remember that customers are only one type of public with which we maintain relationships. Perhaps the best public relations "crises" are the ones that never happen, meaning that full-blown

> Sometimes it's better to advocate rather than to accommodate.

A Crisis Threatens the Future of Maple Leaf Foods: A Classic Study in Crisis Communication

The Arthur W. Page Society is a New York–based professional association for senior public relations and corporate communications executives and educators. Like the CPRS's (Canadian Public Relations Society's) Code of Professional Standards, the Page Society has a set of guidelines for practice. "Page Society members regard these principles as the guidelines by which they, and indeed all communications professionals, should undertake their role."[6]

One of the seven principles is "conduct public relations as if the *whole enterprise* depends on it"; one of the best modern-day illustrations of this principle in action is the 2008 case of Maple Leaf Foods and how the organization handled the communications surrounding the incident.

In August 2008, Maple Leaf Foods was facing a major crisis. Listeria had been found in some of their food products, specifically cold cuts, and people were getting sick and dying.[7] By the time the crisis was over, 22 deaths would be attributed to the contaminated products, and Maple Leaf Foods had a major crisis of confidence on its hands. How could Canadian consumers ever feel safe buying roast beef, corned beef, and other cold cuts for their families knowing Maple Leaf products had caused a number of deaths?

Photo by Deborah Baic/The Globe and Mail via CP Images

Maple Leaf Foods CEO Michael McCain was widely praised for how his company handled the crisis.

Can you think of other examples of crises that were well handled?

The company, which was founded in 1927, was a major employer (approximately 24,000 employees) with plants around the country. On 17 August, the Canadian Food Inspection Agency (CFIA) issued a health hazard alert warning the public not to serve or consume Sure Slice (a Maple Leaf brand) roast beef and corned beef because they may be contaminated with Listeria monocytogenes.[8]

While some organizations seem unsure of how to proceed when faced with a crisis, Maple Leaf took quick and decisive action. Josh Greenberg wrote the following in an article exploring the crisis:

> The Maple Leaf Foods listeriosis outbreak is significant not only because of the health and economic impacts, but also because of how the company communicated in its response. In contrast to organizations that have confronted crisis situations by avoiding and displacing blame, or keeping silent and maintaining a low profile, Maple Leaf opted for a strategy of high visibility.[9]

Maple Leaf president and CEO Michael H. McCain was front and centre throughout the crisis. Following the news of the first death, a camera crew was summoned to Maple Leaf's offices where the president recorded a statement that was aired on all major broadcast media (at Maple Leaf's expense) and was widely viewed on YouTube. The full text of McCain's statement is below:

> My name is Michael McCain. As you may know listeria was found in some of our products. Even though listeria is bacteria commonly found in many foods and in the environment, we work diligently to eliminate it.
>
> When listeria was discovered in the product, we launched immediate recalls to get it off the shelf, then we shut the plant down. Tragically, our products have been linked to illnesses and loss of life. To Canadians who are ill and to families who have lost loved ones, I offer my deepest sympathies. Words cannot begin to express our sadness for your pain.
>
> Maple Leaf Foods is 23,000 people who live in a culture of food safety. We have an unwavering commitment to keeping your food safe with standards well beyond regulatory requirements.
>
> But this week, our best efforts failed and we are deeply sorry. This is the toughest situation we have faced in 100 years as a company. We know this has shaken your confidence in us; I commit to you that our actions are guided by putting your interests first.[10]

Maple Leaf's actions following the discovery of listeriosis were not limited to a single video statement. They communicated openly to stakeholders through the media and directly through online tools, they recalled hundreds of products from the affected plant (not just those found to be contaminated), they shut down and cleaned the plant, and they hired their own food safety inspector.

Continued

As *The Globe and Mail* columnist Tony Wilson pointed out, Maple Leaf's decisive actions following the crisis likely saved the company:

> *First, it admitted it was the company's fault. It admitted it was responsible. It said, in essence, "it's our fault and we're going to fix it." Second, Maple Leaf apologized. It wasn't "wordsmithed" or spin-doctored to deny culpability. The company didn't dodge the issue. It apologized up front in every possible media. Third, it didn't hire a celebrity to deliver the apology, or a blonde actress with very white teeth wearing a lab coat. CEO Michael McCain was the voice and the face of the crisis, and of the apology. Fourth, once Maple Leaf realized the problem was the company's fault, it acted decisively, and transparently.*[11]

The company's response has been lauded as a textbook example of how to handle a crisis by public relations professionals and the media. Toronto-based PR firm Veritas described it as a bold, breathtaking communications play, and Peter Lapinskie of the *Daily Observer* in Pembroke, Ontario, said, "(McCain's) candour at a time when his contemporaries would have scurried behind spin doctors and legal eagles was a refreshing way to address a potentially devastating mistake. I actually trust the man!"[12]

A few months after the crisis began, Michael McCain was named business newsmaker of 2008 by Canadian Press based on his effective handling of the situation. "Conduct public relations as if the whole enterprise depends on it" is one of the seven principles espoused by the Arthur Page Society.

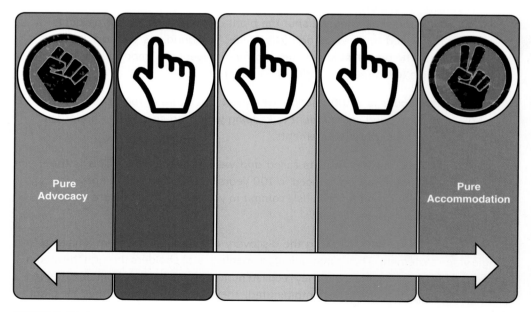

Pure Advocacy

Pure Accommodation

FIGURE 12.1 Continuum of options for managing issues and conflict, according to contingency theory.

Are there situations when pure advocacy or pure accommodation might be appropriate, or are these merely theoretical constructs?

crises are averted with effective communication and issues management—not just with customers, but with all publics.

Managing Issues

Organizations face all sorts of issues that can develop into crises if they are not managed appropriately. **Issues management** is an area of public relations that focuses on proactive monitoring and management to prevent crises from happening.[13]

issues management
Systematic process whereby organizations work to identify and resolve issues before they become crises.

Issues Life Cycle

In order to manage issues, you must first be able to identify them. The earlier you uncover an issue, the more options you will likely have for dealing with a situation. Issues management scholars have outlined several stages in the issue life cycle (see Figure 12.2):

1. Early/potential: when a few people begin to become aware of possible problems
2. Emerging: when more people begin to notice and express concern
3. Current/crisis: when the negative impact on an organization becomes public and pressure on the organization builds
4. Dormant: when the organization has no choice but to accept the long-term consequences

The longer an issue exists without being addressed, the more entrenched publics become in their opposition and the fewer options for strategic response are available to organizations.

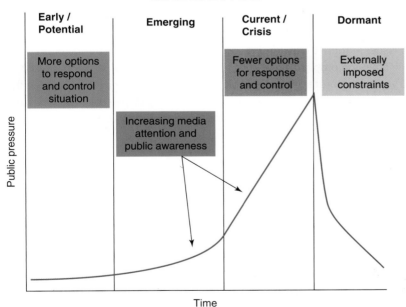

ISSUE LIFE CYCLE

| Early / Potential | Emerging | Current / Crisis | Dormant |

More options to respond and control situation

Increasing media attention and public awareness

Fewer options for response and control

Externally imposed constraints

Public pressure

Time

> Monitor social media to uncover issues sooner and give you more options for dealing with a situation.

FIGURE 12.2 This illustration of the issue life cycle shows how public pressure builds over time as an issue moves from potential to emerging to current/crisis.

Is the Volkswagen "dieselgate" issue dormant now? What role did media coverage play?

The Issue Life Cycle of Volkswagen's Dieselgate

Volkswagen's diesel emissions scandal, dubbed "dieselgate" by some and "the diesel dupe" by others, provides an example of how an issue can grow into a full-blown crisis with major consequences.

Early/Potential

At the earliest stages, issues are often identified first by experts or specialists who pay close attention to small changes in the internal or external environments of organizations. When these experts or specialists perceive a potential problem and people within an organization begin planning to respond in some way, the issue has entered the *early/potential* stage.

In 2012, Arvind Thiruvengadam, an assistant professor at West Virginia University, and a few of his colleagues won a grant from the International Council on Clean Transportation (ICCT) to test the environmental friendliness and fuel efficiency of diesel cars. As part of their research, Thiruvengadam and his team ran emissions tests on a 2012 Volkswagen Jetta and a 2013 VW Passat. In the decade prior, Volkswagen's marketing message had emphasized "clean diesel."[14] Therefore, Thiruvengadam and his team expected to find that these two VW models, which were designed for sale in the United States, would run cleaner than cars sold in other countries with more lax emission standards. Instead, the researchers were surprised to find that the two VWs emitted significantly higher levels of pollutants.

In May 2014, the ICCT alerted the Environmental Protection Agency (EPA) and the California Air Resources board about the unexpected findings. At this point, Volkswagen had a *potential* issue. In fact, it was later revealed that people inside the company had known about the emission problem since 2005, so the early/potential stage for this issue lasted nearly 10 years. Corporate culture likely played a big role in the case. In exploring the role of Volkswagen's management in the circumstances leading to the crisis, *The New York Times* described the company's corporate culture as "confident, cutthroat and insular."[15]

Emerging

In the emerging stage, groups begin to form and take sides on an issue. In their book *Risk Issues and Crisis Management in Public Relations*, Michael Regester and Judy Larkin describe the emerging phase as a time when industry insiders, specialist media, professional interest groups, activist organizations, or any other publics with direct interest begin to notice and to voice concerns or opinions.[16] Media attention may be sporadic in this stage, but if public relations people are monitoring the media, including specialty media like blogs and trade publications, they still may have an opportunity to intervene and begin to formulate plans for action. As mentioned previously, the more an issue develops, the fewer options there are available for proactive management both internally and externally.

There was very little media attention for several months after the fuel efficiency researchers published their results. Volkswagen denied there was a problem and offered other explanations for why results from the road tests did not meet the expected standards.[17] Meanwhile, regulators continued to investigate. The issue was *emerging*.

Current/Crisis

In the current/crisis stage, the issue matures, and pressure builds as the impact of the issue on the organization becomes clear. Public relations people have very little control of the situation at this stage. Strategy options become mainly reactive. According to Regester and Larkin, issues become enduring and pervasive in the current stage. They increase in intensity. In September 2015, the EPA publicly accused VW of using "defeat devices"

AP Photo/Kevin Hagen, File

"We have totally screwed up," announced Volkswagen Group of America's chief executive, Michael Horn, in September 2015.

If you were an owner of one of the cars (or maybe you actually were) affected in "diesel dupe," what could Volkswagen do "to make things right"?

hidden in its diesel cars that manipulated the results of emissions tests. Basically, the devices were software designed to detect when cars were undergoing an emissions test and then improve performance accordingly.[18] Volkswagen had been caught cheating.

On 21 September 2015, Volkswagen Group of America's chief executive, Michael Horn, had to use what should have been an occasion to celebrate—the company's launch event for its 2016 Passat—to issue an apology instead. "Our company was dishonest, with the EPA and the California Air Resources board, and with all of you, and in my German words, we have totally screwed up," Horn told the Brooklyn, New York, audience. "We have to make things right, with the government, the public, our customers, our employees and also very important, our dealers." Volkswagen was amidst a crisis that had spun well beyond its control.

Consider for a moment how you would feel if you owned one of the approximately 11 million affected cars sold by Volkswagen (e.g., VWs, Audis, or Porsches). You've chosen to invest in what you believe to be smart, environmentally friendly technology, only to learn that your now highly devalued car emits "up to nine times the legal limit of smog-produced nitrogen oxide pollutants."[19] Is it safe to say you'd be, um, peeved?

Now think of how dealers and employees felt, not to mention the governments and regulators who were deliberately deceived. When an organization has damaged relationships like this with so many key publics, it is clearly in *crisis* mode. In Volkswagen's case, all they could do at this point was react to a series of painful consequences as they unfolded:

- The company admitted that 11 million of its diesel cars had been "rigged to fool emissions tests," going back to 2005 when it began focusing major marketing efforts on selling diesel cars in the United States.[20]

Continued

- Volkswagen chief executive Martin Winterkorn resigned on 23 September 2015.
- By 25 September 2015, Volkswagen stock had plummeted more than 50 per cent below its 52-week high in March 2015.[21]
- The value of used VW and Audi diesels fell more than 13 per cent in the month following the EPA announcement.[22]
- By late October 2015, more than 350 US lawsuits against Volkswagen had been filed, and legal experts expected many of those suits to be consolidated into mass class action suits. Volkswagen reportedly had set aside $7.3 billion to prepare for the fallout from the crisis, no doubt including the millions of vehicle recalls.[23]
- The company faced the likelihood of regulatory action following investigation from governments across the globe, including Germany, France, Australia, India, China, the European Union, South Korea, and Sweden— just about any country where the diesel cars were sold.
- At the end of 2015, Hans-Dieter Pötsch, chairman of Volkswagen's supervisory board, said in a press conference that an organizational climate of poor ethical standards was partly to blame, and "there was a tolerance for breaking the rules."[24]

Image courtesy of Brandalism.org.uk

Following its diesel crisis, Volkswagen became the target of the "brandalism movement" (e.g., www.brandalism.org.uk) as part of a protest campaign tied to international climate change talks.

How could Volkswagen have responded (if at all)?

Dormant

According to Regester and Larkin, an issue reaches the *dormant* stage when an organization comes to terms with the consequences.[25] This does not mean, however, that the issue is over and gone. Rather, this means that the organization has had to accept, and live with, the consequences of its actions (or inaction). In 2018, the company agreed to pay $290 million to settle claims with Canadian owners involved in a class action lawsuit. Other lawsuits are still pending in Canada and around the world, with billions in settlements already approved.

Proactive Issues Management

Now that we've seen how organizations can get into trouble, let's look at how they can work to prevent issues from turning into crises. Regester and Larkin have outlined a seven-step process for proactive issues management: (1) monitoring, (2) identification, (3) prioritization, (4) analysis, (5) strategic planning, (6) implementation, and (7) evaluation.[26] Notice how these seven steps run parallel to the four-step RACE process presented earlier in this text (Table 12.1).

Table 12.1 Overlap between RACE and Proactive Issues Management

Four-Step Process for Public Relations (RACE)	Seven-Step Process for Proactive Issues Management
Research	Monitoring Identification
Action Planning	Prioritization Analysis Strategic Planning
Communication	Implementation
Evaluation	Evaluation

1. Monitoring

The first step to avoiding crises is to continuously monitor your organization's internal and external operating environments. What is being said about your organization offline, on social media, and in traditional media? Listen carefully at meetings and events, systematically pay attention to internal and external communications, formally and informally analyze media content (including social media), and keep lines of communication open with opinion leaders. Remember that it is just as important to listen to your organization's detractors as it is to listen to supporters. The methods for research outlined in Chapter 5—primary and secondary, quantitative and qualitative, formal and informal—are all ways to monitor the environment. Your goal is to find any early, potential, or emerging issues and turn them into opportunities instead of crises.

It's just as important to listen to detractors as it is to listen to supporters.

One example of systematic monitoring is the practice of responsible supply chain management, which occurs when organizations carefully monitor all stages of production and distribution to ensure that working conditions are safe, wages are fair, and generally high ethical standards of social and environmental responsibility are maintained. This helps organizations avoid public relations crises of the type Nike and Gap faced in the 1990s and 2000s when news broke that their supply chains included child labour and sweatshops.[27]

2. Identification

Once you notice an issue, you'll need to be able to describe it and determine if it is something significant or just a random blip on the radar. Think about financial data. Company stock values rise and fall every day, but that does not mean that every time a company's stock value falls that the organization faces a crisis. Instead, analysts watch data over time and in a broader context to identify trends. Is the daily dip in stock prices part of a larger pattern? Are there other factors in the environment such as legal challenges, competitor activity, potential boycotts, or broader political and economic changes that suggest a trend that needs further attention?

Identifying issues works the same way. Even in a small organization, you have to assess the environment and look for patterns. In a student organization, you might pay close attention to meeting attendance numbers or data on new applications to identify issues with membership. A non-profit might compare year-end or holiday donations from year to year in the context of trends in competition. The website www.yourmembership.com notes that increased competition is becoming a more common issue for established non-profits as smaller non-profits use social media to compete with established organizations for both funds and volunteers.[28]

3. Prioritization

Most organizations have issues. A big part of the *management* in *issues management* is deciding which issues require resources and when. Prioritizing issues means weighing the potential scope and impact of each. When investigating an active *E. coli* outbreak in the United States, the Centers for Disease Control and Prevention (CDC) released a report that linked 53 illnesses in nine states with 47 people who said they had eaten at a Chipotle restaurant. Twenty people were hospitalized.[29] Chipotle was then criticized by some for paying more attention to GMO (genetically modified organism) issues (see Chapter 7) than the more immediate issue of restaurant food-safety procedures.

Some customers faulted Chipotle for not prioritizing its issues well. One twitter user, @producebunny, tweeted, "#Chipotle should pay more attention to food safety than hyping anti-GMOs. Foodborne pathogens are deadlier than GMOs."

How should Chipotle balance its attention to the two issues of GMOs and foodborne illnesses?

4. Analysis

Once issues have been identified and prioritized, they need to be analyzed to determine how they might affect the organization and its publics. Chipotle expected that same-store sales would fall 8–11 per cent in the quarter following the *E. coli* outbreak.[30] Volkswagen's sales dropped 24.7 per cent after its diesel crisis. Volkswagen sold 23,882 cars in November 2015 compared to 31,725 cars in November 2014.[31] Of course, issues management, and public relations in general, is about much more than sales. Analysis should include all sorts of publics besides customers. How, specifically, will employees be affected? Will they have to work longer hours? Earn less pay? Will they face public criticism? If you work for a non-profit organization, you may analyze an issue's impact on volunteers and donors. In a college or university, you would consider students, faculty, staff, and alumni. Each public will have its own specific concerns related to the issue.

5. Strategic Planning

After research and analysis, including the identification of key publics and how the issue will affect them, you can begin developing communication and relationship management strategies for each. If your role in public relations gives you a voice in the management of the organization (let's hope so), you can work on both the strategic action response to the issue and the messages that will be communicated in conjunction with that response. For example, Maple Leaf Foods apologized for the listeriosis outbreak and also announced new food safety procedures that it had developed, including hiring a new food safety officer. Strategy at this stage means considering the specific actions that should be taken as well as who should take these actions, when, and with what resources. Even if the management plan is developed outside of the public relations department, your communication plan must be coordinated with those management operations. Such strategy involves goals, objectives, timelines, and budgets, as outlined in Chapter 6 on planning.

6. Implementation

Implementation includes both action and communication. This is where policies and programs are put into action, and you activate owned, paid, shared, and earned media (Chapter 7). In issues management, the underlying purpose of implementation is to prevent negative outcomes and encourage beneficial ones. In response to sweatshop and child labour problems that arose in the 1990s and persisted well into the 2000s, both Nike and Gap began funnelling considerable resources into preventing further supply chain issues. Nike and Gap now tout their efforts on websites that they host to draw attention to their corporate social responsibility efforts. Nike's site (www.nikeresponsibility.com) includes detailed reports, interactive maps of factory locations, and infographics listing performance goals and progress towards reaching those targets.

Socially responsible management also can be leveraged by organizations of any size to recruit and retain top talent. Millennials regularly report that engaging in socially responsible work is a big draw for employment.[32]

> Ensure your communication plan matches the crisis response action plan, even if the response plan was developed outside of the public relations department.

7. Evaluation

In the evaluation stage, you assess the results, just as you would with any other public relations strategy (Chapter 8). If you're working with clearly articulated goals and objectives from your strategy, you will be able to measure the beneficial outcomes. However, many of the most important results of issues management stem from the crises *prevented*, or negative outcomes averted. These kinds of outcomes can be harder to measure with certainty because they are based on speculation about what might have occurred had the issue not been managed properly. Think of all the car companies that have *not* cheated on emissions tests. Think of all the restaurants that have *not* had *E. coli* outbreaks, or the student groups that maintained membership despite changes in leadership, or the non-profits that rode out bad slumps in the economy, and so on. In some cases, alternate models can be used to illustrate what would have happened if a crisis occurred and had been managed poorly. And this is a happy outcome! Managers, experts, and others with deep knowledge of an organization and its day-to-day and year-to-year options will appreciate knowing they avoided a boycott, illness outbreak, bankruptcy, product recall, lawsuit, embarrassing media scandal, or any other potential crisis. What's more important—and this may be the result of either an issue averted or a crisis that played out all the way—is that evaluation allows you to learn lessons from experience and develop strategies for the future. Evaluation of how one issue was managed informs the first efforts of monitoring for the next one.

Crisis Types

Not all crises are preventable, and how organizations respond to crises should depend on the degree to which people attribute responsibility for the crisis to the organization. Public relations scholars Tim Coombs and Sherry Holladay developed one of the most well-researched and practical theories for crisis management called situational crisis communication theory (SCCT). SCCT is a contingency theory because it suggests that how organizations should respond to crises depends on the situation. Coombs defines an organizational crisis as "a significant threat to organizational operations or reputations that can have negative consequences for stakeholders and/or the organization if not handled properly."[33] When people think that an organization is responsible for a crisis (e.g., Volkswagen), its reputation suffers, and the crisis leads to more anger, less purchase intent, and greater likelihood of negative word of mouth about the organization. While issues management focuses on how to prevent organizational crises, crisis management deals with how to repair damage and rebuild reputation.[34]

Who's to blame? That is the question at the heart of initial crisis assessment. Researchers have identified three main groups of crisis types: victim crises, accident crises, and preventable crises.

Victim Crises

When publics see the organization as a victim, they assign minimal responsibility for the crisis to the organization. Natural disasters such as hurricanes, tsunamis, and earthquakes are prime examples. People outside of an organization can cause victim crises too, such as cases of sabotage, terrorism, or product tampering.

One of the most famous examples of crisis management in the history of public relations stemmed from a victim crisis that arose because of product tampering by someone from outside an organization. In 1982, news broke that six adults and one 12-year-old girl in the Chicago area had died from cyanide poisoning after taking capsules of Extra-Strength Tylenol.[35] Since the bottles of Tylenol capsules that had been tampered with had come from different production facilities but were all purchased in the Chicago area, investigators ruled out sabotage or foul play at Tylenol factories. Police suspected that someone had purchased the bottles from local stores, poisoned the capsules, and then returned the products to store shelves. The murderer was never caught.

Tylenol's parent company Johnson & Johnson cooperated extensively with news media in expressing sympathy and sharing accurate information about both the crimes and the organization's response. At a cost of more than $100 million, Johnson & Johnson quickly pulled more

situational crisis communication theory (SCCT) Theory that proposes effective crisis communication entails choosing and applying appropriate response strategies depending on how much responsibility for the crisis is attributed to the organization by key publics.

organizational crisis A major threat to an organization's operations or reputation.

than 30 million bottles of Tylenol from store shelves. They did not return the product to market until months later after developing now-standard tamper-resistant packaging.[36] The combination of quick, ethical action and communication earned the Tylenol case a place in history as an example of "how a major business ought to handle a disaster."[37]

Rumours are another category of victim crises. Social media have accelerated the pace by which false, damaging information can be spread. For example, McDonald's routinely has to deal with rumours that "pink slime" has been added to its hamburgers or its chicken nuggets. The McDonald's Canada consumer site "Our Food. Your Questions." routinely responds to the pink slime question to reassure stakeholders.

Rumours abound online. Just check the rumour-busting website Snopes.com for daily examples. For example, the NFL did not fine Cam Newton $253,552 for giving away footballs, Pope Francis did not post a selfie to Instagram, and UPS isn't using its planes to smuggle illegal immigrants into the United States. Oh, and Oprah Winfrey is not pregnant.

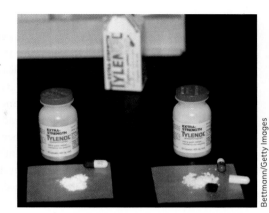

A sample of Extra-Strength Tylenol is presented side by side with a sample of cyanide-laced medicine in a medical examiner's office in October 1982.

Why is this classified as a "victim crisis"? Would Tylenol's response have been different if it were an accident or preventable crisis?

Accident Crises

Accidents happen. Industrial accidents, mechanical failures, or IT crashes could all be considered accidents. In situations like these, an organization may not get a full pass as it would in a victim crisis, because publics still might question the organization's operations. In an industrial accident, were the appropriate safety procedures in place? In a mechanical failure, was the equipment maintained properly? In an information systems crash, were the data backed up in a timely manner? In any of these situations, if people label the source of a crisis as an accident, the amount of responsibility that they attribute to an organization is still relatively low compared to the next category, preventable crises.

Preventable Crises

Consider an airline crash. If investigators determine that an act of terrorism took place, the airline would likely be considered a victim. If, instead, they determine that a mechanical failure was to blame, this could be seen as an accident. If, however, the mechanical failure was due to improper maintenance by the ground crew or a skipped preflight inspection by a pilot, publics would see the crisis as preventable.

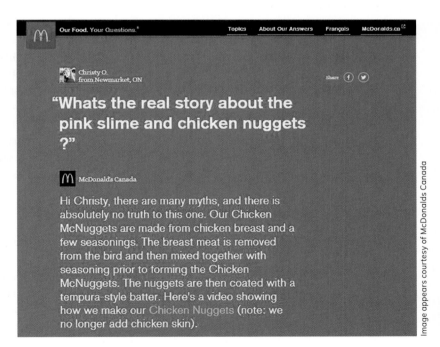

McDonald's often dispels rumours about "pink slime."

Where do you think these rumours come from, and why do they happen?

Use your social media accounts to correct rumours and re-post corrections made by others.

Preventable crises caused by mismanagement, illegal activity, or unethical action are the worst kind for organizations, and they may be intensified when the organization already has a reputation for breaking rules or a history of similar crises. Urban Outfitters faced outrage from African-American community leaders and clergy when it started selling a board game called Ghettopoly in its clothing stores in 2003. It included characters with intentionally misspelled names like "Malcum X" and "Martin Luthor King Jr." One game card read, "You got yo whole neighborhood addicted to crack. Collect $50."[38] The store stopped selling the game but continued to offend people with other poor product choices. More than 10 years later, the store offered a "vintage" Kent State sweatshirt for sale online at $129. The sweatshirt was stained blood red, hauntingly reminiscent of (and insensitive to) the 1970 massacre on campus in which four Kent State students were shot and killed by members of the Ohio National Guard. *The Washington Post* noted, "It seems like every few weeks, Urban Outfitters is in the news for some new controversy."[39] Urban Outfitters issued the following apology, which many find difficult to accept given the company's history: "Urban Outfitters sincerely apologizes for any offense our Vintage Kent State Sweatshirt may have caused. It was never our intention to allude to the tragic events that took place at Kent State in 1970 and we are extremely saddened that this item was perceived as such."

Crisis Response Strategies

In addition to classifying the most common types of organizational crises, Coombs and Holladay offer an outline of crisis response strategies: deny, diminish, rebuild, and reinforce. SCCT recommends selecting a response strategy appropriate to the situation.

Deny Strategies

scapegoating Blaming an outside person or organization for a crisis.

Organizations applying deny strategies aim to absolve themselves of responsibility. They may claim there is no crisis at all or blame another organization or person for the crisis. They may also confront the accuser directly. Scapegoating or attacking the accuser is generally not received well by publics. For example, when Chipotle co-CEO Monty Moran appeared to blame the CDC (Centers for Disease Control and Prevention) for the intensity of its *E. coli* crisis by saying that it was "fueled by the sort of unusual and even unorthodox way the CDC has chosen to announce cases related to the original outbreak," *Fortune* Senior Editor Geoff Colvin characterized the response as "how crisis leadership is *not* done."[40]

Diminish Strategies

Diminish strategies acknowledge the existence of a crisis, but they minimize the organization's responsibility for the crisis or any bad intentions. The organization may also try to reframe the situation. For example, when schools receive media attention for low scores on national standardized tests, they may use a diminish strategy that questions the validity of the tests, claims that the school system is underresourced compared to others, or focuses on how hard teachers are working with so little compensation.

Rebuild Strategies

Crises test relationships. If the heart of public relations is relationship management, then there is perhaps no greater role for public relations in a crisis than rebuilding relationships.

If an organization is responsible for a crisis, one of the most important communications it must issue is a public acceptance of that responsibility. If you realize you've screwed up in an interpersonal relationship and you want to repair the damage, you apologize. The same goes for organization–public relationships.

Apology, accepting responsibility and asking for forgiveness or understanding, is key to your rebuild strategy. That said, we all know that forced apologies come across as fake and insincere. One kid trips another on the playground and laughs. No remorse whatsoever. But then the teacher steps in and forces an apology. The words "I'm sorry" are muttered, but the relationship between the two kids doesn't improve. Adults have the same issues—even CEOs of major companies. When, in 2010, British Petroleum's CEO Tony Hayward stepped in front of a microphone following the largest US marine oil spill ever, he appeared at first to apologize to local communities and families. "I'm sorry. We're sorry for the massive disruption it's caused their lives." But then Hayward delivered one of the most infamous lines in the history of corporate crisis management. "There's no one who wants this over more than I do. I'd like my life back." Hayward later had to issue a statement that apologized for his apology.[41]

An apology that doesn't play well can have a **boomerang effect**, causing more damage than it repairs. Yoga clothing manufacturer Lululemon faced a crisis when then-CEO Chip Wilson suggested that the problem with their yoga pants wasn't a defect—the problem was that the pants didn't suit every body type, hinting that larger women were the issue. Accused of "fat-shaming," Wilson's apology for the remarks made the situation worse.

Relationship management, as discussed throughout this text, is about both communication and action. Apologies go a lot further when they are backed up with behaviour. Maple Leaf Foods communicated continuously, going so far as to print full-page ads a year after the crisis to update stakeholders on their actions. When Domino's Pizza faced an online crisis after a video showing staff contaminating the food went viral, Domino's shut down the store where the incident happened, opened a Twitter account for consumer inquiries, and worked openly with bloggers and reporters. Social media expert Brian Solis suggested that these rebuild strategies helped keep the crisis for Domino's from becoming even worse.[42]

Compensation is another classic rebuild strategy. Organizations may offer products, services, or money to help make amends with publics. When Loblaws issued consumers $25 gift cards after admitting its role in a bread price-fixing scandal, that was clearly a rebuilding strategy (and, as some critics have suggested, perhaps an attempt to head off a class-action lawsuit).

Reinforce Strategies

Another common response to crises is to reinforce relationships. Reminding people of all the good things your organization has

apology Act of taking responsibility for an issue or crisis and seeking forgiveness or understanding.

boomerang effect Unintended consequence of an apology or other attempt to create positive response results instead in a negative response.

compensation Crisis response strategy of offering products, services, or money to help make amends with publics.

Following BP's tragic Gulf of Mexico oil spill, CEO Tony Hayward became the subject of ridicule for saying, "I'd like my life back."

Why might people have responded so negatively to his initial apology?

Bolstering to #Staystrong in the Fight against Cancer

When world-famous cyclist Lance Armstrong was diagnosed with testicular cancer in 1997 at age 25, he started the Lance Armstrong Foundation to raise money to fight cancer. The organization grew fast and became one of the world's most recognizable philanthropic organizations, aided by a partnership with Nike, which honoured Armstrong and the foundation with its iconic yellow Livestrong bracelets. Armstrong won seven Tour de France races between 1999 and 2005, and the foundation grew to more than 100 employees with thousands of volunteers. But then crisis hit when Armstrong fell from grace in 2012.

The United States Anti-Doping Agency (USADA) released a report showing a "systemic, sustained and professionalized doping conspiracy" by Armstrong and his cycling team.[43] Armstrong was forced to vacate his cycling titles, and he resigned as chairman of the foundation, which formally changed its name from the Lance Armstrong Foundation to Livestrong. The foundation had some serious bolstering to do. It launched a campaign around the theme "Stillstrong," which was "intended to remind people that the charity is still operational and providing key services to cancer patients."[44] The charity still operates today, constantly reinforcing its mission and story:

> LIVESTRONG has served millions of people affected by cancer through collaborative programs and direct support services that fill critical financial, emotional, physical and practical gaps in care. Though Lance is no longer involved with LIVESTRONG, he remains the foundation's single biggest donor. The progress he helped generate within the field of cancer survivorship stands as a lasting legacy.[45]

bolstering Attempting to offset reputational damage to an organization during a crisis by emphasizing the good work that the organization has done in the past.

ingratiation A type of reinforcing crisis response strategy in which stakeholders are praised or thanked to win their good favour.

Be careful of issuing apologies or applying ingratiation strategies on social media unless they are clearly sincere and authentic.

done in the past is one way to reinforce a relationship during or following a crisis. This is called **bolstering**.

Ingratiation is another reinforcing strategy. In a crisis, many of an organization's most important relationships are with the people who help to solve the crisis or aid its victims. Thanking first responders, praising volunteers, and expressing appreciation to authorities who are involved in the crisis cleanup are ways organizations work to curry favour with key publics. However, as with apology strategies, ingratiation strategies risk backfiring if they are seen as insincere.

Social Media and Crises

One of the biggest challenges in managing crises is handling the rapid spread of information and the constant demand for that information. Prior to the rise of social media, crisis managers talked about the importance of the "golden hours"—the first few hours after a surprise crisis breaks—when an organization has its best opportunity to try to get out ahead of crisis communication with accurate information. With social media, those hours are reduced to minutes or even seconds. Social media have increased both the volume and speed of communication in crisis situations and opened new channels for both organizations and publics to communicate. Crisis managers may see social media as a blessing (for communicating quickly and directly with publics) and a curse (for fuelling the uncontrolled spread of misinformation and rumours). Recognizing the importance of social media in particular in the ecology of crisis situations, public relations scholars Yan Jin, Brooke Fisher Liu, Julia Daisy Fraustino, and their colleagues developed a **social media crisis communication model (SMCC)** that highlights the interaction among social media, traditional media, and word-of-mouth communication in crisis situations. Think for a minute about a recent organizational crisis that you've heard about. How did you receive the information? There's a good chance that all three sources came into play. You may have heard about the crisis in a conversation with friends or family (word of mouth), seen it on TV or read about it in the newspaper (traditional media), or seen it on Twitter, Facebook, and so on (social media). SMCC emphasizes that these sources are not mutually exclusive. If you learned about a crisis from a friend who used Facebook to re-post and comment on a CNN.com article, this is an example of how word of mouth, traditional media, and social media sources are all integrated in the crisis communication process.

The SMCC identifies three types of social media users for public relations practitioners to pay attention to during a crisis:

1. Influential **social media creators** are among the first to identify crises online and then post about them.
2. **Social media followers** receive their information from the influential creators.
3. **Social media inactives** receive information from traditional media and offline word of mouth. This does not mean that social media are not involved. Instead, what social media inactives learn offline may be informed by what their sources have learned from social media.

By understanding the relationship among these three sources, public relations professionals can think strategically about how an organization communicates during a crisis.

In most cases, it is good practice for the crisis team to centralize the flow of information. Historically, this would be done by using tactics such as periodic press conferences or conference calls that enabled the organization to communicate consistently and accurately with the news media. This is still common practice. Today, however, those news media then report breaking news via print, radio, and television, as well as via social media platforms. SMCC describes one process whereby news media act as influential social media creators who share breaking news with followers on social media in addition to reaching social media inactives with traditional outlets like radio, TV, and newspapers.

SMCC also outlines another process for the spread of information in which the organization itself acts as a social media creator, as when companies set up new Twitter accounts for crisis-specific updates and inquiries. While it's difficult to think of anything either controlled or "centralized" about the wildly crowd-fuelled nature of how major crises break on social media, this doesn't mean public relations people can't play an important role in the process. As representatives with inside knowledge of the latest news related to the crisis, public relations people have the option of becoming influential social media creators. In that role they can work to communicate accurate and useful information directly with followers and indirectly with inactives.

social media crisis communication model (SMCC) Model describing the role of social media influencers, followers, and inactives in spreading information in crisis situations.

social media creators Influential social media users who are among the first to identify and post about crises online.

social media followers Social media users who receive crisis information from social media creators.

social media inactives People who receive crisis information indirectly from social media via traditional media and offline word of mouth.

Voices from the Field

Grant Bastedo

Image Courtesy of Grant Bastedo

Grant Bastedo is an award-winning accredited communications and public relations professional from Regina, Saskatchewan. In his long career, he has spearheaded countless successful communications campaigns, marketing initiatives, community investment projects, and large multifaceted events for clients across Canada.

Grant is known for his innovative approach and his smart use of cutting-edge technologies. He has expertise in developing digital communications strategies and has led portal, website, corporate intranet, and mobile projects for clients including ISC, SIAST, University of Regina, and Saskatchewan Liquor and Gaming Authority (SLGA).

In 2012, he brought together internationally renowned experts and over 400 of Saskatchewan's public and private sector leaders at the Saskatchewan 3.0 Summit. The summit fostered meaningful discussion about the province's digital future and showcased successful digital innovations that are occurring around the globe.

What's the biggest crisis you've ever had to manage?
I managed a lot of crises during my career, but most of those were reputation-based—corporate issues, issues management, weather-related crises—things like that. When I worked with Saskatchewan Polytechnic, I dealt with student-related crises like school closures due to weather, student injuries and deaths, and complaints to the media. Obviously, the Humboldt Broncos accident was the largest crisis I dealt with in my 27 years of practice.

How did you get involved in that crisis?
Everyone in Saskatchewan knew about that accident within hours. Minutes. A colleague of mine headed out

there to help deal with the situation, and because The Humboldt Broncos's board of directors was a client, she called me to help. It is hard to put into words the scale of what was happening there, communications-wise. The accident was on a Friday night, and by Tuesday, almost five days later, the media interest was as high as it had ever been. We had calls from around the world—The New York Times, Sports Illustrated, BBC Australia—you name it. We set up a 1-800 number for media calls and as soon as you put down the phone it would ring again. Everyone had the same questions.

What were some of the challenges you faced in dealing with that situation?
The biggest challenge we faced immediately was how to get information out to the world. The coach and assistant coach were both killed in the crash, so we didn't have the passwords or access to any of the social media accounts. We were starting from scratch. To deal with that, we set up a crisis website, and within four hours we had 200,000 visitors. It was over 1,000,000 by the end of the week.

The whole thing was an incredibly surreal experience—incredibly stressful. We put out four or five news releases a day, and sometimes that didn't seem like enough. The hours were crazy—we worked from 6 a.m. to 1 a.m. every day. Ultimately, I worked on that full-time for about six months.

It must have been an incredibly emotional experience. How did you look after yourself?
Honestly, I didn't anticipate it being as hard as it was. Emotionally, dealing with all the well-wishers from around the world was the hardest part. They would send videos, thought, prayers—those really got to you.

I remember watching a video of a school's jersey day that was sent to us by a Catholic priest, and when I saw those 250 kids having a memorial, the tears just started flowing. There were plenty of moments like that—we would need to take emotional breaks from time to time and just go for a walk and do something different. I don't think we did enough to look after ourselves.

What did you learn from this experience?
So much! For a lot of what we did, we were just winging it; there was no plan in place. That would be my advice to any practitioner, any organization: get a crisis communication plan in place, however simple. Even just the social media passwords and some contact information would have been helpful at the time.

Social media was invaluable, it allows you to communicate with the world quickly. Twitter became our main means of communication; we had 60,000 followers by the time we were done. On Jersey Day, we weren't quite sure how to deal with all of the well-wishers but we knew we needed to acknowledge them, so we simply tweeted "We hear you, we see you, we love you." That was retweeted thousands of times, instantly.

Prior to this, most of what I learned about crisis communication I learned through IABC and CPRS—going to lunch and learns and hearing about cases. I really drew from that learning.

Ethics: Conflicts of Interest

Public relations people are often faced with the challenge of balancing conflicting loyalties among various publics. If conflicts aren't managed well, they can become crises. Some of the most difficult ethical dilemmas that you may face in public relations, however, arise when *you yourself* are one of the parties in a conflict of values involving your organization. The CPRS Code of Professional Standards includes the following principle regarding conflict of interest:

> A member shall not represent conflicting or competing interests without the expressed consent of those concerned, given after a full disclosure of the facts. Members shall not permit personal or other professional interests to conflict with those of an employer client without fully disclosing such interests to everyone involved.

One example of a conflict of interest provided in the code is failing to disclose that you have a major financial interest in a competitor of your organization or client. For example, if you work for Coca-Cola, you wouldn't want to own stock in PepsiCo. However, sometimes conflicts of interest are unavoidable. In *Doing Ethics in Media*, Jay Black and Chris Roberts present a particularly sticky example that they developed as a hypothetical case study from real-world, first-hand experiences.[46]

In the scenario, you work as a public relations officer for a big mill operation in a small town that is facing tough economic times. The company has been good to you. They were very generous and supportive when your spouse (also a company employee) died in an accident at the plant a few years back. They've also rewarded your hard work with a series of promotions. You feel a strong sense of loyalty. But that loyalty is seriously tested when, in a meeting with upper management, you learn that the company's long-term plans include major layoffs at your plant. Thousands will lose jobs. You are upset, but the reasons for layoffs are understandable. Environmental problems and economic forces have made the plant's continued operation unsustainable. You're asked to keep the information confidential so the company will not lose its last major contract and set of work orders.

To make matters worse, you have family members who will be impacted in major ways. Your sister works in real estate and is planning to close some big deals on local homes in the area, and you now know the local real estate market is about to tank because of your company, taking those deals down with it. Your brother-in-law works at the company too, as a shift foreman. What do you do?

What makes this decision so difficult? It's the conflict of interest. On one hand you are a loyal employee and representative of the organization and you have accepted the responsibility of safeguarding confidences to lessen the impact of a crisis. On the other hand, you are very close to your sister and her husband, and your close family ties make it even more difficult to ignore the interests and values of the local community as a public with which you are deeply connected.

One tenet of crisis management that may help both the organizational and personal crisis is "Tell it all and tell it fast." Ralph Barney, a founding editor of *Journal of Mass Media Ethics*, offered this in response to an earlier version of this case when it was first published: "A principled response would be to make public the plans the company has for the plant, thereby demonstrating a willingness to serve larger society."[47] In a case like this, "larger society" includes your family and friends in the community. While you may serve as an advocate for your organization, traditional news media and social media influentials will no doubt serve to advocate for the interests of larger society. If these sources get wind of the story before your company is ready to release it (a common occurrence for organizations that try to keep a crisis secret for too long), your organization will be behind the eight ball.

Social media crisis communication theory suggests that your organization can serve as a primary source of information to publics during a crisis if you act fast enough. Crisis communication researchers have applied the term stealing thunder to describe this strategy. In law, attorneys are known to "steal thunder" when they expose weaknesses in their own cases and address those weaknesses before their opponents have the opportunity to do so.[48]

Negative information spreads extremely fast in the communication ecosystem of traditional media, social media, and word of mouth. But if you work with traditional media and/or act as a social media creator for crisis-related information, it is possible to get ahead of the story and save some people from harm. One possible solution is for the public relations practitioner to apply both crisis communication theory and a deep understanding of the affected publics to make a case to upper management that "telling it all and telling it fast" is a better strategy than prolonged secrecy.

stealing thunder Crisis response strategy in which an organization exposes its own problems (and works to address those problems) before opponents have the opportunity to do so.

In Case You Missed It

While classic principles of conflict management, issues management, and crisis management still hold, social media have increased options for detection, prevention, response, and communication. Social media must be used with a clear understanding of their role in the communication process.

- Respond quickly and appropriately to challenges on social media to prevent issues from becoming crises.
- Sometimes it's better to advocate rather than to accommodate.
- Monitor social media to uncover issues sooner and give you more options for dealing with a situation.

- It's just as important to listen to detractors as it is to listen to supporters.
- Ensure your communication plan matches the crisis response action plan, even if the response plan was developed outside of the public relations department.
- Use your social media accounts to correct rumours and re-post corrections made by others.
- Be careful of issuing apologies or applying ingratiation strategies on social media unless they are clearly sincere and authentic.
- Make yourself and your organization "influential social media creators" by setting up and maintaining crisis-specific social media accounts.

ICYMI

Summary

12.1 Analyze responses ranging from advocacy to accommodation in public relations conflict cases.

In conflict, the action or communication tactic that you choose depends on the specifics of the situation. Contingency theory holds that response options range on a continuum from pure advocacy on one side to pure accommodation on the other.

12.2 Identify stages in the issues life cycle.

Stages in the issue life cycle include (1) early/potential, (2) emerging, (3) current/crisis, and (4) dormant. As issues grow, publics become more active and an organization's options for proactive management become more limited.

12.3 Describe how issues management can prevent or lessen the impact of crises.

The seven-step process for proactive issues management—(1) monitoring, (2) identification, (3) prioritization, (4) analysis, (5) strategic planning, (6) implementation, and (7) evaluation—runs parallel to the four-step RPIE process. Actively monitoring the environment with research increases the likelihood of identifying issues early enough to allow for proactive, strategic public relations rather than reactive, constrained damage control.

12.4 Discuss how traditional media, social media, and offline word of mouth interact in the spread of crisis information.

Traditional news media are still an important source of information in crises, and—as has always been the case—offline word of mouth interacts with news media as people discuss what they learn from news media and as news media report on issues that people discuss. Social media offer greater opportunities for people to discuss and share information inter-personally (online word of mouth) and new channels for traditional media to reach publics. During a crisis, it is useful to identify influential social media creators, who are among the first to identify and post about crises online; social media followers, who receive their information from the influential creators; and social media inactives, who receive information from tradi-tional media and offline word of mouth. Both traditional media and offline word of mouth may be informed by social media activity.

12.5 **Assess competing values in ethical conflicts of interest in the context of public relations issues and crises.**

Public relations professionals face difficult ethical dilemmas when they have a deep personal connection with one of their organization's publics in a conflict or crisis situation. A classic dilemma involves a plant closing that will negatively affect the practitioner's close family and friends. One possible solution is for the practitioner to apply both crisis communication theory and deep understanding of the affected publics to make a case to upper management that "telling it all and telling it fast" is a better strategy than prolonged secrecy.

Discussion Questions

1. Describe a time that you thought an organization was right to advocate instead of accommo-date a key public during a publicly disputed issue. What contingencies of the situation made advocacy a better strategy than accommodation?
2. Select an organization to which you belong (club, school, place of employment, etc.), and then identify one early/potential issue for the organization.
3. Following up on number 2, briefly outline recommendations for how the organization can handle the seven-step process as it relates to that issue.
4. What is the biggest organizational crisis you've seen in the past month? Were you a social media creator, a social media follower, or a social media inactive in the case? How so? What role did the organization play in communicating to you about the crisis?
5. Suppose you find extremely biased information on the Wikipedia page for your organization. This information makes your organization look bad. Technically, anyone can edit Wikipedia en-tries, but why would it be a conflict of interest for you to do so? (You can find hints at en.wikipedia .org/wiki/Wikipedia:Conflict_of_interest and www.instituteforpr.org/wp-content/uploads/ Beutler_WikiPrimer.pdf.)

Further Readings and Online Resources

Issues Management

instituteforpr.org/issues-management/

This long posting on the Institute for Public Relations (IPR) website is the definitive word on issues management. A great starting point if you have a paper to write.

Ongoing Crisis Communication

Coombs, W.T. (2015). *Ongoing crisis communication: Planning, managing, and responding* (4th ed.). Thousand Oaks, California: SAGE.

Timothy Coombs is one of the leading academics in the field of crisis communication, and this book, which explores situational crisis communication theory, is filled with theoretical back-ground and practical, workable strategies for managing crises.

"The Golden Hour": Protect Your Company's Reputation in the First Few Minutes of a Crisis
cw.iabc.com/2014/05/08/golden-hour-protect-companys-reputation-first-minutes-crisis/
> This podcast, featuring crisis communicator James Lukaszewski, explores what a company should do in "the golden hour," which is the first hour after a crisis hits.

Peer-Reviewed Academic Journal Article
Sanderson, J., Barnes, K., Williamson, C., & Kian, E.T. (2016). "How could anyone have predicted that #AskJameis would go horribly wrong?" Public relations, social media, and hashtag hijacking. Public Relations Review, 42(1), 31–7. doi:10.1016/j.pubrev.2015.11.005
> This article explores the social media crisis that ensued when Florida State University decided to launch a social media campaign featuring controversial player Jameis Winston.

Key Terms

Apology   313
Bolstering   314
Boomerang effect   313
Compensation   313
Contingency theory   298
Ingratiation   314
Issues management   303
Organizational crisis   310

Pure accommodation   299
Pure advocacy   298
Responsible supply chain management   308
Scapegoating   312
Situational crisis communication theory (SCCT)   310
Social media creators   315

Social media crisis communication model (SMCC)   315
Social media followers   315
Social media inactives   315
Stealing thunder   318

13

Global

With working principles that include impartiality, independence, and bearing witness, Doctors Without Borders/Médecins Sans Frontières has to carefully consider their communications strategy in each country in which they operate.

Key learning outcomes

13.1 Explain why issues of public access and usage of digital communication technology are critical in planning for global public relations.

13.2 Analyze cases of international public relations involving intercultural communication.

13.3 Compare high-context and low-context communication.

13.4 Apply cultural dimensions (e.g., uncertainty avoidance, masculinity–femininity) to public relations strategy and practice.

13.5 Explain the relationship between intercultural public relations, international public relations, and public diplomacy.

13.6 Discuss the ethics of balanced dialogue in global public relations.

▲ Courtesy of Doctors Without Borders/Médecins Sans Frontières (MSF)

Do you like potstickers? How about gyoza? Maybe you're a fan of ravioli, khinkali, mandoo, momos, pelmeni, kreplach, pieroji, or empanadas. Whether you're in the mood for Chinese, Japanese, Italian, Georgian, Korean, Nepalese, Russian, Jewish, Polish, or Argentine food, respectively, there's a good chance that some form of dumpling will be an option.

The dumpling was *not* an option, however, as an emoji in 2016. We had a pizza emoji 🍕 , a hamburger emoji 🍔 , and a taco emoji 🌮 , but no dumpling emoji. And many people were not happy about it. Enter the Dumpling Emoji Project, which was a campaign "designed to bring together like-minded emoji enthusiasts" to influence a group called the Unicode Consortium to adopt the dumpling emoji 🥟 .[1] The Unicode Consortium is a group of corporations, government organizations, research institutions, and various other tech-savvy associations and individuals that defines universal standards for computer languages. These standards allow people using all sorts of software and operating systems all over the world to communicate with one another. The consortium includes a committee that decides which emojis become available on your smartphone, tablet, or any other device that uses Unicode text. Voting members include Apple, IBM, Oracle, Microsoft, Adobe, Google, Yahoo, Facebook, SAP, the Chinese telecom company Huawei, and the Government of Oman.

Emoji dumplings found advocates in Jennifer Lee, a former *New York Times* tech reporter and co-founder of the digital publishing company Plympton, and designer Yiying Lu. Lee and Lu organized the Dumpling Emoji Project (www.dumplingemoji.org) and launched a Kickstarter campaign that raised more than $12,000 for the cause. They used the money in 2016 to fund international coordination and travel to make their case in person at a meeting of the Unicode Technical Committee in California. The campaign was a success, with the dumpling emoji joining the line-up in June 2017 along with chopsticks, a fortune cookie, and a classic Chinese-food takeout box.

On one hand, the emoji project demonstrates a rather straightforward campaign with a clear goal, well-chosen tactics, a rather small budget, and easily observed outcomes. On the other hand, the emoji project illustrates the interplay of many important facets of global public relations that will be defined and discussed in this chapter, including international communication, intercultural communication, and even, perhaps, some international diplomacy.

Anyone thinking about a public relations career needs to be ready to embrace the globalization of the field, which happens whenever public relations efforts spread across national, geographic, or cultural borders. Fluency in intercultural and international interactions has become a key ingredient in boosting prospects for career success. In this chapter, we

Illustration by Christina Gualy and Yiying Lu, www.dumplingemoji.org

The Dumpling Emoji Project raised more than $12,000 in a campaign to include the dumpling emoji as part of Unicode text.

Why do you think anyone would care so much about the universal availability of a dumpling emoji?

approach the topic of global public relations by considering factors that influence communication between people from different cultures and different nations as well as communication between people from different cultures within the same countries.

Digital Divides—At Home and Abroad

"Let's make Fremont Fiber Optic!"[2] The person who started this discussion thread in the Reddit online social media community was seeking support from neighbours in Fremont, California. The "Redditor" asked others to email the mayor of Fremont and request that the city join the Next Century Cities movement, a group of community leaders seeking faster, cheaper access to the Internet nationwide.

You may wonder if this is a case of #FirstWorldProblems. The "First World problems" meme grew in popularity on social media in the 2000s as a way of mocking complaints about inconveniences like slow Internet speeds in wealthy nations when citizens of poorer, underdeveloped Third World countries face more pressing concerns like widespread hunger, disease, and political oppression. Indeed, half the world doesn't even have access to the Internet.[3] But the Next Century Cities website argues that affordable, reliable high-speed Internet access is not just a luxury or a convenience.[4] According to the group, accessible broadband connections are part of a "necessary infrastructure" in today's world for residents to participate in their communities, for students to learn, for businesses to successfully engage in commerce, and for everyone to share knowledge.[5] In other words, the Internet is necessary to make democracies work.

The term **digital divide** refers to a gap in access to digital information and communication technologies between the "haves" and "have-nots." The digital divide concept is a relative one—meaning that it could be used to describe the difference between populations that are completely wired with the latest fibre optic connections and those that have slower access to the Internet via older technologies, such as dial-up; or, it could be used to describe the relative difference between people with Internet access and those without any access at all. While there is a digital divide between Canada and other (generally poorer) countries, there is also one right here at home. According to a 2015 survey, 91 per cent of Canadians have the Internet at home. Among those who don't, 30 per cent said cost was a barrier, while the other 70 per cent cited a lack of interest or ability.[6]

Another significant digital divide is based on gender. In many countries around the world, women experience significant barriers to technology in general and the Internet specifically. According to data from EQUALS Global Partnership, which is committed to digital equity, there is a gender gap in computer and mobile phone usage in most countries. The largest gender divides are found in Turkey, Palestine, and Morocco.[7]

As public relations practitioners, we have to be careful not to assume that all of our publics are online simply because we ourselves are feeling fully immersed in digital communication. Furthermore, even if our publics have access to the same communication technologies we use, that doesn't mean they are using them to engage us, our organizations, or society at large.

In the 2000s, social scientists started to pay attention to a second type of digital divide. They labelled the first digital divide the **access divide** (the gap between people with access to digital technology and those without access) and identified the second divide based on usage. The **usage divide (or second digital divide)** focuses on differences in how people from

digital divide Gap between those people with relatively little access and use of information and communication technologies and those people with greater access and usage.

> Don't assume that your publics are online simply because you are.

access divide Gap between people with access to digital technology and those without access.

usage divide (or second digital divide) Gap between people who use information and communication technologies for education, self-betterment, civic engagement, etc., and those who use the technologies for less constructive reasons.

different groups (or publics in the case of public relations) actually use the technologies to which they have access. What if every school in a community has computers, but kids aren't using them to learn? What if every household has a high-speed Internet connection, but people are connecting only for games and entertainment?

In planning programs for global public relations, it is essential to consider differences in digital access and usage. Many Canadians are fairly privileged when it comes to communication technology. Recent data show that the majority of Canadians own a smartphone, 90 per cent of Canadians own two or more digital devices, and 80 per cent own three or more. In addition to smartphones, 71 per cent of the Canadians surveyed owned a laptop or netbook, 54 per cent had a tablet or e-reader, and 50 per cent a desktop computer. Of course, the data look different in other nations, but smartphone usage continues to grow around the world.

Smartphone ownership around the world has steadily increased since 2015, with large increases occurring in countries that include Lebanon, Jordan, and the Philippines. Like Internet usage, smartphone ownership varies by age and level of education. The biggest generational divide is in Greece, where 93 per cent of those aged 18 to 36 own a smartphone, compared with 38 per cent of those 37 or older. There is also a significant divide in income levels when it comes to smartphone ownership around the world. The biggest income gap is in Peru, where six in ten of those with higher incomes say they own a smartphone, compared with only 24 per cent of those with lower incomes.

Internet penetration rates are high in North America, Europe and parts of the Asia Pacific
Adults who use the internet at least occasionally or report owning a smartphone

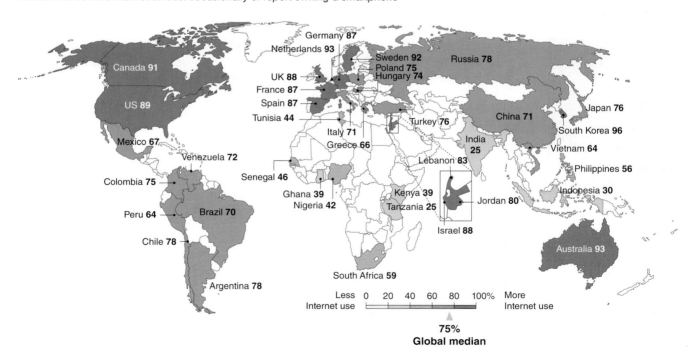

FIGURE 13.1 Data from the Pew Research Center show that Internet access varies widely in different countries.

How might practising public relations in Bangladesh be different from practising public relations in Canada?

Source: Pew Research Center

SAM PANTHAKY/AFP/Getty Images

Technology merges with tradition in India as sisters and brides from the Rabari Samaj community take a selfie on a mobile phone before participating in a mass marriage.

Are selfies a trend that will end soon or are they now a part of our culture that will endure for years to come?

Another important indicator of technology access and use is the speed of Internet connections. To think about Internet access as a simple question of who has it and who doesn't misses the point that communication technology is continuously advancing, and people will always have different levels of access. According to the Speedtest Global Index of August 2018 (it's updated monthly), the fastest mobile download speed worldwide was found in Norway with 63.13 megabits per second (MBPS) compared to the global average, which was 22.99. Qatar, United Arab Emirates, Australia, and Singapore round out the top five fastest countries. Canada clocks in at a respectable 8th, whereas the United States is ranked 45th, behind countries that include Spain, Latvia, and Turkey.

Access speeds vary from province to province, as well. According to a 2016 study, New Brunswick enjoys the fastest average speeds, while Yukon residents face the lowest.

> Think carefully about how your publics are accessing and using communication technology in other parts of the world.

TABLE 13.1 National Rankings for Internet Connection Speeds

Global Rank for Connection Speed (Mobile)	Country	Average Mbps (megabytes per second)
1	Norway	63.13
2	Qatar	63.00
3	United Arab Emirates	56.05
4	Australia	53.51
5	Singapore	53.18
6	Iceland	52.56
7	Netherlands	52.37
8	Canada	51.46
9	Belgium	48.70
10	Luxembourg	48.64
45	United States	28.63

Data from Speedtest's August 2018 *Global Index Report* show that Canada ranks 8th in the world for average connection speeds.
How might practising public relations in Norway be different from practising public relations in the United States?

One Laptop per Child

In 2005, Nicholas Negroponte founded the non-profit One Laptop per Child (OLPC) organization. The organization leveraged $1 billion of investment and partnerships with individuals, UN agencies, and organizations like eBay, Red Hat, Google, and News Corporation to pursue a broad goal of providing a "rugged, low-cost, low-power, connected laptop" computer for each primary-school child in developing nations.[8] Negroponte, who delivered the very first TED talk in 1984 and co-founded the MIT Media Lab in 1985, envisioned a program that would bridge both the access and usage divides. In a 2006 TED talk, he shared a personal anecdote from a remote village in Cambodia:

> I was recently in . . . a village that has no electricity, no water, no television, no telephone, but has broadband internet now. And these kids, their first English word is "Google" and they only know Skype. They've never heard of telephony. They just use Skype. And they go home at night—they've got a broadband connection in a hut that doesn't have electricity. The parents love it, because when they open up the laptops, it's the brightest light source in the house.[9]

Unfortunately, even with an inspirational vision, the program was not as successful as investors, educators, scholars, policy-makers, and designers had hoped.

AP Photo/Martin Mejia

The non-profit One Laptop per Child organization aimed to provide every child in developing nations with a laptop, but even with a billion dollars of investment and an inspiring vision, the initiative struggled.

What lessons does this case provide for public relations?

Continued

The technological difficulty of producing and distributing extremely low-cost laptops was part of the problem. The program originally aimed to produce the OLPC XO model at a price of $100 per laptop, but manufacturers often had to price them at $200 or more. The laptops also were criticized for lacking connection ports for classroom projectors, having limited access to troubleshooting assistance for software issues, requiring expensive replacement parts for hardware, and being made with environmentally hazardous materials.

Cultural issues also presented significant challenges.[10] In Uruguay, for example, a national evaluation of the program after it launched revealed that only 21.5 per cent of teachers reported using the laptops in class daily or near daily, and 25 per cent of the teachers reported using them less than once a week.[11] The program also was deployed in parts of the United States, but results there were equally discouraging. In Birmingham, Alabama, the city invested more than $4 million to provide more than 1,700 fourth- and fifth-graders with laptops. In a survey, however, 80 per cent of the students said they used the laptops either seldom or never.[12]

So, what went wrong? In reviewing the data and reports, UC–Irvine professor Mark Warschauer and Stanford PhD candidate Morgan Ames found the results illustrated how important it is to adapt to local cultures. The OLPC programs struggled, they said, "because they ignored local contexts and discounted the importance of curriculum and ongoing social, as well as technical, support and training."[13]

No one faults the program for its intent and ambition. Even the program's critics also acknowledge that the OLPC program spurred innovation in low-cost computers with more durable, low-power hardware, and collaborative software designed to improve access, use, and education. Nonetheless, analyzing the OLPC's shortfalls yields valuable lessons for designing programs that involve strategic communication across cultures.[14]

As *Business Week's* Bruce Nussbaum wrote, the program broke a cardinal rule of program design by not focusing first on the end users of the laptops. Nussbaum suggested that OLPC would have been more successful if it had involved its primary publics earlier in the planning. "It would have been far better to begin in the villages, spend time there and build from the bottom up."[15] Had teachers, parents, and students been consulted more in the research and planning stages before implementation, OLPC strategists may have been in a better position to tailor the program to needs at the local level. Public relations professionals should apply this type of design thinking that focuses on end users (i.e., key publics) in any kind of planning. Access to technology is perhaps the first concern, but any effective communication strategy also requires careful attention to social and cultural contexts.

While the Internet makes it easy for us to reach publics in our communities and all over the world, access and usage vary greatly from community to community and from nation to nation. Any careful thinking about public relations requires attention to how people access and use communication technology (if they have access at all). Whether communication is wired, wireless, or altogether offline, effective global communication also requires an understanding of cultural contexts.

Public Relations and Culture

Every public has its own cultural dimensions. Naturally, Chinese groups will have different cultural characteristics from German, Pakistani, or American groups. A public composed of mostly Caribbean-born Canadians will differ culturally from African-Canadians, Caucasians, Indigenous peoples, or Greek-Canadians. Of course, the concept of culture applies to any group, not just groups defined by race, ethnicity, or nationality. As more and more families are becoming multiracial, categorizing people by ethnicity will become a less relevant way to understand publics, and shared interests and affinity will become more important.[16]

Canada is often described as a multicultural country. But what do we mean by *culture*?

The Canadian Encyclopedia devotes hundreds of words to the definition, while Statistics Canada openly discusses the challenge of defining *culture* on its website:

> The term "culture" is value-laden and can be defined in many ways. Broadly described, culture can include economic systems, political ideologies and processes, ways of life and social mores, educational institutions, social programs, the environment, technological systems, recreational practices, customs and traditions, artistic and heritage activities, transportation and communication industries, and religious and spiritual activities.

Global Affairs Canada defines *culture* as follows:

> Culture rules virtually every aspect of your life and like most people, you are completely unaware of this. If asked, you would likely define culture as music, literature, visual arts, architecture or language, and you wouldn't be wrong. But you wouldn't be entirely right either. In fact, the things produced by a culture which we perceive with our five senses are simply manifestations of the deeper meaning of culture—what we do, think and feel. Culture is taught and learned and shared—there is no culture of one. And yet, culture is not monolithic—individuals exist within a culture. Finally, culture is symbolic. Meaning is ascribed to behaviour, words and objects and this meaning is objectively arbitrary, subjectively logical and rational. For example, a "home" is a physical structure, a familial construct and a moral reference point—which is distinct from one culture to another.
>
> Culture is vital because it enables its members to function with one another without the need to negotiate meaning at every moment. Culture is learned and forgotten, so despite its importance we are generally unconscious of its influence on the manner in which we perceive the world and interact within it. Culture is significant because as we work with others it both enables us and impedes us in our ability to understand and work effectively together.

The Oxford Dictionary provides a shorter definition, as follows:

> The ideas, customs, and social behaviour of a particular people or society; the attitudes and behaviour characteristic of a particular social group.

culture The ideas, customs, and social behaviour of a particular people or society.

intercultural public relations Management of relationships between organizations and publics of different cultures.

Intercultural Public Relations

If we define a public as a group of people with shared interests (as we did in Chapter 1), then we see how the concept of **culture** applies to just about any public—residents of a town, students in a school, volunteers of a non-profit, a company's top management, or opponents of a political action. While we may think we understand different cultures, when we reach out to people or publics, we have to check our assumptions carefully. **Intercultural public relations** involves the interaction of an organization and publics across cultures.

Case Study

Intercultural Communication and Potty Talk

Intercultural scholar Gary Fontaine has called it "one of the world's most persistent intercultural challenges." Archaeologists study it as a cultural artifact. You would likely approach it carefully when travelling abroad. What is it? It's a toilet. That's right, a potty. And although its function is universal, its design and use can differ significantly from one culture to another.

Now, imagine you work for a company that manufactures and sells toilets, and your job is to promote a new model in a different culture. That's what Swiss manufacturer Geberit asked Danish public relations firm Kragelund Kommunikation to do when it wanted to introduce its AquaClean shower toilet to Denmark. In case you're wondering what a shower toilet is, here's how the AquaClean website explains it: "A shower toilet combines the functionality of a toilet and the cleaning properties of a bidet . . . at

Squatty Potty LLC/Harmon Bros

Publicly discussing bathroom habits presents a number of intercultural challenges, but companies that make bathroom-related products still seek to reach international markets.

What communication strategies cleared these obstacles?

the touch of a button, the concealed spray arm extends and washes you clean with a jet of pleasantly warm water."[17]

In developing strategy, the agency studied Danish and international toilet habits. (Don't ask me how they did this.) They identified some important market challenges, including the high price of the product at €4,500 and lack of consumer knowledge—less than 5 per cent of Danes had a bidet and 0 per cent owned a shower toilet at the time. These challenges were compounded by the fact that Danish consumers tended to think of the toilet as a plumbing item and not a "lifestyle product." In other words, one of the biggest obstacles for Geberit and its public relations agency was cultural. Shower toilets and bidets were "considered oddities and taboos in Scandinavia."[18]

The campaign, which the International Public Relations Network (IPRN) recognized as the overall winner of its business-to-consumer project of the year award, focused on middle- to high-income Danes aged 35 and up. The communication strategy relied on both information and emotion by emphasizing hygienic benefits and promoting cleanliness and well-being.

Kragelund Kommunikation set up opportunities for journalists from newspapers and high-end design magazines to "try the product themselves in exclusive surroundings," including a press trip to Paris. They also partnered with the ritzy Hotel D'Angleterre in Copenhagen, which installed the shower toilets in all of its rooms. Story angles included humour ("The toilet is our armchair"), cleanliness ("We feel unclean despite strong personal hygiene"), business ("Large Swiss corporation aims for Denmark"), and technology ("High tech toilets with fancy features").[19]

The press trip was a success, and the story angles were effective with Danish media. Prominent bloggers also wrote about the product. While most metrics focused on media coverage and impressions, the image of Danish TV host Søren Jensen reporting "with his trousers round his ankles and sitting on an AquaClean toilet in the studio" indicates that a cultural barrier had been breached. The client later extended the campaign to other regions.

Introducing an expensive high-tech toilet to a new culture is one kind of challenge. Another is introducing a low-tech product like the Squatty Potty. Basically a step that slides against the side of a toilet, Squatty Potty allows people to do their business more like people did before modern toilets were commonplace.

Despite the cultural awkwardness of the topic, Squatty Potty's creator Robert Edwards managed to win the opportunity to pitch his idea on ABC's *Shark Tank* in 2015, where he and his mother persuaded Lori Greiner to invest $350,000 in the business. The show's producers had been reluctant to feature a bathroom-related product on the show, but Edwards persisted by emphasizing a health angle. "In our second [audition] tape we really nailed down that Squatty Potty is a health tool," Edwards said in an interview.[20] The Squatty Potty also has been featured on health shows, including *The Doctors* and *The Dr Oz Show*, and has its own Facebook page and Twitter and Instagram accounts, as well as a YouTube video with more than 15 million views. It even was a major YouTube hit with a video of a unicorn and rainbow-coloured softserve ice cream to illustrate "the effects of improper toilet posture and how it can affect your health."[21]

Low-Context versus High-Context Communications

In his classic book *Beyond Culture*, anthropologist Edward Hall distinguished between low-context communication—in which most of the meaning of a message is stated explicitly in the message itself and requires little understanding of context, and high-context communication—in which most of the meaning of a message is based on context or something internal to the communicators rather than being directly stated in the message.[22] Restaurant menus, brochures, web pages, and even course syllabi include very detailed descriptions and instructions and are tools of lower-context communication, while tweeting and text messaging, which are limited to very few words and characters, illustrate well the concept of high-context communication. Like so many other concepts in social science and public relations, however, high- and low-context communication are best thought of as ends on a spectrum rather than two completely separate ideas.[23]

Think about the shortest text message you have ever sent or received. For many this will be a one-letter message: *K*. In the context of a chemistry lab, *K* stands for potassium. In baseball, *K* represents a strikeout. But in text messaging, the single character *K*—the explicit transmitted message—is often used as an abbreviation for *OK*. To understand the actual meaning you have to understand the context. When it works, it may be the most efficient communication tactic ever, bringing a successful communication exchange to a satisfying conclusion with a single keystroke. But according to BuzzFeed's Katie Heaney, *K* is "the one thing you should never text anyone ever." In her eyes it "means you're too lazy to type out just one extra letter," "makes you seem mad," and sends a message that you're on a power trip.[24] The true meaning of *K* totally depends on the context, including the relationship between the sender and receiver.

When organizations develop branding campaigns, they have to be especially sensitive to high-context communication. Branding efforts rely on simple images, icons, logos, words, and brief taglines to communicate enormous amounts of meaning about the organization or its products and services. The meaning depends on context. Branding magic happens when communication strategists successfully align an organization's actions, communication, and culture with the cultural contexts of key publics.

A major part of the inspiration for Nike's successful "Just Do It" campaign (launched in the late 1980s) was a sensitivity to cultural trends in the United States, where obesity and procrastination were becoming more problematic for a large part of the population. According to Nike's former director of marketing insights and planning Jerome Conlon, the campaign developed by Nike's ad agency Wieden+Kennedy needed to reach people beyond highly motivated athletes. The campaign had to appeal to "the actual role that fitness plays in people's lives, the actual experience of really working out, doing aerobics, going on a bike ride, etc.," wrote Conlon.[25] The power of "Just Do It" lies not in the eight letters of text. It emanates from the contextual meaning assigned to it by millions of Nike fans.

The Internet is full of examples of spectacular failures of branding and strategic communication across national and cultural borders. You may have heard about *Coca-Cola* translating to "Bite the wax

Story of my life

This Internet meme captures some of the frustration (and humour) that occurs when cultural contexts clash.

How does this image illustrate high-context and low-context communication styles?

tadpole" in China, or how the Scandinavian vacuum company Electrolux ran a campaign in the United States that "Nothing sucks like an Electrolux." Another classic is that General Motors stumbled in marketing its Chevrolet Nova in Spanish-speaking countries because *no va* translates to "does not go" in Spanish. Ironically, all three of these legends of mis-communication have been taken out of context to some degree over the years.

Coca-Cola did have some difficulty trans-lating its brand name as it sounds ("ko-ka-ko-la") into Chinese characters after entering Hong Kong and Shanghai markets in the 1920s. But when Coca-Cola officially registered its trademark in China in 1928, the series of characters approximated "something palatable

NOTHING SUCKS LIKE AN ELECTROLUX

The most powerful vacs you can buy are in the new 2000 series.

Electrolux is a Swedish company. This ad for British audiences was designed by British ad agency Cogent Elliot.

Do you see it as a cultural gaffe or a clever play on words?

from which one receives pleasure."[26] The Electrolux ad was designed by British ad agency Cogent Elliot for British—not American—consumers and included an intentional pun, with the words on a poster accompanying a picture of the leaning tower of Pisa apparently being sucked towards a vacuum cleaner.[27] On YouTube, you can also find a humorous Electrolux ad, apparently from the 1970s, that includes the tagline at the end.[28] Finally, while *no va* may translate literally to "doesn't go," apparently few Spanish speakers in GM's markets for the car in Mexico and Venezuela were put off by the single word *Nova*. Snopes.com claims that sales even exceeded expectations.[29]

Logos, taglines, and advertising copy are essential to marketing, but public relations also entails a great deal of longer-form communication in the management of relationships between organizations and publics. Public relations professionals are often in charge of "spelling out" an organization's goals, policies, position statements, news, and responses to inquiries. This type of elaboration requires low-context communication.

The distinction between high-context and low-context communication can be useful to people studying and practising international communication. For example, people from Western cultures, such as those from America, Switzerland, Germany, and Scandinavia, *tend to* use more low-context communication. In low-context cultures, web users are more likely to use search features and links to seek specific information and facts about an organization. On the other hand, people from high-context cultures, such as those from Asia, Africa, the Middle East, and Latin America, *tend to* rely more on interpersonal exchanges and social recom-mendations online.[30] One major caution in comparing people using these descriptions (high-context and low-context cultures) is that they are broad generalizations that do not apply to every individual or group within a geographic region. This is why we are careful to emphasize *tend to*, as in, "Europeans *tend to* use more low-context communication than Asians."

> *You will likely deal with both high-context tactics like texts and tweets and low-context communication that spells out your organization's goals, policies, and positions.*

Cultural Dimensions

To avoid stereotyping, public relations professionals (and anyone else communicating across cultural boundaries) should work to understand the various dimensions of any group's culture. Geert Hofstede is a Dutch social psychologist and professor who worked for years

power distance
Cultural dimension
describing the difference
between cultures that
value hierarchy and
authority more and
those that value equal
distribution of power
more.

**individualism–
collectivism** Cultural
dimension describing
the difference between
cultures that value loyalty
to self and immediate
family more and those
that value loyalty to larger
groups and society more.

**uncertainty
avoidance** Cultural
dimension describing
the difference between
cultures that are less
comfortable with
ambiguity (high-
uncertainty avoidance)
and those that are more
at ease with ambiguity.

**masculinity–
femininity** Cultural
dimension describing
the difference
between cultures that
value competition,
achievement, and
material success more
and those that value
care, collaboration, and
modesty more.

**long-term
orientation** Cultural
dimension describing
the difference between
cultures that value long-
held traditions more
and cultures that value
entrepreneurship and
innovation more.

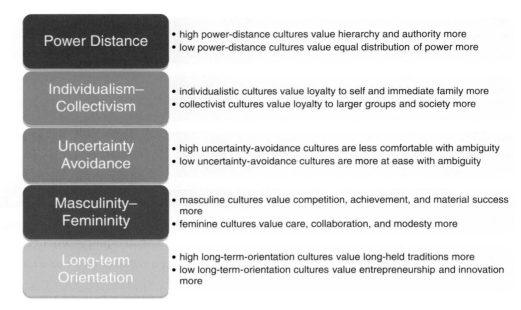

FIGURE 13.2 Hofstede found these cultural dimensions to be helpful in understanding differences in communication styles.

With which cultural dimensions do you identify most? Which would be the hardest for you to adapt to in intercultural public relations?

as a management trainer at IBM. In that role, he travelled around the world and systematically studied how IBMers operated and communicated differently in different cultures. Hofstede identified five major cultural dimensions that have been useful to understand and improve how people of different cultures communicate: power distance, individualism–collectivism, uncertainty avoidance, masculinity–femininity, and long-term orientation (Figure 13.2).[31]

Individuals in high-uncertainty avoidance cultures, for example, are less comfortable with ambiguity. They prefer stricter sets of rules and procedures and seek to define future outcomes as specifically as possible. In low-uncertainty avoidance cultures, individuals are more tolerant of not knowing how things will turn out, but it is important to still include them in conversations about the future. An organization opening a new plant in a high-uncertainty-avoidance culture may be required to present a detailed environmental-impact statement showing exactly how they expect social, natural, and economic environments to be affected.[32] Lower-uncertainty-avoidance cultures are more likely to seek an open-ended dialogue about the organization's plans for a new plant, and so town hall meetings or online forums for public discussion may be more effective ways to communicate plans and discuss options with low-uncertainty-avoidance publics.

Another example is the dimension of masculinity–femininity. Masculine cultures tend to value assertiveness, competition, achievement, and material success, while feminine cultures tend to value care, collaboration, modesty, and quality of life. Consider how masculinity–femininity may play out in gamification, which is a strategy of applying rules and rewards of game playing (points, scoring, competition, collaboration, etc.) to other areas of behaviour. Gamification is becoming more and more common in public relations.

Companies use games and apps to build customer loyalty. Starbucks stars, PC points, and Aeroplan miles are all little incentives that keep people coming back for more from these companies. Non-profits and NGOs (non-governmental organizations) also use games as tactics towards larger goals of social impact. Games for Change (gamesforchange.org) features games like *Never Alone* and *Start the Talk*. *Never Alone* (Kisima Ingitchuna) is a game that allows players to unlock "cultural insights" in the form of short video clips about Iñupiat native Alaskan people if the players overcome in-game obstacles and solve puzzles related to native Alaskan folklore and culture.[33] *Start the Talk* is a role-playing game developed as part of a Substance Abuse and Mental Health Services Administration (SAMHSA) campaign called "Talk. They Hear You." The game is designed to help players learn how to talk to kids about underage drinking.[34]

Gamification strategies that focus on points and competitions may play better as tactics in public relations efforts in masculine cultures, while games that focus on communication, care, and collaboration may appeal more in feminine cultures. However, according to An Coppens, a game designer at Gamification Nation Ltd., games also can be designed with both genders in mind. "For example," she writes, "measure performance based on completion, yet also allow and encourage social support which appeals to empathy and requires mutual respect."[35]

Cultural Intelligence

Unfortunately, merely studying and understanding cultural dimensions is not quite enough to ensure successful intercultural communication. Successful communication takes **cultural intelligence**. London Business School professor Christopher Earley and University of Colorado professor Elaine Mosakowski define *cultural intelligence* as someone's ability to interpret the cultural nuances of others' communications, even as an outsider. "A person with high cultural intelligence can somehow tease out of a person's or group's behavior those features that would be true of all people and all groups, those peculiar to this person or this group, and those that are neither universal nor idiosyncratic."[36]

Earley and Mosakowski identify three sources of cultural intelligence: head (cognitive), body (physical), and heart (emotional/motivational). Fluency in intercultural public relations comes from a combination of head, body, and heart. As professional communicators and managers, public relations professionals succeed with different combinations of the three strengths.

Head (Cognitive)

Learning about high-context and low-context communication through reading is mostly a cognitive endeavour. You can study foreign languages and learn facts about cultures without ever really interacting with others from those cultures. And, while websites and corporate training programs also offer a wealth of knowledge, this type of knowledge is not sufficient to prepare you for all the situations you might encounter.[37] Before setting up a global webinar, international press conference, or site visit to a location where you will be interacting with those from another culture, you'll definitely want to study up. The most valuable learning, however, will come from careful observation and awareness of your surroundings during your actual foray. Earley and Mosakowski recommend developing strategies for this immersive type of cognitive learning:

- Think about what you hope to achieve.
- Learn from your experiences when you encounter something new in a different culture.

gamification Strategy of applying rules and rewards of game playing (points, scoring, competition, collaboration, etc.) to other areas of behaviour such as desired public relations outcomes.

In high-uncertainty-avoidance cultures, it may be wiser to focus on specific outcomes of communication rather than dialogue as an end in itself.

cultural intelligence Ability to adapt, communicate, and interact effectively across cultures by learning and applying cognitive, emotional, and behavioural skills.

Build fluency in intercultural public relations with a combination of head (cognition), body (behaviour), and heart (emotion/motivation).

- Use those experiences to inform future actions and communication.
- Plan ahead for introductions to new people.

Body (Physical)

Physical actions such as body motions, eye contact, and gestures are a huge part of intercultural communication. When do you shake someone's hand? How firmly? Do you ever hug someone in a professional setting? Who sits where at a conference table? How should you dress for an in-person press conference? What about a Skype interview? These are all questions of how you present yourself and interact in a physical sense.

For example, while organizing an event at the Japanese Cultural Center of Hawaii featuring the late senator Daniel K. Inouye as the keynote speaker, the two most important things I had to know in planning for his introduction were physical. First, Inouye, who was a Congressional Medal of Honor winner and the highest-ranking Asian-American government official in US history, had lost his right arm in combat during World War II. Second, Inouye was allergic to pollen. Because we were aware of these physical issues, we made sure that when we presented Inouye with a lei as a symbol of aloha that we gave him a *maile* lei (a lei made with dark green ti leaves without flowers) and, in greeting him, we were careful not to extend our right hands expecting right-handed handshakes.

Heart (Emotional/Motivational)

self-efficacy One's belief that he or she can perform certain behaviours to achieve certain outcomes.

The more experience we have in intercultural interaction, the more confidence we build in our ability to learn and adapt. Social psychologists call this self-efficacy, which is our belief that we can perform certain behaviours to achieve certain outcomes. Prior experiences and successes help us build self-efficacy, which motivates us to persist in difficult situations and learn new strategies, which leads to more success, which leads to more self-efficacy, and so on. It's a virtuous cycle if you can maintain it. Stanford psychologist Albert Bandura identified self-efficacy as a key to social learning, and social learning is what cultural intelligence is all about. People with high emotional or motivational cultural intelligence are confident they can work with others from different cultures and find it relatively easy to adapt to different cultures and unfamiliar cultural situations.

International Public Relations

international public relations Management of relationships between organizations and publics of different nations.

International public relations involves the interaction of an organization and publics across national boundaries. As discussed in Chapter 3, globalization and global connectivity have facilitated more opportunities for intercultural communication and cultural convergence, which is when diverse cultures are imported, exported, exchanged, and mixed. Economic convergence is also a hallmark of globalization. Economic convergence is evident when multinational advertising, marketing, and communication conglomerates like Omnicom, Publicis, or Burson-Marsteller (WPP) conduct their business via subsidiaries operating across the globe.

For organizations practising international public relations, the benefits of globalization include increasing the scope of operations, making more money in new markets, and opportunities for achieving greater social and environmental impact with more diverse publics. But globalization also carries with it greater risks for unintended consequences, negative social and environmental impacts, miscommunication, and faux pas.

Royal Dutch Airlines partners with a dozen other organizations globally including Nike and Accenture as part of a biofuel program that "aims to reduce CO_2 emissions by 20% in 2020 (compared to 2011)."[38] This is an example of an international public relations program designed to help the environment and strengthen the organization's relationships with governments, regulatory bodies, and other international companies over the course of several years. In other cases, however, international public relations issues can arise in a matter of seconds with just a few ill-advised words. When the Netherlands defeated Mexico in World Cup play, Royal Dutch Airlines (@KLM) tweeted "Adios Amigos! #NEDMEX," and accompanied the post with an image of an airport "Departures" sign featuring a caricature of a man with a large moustache, sombrero, and bandana.[39] That tweet created an international public relations problem because publics in Mexico were offended by what the Dutch organization had communicated.[40] One Twitter user responded, "@KLM your brilliant social media experts just lost you the 2nd largest market in Latin America in one tweet, they must feel really clever."[41]

rafapress/Shutterstock.com

Royal Dutch Airlines (@KLM) was criticized for tweeting "Adios Amigos! #NEDMEX" after the Netherlands defeated Mexico in World Cup soccer.

Do you think the tweet caused long-term damage to KLM's business in Mexico? Why or why not?

As discussed in Chapter 3, global conglomerates are advancing the internationalization of public relations with both economic and cultural convergence. However, you don't have to work for an international company like Nike, Accenture, or KLM, or for a global agency like Ketchum (Omnicom) or WPP, to work in international public relations. Even small organizations communicate regularly across national borders.[42]

Public Diplomacy

Public diplomacy is an important subset of international public relations that deals with communication designed to promote national interests. In most cases, this means that the organization, a key public, or both are nations, but in certain cases diplomatic actors may include nonstate organizations such as NGOs or corporations. If you work in communications for a government organization like Global Affairs Canada or for a Canadian embassy or consulate (there are 240 around the world), or if you work for one of these departments' counterparts in another nation, your job will likely entail public diplomacy with the broadest mission of promoting national interests abroad. You may also be involved in public diplomacy working for an NGO or corporation.

Consider the Paris Agreement, which 195 nations adopted to reduce global greenhouse gas emissions at the United Nations Convention on Climate Change in 2015. NGOs such as Greenpeace, World Wildlife Fund, and the Union of Concerned Scientists were not pleased with the agreement, which they felt did not go far enough in limiting the use of fossil fuels.[43] On the other hand, the climate change conference itself was sponsored by corporations such as Michelin, Google, Ikea, SkyPower Global (a solar energy company), and Renault-Nissan

public diplomacy
Subset of international public relations that focuses on promoting national interests.

mediated public diplomacy A nation's strategic use of media to promote its agenda abroad to foreign publics.

relational public diplomacy Engagement between a nation and its foreign publics in cultural exchange and two-way communication with the goal of achieving mutual benefits.

National diplomats celebrated the Paris Agreement on climate change.

What other organizations besides governments participated in the diplomatic efforts as a form of international public relations?

(an alliance of French and Japanese auto-makers).[44] To the degree that these NGOs and corporations worked to influence the nations participating in the negotiations, they were practising public diplomacy as a form of international public relations.

In discussing public diplomacy as a form of public relations, professor Guy Golan defines two key perspectives. First is **mediated public diplomacy**, which is a nation's strategic use of media to promote its agenda and "impact opinions held by targeted foreign audiences."[45] The second approach is **relational public diplomacy**, which is engagement between a nation and its foreign publics in cultural exchange and two-way communication with the goal of achieving mutual benefits. Mediated public diplomacy aligns well with the public information and asymmetrical models of public relations that were outlined in Chapter 2. Relational public diplomacy fits better with two-way models and the symmetrical ideal. Golan recommends integrating the two approaches, using media to gain favourable international coverage that helps set the stage for more interactive relationship-building.

dialogic communication
Exchanges involving people communicating their own views and backgrounds while remaining completely open to seeing the world as others do.

monologic communication
Communication in which one party attempts to impose its view on others.

> Use media to gain favourable exposure that helps set the stage for more interactive relationship-building.

Ethics: Dialogic Ethics

In his 1923 book *I and Thou*, Austrian-born philosopher Martin Buber developed the concept of dialogue to explain how people come to understand their own existence through their interactions and relationships with others. **Dialogic communication** happens when people enter into an exchange with an understanding of their own views and backgrounds but also with complete openness to seeing the world as others do. The growth of the web and social media as tools for public relations has led a number of public relations scholars to focus on the concept of dialogue as an ethical guidepost.

The opposite of dialogic communication is **monologic communication**, in which communicators strive to impose their view on others. Ethicists hold that the day-to-day practice of public relations leans too much towards monologic and not enough towards dialogic. They consider monologic public relations to be less ethical because it treats publics as less important than the powerful organizations conducting public relations. Dialogic public relations facilitates a fairer balance of power.

It's easy to see how dialogue and relational diplomacy can be praised as ethical public relations, but what about monologic, mediated diplomacy when a cause is perceived to be just? As part of its counter-terrorism efforts, the US Department of State ran a social media campaign against ISIS in 2014. The State Department's strategy included a YouTube video that parodied ISIS recruitment efforts. The video mocked ISIS in graphic detail, juxtaposing disturbing images of prisoner crucifixions, mosque bombings, and severed heads with ISIS claims that joining the organization will lead to some kind of promised land. The video concludes with a sarcastic note, "Travel is inexpensive, because you won't need a return ticket!"[46]

The counter-terrorism strategy, which also included anti-ISIS Facebook, Twitter, and Tumblr accounts, was anything but dialogic in its approach to ISIS. Given the circumstances, is this monologic approach ethical?

The decision between monologic and dialogic public relations parallels questions of one-way versus two-way communication (Chapter 2), asymmetrical versus symmetrical public relations (Chapter 2), and advocacy versus accommodation (Chapter 12). Reasonable moral arguments can be made for both sides depending on the circumstances.

In using social media to counter ISIS recruitment efforts, the US Department of State produced a graphic video mocking the terrorist group, showing disturbing images of extreme violence from the terrorist's own videos.

Did the American government go too far? Can this type of persuasive tactic be justified ethically? If so, how? If not, why not?

In global public relations, reaching across cultural and geographical boundaries to get to know one another better takes extra work, but it is a must. Whether you are advocating for a new emoji, delivering educational technology, marketing bathroom goods, or fighting terrorism, successful and ethical public relations requires an understanding that not everyone shares your background and culture. It's crucial that you take the time to learn about what matters most to your publics.

Voices from the Field

Darren Barefoot

Image courtesy of Darren Barefoot

Darren Barefoot is a marketing and communications strategist with a deep understanding of technology and web culture, and with experience deploying complex, innovative digital projects that connect and inspire people to improve their world. Darren advised the United Nations climate change secretariat on digital engagement in the lead-up to the Paris climate talks. Darren is a partner at Capulet, where he has worked on campaigns with MEC, .eco, Ecojustice, Project AWARE, and CPAWS. He's co-author of *Friends with Benefits: A Social Media Marketing Handbook* and *The Noble Arsonist: Stoking Fires and Igniting Movements for NGOs and Companies That Care.*

At the time of writing, Darren was living in France and working with clients from his native Vancouver (where he is still a CPRS member) and around the world.

You live in France but you have clients in Canada and other places in the world. How does that work?
We shift our workday so that we start work after lunch and work into the evening. This enables us to have some overlap with clients everywhere, whether they're in Europe or on either coast in North America. For our North American clients, this also means that we can often send over work for their review while they're sleeping, so it's

Continued

in their inbox first thing in the morning. We've found that this can, in many cases, expedite review and approval cycles.

What kind of global opportunities does a career in public relations offer?

In terms of working globally, I think the main challenge is understanding your market. If you move, for example, from Vancouver to Moscow to do local PR there, you're going to need a while to get up to speed with the local scene (assuming you know the language). The same goes for PR for a particular sector. If you're unfamiliar with, for example, the European manufacturing sector, then you're going to need to build up some knowledge on that front.

But, people need PR everywhere on the planet, so if you've got the background or a patient employer, then opportunities abound.

What does a practitioner have to be aware of when he/she is communicating across languages and cultures?

I'm always very cautious around communicating across language and cultures, unless I'm very familiar with the landscape. My business partner and I lived in Dublin for a while, and she was hired as a PR person for a variety of Irish tech start-ups. They specifically hired her because she had familiarity with the American market, which they wanted to break into. It was challenging for Irish communicators, even though they spoke the same language, if they weren't familiar with American business language.

Plus, of course, there was the accent issue. My partner had to teach one client how to pronounce *palm* (as in *PalmPilot*) in the American style, instead of the Irish *pam*.

What's the most challenging intercultural communication situation you've observed in public relations?

I worked for the United Nations climate change secretariat for a couple of years. The UN often communicates in its six "official" languages (Arabic, Chinese, English, French, Russian, and Spanish), so when we produced communications materials, we often had to have our press releases and reports translated into all six languages. You needed to anticipate this translation in how you wrote the original English version, so that it wasn't too idiomatic or nuanced.

What can students do to prepare for international and intercultural public relations assignments in advance? What kinds of things can they learn only from experience?

Get as much familiarity with your target market(s) as possible. Certainly, I mean reading audience research and the like, but I'd also recommend getting as familiar with the market's culture as well. Read popular books, watch films, and the like.

If students are interning or doing work–study in a foreign location, then I'd recommend connecting with local students and with staff who are from their home country or region. The latter is because those people will have brought a similar perspective to their new destination, and can help guide the student through the often discombobulating entry into a new professional culture.

What do you see as the greatest opportunity for public relations as a field arising from trends in globalization?

I think the greatest opportunity is to be able to work remotely, so that you're not necessarily doing PR where you live. There are challenges to overcome to be successful, but I know plenty of folks who live on one continent and do public relations on another.

Given changes in demographics and technology, how are new public relations practitioners entering the field more prepared? Less prepared?

I'm not sure I have a strong opinion on this. I do occasionally wonder about the impact of machine learning and AI on our field. How many years will it be before every press release or article is written and distributed by a computer? That will come with its own challenges—if everybody is using the same PR bot, then there's going to be a lot more commodification of work. If I were a young PR professional, I'd be keeping an eye on this area.

In Case You Missed It

Almost everyone with an Internet connection can practise some form of international communication. This means navigating intercultural challenges is part of everyday public relations work. Cultural intelligence also comes into play practising public relations offline. Here's some advice culled from the chapter.

- Don't assume that your publics are online simply because you are.
- Think carefully about how your publics are accessing and using communication technology in diverse cultural contexts.

- You will likely deal with both high-context tactics like texts and tweets and low-context communication that spells out your organization's goals, policies, and positions.
- In high-uncertainty-avoidance cultures, it may be wiser to focus on specific outcomes of communication rather than dialogue as an end in itself.
- Build fluency in intercultural public relations with a combination of head (cognition), body (behaviour), and heart (emotion/motivation).
- Use media to gain favourable exposure that helps set the stage for more interactive relationship-building in public diplomacy.

ICYMI

Summary

13.1 Explain why issues of public access and usage of digital communication technology are critical in planning for global public relations.
Internet access and usage vary from community to community and from nation to nation. Even when publics have access to communication technologies, that doesn't mean they are inclined to use them to engage organizations. Cultural factors and offline communication must be considered in planning.

13.2 Analyze cases of international public relations involving intercultural communication.
Any time public relations practitioners communicate across national borders, they are likely communicating across cultures too, and they should plan for intercultural communication challenges. In cases of public relations supporting efforts to market bathroom-related products internationally, successful strategies included focusing on culturally important values in the new markets (e.g., cleanliness and health) and persuading key influencers in other cultures (e.g., TV show hosts, doctors, investors) to publicly endorse the concept.

13.3 Compare high-context and low-context communication.
In high-context communication, most of the meaning conveyed between people lies in the context of the communication or is internal to the communicators. Taglines, tweets, brand logos, and text messages are examples of high-context communication because success in this type of messaging depends so heavily on the context and the meaning assigned by the people involved. In low-context communication, most of the meaning lies in the message itself. Low-context communication requires greater elaboration and detail in composing

messages. Public relations practitioners need to be able to do both and to properly adapt communication styles to publics in context.

13.4 Apply cultural dimensions (e.g., uncertainty avoidance, masculinity–femininity) to public relations strategy and practice.

Understanding cultural dimensions such as power–distance, individualism–collectivism, uncertainty avoidance, masculinity–femininity, and long-term orientation is an important part of cultural intelligence, which involves cognitive skill in designing public relations strategy. But gaining experience and confidence (emotional skill) and learning how to actually behave appropriately (physical skill) in different cultural contexts are also keys to successful practice. Head (cognitive), heart (emotional), and body (physical) are all necessary for excellence in the practice of intercultural public relations.

13.5 Explain the relationship between intercultural public relations, international public relations, and public diplomacy.

Most international public relations involve intercultural communication because different nations have different cultures, but not all intercultural public relations are international because cultures vary widely within national boundaries. Public diplomacy is a subset of international public relations that deals with communication intended to promote national interests.

13.6 Discuss the ethics of balanced dialogue in global public relations.

Dialogic approaches to public relations are commonly held to be more ethical than monologic approaches because dialogue fosters equality and may lead to an understanding of truth that arises from multiple perspectives. Equality and mutual understanding are particularly noble aspirations for international and intercultural communication. Some may argue, however, that monologic public relations that use public relations tactics primarily for persuasion are more effective and ethical when the cause is just, such as in diplomatic efforts against terrorism.

Discussion Questions

1. Do you think digital divides are getting wider or narrower in today's world? Explain with examples or data.

2. Have you ever surprised yourself by adopting a product or service that you didn't expect to like from another country or completely different culture? How were you persuaded to give it a try? Were public relations tactics involved?

3. Identify an organization that is really good at high-context communications, and compare that organization to one that is really strong in low-context communications. Which would you rather work for and why?

4. How would you describe your own cultural preferences, according to Hofstede's model? (You may want to try this resource: geert-hofstede.com/cultural-survey.html.) Which of the dimensions would be hardest for you to adapt in practising intercultural public relations?

5. Explore the web presence of an international embassy (sites like embassy.goabroad.com may be helpful). Explain how the embassy's diplomatic approach is more *mediated* or *relational*, or if it is better described as a mix of the two.

6. In 2017, Trudeau's Liberal federal government set up a website, canada.ca/results, which they said was designed to track progress on government commitments or promises. The opposition parties quickly dismissed the site as propaganda, saying the Liberals were not being truthful regarding the progress on many initiatives.

   What do you think? Is the website the government's attempt to be transparent, or is it a piece of pre-election propaganda? Are there any ethical challenges associated with this site?

Further Readings and Online Resources

Curtin, P.A., & Gaither, T.K. (2007). *International public relations: Negotiating culture, identity, and power.* **Thousand Oaks, CA: SAGE Publications.**

This book, sometimes used as a textbook for international public relations courses, explains public relations techniques and practices in a variety of regulatory, political, and cultural climates. It is a little old, but still relevant.

Public Relations across Cultures
www.aboutpublicrelations.net/ucpayne.htm

In this blogpost, international public relations practitioner Neil Payne shares some practical tips for those working in an international context.

Global Internet Access Is Even Worse Than Dire Report Suggests
www.wired.com/story/global-internet-access-dire-reports/

According to this article published by *Wired*, less than half the world's population has Internet access, leaving an estimated 3.8 billion people behind. This has serious implications for public relations practitioners, especially those working in a global context.

Peer-Reviewed Academic Journal Article
Dhanesh, G.S., & Sriramesh, K. (2018). Culture and crisis communication: Nestle India's Maggi noodles case. *Journal of International Management,* **24(3), 204–14. doi:10.1016/j .intman.2017.12.004**

This article analyzes a crisis faced by Nestle India using the framework of global public relations. What role did culture (the company's and the country's) play in this case?

Key Terms

Access divide   324
Cultural intelligence   335
Culture   330
Dialogic communication   338
Digital divide   324
Gamification   335
High-context
  communication   332
Individualism–
  collectivism   334

Intercultural public
  relations   330
International public
  relations   336
Long-term orientation   334
Low-context
  communication   332
Masculinity–femininity   334
Mediated public
  diplomacy   337

Monologic
  communication   338
Power distance   334
Public diplomacy   337
Relational public
  diplomacy   337
Self-efficacy   336
Uncertainty avoidance   334
Usage divide (or second
  digital divide)   324

14

Careers

Could griping about your job on social media ever be a smart career move? Find out what happened when an entry-level employee gave Yelp a less-than-stellar review.

> ### Key learning outcomes
>
> **14.1** Identify different types of employers for public relations jobs.
>
> **14.2** Assess how different areas of specialization in public relations match your interests, and consider the knowledge and skills that jobs in those areas require.
>
> **14.3** Plan for your own continuing education in public relations including core competencies and evolving skills for a changing media environment.
>
> **14.4** Map a public relations career trajectory from entry level to executive.
>
> **14.5** Discuss ethical dilemmas related to the professional values of competition and loyalty.

When you close your eyes and picture yourself working in public relations, what do you see? Do you picture yourself in a chic urban agency or a tech start-up, surrounded by hipsters and creative geniuses? Are you dressed more formally, working with laser focus on business strategy in a corporate high-rise? Perhaps you're walking the halls of a children's hospital with a therapy dog and a group of reporters. Do you see yourself working quietly, uploading data to a government web page behind the scenes? Or are you leading an environmental protest with a bullhorn and a smartphone, hashtagging the energy of a movement? Jobs in public relations allow you to make a difference in people's lives in a lot of different ways. While no two careers in public relations are alike, and career options are always changing, this chapter offers a look at major types of employers, lists sample jobs from some major areas of specialization, and describes typical responsibilities of practitioners as they move from entry level to the top of the field.

Employers

One of your first major considerations in thinking about a career in public relations is what type of employer you want to work for. Discussed throughout this book are cases and examples of public relations conducted by global agencies, for-profit companies, non-profit organizations, international NGOs (non-governmental organizations), and government agencies. During the course of your career, you may work for organizations as big as Google, Walmart, or the Canadian government, or as small as a two-person business. Or maybe you will start your own firm and become your own boss. As you launch your career, all options are on the table.

Agencies

For many aspiring public relations professionals, an agency job is the first position that comes to mind when they think about starting in the business, and agencies are certainly great places to launch and build careers. Agencies provide corporate clients with specialized services including research, campaign planning and implementation, speech-writing, crisis management, special events, and so on, but most large companies also include in-house public relations departments.

Agencies range in size from two- to three-person shops to the biggest public relations firms in the world like Edelman, Weber Shandwick, FleishmanHillard, and Ketchum. The biggest agencies have tens of thousands of employees spread across offices all over the world. As you can see from the chart in Table 14.1, many of the largest agencies in the world are American, but large Canadian cities like Vancouver, Montreal, and Toronto are also home to many thriving PR agencies. Agencies

Courtesy of Adrien Williams

The uniquely designed offices of Bicom Communications in Montreal have been featured in design magazines around the world. Employees can grab a quick meeting in the Muskoka chairs surrounding a faux firepit.

How do you picture your workplace in public relations?

serve multiple clients, very often in different businesses. This means that if you work for an agency, you'll likely have an opportunity to work on multiple projects for multiple organizations.

In mid-size to large agencies, client work is assigned to account teams. Each client has an account with the agency, and agency employees work on multiple accounts simultaneously. From entry level to executive leadership, traditional jobs in agencies include the following:

- account assistant
- account coordinator
- account executive
- senior account executive
- account supervisor
- director
- vice-president

According to PayScale.com the salary for an entry-level account coordinator in a Canadian agency ranges from $31,495 to around $51,408 with a median of a $38,798.[1]

TABLE 14.1 The world's largest PR agencies, by annual billings

2019	2018	Agency	HQ	Fee Income 2018 ($)	Fee Income 2017 ($)	Growth (Constant Currency)
1	1	Edelman	USA	888,405,000	893,591,000	-0.6%
2	2	Weber Shandwick	USA	840,000,000	800,000,000	5.0%
3	N/A	BCW	USA	723,000,000	709,000,000	2.0%
4	3	FleishmanHillard	USA	605,000,000	570,000,000	6.1%
5	4	Ketchum	USA	545,000,000	550,000,000	-0.9%
6	6	MSL	France	450,000,000	460,000,000	-2.2%
7	7	Hill+Knowlton Strategies	USA	400,000,000	400,000,000	0.0%
8	8	Ogilvy	USA	388,000,000	354,000,000	9.6%
9	9	BlueFocus	China	336,372,995	321,849,607	10.8%
10	11	Brunswick	UK	280,000,000	260,000,000	7.7%

Seven of the largest pr firms in the world are US based, but all of these—except for Brunswick Group at #10—have Canadian offices. Blue Focus, which is based in China, recently purchased a majority stake in the Canadian-based firm Cosette.

Sources: US Department of Defense, International Institute for Strategic Studies, Walmart, McDonald's, NHS Information Services, China National Petroleum Corporation, State Grid Corporation of China, Indian Railways, Indian Armed Forces, Foxconn
* Including franchises (420,000 excluding franchises)

Of course, different agencies offer different salaries and different job titles. Convergence and integration have led many firms to rethink how they organize teams and name positions. The work can be nonstop and involve significant multitasking as employees jump between account projects and urgent client demands, but those who succeed gain experience in a hurry. This combination of jam-packed workdays (and nights), steep learning curves, and fast-growing professional networks also means that there is quite a bit of turnover. It's not uncommon for rising stars to move up through two or three positions in their first few years on the job, and often these job changes include lateral moves from one agency to another.

However, some young professionals find that agency work just isn't for them. Some will move to other careers altogether. Others will go to work doing public relations for other types of organizations, often finding their new positions with the help of contacts they made in agencies.

Corporations

Working in-house as a full-time employee of one company means that your responsibility in managing organization–public relationships is primarily to a single organization. A corporate job on the client side may look like a posh gig—you have only one "client" to serve, the schedule may be more predictable, and pay is often higher. Keep in mind, however, that the person making $50k working in-house very likely has more years of experience than the entry-level account coordinator at an agency.

In addition, while you may have only one client to serve working in-house, you will still be responsible to many publics. Corporate jobs focus on customers (marketing communications), investors (financial relations), government agencies (public affairs), employees (internal relations), and the publics who live wherever companies operate (community relations). Large corporations may employ separate departments for each of these publics and may also hire public relations agencies for help with various functions, but the departments must still work together.

As discussed in Chapter 4, corporate social responsibility (CSR) programs have become more common in response to negative public sentiment about corporations and their impact on society and the environment. CSR efforts are a prime example of the importance of balancing the interests of various stakeholders, even if you work only for a single organization.

Non-profits and NGOs

By definition, non-profit organizations exist to do something other than make money for shareholders. Non-profit work may appeal to people who work hard to support the missions of those organizations, such as health, education, and environmental causes. While non-profits often benefit from the service of volunteers, as strategic organizations they operate with business models that require full-time paid staff.

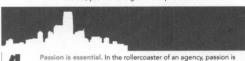

10 Things To Know About Working in an Agency

1. It's a great place to start. Agencies allow you to learn everything about the industry while you work directly with clients. If a next step in life is corporate, an agency background allows you to relate to those from the other side.

2. PR is more than you think. Although a common request from clients is media relations, PR firms offer more than expected. Understanding the core functions and capabilities of your firm will allow you to push the envelope and help your business grow faster than the times.

3. Personal growth is inevitable. In the fast-paced world of an agency, you have no choice but to learn your strengths and weaknesses. You must offer quick and quality work, become accountable and accessible, and push yourself harder than you ever thought was possible, and before you know it, you will have grown as a professional.

4. Passion is essential. In the rollercoaster of an agency, passion is necessary in remaining resilient. Passion engages creativity, ignites progression and allows for business growth.

5. Communication is key. Whether leading account teams, asking questions or exploring new ideas, communication offers opportunities for agencies to surpass the relevant and remain innovative.

6. Managers are like clients. Invest in the relationship to understand how they prefer to work; learn to predict needs and get ahead of asks.

7. Be somebody that others enjoy working with. This can mean being reliable, thoughtful, productive and just being a kind person. Consider your reputation on your teams and with the agency overall.

8. Numbers are part of the job. Research and data matter in making decisions and that means numbers. But it's not calculus so don't run away; train yourself to think about how numbers tell the story or dictate possibilities.

9. Your internal network will grow. Your agency is a gold mine for networking. Find time to meet others with interesting clients or roles you're unfamiliar with to find your passion points and to develop mentors.

10. Become an entrepreneur in your role. Embody a drive to take charge in order to make a difference for clients and internal teams. Seek opportunity to investigate growth and go beyond the requirement. Prove yourself indispensable. Be an eternal learner.

THE PLANK CENTER
FOR LEADERSHIP IN PUBLIC RELATIONS
@PlankCenterPR
plankcenter.ua.edu

Reprinted with permission of the Plank Center for Leadership in Public Relations, University of Alabama.

Agencies provide great learning experiences.

What appeals to you least and most about working in an agency?

Photo by Richard Levine/Corbis via Getty Images

Workers at a Procter & Gamble social media command centre manage the company's #EverydayEffect campaign to highlight its brands' positive effects on consumers.

What other publics besides consumers are important in corporate public relations?

> Public relations jobs in non-profits are just as demanding and require just as much accountability as corporate jobs.

> If you start at an agency, be prepared to move through multiple positions in your first few years.

Public relations jobs in non-profits are often just as demanding and require just as much accountability as corporate jobs. In addition, in many ways the stakes are higher at non-profits because public health, education, social justice, and the environment depend on them.

In general, public relations management in non-profits involves similar strategies and skills as for-profits (media relations and publicity, branding, community relations, public affairs, etc.). However, a major difference between non-profits and corporations is the key publics of donors and volunteers. Fundraising and volunteer management are critical to public relations success at non-profits. Public relations practitioners working in non-profit also need to master the art of partnerships, as their work often involves working with business organizations and/or government agencies.

MADD Canada, for example, works with a long list of corporate sponsors that includes Allstate Insurance, BMO Mastercard, and Uber to pursue its mission of ending impaired driving. They also work with various levels of government and the police, and involve school boards when it comes to educational initiatives.

The starting pay at non-profits tends to be lower than the pay offered in agencies or corporate jobs, and some non-profit public relations roles are performed on a volunteer basis.

NGOs are one type of non-profit. NGOs are organized at local, national, or international levels and advocate for humanitarian and environmental causes. Some NGOs work closely with the United Nations, and their relationships with corporations and governments range from contentious to cooperative.

Government

More than 3.6 million[2] Canadians are employed in the public sector, which includes all economic entities controlled by governments including health care and education. Federal, provincial and territorial, and local governments combined account for almost 40 per cent of total public sector employment, and all levels of government employ public relations and communications specialists.

Federal government jobs tend to be clustered in large cities. Almost one-third (32 per cent) of federal employees work in Ottawa–Gatineau. Montreal has the second-largest number of federal employees, and Toronto, the third-largest.

Many public relations practitioners find the idea of working for a government or government entity attractive. These jobs tend to be more stable, pay well, and offer good benefits. On the flip side, some practitioners will tell you that these jobs lack the excitement and creativity found in agencies, and dealing with the various levels of bureaucracy (especially when it comes to getting work approved) can be frustrating. This, of course, is a generalization—there are many exceptions to this rule, and the director of communications for a large hospital or a large Canadian city will likely tell you his or her job is as exciting and fast-paced as any agency gig.

As noted throughout this book, open communication and access to information about government operations is a foundation of democracies. The "information age" in many ways has opened government information to easier access than ever before (and public relations jobs play a key role in how our societies continue to evolve).

Self-Employment and Small Business

On the opposite end of the spectrum from jobs with enormous government organizations are small businesses—millions of them worldwide. In Canada 8.2 million people are employed by a small business, which is defined as a company with fewer than 99 employees. According to the Canadian government, there are 1.17 million employer businesses in Canada, and almost 98 per cent of these are small businesses. Most of these organizations do not have a full-time position or department labelled *public relations*, but all of them will require managing relationships with publics.

Whether you are writing code, renting sailboats, or wrapping burritos, you'll need to be much more of a generalist in small businesses compared to large companies, non-profits, or government organizations. Instead of specializing in only the

Wangkun Jia/Shutterstock.com

In Canada, the government is a major employer. Globally, governments and large corporations are the world's largest employers.

What appeals to you least and most about working for a large government organization?

Melinna Mills/Canadian Red Cross

The Canadian Red Cross has created Emergency Response Units (ERUs) that can respond quickly to emergencies around the world. To support the ERUs, the Red Cross maintains a roster of 300 professionals including doctors, nurses, and public affairs professionals.

What kinds of public relations skills would be important in public affairs jobs focused on disaster management?

Keith Bedford/Bloomberg via Getty Images

Small business owners, start-ups and self-employed public relations practitioners often work in home offices or "co-working" spaces such as WeWork, which has locations around the world including Vancouver, Toronto, and Montreal.

What do you see as the advantages and disadvantages of this type of work environment?

communication function, you will likely be involved in core operations in addition to building and maintaining relationships with customers, vendors, regulators, banks and investors, and media. If your budget for promotions is small, you may rely more on social media and word of mouth. But good media relations can still lead to big hits in influential channels, if you know how to tell and pitch your stories well (Chapters 4 and 9).

As an owner, operator, partner, or employee of a small business you will be directly responsible to your organization for key management decisions. You will also be directly accountable to publics for the outcomes and effects of those decisions. In this sense, working in a small organization can be seen as one of the purest forms of public relations as a management function. Also, many public relations agencies are small businesses themselves and offer opportunities for internships and entry-level jobs that expose you to all facets of client service work from top to bottom.

The Public Relations Entrepreneur

Many PR professionals also operate their own small businesses—known as a *sole proprietorship*—offering public relations services to companies that require extra help or are too small to warrant a dedicated public relations role. Over the course of a career, it is very common for practitioners to spend some time working as a public relations or communications consultant, either alone or in partnership with one or more practitioner.

Some of these small businesses eventually evolve into larger agencies (which may, in turn, be purchased by an even larger agency), or practitioners may elect to continue to work alone. Either way, practitioners who choose this path will require entrepreneurial skills in addition to public relations skills.

Practitioners who open their own business will need to develop some core business skills in the area of accounting/bookkeeping and human resources.

> *If you work for a small business, you'll need to be much more of a generalist.*

Areas of Specialization

You'll find as many different areas of specialization in public relations as there are different missions of organizations. That said, some of the major categories are health care, sports and entertainment, political and public affairs, financial and entrepreneurial, consumer, and international public relations. Within each category are countless types of public relations jobs.

Public Relations Careers Health Care

Communications Officer

Public relations professionals working in health care often play a role in educating patients or may be involved with the hospital's foundation, which raises money for new buildings and equipment. If you care about children's health, this job might be right for you.

JOB TITLE
Communications Officer, BC Children's Hospital

JOB DESCRIPTION
Your opportunity to champion world-class services provided to seriously ill children and their families in the province of British Columbia.

Reporting to the Manager, Communications for BC Children's Hospital and BC Women's Hospital and Health Centre, you are responsible for providing communications services to build awareness and a positive reputation for BC Children's Hospital's programs, services and achievements. You will create news releases, draft issues notes and key messages for interviews; develop and maintain strong relationships with internal and external stakeholders; and develop and implement communication and event plans for key initiatives.

SAMPLE DUTIES AND RESPONSIBILITIES
- Develop and execute internal and external communication plans that promote and support BC Children's Hospital's excellence in patient care, education, research, prevention, and partnerships
- Produce effective media releases, draft key messages, and issue notes, as well as contribute to online and social media
- Identify and produce digital, video, web, intranet, and social media content, with a particular emphasis on helping to promote program awareness and achievements
- Work with key staff, hospital leadership, and PHSA executives to support change internally and oversee the implementation of corporate identity strategies
- Develop and maintain relationships and coordinate with hospital foundation teams, research institutes, and other associated groups

QUALIFICATIONS
- Bachelor's degree
- At least five years' experience in communications, public relations, journalism, or marketing
- Ability to write a communications plan
- Proven writing skills
- Issues management experience
- The ability to handle highly confidential and sensitive issues with tact and diplomacy
- Experience in proactive public relations, and identifying and executing story opportunities
- Proficiency in social media, including content creation, posting, and distribution

DISCUSSION QUESTIONS
The qualifications for this job include an ability to handle highly confidential and sensitive issues. What might some of these be? As a PR practitioner, would you have the opportunity to meet hospital patients?

This section briefly outlines some major areas of specialization and offers an example job description from each. The job ads all were found online during a brief period, and the openings listed are either entry level or appropriate for someone just a few years out of school. Their purpose is to get you thinking about the experiences you should seek now as you consider your future career options in these areas of specialization.

Photo by Markus Gilliar-Pool/Bongarts/Getty Images

Piotr Trochowski of the German national football team participates in a photo shoot for the German Football Association (DFB).

What appeals to you least and most about working for a sports organization?

> It takes more than enthusiasm to keep up with the 24/7 ups and downs of public relations jobs in sports and entertainment.

grassroots campaign A bottom-up campaign that focuses strategy on mass participation of citizens or political constituents in an effort to influence policy or legislation.

grasstops campaign A campaign that focuses strategy on directly influencing opinion leaders and well-connected individuals such as donors or political party leaders.

Health

The goals of health care are as universal as the human race. From family planning to end-of-life hospice care, governments, NGOs, hospitals, pharmaceutical companies, educational and research institutions, and medical device manufacturers—these are only some of the organizations that have a stake in fighting disease, caring for the ill, and keeping healthy people healthy.

Sports and Entertainment

Sports and entertainment may be one of the hardest areas to break into right after college because so many people would love to work for the athletes and celebrities they already enjoy following. Most are also willing to work very, very hard to get one of those jobs. Moving from fan to employee can be a rewarding transition, but also humbling and exhausting. It takes a lot more than just pastime levels of enthusiasm to keep up with the business side of the 24/7 ups and downs of sports and entertainment.

Sports information directors, for example, are responsible for documenting and promoting the accomplishments of the athletes, teams, and leagues they represent. They provide updated—often real-time—statistics for use by the media. This requires deep knowledge of sports, teams, and athletes. Sports information directors must have strong organizational and analytic skills and a solid understanding of how sports media operate in order to effectively serve a media relations function. Sports and entertainment jobs also include issues and crisis management, marketing and branding, and community relations.

Political and Public Affairs

Strategic campaigns are a core function of public relations, and when people hear the word *campaign* many will think of political campaigns. Political campaigning done well is the epitome of a public communication process that builds strategy from research to achieve measurable outcomes. Some jobs in political public relations last only as long as a candidate is running for office, while others are tied to politicians and organizations that require continuous public relations efforts from term to term and from political initiative to political initiative. Most of us have heard the term **grassroots campaign**, which refers to large groups of citizens who try to influence the political process. Public affairs specialists, on the other hand, will sometimes initiate what are called **grasstops campaigns**, which involve trying to influence opinion leaders and other well-connected individuals.

Public Relations Careers Sports PR

Manager, In-Game Communications

For a die-hard hockey fan, this may seem like a dream job, but it would be a tough one to land and maybe even tougher to succeed. Would you be ready for it?

JOB TITLE

Manager, In-Game Communications, NHL

JOB DESCRIPTION

The Manager, In-Game Communications is a versatile writer who leads the NHL's In-Game Communications team in bringing to life the facts, figures, and story lines from more than 1,300 games each season. The Manager is responsible for guiding storytelling and research, leading and assisting a group of writers, and communicating relevant information to media, Rightsholders, Member Clubs, League executives, and fans in real time during all games.

SAMPLE DUTIES AND RESPONSIBILITIES

- Identify storylines and lead the writing, research, and editing of the NHL Morning Skate, a daily publication that pulls together the NHL's top editorial moments and highlights in a succinct, compelling manner
- Use a deep knowledge of hockey to guide in-game storytelling in real-time and act as the lead for all in-game communications from the public relations team
- Actively contribute to real-time coverage and end-of-night publications while leading 3-5 team members.

- Monitor trending topics and relay information to other members of the Communications team and/or League executives, as necessary.

QUALIFICATIONS

- Proficient writer and editor who can work under tight deadline pressure in a fast-paced environment
- Excellent oral communication and interpersonal skills
- A strong understanding of the League's rule book and a passion for hockey
- Exhibit excellent attention to detail
- Experience with Adobe Photoshop or equivalent considered an asset
- Successful completion of post-secondary education in a relevant discipline
- 3-5 years demonstrable experience working in a similar capacity at a Club or League level or in another fast-paced, live environment
- Understanding of and aptitude for social media, with an emphasis on Twitter and Instagram

DISCUSSION QUESTIONS

How would you demonstrate an aptitude for social media? Which specific publics would you work with as part of the job?

Many political candidates and organizations hire agencies that specialize in political communication. If you're fired up about a candidate or a political cause, or if you think of yourself as a policy wonk and want to make a difference in the technical details of how government operates, political public relations may be for you.

Financial and Entrepreneurial

Financial public relations deals with investor relations, financial media relations, and disclosures of financial information, as discussed in Chapter 4 on relationship management. Employers range from Canada's banks, to large publicly held companies like Berkshire

Public Relations Careers Public Affairs

Manager, Public Affairs

In Canada, health care is publicly funded, so it is important for a hospital to have positive relations with communities and various levels of government. Here's what a public affairs job entails at Trillium Health, a hospital in southern Ontario.

JOB TITLE
Manager, Public Affairs, Trillium Health

JOB DESCRIPTION
Reporting to the Director, Communications and Public Affairs, the Manager, Public Affairs will be responsible for ongoing, strategic engagement with organizational partners, including local, provincial, and federal government officials, colleague organizations, staff, patients, and families, and the communities of Mississauga and West Toronto. Trillium Health is looking for a talented leader who has the ability to create and maintain meaningful collaborative, inclusive engagements across a diverse and growing community, to enhance brand presence and awareness to support an ambitious organizational mission. This individual also has experience building and sustaining brand presence within complex, rapidly changing environments. The successful candidate will work closely with diverse multidisciplinary teams of clinicians, communicators, strategists, and designers building a strong foundation for community relations, ongoing dialogue, and increased partnership.

SAMPLE DUTIES AND RESPONSIBILITIES
- Communicate and collaborate with stakeholders representing diverse skill sets, reporting structures, and backgrounds to develop and implement the most appropriate, inclusive, and effective plan for the organization and community
- Identify and produce required supporting collateral, such as key messages, written communications, speaking notes, briefing notes, and other products
- Manage the various internal stakeholder requirements needed to implement plans

- Develop and monitor evaluation criteria to measure success and impact of partner & community relations efforts
- Participate in developing and managing interactions with the media and contributing to issue management, as required
- Participate in the Communication's On-Call program

QUALIFICATIONS
- 5+ years in government, communications, community relations, and/or engagement
- Strong government and public relations acumen, including deep knowledge of various levels of government
- Experience developing and implementing engagement plans
- Proven experience building and maintaining brand presence to help achieve an organizational mission
- Strong time management skills with minimal need for oversight
- Strong attention to detail
- Strong written and verbal communication skills
- Results-oriented and client-focused with a commitment to excellence

DISCUSSION QUESTIONS
Like many public relations jobs, the ideal candidate for this job will need proven communication skills but also a working knowledge of the government. How could you prepare to demonstrate knowledge of government in an application or interview?

How could you demonstrate experience developing and implementing plans?

Public Relations Careers Government

Communications Consultant

JOB TITLE
Communications Consultant, Government of Saskatchewan

JOB DESCRIPTION
The Communications Branch of the Ministry of Health is seeking an energetic and motivated communications professional to research and produce a variety of written communications materials to support the goals and objectives of the Ministry.

SAMPLE DUTIES AND RESPONSIBILITIES
- provide strategic communications advice and direction for a variety of programs and services
- research and prepare a wide range of written materials including communications strategies, speeches, news releases, media backgrounders, and social media content

- develop and implement communication plans and advertising campaigns
- provide issues management and media relations support as required

QUALIFICATIONS
- Typically, the knowledge required for this position would be gained through completion of post-secondary studies in Communications and/or Journalism, although other relevant education and work experience will also be considered.
- Knowledge of the Saskatchewan health system, the Sitecore content management system, and media relations experience would be an asset.

DISCUSSION QUESTIONS
How does this government job differ from the public affairs job listed earlier?
Who are the audiences this person might target?

Hathaway, General Electric, Samsung Electronics, and Apple, to small start-up businesses raising capital for entrepreneurial endeavours. Agencies also specialize in serving clients with financial public relations needs. If you've got a good mind for business and finance, you can put your communication skills to work in financial public relations.

Consumer

Consumer public relations is one of the most visible segments of public relations, perhaps because it is so closely tied with the advertising and marketing of brands we all know well and products we consume every day. When the key publics of public relations are consumers, opportunities for convergence and integration abound.

The growth of digital, social, and mobile media that reach consumers in so many ways has further blurred the lines between public relations, advertising, and marketing. These media afford us more feedback and information from consumer publics than we've ever had before. This convergence has resulted in entirely new career possibilities for those who "get it" when it comes to communicating in these new contexts. If you're into messaging with the right voice, reading feedback well, turning raw data into useful information, and carrying on conversational communication to build relationships with consumers on a large scale, then you might just be perfect for consumer public relations.

Public Relations Careers Investor Relations

Manager, Investor Relations

Investor relations involves communicating about money and financial issues. Are you ready to be part of the investor relations team for one of Canada's most recognizable organizations?

JOB TITLE
Manager, Investor Relations, Canadian Tire Corporation

JOB DESCRIPTION
Reporting to the Associate Vice-President, Investor, the Manager, Investor Relations supports all investor relations activities for Canadian Tire Corporation. This collaborative role requires a balanced skill set with the ideal applicant being a skilled communicator with a solid foundation in finance or accounting. Investor relations experience is an asset, knowledge of the retail business is nice to have. Areas of focus will include assisting in the development and execution of IR programs and communication materials that support CTC's goal of being the number one retail brand in Canada. This role will help facilitate effective communication between executive management and the investment community, in order to encourage a long-term view of the company, a stable investor base, and ultimately a fair market valuation of Canadian Tire's shares.

SAMPLE DUTIES AND RESPONSIBILITIES
- Plan and deliver key investor relations programs including Quarterly and Annual Disclosures
- Work collaboratively with External Reporting and Communications teams to deliver consistent messaging and flawless execution of quarterly conference calls, press releases, MD&A, and annual general meetings

- Develop and implement a process for continuous monitoring and updates of IR website, mobile app, and performance of stock price
- Play a lead role in preparation and execution of shareholder and analyst engagements—from event planning and management, to content build and post-event reports
- Play a lead role in creating the CFO remarks for the quarterly conference call

QUALIFICATIONS
- Minimum 5–7 years' work experience in financial communications/investor relations with the ability to read, understand, simplify, and communicate complex financial issues and business results
- Excellent communication skills including writing, editing, and proofreading
- Robust process and project management; organization and priority-setting skills
- Strong financial and investment comprehension and analysis skills; solid business acumen and general understanding of capital markets
- Advanced PC skills, including Microsoft Excel, PowerPoint, and Word

DISCUSSION QUESTIONS
Investor relations jobs often pay quite well, as discussed in Chapter 4. What else besides money might motivate you to pursue this career option?
What additional education might be required to work in investor relations?

Public Relations Careers | Consumer PR and Communications

PR and Communications Specialist

PANDORA is a popular jewellery manufacturer and retailer. Founded in 1982 and headquartered in Copenhagen, Denmark, PANDORA employs more than 26,500 people worldwide.

JOB TITLE
PR and Communications Specialist, PANDORA Canada

JOB DESCRIPTION
The PR and Communications Specialist will provide strategic planning and direction relating to the Marketing and Communications for PANDORA Canada. The role is responsible for re-enforcing the Brand, developing and implementing the Brand strategy, and all external and internal communications and will work directly with key fashion influencers, media, and bloggers. The Public Relations & Communications Specialist will ensure all communication and brand messaging aligns with PANDORA regional and global guidelines.

SAMPLE DUTIES AND RESPONSIBILITIES
Branding and Marketing: Devise the PR and Communication strategies with the Marketing Director to maximize PANDORA Brand in the Canadian market in both English and French while promoting the website and creating compelling print and electronic communication, content, and event materials to drive retail store traffic in both languages.

External Communication: Lead the development and management of PANDORA's external communications including directing strategic media relations, social media, projects, and events for key stakeholder relations.

Internal Communication: Direct development, implementation, and evaluation of multi-year communications strategies and plans in order to influence and coordinate internal communications.

Events and Brand Activations: Manage and implement the National Event and sponsorship plan including tracking and updating sales collaterals, contracts, finance documentation, and materials inventory.

QUALIFICATIONS
- Bachelor's degree or Master's degree in Marketing, Communications, or a related field
- Minimum of 3 years of related experience
- Specialized knowledge required in the principles and practices of public relations, marketing, social media, design, communications, publishing, and print applications
- Excellent analytical skills related to policy, budget, and operational issues
- Demonstrated superior understanding of a complex, multi-stakeholder environment and sensitivity to issues of diversity of the population in the Canadian Market

DISCUSSION QUESTIONS
How important is a passion for the brand when applying for a public relations job in consumer products?

PANDORA's head office is in Denmark. How might this role be different from one where the head office is in Canada?

Stuart Ramson/AP Images for M&Ms

Actor Tony Hale shoots videos to announce a campaign for M&Ms in which consumers were invited to try three new peanut flavours and vote for their favourite on the M&Ms website and Facebook pages.

What specific role do you think a social media specialist would play in this type of campaign?

International

All of the previously discussed areas of specialization can involve international work. Health care, sports, entertainment, political, financial, and consumer product organizations and publics are spread all over the world, and, as discussed in Chapter 13, the relationships among them cross national borders more than ever before. Many organizations distinctly identify themselves as global or international and specifically seek employees with a strong desire to work and communicate across countries and cultures.

Education and Continued Learning

You're probably reading this text for one of three reasons: you are taking public relations as a required course for your degree or diploma, you are taking a public relations course as an elective for a related degree plan, or you are interested in public relations work and educating yourself independently. These three reasons represent three common tracks into the field. Practising public relations does not necessarily require a specific degree, but as public-relations–specific diplomas and degree programs are becoming more common, it is increasingly common to see employers asking for these qualifications specifically. Many public sector jobs require a degree as opposed to a diploma, so this should be a consideration as you plan your career.

A typical course sequence for the public relations major includes an introductory course, public relations research, public relations writing, an internship, and a campaigns course. Other common courses in public relations majors focus on public relations case studies, law, ethics, planning, and management.[3]

If you're working on a college diploma or a degree from a college or university, however, keep in mind that your broader education is just as important as your public-relations–specific courses. In its Pathways to the Profession report, CPRS (Canadian Public Relations Society) has clearly identified skills and abilities new public relations graduates will need in addition to core public relations skills such as writing:

> The need for critical thinking, teamwork and analytical ability, along with a strong work ethic and an ability to multitask and manage time effectively under the pressure of competing deadlines, continue to be cited by employers as skills required from new graduates.
>
> There is concern that many new practitioners are unaware of broader current and global events and issues that may have an impact on their organizations. Graduates needto have a higher level of awareness of trends and current events, be

> *Your broader education is just as important as your public-relations–specific courses.*

Public Relations Careers International

Communications and Campaigns Manager

Save the Children is an international NGO working on behalf of children's interests worldwide. This position is located in Burma (Myanmar). Do you think you could make a difference in a faraway corner of the world?

JOB TITLE

Communications and Campaigns Manager, Save the Children

JOB DESCRIPTION

This is a two-year contract position to lead a communication and campaign team in implementing advocacy, media engagement, and digital/social media strategies to raise visibility and support the goals of Save the Children's various programs and brand rollout in Burma.

SAMPLE DUTIES AND RESPONSIBILITIES

- Managing communications team
- Working closely with the Country Director to ensure common messaging
- Promoting campaigns and global advocacy partnerships including international consortiums and fund management teams such as Global Fund, Scaling Up Nutrition Civil Society Alliance (SUN CSA), Tat Lan, and Leveraging Essential Nutrition Actions to Reduce Malnutrition (LEARN)
- Developing innovative ways to communicate to target audiences
- Leading communications in emergency situations
- Branding "Save the Children"

- Producing fundraising materials for donors and public supporters

QUALIFICATIONS

- Bachelor's degree in communications, arts, or any related field, with overseas study experience preferred
- Seven years' experience in public relations, advertising, communications, media management, event management, or related field
- Experience implementing strategic campaigns or advocacy work, preferably overseas
- Excellent communications skills, with Myanmar language skills "a definite asset"
- Ability to speak confidently and deliver key messages to the media and donors
- Understanding of social media engagement, brand management, and an eye for layout and design

DISCUSSION QUESTIONS

Of all the jobs explored in this chapter, this one requires the most global and intercultural experience. What kind of career path do you think the successful applicant will have taken from school to this position? How is the commitment and lifestyle different from the other jobs described in this chapter?

---

more curious and mindfully aware of their environment, government, and community and have an understanding of how these link with one another.

This all makes sense, given the importance of relationship-building, culture, persuasion, management, law, ethics, societal trends, and research to public relations practice.

If you're reading this book independently—or taking advantage of any other professional development resources for that matter—that's a really good sign for your future. Adaptability is a survival strategy for twenty-first-century learners, according to *Future Shock* author Alvin Toffler.[4] We all must be ready to learn, unlearn, and relearn, and that's what will serve

> *Adaptability is a survival strategy for twenty-first-century learning—be ready to learn, unlearn, and relearn.*

us well as the field continues to change. As Ketchum president and CEO Rob Flaherty put it in a keynote presentation to a 2015 industry–educator summit, "Half of everything needed now didn't exist ten years ago."[5]

In thinking about your education, it may be useful to identify core competencies and then to identify the other "half" of what you need to continually adapt to and learn—the half that "didn't exist 10 years ago" and that may change drastically in the next 10 years. New graduates should consider writing the Public Relations Knowledge (PRK) exam, which was designed by to test the overall grasp of concepts and procedures most commonly used in the day-to-day life of junior PR and communication professionals.

After five years of experience, you're eligible to pursue the Accredited in Public Relations (APR)® designation. The accreditation process is designed to test your proficiency in all areas of public relations and communications through rigorous evaluation of the skills and abilities needed to practise at a senior level. While evaluating experience and strategic thinking are the primary focus, it is also important to have a foundation of knowledge of public relations theory and policy issues, plus an understanding of the ethical practice of public relations and comprehension of the standards outlined in the CPRS Code of Professional Standards.

In 2012, public relations blogger and consultant Arik Hanson went out on a limb to suggest "10 Skills the PR Pro of 2022 Must Have."[6] In 2016, he took to his blog to revise the list. No doubt he'll revise his thinking again a few more times before 2022 arrives.[7] Learn, unlearn, relearn. Credit Hanson for his adaptability. What follows is a condensed list (from 10 items down to 5) of what Hanson identifies as key skills for the future. Most of the core competencies are not new, but the contexts for practising them have changed.

1. *Ability to write for both internal and external publics.* You must be able to write clearly for internal communication with employees, volunteers, and so on as well as for owned, paid, shared, and earned media that reach external publics (Chapters 7 and 9). According to Hanson, "PR folks are asked to manage social ad campaigns all the time," and this requires knowledge of paid media services for platforms like Twitter, LinkedIn, Facebook, and Instagram.

2. *Multimedia production skills.* Online video may be the first format that comes to mind, but audio shouldn't be overlooked, either as content in its own right or as part of a multimedia mix (Chapter 10). An eye for the visual appeal of still photography and logo design also is important. Hanson notes that many firms and brands have creative departments specifically tasked with developing a compelling and consistent visual style, but that practitioners with a good feel for positioning brands visually are in demand to "fill in the gaps," especially in organizations that aren't big enough to employ entire departments for this function.

3. *Ability to manage social media content.* Managing social media content systems means knowing how to tag, organize, and sometimes repurpose content for different contexts and platforms. Content should be both "searchable and findable." Managing social media also requires a thorough understanding of analytics (Chapter 8). Facebook Insights and Google Analytics are examples of easily accessible sources of large amounts of customizable data, and people who can take that data and translate it into actionable ideas are in high demand.

4. *Analyzing and presenting data that make sense to management and clients.* Digital and social media can be treasure troves of data on publics and how they engage organizations, but making sense of that data in a way that informs strategy is critical (Chapter 6). Public relations practitioners who can report data with "context, actionable intelligence and clearly articulated next steps" will shine in modern organizations. Hanson acknowledges that analysis and reporting always have been essential in public relations, but the availability of such large amounts of data elevates the importance of being able to convert raw data into useful knowledge.

5. *Collaborating online.* Be prepared to work with geographically dispersed teams within your organization to complete projects and tasks (Chapter 13). If you've ever worked on a challenging group project for an online class, you know that managing workflow, deadlines, communication tools, and cultural expectations can be frustrating. Take heart that much of what you learned from the process will be helpful to you when you work with dispersed teams in your career ahead. Digital collaboration also will be key to your communication with external publics, particularly in building online communities and collaborating with influential individuals across social media platforms. Hanson calls it "influencer outreach" and notes that building and maintaining these relationships with external publics requires an ability to identify the right people and a sensitivity to the culture of online communities and their leaders—"knowing how to approach them—without offending them."

Career Tracks and Roles

Typically, PR practitioners begin their careers in a role with a tactical focus on writing and producing before moving into more strategic aspects of research and analysis and, finally, relationship management. Long before the rise of social media, research suggested that public relations practitioners could be broadly described as fulfilling either a technician role or a management role.[8] Public relations technicians of the twentieth century primarily focused on producing and disseminating communication tactics such as brochures, news releases, speeches, and photographs. While these tactics have evolved into more digital formats, the idea endures that technicians focus more on production and dissemination, and managers organize strategy and make decisions. Those in management roles are held more accountable for program outcomes.

As you move through a career in public relations, you'll be involved with both roles, but as an intern or entry-level employee you will most likely start as a technician. Your title will not be technician, but your main responsibilities will likely be assigned based on strategy and decisions made by others. While some highly talented practitioners will make a career out of their expertise in the technical side of public relations (e.g., web design, app development, writing, multimedia, analytics), most eventually move into jobs that involve a greater degree of management.

The line between technicians and managers is a blurry one. When San Diego State University professor and public relations management expert David Dozier developed the concept, he was careful to explain that the terms do not describe completely separate categories but, rather, *predominant* roles. Some people predominantly perform technical functions and others predominantly practise management functions.

technician role Concept describing those in public relations who primarily implement decisions of others in an organization including writing, production, and dissemination of communication tactics.

management role Concept describing those in public relations who primarily develop strategy, participate in organizational decision-making, and are held accountable for program outcomes.

CEO versus New Hire: Who Wins?

After completing a degree in English literature from California State University–Long Beach, Talia Jane headed north to the San Francisco Bay area to pursue a career in media. Jane's job seemed promising at first. Even though her prior experience was primarily tutoring and freelancing as a writer, Jane landed an interview with Yelp/Eat24 and was hired on the same day that she interviewed.[9] (Eat24 is a food delivery app purchased by Yelp.)

Although her goal was to work in a media job at Yelp and "be able to make memes and twitter jokes about food," Jane took the entry-level job in customer service to get started. But the pay was low. So low, she wrote in a letter to Yelp CEO Jeremy Stoppelman, that she could afford to eat only free food at work and from a 10-pound bag of rice at home. Her salary, which she calculated to be $8.15 per hour after taxes, was not enough to make ends meet: "Because 80 percent of my income goes to paying my rent. Isn't that ironic? Your employee for your food delivery app that you spent $300 million to buy can't afford to buy food."[10]

Within a few hours of posting her letter on Medium, Jane was fired. Stoppelman later tweeted that Jane's firing was not related to the Medium post, but Jane said in a BuzzFeed News interview that her manager and HR representative had told her that her post violated the company's code of conduct.[11]

Meanwhile, Jane's case caught lots of attention on social media. Thousands of people took her side by commenting on her Medium post, supporting her on Twitter, or donating to PayPal and Square Cash accounts that she posted at the end of her

Yelp entry-level employee Talia Jane went public on Medium to get her CEO's attention about her low pay. It worked. And she was fired.

Do you admire what she did? Why or why not?

letter. One supporter set up a GoFundMe account, "Help A YELP/EAT24 Employee EAT/LIVE," and raised $2,755 in 28 days from 80 donors.[12]

Others were not as sympathetic. Internet users found Jane's Instagram and Tumblr accounts and commented wryly on her ability to make (and post pictures of) prosciutto brie garlic biscuits and margarita–, mint-julep–, and piña-colada–flavoured cupcakes. The pictures she posted of a bottle of Bulleit Bourbon that had been delivered to her didn't help her case in the court of public opinion either.

In a blog on the website Ranker titled "Pictures From Talia's Instagram That Aren't Rice," Ranker user Ariel Kana re-posted 26 of Jane's photos. "It was a simple dream, really: To work in media, live in her own apartment, and be able to afford to eat a variety of foods," wrote Kana in the sarcastic post. But "armed only with a degree in English literature, a supportive father, and a coveted job in San Francisco at one of the internet's most visited websites, that dream could never become a reality."[13]

Jane defended her position, claiming that her posts on Instagram were designed to make it seem like she was thriving when the reality was otherwise, so people wouldn't worry about her.[14] In weighing the case, tech industry career consultant Gayle Laakmann McDowell wrote for Forbes.com that Jane's post was "Maybe unwise for her future career, but somewhat admirable that she was willing to do it anyway."[15]

In the early 1990s, the PRSA (Public Relations Society of America) Foundation published a career guide that outlined five levels of professional growth: technician, supervisor, manager, director, and executive (Figure 14.1).[16] While this study was undertaken in the United States, it holds true for the industry in Canada as well. In the past quarter-century, the media environment has changed drastically, and the lines between manager and technician roles have continued to blur, but the general order of responsibilities still applies remarkably well.

Technicians still focus on writing, editing, and producing. Supervisors build on those craft skills as they become more involved in planning, budgeting for, and scheduling their own efforts as well as the work of technicians. Managers take on more planning and organizing responsibilities as they move into leadership positions that require them to evaluate outcomes, solve problems, and consult others on decisions that affect the organization and its publics. Directors are in charge of larger staffs and entire organizational management functions defined by the organization's main constituencies (e.g., VP of internal communications, director of public affairs, and VP of university relations). Top executives in public relations agencies may hold the title of CEO or president. Top corporate and non-profit public relations positions may be called executive vice-president or senior vice-president or executive director. These executives are responsible for the overall mission and vision of an organization and accountable for the organization meeting its annual goals.

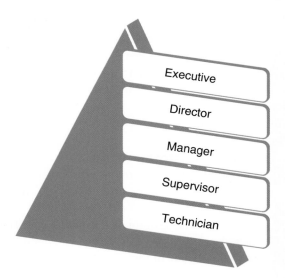

FIGURE 14.1 Five levels of professional growth, as outlined in a 1993 PRSA career guide.

How have social media changed the way technicians do their jobs? Have social media changed the way executives do their jobs?

Voices from the Field

Lesley Chang

Lesley Chang is the communications manager at Tourism Richmond, where she delights in showing off her hometown to media from Canada and around the world.

After completing a certificate in computer information systems, Chang re-thought her career aspirations, and decided to study public relations at Kwantlen Polytechnic University, a decision she describes as "the best decision ever." While still at school, she started freelancing in media relations, which helped her build relationships with the media and hone her skills in pitching story ideas.

An active CPRS member and past board member, she recently participated in the mentorship program. When she isn't busy scouting out new restaurants and attractions in Richmond, Chang runs a public relations, communications, and marketing job board on Twitter, @BestJobsInVan.

What was your first job in public relations?
My first full-time public relations job was actually in integrated marketing communications at a travel agency. Throwing marketing into the mix was a brand-new challenge; it was very visual and brand oriented. I gained experience in internal comm, brand copywriting, and advertising.

What came after that?
I landed a job with a public relations agency, National. There, I learned a lot about PR and corporate communications.

Agency is great for new practitioners. The big agencies all operate very differently. You need to do your research and look at the client list and see if it's a good fit for you. I also worked at another agency which was more events-focused. Working on large-scale projects such as the Squamish Valley Music Festival and the Vancouver International Auto Show gave me a real appreciation for event management.

What do you do now, at Tourism Richmond?
The majority of my time is spent on media relations—working with travel writers, freelancers, and social media influencers. Building relationships is about 80 per cent of my job.

I get to meet media from the around the world, which can be very exciting. And, depending on their assignment, I get to take them places. For one assignment I went birdwatching, which was new for me. If they're into food, they've certainly come to the right city! We have a fisherman's wharf where you can buy fish right off the boat. One time I was with a journalist and we walked up to an uni (sea urchin) boat and bought some uni. We then walked over to a store, opened it up right there and ate it. We loved it!

I was really lucky to land this role. I get to put the city I grew up in on the world stage.

What's a typical day like for you?
Of course, there is no typical day, but I do spend a lot of time on email fielding media requests. Some days I conduct fam (familiarization) tours for media, either one-on-one or in groups. I also spend a great deal of time working with local stakeholders, story mining. I speak Mandarin, which helps me talk to local restaurants and business owners.

What's the most exciting part of your job?
It's pretty exciting when you get to see your work in print. I recently worked with *The New York Times* on a feature article—that was a huge highlight of my career. But what I really enjoy is getting out there, seeing what's new, what's opening. That's what gets me going. The media want to cover something new and original, they don't want you pushing a message. (You can read *The New York Times* article at www.nytimes .com/2018/06/04/travel/richmond-bc-asian-chinese-food-restaurants.html.)

You run a job board for public relations and marketing positions. How do you see entry-level public relations positions changing?
There's still a demand for the basics—writing, communication skills, and hard work. But we're starting to see more social media and digital marketing jobs. It's also really important that you understand the metrics.

What's the biggest misperception of public relations jobs you've come across from people outside of public relations?
A lot of people don't really understand what PR is, until someone points it out, or if you're in a crisis. Some people boil it down to how your organization relates to the public, but it's so much more than that. It's finding the right people to tell the right story to the right audience. Once you get those three things down, you'll see some magic happen.

Ethics: Competition, Loyalty, and Job Changes

As you climb the public relations pyramid from entry level into management, you'll switch jobs and employers. A lot. Most people entering the workforce don't expect to stay in any one job for much longer than three years. Mid-career employees also recognize that switching jobs is often the key to raising earnings and moving up in management. An average annual raise within a company is about 3 per cent,[17] while employees switching jobs expect a 10–20 per cent increase in salary.[18]

There was a time when changing jobs every two or three years was seen as suspicious, indicating a flighty work ethic, difficulty getting along with colleagues, or a lack of loyalty. "That stigma is fast becoming antiquated," according to *Fast Company's* Vivian Giang, "especially as millennials rise in the workplace with expectations to continuously learn, develop, and advance in their careers."[19] Some have even argued that frequent job hoppers are *more* loyal because they are willing to work harder for their current colleagues to make a stronger positive impression during the relatively short time that they work with an organization.[20]

All that job hopping, however, creates ethical challenges. While it is healthy and competitive to shift your loyalty to your new organization when you get a new job, what does that mean for your loyalty to your prior employer and co-workers?

The CPRS Code of Professional Standards makes several references to the concepts of loyalty, competition, and respecting client confidentiality. Ethical dilemmas may arise when loyalty to colleagues from prior jobs conflicts with responsibility for fair competition in a new job.

As a legal matter, many employees sign employment contracts that include **non-compete clauses** that prohibit them from working for competitors or sharing competitive information such as trade secrets. However, with so much personnel movement between and among agencies and clients, ethical dilemmas are hard to avoid, even when the legal issues are clear.

For example, suppose you work for an agency and then leave that agency to work for one of the agency's clients. That's a common job change that normally would not raise many ethical issues. But what if a year later your organization—the client—decides to consider bids from other agencies? Do you help your former agency colleagues by giving them a heads-up

non-compete clause Part of an employment contract that restricts employees from working for competitors or sharing competitive information such as trade secrets even after they no longer work for the organization.

de-focus/Shutterstock.com

Non-competition or non-compete agreements define expectations in legal terms for employees who change jobs.

Beyond legal obligations, what kinds of ethical dilemmas might you face as you change from one employer to another in public relations?

on what they should do to keep the account? If so, do you give that same information to other agencies bidding for the work? Which course of action represents dealing fairly with past or present employers, as the CPRS Code of Professional Standards suggests?

Competition is also an important principle to honour in recruiting talent for an organization. It may be tempting to hire employees away from other organizations as a way to gain a competitive advantage, but that could be seen as violating the CPRS Code of Professional Standards, which states that "a member shall deal fairly with past or present employers/clients, fellow practitioners and members of other professions."

Earlier in your career your ethical dilemmas may revolve mostly around your own role and personal and professional values as they relate to those with whom you work and compete most closely. As you move into management and become more responsible for others in your organization, your ethical responsibility expands. When you begin to approach executive levels, you must grow the scope of your ethical attention along with your career responsibilities. This ethical growth includes careful consideration about how your decisions drive your entire organization and affect your publics. Done right, ethical public relations management benefits individuals, groups, organizations, and even entire societies. Done right, ethical public relations elevates the practice to a profession.

Ongoing Professional Development

Graduating with a diploma or a degree in public relations is only the first step. Once you're working in public relations, you'll need to make a concerted effort to stay up to date. Professional associations such as CPRS and IABC (International Association of Business Communicators) are designed to allow professionals to meet other professionals (networking) and provide ongoing professional development at a reasonable cost. You may also want to consider additional public relations education at the degree or master's level. Depending on where your career takes you, you might also consider courses in other disciplines such as business, web development, or marketing.

When it comes to a career in public relations, you never know what kind of knowledge is going to come in handy. Your next client might be a restaurant chain or a company that makes semiconductors—the more you know, the better you'll be able to relate to your clients and develop practical, workable strategies.

In Case You Missed It

No two career trajectories will be the same in public relations, but that doesn't mean you can't prepare for the journey. Here are some general tips to consider as you weigh your career options.

- If you start at an agency, be prepared to move through multiple positions in your first few years.
- Public relations jobs in non-profits are just as demanding and require just as much accountability as corporate jobs.
- If you work for a small business, you'll need to be much more of a generalist.
- It takes more than enthusiasm to keep up with the 24/7 ups and downs of public relations jobs in sports and entertainment.
- Your broader education is just as important as your public-relations–specific courses.
- Adaptability is a survival strategy for twenty-first-century learning—be ready to learn, unlearn, and relearn.

Summary

14.1 Identify different types of employers for public relations jobs.

All types of organizations can benefit from some form of public relations. Most public relations positions are with agencies, large businesses and corporations, non-profits, NGOs, and military and government agencies. Some individuals work in public relations while also performing other core functions in small businesses, start-ups, or self-owned operations.

14.2 Assess how different areas of specialization in public relations match your interests, and consider the knowledge and skills that jobs in those areas require.

Major specialty areas of public relations are health, sports and entertainment, political and public affairs, financial and entrepreneurial, consumer, and international. This list is not exhaustive, and within each category are countless types of public relations jobs. Many of the jobs require some of the same skills.

14.3 Plan for your own continuing education in public relations including core competencies and evolving skills for a changing media environment.

Public relations degree programs offer a series of specific public relations courses designed to prepare students for entry into the field. However, given the importance of relationship-building, culture, persuasion, management, law, ethics, societal trends, and research, a foundation in liberal arts, social sciences, business, and language is also important to help you understand your role in society. Willingness to continually learn beyond school is also critical as media and society change rapidly.

14.4 Map a public relations career trajectory from entry level to executive.

Although specific job titles and tools may vary and change, the following five levels of professional growth still represent a general career progression in public relations: (1) technician, (2) supervisor, (3) manager, (4) director, and (5) executive. Technicians primarily implement decisions of others, including writing and production of communication tactics. Managers become more responsible for developing strategy and participating in organizational decision-making, and they are held more accountable for program outcomes.

14.5 Discuss ethical dilemmas related to the professional values of competition and loyalty.
The CPRS Code of Professional Standards makes several references to the concepts of loyalty, competition, and respecting client confidentiality. Ethical dilemmas may arise when loyalty to colleagues from prior jobs conflicts with responsibility for fair competition in a new job. For example, when working for a company that is accepting bids from agencies, you have to be careful not to give any unfair advantage to an agency for which you used to work. The goal is to promote fair competition and respect among professionals.

Discussion Questions

1. Pick three organizations you would like to work for, and research their job openings. Do any of them list public relations or related jobs? If so, pick the one job that appeals to you most. (If you can't find a public-relations–related job opening, keep searching organizations that you like until you find one.) What are the primary duties of the position?

2. Which area of specialization (health, sports, entertainment, political, financial, etc.) appeals most to you, and why? How would a public relations job in that field be similar to and different from other areas of specialization?

3. Find a specific job ad describing a position in public relations that you would like to have three to five years from now. Carefully review the qualifications. Which qualifications do you meet now? Which ones don't you meet? What, specifically, can you do in the next three to five years to make yourself competitive for that type of job?

4. Carefully observe an organization's social media accounts. In what ways are the people running those accounts serving a technician role? In what ways are they serving a management role?

5. Describe a time that you've been in a position (in games or school or work) where you were responsible for ensuring fair competition despite your loyalty to one of the competitors. Did competition trump loyalty? Why (or why not)? Would you use the same moral reasoning in a professional career in public relations?

Further Readings and Online Resources

Career Advice for Communications Students
marketingmag.ca/advertising/passport-to-pr-career-advice-for-communications-students-140597/
This article, published in *Marketing*, provides a round-up of advice from Toronto public relations practitioners. Hint: there's lots of talk about networking.

What It Is Really Like to Work in PR
gentwenty.com/what-it-is-really-like-to-work-in-pr/
This blogpost features an interview with a young professional who gives you the straight goods on a career in public relations.

5 Major Differences between Agency and In-House PR
www.prdaily.com/5-major-differences-between-agency-and-in-house-pr/
This blogpost on "Ragan's PR Daily" explores the differences between agency and in-house or corporate public relations jobs.

Peer-Reviewed Academic Journal Article

Taylor, R.E. (2016). I like to plan events: A document analysis of essays written by applicants to a public relations program. *Journalism & Mass Communication Educator, 71*(1), 84–94. doi:10.1177/1077695815584060

Why did you decide to study public relations? This article explores some of the reasons students choose public relations education.

Key Terms

Grassroots campaign 352	Management role 361	Technician role 361
Grasstops campaign 352	Non-compete clause 365	

CPRS Checklist for APR Designation

The Accreditation in Public Relations (APR) designation is used by both the American and Canadian Public Relations Societies to differentiate members who have successfully completed the APR process and exam. Seeing APR after someone's name signifies a level of professional competence, expertise, and personal and professional dedication and values.

In Canada, the APR process can be undertaken only by members with at least five years of experience. CPRS has provided the following self-assessment checklist to determine if members are ready to begin the APR process:

	I must have a minimum of five years public relations practical work (and/or teaching) experience where I have been exposed to a broad range of communications activities.
	I must have the ability to communicate well both orally and in writing in one of Canada's two official languages.
	I must be able to write clearly and concisely in plain language and demonstrate that I am competent in grammar, spelling and punctuation.
	I must have a solid theoretical working knowledge of communications principles; including but not limited to: the RACE formula, communications planning, linking goals and objectives to outcomes, media relations, crisis communications, stakeholder identification.
	I must have taken on progressively more responsible roles on behalf of my employer and/or clients; have had experience in planning, guiding and directing projects, activities and/or people toward the fulfillment of strategic objectives; and in developing the strategies themselves.
	I am comfortable in a setting when tasked to draw on my experience and best practices to evaluate challenging situations, and where I am called upon to provide my counsel and insights on matters of a strategic nature as they relate to the organization(s) I work with or for.
	I have been able to hone my skills as a public relations generalist through my work and volunteer experience.
	I have experience dealing with a broad range of issues, publics and situations.
	If I am an educator, I have taken on a leadership role to develop and/or to improve program/course curriculum, delivery and assessment.
	I have reviewed the suggested reading list on the CPRS Accreditation web site. I am familiar with the Accreditation Handbook.

	I am confident in my knowledge and understanding of public relations theories.
	I can cite examples from my work or volunteer activities of how I might apply a theoretical challenge.
	I have earned a reputation as a "go to" practitioner among my peers, and my view or guidance is often sought by others due to my ability to think strategically, act calmly in crisis situations, or come up with practical solutions to problems.
	I follow local, regional, national and international current events.
	I am able to think on my feet to formulate plausible, rational and insightful responses to ethics questions.
	I would welcome mentoring (formally or informally) by an accredited public relations practitioner who would willingly share his/her senior public relations experience and knowledge.
	If I am an educator, I encourage students to volunteer in the community and in the public relations profession. I lead them by example, being active in the community and in the profession as a volunteer.
	I believe attaining my APR is as important to me personally as it could be professionally; recognizing that it may not have a direct impact on my career development or financial remuneration.
	I am committed to participating in lifelong learning and involvement in the discipline, industry or profession, as it is very important to maintain the APR designation once I attain it.

Source: Republished with permission of the Canadian Public Relations Society

B CPRS Code of Professional Standards

Members of the Canadian Public Relations Society are pledged to maintain the spirit and ideals of the following stated principles of conduct, and to consider these essential to the practice of public relations.

Code of Professional Standards

1. **A member shall practice public relations according to the highest professional standards.**
   - Members shall conduct their professional lives in a manner that does not conflict with the public interest and the dignity of the individual, with respect for the rights of the public as contained in the Constitution of Canada and the Charter of Rights and Freedoms.

2. **A member shall deal fairly and honestly with the communications media and the public.**
   - Members shall neither propose nor act to improperly influence the communications media, government bodies or the legislative process. Improper influence may include conferring gifts, privileges or benefits to influence decisions.

3. **A member shall practice the highest standards of honesty, accuracy, integrity and truth, and shall not knowingly disseminate false or misleading information.**
   - Members shall not make extravagant claims or unfair comparisons, nor assume credit for ideas and words not their own.
   - Members shall not engage in professional or personal conduct that will bring discredit to themselves, the Society or the practice of public relations.

4. **A member shall deal fairly with past or present employers / clients, fellow practitioners and members of other professions.**
   - Members shall not intentionally damage another practitioner's practice or professional reputation. Members shall understand, respect, and abide by the ethical codes of other professions with whose members they may work from time to time.

5. **Members shall be prepared to disclose the names of their employers or clients for whom public communications are made and refrain from associating themselves with anyone who would not respect such policy.**
   - Members shall be prepared to disclose publicly the names of their employers or clients on whose behalf public communications are made. Members shall not associate themselves with anyone claiming to represent one interest, or professing to be independent or unbiased, but who actually serves another or an undisclosed interest.

6. **A member shall protect the confidences of present, former, and prospective employers/ clients.**
    - Members shall not use or disclose confidential information obtained from past or present employers/clients without the expressed permission of the employers/clients or an order of a court of law.

7. **A member shall not represent conflicting or competing interests without the expressed consent of those concerned, given after a full disclosure of the facts.**
    - Members shall not permit personal or other professional interests to conflict with those of an employer/client without fully disclosing such interests to everyone involved.

8. **A member shall not guarantee specified results beyond the member's capacity to achieve.**

9. **Members shall personally accept no fees, commissions, gifts or any other considerations for professional services from anyone except employers or clients for whom the services were specifically performed.**

Source: Republished with permission of the Canadian Public Relations Society

C The IPRA Code of Conduct

The IPRA Code of Conduct is an affirmation of professional and ethical conduct by members of the International Public Relations Association and recommended to public relations practitioners worldwide.

The Code consolidates the 1961 Code of Venice, the 1965 Code of Athens, and the 2007 Code of Brussels.

1. **RECALLING** *the Charter of the United Nations which determines "to reaffirm faith in fundamental human rights, and in the dignity and worth of the human person"*;
2. **RECALLING** *the 1948 "Universal Declaration of Human Rights" and especially recalling Article 19*;
3. **RECALLING** *that public relations, by fostering the free flow of information, contributes to the interests of all stakeholders*;
4. **RECALLING** *that the conduct of public relations and public affairs provides essential democratic representation to public authorities*;
5. **RECALLING** *that public relations practitioners through their wide-reaching communication skills possess a means of influence that should be restrained by the observance of a code of professional and ethical conduct*;
6. **RECALLING** *that channels of communication, such as the Internet and other digital media, are channels where erroneous or misleading information may be widely disseminated and remain unchallenged, and therefore demand special attention from public relations practitioners to maintain trust and credibility*;
7. **RECALLING** *that the Internet and other digital media demand special care with respect to the personal privacy of individuals, clients, employers, and colleagues*;

In the conduct of public relations practitioners shall:

1. **Observance**
   Observe the principles of the UN Charter and the Universal Declaration of Human Rights;
2. **Integrity**
   Act with honesty and integrity at all times so as to secure and retain the confidence of those with whom the practitioner comes into contact;
3. **Dialogue**
   Seek to establish the moral, cultural, and intellectual conditions for dialogue, and recognise the rights of all parties involved to state their case and express their views;

4. **Transparency**

   Be open and transparent in declaring their name, organisation, and the interest they represent;

5. **Conflict**

   Avoid any professional conflicts of interest and disclose such conflicts to affected parties when they occur;

6. **Confidentiality**

   Honour confidential information provided to them;

7. **Accuracy**

   Take all reasonable steps to ensure the truth and accuracy of all information provided;

8. **Falsehood**

   Make every effort to not intentionally disseminate false or misleading information, exercise proper care to avoid doing so unintentionally, and correct any such act promptly;

9. **Deception**

   Not obtain information by deceptive or dishonest means;

10. **Disclosure**

    Not create or use any organisation to serve an announced cause but which actually serves an undisclosed interest;

11. **Profit**

    Not sell for profit to third parties copies of documents obtained from public authorities;

12. **Remuneration**

    Whilst providing professional services, not accept any form of payment in connection with those services from anyone other than the principal;

13. **Inducement**

    Neither directly nor indirectly offer nor give any financial or other inducement to public representatives or the media, or other stakeholders;

14. **Influence**

    Neither propose nor undertake any action which would constitute an improper influence on public representatives, the media, or other stakeholders;

15. **Competitors**

    Not intentionally injure the professional reputation of another practitioner;

16. **Poaching**

    Not seek to secure another practitioner's client by deceptive means;

17. **Employment**

    When employing personnel from public authorities or competitors take care to follow the rules and confidentiality requirements of those organisations;

18. **Colleagues**

    Observe this Code with respect to fellow IPRA members and public relations practitioners worldwide.

IPRA members shall, in upholding this Code, agree to abide by and help enforce the disciplinary procedures of the International Public Relations Association in regard to any breach of this Code.

Source: By kind permission of the International Public Relations Association. www.ipra.org. IPRA—leading trust and ethics in global communication.

D IPR Ethical Standards and Guidelines for Public Relations Research and Measurement

Preface

This statement of ethical standards and guidelines for public relations research was developed by a team of the Institute for Public Relations Measurement Commission headed by Shannon Bowen, PhD; John Gilfeather; and Brad Rawlins, PhD, and approved by the IPR Measurement Commission.

Ethics Statement

The duty of professionals engaged in research, measurement, and evaluation for public relations is to advance the highest ethical standards and ideals for research. All research should abide by the principles of intellectual honesty, fairness, dignity, disclosure, and respect for all stakeholders involved, namely clients (both external and internal), colleagues, research participants, the public relations profession, and the researchers themselves.

This statement is based on and promotes the following Core Values:

- Autonomy
- Respondent rights
- Dignity
- Fairness
- Balance
- Duty
- Lack of bias
- Honesty
- Not using misleading information or "cherry picking" data
- Full disclosure
- Discretion
- Judgment
- Protection of proprietary data
- Public responsibility
- Intellectual integrity
- Good intention
- Valuing the truth behind the numbers
- Reflexivity (put self in other's place)
- Moral courage and objectivity

Source: Republished with permission of the Institute for Public Relations

Notes

Chapter 1

1. James E. Grunig and Todd Hunt, *Managing Public Relations* (New York: Holt, Rinehart, and Winston, 1984), 6.

2. Glen M. Broom and Bey-Ling Sha, *Cutlip and Center's Effective Public Relations*, 11th ed. (Upper Saddle River, NJ: Prentice Hall, 2013), 5.

3. http://www.latimes.com/entertainment/tv/showtracker/la-et-st-kerry-washington-olivia-pope-scandal-role-model-20150805-story.html.

4. "Government of Canada Professional Occupations in Public Relations and Communications," accessed January 30, 2019, http://noc.esdc.gc.ca/English/noc/ProfileQuickSearch.aspx?val=5&val1=5124&ver=06.

5. Robert L. Heath, "Issues Management: Its Past, Present and Future," *Journal of Public Affairs* 2, no. 4 (2002): 209–14.

6. https://www.mec.ca/en/article/outside-is-for-everyone.

7. W. Timothy Coombs, *Ongoing Crisis Communication: Planning, Managing, and Responding*, 4th ed. (Thousand Oaks, CA: SAGE, 2015).

8. https://www.ualberta.ca/community-relations.

9. https://www.cbc.ca/news/indigenous/trans-mountain-consultation-extension-judy-wilson-1.5103341.

10. "CPRS Public Relations Definition," Canadian Public Relations Society, accessed December 12, 2018, https://www.cprs.ca/About.aspx.

11. "Crowdsource," *Oxford Dictionaries*, accessed July 12, 2014, http://oxforddictionaries.com/us/definition/american_english/crowdsource?q=crowdsourcing.

12. "Snapshot: #PRDefined Word Cloud-Day 12," Public Relations Defined, accessed July 12, 2014, http://prdefinition.prsa.org/index.php/2011/12/02/snapshot-of-the-public-relations-defined-initaitve-submission-day12/.

13. "About Greenwashing," Greenwashing Index, accessed July 12, 2014, http://www.greenwashingindex.com/.

14. Greenwashing Index, accessed July 12, 2014, http://www.greenwashingindex.com/about-greenwashing/#score.

15. Pamela J. Brubaker, "Arthur W. Page: A Man of Vision, Valor, and Values," in *Words from a Page in History* (University Park, PA: Arthur W. Page Center for Integrity in Public Communication, 2011), 5–9.

16. Brad Rawlins, "Give the Emperor a Mirror: Toward Developing a Stakeholder Measurement of Organizational Transparency," *Journal of Public Relations Research* 21, no. 1 (2008): 71–99, 75.

17. John Vernon Pavlik and Shawn McIntosh, *Converging Media: A New Introduction to Mass Communication* (New York: Oxford University Press, 2011), 365.

18. Anne Landman, "BP's 'Beyond Petroleum' Campaign Losing Its Sheen," The Center for Media and Democracy's PR Watch, May 3, 2010, accessed July 12, 2014, http://www.prwatch.org/node/9038.

19. Elizabeth Shogren, "BP: A Textbook Example of How Not to Handle PR," NPR.org, April 21, 2011, http://www.npr.org/2011/04/21/135575238/bp-a-textbook-example-of-how-not-to-handle-pr.

20. Robert Kendall, *Public Relations Campaign Strategies*, 2nd ed. (New York: HarperCollins, 1996), 527.

21. "PWC—Explore the Survey Themes, Total Retail Report," accessed July 12, 2018, https://www.pwc.com/ca/en/industries/retail-consumer/publications/total-retail-report/total-retail-survey-themes.html#engage.

22. Tom Kelleher, "Conversational Voice, Communicated Commitment, and Public Relations Outcomes in Interactive Online Communication," *Journal of Communication* 59, no. 1 (2009): 172–88.

23. Robert Strohmeyer, "How to Deal with Yelp Disasters," *PC World*, May 31, 2011.

24. Rosa Marchitelli, "Negative Online Reviews Led to Threats of Legal Action from Targeted Businesses," posted October 20, 2014, http://www.cbc.ca/news/canada/british-columbia/negative-online-reviews-led-to-threats-of-legal-action-from-targeted-businesses-1.2803572.

25. Arthur W. Page, "Speech Presented at the Bell Telephone System's General Manager Conference—May 1931," The Arthur W. Page Center at Penn State, accessed July 13, 2014, http://thepagecenter.comm.psu.edu/index.php?option=com_content&view=article&id=413:speech14&catid=36.

26. Harold Burson, "Is Public Relations Now Too Important to Be Left to Public Relations Professionals?," lecture delivered to the Institute for Public Relations, London, October 20, 2004.

27. "Ethics and Public Relations," Institute for Public Relations, accessed July 13, 2014, http://www.instituteforpr.org/topics/ethics-and-public-relations/.

28. Philip M. Seib and Kathy Fitzpatrick, *Public Relations Ethics* (Fort Worth, TX: Harcourt Brace College Publishers, 1995).

29. "About Todd Defren," PR Squared, accessed July 13, 2014, http://www.pr-squared.com/index.php/about.

30. Todd Defren, "Tweeting under False Circumstances: Social Media Ethical Dilemmas," PR Squared, accessed July 13, 2014, http://www.pr-squared.com/index.php/2010/01/tweeting-under-false-circumstances-social-media-ethical-dilemmas.

31. Defren, "Tweeting under False Circumstances."

Chapter 2

1. James E. Grunig and Todd Hunt, *Managing Public Relations* (New York: Holt, Rinehart and Winston, 1984), 4.

2. Ibid., 21.

3. Benjamin Reiss, "PT Barnum, Joice Heth and Antebellum Spectacles of Race," *American Quarterly* 51 (1999): 78–107.

4. Phineas Taylor Barnum, *Life of PT Barnum* (Buffalo, NY: The Courier Company Printers, 1886), 38.

5. http://brandchannel.com/2015/12/16/kfc-hong-kong-tvb-awards-121615/.

6. http://www.thewrap.com/ellen-degeneres-oscars-pizza-party-sparks-sales-surge-pizzeria/.

7. Scott M. Cutlip, *The Unseen Power: Public Relations, a History* (Hillsdale, NJ: Lawrence Erlbaum Associates, 1994), 40.

8. Ray Eldon Hiebert, *Courtier to the Crowd: The Story of Ivy Lee and the Development of Public Relations* (Ames: Iowa State University Press, 1966), 45.

9. Cutlip, *The Unseen Power*, 41.

10. Ibid., 44.

11. Hiebert, *Courtier to the Crowd,* 48.

12. http://www.wired.com/wired/archive/15.04/wired40_ceo.html.

13. Cutlip, *The Unseen Power*, 53.

14. https://www.linkedin.com/jobs/view/604011355/.

15. "Public Affairs Officer," Government of Canada, accessed January 30, 2019, https://www.canada.ca/en/department-national-defence/services/caf-jobs/career-options/fields-work/administration-support/public-affairs-officer.html.

16. http://www.prmuseum.com/bernays/bernays_video_bacon.html.

17. Edward Bernays, *Biography of an Idea: Memoirs of Public Relations Counsel Edward L. Bernays* (New York: Simon and Schuster, 1965), 386.

18. Ibid., 387.

19. Ibid., 387.

20. Vanessa Murphree, "Edward Bernays's 1929 'Torches of Freedom' March: Myths and Historical Significance," *American Journalism* 32, no. 3 (2015): 258–81.

21. Grunig and Hunt, *Managing Public Relations,* 39.

22. Cutlip, *The Unseen Power*.

23. Arthur W. Page, "Speech to the Public Relations Conference of Chesapeake & Ohio Railway Company, October 27, 1939," accessed August 2, 2013, http://thepagecenter.comm.psu.edu/index.php/research-resources/page-speeches/402-speech25.

24. James E. Grunig, "Two-Way Symmetrical Public Relations: Past, Present, and Future," in *Handbook of Public Relations*, ed. Robert L. Heath (Thousand Oaks, CA: Sage, 2001), 12.

25. Robert E. Brown, "St. Paul as a Public Relations Practitioner: A Metatheoretical Speculation on Messianic Communication and Symmetry," *Public Relations Review* 29 (2003): 1–12.

26. Margaret Opdycke Lamme and Karen Miller Russell, "Removing the Spin: Toward a New Theory of Public Relations History," *Journalism & Communication Monographs* 11 (2010): 279–361.

27. Brown, "St. Paul as a Public Relations Practitioner," 232.

28. http://njop.org/resources/social-media-for-synagogues/jewish-treats-top-ten-jewish-influencer-awards/.

29. http://www.islamographic.com.

30. Lamme and Russell, "Removing the Spin," 279–361; Scott M. Cutlip, *Public Relations History: From the 17th to the 20th Century: The Antecedents* (Mahwah, NJ: Erlbaum, 1995).

31. Scott M. Cutlip, *Public Relations History: From the 17th to the 20th Century: The Antecedents* (Mahwah, NJ: Erlbaum, 1995).

32. A. Thurlow and A.R. Yue, "A Brief History of Public Relations in Canada," in *Fundamentals of Public Relations and Marketing Communications in Canada*, eds. Leah-Ann Lymer and William W. Carney (Edmonton, Alberta: Pica Pica Press, 2015).

33. Nancy M. Sheehan, "The WCTU and Educational Strategies on the Canadian Prairie," *History of Education Quarterly* 24, no.1 (Spring 1984): 109.

34. http://www.thecanadianencyclopedia.ca/en/article/sir-clifford-sifton/.

35. http://www.jobvite.com/wp-content/uploads/2015/09/jobvite_recruiter_nation_2015.pdf.

36. Tom Kelleher and Kaye Sweetser, "Social Media Adoption among University Communicators," *Journal of Public Relations Research* 24 (2012): 113.

37. Günter Bentele and Ivonne Junghänel, "Germany," in *Public Relations and Communication Management in Europe*, eds. Betteke Van Ruler and Dejan Verčič (Berlin: Mouton de Gruyter, 2004). Cited in Lamme and Russell, 288.

38. Karl Nessman, "Austria," in Van Ruler and Verčič. Cited in Lamme and Russell, 288.

39. Paul F. Lazarsfeld and Robert K. Merton, "Mass Communication, Popular Taste and Organized Social Action," in *The Communication of Ideas*, ed. Lyman Bryson (New York: Harper & Bros, 1948). Reprinted in Paul Marris and Sue Thornham, *Media Studies: A Reader*, 2nd ed. (New York: NYU Press, 2000), 20.

40. http://www.npr.org/blogs/parallels/2013/05/14/183966785/for-palestinians-googles-small-change-is-a-big-deal.

41. Lamme and Russell, "Removing the Spin," 340.

42. Patrick Lee Plaisance, "Transparency: An Assessment of the Kantian Roots of a Key Element in Media Ethics Practice," *Journal of Mass Media Ethics* 22 (2007): 187–207.

43. Grunig and Hunt, *Managing Public Relations,* 34.

44. http://www.oxforddictionaries.com/us/definition/american_english/objective?q=objective.

45. http://www.journalism.org/resources/principles-of-journalism/.

46. "Ethics Guidelines," The Canadian Association of Journalists, accessed January 30, 2019, http://caj.ca/content.php?page=ethics-guidelines.

47. Genevieve McBride, "Ethical Thought in Public Relations History: Seeking a Relevant Perspective," *Journal of Mass Media Ethics* 4, no. 1 (1989): 5–20, p. 15.

48. *Lewiston Evening Journal*, July 12, 1934, p. 5, news.google.com.

Chapter 3

1. Henry Jenkins, *Convergence Culture: Where Old and New Media Collide* (New York: New York University Press, 2006), 14.

2. Ibid.

3. Henry Jenkins, "Convergence? I Diverge," *Technology Review* 104, no. 5 (2001): 93.

4. http://www.theglobalist.com/globalization-and-cultural-convergence/.

5. Henry Jenkins, *Convergence Culture: Where Old and New Media Collide* (New York: New York University Press, 2006), 18.

6. http://www.businessinsider.com/vladimir-putin-nyt-op-ed-ketchum-pr-2013-9.

7. http://www.thefreelibrary.com/Omnicom+Group+acquisition+of+Ketchum+Communications.-a017999670.

8. http://www.omnicomgroup.com/home.

9. http://adage.com/article/special-report-super-bowl/super-bowl-50-ad-chart-buying-big-game-commercials/301183/.

10. http://adage.com/article/special-report-super-bowl/super-bowl-50-ad-chart-buying-big-game-commercials/301183/.

11. E. Jerome McCarthy, *Basic Marketing: A Managerial Approach* (Homewood, IL: Richard D. Irwin Inc., 1960).

12. https://www.youtube.com/watch?v=xPwUSannP8Y.

13. http://www.wommapedia.org/#section1.

14. http://www.youtube.com/watch?v=Fz22PfPxoXI.

15. https://www.ae.com/aerie/stylegallery/.

16. Bob Lauterborn, "New Marketing Litany; Four P's Passe; C-Words Take Over," *Advertising Age*, October 1, 1990, 26.

17. Henry Ford and Samuel Crowther, *My Life and Work* (Sydney: Cornstalk Publishing, 1922), 72.

18. *Portlandia*, "Is It Local?," Season 1, Episode 1, http://www.ifc.com/portlandia/videos/portlandia-is-it-local.

19. http://www.cluetrain.com/book/markets.html.

20. http://contentmarketinginstitute.com/what-is-content-marketing/.

21. http://mashable.com/2012/12/19/red-bull-content-marketing/.

22. http://www.shiftcomm.com/2013/11/2014-will-be-the-year-of-brand-journalism/.

23. http://www.commpro.biz/social-video/views-you-can-use/chrysler-group-vide/.

24. Susan Robertson, "TV Providers Paid to Carry Russia 'Propaganda' Channel: Kremlin's State-Funded RT Is Available in More Than Half of Canadian Homes with Television Packages," *The Globe and Mail*, December 21, 2017.

Chapter 4

1. John A. Ledingham and Stephen D. Bruning (eds.), *Public Relations as Relationship Management: A Relational Approach to the Study and Practice of Public Relations* (New York: Routledge, 2000), xii–xiii.

2. Linda Childers Hon and James E. Grunig, "Guidelines for Measuring Relationships in Public Relations," The Institute for Public Relations, accessed July 21, 2014, http://www.instituteforpr.org/wp-content/uploads/Guidelines_Measuring_Relationships.pdf.

3. https://abacusdata.ca/canadians-are-ready-for-legal-cannabis/.

4. Childers Hon and Grunig, "Guidelines for Measuring Relationships."

5. Elizabeth L. Toth, "From Personal Influence to Interpersonal Influence: A Model for Relationship Management," in *Public Relations as Relationship Management: A Relational Approach to the Study and Practice of Public Relations* (New York: Routledge, 2000), 205–19.

6. "Media," *Oxford Dictionaries*, accessed July 21, 2014, http://www.oxforddictionaries.com/us/definition/american_english/media?q=media#media.

7. Peter Himler, "Media Relations Is Dead. Long Live Media Relations," PRSAY, accessed July 22, 2014, http://prsay.prsa.org/index.php/2014/01/15/media-relations-is-dead-long-live-media-relations/.

8. "Worksheet 1.1: What Is Newsworthy?," PBS News Student Reporting Labs, accessed April 3, 2016, http://www.studentreportinglabs.com/sites/default/files/Worksheet%201.1.pdf.

9. "Rising Medical Solutions Named National Case Management Awards Finalist," *PR Newswire*, accessed July 22, 2014, http://www.prnewswire.com/news-releases/rising-medical-solutions-named-national-case-management-awards-finalist-250216211.html.

10. "C. Anthony Harris Achieves New Heights with ViSalus," *PR Newswire*, accessed July 22, 2014, http://www.prnewswire.com/news-releases/c-anthony-harris-achieves-new-heights-with-visalus-250217571.html.

11. Richard D. Waters, Natalie T.J. Tindall, and Timothy S. Morton, "Media Catching and the Journalist–Public Relations Practitioner Relationship: How Social Media Are Changing the Practice of Media Relations," *Journal of Public Relations Research* 22, no. 3 (2010): 241–64.

12. Jennifer G. Hanford, "5 Fantastic Examples of B2B Social Media Marketing," *Social Media Today*, accessed July 22, 2014, http://socialmediatoday.com/jenniferhanford/2094261/five-fantastic-examples-b2b-social-media-marketing.

13. "Best Companies to Work For 2014," *Fortune*, accessed July 22, 2014, http://money.cnn.com/magazines/fortune/best-companies/2014/methodology/index.html?iid=BC14_sp_method.

14. Nan S. Russell, "Reality Check: Do You Know the Impact of Trust?" *Psychology Today*, accessed July 22, 2014, http://www.psychologytoday.com/blog/trust-the-new-workplace-currency/201210/reality-check-do-you-know-the-impact-trust.

15. Taylor Short, "3 Ways Intel Gets Employees to Trust (and Adhere to) Their BYOD Security Program," accessed July 22, 2014, http://hello-operator.softwareadvice.com

/3-ways-intel-gets-employees-to-trust-their-byod-program-1113/.

16. Linjuan Rita Men, "Engaging Employees: Effectiveness of Traditional vs. New Media Channels," Institute for Public Relations, accessed July 22, 2014, http://www.instituteforpr.org/2013/10/engaging-employees-effectiveness-traditional-vs-new-media-channels/.

17. https://www.payscale.com/research/CA/Job=Investor_Relations_Manager/Salary.

18. "About Us," National Investor Relations Institute, accessed July 22, 2014, http:// www.niri.org/about/mission.cfm.

19. Alexander V. Laskin, "The Value of Investor Relations: A Delphi Panel Investigation," http://www.instituteforpr.org/wp-content/uploads/2007_Laskin.pdf, 21–22.

20. http://www.natureconservancy.ca/en/who-we-are/mission-values/.

21. https://www.heartandstroke.ca/what-we-do/our-impact/our-story.

22. http://www.carp.ca/2008/06/20/carp-mission-statement/.

23. Julie O'Neil, "The Link between Strong Public Relationships and Donor Support," *Public Relations Review* 33, no. 1 (2007): 99.

24. Richard D. Waters, "Measuring Stewardship in Public Relations: A Test Exploring Impact on the Fundraising Relationship," *Public Relations Review* 35, no. 2 (2009): 113–19.

25. Ibid., 116.

26. Kathleen S. Kelly, *Effective Fund-Raising Management* (Mahwah, NJ: Lawrence Erlbaum Associates, 1998), 441.

27. "Issue," *Oxford Dictionaries*, accessed July 22, 2014, http://www.oxforddictionaries.com/us/definition/american_english/issue?q=issue.

28. Larissa Grunig, "Activism: How It Limits the Effectiveness of Organizations and How Excellent Public Relations Departments Respond," in *Excellence in Public Relations and Communication Management*, ed. J. E. Grunig (Hillsdale, NJ: Lawrence Erlbaum, 2009), 504.

29. "Interbrand—Best Global Brands," Interbrand, accessed July 25, 2014, http://www.interbrand.com/it/best-global-brands/2013/Coca-Cola.

30. "Are All Calories Created Equal?," Arthur W. Page Society, accessed July 25, 2014, http://www.awpagesociety.com/wp-content/ uploads/2014/03/Coca-Cola_CaseStudy.pdf.

31. "Coca-Cola's Global Commitments to Help Fight Obesity," The Coca-Cola Company, accessed July 25, 2014, http://www.coca-colacompany.com/coming-together/infographic-illustrating-coca-colas-global-commitments-to-help-fight-obesity.

32. https://www.cbc.ca/news/health/coke-s-obesity-ad-campaign-criticized-1.1336391.

33. http://www.nielsen.com/us/en/press-room/2015/consumer-goods-brands-that-demonstrate-commitment-to-sustainability-outperform .html.

34. "New Study Shows Strong CSR Boosts Profits," *Bulldog Reporter*, accessed July 25, 2014, http://www.bulldogreporter.com/dailydog/article/pr-biz-update/new-study-shows-strong-csr-boosts-profits-majority-of-companies-incre.

35. https://www.cbc.ca/news/politics/senate-obesity-sugar-tax-1.3471469.

36. https://www.cbc.ca/news/politics/senate-obesity-sugar-tax-1.3471469.

Chapter 5

1. John E. Marston, *The Nature of Public Relations* (New York: McGraw-Hill, 1963).

2. Jerry Hendrix, Darrell Hayes, and Pallavi Kumar, *Public Relations Cases* (Boston: Cengage Learning, 2013).

3. Sheila Clough Crifasi, as cited in Fraser P. Seitel, *The Practice of Public Relations*, 12th ed. (Upper Saddle River, NJ: Pearson, 2014).

4. "Silver Anvil Search," Public Relations Society of America, accessed April 4, 2016, http://www.prsa.org/Awards/Silver-Anvil/Search.

5. Laurie J. Wilson and Joseph D. Ogden, *Strategic Communications Planning for Effective Public Relations & Marketing* (Dubuque, IA: Kendall Hunt, 2008).

6. "Silver Anvil Search," Public Relations Society of America, accessed September 21, 2014, http://www.prsa.org/Awards/SilverAnvil/Search.

7. https://www.wawanesa.com/canada/about-us/about-mission .html.

8. Tom Kelleher, "Conversational Voice, Communicated Commit-ment, and Public Relations Outcomes in Interactive Online Communication," *Journal of Communication* 59, no. 1 (2009): 172–88.

9. Kara Swisher, "Here's the Internal Yahoo No-Work-from-Home Memo for Remote Workers and Maybe More," All Things D, accessed September 12, 2014, http://all thingsd.com/20130222/physically-together-heres-the-internal-yahoo-no-work-from-home-memo-which-extends-beyond-remote-workers/.

10. Kurt Lewin, *Field Theory in Social Science* (New York: Harper & Row, 1951), 169.

11. "Net Neutrality: What You Need to Know Now," Free Press, accessed September 12, 2014, http://www.savetheinternet .com/net-neutrality-101.

12. Reed Hastings, March 20, 2014 (2:00 p.m.), comment on Netflix US & Canada Blogs, "Internet Tolls and the Case for Strong Net Neutrality," accessed September 12, 2014, http://blog.netflix.com/2014/03/internet-tolls-and-case-for-strong-net.html.

13. https://www.fcc.gov/document/fcc-adopts-strong-sustainable-rules-protect-open-internet.

14. http://www.freepress.net/press-release/106826/historic-win-internet-users.

15. Mieczysław Radochoński and Anna Radochońska, "Attitudes of the Polish University Students Toward Voluntary Blood Donation," *Rzeszow* 4 (2007): 329–34.

16. Lorenz Goette and Alois Stutzer, "Blood Donations and Incentives: Evidence from a Field Experiment," *IZA Discussion Papers*, no. 3580 (2008), accessed September 4, 2014, http://www.econstor.eu/bitstream/10419/35271/1/57333479X.pdf.

17. Don W. Stacks, *Primer of Public Relations Research* (New York: Guilford Press, 2010).

18. David Silverman, *Interpreting Qualitative Data: Methods for Analyzing Talk, Text and Interaction* (London: Sage, 2006).

19. David L. Morgan, *Focus Groups as Qualitative Research*, Vol. 16 (Thousand Oaks, CA: Sage, 1997), 11.

20. Bank of Canada. "The Impact of Minimum Wage Increases on the Canadian Economy," accessed January 15, 2018, https://www.bankofcanada.ca/wp-content/uploads/2017/12/san2017-26.pdf.

21. Armine Yalnizyan. "Why a $15 minimum wage is good for business," posted June 2, 2017, https://www.macleans.ca/economy/economicanalysis/why-a-15-minimum-wage-is-good-for-business/.

22. Shannon A. Bowen and Don W. Stacks, "Understanding the Ethical and Research Implications of Social Media," in *Ethical Practice of Social Media in Public Relations*, ed. Marcia W. DiStaso and Denise Sevick Bortree (New York: Routledge, 2014), 219.

23. "Ethical Standards and Guidelines for Public Relations Research and Measurement 2012," Institute for Public Relations, accessed September 18, 2014, http://www.instituteforpr.org/wp-content/uploads/Ethical-standards-and-guidelines-for-public-relations-research-ver-1.1.pdf.

Chapter 6

1. Lucy Townsend, "How Much Has the Ice Bucket Challenge Achieved?," *BBC News Magazine*, September 1, 2014, http://www.bbc.com/news/magazine-29013707.

2. "The ALS Association Expresses Sincere Gratitude to Over Three Million Donors," The ALS Association, accessed February 8, 2015, http://www.alsa.org/news/media/press-releases/ice-bucket-challenge-082914.html.

3. "Star Remains at Top of GTA Readership, Numbers Show," *Toronto Star*, April 14, 2016, https://www.thestar.com/news/gta/2016/04/14/star-remains-at-top-of-gta-readership-numbers-show.html.

4. *The Globe and Mail* Media Kit, accessed July 12, 2018, http://globelink.ca/wp-content/uploads/2017/12/Globe-Newspaper-MediaKit-National-2018.pdf.

5. "Goal Flow: Flow Analysis of Goals and Funnels," Google, accessed November 26, 2014, https://support.google.com/analytics/answer/1686005?hl=en.

6. Neil Patel, "The Marketer's Guide to Tumblr," *KISSmetrics*, accessed November 26, 2014, https://blog.kissmetrics.com/the-marketers-guide-to-tumblr/.

7. "About Us/Vision, Principles & Strategy," Water Supply & Sanitation Collaborative Council, accessed November 26, 2014, http://www.wsscc.org/about-us/mission-strategy-values.

8. Jelena Vucjic and Pavani K. Ram, *Handwashing Promotion: Monitoring and Evaluation Module*, UNICEF, accessed November 26, 2014, http://www.globalhandwashing.org/sites/default/files/UNICEF%20M%26E%20Toolkit%20Final%2011-24%20Low%20Res.pdf.

9. Ibid., 8.

10. Ibid.

11. Ronald D. Smith, *Strategic Planning for Public Relations* (Mahwah, NJ: Lawrence Erlbaum Associates, 2006), 240.

12. James Lukaszewski, "Finding Your First Job in Public Relations: How Agency Billing & Salaries Work," accessed November 26, 2014, http://www.e911.com/pr/PartII_HowAgenciesWork.pdf.

13. Ameet Ranadive, "Demystifying Programmatic Marketing and RTB," *Medium*, accessed November 26, 2014, https://medium.com/@ameet/demystifying-programmatic-marketing-and-rtb-83edb8c9ba0f.

14. "Results of 4A's 2011 Television Production Cost Survey," American Association of Advertising Agencies, accessed November 26, 2014, http://www.aaaa.org/news/bulletins/pages/tvprod_01222013.aspx.

Chapter 7

1. "Food with Integrity," Chipotle, accessed March 5, 2015, https://www.chipotle.com/en-US/fwi/fwi.aspx.

2. "We Treat Them Like Animals," Chipotle, accessed March 5, 2015, https://www.chipotle.com/en-US/fwi/animals/animals.aspx.

3. Matt Krantz, "How Chipotle Is Eating McDonald's Lunch," *USA Today*, January 22, 2015, http://americasmarkets.usatoday.com/2015/01/22/how-chipotle-is-eating-mcdonalds-lunch/.

4. Roberto A. Ferdman, "Why Chipotle's Pork Problem Is a Bad Sign for Its Future," *The Washington Post*, January 14, 2015, http://www.washingtonpost.com/blogs/wonkblog/wp/2015/01/14/why-chipotles-pork-problem-is-a-bad-sign-for-its-future/.

5. Erin Mosbaugh, "#Carnitasgate: Chipotle Not Serving Pork at One-Third of Its Restaurants," *First We Feast*, accessed March 5, 2015, http://firstwefeast.com/eat/carnitasgate-chipotle-not-serving-pork-at-one-third-of-its-restaurants/.

6. *APR Study Guide for the Examination for Accreditation in Public Relations*, Universal Accreditation Board, 2010, accessed March 5, 2015, http://www.praccreditation.org/resources/documents/apr-study-guide.pdf.

7. Emma Prestwich, "Doug Ford Sure Disliked A Lot of Questions in This CBC Interview," *Huffington Post*, March 3, 2018, https://www.huffingtonpost.ca/2018/03/13/doug-ford-sure-disliked-a-lot-of-questions-in-this-cbc-interview_a_23384590/.

8. "LinkedIn Ads—Frequently Asked Questions," LinkedIn, accessed March 5, 2015, http://partner.linkedin.com/ads/info/Ads_faqs_updated_en_US.html.

9. Garett Sloane, "Snapchat Is Asking Brands for $750,000 to Advertise and Won't Budge," *Adweek*, accessed March 5, 2015, http://www.adweek.com/news/technology/snapchat-asks-brands-750000-advertise-and-wont-budge-162359.

10. "In Memoriam: John W. 'Jack' Felton, APR, Fellow PRSA," *Public Relations Tactics*, accessed March 5, 2105, http://www.prsaorg/Search.Results/view/10186/105/In_Memoriam_John_W_Jack_Felton_APR_Fellow_PRSA.

11. Christopher Heine, "Arby's Dishes on Awesome Pharrell Williams Tweet," *Adweek*, accessed March 5, 2015, http://www.adweek.com/news/technology/arbys-dishes-awesome-pharrell-williams-tweets-156149.

12. Christopher Ratcliff, "A Look Inside GoPro's Dazzling You-Tube Strategy," *Econsultancy*, accessed March 5, 2015, https://

econsultancy.com/blog/64370-a-look-inside-gopro-s-dazzling-youtube-strategy.

13. Rosencratzinpants, Twitter post, November 22, 2011, https://twitter.com/PuppyOnTheRadio/status/1388737293326-86848.

14. Rob Taylor, "Epic Fail for Qantas Twitter Competition," *Reuters*, November 22, 2011, http://www.reuters.com/article/2011/11/22/us-qantas-idUSTRE7AL0HB20111122.

15. *APR Study Guide for the Examination for Accreditation in Public Relations*, Universal Accreditation Board, 2010, accessed March 5, 2015, http://www.praccreditation.org/resources/documents /apr-study-guide.pdf, 18.

16. "Search Engine Optimization," *Wikipedia, the Free Encyclopedia*, accessed March 5, 2015, http://en.wikipedia.org/w/index.php?title=Search_engine_optimization&oldid=648870961.

17. "Steps to a Google-Friendly Site," Google, accessed March 15, 2015, https://support .google.com/webmasters/answer/40349?hl=en.

18. Rebekah Iliff, "Why PR Is Embracing the PESO Model," *Mashable,* December 5, 2014, http://mashable.com/2014/12/05/public-relations-industry/.

19. Ibid.

20. Ibid.

21. Eric Deggans, "Diversity: The Gateway to Accuracy and Fairness in Media," in *Doing Ethics in Media: Theories and Practical Applications*, ed. Jay Black and Chris Roberts (New York: Taylor & Francis, 2011), 155.

22. "Agencies Must Find Answers for a Lack of Diversity," *PRWeek*, May 1, 2011, http://www.prweek.com/article/1264390/agencies-find-answers-lack-diversity.

23. Rosanna M. Fiske, "PRSA Committed to Increasing Diversity in Public Relations—*PRWeek* Letter to the Editor," PRSA, June 14, 2011, http://media.prsa.org/article_display.cfm?article_id=2136.

24. Jay Black and Chris Roberts (eds.), *Doing Ethics in Media: Theories and Practical Applications* (New York: Taylor & Francis, 2011), 151.

25. CBC News, "'Because It's 2015': Trudeau Forms Canada's 1st Gender-Balanced Cabinet," posted November 4, 2015, https://www.cbc.ca/news/politics/canada-trudeau-liberal-government-cabinet-1.3304590.

26. Lysiane Gagnon, "Trudeau's Diverse Cabinet Not a True Canadian Portrait," *The Globe and Mail,* November 11, 2015, https://www.theglobeandmail.com/opinion/trudeaus-diverse-cabinet-not-a-true-canadian-portrait/article27200206/.

27. "Kimberly-Clark Names Sue Dodsworth Global Diversity Officer," Kimberly-Clark, November 1, 2010, http://investor .kimberly-clark.com/releasedetail.cfm?releaseid=525475.

28. Molly Petrilla, "How Analytics Helped Kimberly-Clark Solve Its Diversity Problem," *Fortune*, December 10, 2014, http://fortune.com/2014/12/10/kimberly-clark-dodsworth-diversity/.

29. Ibid.

30. "Kimberly-Clark Initiative Wins 2014 Catalyst Award," Kimberly-Clark, accessed January 29, 2014, http://investor .kimberly-clark.com/releasedetail.cfm?ReleaseID=821885.

Chapter 8

1. "PR Software, Marketing, and Media Relations Software and Services," Cision, accessed May 14, 2014, http://www.cision .com/us/.

2. "Say Goodbye to Media Monitoring and Hello to cliQ," iQ Media, accessed May 14, 2015, http://go.iqmediacorp.com/cliq.

3. "LexisNexis Newsdesk—Media Monitoring Solution," LexisNexis, accessed May 14, 2015, http://www.lexisnexis .com/en-us/products/newsdesk.page.

4. "Media Relations Rating Points," CPRS, accessed July 15, 2019, https://www.cprs.ca/Join-us/Media-Relations-Rating-Points.

5. Andrew Rice, "Does BuzzFeed Know the Secret?," *New York Magazine,* April 7, 2013, http://nymag.com/news/features/buzzfeed-2013-4/.

6. Caroline Lees, "How Does Mashable Compete with New York Times?" *INMA Conference Blog*, March 26, 2015, http://www.inma.org/blogs/conference/post.cfm/how-does-mashable-compete-with-new-york-times-big-data.

7. Lisa Arthur, "What Is Big Data?," *Forbes*, August 15, 2013, http://www.forbes.com/ sites/lisaarthur/2013/08/15/what-is-big-data/.

8. Seth Duncan, *Using Web Analytics to Measure the Impact of Earned Online Media on Business Outcomes: A Methodological Approach* (Gainesville, FL: Institute for Public Relations), accessed May 14, 2015, http://www.instituteforpr.org/wp-content/uploads/Seth_Duncan_Web_Analytics.pdf.

9. "Summit Agrees Framework of Global Programme Measurement Standard," International Association for Measurement and Evaluation of Communication, June 21, 2010, http://news.cision.com/amec/r/summit-agrees-framework-of-global-programme-measurement-standard,c498800.

10. "Barcelona Principles 2.0 Launched," International Association for Measurement and Evaluation of Communication, accessed September 3, 2015, http://amecorg.com/2015/09/barcelona-principles-2-0-launched-result-of-cross-industry-collaboration/.

11. "The Barcelona Declaration of Research Principles," Institute for Public Relations, June 18, 2010, http://www.instituteforpr .org/the-barcelona-declaration-of-research-principles/.

12. "Google Brand Lift—Measuring Interest in Your Brand," Google, accessed November 21, 2014, https://www.youtube .com/watch?v=gYJQMRSbMlc.

13. "The Barcelona Declaration of Research Principles," Institute for Public Relations, June 18, 2010, http://www.instituteforpr .org/the-barcelona-declaration-of-research-principles/.

14. "Hiring Veterans and Military Spouses," Starbucks Coffee, November 5, 2013, https://www.youtube.com/watch?v=61aMc8tsAD4.

15. Joshua Williamson, "I am #TheSomebody who perseveres . . . ," [Twitter Post], April 21, 2015, https://twitter.com/ThatJoshuaDude/status/590676200344915968.

16. Lesley Wright, "I'm #TheSomebody who will be the first in my family . . . ," [Twitter Post], April 20, 2015, https://twitter.com/lesleyuf/status/590354132680237056.

17. Andre Manning and David Rockland, "Understanding the Barcelona Principles," *The Public Relations Strategist,* March 21, 2011, http://www.prsa.org/Intelligence/TheStrategist/Articles/view/9072/1028/Understanding_the_Barcelona_Principles.

18. Joel Best, *Damned Lies and Statistics: Untangling Numbers from the Media, Politicians, and Activists* (Berkeley: University of California Press, 2012).

19. Ibid., 5.

20. John Stauber and Sheldon Rampton, *Toxic Sludge Is Good for You: Lies, Damn Lies and the Public Relations Industry* (Monroe, ME: Common Courage Press, 1995).

21. David Michaelson and Don W. Stacks, "Standardization in Public Relations Measurement and Evaluation," *Public Relations Journal* 5, no. 2 (2011): 1–22; Shannon A. Bowen and Don W. Stacks, "Toward the Establishment of Ethical Standardization in Public Relations Research, Measurement, and Evaluation," *Public Relations Journal* 7, no. 3 (2013): 1–28.

Chapter 9

1. http://thelisticles.net/simple-things-wrong/557598/.

2. http://www.cracked.com/article_20559_the-6-most-ridiculous-things-people-claimed-to-legally-own_p2.html.

3. "Listicle," *Wikipedia, The Free Encyclopedia*, accessed May 21, 2015, http://en.wikipedia.org/w/index.php?title=Listicle&oldid=659813869.

4. http://www.forbes.com/sites/stevedenning/2014/08/29/five-reasons-why-millennials-love-listicles/.

5. http://mag.uchicago.edu/arts-humanities/listicle-literary-form.

6. Craig E. Carroll, *The Handbook of Communication and Corporate Reputation* (Oxford, UK: Wiley-Blackwell, 2013), 4.

7. Brian Solis and Deirdre K. Breakenridge, *Putting the Public Back in Public Relations: How Social Media Is Reinventing the Aging Business of PR* (Upper Saddle River, NJ: FT Press, 2009), 102.

8. Ann Wylie, "One More Phrase to Avoid: Enough Already with the 'At XX, We . . .' Construction," *PR Tactics* 22, no. 3 (March 2015): 7.

9. http://www.ncaa.org/champion/will-and-way.

10. William Zinsser, *On Writing Well: The Classic Guide to Writing Nonfiction* (New York: HarperPerennial, 1998), 62.

11. http://www.ncaa.org/champion/will-and-way.

12. "Melissa Kleinschmidt, APR, on College Athletics, Strategy and Storytelling," *PR Tactics* 22, no. 3 (March 2015): 10.

13. "Melissa Kleinschmidt, APR, on College Athletics, Strategy and Storytelling," *PR Tactics* 22, no. 3 (March 2015):10.

14. http://www.newyorker.com/magazine/2015/06/01/off-diamond-head-finnegan.

15. http://www.bbc.com/news/world-asia-32987622.

16. http://pages.instant.ly/bumble-bee-seafoods-testimonial.html.

17. Meta G. Carstarphen and Richard H. Wells, *Writing PR: A Multimedia Approach* (Boston: Pearson, 2004).

18. https://twitter.com/marjoriemliu/status/606122784654299136.

19. https://twitter.com/mattbertz/status/606115220524662784.

20. http://www.tsb.gc.ca/eng/medias-media/communiques/marine/2018/m16p0378-20180531.asp.

21. http://bst-tsb.gc.ca/eng/medias-media/fiches-facts/m16p0378/m16p0378-20180531-02.asp.

22. http://www.rbc.com/newsroom/news/2018/20180703-rbc-reach.html.

23. http://www.rbc.com/newsroom/news/2018/20180703-rbc-reach.html.

24. http://www.rbc.com/newsroom/news/2018/20180703-rbc-reach.html.

25. Brian Solis and Deirdre K. Breakenridge, *Putting the Public Back in Public Relations: How Social Media Is Reinventing the Aging Business of PR* (Upper Saddle River, NJ: FT Press, 2009), 155.

26. http://www.merriam-webster.com/word-of-the-year/2004-word-of-the-year.htm.

27. http://blogs.law.harvard.edu/whatmakesaweblogaweblog.html.

28. http://mashable.com/2010/07/20/corporate-blogging-tips/.

29. http://www.cnn.com/2014/04/10/business/china-weibo-user-base/index.html.

30. http://www.edelman.com/post/friday5-twitter-vs-sina-weibo/.

31. "Search Engine Optimization," *Wikipedia, The Free Encyclopedia*, accessed March 5, 2015, http://en.wikipedia.org/w/index.php?title=Search_engine_optimization&oldid=648870961.

32. https://support.google.com/webmasters/answer/66358?hl=en.

33. http://goinswriter.com/seo-pages/.

34. https://support.google.com/webmasters/answer/40349?hl=en.

35. Abel Meeropol, "Strange Fruit" (Commodore Records, 1939); Lewis Allan, *Strange Fruit* (New York: Edward B. Marks Music Corporation, 1940).

36. http://www.statesman.com/news/business/austin-pr-firm-changing-name-some-say-was-racially/njNHB/.

37. Ibid.

38. Ibid.

39. Jay Black and Chris Roberts, *Doing Ethics in Media: Theories and Practical Applications* (New York: Taylor & Francis, 2011).

Chapter 10

1. Patrick J. Lynch and Sarah Horton, *Web Style Guide*, 3rd ed., http://www.webstyleguide.com/.

2. http://www.forbes.com/sites/robertwynne/2014/01/20/how-to-write-for-public-relations/.

3. http://www.prdaily.com/Main/Articles/10798.aspx.

4. http://www.wsj.com/articles/in-photo-sharing-every-picture-tells-a-story-when-it-has-the-right-caption-1423007365.

5. http://www.cision.com/us/2014/07/pr-goes-pinterest-3-campaigns-to-inspire-you/.

6. James E. Grunig and Todd Hunt, *Managing Public Relations* (New York: Holt, Rinehart and Winston, 1984), 470.

7. http://www.prdaily.com/Main/Articles/5_creative_ways_brands_use_Snapchat_16717.aspx.

8. http://mashable.com/2014/02/24/snapchat-study-college-students/.

9. http://www.entrepreneur.com/article/238624.
10. http://infocus.gettyimages.com/post/new-embed-lets-you-share-tens-of-millions-of-images.
11. http://digg.com/originals/why-audio-never-goes-viral.
12. http://mediaincanada.com/2018/01/31/can-you-guess-how-much-radio-canadians-listen-to/.
13. http://mediaincanada.com/2017/06/06/as-alternative-services-gain-popularity-radio-remains-dominant-study/.
14. http://www.cbsnews.com/videos/new-hope-for-inmate-from-serial-podcast/.
15. Scott M. Cutlip, H. Center Allen, and M. Broom Glen, *Effective Public Relations*, 8th ed. (Englewood Cliffs, NJ: Prentice-Hall, 2000), 317.
16. https://www.omnicoreagency.com/youtube-statistics/.
17. https://www.omnicoreagency.com/snapchat-statistics/.
18. http://www.ragan.com/Main/Articles/44483.aspx.
19. http://www.prdaily.com/Main/Articles/3_ways_to_make_captivating_videos__18966.aspx.
20. https://www.brainshark.com/ideas-blog/2013/January/what-types-of-video-marketing-content-works-for-pinterest.
21. http://www.nytimes.com/2015/08/13/technology/personaltech/vertical-video-on-the-small-screen-not-a-crime.html.
22. Ibid.
23. http://www.adweek.com/socialtimes/beyond-periscope-and-meerkat-the-state-of-live-streaming-video/620195.
24. https://www.elance.com/r/contractors/q-Video%20Production.
25. http://www.makerstudios.com/about.
26. https://www.snapchat.com/geofilters.
27. http://www.fritolay.com/company/media/media-article/2016/04/21/cracker-jack-popcorn-calls-play-ball-and-unveils-new-prize-inside.htm.
28. https://www.facebook.com/crackerjack/photos/a.138381416350587.1073741827.133794093475986/49557238063148 7/?type=3&comment_id=496069930581732&comment_ tracking={%22tn%22%3A%22R%22}.
29. Ibid.
30. http://www.chicagotribune.com/business/columnists/ct-rosenthal-cracker-jack-0501-biz-20160429-column.html.
31. J.G. Blumler, "The Role of Theory in Uses and Gratifications Studies," *Communication Research* 6, no. 1 (1979): 9–36.
32. Ruth Avidar, Yaron Ariel, Vered Malka, and Eilat Chen Levy, "Smartphones and Young Publics: A New Challenge for Public Relations Practice and Relationship Building," *Public Relations Review* 39, no. 5 (2013): 603–5.
33. https://www.emarketer.com/public_media/docs/eMarketer_ Cross_Device_Trends_Roundup.pdf.
34. http://www.apple.com/watch/.
35. Jay Black and Chris Roberts, *Doing Ethics in Media: Theories and Practical Applications* (New York: Taylor & Francis, 2011), 242.
36. http://techcrunch.com/2015/06/02/apples-tim-cook-delivers-blistering-speech-on-encryption-privacy/.

Chapter 11

1. M.J. Simon, *Public Relations Law* (New York: Appleton-Century-Crofts, 1969).
2. Ibid.
3. J.Z. Philips, "The Contentious Relationship between PR and Legal," 2017, http://www.mediabullseye.com/2017/04/the-contentious-relationship-between-pr-and-legal.
4. Ibid.
5. Simon, *Public Relations Law*.
6. Philips, "The Contentious Relationship between PR and Legal."
7. The Constitution Act, 1982, Schedule B to the Canada Act 1982 (UK), 1982, c11.
8. Ibid., s.2.
9. *R v. Keegstra*, [1990] SCR 697.
10. Simon, *Public Relations Law*.
11. The Constitution Act, 1982, Schedule B to the Canada Act 1982 (UK), 1982, c11, s.1.
12. L.W. Sumner, *The Hateful and the Obscene: Studies in the Limits of Free Expression*. (Toronto: University of Toronto Press, 2004).
13. Libel and Slander Act, RSO 1990, c. L.12.
14. P.A. Downard, *The Law of Libel in Canada*, 2nd ed. (LexisNexis Canada, 2010).
15. Ibid.
16. "Defamation: Libel and Slander," https://www.cbabc.org/For-the-Public/Dial-A-Law/Scripts/Your-Rights/240.
17. Downard, *The Law of Libel in Canada*.
18. Ibid.
19. Ibid.
20. http://www.dmlp.org/sites/citmedialaw.org/files/2009-03-26-Simorangkir%20Complaint.pdf.
21. http://www.dmlp.org/sites/citmedialaw.org/files/2009-03-26-Simorangkir%20Complaint.pdf.
22. *Social Media and Internet Law: Forms and Precedents* (Markham, Ontario: LexisNexis Canada, 2014).
23. Ibid.
24. Hayman, A. a. J. R., J., "Intellectual Property and the Internet," 2016, https://www.cbapd.org/details_en.aspx?id-on_16tec0609c.
25. *Mudford v. Smith*, 2009 CanLII 55718 (ON SC)
26. L. Eggertson. "Cyber-libel: Defamation on a Keyboard," *Toronto Star*, May 4, 2011, https://www.thestar.com/business/2011/05/04/cyberlibel_defamatin_on_a_keyboard.html.
27. "Defamation: Libel and Slander," https://www.cbabc.org/For-the-Public/Dial-A-Law/Scripts/Your-Rights/240.
28. Ibid.
29. Ibid.
30. Ibid.
31. Ibid.
32. Ibid.
33. Hayman, "Intellectual Property and the Internet."
34. *Crookes v. Newton*, [2011], SCC 33412.
35. M. Drucker, "Canada v. American Defamation Law: What Can We Learn from Hyperlinks," *Canada-United States Law Journal*, 38, no. 1 (2013).

36. U. Connolly, "Multiple Publications and Online Defamation: Recent Reforms in Ireland and the United Kingdom," *Mararyk University of Journal of Law and Technology* 6, no. 1 (2012): 35.

37. Drucker, "Canada v. American Defamation Law."

38. *Crookes v. Newton*, [2011] SCC 33412.

39. Hayman, "Intellectual Property and the Internet."

40. Canada, O.o.P.C.o., "What Is Intellectual Property?," November 2, 2015, https://www.ic.gc.ca/eic/site/cipointernet-internetopic.nsf/eng/h_wr03685.html.

41. Ibid.

42. Copyright Act, RSC, 1985, C-42, Government of Canada.

43. Canada, O.o.P.C.o., "*What Is Intellectual Property?*"

44. L.A. Lymer and W.W. Carney, *Fundamentals of Public Relations and Marketing Communications in Canada* (Edmonton, AB: Pica Pica Press, 2015).

45. C. Myers, "Protecting Online Image in a Digital Age: How Trademark Issues Affect PR Practice," *Research Journal of the Institute for Public Relations* 3, no.1 (2016): 1.

46. Lymer and Carney, *Fundamentals of Public Relations*.

47. http://turnitin.com/en_us/what-we-offer/originality-checking.

48. C. Alphonso, "Former TDSB Director Guilty of Plagiarizing His PHD, Panel Says," *The Globe and Mail*, 2017.

49. http://memeburn.com/2015/09/top-south-african-instagrammer-accused-of-plagiarism/.

50. https://memeburn.com/2015/09/instagrammer-skye-grove-suspended-from-cape-town-partnership-pending-investigation/.

51. http://memeburn.com/2015/09/instagram-plagiarism-scandal-skye-grove-apologises-deletes-herself-off-internet/.

52. http://memeburn.com/2015/09/instagrammer-skye-grove-suspended-from-cape-town-partnership-pending-investigation/.

53. Copyright Act, RSC, 1985, C-42, Government of Canada.

54. Office of Consumer Affairs (OCA). Innovation, Science, and Economic Development Canada, http://www.ic.gc.ca/eic/site/oca-bc.nsf/eng/ca02920.html.

55. W. Comcowich, W., "How Video Live Streaming Fits into PR & Marketing," April 8, 2016, https://glean.info/how-video-live-streaming-fits-into-pr-marketing/.

56. *Rains v. Molea*, 2013 ONSC 5016.

57. Ibid.

58. Hayman, "Intellectual Property and the Internet."

59. Ibid.

60. Office of Consumer Affairs (OCA). Innovation, Science, and Economic Development Canada, http://www.ic.gc.ca/eic/site/oca-bc.nsf/eng/ca02920.html.

61. Copyright Act, RSC, 1985, C-42, Government of Canada.

62. *CCH Canadian Ltd. v. Law Society of Upper Canada*, 2004 SCC 29320.

63. Cameron Hutchinson, "Digital Copyright Law," *Hyperlink*, 2016, https://en/oxforddictionaries.com/defintion/hyperlink.

64. *Social Media and Internet Law: Forms and Precedents* (Markham, Ontario: LexisNexis Canada, 2014).

65. Ibid.

66. *R v. Spencer,* 2014 SCC 43, [2014] 2 SCR 212.

67. D. Vallieres, "Seclusion Intrusion: A Common Law Tort for Invasion of Privacy," *Litigation and Employment Bulletin* (2012), https://mcmillan.ca/seclusion-intrusion-a-common-law-tort-for-invasion-of-privacy.

68. *Jones v. Tsigei*, 2012 ONCA 32.

69. Lindsay, A. Wasser, "Seclusion Intrusion: A Common Law Tort for Invasion of Privacy." *Litigation and Employment Bulletin* (2012), https://mcmillan.ca/seclusion-intrusion-a-common-law-tort-for-invasion-of-privacy.

70. *Jones v. Tsigei*, 2012 ONCA 32.

71. "Privacy and the Canadian Media: Developing the New Tort of 'Intrusion upon Seclusion' with Charter Values," *The Western Journal of Legal Studies* 2, no. 1 (2012).

72. C.S. Penn, Shift Communications. June 28, 2017, https://www.shiftcomm.com/blog/what-is-investor-relations/.

73. Ibid.

74. Kristine Owram, "Can Uber Bury Its PR Disasters Once and for All and Prove It's a Force for Good?" *The Financial Post*, 2015, https://business.financialpost.com/transportation/can-uber-prove-its-a-force-for-good-and-bury-its-pr-disasters-once-and-for-all.

75. "What Is Material Non-public Information?," https://corporatefinanceinstitute.com/resources/knowledge/finance/material-non-public-information.

76. "Canada's First Criminal Conviction for Illegal Insider Trading," 2010, http://www.millerthomson.com/en/publications/communiques-and-updates/securities-practice-notes/spring-2010-securities-practice-notes/canadas-first-criminal-conviction-for-illegal-2/.

77. Canadian Radio-television and Telecommunications Commission, https://crtc.gc.ca/eng/home-accueil.htm.

78. Ibid.

79. Ibid.

80. "Canada's Anti-Spam Legislation," http://fightspam.gc.ca/eic/site/030.nsf/eng/home.

81. L. Weston, "Webinar—Canadian Anti-Spam Legislation," https://cprs.ca/prodev/webinar/CASL.aspx.

82. Ibid.

83. CPRS, https://www.cprs.ca/about.aspx.

84. Ibid.

85. https://www.law.cornell.edu/wex/trade_secret.

86. Canadian Intellectual Property Office, "What Is a Trade Secret?," https://www.ic.gc.ca/eic/site/cipointernet-internetopic.nsf/eng/wr03987.html.

87. *R v. Ghomeshi*, 2016 ONCJ 155.

88. Ibid.

89. Kevin Donovan, "Jian Ghomeshi Dumped by PR Firm over 'Lies,' Sources Say," 2014, https://www.thestar.com/news/gta/2014/10/30/jian_ghomeshi_dumped_by_pr_firm_over_lies_sources_say.html.

90. Ibid.

91. Carla Shore, "Lying to Your PR Firm Is a Good Way to Lose Your PR Firm," 2014, https://carlashore.wordpress.com/tag/jian-ghomeshi/.

92. Ibid.

93. B. Reid, "Social Media Connections Might Be Trade Secrets," *The Huffington Post*, 2014, https://www.huffingtonpost.com/brad-reid/social-media-connections_b_5986534.html.

94. D. Ciraco, "Who Owns That Social Media Account?," April 25, 2017.

95. Ibid.

Chapter 12

1. http://www.davecarrollmusic.com/music/ubg/story/.

2. http://www.huffingtonpost.com/2009/07/24/united-breaks-guitars-did_n_244357.html.

3. http://business.time.com/2013/09/03/man-spends-more-than-1000-to-call-out-british-airways-on-twitter/.

4. http://www.humansofnewyork.com/post/43997717109/i-am-a-street-photographer-in-new-york-city.

5. Amanda E. Cancel, Michael A. Mitrook, and Glen T. Cameron, "Testing the Contingency Theory of Accommodation in Public Relations," *Public Relations Review* 25, no. 2 (1999): 171–97; Sarah Strasburg, Samuel M. Tham, and Glen T. Cameron, "Taming Contingency Theory: Creating a Quantitative Decision Tool Using Decision Theory and Game Theory in Conflict Management," *Proceedings of the 18th International Public Relations Research Conference* (2015): 331.

6. https://page.org/site/the-page-principles.

7. Josh Greenberg and Charlene Elliott, "A Cold Cut Crisis: Listeriosis, Maple Leaf Foods, and the Politics of Apology," *Canadian Journal of Communication*, 34, no. 2 (2009): 189.

8. Ibid.

9. Ibid.

10. https://www.youtube.com/watch?v=zIsN5AkJ1AI.

11. https://www.theglobeandmail.com/report-on-business/small-business/sb-growth/the-best-legal-advice-is-often-an-apology/article626797/.

12. Greenberg and Elliott, "A Cold Cut Crisis."

13. Elizabeth Dougall, "Issues Management," Institute for Public Relations, December 12, 2008, http://www.instituteforpr.org/issues-management/.

14. http://www.reuters.com/article/2015/09/22/us-usa-volkswagen-emission-idUSKCN0RL2EI20150922#0uoPtue9HzrAyxoo.97.

15. http://www.nytimes.com/2015/12/14/business/the-engineering-of-volkswagens-aggressive-ambition.html.

16. Michael Regester and Judy Larkin, *Risk Issues and Crisis Management in Public Relations: A Casebook of Best Practice*, 3rd ed. (London: Kogan Page Publishers, 2005), 51.

17. www.nytimes.com/interactive/2015/10/23/business/international/vw-scandal-timeline.html.

18. http://www.bbc.com/news/business-34324772.

19. http://www.wired.com/2015/11/vw-epa-3-liter-audi-porsche-emissions/.

20. http://www.nytimes.com/2015/12/11/business/international/vw-emissions-scandal.html?_r=0.

21. http://money.cnn.com/2015/09/24/investing/volkswagen-vw-emissions-scandal-stock/.

22. http://fortune.com/2015/10/08/volkswagen-scandal-fallout/.

23. http://www.nytimes.com/2015/10/27/business/lawyers-jostle-for-lead-position-in-volkswagen-diesel-suits.html.

24. http://www.nytimes.com/2015/12/11/business/international/vw-emissions-scandal.html?_r=0.

25. Regester and Larkin, *Risk Issues and Crisis Management*.

26. Ibid.

27. http://www.nytimes.com/2000/01/26/us/anti-sweatshop-movement-is-achieving-gains-overseas.html.

28. http://www.yourmembership.com/articles/166/How-Nonprofits-Turn-Seven-Important-Issues-into-Opportunities.htm.

29. http://www.cdc.gov/ecoli/2015/o26-11-15/index.html.

30. http://www.bloomberg.com/news/articles/2015-12-04/chipotle-rescinds-16-forecast-after-e-coli-scare-crushes-sales.

31. http://www.usatoday.com/story/money/cars/2015/12/01/emissions-scandal-crushes-volkswagen-sales-november/76605062/.

32. http://www.forbes.com/sites/jeannemeister/2012/06/07/corporate-social-responsibility- a-lever-for-employee-attraction-engagement/;http://www.thecro.com/topics/25115/how-to-recruit-and-retain-millennial/#sthash.KlguNCXg.dpuf.

33. http://www.instituteforpr.org/state-crisis-communication-evidence-bleeding-edge/.

34. W. Timothy Coombs and Sherry J. Holladay, *PR Strategy and Application: Managing Influence* (Chichester, UK: Wiley-Blackwell, 2010), 248.

35. http://www.foxnews.com/us/2013/09/28/chicago-tylenol-murders-remain-unsolved-after-more-than-30-years.html.

36. http://www.nytimes.com/2013/10/30/business/lawrence-g-foster-dies-at-88-helped-lead-tylenol-out-of-cyanide-crisis .html.

37. https://www.washingtonpost.com/archive/business/1982/10/11/tylenols-maker-shows-how-to-respond-to-crisis/bc8df898-3fcf-443f-bc2f-e6fbd639a5a3/.

38. http://usatoday30.usatoday.com/news/nation/2003-10-09-ghettopoly_x.htm.

39. https://www.washingtonpost.com/news/morning-mix/wp/2014/09/15/urban-outfitters-red-stained-vintage-kent-state-sweatshirt-is-not-a-smart-look-this-fall/.

40. http://fortune.com/2015/12/11/chipotle-ecoli-crisis-management/.

41. http://www.reuters.com/article/us-oil-spill-bp-apology-idUSTRE6515NQ20100602.

42. http://adage.com/article/news/crisis-pr-assessing-domino-s-reaction-youtube-hubub/136086/.

43. http://theconversation.com/spin-lance-armstrongs-confession-and-livestrongs-future-11616.

44. http://www.prnewsonline.com/water-cooler/2013/05/30/livestrong-foundation-communications-team-struggles-to-overcome-negative-impact-of-lance-armstrong/.

45. http://www.livestrong.org/who-we-are/.

46. Jay Black and Chris Roberts, *Doing Ethics in Media: Theories and Practical Applications* (New York: Taylor & Francis, 2011).

47. Ralph Barney, "Cases and Commentaries" *Journal of Mass Media Ethics* 1, no. 1 (1985): 80.

48. http://www.instituteforpr.org/crisis-management-communications/.

Chapter 13

1. http://www.dumplingemoji.org.
2. https://www.reddit.com/r/Fremont/comments/3cu15w/lets_bring_gigabit_internet_to_fremont/.
3. http://www.techtimes.com/articles/87039/20150923/more-than-half-the-worlds-population-still-doesnt-have-internet-access-says-un.htm.
4. http://nextcenturycities.org/.
5. http://nextcenturycities.org/about-ncc/.
6. https://www.ipsos.com/en-ca/one-ten-9-canadians-do-not-have-internet-access-home.
7. https://www.equals.org.
8. http://one.laptop.org/about/mission.
9. https://www.ted.com/talks/nicholas_negroponte_on_one_laptop_per_child/transcript?language=en.
10. http://www.bu.edu/writingprogram/journal/past-issues/issue-3/shah/.
11. Mark Warschauer and Morgan Ames, "Can One Laptop per Child Save the World's Poor?" *Journal of International Affairs* 64, no. 1 (2010): 33.
12. http://blog.al.com/spotnews/2010/07/study_shows_majority_of_birmin.html.
13. Warschauer and Ames, "Can One Laptop per Child Save the World's Poor?"
14. https://www.lexico.com/en/definition/culture.
15. http://www.businessweek.com/innovate/NussbaumOnDesign/archives/2007/09/its_time_to_cal.html.
16. http://www.nielsen.com/us/en/insights/news/2015/uncommon-sense-back-to-the-future-perspectives-on-thriving-in-2020.html.
17. http://www.geberit-aquaclean.com/en_uk/dusch_funktion/duschfunktion.html.
18. www.iprn.com/project-of-the-year-2013-winner-turning-taboo-into-a-trend/.
19. www.iprn.com/project-of-the-year-2013-winner-turning-taboo-into-a-trend/.
20. http://heavy.com/entertainment/2014/11/squatty-potty-poop-toilet-stool-shark-tank-products-season-6-100th-episode/.
21. https://www.youtube.com/watch?v=YbYWhdLO43Q.
22. Edward Twitchell Hall, *Beyond Culture* (New York: Anchor, 1989), 91.
23. Ibid, 91.
24. http://www.buzzfeed.com/katieheaney/the-one-thing-you-should-never-text-anyone-ever.
25. www.brandingstrategyinsider.com/2015/08/behind-nikes-campaign.html.
26. Ilan Alon, Romie F. Littrell, and Allan K.K. Chan, "Branding in China: Global Product Strategy Alternatives," *Multinational Business* Review 17, no. 4 (2009): 123–42.
27. http://adland.tv/ooh/nothing-sucks-electrolux-billboard-uk-1991.
28. https://www.youtube.com/watch?v=yZrQqnRhmZ0.
29. http://www.snopes.com/business/misxlate/nova.asp.
30. Marieke De Mooij, *Global Marketing and Advertising: Understanding Cultural Paradoxes* (Thousand Oaks, CA: Sage, 2013).
31. Geert Hofstede, *Culture's Consequences: Comparing Values, Behaviors, Institutions and Organizations across Nations* (Thousand Oaks, CA: Sage, 2001).
32. http://web.evs.anl.gov/uranium/eis/whatiseis/index.cfm.
33. http://www.gamesforchange.org/play/never-alone-kisima-ingitchuna/.
34. http://www.gamesforchange.org/play/start-the-talk-underage-drinking/.
35. http://gamificationnation.com/friday-feminine-gamification-viewpoint-motivation-work/.
36. https://hbr.org/2004/10/cultural-intelligence.
37. Ibid.
38. http://news.klm.com/abn-amro-new-partner-in-klms-corporate-biofuel-programme/.
39. http://time.com/2938225/klm-royal-dutch-airlines-gael-garcia-bernal-world-cup/.
40. http://www.prdaily.com/Main/Articles/16919.aspx.
41. https://twitter.com/PacoSaiso/status/483316208985337856?ref_src=twsrc%5Etfw.
42. Krishnamurthy Sriramesh and Dejan Vercic (eds.), *The Global Public Relations Handbook: Theory, Research, and Practice* (Mahwah, NJ: Lawrence Erlbaum), xxv.
43. http://www.climatechangenews.com/2015/12/12/cop21-ngos-react-to-prospective-un- paris-climate-deal/.
44. http://www.cop21.gouv.fr/en/partners/business-and-sponsors/.
45. Guy J. Golan, Dennis F. Kinsey, and Sung-Un Yang (eds.), *International Public Relations and Public Diplomacy: Communication and Engagement* (New York: Peter Lang, 2014), 5.
46. http://www.dailymail.co.uk/news/article-2745875/War-Twitter-State-Department-releases-mock-ISIS-recruitment-film-bid-counter-terror-groups-online-pursuit-Westerners.html.

Chapter 14

1. September 2018 data.
2. 2011 data.
3. https://www.cbc.ca/news/canada/ottawa/federal-public-servants-in-ottawa-on-rise-1.3927997
4. https://www.ic.gc.ca/eic/site/061.nsf/eng/h_03090.html.
5. http://www.commpred.org/_uploads/report2-full.pdf.
6. Alvin Toffler, *Future Shock* (New York: Bantam, 1990).
7. http://www.commpred.org/_uploads/industry-educator-summit-summary-report.pdf.
8. http://www.arikhanson.com/2012/06/19/10-skills-the-pr-pro-of-2022-must-have/.
9. David M. Dozier, "The Organizational Roles of Communications and Public Relations Practitioners," in *Excellence in Public Relations and Communication Management*, ed. James Grunig (Mahwah, NJ: Lawrence Erlbaum, 1992), 327–55.
10. http://www.prsa.org/jobcenter/career_resources/resource_type/tools_tactics/CareerGuidePRSAFoundation/Career_Guide.pdf.
11. https://medium.com/@taliajane/an-open-letter-to-my-ceo-fb73df021e7a#.c3m0iojso.
12. https://medium.com/@taliajane/an-open-letter-to-my-ceo-fb73df021e7.

13. http://www.buzzfeed.com/davidmack/talia-jane-vs-yelp.

14. https://www.gofundme.com/Help-A-Yelper-EAT.

15. http://www.ranker.com/list/talia-jane-instagram-photos/ariel-kana.

16. http://www.arikhanson.com/2016/02/29/10-skills-the-pr-pro-of-the-future-will-need-revised/.

17. http://qz.com/622232/the-yelp-employee-who-was-fired-after-her-incendiary-open-letter-to-the-ceo-speaks-out/.

18. www.forbes.com/sites/quora/2016/02/26/does-talia-jane-deserve-the-backlash-from-her-open-letter-to-jeremy-stoppelman-yelps-ceo/.

19. http://money.cnn.com/2015/08/10/pf/pay-raise/.

20. http://www.forbes.com/sites/cameronkeng/2014/06/22/employees-that-stay-in-companies-longer-than-2-years-get-paid-50-less/.

21. http://www.fastcompany.com/3055035/the-future-of-work/you-should-plan-on-switching-jobs-every-three-years-for-the-rest-of-your-.

22. http://www.cbsnews.com/news/why-job-hoppers-make-the-best-employees/.

Glossary

A/B testing Experiment in which one group of participants is randomly assigned to see one version of a message and another group is randomly assigned to see a second version. Results are then compared to test the effectiveness of message variations.

Access divide Gap between people with access to digital technology and those without access.

Accredited Business Communicator (ABC) An IABC credential used to recognize accredited communicators until 2013.

Accredited in Public Relations (APR) Credential awarded by CPRS and other professional communication organizations around the world to those who have demonstrated competency in the knowledge, skills, and abilities required to practise public relations effectively.

Active publics People who behave and communicate actively in response to a problem or issue.

Advertising Media space purchased by sponsors to persuade audiences; or the practice of planning and producing this service.

Advertising value equivalency (AVE) A calculation of the value of news or editorial coverage based on the cost of the equivalent amount of advertising space or time.

Advertorial Paid advertising that is presented in the form of editorial content.

Advocacy Public promotion of a cause, idea, or policy.

Algorithm A formula or set of steps for solving a problem. A computer algorithm can be the series of steps used in automated message testing and placement.

Analytics Researching online data to identify meaningful patterns. In strategic communication, analytics often focus on how web traffic leads to behavioural results such as sharing information or making online purchases.

Anchor text Clickable text that provides a hyperlink.

Apology Act of taking responsibility for an issue or crisis and seeking forgiveness or understanding.

Asymmetrical model Model of public relations in which communication is two-way but unbalanced, with the organization using research/feedback in an effort to persuade publics to change attitudes or behaviours.

Attitudinal Having to do with affect, emotion, favour, or disfavour towards an organization, brand, product, service or idea.

Authenticity The degree to which one communicates reliably, accurately, and true to his or her own character and the character of the organization that he or she represents.

Automated copy testing Using computer programs to automate the process of testing digital messages such as promotional copy.

Autoplay Feature that enables automatic playing of videos or other multimedia elements on users' devices.

Aware publics People who recognize that they are affected by a problem or issue in their environment.

Backgrounder Writing tactic used to give depth and context as background information for news stories.

Backlinks Incoming links that direct web users to a web page from another web page.

Banner ads Advertisements on web pages designed to encourage users to click to reach an advertiser's site.

Behavioural Having to do with observable human action.

Benchmarking Process of setting a point for comparison with eventual program results in order to observe change over time. (Benchmarking can also be used to make performance comparisons with other organizations or industry standards.)

Big data Large amounts of data from traditional and digital sources that can be used for ongoing discovery and analysis of media content and human behaviour.

Billable rate Amount that an agency or firm charges clients per hour of an employee's time.

Black box fallacy False notion that predicts most human communication needs will eventually be satisfied with a single device.

Blog Online post (or web log) with reflections, comments, and often links provided by the writer.

Bolstering Attempting to offset reputational damage to an organization during a crisis by emphasizing the good work that the organization has done in the past.

Boomerang effect Unintended consequence of an apology or other attempt to create positive response results instead in a negative response.

Bounce rate In online strategy, the percentage of visitors who visit a site but then leave the site instead of continuing towards other goals as defined by the strategist.

Brand journalism Application of journalistic skills to produce news content for an organization to communicate directly with its publics without going through a third-party news organization.

Brochureware Web pages that present essentially the same material as printed materials such as brochures.

Business to business (B2B) The relationship between a business and other businesses.

Business to consumer (B2C) The relationship between a business and the end users or consumers of its product or services.

Canadian anti-spam legislation (CASL) Law that protects Canadians from spam messages, hacking, malware, harmful software, and any other forms of privacy invasion.

Canadian Press (CP) style Rules of writing (including grammar, capitalization, and punctuation) published by the Canadian Press news agency. These rules are the standard for public relations writing in Canada.

Canadian Radio-television and Telecommunications Commission (CRTC) The administrative tribunal that regulates and supervises broadcasting and telecommunications in the public interest.

Clickbait Promotional or sensational Internet content designed primarily to entice users to visit another website.

Click-through rate Percentage of users who view an ad on the web and click on it to reach an advertiser's site.

Clipping services Businesses that monitor print and electronic media for mentions of clients in local, national, or international outlets; see also **media monitoring services**.

Code-switching Alternating between two or more languages or cultural styles.

Cognitive Having to do with mental processes such as thinking, knowing, perceiving, learning, and understanding.

Commercial electronic messages (CEM) Any electronic message that encourages participation in a commercial activity, regardless of whether there is an expectation of profit.

Communal relationships Relationships in which each party gives benefits to the other and a primary motivation for each is the other's benefit.

Communication Management Professional (CMP) Credential awarded by IABC to recognize communicators at the generalist/specialist level.

Community consultation When an organization seeks input from community members who may be impacted by any decisions or actions taken by that organization.

Community relations The efforts made by an organization to build strong relationships with members of the immediate community.

Compensation Crisis response strategy of offering products, services, or money to help make amends with publics.

Consequentialism Results-based system of ethics that holds that the best ethical decision is the one leading to the best outcomes or impacts.

Constraint recognition When people detect a problem or situation in their environment but perceive obstacles that limit their behaviour to do anything about it.

Content analysis A systematic method for analyzing recorded information such as audio, video, or text.

Content marketing Development and sharing of media content to appeal to consumers as part of an indirect marketing strategy in which consumers are drawn primarily to media content instead of directly to the product being marketed.

Contingency theory A theory that proposes that the best course of action in any situation depends on the specifics of the situation.

Control group A group of subjects or people in an experiment that do not receive or are not exposed to a treatment for the purpose of comparison.

Controlled media Channels of communication that allow public relations practitioners to write, edit, produce, and distribute messages as they see fit.

Conversational voice An authentic, engaging, and natural style of communication that publics perceive to be personable.

Conversion rate In online strategy, the number of goals reached divided by the number of unique visitors to a site.

Cookie A text file stored on a user's computer that is used to track and remember the user's activity online.

Copyright A form of intellectual property that gives one exclusive legal rights to produce, reproduce, publish, or perform an original work.

Copyright infringement Use of protected works without proper permission from the copyright holder.

Corporate advertising Paid media designed to promote an organization as a whole rather than sell a particular service, product, or product category (also sometimes called institutional advertising).

Corporate social responsibility (CSR) Companies' commitment of resources to benefit the welfare of their workforce, local communities, society at large, and the environment.

Cost per thousand (CPM) A measure of advertising reach that represents the cost of an advertisement relative to the estimated size of the audience.

Creative Commons Non-profit organization that encourages fair and legal sharing of content by helping content creators make their work available with clear terms and conditions.

Crisis communication The communication function that deals with undetected problems and sudden crises.

Crowdsource To obtain information or input into a particular task or project by enlisting the services of a number of people, either paid or unpaid, typically via the Internet.

Cultural appropriation The act of taking or using things from a culture that is not your own, especially without showing that you understand or respect that culture.

Cultural convergence When various forms of culture are exchanged, combined, converted, and adapted. On a global scale, this phenomenon has accelerated with the growth of digital media.

Cultural hegemony The imposition of social, political, or economic ideals on subordinate groups in society.

Cultural intelligence Ability to adapt, communicate, and interact effectively across cultures by learning and applying cognitive, emotional, and behavioural skills.

Culture The ideas, customs, and social behaviour of a particular people or society.

Customer relationship management (CRM) Process of tracking and forecasting customers' interactions with an organization, often leveraging data for sales support.

Cyber libel Libel in an online context.

Dateline Text at beginning of news story that describes when and where a story occurred (e.g., "BEIJING, 16 June—").

Defamation False communication that harms someone's reputation.

Delayed lead A style of beginning a story without summarizing the story's main points in a way that entices readers to continue reading.

Demographics Data describing objective characteristics of a population including age, level of income, or highest educational level obtained.

Deontological ethics System of decision-making that focuses on the moral principles of duty and rules.

Dialogic communication Exchanges involving people communicating their own views and backgrounds while remaining completely open to seeing the world as others do.

Digital divide Gap between those people with relatively little access and use of information and communication technologies and those people with greater access and usage.

Digital watermarking Information embedded into digital audio and video signals that can be used to track when and where the content is delivered.

Distributed public relations Intentional practice of sharing public relations responsibilities among a broad cross-section of an organization's members or employees, particularly in an online context.

Direct lead A style of beginning a news story that summarizes the story's main points (e.g., who, what, where, when, why, how) in the first sentence or two.

Diversity Inclusion of different types of people and different types of views.

Dominant coalition Group of people with the greatest influence in determining how an organization operates and pursues its mission.

Economic convergence When various media organizations and functions are merged under a single ownership structure. This form of media convergence is different from the term economists use to describe trends in world economies.

End-user license agreements (EULA) Legal agreement between a software provider and the person using the software.

Ethics Moral principles that govern a person's or group's behaviour.

Exchange relationships Relationships in which each party gives benefits to the other with the expectation of receiving comparable benefits in return.

Explainer video Video produced to demonstrate a product, service, or process.

External publics Groups of people that exist mostly outside of an organization and have a relationship with the organization.

Eye tracking Process of measuring eye movements to determine where people are focusing; often used in website testing.

Fact sheet Short (often one-page) document that presents factual information in concise format.

Fair dealing An exception to copyright laws for the purposes of research, private study, education, parody, satire, review criticism, or news reporting.

Feature story A story that explores some angle of an event, a person's life, an organization, or a place.

Feedback Information returned from the environment in response to an organization's action or communication that can be used for continuous adjustment and improvement of the organization.

First-party data Data on user or consumer behaviour that is collected by an organization from the people who use the organization's websites or online services.

Flaming Hostile communication among Internet users.

Flash mob When a group of people plans and executes a surprise public event or performance that is usually organized via electronic media and unanticipated by those who are not participants.

Formal research Research designed with clear rules and procedures for collection and analysis of information.

Formative research Research conducted at the beginning of the planning process, or during the implementation of a plan.

Freedom of Information and Protection of Privacy Act (FIPPA) A Canadian law passed to ensure that the government makes its information accessible to citizens.

Freelancers People who work on a project-by-project basis instead of working more permanently for a single employer (e.g., freelance writers, photographers, video producers).

Frequency The average number of times people in an audience are exposed to a particular message in a defined period.

Functional magnetic resonance imaging (fMRI) Tests that use magnetic fields to generate images of brain activity, including responses to communication and media stimuli.

Funnel A model for tracking how people move from exposure and awareness to action, particularly in online marketing where the goal is to convert a large number of web page viewers to sales leads or purchases.

Gamification Strategy of applying rules and rewards of game playing (points, scoring, competition, collaboration, etc.) to other areas of behaviour such as desired public relations outcomes.

General public A non-specific term that can refer to everyone in the world.

Geofilter Feature of social media (particularly Snapchat) that encourages communication among users within a specified geographic area by allowing users to post images with location-specific overlays.

Geolocation Function of communication devices that identifies the specific geographic location of the device.

Glass ceiling Metaphor used to describe a present but unseen barrier to promotion for women and minorities.

Goals Statements that indicate a desired result for public relations efforts. In strategic planning, goals are more specific than the organization's mission but more general than objectives.

Golden mean Ethical doctrine holding that the best courses of action are found between extremes.

Golden rule Ethic of reciprocity—treat others as you would like to be treated yourself.

Government relations A specialized branch of public relations that helps organizations form better relationships with governments at all levels.

Grassroots campaign A bottom-up campaign that focuses strategy on mass participation of citizens or political constituents in an effort to influence policy or legislation.

Grasstops campaign A campaign that focuses strategy on directly influencing opinion leaders and well-connected individuals such as donors or political party leaders.

Greenwashing When an organization spends more resources claiming to be "green" through publicity, advertising, and marketing than actually implementing practices that minimize environmental impact.

Hashtag A word or phrase (with no spaces) preceded by the hash symbol (#) that users can include in posts to categorize information online. Many social media platforms allow users to search or filter news feeds for information identified with the tag.

High-context communication Exchanges in which most of the meaning conveyed between people lies in the context of the communication or is internal to the communicators.

Human interest A personal or emotional storytelling angle that focuses on the human condition.

Impacts The broadest and furthest-reaching results of public relations efforts, often stated in terms of societal benefit.

Impression management Process in which people influence perceptions of themselves or their organizations by regulating and controlling information in social interactions.

Impressions A measure of the number of people exposed to a message.

Inbound marketing Marketing strategy that focuses on tactics for attracting customers with useful, entertaining, or valuable information that customers find on blogs, search results, and other forms of online and social media.

Independence In public relations ethics, the value of autonomy and accountability in providing objective counsel.

Individualism–collectivism Cultural dimension describing the difference between cultures that value loyalty to self and immediate family more and those that value loyalty to larger groups and society more.

Infographics Visual presentations designed to communicate information simply and quickly with combinations of images, charts, tables, or text.

Informal research Research conducted without clear rules or procedures, which makes the findings difficult to replicate or compare to other research or situations.

Ingratiation A type of reinforcing crisis response strategy in which stakeholders are praised or thanked to win their good favour.

In house When public relations people are employed directly within an organization rather than working for an external agency or contracted as independent consultants.

Initial public offering (IPO) Financial event in which a private company offers sale of stocks to public investors for the first time.

Insider trading When a company's employees or executives buy and sell stock in their own organization or share information with others who buy or sell before the information has been made public.

Integrated communication Communicating with publics consistently across organizational functions including public relations, advertising, marketing, and customer service.

Integrated marketing communication Strategic coordination of communication functions such as marketing, advertising, and publicity to achieve a consistent concept in consumers' minds.

Intellectual property The creation of the mind.

Intercultural public relations Management of relationships between organizations and publics of different cultures.

Internal publics Groups of people with shared interests within an organization.

International public relations Management of relationships between organizations and publics of different nations.

Internet of things (IoT) Global network of physical objects that are connected to one another in a way that enables them to communicate with one another and the Internet at large.

Inverted pyramid A style of newswriting in which the most important information is presented at the broad top of a story and narrower supporting details are written below.

Investor relations Management of relationships between an organization and publics in the financial community—for example, investors, analysts, and regulators.

Issue An important topic or problem that is open for debate, discussion, or advocacy.

Issues management An anticipatory, strategic management process that helps organizations detect and respond appropriately to emerging trends or changes in the socio-political environment. Ideally, issues are managed and/or resolved before they become crises.

Landscape orientation Images or video framed so that width is greater than height, like traditional movies.

Latent publics People who are affected by a problem or issue but don't realize it.

Legislative relations Management of relationships between an organization and lawmakers, staffers, and others who influence legislation.

Level of involvement The degree to which people feel or think that a problem or issue affects them.

Libel False written communication that injures someone's reputation.

Likert-type items Questionnaire items that ask people to respond to statements with a range of defined response options such as the range from "strongly disagree" to "strongly agree."

Limitation period The two-year interval within which a plaintiff is able to sue for libel.

Listening Deliberately paying attention to and processing what others are communicating. In public relations and organizational communication, this means processing feedback.

Listicle An online article presented in the format of a numbered or bulleted list.

Lobbying Working to influence the decisions of government officials on matters of legislation.

Long-term orientation Cultural dimension describing the difference between cultures that value long-held traditions more and cultures that value entrepreneurship and innovation more.

Low-context communication Exchanges in which most of the meaning of messages is stated explicitly in the messages and requires little understanding of context.

Loyalty A sense of obligation or support for someone or something, including both organizations and publics.

Management function Part of an organization involved in its overall leadership and decision-making, guiding how the organization operates in its environment, rather than merely following the instructions of others.

Management role Concept describing those in public relations who primarily develop strategy, participate in organizational decision-making, and are held accountable for program outcomes.

Marketing Business of creating, promoting, delivering, and selling products and services.

Marketing mix Combination of product, price, place, and promotion strategies in support of profitable exchange.

Market skimming Marketing strategy that starts with higher prices for early adopters of unique products and services and then lowers prices later to sell to a broader base of consumers when competitors enter the market.

Masculinity–femininity Cultural dimension describing the difference between cultures that value competition, achievement, and material success more and those that value care, collaboration, and modesty more.

Mashups Media presentations created by combining two or more pre-existing elements from different sources.

Material nonpublic information Any information that could influence the market value of a company or its products.

Media catching When journalists post queries online inviting public relations people or others with relevant information or expertise to respond. Public relations people "catch" these opportunities rather than "pitching" story ideas to journalists.

Media gatekeepers People or processes that filter information by deciding which content is published, broadcasted, posted, shared, or forwarded.

Media kits Packages of information assembled by public relations people for news media. Common contents include news releases, fact sheets, backgrounders, position papers, photos, graphics, and so on.

Media monitoring services Vendors that assist public relations practitioners in the collection, analysis, and reporting of media data for evaluation; see also **clipping services**.

Media planning Choosing media channels to achieve strategic communication goals and objectives. Media planning drives advertising purchases.

Mediated public diplomacy A nation's strategic use of media to promote its agenda abroad to foreign publics.

Meta tags Text used to describe a web page to search engines.

Microblog A shorter blog post limited by space or size constraints of the delivery platform.

Mission Overall reason an organization exists.

Mission statement A formal statement of an organization's steady, enduring purpose.

Monologic communication Communication in which one party attempts to impose its view on others.

Morgue Storage space for archived files of old stories, notes, and media materials kept by news organizations.

Multimedia The combination of any two or more forms of media such as text, graphics, moving images, and sounds.

Multiple publication rule In defamation, each sale or delivery of a single copy of a newspaper, magazine, or book is a separate publication for which the injured plaintiff has a distinct cause of action.

Multipliers Formulae applied to circulation or other media reach numbers based on assumptions that more than one person will be exposed to each copy of a message or that being covered as part of a news story is more valuable than paid advertising in the same media space.

Native advertising Paid advertising that is presented in the form of the media content that surrounds it. Advertorials are a type of native advertising, as are promoted tweets, sponsored posts, and so on. Native advertising should be labelled as "advertising," "paid content," "sponsored," etc.

Natural links Hyperlinks to a web page that are provided by other people who see value in the content of the page, as opposed to links that are posted for the primary purpose of manipulating search engines.

Net neutrality When data transmitted on the Internet is treated equally by governments and service providers in a way that does not slow down, speed up, or manipulate traffic to create a favourable business environment for some organizations or users over others.

News release A statement of news produced and distributed on behalf of an organization to make information public. Traditionally news releases (aka press releases) have been issued to news media with the intent of publicizing the information to the news organization's readers, listeners, or viewers.

Newsworthiness Standard used to determine what is worth covering in news media.

Non-compete clause Part of an employment contract that restricts employees from working for competitors or sharing competitive information such as trade secrets even after they no longer work for the organization.

Non-governmental organization (NGO) A group of people organized at the local, national, or international level, often serving humanitarian functions and encouraging political participation. NGOs can be large and involved in international development work such as CARE Canada or Médecins Sans Frontières/Doctors Without Borders Canada, or can be focused on a specific region or concern such as the Yukon Conservation Society.

Non-participant observation Research method in which the researcher avoids interaction with the environment or those being observed.

NSFW Shorthand for "not safe/suitable for work."

Objectives Statements that indicate specific outputs or outcomes desired. In strategic public relations, objectives are specific steps taken to achieve broader goals.

Objectivity State of being free from the influence of personal feelings or opinions in considering and representing facts.

Ontario Securities Commission A Canadian regulatory body that administers and enforces compliance with securities legislation.

Organic search results Search engine results that are generated because of their relevance to the search terms entered by users and not resulting directly from paid placement as advertising.

Organization A group of people organized in pursuit of a mission, including businesses, non-profits, NGOs, clubs, churches, unions, schools, teams, and government agencies.

Organizational crisis A major threat to an organization's operations or reputation.

Organizational culture The unique character of an organization composed of beliefs, values, symbols, and behaviours.

Original digital video Video that is recorded, produced, and uploaded digitally for sharing online, as opposed to video originally produced for other channels like television or theatres.

Outcomes Observable results of public relations work.

Outputs Tasks or work attempted and completed, including communication tactics produced. Outputs can be completed without necessarily leading to meaningful results (i.e., outcomes).

Overhead expenses Costs of running a business that are not directly related to the product or services delivered.

Participant observation Research method in which the researcher deliberately interacts with the environment and those being observed.

Participatory culture A culture in which private citizens and publics are as likely to produce and share as they are to consume; commonly applied in mediated contexts in which consumers produce and publish information online.

Participatory media Media in which publics actively participate in producing and sharing content.

Pay per click Model of media sales in which advertisers, marketers, or sponsors pay an online publisher or website owner for each time the sponsored message or advertisement is clicked.

PESO (or PESO model) refers to the mix of paid, earned, shared, and owned content

PIPEDA (Personal Information Protection and Electronic Documents Act) A federally created piece of legislation that applies to organizations that collect, use, or disclose personal information in the course of commercial activity in provinces without substantially similar legislation.

Pitching When a public relations person approaches a journalist or editor to suggest a story idea.

Plagiarism Presenting someone else's words or ideas as one's own.

Planning Forethought about goals and objectives and the strategies and tactics needed to achieve them.

Post production Process in media production that occurs after raw audio, video, or images have been recorded—includes editing, combining media elements, transitions, and special effects.

Power distance Cultural dimension describing the difference between cultures that value hierarchy and authority more and those that value equal distribution of power more.

Pre-roll advertising A commercial ad displayed as online video before the desired video is shown.

Press agentry/publicity model Model of public relations in which communication is mostly one-way, sometimes initiated by an organization with little concern for accuracy or completeness in order to gain the attention of publics.

Primary publics Groups of people identified as most important to the success of a public relations campaign or program.

Primary research Systematic design, collection, analysis, and application of original data or observation.

Proactive A management style that is anticipatory, change-oriented, and self-initiated to improve the organization's environment and its future.

Problem or opportunity statement A concise written summary of the situation that explains the main reason for a public relations program or campaign.

Problem recognition When people detect a problem or situation in their environment and begin to think about it.

Pro bono Public relations work conducted as a public service without fee or payment.

Professional convergence When various functions of professional communication such as publicity, advertising, online services, and marketing are combined to improve strategy.

Programmatic media buying Automated media buying that is preprogrammed so that advertising purchases are completed when certain criteria set by buyers (marketers) and sellers (media) are met. Programmatic media buying commonly occurs via computer-run, real-time auctions.

Propaganda The spread of information used to promote or support a particular point of view. In modern use, the term usually refers to false, misleading, or exaggerated information.

Proselytizing When members of publics advocate or promote to others the goals and objectives of a communication strategy. Proselytizing is a key part of campaigns going viral.

Pseudo-event An event organized primarily for the purpose of generating media coverage.

Psychographics Data describing psychological characteristics of a population including interests, attitudes, and behaviours.

Public affairs A broader practice related to public relations that also deals with the public and special interest groups.

Publication Any act that has the effect of transferring defamatory information to a third person.

Public diplomacy Subset of international public relations that focuses on promoting national interests.

Public domain Works of intellectual property for which the copyright has expired, the creator has forfeited rights, or copyright laws do not apply, making the works freely available for public use.

Public information model Model of public relations in which communication is mostly one-way, initiated by an organization to inform publics with truthful and accurate information.

Publicity Unpaid media coverage, or the practice of deliberately planning and producing information and activities to attract this coverage.

Public relations Management of communication between an organization and its publics, or the strategic communication process that builds mutually beneficial relationships between organizations and their publics.

Publics Groups of people with shared interests. An organization's publics either have an effect on the organization, are affected by the organization, or both.

Pure accommodation Stance in issues management in which a public relations practitioner fully concedes to a public's demands.

Pure advocacy Stance in issues management in which a public relations practitioner firmly pleads an organization's case without compromise.

Qualitative research Research that results in in-depth description and understanding without relying on the use of numbers or statistics to analyze findings.

Quantitative research Research that results in numerical or statistical data and analysis.

Reach Percentage or number of people exposed to a message at least once via a specific communication channel during a defined period of time.

Reactive A management style that responds mainly to problems as they arise rather than anticipating them and averting them.

Relational maintenance strategies Ways of building and sustaining mutually beneficial relationships between organizations and publics.

Relational public diplomacy Engagement between a nation and its foreign publics in cultural exchange and two-way communication with the goal of achieving mutual benefits.

Reliability Consistency and precision of a particular research technique.

Replicability The ability to perform a research procedure or experiment repeated times to attain comparable results.

Reputation management Acting and communicating—often in writing—to influence an organization's reputation as part of a process that includes planning, analyzing feedback, and evaluating.

Responsible supply chain management Careful monitoring of product production and distribution to ensure that generally high ethical standards of social and environmental responsibility are maintained.

Scapegoating Blaming an outside person or organization for a crisis.

Search advertising Paid placement of advertising on search-engine results pages. Ads are placed to appear in response to certain keyword queries.

Search engine optimization (SEO) Process of improving the position of a specific website in the organic search results of search engines.

Secondary publics Groups of people who are important to a public relations campaign or program because of their relationship with primary publics.

Secondary research Collection, summary, analysis, or application of previously reported research.

Selective attention Process of filtering information by focusing on some stimuli in the environment while ignoring others.

Self-efficacy One's belief that he or she can perform certain behaviours to achieve certain outcomes.

Situational crisis communication theory (SCCT) Theory that proposes effective crisis communication entails choosing and applying appropriate response strategies depending on how much responsibility for the crisis is attributed to the organization by key publics.

Situational theory of publics The theory that the activity of publics depends on their levels of involvement, problem recognition, and constraint recognition.

Situation analysis A report analyzing the internal and external environment of an organization and its publics as it relates to the start of a campaign or program.

Slander False oral communication that injures someone's reputation.

Snackable content Easy-to-consume pieces of content that are available on the go.

Social media creators Influential social media users who are among the first to identify and post about crises online.

Social media crisis communication model (SMCC) Model describing the role of social media influencers, followers, and inactives in spreading information in crisis situations.

Social media followers Social media users who receive crisis information from social media creators.

Social media inactives People who receive crisis information indirectly from social media via traditional media and offline word of mouth.

Social media release A news release that applies the conventions of social media and includes content designed for social media distribution and sharing.

Spambots Computer programs that automatically send unsolicited email or post comments in online forums.

Spin Disingenuous strategic communication involving skewed interpretation or presentation of information.

Status conferral When media pay attention to individuals and groups and therefore enhance their authority or bestow prestige to them.

Stealing thunder Crisis response strategy in which an organization exposes its own problems (and works to address those problems) before opponents have the opportunity to do so.

Stock images Images that are professionally produced for selling or sharing, commonly available in searchable databases.

Story placement The outcome of a successful pitch, when a story involving a public relations practitioner's organization or client is covered in the news media.

Strategic Communication Management Professional (SCMP) Credential awarded by IABC to recognize senior communicators who have reached an accepted standard of knowledge and proficiency in their chosen field.

Strategic decision-making Daily management and communication decisions made with mindfulness of the objectives, goals, and mission of the organization.

Strategy Underlying logic that holds a plan together and offers a rationale for why it will work.

Summative research Research conducted at the end of a campaign or program to determine the extent that objectives and goals were met.

SWOT analysis Description and discussion of an organization's internal strengths and weaknesses and its external opportunities and threats.

Symmetrical model Model of public relations in which two-way communication is mostly balanced, with the organization as likely to change attitudes or behaviour as its publics.

Tactical decision-making Daily management and communication tactics implemented without consideration of the strategic objectives, goals, and mission of the organization.

Tactics Specific actions taken and items produced in public relations.

Target audience Group of people strategically identified for their propensity to consume an organization's products, services, or ideas.

Technician role Concept describing those in public relations who primarily implement decisions of others in an organization including writing, production, and dissemination of communication tactics.

Technological convergence (aka digital convergence) When information of various forms such as sound, text, images, and data are digitized, affording communication across common media.

Tertiary publics Groups of people who indirectly influence or are indirectly affected by a public relations campaign or program.

Third-party credibility Assumption that information delivered from an independent source is seen as more objective and believable than information from a source with a vested interest in persuasion.

Third-party data Data on user behaviour that is collected or aggregated by one organization and sold to another organization.

Trademarks Words, sounds, or designs used to distinguish goods and services from those of others in the marketplace.

Trade secret Business information that is not generally known to the public and not readily available to others who could profit from its disclosure or use.

Transmedia storytelling Telling a story across multiple platforms like games, web pages, apps, social media, and traditional media.

Transparency 1. Deliberate attempt to make available all legally reasonable information for the purpose of enhancing the reasoning ability of publics. **2.** In research, openness in describing and explaining methods.

Treatment group A group of subjects or people in an experiment that receive or are exposed to a treatment.

Two-way communication When both parties send and receive information in an exchange, as opposed to the one-way dissemination of information from an organization to its publics.

Uncertainty avoidance Cultural dimension describing the difference between cultures that are less comfortable with ambiguity (high-uncertainty avoidance) and those that are more at ease with ambiguity.

Unconferences Meetings or conferences organized by their participants for active peer-to-peer exchange of ideas and information. Unconferences are less structured and more participatory (e.g., fewer one-to-many presentations) than traditional conferences.

Uncontrolled media Channels of communication that are outside of the control of public relations practitioners.

Usage divide (or second digital divide) Gap between people who use information and communication technologies for education, self-betterment, civic engagement, etc. and those who use the technologies for less constructive reasons.

User-centred design Process by which media, messages, and other products and services are developed with continuous and deliberate attention to how end users will experience them.

Uses and gratifications Approach to studying communication that focuses on how people use media and the gratifications they seek from media, as opposed to studying the effects of media on people as passive audiences.

Utilitarianism Principle that the most ethical course of action is the one that maximizes good and minimizes harm for people.

Validity Accuracy of a particular research technique in measuring or observing what the researcher intends to measure or observe.

Values Ideally, the core priorities in the organization's culture; they represent how people should act in the organization.

Vertical video Video framed in an orientation in which height is greater than width.

Video news release A news release that provides broadcast journalists with pre-produced news packages including audio and video material.

Vision Often aspirational, this is a vivid description of the organization as it effectively carries out its mission.

Word-of-mouth promotion Passing of information and recommendations from person to person.

Index

Note: Page numbers in bold indicate definitions.